Information Technology and Economic Development

Yutaka Kurihara
Aichi University, Japan

Sadayoshi Takaya
Kansai University, Japan

Hisashi Harui
Kwansei Gakuin University, Japan

Hiroshi Kamae
Hitotsubashi University, Japan

Information Science
REFERENCE

INFORMATION SCIENCE REFERENCE

Hershey · New York

Acquisitions Editor:	Kristin Klinger
Development Editor:	Kristin Roth
Senior Managing Editor:	Jennifer Neidig
Managing Editor:	Sara Reed
Copy Editor:	Shanelle Ramelb
Typesetter:	Jamie Snavely
Cover Design:	Lisa Tosheff
Printed at:	Yurchak Printing Inc.

Published in the United States of America by
Information Science Reference (an imprint of IGI Global)
701 E. Chocolate Avenue, Suite 200
Hershey PA 17033
Tel: 717-533-8845
Fax: 717-533-8661
E-mail: cust@igi-pub.com
Web site: http://www.igi-pub.com/reference

and in the United Kingdom by
Information Science Reference (an imprint of IGI Global)
3 Henrietta Street
Covent Garden
London WC2E 8LU
Tel: 44 20 7240 0856
Fax: 44 20 7379 0609
Web site: http://www.eurospanonline.com

Library of Congress Cataloging-in-Publication Data

Information technology and economic development / Yutaka Kurihara ... [et al.] editors.

p. cm.

Summary: "This book examines the impact IT has on politics, education, sociology, and technology. IT has already changed the face of many business activities and has prospects for future development. This book focuses on the benefits of IT for developing countries, whose problems must be solved, and obstacles overcome in order to further IT advancement"--Provided by publisher.

Includes bibliographical references and index.

ISBN 978-1-59904-579-5 (hardcover) -- ISBN 978-1-59904-581-8 (ebook)

1. Information technology--Economic aspects. 2. Economic development. I. Kurihara, Yutaka, 1962-

HC79.I55I5373 2008

303.48'33--dc22

2007007285

British Cataloguing in Publication Data
A Cataloguing in Publication record for this book is available from the British Library.

Table of Contents

Section II
Domestic and Global Markets in the IT Age

Section III
Innovative Engineering in IT

Section IV
Socioeconomic Development in the IT Age

Detailed Table of Contents

Section I
Towards Sustainable and Permanent Economic Growth

Chapter I

In this chapter, we mention that a digital divide could bring about an income divide both within a country and between countries. The more the uses of the Internet diffuse, the more the divide may introduce serious concerns. From a macroeconomic point of view, the increase in the digital divide diminishes ICT investments and delays the innovation of ICT. As a result, we propose that the public policies of each government provide the devices of ICT as social capital and infrastructure. On the global stage, the digital divide exists between developed and developing countries. Therefore, international provision of the digital devices should be achieved through a cooperative effort between developed countries and international organizations.

Chapter II

Within the last decades, there was a very high level of increase in information technology production. This production successfully speeds up technological changes in only developed countries. Such a situation results in the use of existing knowledge as input in the production of new knowledge in a monopoly of developed countries. Developing countries are, however, still struggling with their own sociopolitical and/or socioeconomic problems. This process creates a bigger technological gap between developed and developing countries. One of the reasons for this is a lack of physical and human capital in developing countries. This is a common problem in the world and necessary precautions should be taken in a timely manner. This study discusses the problematic issues of information technology creation in both developed and developing countries and suggests some solutions.

Chapter III

The purpose of this chapter is to investigate IT promotion policies for economic development in Malaysia and to analyze results of those policies. In addition, the author attempts to draw policy suggestions for developing countries in order to encourage their economic development. This chapter reveals disparities in the sector and region that exist even though the government has a strong concern regarding ICT-supported ICT development. From this analysis, three policy implications for other developing countries are suggested. First, government commitment can contribute to ICT development. Second, the government needs to develop ICT through a strategic and gradual approach. Third, the government needs to pay careful attention to ICT disparities that may arise in the process of ICT development for stable economic development.

Chapter IV

Since the early 1990s, the government has emphasised the ICT sector as a new engine of growth and development. The Multimedia Super Corridor (MSC), which was developed in 1996, was regarded as a main vehicle and catalyst for ICT-sector development. Since there were many new institutions established by the government, it some how had complicated and decreased efficiency in expanding the industry. ICT-related courses at public and private institutions were not developed well enough to meet the market demand. Consequently, the human factor, which was a major component for ICT development, was not fully utilised in research and development, therefore reliance on foreign technology remained a critical issue. These have slowed the progress of ICT development. This chapter will discuss the ICT-sector development policy in a broad view and try to analyse critically to what extent the development of the ICT sector has contributed to economic development in Malaysia.

Chapter V

This study analyzes the impact of macroeconomic announcements on the conditional volatility of Japanese government bond (JGB) futures returns. As information technology continues to develop, the arrival and the processing of new market-related information become more rapid. Using high-frequency data of JGB futures, we find that announcement shocks influence the dynamics of bond market volatility. Our results provide empirical evidence that the JGB futures market does not immediately incorporate implications of macroeconomic announcement news. The volatility of JGB futures returns persists for a while. Moreover, after distinguishing among types of shocks, volatility is asymmetric. Negative shocks have a stronger impact on subsequent volatility than do positive shocks.

Chapter VI

New information technologies, including E-commerce and the Internet, have brought fundamental changes to 21st century businesses by making more and better information available quickly and inexpensively. Intelligent enterprises are those firms that make the most from new information technologies and Internet business solutions to increase revenue and productivity, hold down costs, and expand markets and opportunities. In this chapter, the macroeconomic benefits that intelligent enterprises can have on the U.S. economy are explored. We find that the U.S. economy has become less volatile, with demand volatility nearly matching sales volatility, particularly in the durable goods sector. Evidence also suggests that firms are utilizing new information technologies to lower inventory levels relative to sales, leading to higher productivity growth, lower prices, and more competitive markets.

Section II
Domestic and Global Markets in the IT Age

Chapter VII

This chapter examines the global implications from recent reserve accumulation in Asia. Advances in information technology and the closer integration of world markets have complicated economic policy making by increasing countries' vulnerability to capital account crises and introducing new channels of risk transmission. To safeguard against these developments, many countries accumulated unprecedented levels of international reserves. Current account deficits in some industrial countries have supported such reserve accumulation, in particular for Asian countries that have promoted export-led growth underpinned by competitive exchange rates. Asian economies have been willing to absorb the cost of reserve accumulation rather than adjusting their exchange rate levels. This strategy, however, has increased the likelihood of protectionist measures from abroad, which could lead to contractions in trade and output. Moreover, these dynamics may transition to a generalized real appreciation of the major Asian currencies, while mounting pressure for a reduction of the U.S. fiscal deficit to sustainable levels.

Chapter VIII

This chapter describes the development of the stock market in Thailand since it was established in 1975. During these 30 years, the stock market in Thailand has introduced computer systems to facilitate investors and listed companies both in financial data and administrative work. Particularly, the Internet trading system has been introduced to enhance market growth. This can be traced from the increasing volume of trade each day. The growth of the Thai stock market has changed the structure of Thai economy and affects the economic development of Thailand.

Chapter IX

The objective of this chapter is to provide students and managers with a holistic view into the different factors that influence online banking adoption and to use the study's findings to develop strategies for managers on how to maximize the rate of Internet banking adoption. Research done with a sample size of 450 Spanish Internet users has highlighted that Internet banking adoption is more likely in young, highly educated, and high-income consumers. Internet affinity, online use experience, and some perceived benefits are also key drivers of online financial-services-purchase decision making. Perceived financial, social, and psychological risk negatively influences the use of online banking services.

Chapter X

As the trend of ICT development is gaining larger influence over countries' development and growth, e-commerce plays an important role in enhancing the growth of several developed and developing economies over the 21st century. This chapter aims to build the analytical base to support the importance of the development of e-commerce by investigating the role and contribution of e-commerce to economic growth and development. The chapter first investigates past contributions of e-commerce to economic growth in developed countries. Second, past research findings and frameworks are utilized to investigate the contribution of e-commerce toward economic growth, focusing on the case of e-commerce in Thailand. The study found that e-commerce plays an important role in enhancing the economic growth of Thailand. Two important findings supported the growth of e-commerce. First is the increase in sales generated by the use of e-commerce. Second, e-commerce induces the productivity development of firms through higher competition and innovation.

Chapter XI

Vietnam has been advancing toward a market economy since 1986. Industrialization has progressed with a high rate of growth. One of the factors of the economic growth of Vietnam has been FDI. Japanese companies are among those that have a strong interest in Vietnam. Japanese companies are recently taking note of Vietnam's IT and software industries. Now, however, interest is increasing in offshoring as a means for developing in this sector.

Section III
Innovative Engineering in IT

This chapter discusses the relationship between the use of information and communication technologies and transaction costs within micro, small, and medium-sized enterprises (MSMEs). The fundamental problem in this relationship is the asymmetric distribution of information. This asymmetry leads to problems such as adverse selection and moral hazards. Thus, the links between ICTs and the improvement of economic performance can be explained based on the capability of these technologies in reducing information asymmetries and therefore increasing firms' competitiveness. In the case of MSMEs, implementing new ICTs help diminish their frequent lack of information. However, the reduction of transaction costs and their better performance depend not only on the use of ICTs, but also on the integration of these technologies in the strategies and day-to-day activities of the MSMEs. For this reason, the training of the personnel and management is crucial when implementing ICTs in these firms.

It is generally accepted that knowledge has become a third major factor of production, in addition to the traditional factors, labour and capital. Information technology production is a significant factor in the knowledge economy, both because it is a major enabler of that economy, and because it is itself highly knowledge-intensive. Many countries around the world are looking for ways to promote the development of the knowledge economy, and information technology industries in particular. An important question is to what extent and how small developed countries might succeed in this endeavour. This chapter suggests a modified and more comprehensive version of the Ein-Dor, Myers, and Raman (1997) model of information technology (IT) industry success in small developed countries. Whereas the earlier model of IT industry success was based solely on the macroeconomic theory of Grossman and Helpman (1991), the revised model suggested here incorporates Romer's (1990) work in New Growth Economics. A significant advance over earlier work in this area is the use of both longitudinal and time slice data. This chapter provides an in-depth analysis of the IT industry in four countries over a five-year period: Finland, Israel, New Zealand, and Singapore. It analyses some changes that occurred over the period 1994 through 1998 and thus provides a reasonably comprehensive picture of the factors affecting the production of IT in these small developed countries. Our study reveals that four of the five endogenous variables which were studied have a close relationship to the development of IT industries in small developed countries. These variables are: research and development, technological infrastructure, firm strategies, and capital availability. On the other hand, domestic IT use does not seem to be a major factor in IT industry development. Our analysis thus largely supports the more comprehensive model of IT industry success. These findings should be of interest to both researchers and policy makers seeking to develop the knowledge economy and information technology industries in particular.

Chapter XIV

The development of science and technology enhances the economy. However, it also involves many environmental problems. In China, as a developing country, the concentration of the population in cities causes several things. The first is an ecological crisis caused by the environmental problems. On the other hand, with the help of IT, we can monitor the environment in real time online. IT provides so many methods to analyze the data and to control the pollution. So many environmental information systems for environmental impact assessment and environment management have been developed. Making mathematic models to simulate the environment's change, such as to simulate the diffusion of gas in the air, is very helpful for environment impact assessment and environment protection. Information technology is very helpful in handling environmental information.

Section IV
Socioeconomic Development in the IT Age

Chapter XV

The statements, "Life educates," and, "Education is life," are correct in general, but when a formal system of education is organized, society selects from all those cultural experiences to which the child is exposed those aspects of its culture that it regards as most valuable for its own coherence and survival. The power of information technology should be harnessed to plan, design, and execute projects that address the United Nations Millennium Development Goals, especially poverty reduction and the reduction of child mortality, and to promote sustainable development to improve the quality of life in the developing world. The rest of the chapter highlights some of the global problems, issues, and ongoing efforts to solve some of the problems and justify the need for an International Institute for Knowledge Management to specifically focus on the UN Millennium Development Goals.

Chapter XVI

With its constant development and completion of function, and its fast popularization in the world, the impact of computer technology on the mechanical industry of China is more and more far reaching. CAD, CAM, CAE, CIMS, computer controlling, and network information play a very important role in the rapid development and promotion of the quality of the mechanical industry in China. The application of computer technology has made enormous contributions to the improvement of the manufacturing industry and economic development of China. In this chapter, the application situation of CAD, CAM, CAE, CIMS, computer controlling, and network information technology in the mechanical industry of China is analyzed.

Chapter XVII

As ICT-enabled services such as e-government initiatives diffuse globally, it is becoming clear that some nations are not faring as well as others. Yet, the notion of e-government stands to benefit the sorts of countries that are lagging behind the most. Here, we examine the relationships between economic climates and national cultural factors on the one hand, and e-government readiness on the other. Our results showed significant relationships between nations' economic climates, some cultural dimensions, and e-government readiness. We discussed our findings in the context of three relevant socioeconomic theories. We also highlighted the study's implications for researchers, policy makers, and governments.

Chapter XVIII

Information and communication technologies (ICTs) have become ever more prevalent in the last decade. ICTs profoundly affect both global and national economies. Nevertheless, the common view in the literature is that the development of ICTs has been mostly limited to developed countries and has been relatively slower in the rest of the world. There are many factors affecting the acceptance and use of ICTs in developing countries. Although one of the most appealing research areas in recent years is the technology acceptance of consumers, there is a little evidence that the findings of the majority of the technology acceptance studies carried out in developed countries could be generalized to developing countries. In this study, it is aimed to investigate why Turkish people use the Internet. After summarizing the recent household ICT usage statistics, the most popular online activities offered by the top 100 Turkish Web sites are analyzed

Chapter XIX

The rapid growth of technological advances in recent years has opened a completely new dimension to progress in education and training. The emergence of e-learning has created not only business and educational opportunities, but also significantly improved the standard of the society. This chapter explores the implementation of e-learning and its impact on a community, similar to a university or corporate setup. To this aim, a brief introduction into e-learning technology and an example of using the Blackboard Learning System are brought forth, along with some critical success factors. Projecting the e-learning advantages along with the digital library concepts, the economic benefits of such implementation are highlighted. The discussion then moves to the perspective of students and teachers on e-learning. As the trend in the technological world is moving toward mobility, the wireless e-learning perception is also conferred. In the concluding remarks, e-learning implementation is noted as a positive endeavor to boost economic growth.

Chapter XX

This chapter discusses the importance of increasing the number of women who are active in science-related fields, especially in science and technology, because of the microlevel profit that will be derived by individual women and the macrolevel benefit stemming from the effective use of human resources in society. Furthermore, it considers whether women's colleges could play a key role in training and educating capable women in these fields. The chapter also stipulates the significance of women's colleges and their entry into science-related fields and investigates the educational practices adopted by such colleges. The conclusion drawn from the discussion is that it is essential for women's colleges that have entered into these fields to ensure that the significance of their existence is recognized, that their educational practices are based on this recognition, and that such a coherent and meaningful practice will enable these colleges to produce capable women who will play an active role in and contribute to society.

Chapter XXI

This chapter discusses the potential challenges and benefits of information technology and economic development in Sri Lanka by reviewing the awareness and readiness of the selected opportunities. This chapter also identifies the enabling factors and bottlenecks, and forecasts the future growth of ICT developments in Sri Lanka as a host in Asia. Furthermore, developing ICT, professional services, and offshoring opportunities should be a high priority for the development strategy of the country. This chapter presents the findings from the survey that assessed the potential for ICT in Sri Lanka. Sri Lanka is an island state of contrasts in terms of its economic development and ICT capability. Research on a Web survey of government institutes revealed that 30% of ministries in the country do not have Web sites or may not have Web access since they are inactive. 38% of the ministries are still in the infant stage, and information available on Web pages is often little in content and limited to a few pages. Only about 17% of ministries offer interactive Web content, where users have access to regularly updated information, can communicate through e-mail, and can download government documents through the Internet. 15% of the ministries provide some online services to the citizens. Public- and private-sector economic entities do not develop Web sites in the local language; all Web sites are in English even though 80% of the population depend on their own local language. The majority in Sri Lanka do not speak English.

This paper examines the influence of socioeconomic factors on the employment, payroll, and number of enterprises of three technology sectors for counties in California. Based on correlation and regression analyses, the results reveal that factors that are important correlates of technology sectors are professional/ scientific/technical services, other services, and educational services, ethnicity, and college education. As a whole, the findings emphasize the importance of the association of socioeconomic factors with the per capita magnitude of the technology sectors. The paper suggests steps that can be taken by the state of California and its county and local governments to foster technology and reduce the digital divide.

Over recent years, the circumstances surrounding regional cultural assets have been significantly changed. A series of IT promotion projects implemented by the national government since the early 2000s have intensified regional initiatives in managing digital content of cultural assets. Behind this, there has been a growing expectation toward regional development through wide dissemination and proactive use of cultural information resources. In reality, though, many challenges still remain to become a driving force of regional economy. This means, in practice, a more strategic approach should be taken in the management of human, financial, and information resources. Using Kamakura as a case study, we present an integrated model that develops the underlying value of cultural assets into regional economic strength.

Foreword

Most countries achieved annual growth at a rate of more than 10% during the 1950s and 1960s. Recent advances in developing countries have also been remarkable. Information technology has played a large role in economic development in many fields. The trend toward growth and advancement, however, has not been accelerated in one area. Although the pace of growth is still high compared to that of other fields and industries, improvement in people's standards of living lately has been slowing down in most countries. We cannot say that the advancement of IT has brought with it great profits and high utilization as once expected despite the large potential for economic growth using IT. Obstacles in the attainment of such growth have slowed our progress. What should we do? How should IT change to contribute to economic development? What policies should the authorities implement? Little research has been conducted in this field. The 23 chapters from many countries in this book tackle this issue and provide important ideas and suggestions. We are confident that this book answers readers' demands for information on how to overcome these obstacles so that we can maximize the potential for the contribution of IT to worldwide economic growth and well-being.

April 2007
Editors: Yutaka Kurihara, Aichi University, Japan
Sadayoshi Takaya, Kansai University, Japan
Hisashi Harui, Kwansei Gakuin University, Japan
Hiroshi Kamae, Hitotsubashi University, Japan

Preface

INFORMATION TECHNOLOGY AND ECONOMIC DEVELOPMENT: WHERE DO WE STAND?

The world economy experienced dramatic growth following World War II. In Asia, that growth was delayed, and recent development has been spectacular. Central and Eastern European countries have achieved high economic growth and have attracted much attention. Some people foretell of the coming of the "Asian era." Growth rates have been quite high in some countries. Not only newly industrialized economies (NIEs) countries but also those in Association of Southeast Asian Nations (ASEAN) are experiencing remarkable growth, as did Latin American countries in the 1990s. Many African countries also embraced economic growth starting in the mid-1990s. Among the diverse reasons for this growth are the stable and sound social systems that contributed to the development. However, we must note that information technology (IT) or information and communication technology (ICT) has played a significant role in many fields. IT and its use have created major changes and new opportunities. IT, including the Internet, has enormous potential to enrich the lives of people (OECD, 2002). These technologies contribute to the development of business opportunities and distribute information, education, and ideas around the world rather easily. IT also helps in terms of increasing efficiency and speed in the workplace and in the home.

However, IT can be used more effectively to accelerate economic development. For many countries, especially many developing countries, the potential of IT to enhance economic development has not been fully tapped. Although many studies have attempted to analyze the underlying problems, they have yet to be fully examined.

Research have been conducted in very limited or isolated areas. Broader research should be undertaken to examine underlying problems from diverse and broad perspectives. The linkage among IT-related fields we propose as a necessary target of research. There is a strong need for investigating how various aspects of IT influence economic development. This book provides a broader, more comprehensive perspective than existing works in the examination of the relationship between IT and economic development.

The relationship between economic development and IT merits attention in many cases and fields. Some countries have ample natural resources whereas others are limited. Knowledge and wisdom are the key resources of a bright economic future. IT, an area that relies little on natural resources and heavily on brain funds of wisdom and intellectual resources, occupies a central position in the constellation of factors and activities that contribute to economic development. On the other hand, remarkable economic growth has broadened the gap between the rich and the poor. IT can reduce this divide. However, it is important to consider how IT can be converted into useful knowledge.

A well-known theory, the theory of comparative advantage, is relevant to the field of international economics. In an age of global economics, IT is an important determinant of competitiveness and growth of both industries and countries. The role of traditional sources of comparative advantage in determining international competitiveness decreases as it is replaced by access to IT and knowledge.

Unfortunately, in many countries IT is still under-developed, but there is much room for further growth (IMF, 2001). The benefits of IT for developing countries seem less clear-cut. In our editors' field of monetary economics, we cannot forget the 1997 economic crisis in Asia. Some countries' currencies suffered large fluctuation, producing economic and political instability. The contagion of the currency crisis to other countries was also serious. In the past, similar phenomena had occurred in Latin American countries. Enhancements of efficiency and speed engendered by IT development have greatly increase the volume of fund transfers. Instability of financial and economic conditions, along with the development of financial engineering, has created a crisis. Beyond such financial phenomena, has IT brought wealth to developing countries? In its early stages, IT seemed to improve efficiency and competitiveness and promised a better life for people.

From the view of policy authorities, attempts to improve the delivery of IT should stress the importance of successful transition to well-regulated and competitive service provision to attract needed investment (World Bank, 2006). Promoting the spread of the Internet, for example, is insufficient. Many problems must be solved and obstacles overcome in developing countries for further enhancement of the contribution of IT to society.

What are the reasons behind this lack of development? Where do we stand? Where should we go? The book addresses these issues and future options for growth that are not limited to economics nor to the cases of developing economies. We examine IT impact on various fields, such as politics, education, sociology, technology. The complexities of national and international trade and finance render it impossible to detail this theme fully in a limited volume; our intent, therefore is to contribute to the analysis as much as possible.

Scholars in diverse fields (economics, IT, business/marketing), policy makers, and business persons with both domestic and international interests are the target audience for the book. We believe that this book will satisfy all readers.

Finally, we would like to introduce the content of this book. This book is divided into four sections as described below:

Section I: *Towards Sustainable and Permanent Economic Growth*. The world economy, including that in developing countries, still has much potential for growth. Attaining growth and maintaining it using IT has some important key points. On the other hand, IT has shifted the structure of economy. Globalization is ongoing. We find solutions in IT for sustainable and permanent economic growth from various aspects. This part considers future directions toward growth.

Section II: *Domestic and Global Markets in the IT Age*. IT has also affected market structure. Sound, active markets produce growth. IT has changed market and business activities and still has important prospects for future development. This part focuses on various markets and analyzes not only commodity markets but also service markets, including financial and stock markets.

Section III: *Innovative Engineering in IT*. IT development has been ongoing in various fields. Without it, economic development would be impossible. Also, economic growth will be engineered by knowledge using IT. This part also discusses environmental issues, which are serious all over the world; introduces recent innovations in IT; and analyzes how to encourage economic development using IT effectively and adequately.

Section IV: *Socioeconomic Development in the IT Age*. This critical aspect of economic development has not been fully analyzed. Recent advances in IT are becoming central to the process of socioeconomic development. IT provides efficient means of using human capabilities and institutional facilities of countries in both private and public sectors. The contribution of IT is not confined to economic, business, and technology fields. The world is rapidly moving toward knowledge-based social and economic structures. This section also examines e-learning.

Our editors collected 23 interesting, high quality articles from widely published and respected authors who have contributed greatly in their respective fields. Each article constitutes a chapter in this book and is described below.

Section I: *Towards Sustainable and Permanent Economic Growth*

Chapter I: *The Evolution of ICT, Economic Development, and the Digitally-Divided Society*. This chapter focuses on the digital divide effects on economic development and social dynamics. Continuing worldwide evolution of Information and Communication Technology since the 1990s may achieve broad convenience for people, but also may contributed to the economic divide between those with digital devices and those without them. New technology such as ICT has two phases in developing economies: inducing new demands and reducing disparity in and between countries. The author constructs a dynamic model that describes the dynamics of the digital divide and economic developments.

Chapter II: *Information Technology and Economic Development in Development Countries*. Rapid changes and globalization force countries to change their economic structures and the way their developments work. Although the wave of IT based on the economic developments of developed countries seems to be leaping to underdeveloped and developing countries and triggering global competition, there are some concerns. Although IT-based economic development takes place in developed countries in a modern and knowledge-based manner, the same situation does not occur in underdeveloped and developing countries. This chapter considers how to improve economic welfare in all countries.

Chapter III: *IT Promotion Policies for Economic Development: The Case of Malaysia*. This chapter investigates IT promotion policies for economic development and analyzes outcomes of those policies in Malaysia. This case study provides developing countries with some potentially useful lessons. The author attempts to draw policy suggestions for developing countries to encourage their economic development by showing how Malaysia has promoted an IT-based economy and discussing whether IT has been beneficial to the Malaysian economy.

Chapter IV: *Information and Communication Technology and Economic Development in Malaysia*. Policy-makers are concerned about many issues with respect to the ICT industry in Malaysia. There is some possibility that over-emphasis on the ICT sector, particularly by government and the market, has increased unemployment. This chapter discusses to what extent the ICT sector has contributed to economic development in Malaysia.

Chapter V: *Macroeconomic Announcements, Asymmetric Volatility, and IT: Evidence from JGB Futures*. This chapter analyzes the impact of macroeconomic announcements on the conditional volatility of JGB futures returns. As IT continues to develop, the arrival and processing of new market-related information becomes increasingly rapid and its impact expands. Using high-frequency data for JGB futures, the chapter points to the influence of announcement shocks on the dynamics of bond market volatility and provides empirical evidence that the JGB futures market does not immediately incorporate implications of macroeconomic announcement news. The volatility of JGB futures returns persists for a while. Moreover, after distinguishing among types of shocks, volatility is asymmetric. Negative shocks have a stronger impact on subsequent volatility than do positive shocks.

Chapter VI: *The Macroeconomic Benefits of Intelligent Enterprises*. Information technologies, including e-commerce and the Internet, have brought fundamental changes to 21st century businesses by making more and better information available quickly and inexpensively. This chapter analyzes the macroeconomic benefits that intelligent enterprises can have on the U.S. economy. They find that the U.S. economy has become less volatile, with demand volatility nearly matching sales volatility, particularly in the durable goods sector. The evidence also suggests that firms are utilizing new information technologies to lower inventory levels relative to sales, leading to higher productivity growth, lower prices, and more competitive markets.

Section II: *Domestic and Global Markets in the IT Age*

Chapter VII: *International Reserves Accumulation: Some Lessons from Asia.* The chapter examines the implications of the reserve accumulation process in Asia. Current account deficits in major industrial countries have supported third-country reserve accumulation as these countries have promoted export-led growth underpinned by competitive exchange rates. Asian economies have been willing to absorb the cost of reserve accumulation to maintain favorable exchange rate levels. This strategy has increased the likelihood that protectionist measures may surface from abroad, which may have substantial economic costs. These dynamics are likely to transition to a generalized, real appreciation of the major Asian currencies and efforts to reduce the U.S. fiscal deficit over the longer term. Under this condition, this chapter examines suitable macroeconomic policies for development.

Chapter VIII: *IT and Thai Stock Market Development.* This chapter describes the development of the stock market in Thailand. For more than thirty years, the Thai stock market has introduced computer systems to facilitate investors and listed companies both in financial data and administrative work. In particularly, the Internet trading system has been introduced to enhance market growth. This can be traced to the increasing volume of trade each day. The growth of Thai stock market has changed the structure of that nation's economy and has affected its economic development.

Chapter IX: *Key Drivers of Internet Banking Adoption: The Case of Spanish Internet Users.* New technologies encourage the use and development of new shopping methods, such as online and mobile shopping, which favor economic growth and provide companies and consumers with additional benefits with respect to traditional shopping channels. In the world of banking, developments in IT have led to significant improvements. This chapter offers an insight into online banking in Spain. Distinct differences and common trends between Spain and other countries are observed with clear indications of marketing strategies deployed by service providers.

Chapter X: *E-Commerce Contribution to Economic Growth: The Case of Thailand.* This chapter analyzes the role of e-commerce in economic development in developing economies, particularly Thailand. The author considers the linkage between e-commerce and economic development to provide a framework for the study and conducts an empirical investigation of the contribution of e-commerce to economic development in Thailand using a combination of quantitative and qualitative analysis framework.

Chapter XI: *IT and Software Industry in Vietnam.* Recently in Vietnam's IT industry, so called "offshore development," such as performing software development of Japanese companies abroad, has attracted much attention. Japanese companies are also becoming interested in Vietnam as an IT base for software that ranks next to China and India. IT development in Vietnam has been ongoing. This chapter focuses on the cases of Japan and Vietnam and considers their problems.

Section III: *Innovative Engineering in IT*

Chapter XII: *The Influence of New Information and Communication Technologies on Transaction Costs of Micro-, Small- and, Medium-Sized Enterprises.* Microenterprises are more significant in number than small, medium, and large enterprises (SMEs) in Indonesia. On the other hand, IT is the one solution alternative for SMEs in Indonesia, including microfinance. This chapter presents a lesson learned regarding microfinance management from some developed countries that have achieved relative success in microfinance empowerment. The authors focus on the organization model for microfinance, including benefits of IT, and analyzes the prototype model of the Internet in microfinance management in Indonesia.

Chapter XIII: *Information Technology Industry Development and the Knowledge Economy.* Knowledge has become a third major factor of production, in addition to the traditional factors—labor and capital. Many countries around the world are looking for ways to promote the development of the knowledge economy, and information technology industries in particular. This chapter provides an in-depth analysis of the IT industry in four countries over a five-year period: Finland, Israel, New Zealand and Singapore. Their study reveals that four of the five endogenous variables studied have a close relationship to the development of IT industries in small developed countries. These variables are research and development, technological infrastructure, firm strategies, and capital availability.

Chapter XIV: *Information Technology and Environment.* Although our economy and our society are being built on decentralized information networks of interaction powered by the Internet and IT, the spatial pattern of human settlement is characterized by an unprecedented territorial concentration of population and activities. The largest metropolitan settlements in the world are certainly already in the so-called developing world and this will be increasingly the case. More than half of the projected population growth of China, a developing nation, will take place in cities. This chapter employs mathematic models to simulate the environment change. Using IT is important to solving the problems associated with this new phenomenon.

Section IV: *Socioeconomic Development in the IT Age*

Chapter XV: *International Institute for Knowledge Management.* The primary function of formal education has always been to induct the young people into the culture of the community, society, or nation. Life educates and education in life is correct in general, but, when a formal system of education is organized, society selects from all of those cultural experiences to which the child is exposed those aspects of its culture regarded as most valuable for their own coherence and survival. This chapter illustrates this concept and provides economic and other views that are important factors for development.

Chapter XVI: *Application of Computer Technology in Mechanical Industry of China.* With the constant development and constant completion of function, and its rapid popularization in the world, the impact of computer technology on China's mechanical industry is more and more far-reaching. CAD/CAM/CAE, CIMS, computer controlling and network information play a very important role in the development and promotion of a quality mechanical industry in China. Application of computer technology has made enormous contributions to improving manufacturing at the industry level and economic development in that country. This chapter analyzes the application situation of CAD/CAM/CAE technology, CIMS, computer control and network IT in China's mechanical industry of China.

Chapter XVII: *A Study of the Relationships between Economic Climates, National Culture, and E-Government Readiness: A Global Perspective.* Despite the importance of e-government, little research has been done on the subject. This chapter develops a conceptual model that highlights the influence and impact of the contextual and cultural factors on e-government adoption. The chapter describes the nature of relationships in the authors' conceptual model and theorizes the reasons for the existence variation in different economies. The conclusions are pertinent both to academia and policy-makers.

Chapter XVIII: *Society and World Wide Web in Developing Countries: The Case of Turkey.* Turkey is the site of some interesting characteristics in IT-related industry. This chapter provides a review of the literature on Internet and e-commerce adoption in developing countries and discusses existing infrastructure and demographic details of Turkey. Moreover, to identify the profile of Turkish Internet users, this chapter provides the results of detailed investigations into types of popular Web sites, number of visits, and time spent on the net. Using the findings, the author provides suggestions for strategies to promote electronic commerce.

Chapter XIX: *E-Learning Implementation and Its Diverse Effects.* This chapter investigates how e-learning programs contribute to society by promoting economic growth and analyzes a survey performed at a Malaysian university to explore into the general attitudes toward e-learning and the relation between these attitudes and those toward new technologies. This chapter takes a look at the overall university experience in relation to the e-learning initiative and shows how e-learning systems may foster economic growth.

Chapter XX: *The Significance of the Existence of Women's Colleges and Their Entry into Science-Related Fields.* This chapter reviews discussions on the relationship between mathematical sciences and gender in higher education. The chapter explores the problem of digital divide in terms of gender and provides implications for the economy at both individual and social levels.

Chapter XXI: *Potential Challenges and Benefits of Information Technology and Economic Development in Sri Lanka.* This chapter discusses potential challenges and benefits of implementing e-learning in Sri Lanka by reviewing the awareness and readiness of selected higher educational institutions. Awareness of e-learning among educational institutions is very high, but their investment in developing e-learning applications is poor according to the survey. Most of them use Internet-related e-learning sites just for the sake of it and not for real online learning. There is a trend to create Web sites at most of the institutions. The author considers and suggests an appropriate model for e-learning in Sri Lanka.

Chapter XXII: *Socioeconomic Influence on Information Technology: The Case of California.* This chapter examines the influence of socio-economic factors on the employment, payroll, and number of enterprises of three technology sectors for counties in California. It shows that factors that are important correlates of technology sectors are professional/scientific/technical services, other services, and educational services, ethnicity, and college education. As a whole, the findings emphasize the importance of the association of socio-economic factors with the per capita magnitude of the technology sectors. This chapter suggests steps that can be taken by the state of California and its county and local governments to foster technology and reduce the digital divide.

Chapter XXIII: *Strategies for Cultural Economic Development in Kamakura: Managing Digital Contents and Cultural Assets.* This chapter explores an IT-based approach to managing cultural assets that can lead to local economic growth and examines how cultural assets can be leveraged to boost regional economy as well as how IT can be employed for this purpose. Emphasis is on creating a regional self-aid and support system that involves development of and ensuring high-quality human capital, enhancement and retention of the values of cultural resources, and creation and maintenance of a highly reliable and sustainable networking environment.

REFERENCES

IMF (2001). *World Economic Outlook 2001.*
OECD (2002). *OECD Economic Studies, 34*(1).
World Bank (2006). *Information and Communications for Development 2006.*

Acknowledgment

The editors would like to acknowledge the support of all involved in the collection and review process of this book. Without their diligent support, the project could not have been successfully completed. Not only "blind referees" but also some authors of chapters included in this book served as referees for articles written by other authors. We extend our gratitude to all of those who provided constructive and comprehensive reviews. Especially, we thank Akihiro Amano, Christopher Decker, Nobuyoshi Yamori, Masayuki Susai, Hiroshi Moriyasu, Guofeng Sun, Davis Simon, Miori Mary Motomori, Mary Toner, Glenn Anderson, Takashi Kubota, and Manami Fujishiro.

A special thanks goes to staff members at IGI Global, whose contributions throughout the process, from inception of the initial idea to final publication, have been invaluable. They have contributed much to the completion of this book. In particular, we would like to thank Jan Travers and Meg Stocking, who continuously prodded via e-mail to keep the project on schedule and Mehdi Khosrow-Pour, whose enthusiasm motivated us initially to accept his invitation to take on this project.

Financial support from Postal Life Insurance Foundation of Japan, Zengin Foundation for Studies on Economics and Finance (Japanese Bankers Association), Japan Post Research Institute, Aichi University (C-130), and University of Valencia (UV-AE-06-46) were also appreciated.

Finally, we wish to thank all of the authors for their insights and excellent contributions to this book.

April 2007
Editors: Yutaka Kurihara, Aichi University, Japan
Sadayoshi Takaya, Kansai University, Japan
Hisashi Harui, Kwansei Gakuin University, Japan
Hiroshi Kamae, Hitotsubashi University, Japan

Section I
Towards Sustainable and Permanent Economic Growth

Chapter I
The Evolution of ICT, Economic Development, and the Digitally–Divided Society

Sadayoshi Takaya
Kansai University, Japan

ABSTRACT

In this chapter, we mention that a digital divide could bring about an income divide both within a country and between countries. The more the uses of the Internet diffuse, the more the divide may introduce serious concerns. From a macroeconomic point of view, the increase in the digital divide diminishes ICT investments and delays the innovation of ICT. As a result, we propose that the public policies of each government provide the devices of ICT as social capital and infrastructure. On the global stage, the digital divide exists between developed and developing countries. Therefore, international provision of the digital devices should be achieved through a cooperative effort between developed countries and international organizations.

INTRODUCTION

Currently, the global information society achieves progress by the development of information and communication technology. ICT offers the global society several conveniences, such as communication measures among countries and/or local areas, Web systems for businesses, online trading of securities, and distance learning.

ICT has the characteristics of a general-purpose technology (GPT); that is, it has the two qualities of compatibility and applicable innovation as identified by Helpman and Trajtenberg (1994). A GPT has broad compatibility across many industrial fields, for example, the steam engines of the 18th century. Furthermore, a GPT encourages the creation of new technologies based on its own core technology. Through such move-

Figure 1. Contribution of ICT investment to GDP growth 1990-1995 and 1995-2003. Source: OECD Productivity Database, September 2005 (www.oecd.org/statistics/productivity)

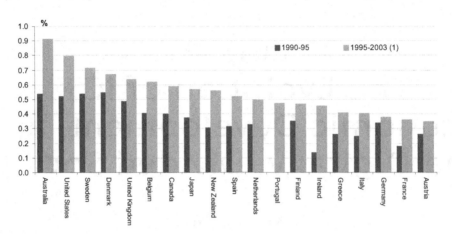

Note: (1) 1995-2002 for Australia, France, Japan, New Zealand, and Spain.

ments, the core technology diffuses across many industries. Presently, in what is known as the IT revolution, ICTs are widely used by citizens, firms, and governments across the world. At the same time, ICTs create applied technologies in many fields. Looking back at this age from the future, one might well regard the ICT as being a GPT.

Figure 1 presents the contributions of ICT investment to gross domestic product (GDP) growth in Organization for Economic Cooperation and Development (OECD) countries during 1990 to 1995 and 1995 to 2003. From this figure, we can observe that ICT could contribute to increasing the growth rate in developed countries. Because ICT investment includes two aspects—increase in demand and technological change in the supply side—this contribution may not stem solely from innovations by ICT. Nevertheless, ICT may be one of the factors in growth engines.

We would like to suggest that there are two perspectives on ICT. One is the perspective of ICT as development infrastructure; the other is that of ICTs as communication measures. From the first perspective, networks provide the production factor and nurture human capital. This perspective is based on the view that ICT is an infrastructure of economic development that is related to the supply side of economies, not the demand side. Developments of ICT provide new information, knowledge, and education to nurture highly qualified human capital. This argument is based on the endogenous growth theory,[1] which suggests that economic growth is driven by the accumulation of knowledge. Since this theory regards knowledge as capital, economic development progresses if the development of ICT contributes to the diffusion and deepening of knowledge.

On the other hand, the perspective of ICTs as communication measures is related to the demand side of the economy. Horrigan (2002) suggests that the notion of social capital is linked to the concept of measures as reducing transactions costs by access to ICT. ICT is, then, proposed to be social capital. The Internet provides facilities of the network of information exchange that can promote businesses and consumptions.

When, however, people use tools innovated by ICT, a burden is imposed on them. Their ability to use the devices, therefore, depends on whether or not they can bear the burden. Furthermore, their ability to use the devices depends on where they reside because regional differences exist with regard to the uses of the devices, such as the Internet. Due to these reasons, the uses of digital devices depend on incomes and areas of residence. As a result, the digital divide, which causes the difference with regard to the uses of digital devices, may become an issue in both the global and local society.

The concept of the digital divide was first used in a 1999 report entitled *Falling through the Net: Defining the Digital Divide* by the Department of Commerce in the United States. This concept includes the difference in the availability of the Internet and/or broadband Internet as well as the disparity of information literacy by region, country, and/or individual.

For our purposes, we use the concept of the digital divide to imply the disparity of information literacy and availability. Furthermore, a person under a digitally divided society faces some challenges in accessing the private and public services supplied through the Internet.[2]

In former studies of economic effect by ICT, Jorgenson and Stiroh (2000) estimated that average labor productivity in the United States grew at 2.4% annually during 1995 to 1998. They concluded that there was little evidence of ICT's effect on production. Gordon (2000) found that ICT led to price-induced substitution and rapid investment in ICT devices. He concluded, therefore, that ICT capital was deepening in the 1990s. Bailey and Lawrence (2001) found empirical evidence for the effect of ICT development on higher productivity in service industries. These empirical works implicate that access to ICT products is important for development, and ICTs also reduce the real costs of ICT equipment to increase the economic welfare of persons who can easily access ICT devices.

Casselli and Coleman (2001) found that computer skill is positively related to the level of human capital. Openness of trade, high rates of investment, and low share of agriculture in GDP had a positive relationship to computer use. Their findings are important because human capital is complementary to computers

On the other hand, there are only a few effects of the digital divide on economic growth or development. Sidorenko and Findlay (2001) discussed the concept of digital divide in a global economic context, related to the economic growth theory and the evolution of technology in East Asia. They suggested that an appropriate policy for bridging the digital divide could bring about considerable gain in East Asia through openness in trading ICT products and through policy cooperation.

Wong (2002) estimated the scope of the economic effect of the divide in East Asia, despite the region having captured a high share of the global production of ICT goods. He found that a significant digital divide exists between the five leading countries in East Asia and the other seven developing countries.

Antonelli (2003) examined the composition effects stemming from the interaction between the direction of technological change and relative factor prices. He also suggested that these effects are necessary in order to understand the economics of new ICT in the global economy because of the significance of the digital divide.

Mariscal (2005) investigated the appropriate policy to address the digital divide. He classified different policy trajectories recommended by the literature on telecommunications development. He investigated the case of a developing country to use it as an analytical framework.

Most of these previous studies are empirical, not theoretical. Our work involves a mathematically theoretical approach through the construction of a simple economic growth model. The purpose of this chapter is to clarify the macroeconomic effects of the digital divide. If the digital divide in a digital economy progresses, the divide may result in a decrease in the aggregate economic demand. If this is the case, the divide should be resolved using political initiatives.

The remainder of this chapter is divided as follows. First, ICT diffusion and division in the global economy is explained. Then we illustrate a static economic model to clarify the macro-economic effects of digital divides. Next, the implementation of public policies is suggested. Finally we conclude the chapter.

ICT DIFFUSION AND DIVISION IN THE GLOBAL ECONOMY

Since the late 1990s, the Internet has come to be widely used, particularly in the industrialized societies. The Internet has provided not only useful services of communication among individuals, but also new business opportunities for many private companies. For instance, a worker who gains ac-

Table 1. Basic data on ICT diffusion. Source: International Telecommunication Union, "The Portable Internet 2004"

	Japan	the United States	United Kingdom	Germany	France	Korea
volume of computer per 100	38.2	65.9	40.6	43.1	34.7	55.8
diffusion rate of internet(%)	48.3	55.1	42.3	53.6	36.6	61
quantity of contracts of broadband(million	1491.7	2715.1	182.1	456	336.1	1117.9

Table 2. Differences in ICT use among country groups. Data source) ITU http://www.itu.int/ITU-D/ict/statistics/index.html. Access August 1 ,2006.

		Internet		PC
		Hosts per million	Users per 100inhab.	Users per 100inhab.
Africa	average	6.56	3.51	3.42
	high	77.52	26.08	36.31
	low	0.01	0.09	0.07
Latin America	average	118.62	17.72	11.72
	high	1837.90	62.90	52.31
	low	0.05	1.32	1.57
North America	average	3878.01	62.68	73.02
	high	6645.16	63.00	76.22
	low	1110.85	62.36	69.82
Middle East	average	66.48	12.41	13.95
	high	789.56	46.63	73.40
	low	0.01	0.14	0.83
Industrial economies in Asia	average	879.96	49.57	47.48
	high	1389.65	65.68	62.20
	low	1.74	32.24	19.16
Developing Asia	average	7.78	3.49	2.60
	high	58.13	11.25	11.86
	low	0.05	0.08	0.26
EU countries	average	760.14	45.62	39.36
	high	3334.42	75.46	76.14
	low	70.50	17.81	8.98
Non- EU Euroepan countries	average	451.94	25.85	18.06
	high	4758.60	77.00	82.33
	low	0.03	0.10	1.17
Oceania countries	average	436.81	17.95	16.56
	high	1978.27	65.28	68.90
	low	1.05	0.61	0.67

cess to a personal computer (PC) and the Internet will find it easy to secure a higher paying job. Moreover, many companies can get opportunities to tackle new businesses in ICT fields.

Table 1 charts the current aspects of ICT diffusion in leading ICT countries. With regard to the number of computers per 100 persons, the United States is the highest, followed by Korea.

However, with regard to the diffusion rate of the Internet, Korea ranks first, with the United States being second. With regard to the number of contracts for broadband Internet, the country with the highest diffusion is the United States with Japan being second. Diffusions of the PC, the Internet, and broadband Internet vary even among the leading countries.

Table 3. Regional ICT indicator of Japan in 2005. Data (source), white paper information and communications in Japan, 2005. Ministry of Internal Affairs & Communications.

	Diffusion rate of Internet 1)	Ratio of volume of broadband contract to total households 2)	Diffusion rate of mobile Internet 3)	Ratio of occupied person in ICT industry 4)
Hokkaido	45.0	17.5	35.9	1.9
Aomori	26.8	16.8	23.5	0.8
Iwate	31.5	17.5	27.9	1.0
Miyagi	43.5	24.7	32.9	2.1
Akita	36.4	19.9	20.7	0.8
Yamagata	44.2	24.2	30.5	1.1
Fukushima	39.0	17.2	36.0	1.0
Ibaragi	44.0	23.9	35.3	1.8
Tochigi	48.8	25.2	43.0	1.2
Gunma	45.1	24.0	37.3	1.7
Saitama	53.6	32.0	43.9	3.6
Chiba	53.6	31.1	41.8	4.4
Tokyo	62.2	37.7	49.8	6.8
Kanagawa	59.7	36.7	44.0	5.5
Yamanashi	43.4	27.2	35.7	1.6
Niigata	53.0	22.3	39.1	1.3
Nagano	43.8	25.6	31.5	1.5
Toyama	30.0	32.8	30.0	1.4
Ishikawa	38.0	26.5	34.0	2.0
Fukui	38.0	33.3	31.5	1.5
Gifu	42.9	24.6	36.3	1.2
Shizuoka	50.9	33.5	33.8	1.6
Aichi	49.5	32.4	40.0	2.0
Mie	50.9	33.3	35.8	1.2
Shiga	49.6	24.1	38.0	1.1
Kyoto	52.7	28.5	40.6	1.8
Osaka	56.6	30.8	41.9	2.7
Hyogo	52.3	28.9	39.5	2.0
Nara	57.5	29.8	48.8	2.3
Wakayama	45.6	20.4	35.9	1.1
Totori	46.8	20.4	37.7	1.0
Simane	48.3	17.4	41.9	1.0
Okayama	50.3	24.4	34.8	1.6
Hiroshima	53.0	21.2	43.1	2.0
Yamaguch	44.8	19.5	36.0	0.8
Tokushima	38.0	21.8	32.0	1.1
Kagawa	71.7	24.3	48.3	1.2
Ehime	42.6	20.5	31.7	1.4
Kochi	41.6	14.3	34.5	1.1
Fukuoka	51.5	22.9	39.1	2.6
Saga	34.7	18.6	32.0	0.9
Nagasaki	36.4	17.7	27.3	0.9
Kumamotc	41.5	25.5	35.9	1.5
Oita	40.7	20.5	31.3	1.1
Miyazaki	43.5	16.9	31.3	1.0
Kaqoshima	31.8	10.4	26.7	0.7
Okinawa	31.3	18.3	22.9	1.8
Average	45.5	24.2	35.8	1.7
variance	9.0	6.2	6.5	1.2

unit: percentage

Furthermore, Table 2 indicates the regional differences in the diffusion of the Internet and PC; it displays the Internet usage indicator by the International Telecommunication Union (ITU). This table indicates the disparity in Internet usage among country groups categorized according to income level. People in low-income countries do not have easy access to PCs, the Internet, and/or broadband. This condition creates a divide between people in the high- and low-income groups with regard to their current income and their potential to earn higher incomes in the future.

For example, the highest average number of hosts for Internet networks is in North America; this is followed by the industrial economies in Asia, including Malaysia, Korea, Hong Kong, Japan, Singapore, and Taiwan. The number of network hosts is an important indicator because the data indicate the degree of ICT as well as the degree of dependence on hosts in the home country that is needed in order to connect to the Internet. In the case of the average number of PC users, North America ranks the highest, followed by the industrial countries in Asia and subsequently by the EU (European Union) countries. The average numbers of Internet hosts and users, and PC users in developing Asian and African countries are very low; this is in conjunction with the fact that the per capita GDP of these countries is also low.

These data imply that the digital divide exists in the global society and it is caused by the disparity in income. Since the infrastructure of the Internet—that is, the hosts and the network of the Internet—and personal computers place an enormous expense on individuals, companies, and even governments, low-income countries are unable to afford the costs and shoulder the burden. For this reason, the diffusion of the Internet in low-income countries is low, which may make it difficult to boost the growth of these economies. If the digital divide exists, it may create an income divide on a global scale.

Table 3 shows the aspects of the digital divide in Japan, which has local differences with regard to the use and the diffusion of the Internet. Although Japan is one of the leading countries in ICT fields, the disparity of the Internet environment exists in this country. From this example, we infer similar conditions in other countries. In developing countries, these conditions may be cause for more serious concern.

In order to clearly highlight the digital divide, we estimated a cross-country relationship between the diffusion of PC use and per capita income in 2004. The sample consists of 160 countries and the method used is the ordinary least squares method. The estimated equation is as follows:

$$\log(PC_i) = c_1 + \alpha_1 \log(GDP2004_i) + u_1, \quad (1)$$

where i country's PC_i denotes PC users per 100 inhabitants, $GDP2004_i$ is i country's per capita GDP in 2004, and u_1 is the error term. Furthermore, we estimated the cross-country relationship between the diffusion of the use of the Internet and per capita GDP. The estimated equation is as follows:

$$\log(Internet_i) = c_2 + \alpha_2 \log(GDP2004_i) + u_2, \quad (2)$$

where $Internet_i$ denotes i country's Internet users per 100 inhabitants and u_2 stands for the error term. Tables 4-1 and 4-2 display the results. The per capita GDP significantly affects the use of the PC and the Internet in 160 countries. Therefore, the higher the income, the greater the diffusion of the PC and the Internet. Such results show that the diffusion of ICT implies the burden of a large amount of expense because people should pay more in order to catch up in using the new digital devices. In addition, we chart the graphs of the relationship between per capita GDP and the diffusion of the PC, as well as between per capita GDP and the diffusion of the Internet. From these figures, we can easily infer that these diffusions are positively correlated with per capita GDP.

However, if the diffusion divide is transitory, the so-called digital divide poses no problem.

Table 4-1. Estimation results of diffusion of the PC

Dependent Variable: LOG(PC)				
Included observations: 160				
Variable	**Coefficient**	**Std. Error**	**t-Statistic**	**Prob.**
C_1	0.7046	0.0716	9.8408	0.0000
α_1	0.9084	0.0361	25.111	0.0000
Adjusted R-squared	0.7984	S.D. dependent var		1.6737
Log likelihood	-180.3214	F-statistic		630.5789
Durbin-Watson stat	1.9086	Prob(F-statistic)		0.000000

Table 4-2. Estimation results of diffusion of the Internet

Dependent Variable: LOG(INTERNET)				
Included observations: 160				
Variable	**Coefficient**	**Std. Error**	**t-Statistic**	**Prob.**
C_2	0.9456	0.0779	12.137	0.0000
α_2	0.8831	0.0400	22.065	0.0000
Adjusted R-squared	0.7275	S.D. dependent var		1.72887
Log likelihood	-239.8867	F-statistic		486.8850
Durbin-Watson stat	1.9749	Prob(F-statistic)		0.000000

For instance, advanced technologies such as ICT have a tendency to be more developed in a few industrial countries. Thereafter, other developed and developing countries obtain those advanced technologies, which subsequently results in high levels of growth in those countries, similar to the leading industrial countries. This is known as the flying-geese pattern of development. If the pattern is applied at the current stage, the digital divide will be merely a transitory problem. Therefore, there is no need for governments or industrial organizations to reach a solution to the divide problem.

Until now, the trend was unclear; however, we estimated the relationship between the diffusion of the PC and the Internet and income disparity from the average value. The estimated equations are as follows:

$$\log(std\_GDP2004_i) = c_3 + \alpha_3 \log(PC_i) + u_3 \tag{3}$$

$$\log(std\_GDP2004_i) = c_4 + \alpha_4 \log(Internet_i) + u_4 \tag{4}$$

where *std_GDP*2004$_i$ denotes i country's deviation of GDP from the average of 160 countries in 2004. Equation (3) suggests that the diffusion of the PC may cause deviation of GDP from the global average value, and equation (4) suggests that the diffusion of the Internet may bring about the deviation. Therefore, coefficients c_3 and c_4 are supposed to be positive.

Table 5-1 presents an estimation result of equation (3). According to Table 5-1, the diffusion of the PC may contribute to the disparity of GDP in the global society. Table 5-2 also presents an estimation result of equation (4). According to

Table 5-2, the diffusion of the Internet may also lead to gaps in GDP.

Since we can easily anticipate the progress of PC and Internet uses, the gaps of GDP may also expand further. However, simple market mechanisms, which remain unaccounted for in the global economy, are not the panacea for the digital divide. Consequently, should the divide be narrowed regardless of the efforts involved? If not, should it be permitted to exist even if it may be serious? Our response is that the divide should be resolved because GDP gaps by the divide may cause a decrease in the aggregate

Table 5-1. Estimation results of Income Divides 1

Dependent Variable: (STD_GDP)				
Included observations: 160				
Variable	**Coefficient**	**Std. Error**	**t-Statistic**	**Prob.**
C_3	-17.963	1.1294	-15.905	0.0000
α_3	5.8156	0.4776	12.176	0.0000
Adjusted R-squared	0.4746	S.D. dependent var		14.0134
Log likelihood	-611.8865	F-statistic		148.2445
Durbin-Watson stat	1.9673	Prob(F-statistic)		0.000000

Table 5-2. Estimation results of Income Divides 2

Dependent Variable: (STD_GDP)				
Included observations: 160				
Variable	**Coefficient**	**Std. Error**	**t-Statistic**	**Prob.**
C_4	-21.084	1.8064	-11.672	0.0000
α_4	6.5234	0.6371	10.239	0.0000
Adjusted R-squared	0.5352	S.D. dependent var		15.2848
Log likelihood	-702.6269	F-statistic		215.1598
Durbin-Watson stat	1.9484	Prob(F-statistic)		0.000000

demands in the global economy. Because ICT has the distinct feature of progressing rapidly, some persons, companies, or countries will be unable to keep pace with the progress pertaining to the usage and the developments. As a result, the rapid progress may bring about an impoverishment in the case of a majority of people or countries. If this scenario actualizes, the global economy will shrink. The next section illustrates this scenario more clearly using a simple static model.

THEORETICAL MODEL

In this section, we theoretically examine the effects of ICT diffusion and divisions on economic development as this chapter represents effects of economic activity by evolution of technology because there could be a positive relationship between technological developments and economic progress. For the purpose of the investigation, we construct a simple static economic model.

Our model is composed of the demand and supply sides. The demand side consists of two strata: well-trained persons who easily access ICT, and less-trained persons who rarely access ICT.

$$m + n = 1 \qquad (5)$$

In equation (5), m denotes the population of less-trained persons and n that of well-trained persons. The total population is assumed to be fixed as one. The population of well-trained persons is assumed to be a decreasing function of technology. The development of technology leads users to obtain advanced training for new digital devices and computer applications, and higher information literacy. Consequently, in accordance with the development of technology, well-trained persons n are assumed to decrease:

$$n = \theta(T), \qquad (6)$$

$$\theta_T' < 0, \; \theta_{TT}' < 0$$

where T is the accumulation of technology. Aggregate demand D is the sum of the incomes of less-trained and well-trained persons.

$$D = mY_m + nY_n \qquad (7)$$

In equation (7), Y_m denotes the income of less-trained persons and Y_n that of well-trained persons. Furthermore, both incomes depend on the accumulation of technology as follows:

$$Y_m = \alpha_m T - l_m T^2 \qquad (8)$$

and

$$Y_n = \alpha_n T - l_n T^2. \qquad (9)$$

Equation (8) represents the income function of less-trained persons, which is a positive coefficient function α_m of T and a negative square function with coefficient l_n. The former term represents the contribution of T to income. In other words, α_m is the income multiplier of technology. The latter term denotes the marginal cost of training or education, which we assume to be the square function of T.

Equation (9) is the income function of well-trained persons, whose components are similar to those in equation (8), with the exception of the coefficient. In addition, we assume the magnitude of coefficient α_m, α_n as follows:

$$\alpha_n > \alpha_m. \qquad (10)$$

Equation (10) implies that the contribution of T to well-trained persons' income is higher than that of the less-trained persons. Since a well-trained person can achieve a higher income, he or she has an incentive to obtain training for ICT by paying its marginal cost.

We do not assume the magnitude of marginal cost,

$$l_n - l_m \sim 0.$$

Here, we show effects of technology on aggregate demand as follows, see equations (11) and (12).

Next, we present the supply side of our model. A representative firm infinitely maximizes its profit by investment, subject to technology innovation dynamics; that is:

$$Max \ \pi \qquad (13)$$

$$\text{s.t. } \pi = D - \frac{cI^2}{2} \qquad (14)$$

Here, π denotes the profit function in equation (13). The profit function is defined in equation (14), in which the second term represents the adjustment function of investment, which is supposed to be a quadratic form function. In addition, we assume the innovation function caused by investments I as follows:

$$T = \beta I. \qquad (15)$$

Equation (15) indicates that increases of private investments induce developments in information and communication technology; therefore, it is assumed that $\beta > 0$.

From equations (13), (14), and (15), we can easily obtain the FOC as follows:

$$\frac{\partial \pi}{\partial I} = D_T \beta - cI = 0. \qquad (16)$$

We can rewrite equation (16) as the following:

$$I^* = \frac{\beta}{c} D_T, \qquad (17)$$

where the asterisk denotes the equilibrium value. By using equation (17), we can obtain equilibrium technology and equilibrium aggregate demand as follows:

$$T^* = \frac{\beta^2}{c} D_T \qquad (18)$$

and

$$D^* = \left[m\left(\alpha_m - \frac{l_m \beta^2}{c} D_T \right) + n\left(\alpha_n - \frac{l_n \beta^2}{c} D_T \right) \right] \frac{\beta^2}{c} D_T \qquad (19)$$

From the above equations, the equilibrium investments, equilibrium technology, and equilibrium aggregate demand depend on the marginal demand of change of technology. If D_T is zero, due to an enlargement of the disparity between less-trained and well-trained persons, the development of technology is zero; therefore, the aggregate demand is also zero.

Equation 11.

$$\frac{\partial D}{\partial T} = n(\alpha_n - \alpha_m) + \alpha_m - \left\{ (1-n)l_m + nl_n \right\} T + \theta'_T \left\{ (\alpha_n - \alpha_m)T - (l_n - l_m) \right\} \equiv D_T \geq 0$$

Equation 12.

$$\frac{\partial^2 D}{\partial T^2} = -\left\{ (1-n)l_m + nl_n \right\} + \theta'_T (\alpha_n - \alpha_m) + \theta''_{TT} \left\{ (\alpha_n - \alpha_m)T - (l_n - l_m) \right\} \equiv D_{TT} \sim 0$$

The implications of our economic model are that the regional digital divide causes decreases of aggregate demands in the domestic dimension, and the international digital divide causes decreases of global demands in the international dimension. If ICT develops further, it is possible to diminish local and global demands, which in turn would bring about stagnancy to ICT innovation itself.

IMPLICATIONS FOR GLOBAL ECONOMY AND DOMESTIC SOCIAL DYNAMICS

In the previous sections, we mentioned that the digital divide exists in the global economy, and it may induce a blockage in the development of technologies. Consequently, in this chapter, we argue for a policy analysis that would address this digital divide. From the perspective of the market economy, the digital divide is resolved through market mechanisms. That is to say, the market forces should drive the deployment of ICT. A competitive force will encourage technological innovation, and the prices of information and communication will decrease for many people (Moschella & Atkinson, 1998). Therefore, public policy should be used to promote competition in the fields of Internet and communication, for example, in order to promote universal access services and to liberalize the regulations of the Internet and communications. Active competition causes redistribution between digitally divided people.

However, ICT is a GPT whose versatility is considerably high among many industries. This technology has externality in economies. From the perspective of economic theory, the market mechanism does not function effectively to bring about sufficient redistribution. Furthermore, the externality of ICT has two aspects, namely, economic developments and communication measures. The former indicates that ICT contributes directly to economic development by the creation of new businesses and a decrease of transaction costs. The latter indicates that ICT promotes individual and corporate communications at less cost to promote economic growth. With regard to the former aspect, ICT is the infrastructure for development. On the other hand, with regard to the latter aspect, ICT is a social capital for communication.

From the perspective of ICT as infrastructure for development, public policies promote ICT by, for example, supporting the consumption of information and communication services, and/or investing in ICT infrastructure such as LAN (local area network) and public access points. From this perspective, public policies are needed to promote the growth of the entire spectrum of ICT networks, equipment, and infrastructure.

On the other hand, the perspective of ICT as communication measures and social capital is related to the demand side of the economy. From this perspective, public policies must provide the networks in order to activate communication in the community.[3] These promote the consumption of digital devices such as mobile phones and PCs, and create investments in digital equipment for offices and factories, such as LANs, mobile PCs, and online systems of orders via the Internet. ICT as social capital, therefore, contributes to economic growth through the enlargement of aggregate demands.

Although the supply side is an important factor for growth in the long run, the demand side is a crucial factor for economic stability in the short run. Both sides interact in each time definitively. Public policies should promote the diffusion of communication methods of ICT in order to provide easy access to them by many users, regardless of their income and/or regional differences. Thus, not only will each government cope with digital divides as a local problem, but international cooperation by the governments and international organizations will also tackle digital divides as a global problem. All governments can support the public provision of information and communication infrastructures by their respective public budgets. While cooperating internationally, developed countries should act as leaders to finance the ICT infrastructures in developing countries in order to bridge the gap in the uses of digital devices. These policies may improve digital circumstances not only in developing countries, but also in developed countries through a global increase in the demand for digital devices.[4]

CONCLUSION

In this chapter, we stated that a digital divide could cause an income divide within a country and between countries. The more the uses of the Internet diffuse, the more serious concerns the divide may introduce. From a macroeconomic point of view, the increase in the digital divide diminishes ICT investments and delays the innovation of ICT. As a result, we propose that the public policies of each government provide the devices of ICT as social capital and infrastructure. On the global stage, the digital divide exists between developed and developing countries. Therefore, international provision of the digital devices must be achieved through a cooperative effort between developed countries and international organizations.

REFERENCES

Antonelli, C. (2003). The digital divide: Understanding the economics of new information and communication technology in the global economy. *Information Economics and Policy, 15*, 173-199.

Bailey, M. H., & Lawrence, R. Z. (2001). Do we have a new economy? *American Economic Review, 91*, 308-312.

Collier, P. (1998). *Social capital and poverty: Social capital initiative* (Working paper No. 4). Washington, DC: The World Bank.

Gordon, R. J. (2000). Does the "new economy" measure up to the great inventions of the past? *Journal of Economic Perspectives, 14*, 49-74.

Helpman, E., & Trajtenberg, M. (1994). *A time to sow and a time to reap: Growth based on general purpose technologies* (NBER Working Paper Series No. 4854).

Horrigan, J. (2002). Online communities: Networks that nurture long-distance relationships and local ties. *Pew Internet and American Life Project.* Retrieved September 1, 2006, from http://207.21.232.103/pdfs/PIP_Communities_Report.pdf

Jorgenson, D. W., & Stiroh, K. J. (2000). Raising the speed limit: US economic growth in the information age. *Brookings Papers on Economic Activity, 1*, 125-235.

Mariscal, J. (2005). Digital divide in a developing country. *Telecommunications Policy, 29*, 409-428.

Moschella, D., & Atkinson, R. D. (1998). *The Internet and society: Universal access, not universal service.* Washington, DC: Progressive Policy Institute.

Romer, P. (1986). Increasing returns and long run growth. *Journal of Political Economy, 94*, 1002-1037.

Sidorenko, A., & Findlay, C. (2001). The digital divide in East Asia. *Asia-Pacific Economic Literature, 15*, 18-30.

Wong, P. K. (2002). ICT production and diffusion in Asia: Digital dividends or digital divide? *Information Economics and Policy, 14*, 167-187.

ADDITIONAL READING

Helpman, E. (Ed.). (1998). *General purpose technologies and economic growth.* Cambridge, MA: MIT Press.

Katz, M., & Shapiro, C. (1985). Network externalities, competition, and compatibility. *American Economic Review, 75*, 424-440.

Lenhart, A., & Horrigan, J. B. (2003). Re-visualizing the digital divide as a digital spectrum. *IT & Society, 1*, 23-39.

Liu, M.-c., & San, G. (2006). Social learning and digital divides: A case study of Internet technology diffusion. *Kyklos, 59*(2), 307-321.

Quibria, M. G., Ahmed, S. N., Tschang, T., & Reyes-Macasaquit, M. L. (2003). Digital divide: Determinants and policies with special reference to Asia. *Journal of Asian Economics, 13*, 811-825.

Robinson, J. P., Dimaggio, P., & Hargittai, E. (2003). New social survey perspectives on the digital divide. *IT & Society, 1*, 1-22.

Shapiro, C., & Varian, H. R. (1999). *Information rules: A strategic guide to the network economy.* Boston: Harvard Business School Press.

ENDNOTES

1   This theory was mainly proposed by Romer (1986).

2   The divide includes two phases: an international divide between developed and developing countries, and a domestic phase where the divide exists between highly diffused areas and lesser ones. As we discuss, our investigation sheds light on these phases through the simple economic model.

3   Collier (1998) conducted an empirical study on telephone networks that would activate the requisite social interaction in the community.

4   This was pointed out in our model.

Chapter II
Information Technology and Economic Development in Developing Countries

Muhammed Karatas
Mugla University, Turkey

Selahattin Bekmez
Mugla University, Turkey

ABSTRACT

Within the last decades, there was a very high level of increase in information technology production. This production successfully speeds up technological changes in only developed countries. Such a situation results in the use of existing knowledge as input in the production of new knowledge in a monopoly of developed countries. Developing countries are, however, still struggling with their own sociopolitical and/or socioeconomic problems. This process creates a bigger technological gap between developed and developing countries. One of the reasons for this is a lack of physical and human capital in developing countries. This is a common problem in the world and necessary precautions should be taken in a timely manner. This study discusses the problematic issues of information technology creation in both developed and developing countries and suggests some solutions.

You may not swim two times in the same river, because every time you go into that river, there will be a different flow of water passing over you. Today's world is different than yesterday's world; and tomorrow's world will be different than that of today as well.

Heracleitus

INTRODUCTION

There are some changes occurring in the 21st century, particularly in the circle that information technologies incorporate, with economic developments in fast pace. As a matter of fact, the concept of change is not novel but is a process that has existed since the beginning of the world. The real difference between the past and the present is the dimension and the speed of change. For instance, it is a well-known fact that the amount of knowledge that has been produced in the last 20 years is twice the knowledge produced since the early years of the world. Indeed, it is also known that 85% of the scholars on earth are living at present. Thus, the revolutionary developments in knowledge production, its storage, its distribution, and its conversion are the determinants of the era. It worths mentioning here that, while we are analyzing the problem of underdevelopment, we use the terms *knowledge* and *information* in an exchangeable manner, although there are some nuances between them.

Rapid changes and globalization force countries to change their economic structures and the way their developments work. Although the wave of IT-based economic developments of developed countries seems to be leaping to underdeveloped and developing countries to trigger global competition, there are still some concerns. Although IT-based economic development takes place in developed countries in a modern and knowledge-based manner, the same situation does not really happen in underdeveloped and developing countries. Indeed, one can state that the globalization arguments of developed countries with a high level of economic development performance cause pressure on underdeveloped and developing countries, especially in commercial, political, and cultural areas. In this sense, it cannot be accepted ethical and rational to state that globalization increases worldwide competition and improves economic welfare in all countries in order to make national businesses vulnerable and defenseless.

The tremendous increase of knowledge production successfully speeds up technological changes in only developed countries. Such a situation results in the use of existing knowledge as input in the production of new knowledge in a monopoly of developed countries. The concepts of globalization, hence, presently negatively affect

and will remain harmfully affecting underdeveloped and developing countries as they have done in the past.

In the light of aforementioned discussions, the relationship between economic development and information technology will be thoroughly analyzed in this study. The discussions will focus on the following:

- The problems that underdeveloped and developing countries confront due to change and globalization.
- Technology production and transition to a knowledge economy in economic development.
- The differences that economic development causes in underdeveloped and developing countries.
- The utilization of information technologies in economic development.
- Economic development and IT-related regional development policies of developing countries.
- Industrialization policies in underdeveloped and developing countries.
- The importance of human capital for economic development.

The discussions of this study will concentrate on the crucial role of information technology in the economic development of countries, and the relationship between economic development and technological innovations.

PROBLEMS DEVELOPING COUNTRIES FACE AND TERMINOLOGY OF UNDERDEVELOPMENT

Before beginning a formal and detailed analysis, it is worthwhile giving some characteristics of developing countries; they all have the following:

- Lower income levels
- Poverty
- Unbalanced distribution of income
- High population growth
- Problems in industrial sectors
- Low education levels
- Insufficient health services

Other common factors that result in problems in developing countries can be analyzed under three main titles.

Economic Factors
- No economic development strategy
- Sectoral and regional distribution of investment unbalanced
- Geographical restrictions on production
- Sectoral structure of the economy
- Unemployment

Political Factors
- Political structure of the country
- Restrictions on the quality of organizations
- Political preferences of the electorate (if any)

Sociocultural Factors
- Education level
- Unequal opportunities for different regions or groups
- Traditions and customs

In summary, one can say that, in developing countries, both the reasons of poverty and the magnitudes that affect poverty are interconnected. Thus, long-term policy applications should be adopted in order to create sustainable development in these countries. Some of the basic necessities for these countries can be stated as follows:

- The quality of labor should be increased.
- Physical capital should be increased.

- Natural resources should be efficiently used.
- Entrepreneurially talented people should be encouraged.
- Technological progress should be adopted.

These are very important factors for developing countries to face the developing world. These factors should come together in order for a developing country to have harmonized development. Also, information technology and its related derivatives should be formed accordingly.

INFORMATION ACCUMULATION AS A STIMULANT FACTOR FOR ECONOMIC DEVELOPMENT

We have to make a very good analysis of the term *change* in order to grasp a better understanding of the problems that developing countries are facing today. Especially when talking about IT-development-related issues, it is very important that the term *change* and its components are defined and analyzed very seriously. There are two kinds of change that we may discuss here: a positive change that is called economic development, and a negative change that is called economic crisis.

Heracleitus claims that everything is in the process of changing, which is why it is impossible to analyze the objectivity of the world itself. In order for us to analyze the objectivity of an entity, that entity must keep its own structure as is. This is not the case for the real world, however. Thus, one must be very cautious about analyzing the existing world for different time periods. Some other philosophers and writers used different terms interchangeably to describe the changing world, such as the following:

- Growth
- Innovation
- Development

- Modernization
- Technology

Before we proceed further, it is worthwhile giving very short definitions and economic meanings of the concepts above.

Growth refers to an increase in production and per capita income. Innovation refers to a new way of organizing an entity so that it produces better solutions for the needs of the community. Development refers to a planned behaviour affecting the quality of life. In other words, in order for us to talk about the development concept, both an increase in income and also a better distribution of income must be obtained. In addition to this, it also includes a more efficient use of factors such as capital and labor. Modernization refers to a mental change as well as a change in tools and equipment used in the production process. The last term, technology, refers to the knowledge and information produced to increase the effectiveness or productivity of inputs. In other words, it is a mental effort that creates an increase in the input-output ratio.

All these terms imply direction, an ideal, and a value in the interpretation of them. In other words, they all show ripeness and maturity so that people may form a connected bridge when they are analyzing the relationship between the past and future. In fact, although some authors use the terms mentioned above interchangeably, the term *change* itself contains all in it.

Social and economic changes always happen with changes in information, technology, and social values. For instance, events and aspects such as geographical and demographical factors, influenced leaders, military coups, wars, religion, and education cause change in the structure of nations. The most important factors that cause the structural changes in today's world are technological innovations, population growth, administrational changes, and mass-communication tools such as radio, TV, and the Internet (Karataş, 2003).

Developing countries face changes in the following in the process of economic development:

- The structure of the economy
- The production process
- Technology
- Mass-communication tools
- Social roles and positions
- Education systems
- Social values and customs
- Culture and linguistics
- Sexual behaviours and customs
- Family and relative relations
- Populations growth rate
- Religious organizations

Table 1. Information accumulation as the main component of development

Human Being	Invention of Wheel	Plough	Machine	Computer	Information Technology
Starting point of technology and information accumulation	a) First home devices b) Invention of fire c) Invention of wheel	a)Domestication of animals b) Cultivation of soil	Steam machines	Computer	New economy
	Primitive communities	Agricultural communities	Industrial communities	Far-industrial communities	Information communities
Mental Labor → Information → Growth → Welfare Increases → Economic Development					

In addition to the factors above, there are some factors that directly affect economic development and, thus, cause an increase in the life standards of developing countries. These are the following:

- Socioeconomic infrastructure
- Education level
- Technology level of the country
- The quality and quantity of the entrepreneurs of the country
- Labor efficiency
- The working environment
- The renovation absorption capacity of the community

These factors are very important for a developing country to become a developed one since they play a very crucial role in the development of information technology infrastructure. As can be seen from Table 1, social changes started in the very early phases of human beings, and these changes continue in today's world increasingly and diversely.

The Transformation of Information to Technology: The Relationship among Human Capital, Technological Innovations, and Investment

Economic development is related to capital accumulation and the labor force; however, economic innovation is related to factor proportionality (Todaro, 1989). Capital accumulation, in a broader sense, implies the level of physical capital as well as human capital. An increase in physical capital is not more important than an improvement in human capital for the economic development process (Kaplinsky, 1990) since technological improvements and innovations can only be achieved by a certain level of human capital. So, human capital can be considered the main (if not the only) factor in economic development (Todaro, 1989). Also, both the production and use of technology requires a skilled labor force that is able use new methods and has problem-solving ability. Even just for this specific reason, human capital has a very high level of importance in economic development (UNCTAD, 1972). The widespread use of information technology is a very crucial reason for the 40% increase of the skilled labor force from 1970 to today (Chun, 2003).

The production of information hastens technological changes since a main input to produce a new technology is previously created information. In other words, past information is an input for present information, and thus, it will also become an input for new technology creation. This process creates diffusion, and diffusion is a dynamic process. Diffusion may not be seen very clearly unless there are also permanent changes in the political and administrative structure of countries (Piek, 1998). In order for the diffusion to be felt, there must also be a very high number of skilled labor workers in that country. The reason for this is because developing countries must focus on high-tech productions in order to become a developed country. Since they do not have enough capital accumulation, foreign investors move their capital into these countries as long as the rate of return on capital is high enough and there is enough skilled labor for them to run their businesses (Lall, 1992). Technical capacity, in a broader sense, implies increases in the economic activities of the skilled labor force over time, and this, of course, implies increases in human capital (Piek, 1998).

Some local factors such as customs and traditions, the demographic and population structure, and social capital also affect the economic development of a country (Mohannak & Turpin, 2002). Since these factors directly affect economic development, developing countries must be very careful and should take necessary precautions when they are imposing a new information (or technology) into their regions. A country that is open to the world markets gains a more flexible and dynamic administrative structure, and becomes more advantageous in world competition. For these reasons, the administrative talents and creativity of the employees in developing countries are even more important (Wu, 1996).

Firms, as individual entities, are also using technology and combining it with experience. They also see technology combined with experience as a very effective power for their activities (Edvinsson & Malone, 1997). Developed countries give a very high level of importance to education as well as other areas related to information technology. For instance, most of the developed countries focus on human capital based on individual abilities and technological progress. Again, for the developed countries, human capital and light infrastructural resources become two of the main stimulants for economic development (Grossman, 1990). For this reason, individuals must add new things to their knowledge in order to have continuous development in their ability (Croix & Doepke, 2004). If this has not been done in a country, that country may be restricted by low ability. In other words, a developed country with a

low-ability labor force may find itself in very deep problems. Thus, as it is stated in the literature, physical capital must always be combined with human capital (Nichell & Nicolitsas, 2000).

Figure 1 shows a historical scheme for economic development and its relationship with investment, innovation, and human capital. There are three stages in the graph. The first stage explains that investments are very important for economics development. Also, innovations must continue in order for investments to be productive. If this relationship ceases in a certain time, the effectiveness of investments on economic development will decrease. In other words, the investment and innovations relationship must be a continuous one. This continuous relationship can be formed with human capital. Individual abilities and efforts create innovations, and innovations create economic developments. Individual firms also participate in this process because they should be producing cost-effective (low-price) and newer products in order to compete with the changing world. One of the ways that firms participate in

Figure 1. Stages of economic development and the relationship between investment, innovation, and human capital (Source: Karataş & Deviren, 2005)

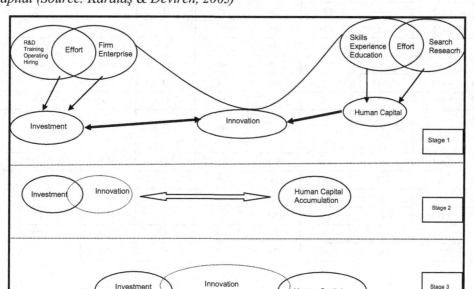

this process is to have R&D (research and development) budgets. This process encourages talented people to produce new ideas and innovations, and thus makes their companies more powerful in the global world. With this, the first stage ends.

The second stage assumes that, due to R&D activities in the first stage, firms have more information about the innovations. These innovative progresses become the vision of the firms in the second stage. In other words, the firm and innovation become interrelated, and human capital is supporting and assuring the continuation of this relation. For these reasons, there is sufficient amount of human capital for the firms, and also there are obvious indications of productivity increases due to innovations and a higher level

Table 2. Numbers in communications in selected countries (Source: World Bank World Development Indicators 2006, 2006)

	Electric Power		Telephones						
	Consumption per capita 2003 (kWh)	Transmission and distribution losses 2003 (% of output)	Access				Quality	Affordability and efficiency	
The Top Developing Countries			Fixed main lines per 1,000 people 2004	Mobile subscribers per 1,000 people	Population covered by mobile telephony (%) 2004	International voice traffic minutes per person 2004	Faults per 1,00 main lines 2004	Total telecommunications revenue (% of GDP) 2004	Total telephone subscribers per employee 2004
China	1,379	6	241	258	73	6	...	3.2	656
India	435	27	41	44	41	3	126.0	1.9	...
Turkey	1,656	17	267	484	68	32	30.4	3.0	664
Russia	5,480	12	256	517	78	15	...	3.2	193
Thailand	1,752	7	107	430	92	12	2.5	3.6	...
Egypt	1,127	12	130	105	91	23	0.1	3.4	274
Mexico	1,801	15	174	370	86	82	1.7	2.7	505
Malaysia	3,061	5	179	587	96	85	40.0	4.4	728
Poland	3,329	10	322	605	98	61	17.2	3.5	603
Brazil	1,883	17	230	357	68	12	1.6	4.0	...
Some Developing Countries									
Jamaica	2,481	9	189	832	95	233	39.7	5.5	345
Pakistan	408	25	30	33	45	11	...	2.1	97
Sri Lanka	325	18	51	114	40	20	6.8	2.2	166
Argentina	2,185	15	227	352	95	40	...	2.4	625
Madagascar	...	...	3	18	30	1	59.6	12.5	93
Ghana	248	12	14	78	28	15	67.4	5.2	137
Papua New Guinea	...	...	11	3	...	8	...	2.3	...
Colombia	834	19	195	232	74	44	33.0	4.9	...

of human capital. When this link between innovations and human capital explained above has been noticed, the second phase ends.

In the last stage, the combined effects of human capital, innovations, and investment make both the firms and the individuals better off, and thus life standards increase and economic developments take place. This last stage has very unique characteristics. It is the last stage, but also it is the fundamental stage for continued economic development. If the combined effects and relations of human capital, innovations, and investments do not harmonically continue, economic development suddenly ceases.

The Importance of Information Technology for Economic Development

Technological change in the world affects people's development abilities over time. Some managers, technicians, and engineers become less and less useful due to the lack of ability in adopting new techniques used in organizations. This problem is being seen in countries with a higher level of computerizing technologies. However, this problem is not completely redundant for developing countries. For instance, some regions are dynamic and synergistic. These regions are very important for the agents who have innovative and creative abilities. These agents typically are not always investors, but also powerful politicians, business leaders, university officials, or other social leaders. The main and the most important problem here, however, is bringing all these agents together on the same platforms, and acceptably forcing (or persuading) each to act as if it is only one part of the same body (Goldstein & Luger, 1993).

Table 2 gives some information in regard to the factors that become effective for the development process in some developing countries. The table basically contains some data regarding power and communication information to show the way that countries have taken in the economic development process.

Information Infrastructure and its Importance for Developing Countries

The foundations of socioeconomic development and change in a society lean on technological innovations. For instance, education, information, and technology are the main factors for structural change in industrial communities. In other words, in order for a society to progress in economic and social development, it needs higher technology; higher human capital, which is basically the quality of the labor force; and information. These factors, then, are being used in the production process.

There are some limitations, however. Creating and capturing information are not easy tasks themselves. The communities must internalize and use the information. On the other hand, when the information has been used, it will be a public good in some sense. If that community does not have a legal and structural background, then creating information will be only a sunk cost for the institutions. Developing countries must first create a structural adjustment in their legal systems to hasten the information technology creation process.

Table 3 gives science- and technology-related numbers for some of the top developing countries and also other developing countries.

Developed countries allocate more and more of their budgets to information technology. In order for information technology to develop, more investment must be put to human capital, which is basically, among other things, the education level. However, when higher human capital combines with physical capital, then that country can produce technology-oriented products and create innovations. Innovations always have higher-value-added opportunities for outputs produced. Development does not mean, however,

Table 3. Science- and technology-related numbers for selected countries (Source: World Bank World Development Indicators 2006, 2006)

The Top Developing Countries	Researchers in R&D per 1 million people 1996-2004	Technicians in R&D per 1 million people 1996-2004	Scientific and technical journal articles 2001	Expenditures for R&D (% of GDP) 1996-2003	High-technology exports ($ millions) 2004	High-technology exports (% of manufactured exports) 2004	Royalty and license-fee receipts ($ millions) 2004	Royalty and license-fee payments ($ millions) 2004	Patent applications filed by residents 2002	Patent applications filed by nonresidents 2002	Trademark applications filed by residents 2002	Trademark applications filed by nonresidents 2002
China	663	...	20,978	1.31	161,603	30	236	4,497	40,346	140,910	321,034	57,597
India	119	102	11,076	0.85	2,840	5	25	421	220	91,704	...	...
Turkey	341	37	4,098	0.66	1,064	2	0	362	550	250,492	28,209	7,611
Russian Federation	3,319	557	15,846	1.28	3,432	9	227	1,094	24,049	96,315	29,279	14,215
Thailand	286	115	727	0.24	18,203	30	14	1,584	1,117	4,548	...	...
Egypt	...	...	1,548	0.19	15	1	100	108	627	798	0	2,496
Mexico	268	96	3,209	0.42	31,832	21	92	805	...	94,116	40,141	18,509
Malaysia	299	58	494	0.69	52,868	55	20	782	2,324	...	...	...
Poland	1,581	282	5,686	0.56	1,932	3	27	880	6,521	92,176	12,355	11,607
Brazil	344	332	7,205	0.98	5,929	12	114	1,197		95,225	81,036	13,218
Some Developing Countries												
Jamaica	...	...	44	0.07	3	0	10	9	15	54	663	1,433
Pakistan	86	13	282	0.22	150	1	10	95	58	0	5,342	1,560
Sri Lanka	181	44	76	0.18	60	1	...	...	0	89,759	...	...
Argentina	720	316	2,930	0.41	749	8	58	483	0	6,634	30,839	12,007
Madagascar	15	45	...	0.12	1	1	1	13	4	89,526	162	293
Ghana	...	...	90	...	8	4	0	0	0	177,371	...	...
Papua New Guinea	...	...	36	...	47	39	...	...	...	...	...	...
Colombia	109	77	324	0.17	347	6	7	82	52	87,859	7,265	7,096

an increase in value-added outputs only; it also means an increase in community health, the life expectancy of the people, the number of live births, and so forth. Thus, developing countries, as they are struggling to increase information technology, should also be considering some innovations for these mentioned issues as well.

Data show that, even though some developing countries allocate considerable amount of money to education, they cannot reach a higher education level. This is true for many developing countries, especially at the high school level. The reason for this is because the personal income level is too low in these countries; children are working and contributing to the household budget instead of attending school. One solution for this problem is given by the Turkish government. With funds from the IMF (International Monetary Fund), it gives money to parents in low-education-level regions who are putting their children into school instead of having them go to work. This has created considerable increases in the education level of those regions.

According to Drucker (1995), without mental effort, no innovations can be created. Thus, the source of welfare is information. With these innovations, an increase in per capita income will be experienced, and innovations will be created. In other words, physical and human capital are interconnected for economic development.

Information technology also implies more research centres, data banks, and other Web systems, which can connect people with very low costs. Mobile communication tools, computer-related activities, cable televisions, and so forth need considerable amounts of physical capital as well, and they are mostly the "musts" of IT-oriented life. These investments must be made very quickly, and also the regional distributions of these investments must be fair. We used the word *quickly* because the source and variety of information changes very quickly, and thus making the best use of these investments requires very agile actions.

Since information technology contains both social and physical capital, it is used for dwelling and construction-related industries as well. Because the dwelling and construction industry is one of the main markets in which IT-related activities take place, and because it is a market in which the producer and consumer meet each other, the infrastructure of this area is very important for efficient economic development (Erkan, 1998).

As explained previously, these innovation-related activities require considerable amount of investment, which developing countries have a problem finding. Financial problems are one of the main vicious cycles for developing countries. They basically cannot afford investing in these areas, and foreign investors are hesitant to invest because these countries have not completed their administrative and legal procedures yet. In some cases, the political structure of the country does not even allow such procedures to be completed.

When the process taken by developed countries is investigated very carefully, one can easily see that the development process started with the increased use of computers. For this reason, information technology is used in very limited areas first, and then all over the country. Computerized systems spread over the whole world by increased public investment in this area. So, in order for information to be created, used, and kept if necessary, countries should change their institutional and administrative structures as well. Most developed countries, as a matter of fact, did this. This, itself, is not enough, however; the investments made and information created must be organized, too. This means that instead of having small investments in different areas, there should be big amounts of investment in certain areas so that when they develop, these sectors might create spill over in other sectors.

Table 4 gives some numbers of daily newspapers and household televisions bought for some selected countries.

Table 4. Daily newspapers and televisions for selected countries (Source: World Bank World Development Indicators 2006, 2006)

	Daily newspapers per 1,000 people 2000	Households with televisions (%) 2004
The Top Developing Countries		
China	59	91
India	60	37
Turkey	...	...
Russian Federation	...	98
Thailand	197	92
Egypt	31	95
Mexico	94	92
Malaysia	95	98
Poland	102	92
Brazil	46	90
Some Developing Countries		
Jamaica	...	70
Pakistan	39	39
Sri Lanka	29	32
Argentina	40	97
Madagascar	5	8
Ghana	14	21
Papua New Guinea	...	...
Colombia	26	92

It is also very important for a developing country to have more personal computers and a higher Internet access level per person. Table 5 gives detailed information for selected countries.

There is one very important factor to mention here, however. The information technology infrastructure in developing countries causes less damage to ecological harmony when it is compared to that of developed countries. Also, in most cases, information technology infrastructure creates more positive externalities in developing countries because information is more mobile compared to land and capital, and it usually cannot be privately owned in these countries (Erkan, 2000). IT-related improvements bring new techniques to economic activities such as production, consumption, and

resource and income distribution. This causes efficiency increases. In other words, IT-related developments create a stimulated impact in economic structure.

In the industrialized world, reaching goods and services is mostly directly related to the income level of the consumers, but in the information age, which is one step ahead of the industrial age, this is not the case. Due to information-sharing and communication devices, reaching goods and services is not so directly related to the income level of the consumers anymore. Consumers can reach all the goods and services a lot faster with lower cost in the information age. Since people obtain goods and services faster and cheaper, they start allocating their fixed income to other

Table 5. Personal computers and Internet access for selected countries (Source: World Bank World Development Indicators 2006, 2006)

	Personal Computers and the Internet						
	Access			Quality		Application security	Affordability
The Top Developing Countries	Personal computers per 1,000 people 2004	Internet users per 1,000 people 2004	Schools connected to the Internet (%) 2004	Broadband subscribers per 1,000 people 2004	International Internet bandwidth bits per capita 2004	Internet servers per 1 million people November 2005	Price basket for Internet ($/month) 2003
China	41	73	...	16.5	57	0	10.1
India	12	32	...	0.6	11	1	8.7
Turkey	52	142	40	0.8	124	17	19.8
Russian Federation	132	111	65	0.9	100	2	10.0
Thailand	58	109	37	0.2	47	5	7.0
Egypt	32	54	66	0.4	19	1	5.5
Mexico	108	135	60	3.1	108	8	22.6
Malaysia	197	397	...	10.1	128	15	8.4
Poland	193	236	90	32.7	560	22	15.7
Brazil	105	120	50	12.4	149	14	28.0
Some Developing Countries							
Jamaica	63	403	10	9.6	...	14	43.5
Pakistan	5	13	...	0.0	5	0	15.6
Sri Lanka	27	14	...	0.1	17	2	15.1
Argentina	96	133	...	13.5	319	11	13.3
Madagascar	5	5	...	0.0	2	0	67.3
Ghana	5	17	1	0.0	1	0	43.8
Papua New Guinea	64	29	...	0.0	1	1	20.0
Colombia	67	80	50	2.8	124	4	18.6

consumptions they were not able to consume before. This in turn brings welfare increases to all of society.

Since technological structure changes very fast in the information age, developing countries may have been negatively affected by this process. If these countries cannot develop some supporting activities that renew the existing information, then they might face an information deterioration process. This means that the old informa-tion they have will start depreciating, and at the end, it may not produce enough solutions for the continuing process of development. Basically, the old information becomes useless in solving existing problems.

In addition to all these, the information age may cause some other problems if they are not previously noted. These are as follows (Şanlısoy, 1999):

- If information is gathered and distributed by specific firms, there is the risk that the information sector will have a monopolistic (oligopolistic) structure.
- Since it is very expensive to obtain information in developing countries, some people or groups may become the information elite and solicit the remaining sectors.
- Critical information may be black-marketed if the copyright system of the country is not effective.
- Since there is an insufficient number of specialists, there may be some user-related errors.
- There may be misuse of information.
- Environment-related problems may arise due to technological progress.
- Physical and social problems may arise due to technological progress.
- The information age may bring a higher frequency of problems to developing countries.
- Monopolistic companies may exist due to information accumulation.

Importance of Technological Advances in Economic Development

The economic recession of the last two decades left its place to a dynamic process of economic growth in developing countries since information-based competition became more and more important in international trade. However, some Organization for Economic Cooperation and Development (OECD) countries could not reach a certain level of economic growth within the last decade, and thus they did not invest in information technology as they should have. Some countries aware of the importance of the technological process, however, left government R&D expenditures out of the budget cuts and also applied tax cuts for privately managed R&D expenditures (OECD, 2004). With this, governments try to construct a good connection between publicly and privately owned R&D companies so that they can share information amongst themselves.

In order to have a better understanding of why some countries were able to develop and others were not, it is better to look at those countries' economic and social histories. Freeman and Soete (1997) may shed some light on current and past conditions of the world economies. As it is explained very clearly in their work, there are stages for economic and social development. Although these stages cannot certainly be applied to all countries of the world, they are generally true for most instances. Underdeveloped or developing countries are mostly stuck in one of these stages and cannot pass to the next stage.

The difference in development level increases between developing and developed countries. This is because new technology adopted stimulates R&D expenditures, R&D expenditures stimulate new technology, and new technology creates and accumulates information. While developed countries show a higher level of growth, developing countries show a lower level of growth due to economic, social, and political reasons. This situation causes the gap between these countries to become even bigger.

Today's leading developed countries have some common characteristics of their own. For instance, they all have the following:

- A higher education level
- A strong economic and institutional structure
- Advanced technological progress
- Military power
- A higher level of growth rate

Table 6 shows information and communication technology expenditures of selected countries.

Figure 2 indicates that the maximum amount of Internet use is seen in higher-income-level regions. Among these regions, Europe and Central Asia have the highest level of Internet use. Internet use becomes higher or lower depending

Table 6. Information and communication technology expenditures of selected countries (Source: World Bank World Development Indicators 2006, 2006)

	Information and Communication Technology Expenditures	
The Top Developing Countries	**% of GDP 2004**	**$ per Capita 2004**
China	4.4	66
India	3.8	24
Turkey	6.9	293
Russian Federation	3.3	135
Thailand	3.6	91
Egypt	1.4	15
Mexico	3.0	196
Malaysia	6.7	316
Poland	4.3	270
Brazil	6.3	208
Some Developing Countries		
Jamaica	11.8	395
Pakistan	7.1	45
Sri Lanka	5.9	61
Argentina	5.6	224
Madagascar	...	...
Ghana	...	...
Papua New Guinea	...	...
Colombia	8.3	180

Figure 2. Internet use among regions (per 1,000 people in 2004; Source: World Bank World Development Indicators 2006, 2006)

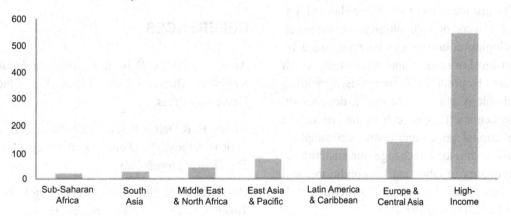

upon the economic development of the country. Developing countries must allocate more and more resources for information technology and more interaction with the world. Also, human capital must be increased by allocating more and more resources for education and training activities. The faster the adaptation to the world, the faster the development will be for developing countries.

CONCLUSION

It is very easy to follow employee performance, changes in the global markets, and the effectiveness of various techniques in the information age. It is also easier for investors to obtain information with various institutional linkages. Thus, developing countries must form these institutional linkages as fast and as efficient as they can since these linkages are a very fundamental portion of economic and social development. Increasing production efficiency will be continued if and only if economic institutions are investing in information technology and human capital.

This study tries to examine the problematic structure of information technology in developing countries. Within this context, the study evaluated the reasons for underdevelopment, and the future perspectives and solutions for the existing underdevelopment problems of the related countries. For instance, in our study, we claimed that regional effects of technological development in developing countries can be recognized by a higher level of income and investment, which are created by productivity increases. Spreading the technology obtained, however, depends on some systematic factors such as the production of new capital goods and spare-part supplies. With this technological change, the structure of capital, quality of labor, market conditions, and sociopolitical and institutional structures will change as well (Eser, 1993).

We also discussed that technological innovations result in cost-reducing effects in the production process. In the global world, market conditions are getting more and more competitive; thus, R&D expenditures in developed countries contribute very much to economic development. However, R&D expenditures started decreasing in some developed countries in the last three decades due to enough developments in communication and information technology, and to an increased level of biotechnology and advanced equipment (Şahin, 1997). Technological progress in developing countries, however, continues to exist as a result of adapting imported technologies into the domestic structure. In most cases, though, government policies and market distortions created big problems for development in these countries. Also, there is not enough capital to renew the existing technology.

Thus, the main problems in developing countries are to have capital to support existing technology and human capital to create alternative ways of existing technology to function well enough. Governments should form their socioeconomic structures in such a way that it makes both physical and human capital accumulation a lot easier. Otherwise, the technological gap between developing and developed countries will continue to exist, maybe in a wider and broader sense.

REFERENCES

Acar, Y. (2002). *İktisadi büyüme ve büyüme modelleri*. Bursa, Turkey: Vipas, A.S. Uludag University Press.

Arısoy, E., & Demir, R. (2001). Eğitim, haberleşme ve ticari serbestliğin ekonomik büyümeye katkısı. *Dış Ticaret Dergisi, 23*.

Bozkurt, V. (1996). *Enformasyon toplumu ve Türkiye*. Istanbul, Turkey: Sistem Press.

Chun, H. (2003). Information technology and the demand for educated workers: Disentangling the impacts of adoption versus use. *The Review of Economics and Statistics, 85*(1).

Croix, D., & Doepke, M. (2004). Public versus private education when differential fertility matters. *Journal of Development Economics, 73*(2), 607-629.

Drucker, P. (1995). *Gelecek için yönetim* (F. Üçcan, Trans.). Ankara, Turkey: Türkiye İş Bankası Press.

Edvinsson, L., & Malone, M. M. (1997). *Intellectual capital: Realizing our company's true value by finding its hidden brainpower.* New York: Harper Collins Publishing.

Erkan, H. (1998). *Bilgi toplumu ve ekonomik gelişme.* Ankara, Turkey: Türkiye Is Bankasi Cultural Press.

Erkan, H. (2000). *Bilgi uygarlığı için yeniden yapılanma.* Ankara, Turkey: Imge Publishing.

Ertek, T. (2006). *Temel ekonomi.* Istanbul, Turkey: BETA Publishing Co.

Eser, U. (1993). *Türkiye'de sanayileşme.* Ankara, Turkey: Imge Publishing.

Fischer, S., Rudiger, D., & Richard, S. (1988). *Economics.* New York: McGraw-Hill Publishing Company.

Freeman, C., & Soete, L. (1997). *Yenilik iktisadı* (E. Türkcan, Trans.). Ankara, Turkey: Tubitak Press.

Goldstein, H. A., & Luger, M. I. (1993). Theory and practice in high-tech economic development. In R. D. Bingham & R. Mier (Eds.), *Theories of local economic development* (pp.147-169). SAGE Publications.

Grossman, G. M. (1990). Promoting new industrial activities. *OECD Economic Studies, 14*, 87-125.

Han, E., & Kaya, A. A. (1999). *Kalkınma ekonomisi teori ve politika.* Eskişehir, Turkey: Etam Matbaası Press.

Ilyasoğlu, E. (1997). *Türk bilgi teknolojisi ve gümrük birliği.* Ankara, Turkey: Türkiye Is Bankası Press.

Jones, C. I. (2001). *Iktisadi buyumeye giris* (A. Sanlı & T. Ismail, Trans.). Istanbul, Turkey: Literature Press.

Kaplinsky, R. (1990). *The economies of small: Appropriate technology in a changing world.* London: Intermediate Technology Publications.

Karataş, M. (2003). Sosyo-ekonomik gelişmede yapısal değişim. *Stratejik Araştırmalar Dergisi, 1*, 169-190.

Karataş, M., & Bekmez, S. (2005). Türkiye'nin iktisadi gelişmesinin dış ticaret ve teknolojik ilerleme açısından değerlendirilmesi. *Celal Bayar Üniversitesi İktisadi ve Idari Bilimler Fakultesi Yönetim ve Ekonomi Dergisi, 12*(2), 105-126.

Karataş, M., & Deviren, V. N. (2005). Türkiye'nin iktisadi gelişmesinin beşeri sermaye içerikli solow modeli açısından bir değerlendirmesi. *İktisat İşletme ve Finans Dergisi, 233*, 68-87.

Kaslıval, P. (1995). *Development economics.* Cincinnati, OH: Thomson Publishing.

Kaya, A. A. (2000). *Yeniliğe dayalı endüstriyel kalkınma ve Türkiye.* Unpublished manuscript, Ege University, Faculty of Economics and Administrative Science, Izmir, Turkey.

Kirmanoğlu, H. (2000). Beşeri kalkınma ve eğitim: Sağlık hizmetleri. *İktisat Dergisi, 397-398.*

Lall, S. (1992). Technological capabilities and industrialization. *World Development, 20*(2), 86-165.

Mohannak, K., & Turpin, T. (Eds.). (2002). *Innovation knowledge systems and regional development*. Edward Elgar Publishing.

Nichell, S., & Nicolitsas, D. (2000). Human capital, investment and innovation: What are the connections? In R. Barrell, G. Mason, & M. O'Mahony (Eds.), *Productivity, innovation and economic performance*. Cambridge University Press.

Organization for Economic Cooperation and Development (OECD). (2004). *Science, technology and industry: Outlook 2004.*

Piek, H. (1998). *Technology development in rural industries*. London: Intermediate Technology Publications Ltd.

Şahin, S. (1997). *Türkiye'de bilim ve teknoloji politikası*. Istanbul, Turkey: Gocebe Press.

Şanlısoy, S. (1999). Bilgi toplumunda ortaya çıkabilecek sorunlar. *D.E.Ü. İktisadi ve İdari Bilimler Fakültesi Dergisi, 14*(2), 169-184.

Soyak, A. (1996). *Teknolojik gelişme ve özelleştirme*. Istanbul, Turkey: Ekonomiye Yaklaşım.

State Institute of Statistics (DIE). (2002). *Yoksulluk çalışması: 2002*. Ankara, Turkey.

Todaro, M. P. (1989). *Economic development in the third world*. Longman Group Ltd.

Turpin, T., Xielin, L., Garrett-Jones, S., & Burns, P. (Eds.). (2002). *Innovation, technology policy and regional development*. Edward Elgar Publishing.

UNCTAD. (1972). *Guidelines for the study of the transfer of technology*. New York: United Nations Press.

World Bank world development indicators 2006. (2006) Retrieved July 13, 2006, from http://devdata.worldbank.org/wdi2006/contents/Section5.htm

Wu, Y. (1996). *Productive performance in Chinese enterprises*. St. Martin's Press, Inc.

http://www.die.gov.tr

http://www.imf.org

http://www.oecd.org

http://www.un.org.tr/undp_tur/docs

http://devdata.worldbank.org

Chapter III
IT Promotion Policies for Economic Development:
The Case of Malaysia

Rika Nakagawa
Institute of Developing Economies, Japan

ABSTRACT

The purpose of this chapter is to investigate IT promotion policies for economic development in Malaysia and to analyze results of those policies. In addition, the author attempts to draw policy suggestions for developing countries in order to encourage their economic development. This chapter reveals disparities in the sector and region that exist even though the government has a strong concern regarding ICT-supported ICT development. From this analysis, three policy implications for other developing countries are suggested. First, government commitment can contribute to ICT development. Second, the government needs to develop ICT through a strategic and gradual approach. Third, the government needs to pay careful attention to ICT disparities that may arise in the process of ICT development for stable economic development.

INTRODUCTION

Information technology is having a great impact on our society and economy. In the context of developing countries, because IT is expected to become an engine of growth, it thus becomes essential for economic development. It is also thought that IT will be important for economic development by improving human resources and reducing transaction costs in business and public administration. Furthermore, IT may provide a shortcut for some countries to catch up with developed countries. Therefore, governments of developing countries are trying to promote IT-based economies.

There are two channels for IT to stimulate economic growth in developing countries: export and investment. Exports of manufactured IT products can be a contributing factor in promotion of economic growth. However, this is sometimes difficult for developing countries because it takes time to promote IT manufacturing industries. Through the second channel, investment in IT equipment in companies, it is possible for developing countries to make business and production procedures more effective and efficient and to increase their economic growth rate. This second method may be more feasible politically for developing countries, such as Malaysia; therefore, the latter issue is mainly addressed in this chapter.

Since the mid-1990s, the government of Malaysia has emphasized the importance of IT for the country's economic development and has implemented several policies for a more effective and efficient economy. In order for the country to become a developed country by 2020, the Malaysian government has taken a strong initiative and introduced a strategic policy package.

The purpose of this chapter is to investigate IT promotion policies for economic development in Malaysia and to analyze the results of those policies. In addition, this study finds some potentially useful lessons and draws policy implications for developing countries.

The structure of this chapter is as follows. The following section reviews past literature regarding impacts of IT on economic development and the role of the government in IT diffusion. The third section explains IT promotion policies after the late 1990s in Malaysia. The fourth section analyzes outcomes of the country's promotion policies at three levels: the country level, sector level, and state level. The final section consists of concluding remarks and policy implications.

PRODUCTIVITY, IT, AND THE ROLE OF THE GOVERNMENT: LITERATURE REVIEW

It has been considered that IT has great impact on an economy. IT does not necessarily affect all industries, but it is possible for IT to affect not only production processes, including R&D (research and development) and marketing, but also general administration. Freeman (1992) argued that communication technology, along with IT, has significant impacts on the economy and it is possible to improve the efficiency of every function within each company or industry. In addition to this, the development of IT has two different impacts on employment. If a company succeeds in making routine work efficient by introducing IT, the company can reduce the number of employees in order to reduce labor costs. On the other hand, labor demand in the IT sector increases as the IT sector develops (Fukuda, Sudo, & Hayami, 1997). As Mody and Dahlman (1992) indicate, these arguments imply that investments in IT by the private and public sectors lead to an improvement of productivity and make it possible to change social or economic structures in a country.

Since the IT revolution in the 1980s, many economists have paid attention to IT and productivity. One important trigger for economists in discussing IT and its impact on the economy was a remark by Solow (1987), who pointed out that, although people felt that productivity was increased by computers, in fact, the growth rate of labor productivity slowed down in industrialized countries, in particular the United States. This phenomenon, the so-called productivity paradox of computers, became a big debate in the United States and raised the question of how to explain the relationship between computers and productivity.

Since then, many studies have tackled the productivity paradox.[1] Empirical studies about productivity and IT can be classified into three categories. The first category is the aggregate-level study, which is trying to find reasons why the growth rate of labor productivity declined in developed countries despite the diffusion of IT. The second category is the industrial-level study, and the third one is the firm-level study. The last two focus more on microlevel effects and try to show how the productivity of each industry or each firm improved after the introduction of IT.

In the aggregate-level studies, the focus was on revealing reasons for the decrease in the growth rate of labor productivity in the United States from the 1970s. Griliches (1988) found that the sharp increase in the price of oil was a major factor in weak labor productivity. In 1973 and 1979, oil prices soared, and this had a negative impact on the economic growth rate. Macroeconomic shocks caused a decrease in the overall output of the economy and in labor productivity. This argument focused on factors that affected business cycles rather than on relationships between factors of production and output growth.

To make the relationship between factors of production and economic growth clear, the productivity debate in the United States was narrowed down to the impacts of IT or computers on output growth. Oliner and Sichel (1994) analyzed output growth in the United States from 1970 to 1992 in terms of computer investment in companies. This study found only a small contribution of computer hardware toward output growth. The reason was that the proportion of computer investment to the total investment in equipment was small. This paper also mentioned that other important factors related to computers, such as software and labor inputs, were not included. This implies that there was a possibility of measurement errors, as noted by Baily and Gordon (1988).

Aggregate- and industry-level studies failed to prove a positive contribution of IT toward output and found a weak relationship between the two. Firm-level studies, however, came to the conclusion that computer or information technology could support the output of each firm (Brynjolfsson & Hitt, 1996; Lehr & Lichtenberg, 1999). Brynjolfsson and Hitt analyzed firm-level data from 1987 to 1991 and found evidence that computers supported the output of each firm in the observation period. They concluded that by 1991, it was no longer possible to see the productivity paradox.

The significance of firm-level studies is showing that it is possible for IT to become a contributing factor toward better productivity and economic growth, although these relationships were not clear in the aggregate-level and industry-level analyses. In other words, in investigating whether the diffusion of IT can be an engine for growth, microdata analysis may be tenable. This type of analysis, however, is not easy in research on developing countries because data and information are difficult to access. The most serious problem is that capital stock data or sufficient data to estimate capital stock are not available. Therefore, most studies focused on developing countries have been carried out with aggregate data or industry data. Kraemer, Gurbazani, and King (1992, 1994) indicated that from an aggregate data analysis of Asia-Pacific countries, expenditures on computers correlated positively with the level of economic development and productivity in each economy. In addition, they discussed the role of the government in stimulating computer spending and concluded that overall spending on computers was not much affected by government policies. On the other hand, Mody and Dahlman (1992) pointed out that effective IT planning by the government was critical. They insisted that the Asian newly industrialized economies (NIEs), such as Singapore and South Korea, succeeded in the diffusion of ICT because governments invested in ICT infrastructure to foster ICT diffusion. Furthermore, the IT absorption capabilities of companies in NIEs were supported by education or training institutions established by the government.

These studies provide us with important implications. First, ICT can be a push factor in economic development even in developing countries. Second, the role of the government can be crucial, and policies for developing telecommunications, computer networks, and human resources are effective.

It is not surprising that the role of the government in developing ICT-related infrastructure and human resources is significant because the infrastructure, such as computer networks and telecommunications, and IT training are a kind of public goods. Once ICT-related infrastructure is developed throughout a country, many people benefit from the infrastructure. This is called positive externality, which occurs when an action that affects others can be taken by an individual or company without paying for a beneficial outcome (Stiglits & Walsh, 2002). In addition to this, it is often said that the private sector is not willing to spend on a suitable ICT infrastructure because of the large setup cost. The industry with large fixed costs and small marginal costs has a tendency toward a natural monopoly (Varian, 2003). The ICT-related infrastructure industry is a typical case. The private sector may suffer heavy investment losses if the business fails. Even though the business succeeds, it takes a long time to make a profit on the investment. This leads an industry to less competition and finally results in a natural monopoly. In the case of most natural monopolies, the government controls or operates them. Regarding human resource development, it takes a long time to promote computer literacy and train IT professionals. As a consequence, private companies are apt not to spend much on IT training. The government is the best supplier of an IT-friendly environment.

IT PROMOTION POLICIES AND INSTITUTIONAL DEVELOPMENT IN MALAYSIA

In Malaysia, IT development policies have been implemented in accordance with national development plans. The Malaysia Plans contain detailed strategies to be executed for economic development. In other words, what the government should do for 5 years is embodied in each Plan.

Since the mid-1980s, the government has emphasized that Malaysia should improve technology and focus on IT; however, it was only from the 1990s that the government began to have a commitment to the development of IT. In the *Sixth Malaysia Plan* (1991-1995), technology in the manufacturing sector was emphasized because advances in technology could improve the productivity of the sector. In addition, this plan placed emphasis on technology in R&D. Based on the *Sixth Malaysia Plan*, the government focused on the development of IT infrastructure and human resources (Table 1). The most remarkable policy in this period was the establishment of a think tank and advisor to the government on ICT development: the National Information Technology Council.

The next significant policy was that the government, under the National Productivity Council (Incorporation) (Amendment) Act of 1991,[2] incorporated an institution to conduct research on productivity in the country, namely, the National Productivity Corporation (NPC). The NPC has initiative in five areas: implementing productivity and quality management systems, improving national productivity through benchmarking activities, intensifying the application of information technology, upgrading skills and human resources, and improving quality products through research and development (Ismail, 1999). It is noteworthy that the NPC insisted IT would make business more efficient and improve productivity.

Along with these strategies, the NPC drew up an action plan for enhancing productivity growth.[3]

In the *Seventh Malaysia Plan* (1996-2000), the government strived to change the quality of economic growth from input-driven to productivity-driven growth. The plan laid stress on a knowledge-based economy and total factor productivity (TFP).[4] TFP shows how much change in total output can be attributed to change in technology. Therefore, an improvement in TFP means progress in technology, which leads to an efficient, knowledge-based economy. It is critical for a small country like Malaysia, with limited labor and capital, to pursue better TFP for economic development (Government of Malaysia, 1996).

In order to foster better TFP, the government has focused on information technology.[5] The *Seventh Malaysia Plan* proposed several policies concerning IT development, for example, the diffusion of IT, the development of the Multimedia Super Corridor (MSC), the education and training of IT manpower, the review of laws and regulation, the promotion of local IT companies, and the enhancement of IT awareness (Government of Malaysia, 1996).

During the *Seventh Malaysia Plan* period, the government continued its efforts in the development of ICT infrastructure and human resources. Along with these efforts, the country established the MSC to promote the IT industry. To attract companies not only in Malaysia but also in the world, the government provided several incentives (MSC status) for companies.[6]

Electronic commerce was a new issue that the government emphasized. Through online business, it is possible for rural people to have access to markets all over the country; this can be beneficial for many people and make a business efficient. Therefore, the government pushed to develop an environment conducive to e-commerce, including an e-payment system and laws and regulations for e-business (Table 1).

In the *Eighth Malaysia Plan* (2001-2005), the government declared continuous efforts to develop communication technology in addition to information technology. Eight overall goals regarding the development of information and communication technology were presented: promoting the country as a global IT hub, upgrading ICT infrastructure, developing human resources in ICT, enhancing e-commerce, promoting local content companies, developing the MSC, encouraging ICT-based small and medium-sized enterprises, and fostering R&D activities in the ICT sector.

In this period, the government started new policies, such as e-learning, content development, and information security, in addition to ICT physical infrastructure and human resource development. Among the new policies, the government took a constructive attitude toward information security because the country had incomplete legal infrastructure regarding ICT abuse or misuse. Therefore, through the authority of the government, a framework was developed for information security, and several organizations were set up to provide people with services related to technical assistance and solutions for problems of ICT abuse or misuse (Table 1).

Investment in ICT, its Development, and Productivity

Country-Level Analysis

In Malaysia, the government has played a significant role in the development of ICT. The main purpose of policies implemented by the government was to improve TFP and the efficiency of the economy. The government encouraged investments in IT, and the growth rate of IT investments steadily increased, except in 1998. In addition, the growth rate of gross capital formation was unstable, with negative growth in 1998, 1999, 2001, and 2002 (Figure 1). One reason the growth rate of investments was negative in 1998 was the influence of the economic crisis following the Asian currency crisis. Investments in IT recovered quickly, and since 1999, the growth rate

Table 1. ICT-related policies

Sixth Malaysia Plan 1991-1995

Infrastructure for IT

+ Issued telecommunications network licences to 6 telecommunications operators

+ Launched the JARING Project to promote information exchange and database development through access to the internet

Human Resource Development for IT

+ Provided training at the basic degree and diploma levels in IT-related courses National Information Technology Council

+ Initiated the process of formulating a national IT plan and identifying key programs

Seventh Malaysia Plan 1996-2000

Infrastructure for Communications

+ Invested in communication infrastructure, such as fiber optics, satellite and cellular technology

+ Granted six internet service providers

Human Resource Development for ICT

+ 170 private institutions and 28 public institutions offered ICT courses

+ Established Multimedia University

Development of the Multimedia Super Corridor

+ Established MSC in 1996 and provide several incentives, named MSC Status (as of 2000, 429 companies were granted MSC status, in which 274 were Malaysian-owned companies)

+ Established five cyber-cities: Cyberjaya, Technology Park Malaysia, University Putra Malaysia-Malaysian Technology Development Corporation, Petronas Twin Towers, and KL Tower

+ Introduced MSC flagship applications: E-government, Smart schools, Multipurpose cards, Telehealth, R&D cluster, Entertainment village

E-Commerce

+ Organized a National E-Commerce Committee to formulate a framework of promoting and coordinating the development of E-commerce

+ Undertook a study on E-Commerce Strategic Directions for Malaysia

+ Local companies started their business on-line through E-commerce-enabled websites

+ Bank Negara Malaysia created a plan of on-line payment system (Malaysian E-Payment Systems)

+ Enacted various laws and regulations which were related to E-commerce

Funds for the ICT Industry

+ Established a RM500 million ICT Fund for high-technology and ICT-based firms

+ Established MSC Venture Corporation for small and medium sized enterprises

+ Opened the Malaysian Exchange of Securities Dealing and Automation Quotation (MESDAQ) for technology and high-growth companies

National IT Agenda

+ Launched the Five Strategic Thrusts Agenda (E-Economy, E-Publilc Services, E-Community, E-Learning, E-Sovereignty)

+ Established the Strategic Thrusts Implementation Committee and implement 30 Projects

+ Held Information Society conference and exposition events annually

+ Established the Demonstrator Applications Grant Scheme and implemented 37 Community-based projects under the scheme

continued on following page

Table 1. continued

Eighth Malaysia Plan 2001-2005

Infrastructure for ICT

+ Established fixed phone lines, public payphones and Internet in rural and remote areas, such as schools clinics and libraries (Universal Service Provision Fund)

+ Launched National Broadband Plan to provide broadband services throughout the country

+ Liberalized the telecommunications industry

+ Reviews and upgraded laws, regulations, and tariff structure to facilitate the USP programs

+ Issued the Malaysian Information, Communications and Multimedia Services Blueprint and suggested guidelines for the key

Human Resource Development for ICT

+ Provided the Undergraduate Skills Programe and the MSC Intership Programe for new ICT graduates

+ Disbursed for RM176 million to ICT-related training places and centers under the Human Resource Development Fund

Development of the Multimedia Super Corridor

+ Established 500 shared services and outsourcing companies by the end of 2005

+ Developed computer-based systems to generate business opportunities for the private sector

+ Established MSC office in Saudi Arabia and China

E-Commerce

+ Facilitated Internet banking services and the MSC E-Business Programe for B2B and B2C online business

+ Prepared new legislation; the Electronic Transaction Bill, the Electronic Government Activities Bill and the Personal Data Protection Bill

Funds for ICT Development

+ Disbursed a total of RM1.1 billion to ICT and high growth sectors (Malaysia Debt Ventures Bhd.)

+ Provided ICT-related ventures with financing facilities for RM82.6 million (Venture Capital Management Bhd.)

+ Launched a number of ICT-related financial schemes to accelerate ICT usage (Commercialization of Research and Development Fund and the Small and Medium Industries Development Corporation)

+ Funded 51 projects (RM79.7 million) related to creating, developing and promoting new ICT applications (Demonstrator Application Grant Scheme)

Information Security

+ Initiated the preparation of a National Information Security Framework to address the requisite legislative, reguratory and technical aspects

+ Provided services of computer forensics, acculturation programs, policy research, security Advisory and assessment of security solutions (National ICT Security and Emergency Response Center)

+ Opened the national ICT Security and Emergency Response Center to provide services of computer forensics, policy research, security advisory and assessment of security solutions

+ The national ICT Security and Emergency Response Center provided services of computer forensics, acculturation programs, policy research, security advisory and assessment of security solutions

+ Organized the Malaysian Computer Emergency Response Team to provide Internet users with a platform to deal with security breaches, misuse and abuse of the Internet

Narrowing the Digital Divide

+ Established 217 telecenters for universal Internet access in rural communities

+ Provided 78 computer literacy classes for IT education

+ Launched One Home One PC Project to promoted ownership of personal computers

+ Undertook a study on a National Strategic Framework for Bridging the Digital Divide

Promoting R&D in ICT

+ Approved 192 ICT-related R&D projects for 46 million under the Intensification of Research in Priority Areas Program

+ Approved 27 ICT-related projects for RM28 million under the Industry Research and Development Grant Scheme

continued on following page

Table 1. continued

E-learning
+   Started Elearning and smart school community projects (Multimedia Development Corporation)
+   Set up a National E-Learning Consultative Committee to advise and monitor E-learning programs
Fostering Local Capabilities in Content Development
+   Opened the MSC Creative Applications and Development Center for R&D activities in high value added content development

Sources: Government of Malaysia (1996, 2001a, 2006)

Figure 1. Growth rate of gross capital formation and IT spending

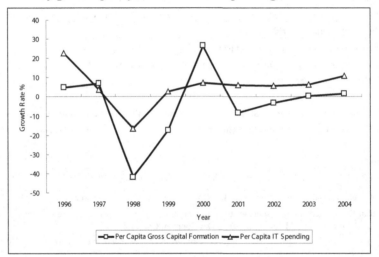

Sources: Author's calculation based on data retrieved July 5, 2006 from the Association of the Computer and Multimedia Industry of Malaysia, Web site (www.pikom.org.my) and Bank Negara Malaysia (2006).

has been positive even during the downturn in the world economy due to the collapse of the IT bubble in 2001. Furthermore, the growth rate of IT spending has been stable and has grown more than the growth rate of gross capital formation. It is clear that Malaysia has been positive about IT investments.

From the time that ICT promotion policies were initiated in the *Sixth Malaysia Plan*, the government has committed itself to promoting infrastructure and human resource development for ICT. As shown in Table 2, it is clear that the continuous efforts of the government have contributed toward both a well-developed ICT

infrastructure and a business environment of ICT that is superior to that found in East Asia and the Pacific. It is noteworthy that the rating of government prioritization of ICT in 2002 was 5.9; this means that the government took a strong initiative in carrying out ICT development plans.

Sector-Level Analysis

In case of investments in IT by selected sectors (Table 3), the banking and finance sector actively invested in IT in the 1990s. The ratio of IT spending to total spending in the banking and finance sector shows 39% in 1990 and 27.2% in 1995.

Table 2. Diffusion of ICT in Malaysia

		Malaysia		East Asia & Pacific[1]
ICT Infrastructure, Computers & Internet		**1995**	**2001**	**2001**
Telephone mainlines	(per 1,000 people)	166	196	110
Mobile phones	(per 1,000 people)	50	314	97
Personal computers	(per 1,000 people)	37.3	126.1	19.1
Internet users	(thousands)	40.0	6,500.0	50,901.8
ICT Business & Government Environment[2]		**1995**	**2002**	**2002**
Broadband internet access availability		--	3.4	3.4
Local specialized IT services availability		--	3.9	4.0
Government online services availability		--	3.3	2.7
Laws relating to ICT use		--	4.8	3.5
Government prioritization of ICT		--	5.9	4.9

Notes: 1. According to the classification of the World Bank, East Asia & Pacific includes American Samoa, Cambodia, China, Fiji, Indonesia, Kiribati, Dem. Rep. of Korea, Lao PDR, Malaysia, Marshall Islands, Fed. Sts. of Micronesia, Mongolia, Myanmar, Northern Mariana islands, Palau, Papua New Guinea, Philippines, Samoa, Solomon Islands, Thailand, Timor-Leste, Tonga, Vanuatu, Vietnam. 2. Rating from 1 to 7, with 7 the highest/best. Source: Data retrieved March 1, 2006, from World Bank, Web site (www.worldbank.org).

In 2000, the ratio dropped to 14%. On the other hand, the manufacturing sector has increased its ratio since 2000. The manufacturing sector has been the most active sector in investing in IT, although the ratio of spending to output was only 1.1% or 1.2%.

The government is also an active investor in IT. The ratio of IT spending to total spending is between 9% and 11%, and not much different from the distributive-trade and telecommunications and transportation sectors. However, the ratio of IT spending to output is relatively high when compared with that in other sectors, with the ratio being higher than the country average since 1995. In 1995, the government spending rate was 2.3%, with the country average being 1.7% in the same year. The government took the lead in investing in IT and tried to make government operations efficient.

On the other hand, investment in IT is relatively small in the distributive-trade sector; the ratio of IT spending to total spending has been only 11% since 2000. The ratio of IT spending to output was 1.6% in 2003; this ratio is below the country's average.

In labor productivity, a high growth rate is observed in the manufacturing sector except in the year 2001. In that year, the IT bubble in the United States burst and the world economy slowed down. Malaysia was involved in this and IT production decreased. The growth rate of labor productivity in the whole country was -4.3% and that of the manufacturing sector was -12.7%.

In the case of the distributive-trade sector, the growth rate of labor productivity was low compared to the other sectors. In addition, the rate was negative from 2000 to 2003.

One reason why the manufacturing sector has been the most active investor in IT since 2000 is that the Malaysian government emphasized the manufacturing sector as a priority and facilitated the introduction of IT in that sector. In addition to this, as has been noted, the government established the MSC to attract world-class IT companies. IT

Table 3. IT spending and labor productivity in selected sectors

	1990	1995	2000	2001	2002	2003
Manufacturing						
Output (RM million)	28,847	58,684	111,900	101,735	110,561	122,706
IT Spending (RM million)	78	494	1,182	1,170	1,290	1,416
Ratio to Total IT Spending in the Country (%)	6.0	13.1	20.0	18.0	18.0	18.0
Ratio to Output (%)	0.3	0.8	1.1	1.2	1.2	1.2
IT Spending per Employee (RM)	59	277	556	536	624	664
Labor Productivity (RM)	21.6	33.0	52.6	46.6	53.4	57.6
Growth Rate (%)	n.a.	n.a.	10.9	-12.7	12.7	6.5
Banking & Finance						
Output (RM million)	10,707	25,758	40,300	41,544	45,806	47,208
IT Spending (RM million)	507	1,026	827	910	1,000	1,101
Ratio to Total IT Spending in the Country (%)	39.0	27.2	14.0	14.0	14.0	14.0
Ratio to Output (%)	4.7	4.0	2.1	2.2	2.2	2.3
IT Spending per Employee (RM)	1,962	2,821	1,791	1,586	1,568	1,754
Labor Productivity (RM)	41.4	70.8	87.2	72.4	71.8	75.2
Growth Rate (%)	n.a.	n.a.	4.5	-18.2	-2.5	3.5
Government						
Output (RM million)	11,149	16,780	22,576	24,104	27,450	29,643
IT Spending (RM million)	156	380	532	715	790	865
Ratio to Total IT Spending in the Country (%)	12.0	10.1	9.0	11.0	11.0	11.0
Ratio to Output (%)	1.4	2.3	2.4	3.0	2.9	2.9
IT Spending per Employee (RM)	n.a.	n.a.	n.a.	1,076	1,190	1,298
Labor Productivity (RM)	n.a.	n.a.	n.a.	36.3	41.4	44.5
Growth Rate (%)	n.a.	n.a.	n.a.	n.a.	12.1	6.3
Distributive Trade						
Output (RM million)	16,171	34,132	47,849	48,726	50,937	52,654
IT Spending (RM million)	91	304	650	715	787	865
Ratio to Total IT Spending in the Country (%)	7.0	8.1	11.0	11.0	11.0	11.0
Ratio to Output (%)	0.6	0.9	1.4	1.5	1.5	1.6
IT Spending per Employee (RM)	75	222	363	350	372	387
Labor Productivity (RM)	13.3	24.9	26.7	23.8	24.1	23.5
Growth Rate (%)	n.a.	n.a.	-1.5	-12.0	-0.7	-3.4
Telecommunications & Transportation						
Output (RM million)	7,026	14,964	22,263	23,636	25,126	26,919
IT Spending (RM million)	n.a.	n.a.	650	715	787	865
Ratio to Total IT Spending in the Country (%)	n.a.	n.a.	11.0	11.0	11.0	11.0
Ratio to Output (%)	n.a.	n.a.	2.9	3.0	3.1	3.2
IT Spending per Employee (RM)	n.a.	n.a.	1,538	1,527	1,584	1,796
Labor Productivity (RM)	23.3	41.7	52.7	50.5	50.6	55.9
Growth Rate (%)	n.a.	n.a.	7.5	-5.5	-1.5	9.2
Malaysia						
Output (RM million)	119,081	222,473	343,215	334,405	362,012	395,017
IT Spending (RM million)	1,300	3,800	5,910	6,501	7,151	7,866
Ratio to Output (%)	1.1	1.7	1.7	1.9	2.0	2.0
IT Spending per Employee (RM)	194	497	634	695	749	797
Labor Productivity (RM)	17,813	29,101	36,819	35,738	37,936	40,023
Growth Rate (%)	n.a.	n.a.	6.5	-4.3	4.3	4.3

Note: n.a. = not available. Sources: Author's calculation based on data from Government of Malaysia (1996), Ministry of International Trade and Industry (2004), International Labor Office (1999, 2004).

manufacturing companies need IT equipment and IT-related intangible assets such as software to produce IT products. Therefore, IT investments in the manufacturing sector expanded compared to the distributive-trade sector. As a consequence, the positive attitude of the government toward the manufacturing sector has contributed to an increase in IT investments and better labor productivity; however, a disparity among sectors has arisen in Malaysia.

State-Level Analysis

Tables 4 and 5 show the situation regarding economic and ICT-related indicators in each state. In these tables, all states and federal territories are classified according to per capita state

gross domestic product (GDP). It is obvious that the relatively less developed states are Sabah, Sarawak, and those mainly in the eastern and northern parts of the Malay Peninsula, and the more developed states are concentrated mainly in the center, south, and one part of the northern area of the peninsula.

States in which the per capita state GDP is relatively low have less developed basic ICT systems, such as telephone and electricity, that people need in order to be benefited by ICT. Internet subscribers in less developed states are fewer than those in more developed states. A large number of Internet subscribers are in the central area; the share is more than 50% in Slangor and Kuala Lumpur. With the exception of Sabah, in the less developed states, the number of subscribers per

Table 4. Development Index (1990=100)

	Region	Per Capita GDP		Telephones per 1,000 Population		Population Provided Electricity	
		1990	2000	1990	2000	1990	2000
More Developed States		104.4	133.8	106.6	134.2	105.0	135.9
Johor	South	97.0	128.5	101.2	130.9	99.1	135.9
Melaka	Central	100.1	131.2	99.0	130.7	107.6	135.9
Negri Sembilan	Central	94.9	126.8	99.7	129.9	106.8	135.9
Perak	North	95.1	127.4	97.9	130.5	99.1	135.9
Pulau Pinang	North	106.4	140.0	108.6	140.8	106.8	135.9
Selangor[1]	Central	113.4	133.7	113.3	147.8	107.6	135.9
Federal Territory Kuala Lumpur	Central	120.6	154.1	126.4	128.8	107.6	135.9
Less Developed States		94.6	123.9	93.4	117.8	95.0	128.1
Kedah	North	88.3	120.9	92.0	115.9	100.9	135.9
Kelantan	East	94.3	116.8	89.6	115.4	95.0	135.9
Pahang	East	94.2	123.1	93.2	122.4	103.8	135.9
Perlis	North	90.1	123.7	94.7	115.9	106.8	135.9
Sabah[2]	Borneo	96.2	121.2	95.9	115.9	77.2	107.7
Sarawak	Borneo	99.2	126.7	96.9	120.1	79.5	109.1
Terengganu	East	108.2	142.3	91.6	119.0	102.1	135.9
Malaysia		100.0	129.5	100.0	126.0	100.0	132.0

Notes: 1. Includes Federal Territory Putrajaya. 2. Includes Federal Territory Labuan. Source: Government of Malaysia (2001b), p. 109.

Table 5. Internet subscribers by state (Year 2000)

	Region	Total Subscribers	Share (%)	Subscribers per 1,000 Population
More Developed States		706,479	80.6	
Johor	South	77,747	8.9	30.3
Melaka	Central	17,234	2.0	28.6
Negri Sembilan	Central	22,373	2.6	27.0
Perak	North	55,345	6.3	27.3
Pulau Pinang	North	63,648	7.3	51.9
Selangor[1]	Central	335,262	38.2	84.9
Federal Territory Kuala Lumpur	Central	134,870	15.4	103.9
Less Developed States		170,294	19.4	
Kedah	North	28,494	3.2	18.1
Kelantan	East	16,101	1.8	12.5
Pahang	East	21,682	2.5	18.0
Perlis	North	3,710	0.4	18.7
Sabah[2]	Borneo	42,047	4.8	35.8
Sarawak	Borneo	43,219	4.9	21.5
Terengganu	East	15,041	1.7	17.1
Malaysia		876,773	100.0	39.5
Mean		62,627		35.4
Median		35,271		27.2

Notes: 1. Includes Federal Territory Putrajaya. 2. Includes Federal Territory Labuan. Source: Government of Malaysia (2006), p.368.

1,000 people is less than the country's mean of 27.2.[7] Although the government of Malaysia has committed itself to facilitating key infrastructure, there is regional disparity not only in income but also in IT promotion.

CONCLUDING REMARKS AND POLICY IMPLICATIONS

In this study, the author looked at IT promotion policies and analyzed their outcomes in Malaysia. In the review of literature, it is portrayed that firm-level studies focused on developed countries successfully showed relationships between IT and economic development; however, it is not easy to do research regarding developing countries because reliable data and information are difficult to access. Capital stock data are not available in Malaysia; this study was conducted from the viewpoint of the aggregate level. In addition to this, the author tried to analyze the outcome of government policies on the basis of other evidence by utilizing sector-level and state-level data.

The government of Malaysia began to mention strategic development plans of IT in the *Sixth Malaysia Plan* (1991-1995). In order to improve TFP, the government emphasized R&D activities and IT, IT-related infrastructure, and IT-related human resource development. The *Eighth Malaysia Plan* (2001-2005) stressed communication in addition to IT. The government expected information and communication technology to become one of the major engines of economic development.

Based on this idea, Malaysia promoted IT-related infrastructure and human resources. For human resource development, the government encouraged e-learning. Furthermore, the government recognized the importance of security. Therefore, legal infrastructure and a framework of IT security were introduced.

The government's strong concern regarding ICT-supported ICT development in Malaysia is shown by the statistics in this chapter; however, new problems have arisen. This chapter reveals disparities in sectors and regions. In the sector-level analysis, the manufacturing sector and the financial sector were the most active investors in ICT, whereas the distributive sector was relatively less developed in terms of ICT development. In the state-level analysis, relatively poor states have less developed basic ICT systems, such as telephone and electricity, that people need in order to be benefited by ICT. Internet subscribers in less developed states are fewer than those in more developed states. In Malaysia, these issues should be addressed as the next step toward a knowledge-based economy.

From these analyses, this chapter suggests three policy implications for other developing countries. First, government commitment can contribute to ICT development. ICT is a sort of public goods, and a large amount of investment is needed for basic ICT infrastructure. In developing countries, it is difficult for the poor private sector to promote ICT. Second, the government needs to develop ICT through a strategic and gradual approach. In this sense, the government needs an appropriate development plan in keeping with the development stages of the country. Third, the government needs to pay careful attention to ICT disparities that may arise in the process of ICT development. This may be an important point in pursuing stable economic development.

REFERENCES

Abdulai, D. (2004). *Can Malaysia transit into the k-economy?: Dynamic challenges, tough choices and the next phase.* Selangor, Malaysia: Pelanduk Publications.

Baily, M. N., & Gordon, R. J. (1988). The productivity slowdown, measurement issues, and the explosion of computer power. *Brookings Papers on Economic Activity, 2*, 347-431.

Bank Negara Malaysia. (2006, March). *Monthly Statistical Bulletin.*

Brynjolfsson, E., & Hitt, L. (1996). Paradox lost?: Firm-level evidence on the returns to information systems spending. *Management Science, 42*(4), 541-558.

Brynjolfsson, E., & Yang, S. (1996). Information technology and productivity: A review of the literature. *Advances in Computers, 43*, 179-214.

Freeman, C. (1992). *The economics of hope: Essays on technical change, economic growth and the environment.* London: Printer Publishers.

Fukuda, Y., Sudo, O., & Hayami, H. (1997). *Economics of information.* Tokyo: Yuhikaku.

Government of Malaysia. (1996). *Seventh Malaysia plan 1996-2000.* Kuala Lumpur, Malaysia: Percetakan Nasional Malaysia.

Government of Malaysia. (2001a). *Eighth Malaysia plan 2001-2005.* Kuala Lumpur, Malaysia: Percetakan Nasional Malaysia.

Government of Malaysia. (2001b). *The third outline perspective plan 2001-2010.* Kuala Lumpur, Malaysia: Percetakan Nasional Malaysia.

Government of Malaysia. (2006). *Ninth Malaysia plan 2006-2010.* Kuala Lumpur, Malaysia: Percetakan Nasional Malaysia.

Griliches, Z. (1988). Productivity puzzles and R&D: Another nonexplanation. *Journal of Economic Perspectives, 2*(4), 9-21.

Ibrahim, A., & Goh, C.C. (1998). *Multimedia super corridor.* Kuala Lumpur, Malaysia: Leeds Publications.

International Labor Office. (1999). *Yearbook of labor statistics.* Geneva, Switzerland: Author.

International Labor Office. (2004). *Yearbook of labor statistics.* Geneva, Switzerland: Author.

Ismail, A. (1999). Malaysia. In Asian Productivity Organization (Ed.), *Changing productivity movement in Asia and Pacific: Challenges and lessons* (pp. 170-191). Tokyo: Asian Productivity Organization.

Kraemer, K. L., Gurbazani, V., & King, J. L. (1992). Economic development, government policy, and the diffusion of computing in Asia Pacific countries. *Public Administration Review, 52*(2), 146-156.

Lehr, B., & Lichtenberg, F. (1999). Information technology and its impact on productivity: Firm-level evidence from government and private date sources, 1977-1993. *The Canadian Journal of Economics, 32*(2), 335-362.

Mahathir, M. (1998). *Excerpts from the speeches of Mahathir Mohamad on the multimedia super corridor.* Selangor, Malaysia: Pelanduk Publications.

Ministry of International Trade and Industry. (2004). *Malaysia international trade and industry report 2004.* Kuala Lumpur, Malaysia: Ampang Press.

Mody, A., & Dahlman, C. (1992). Performance and potential of information technology: An international perspective. *World Development, 20*(12), 1703-1719.

Oliner, S. D., & Sichel, D. E. (1994). Computers and output growth revisited: How big is the puzzle? *Brookings Papers on Economic Activity, 2,* 273-334.

Solow, R. M. (1987, July 12). We'd better watch out. *The New York Times Book Review,* p. 36.

Stiglits, J. E., & Walsh, C. E. (2002). *Economics* (3rd ed.). New York: W. W. Norton & Company.

Varian, H. R. (2003). *Intermediate microeconomics: A modern approach.* New York: W. W. Norton & Company.

ENDNOTES

[1] Brynjolfsson and Yang (1996) provide a comprehensive literature review regarding this issue.

[2] This institution was started as the National Productivity Center in 1962, a joint project of the United Nations Special Fund and the government of Malaysia. The government has improved and enhanced the function of this institution and finally approved the National Productivity Corporation becoming a federal statutory organization (Ismail, 1999).

[3] In addition to this, the NPC launched a 3-year campaign (1997-1999) for accelerating productivity growth. The NPC plays an important role in productivity enhancement in Malaysia.

[4] The orthodox explanation is that total output results from the stock of capital (both human and physical), supply of labor, and another factor that cannot be explained by the two. Economists consider that the last factor is almost the same as technology and call it TFP.

5   Research and development activities are also addressed. To foster R&D and make a tight linkage between research institutions and business entities, the government established University Putra Malaysia-Malaysian Technology Development Corporation.

6   As of the end of 2000, 429 companies were granted MSC status. For details about the MSC, please refer to Ibrahim and Goh (1998) and Abdulai (2004). Mahathir (1998) is a collection of Dr. Mahathir's speeches on the MSC.

7   One reason for the number of Internet subscribers per 1,000 people being so high in Sabah, categorized as a less developed state, is that the statistics include the Federal Territory of Labuan. In Labuan, there is an offshore banking center where many foreign financial institutions are doing business; these institutions are ICT intensive.

Chapter IV
Information and Communication Technology and Economic Development in Malaysia

Mohamed Aslam
University of Malaysia, Malaysia

ABSTRACT

Since the early 1990s, the government has emphasised the ICT sector as a new engine of growth and development. The Multimedia Super Corridor (MSC), which was developed in 1996, was regarded as a main vehicle and catalyst for ICT-sector development. Since there were many new institutions established by the government, it some how had complicated and decreased efficiency in expanding the industry. ICT-related courses at public and private institutions were not developed well enough to meet the market demand. Consequently, the human factor, which was a major component for ICT development, was not fully utilised in research and development, therefore reliance on foreign technology remained a critical issue. These have slowed the progress of ICT development. This chapter will discuss the ICT-sector development policy in a broad view and try to analyse critically to what extent the development of the ICT sector has contributed to economic development in Malaysia.

INTRODUCTION

In 1991, the Malaysian government launched Vision 2020, with one of its main goals for Malaysia to become a fully developed nation by the year 2020. En route to achieving this goal, the information and communication technologies had been identified as one of the key sectors to realize this goal. This sector has been regarded and emphasized as a new sector of future economic growth and development. The sector had been included in the *Sixth Malaysia Plan* (6MP) for development within 5 years from 1991 to 1995. However, a bold policy and the necessary infrastructure and environment for the development of ICT was developed during the *Seventh Malaysia Plan* (7MP, development period from 1996-2000). Under the *Ninth Malaysia Plan* (9MP, development period from 2006-2010), the government has almost doubled its allocation for the ICT sector to RM13 billion compared to RM7.8 billion in the *Eighth Malaysia Plan* (8MP, development period from 2001-2005)(Table 1). Part of the allocation, about RM3.7 billion (in 8MP, the amount was RM2.4 billion), will be used to boost ICT capacity in government agencies and bridge the digital divide between urban and rural agencies.

To strengthen ICT development, in 1996 the government had initiated and established the Multimedia Super Corridor (MSC) managed by the Multimedia Development Corporation (MDC). Since then, the MSC has grown into a thriving dynamic ICT hub, hosting more than 900 multinational foreign-owned and homegrown Malaysian companies focused on multimedia and communications products, solutions, services, and research and development (R&D). The government has planned for the second phase of MSC and four new cybercities, which will be developed under 9MP. The number of MSC-status companies is projected to grow from 1,421 as of 2004 to some 4,000 by 2010, and these are expected to create some 100,000 new jobs and generate about 1,400 new intellectual properties.

In order to support the country's ICT development plan and fulfill Vision 2020, the education system is in the process of being transformed to create a new generation of more creative and innovative Malaysians who are adept with new technologies and able to access and manage the information explosion. ICT-enabled smart schools act as a catalyst within this process. The first phase of implementation began in 1999 with 90 schools. Also, to foster the ICT industry in the short term, tertiary education, particularly computer science and engineering faculties, has been restructured

by not only focusing on hardware matters but also focusing on software development. This is to ensure human capital for the ICT industry in various specialities adequate to meet the demand.

In fact, the ICT sector has been a main industry and a main component of economic growth since the early 1970s. The introduction of export-oriented industries with emphasis on electrical and electronics (E&E) industries and supported by the heavy inflow of foreign direct investment (FDI) in the sector has expanded it. The expansion of the foreign-owned E&E industries has spilled over into the domestic economy, whereby many local support industries and IT-related firms have been developed. Consequently, the demand on labour for both skilled and unskilled workers has increased very significantly. The ICT industry's export performance has been increasing steadily over the years from RM35.3 billion in 1998 to about RM61 billion in 2005 (about 50% of the total manufacturing goods). Major export destinations were the traditional markets such as the USA, Japan, Singapore, and Hong Kong. On the other hand, domestic spending on ICT material reached RM36 billion in 2004. To enhance trade in the ICT sector, e-commerce trading has been promoted and developed.

With respect to the ICT industry, there are many issues that have emerged and worry policy makers. Too much emphasis on the ICT sector, particularly by the government and by the market, has created and increased unemployment for ICT graduates either at the first degree or certificate level, including diploma holders. This has some how retarded the smooth development and progress of the ICT sector. The economic crisis from 1997 to 1999 has also slowed the ICT industry's development. Many companies that are ICT related, foreign as well as local, have closed operations and moved to China in particular. This is a cost to the economy. The government has revised and further liberalized the investment incentives for the ICT industry to reattract old firms and attract new ones to be established in the country. The Third Industrial Master Plan, which was launched in August 2006, gave greater concentration on the ICT sector besides services related to the manufacturing sector.

Government Policies on ICT-Sector Development

The government has been committed to developing the ICT sector since the 6MP. It has established various agencies related to ICT, and each agency has introduced policies promoting ICT development within the jurisdiction of the particular agency, such as the Malaysian Institute of Microelectronic Systems (MIMOS), the National Information Technology Agenda (NITA), the National Information Technology Council (NITC), and the Ministry of Energy, Communications, and Multimedia (MECM; Table 2). Too many policies were formulated by the federal government, and the agencies have some how increased in redundancy and created inefficiencies in developing the ICT sector.

The seriousness of the government in promoting the ICT sector can be seen from the government's allocation for the sector. The government has increased allocation from RM2.125 billion under the 8MP to RM5.734 billion under the 9MP. The large amount of allocations is invested in the computerisation of ministries and government agencies. This huge amount of funds is in line with the government's plan to increase paperless transactions, reduce operating costs in the future, and speed up the processing of applications and any matters related to government. To meet the aims, the government has increased allocation to the e-government subarea of the MSC multimedia application from RM537.7 million in the 8MP to RM572.7 million under the 9MP, (Table 1). Another vital project is Bridging the Digital Divide, which also received a huge amount of government allocation. The allocation of the project has been increased from RM1.1 billion in the 7MP to RM3.7 billion in the 9MP. Even though the federal government allocation to ICT

Table 1. Development expenditure and allocation for ICT-related programmes, 1996-2010 (RM million; Source: Government of Malaysia, 2001, p. 388; Government of Malaysia, 2006, p. 154)

Programmes	7MP	8MP	9MP
Computerisation of Government Agencies	1,641.8	2125.0	5,734.2
Bridging the Digital Divide	1,098	2,433.1	3,710.2
Schools	945	2,145.1	3,279.2
Communications Infrastructure Service Provision Programme	119.8	254.0	150.0
Telecenters	33.2	18.1	101.0
ICT Training/Services	-	15.9	180.0
ICT Funding		1,125.6	1,493.0
MSC Multimedia Applications	1,824.9	1,153.1	1,100.5
E-Government	434.8	537.7	572.7
Smart Schools	401.1	363.9	169.8
Telehealth	400.0	91.8	60.0
Government Multipurpose Card, etc.	589	159.7	298.0
MSC Development	-	320.8	377.0
ICT Research and Development	300.0	727.5	474.0
Other	294.4	-	-
Total	5,159.1	7,885.1	12,888.9

has increased over the years, the government's spending is about 6% compared to the global average government ICT spending of 15%.

Government Agencies and Policies on ICT Development

As mentioned, there are many agencies that have been developed by the government that have established a law related to ICT. Also, a trade association was formed among ICT firms (Table 2). In this section we will focus on the government think tank on ICT, the National Information Technology Council, which was established in 1994. The NITC was responsible for formulating the National Information Technology Agenda, which was launched in 1996. NITA provides a comprehensive framework for ICT development. The primary objective of NITA is to ensure a co-ordinated and integrated approach in developing the ICT industry more systematically and also to transform the Malaysian society into a value-based knowledge society. The government has adopted NITA as a major strategy for national development and nation building through the ICT sector. NITA proposed a trisectoral smart partnership between the public, private, and community-interest sectors, where all parties win. A two-prong strategy of combining top-down and bottom-up approaches for planning and implementation is recommended (refer to subsection on MSC).

The National ICT Framework under NITA is combining people (human resource), infrastructure (both hard and soft infrastructure), and appli-

Table 2. ICT sector: Institutional development (Source: MDC, 2003)

Agencies	Function/Role
Malaysian Institute of Microelectronic Systems (MIMOS Berhad)	Established on January 1, 1985, then corporatised on November 1, 1996. Deals with research and development (wafer and chip technology). Plays a crucial role in developing ICT. An Internet service provider (Jaring).
National Information Technology Council (NITC)	Established in 1994. A government think tank. Advising and recommending policy on ICT development.
Ministry of Energy, Communications, and Multimedia (MECM)	Established on November 1, 1998. To develop the communications and multimedia industry based on the concept of the convergence of the telecommunications, broadcasting, and computing services.
Malaysian Communications and Multimedia Commission (MCMC)	Established on November 1, 1998. Responsible for regulating the broadcasting industries, ICT, and telecommunications in accordance to the Communications and Multimedia Act of 1998. A sole regulating authority for all communication and multimedia industries.
Multimedia Developed Corporation (MDC)	MDC was established to assist the government in developing and managing the MSC. A one-stop shop for investors.
Association of the Computer and Multimedia Industry Malaysia (PIKOM)	A voluntary self-funding trade association representing the ICT industry. The number of members is about 370 companies. Members control about 400 firms and represent about 80% of the total ICT trade in the country.
Legislation Supports	The Digital Signature Act of 1997, which governs electronic signatures. The Computer Crimes Act of 1997, which outlaws the fraudulent use of computers and other related cybercrime. The Electronic Government Act of 1997, which regulates communication within the public sector. The Multimedia Convergence Act of 1997, which streamlines communication, information, and broadcasting services. The Telemedicine Act of 1997, which allows for the promotion of medical services. The Communications and Multimedia of Act 1998, which facilitates the orderly development of the multimedia industries, in particular the contents industry, and replaces existing inadequate legislation. The Intellectual Property Protection Act of 1998, which protects copyright laws.

cations and content (product) development. NITA places the human factor as the main element; all citizens need access to information in an equitable manner. The second element of infrastructure is seen in terms of both the hard and soft infrastructure. The hard infrastructure is the computer hardware and the relevant telecommunication components. The soft infrastructure includes databases, networks, laws, and regulations. The applications and content element emphasises the importance of developing applications in IT and encouraging local product development.

Under the 7MP, the government indirectly based its policy on ICT development on NITA. The policy formulated by the federal government under the 7MP was regarded as a concrete policy in promoting, developing, and expanding the ICT infrastructure, and to promote the extensive application of ICT and accelerate ICT usage in the various sectors of the economy. The document elucidates several national strategies on ICT as listed below:

- Develop a national plan to ensure a more systematic approach to manage the development of ICT through NITA and the Multimedia Super Corridor.
- Increase and enhance IT education and training.
- Expand and upgrade the communications infrastructure to increase accessibility.
- review laws and regulations to promote the growth of electronic communities and the development of a continuous learning environment.
- Promote the development of e-commerce, indigenous contents, and the local IT industry, especially the software and knowledge products industries, to generate new growth opportunities.
- Review and improve the national innovation systems to generate R&D output capable of driving the knowledge economy.

Multimedia Super Corridor

Under the 7MP, the government established the Multimedia Super Corridor on August 1, 1996. The development of the MSC was the main outcome of NITA and the government policy in developing the ICT sector. The initiative of MSC came with a two-prong strategy. The strategies are to transform the Malaysian economy from one of manufacturing and primary commodities to software and services, and to create an ideal environment for global ICT companies to use as their regional hub and test bed, becoming a catalyst for a highly competitive cluster of homegrown ICT companies that can become world-class over time.

Development of the MSC is a government long-term project that was initiated to run from 1996 up to 2020. This long-term period is divided into three phases. The first phase covers 1996 to 2004, during which the government would develop the MSC area. The second phase covers 2004 to 2010. This phase will link the MSC to other cybercities in Malaysia. Finally, the third phase covers 2010 to 2020, during which the government hopes to realise the objective of transforming Malaysia into a knowledge society.

In the first phase, the government developed the MSC center, which is located south of the Kuala Lumpur City Center. Two smart cities, namely Putrajaya and Cyberjaya, were developed in the MSC. Putrajaya is the new seat of the federal government and administrative capital of Malaysia, where the concept of electronic government is introduced. Cyberjaya was planned as an intelligent city with multimedia industries, R&D centers, a multimedia university, and operational headquarters for multinationals using multimedia technology for their worldwide manufacturing and trading activities. The MSC was built upon a 2.5- to 10-gigabit digital optical fibre backbone enabling direct high-capacity links to Japan, the USA, and Europe (MDC, 1996). The MSC was developed to attract world-class technology-led companies to Malaysia and to develop local industries; to create a multimedia utopia that offers a productive, intelligent environment within the multimedia value chain of goods and services that will be produced and delivered across the globe; to offer a place of excellence with multimedia-specific capabilities, technologies, infrastructure, legislation, policies, and systems for competitive advantage; to establish a center for invention, research, and other multimedia developments; and to create a global community living on the leading edge of the information society, and a world of smart homes, smart cities, smart schools, smart cards, and smart partnerships (MDC, 1996).

To ensure the realisation of the MSC, the government introduced the MSC Bill of Guarantees. Under the Bill of Guarantees, the Malaysian government commits the following to companies with MSC status:

- Provide a world-class physical and information infrastructure.
- Allow unrestricted employment of local and foreign knowledge workers.
- Ensure freedom of ownership by exempting companies with MSC status from local ownership requirements.
- Give the freedom to source capital globally for MSC infrastructure and the right to borrow funds globally.
- Provide competitive financial incentives (no income tax up to 10 years or an investment tax allowance of up to 5 years will be granted).
- Become a regional leader in intellectual property protection and cyberlaws.
- Ensure no Internet censorship.
- Provide globally competitive telecommunication tariffs.
- Tender key MSC infrastructure contracts to leading companies willing to use the MSC as their regional hub.
- Provide a high-powered implementation agency to act as an effective one-stop supershop.

The Multimedia Development Corporation, the agency that manages the MSC, is the one-stop shop for Malaysian and international companies that are prepared to set up operations within the MSC or otherwise contribute significantly and strategically to the MSC's development. A company seeking MSC status must fulfill three criteria. The company must (a) be a provider or a heavy user of multimedia products and services, (b) employ a substantial number of knowledge workers, and (c) be able to transfer technology and knowledge to Malaysia, or otherwise contribute to the development of the MSC and the Malaysian economy.

Since the development of the MSC in 1996 until 2000, there have been 326 companies that have received MSC status, and 192 of these companies are fully owned by Malaysians. In 2005, the number increased to 1,421 companies, of which 1,033 firms were fully locally owned and 349 firms were fully foreign owned. Since the early phase of the MSC produced remarkable results, the government plans to develop MSC's second phase (MSC II) under the 9MP. Under the second phase, the government plans to build new MSC cybercities in the states of Perak, Melaka, Johor, and Sarawak. The proposed development is expected to bring in 250 additional multinational companies (Government of Malaysia, 2006). The number of MSC-status companies is projected to increase from 1,421 in 2005 to 4,000 by 2010, generating 100,000 jobs nationwide and 1,400 intellectual properties.

Progress and an Assessment of ICT Development since the 1990s

Since the government introduced the national development and expansion of the ICT industry in 1996, it has been very committed and serious on the matter, and this can be seen by looking at the government expenditure, which has increased quite tremendously (Table 3). In terms of spending on ICT usage, the government expenditure has increased from RM159 million in 1990 to RM2.2 billion in 2005 (Table 3). The government policy and expenditure allocation has in turn accelerated private-sector expenditure on ICT. In 1995, the total expenditure on ICT was RM1.3 billion. The figure increased to RM3.8 billion in 1995, to RM25.6 billion in 2000, and to about RM32.2 billion in 2005. The main industry that has increased expenditure significantly is the manufacturing sector; its expenditure has increased from 6% of the total economy expenditure in 1990 to about 45% in 2005. Other sectors that have increased the usage of ICT are wholesale and retail trade, transport and communications, finance and business services, and consumer spending on ICT products (Table 3).

Figures in parentheses are the percentage of expenditure of each sector of the total expenditure of the period.

Expenditure on ICT by consumers (society) has increased. Since 1995, it has increased by more than 7,000%. In 2005, consumers spent about RM8.1 billion on ICT-related products. The expansion of consumer expenditure on ICT-related products is clearly indicated in Table 4. The number of people who bought computers has increased from 0.8 million people in 1996 to about 5.7 million in 2005. Indicators of IT us-

Table 3. ICT expenditure by sector, 1990-2005 (RM million; Source: Government of Malaysia, 1996, p. 479; Government of Malaysia, 2001, p. 365; Government of Malaysia, 2006, p. 136)

Sector	1990	1995	2000	2004	2005
Agriculture	26 (2.0)	76 (2.0)	200 (0.8)	128 (0.4)	138 (0.4)
Mining	234 (18.0)	380 (10.1)	222 (0.9)	224 (0.7)	234 (0.7)
Manufacturing	78 (6.0)	494 (13.1)	12,188 (47.5)	13,652 (45.6)	14,367 (44.6)
Utilities	39 (3.0)	266 (7.0)	378 (1.5)	430 (1.4)	470 (1.5)
Construction	-	-	112 (0.4)	126 (0.4)	135 (1.5)
Wholesale and Retail Trade	91 (4.0)	304 (8.1)	1,585 (6.2)	1,735 (5.8)	1,870 (5.8)
Transport and Communications[1]	39 (3.0)	114 (3.0)	1,221 (4.8)	1,581 (5.3)	1,770 (5.5)
Finance and Business Services	507 (39.0)	1,026 (27.2)	1,894 (7.4)	2,563 (8.6)	2,845 (8.8)
Government	156 (12.0)	380 (10.1)	1,389 (5.4)	1,981 (6.6)	2,245 (7.0)
Consumers	-	76 (2.0)	6,314 (24.6)	7,440 (24.9)	8,104 (25.1)
Other Services[2]	130 (10.0)	657 (17.4)	140 (0.5)	62 (0.2)	70 (0.2)
Total	1,300	3,773	25,643	29,922	32,248

Notes: [1] Includes telecommunications services

[2] Includes businesses providing personal, repair, cultural, recreation and entertainment, health care, legal, educational, social, and professional services

Table 4. Selected ICT indicators (Source: Ministry of Finance, 2001, 2002, 2006)

Indicator	1996	1998	2000	2001	2002	2003	2004	2005
Telecommunications								
Number of cellular phone subscribers (thousands)	1,363	2,149	5,122	7,385	9,053	11,124	14,611	19,545
Number of Internet dial-up subscribers (thousands)	64	405	1,659	2,113	2,614	2,881	3,293	3,672
Information Technology								
Personal computers actively installed (millions)	0.8	1.4	2.2	3.0	3.6	4.2	4.9	5.7
Number of computers per 1,000 people	50	60	94	125	145	166	192	218
Broadband subscribers (thousands)	-	-	-	-	19.3	110.4	252.5	490.6

age in society have increased from 50 per 1,000 people in 1996 to 218 per 1,000 people in 2005. In line with IT usage, Internet subscription by society has increased quite remarkably. Internet dial-up subscription also increased from 64,000 people to 3.7 million people in 2005 (Table 4). The Internet was first introduced in Malaysia in the mid-1990s with MIMOS as the sole provider of Internet service. In the late 1990s, the government liberalized the sector by allowing more network-based companies to provide Internet service. At present, there are six network-based companies that have been licensed to provide Internet service in the country, namely, MAXIS, DIGI, TT.DOT. COM, CELCOM, TELEKOM, and PRISMANET. However, only three network-based companies provide Internet service, namely, JARING (under MIMOS), TMNet (under TELEKOM), and MaxisNet (under MAXIS). In terms of subscribers registered with JARING and TMNet, the number increased 10 times from 42,000 in 1995 to 425,320 in 1998, and reached about 1.68 million in 2002 (Yusuf & Radzi, 2003). In terms of users of the Internet, the number has increased from 30,000 in 1995 to 4.8 million in 2001 (Minges & Gray, 2002). The penetration rate has increased from 0.1% in 1991 to 20.2% in 2001 (Minges & Gray, 2002). A survey by the International Data Corporation

in 1999 indicated that households constituted the largest group using the Internet, comprising 64% of total users, followed by users in the education and business sectors who comprised 24% and 12%, respectively (MDC, 2003). The survey also showed that subscribers were concentrated in the urban areas, particularly in the Federal Territory of Kuala Lumpur, Johor Bahru, Petaling Jaya, and Penang. The growing market of ICT in the country provides incentives for local firms to invest further in telecommunication. Currently, there are six licensed telecommunication companies in Malaysia, but only five in operation, providing telephony services. During 1996 to 1999, telecommunications operators upgraded and improved their services through investments in telecommunication infrastructure, comprising fibre optics, satellites, and wireless technology. As a result, the backbone of the information superhighway was formed, which was capable of supporting extensive public, educational, and business applications. In addition, the country also registered a market penetration rate of 10 cellular phones for every 1,000 people, which was one of the highest in the developing world (MDC, 2003). The number of mobile phone customers is expected to break the 6 million mark or 250 for every 1,000 people by 2005 (MDC, 2003).

Investment and Export

The investment incentives such as tax breaks, MSC status, and capital allowance that have been provided by the government have managed to attract local and foreign capital into the ICT sector. In the broad category of the ICT sector, that is, the E&E sector, investment has increased from 39% of the total investment in 1996 to 40% in 2005. The electronics goods exported in 1996 was 62% of the total export of manufactured goods, with 34.1% coming from the semiconductor industry followed by electronics equipment and parts. In 2005, exports of E&E goods increased to 73.4% and semiconductor industries contributed about 32%, while 42% came from firms producing electronics equipment and parts (Table 5). Major export destinations were the traditional markets such as the USA, Japan, Singapore, and Hong Kong. Malaysia was a net exporter of ICT products worth RM28.3 billion in 2002 and RM33.8 billion in 2003 (Malaysian Industrial Development ment Authority [MIDA], 2005). Imports of ICT products, which consist of computers, servers, mainframes, and telecommunication equipment, totaled RM18.6 billion in 2002 and RM18.0 bil-

lion in 2003 (MIDA, 2005). Major imports for computers and computer peripherals were sourced from China, Singapore, and the USA, while telecommunications products were imported mainly from China, Japan, and Korea. Major import items were thermionic valves and tubes, parts for office machines, electrical apparatuses, and measuring, checking, and controlling instruments. The items most imported were thermionic valves and tubes, whose worth has increased from RM45.8 billion in 1997 to RM105.7 billion in 2005 (Ministry of Finance, 2006). The presence of foreign firms made Malaysia a net exporter of computers and computer peripherals valued at RM22.1 billion in 2002 and RM22.6 billion in 2003. Malaysia currently ranks third in the world for the production of HDD for desktop computers (MIDA, 2005).

In the case of investment in the MSC zone, the value increased from RM3.16 billion in 2001 to RM5.11 billion in 2005 (Table 6). As mentioned in the previous section, in 2005, the number of firms that were ICT related was 1,421; about 1,033 were fully locally owned while about 349 were fully foreign owned. There were more than 50 international world-class companies that received MSC status such as NTT, Fujitsu, IBM, Sun Mi-

Table 5. Exports of ICT-related products (percentages; Source: Bank Negara Malaysia, 2006)

Products	1996	2000	2003	2005
Electronics	62.0	72.4	75.1	73.4
Semiconductors	34.1	30.9	38.2	31.8
Electronics equipment & parts	27.9	41.5	36.9	41.6
Electrical machinery & appliances	38.0	27.6	24.9	26.6
Consumer products	19.1	11.5	8.8	8.1
Industrial & commercial products	10.1	10.3	9.1	10.2
Industrial machinery & equipment	8.2	5.5	6.1	7.3
Household electrical appliances	0.6	0.3	0.9	1.0
Total E&E exports (RM billion)	104.3	230.4	222.9	282.8
Percentage of total exports	65.8	72.5	67.9	65.8

crosystems, Microsoft, Oracle, Ericsson, Nokia, Siemens, and Dell. Until 2003, the activities of MSC-status firms range from software development, Internet-based business, and hardware and electronics design to education and training, as

shown in Figure 1. The exports of the MSC-status firms were about RM1.57 billion in 2005. The revenue of the firms in the same year was about RM7.21 billion (Table 6). The firms involved in the research and development area had spent

Figure 1. MSC-Status by Type of Activity, 2003

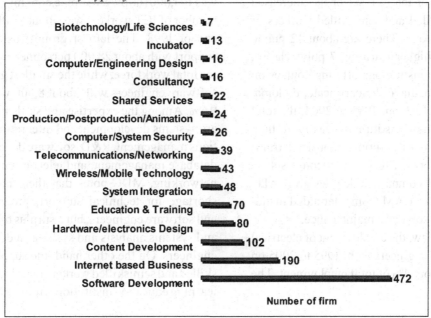

Source: Multimedia Development Corporation (MDC), 2005. www.mdc.com.my

Table 6. MSC indicators, 2001-2010 (Source: Government of Malaysia, 2006, p. 145)

Category	2001	2005	2010
MSC-status company (number)	621	1,421	4,000
Locally owned	410	1,033	-
Foreign owned	198	349	-
Joint venture (50/50)	13	39	-
Job creation (number)	14,438	27,288	100,000
Knowledge workers	12,169	24,252	-
Others	2,269	3,036	-
Investment (RM billion)	3.16	5.11	12
Revenue (RM billion)	-	7.21	69
Exports (RM billion)	-	1.57	2.5
R&D expenditure (RM million)	-	670	1,000
IPs registered (number)	-	119	1,400

about RM680 million. The expansion of the industry has created jobs, from 14,438 in 2001 to 27,288 in 2005. The majority of workers that have been employed by the firms are knowledge workers (ICT).

Human Resource Development

The expansion of the ICT sector has increased demand on skilled and semiskilled workers or knowledge workers. There are about 12 public institutions of higher learning, 7 polytechnics, and 154 private institutions offering courses on ICT and multimedia at the certificate, diploma, and degree levels. From 1995 to 2004, the total enrollment at these institutions was more than 80,000 students. In addition, industrial training institutes conduct ICT-related courses such as architectural computer-aided design (CAD), mechanical CAD, CAM (computer-aided manufacturing), and computer maintenance.

In a broad view, the employment of electrical and electronics engineers from 1995 to 2005 on average was about 4% of total employment. The employment of assistant engineers in the same field on average was about 10% of total employment (Table 7). According to statistics from the MDC, the estimated net demand for ICT manpower between 1998 and 2005 in five occupations (technical support, programmers, business/system analysts, software engineers, and systems/hardware engineers) was 108,000 while the supply was 104,000 (http://www.mdc.com.my). The total number of ICT workers was about 87,000 by the end of 1998. The largest group was technical support with about 28,000 personnel or 32.2% of the total workforce, while the smallest group was software engineers with about 8,000 workers or 9.6%. Among the expertise and skills in demand are systems development and integration, operations management, R&D, software development, database management, and telecommunications networking. MDC notes that there is a labour shortage for technical support, programmers, and software engineers, but a surplus of business and systems analysts and systems and hardware engineers. On the other hand, the supply of ICT skilled and semiskilled workers from local higher learning education institutions from 1995 to 2005

Table 7. Employment of engineers (Source: Government of Malaysia, 1996, p. 121; Government of Malaysia, 2001, p. 95)

Occupation	1995		2000		2005	
Engineers	55,254[1]	(12.1)	61,034	(10.4)	108,400	(12.6)
Civil	16,695	(3.6)	20,711	(3.5)	27,500	(3.2)
Electrical & Electronics	15,759	(3.4)	21,064	(3.6)	38,600	(4.5)
Mechanical	12,583	(2.7)	16,082	(2.7)	29,800	(3.5)
Chemical	1,037	(0.2)	3,177	(0.5)	12,500	(1.5)
Engineering Assistants	92,082[2]	(20.1)	143,220	(24.4)	247,739	(28.9)
Civil	25,971	(5.7)	25,973	(4.4)	71,401	(8.3)
Electrical & Electronics	40,023	(8.7)	65,353	(11.1)	103,856	(12.1)
Mechanical	18,706	(4.1)	50,020	(8.5)	67,073	(7.8)
Chemical	1,425	(0.3)	1,874	(0.3)	5,409	(0.6)

Notes: [1] *including unspecified engineers (8,509)*

[2] *including unspecified assistants (5,957)*

was about 9,500 workers a year. By 2006, the total number of workers should exceed 104,500 workers. Therefore, the figures produced by the MDC are overestimated. With the total ICT graduates that are produced by public and private higher learning institutions, more than 30% of the graduates were unemployed by 2006.

The government realised that there is an increasing demand and shortage of certain skills in the ICT sector due to new developments in the ICT industry. However, the public and private institutions are slow in improving and developing new courses to meet the current demand. In general, the institutions offer a basic curriculum in ICT courses. To overcome the situation, the government, particularly the Ministry of Human Resource and the Ministry of Education, is trying to match the supply of skilled human resources with the needs of the ICT sector. Moreover, the government has encouraged more training courses provided by employers, as well as encouraging local higher learning institutions to embark on more courses related to ICT. The government set up the Human Resource Development Fund (HRDF) to provide reimbursements for ICT-based training (offered by ICT-related firms and private colleges) to ensure that there is continuous upgrading of ICT knowledge and skills among the working population. During the period of 1996 to 1998, a sum of RM64.8 million or 14.6% of the total HRDF disbursements were utilised for ICT-based courses. In May 1998, the HRDF introduced the Training Scheme for Retrenched Workers. Under this scheme, a sum of RM846,000 was provided to finance 203 courses or 36% of the ICT courses approved at the certificate and diploma levels.

Figures in parentheses are the percentage of engineers (and assistants) of total employment.

CONCLUSION

ICT development, which was planned under the 6MP and embarked on since the 7MP, has pro-

duced overwhelming results. The impetus of the plan and policies were somehow retarded from 1997 to 1999 due to the impact of the financial crisis that hit in July 1997; however, the crisis has not stopped the federal government from achieving the ICT development plan. Since the 6MP, the development budget for the ICT-related sector has increased dramatically. The eagerness and seriousness of the government is evident in the national development report in terms of the increase of ICT usage in government services and in school. Furthermore, the government has received support from foreign firms. The investment by foreign firms that are ICT related has increased significantly. In fact, the overwhelming response from the local and foreign firms has encouraged the government to proceed to the second phase of MSC development and to develop a few more cybercities in selected states in Malaysia.

We do not deny that the development of the ICT sector, particularly through the development of the MSC, has induced the sector development in terms of investment, exports, and labour absorption. However, there are a few shortcomings in the development. First, the development of the ICT sector has established many institutions with different policies and roles, and there were more than seven main rules and regulations related to ICT. In certain circumstances, roles of the agencies were overlapping each other, for instance, the roles of the MECM, MDC, and MCMC. Which agency has the right to approve and issue telecommunications licenses? Which agency handles rules and regulations, and which agency has the right to enforce rules that have been established? The government should streamline and provide clear guidelines, roles, and functions of the agencies that have been established to avoid any redundancy, attract more investors, and become more private-sector friendly. The second shortcoming is related to human resource development. The development of the ICT industry, for instance, in the software and hardware areas (Figure 1), requires high-skilled workers. Public and private institutions have produced an ample workforce for the sector; however, most of the MSC-status firms have employed foreign workers, subsequently creating unemployment for local ICT graduates, of which more than 30% were unemployed. The oversupply of ICT graduates is attributed to weak planning by the education ministry; furthermore, the curriculum of the ICT courses that are offered by the higher education learning institutions do not meet the market demand. Most institutions produced a workforce knowledgeable in how to handle and manage ICT rather than in how to create, invent, and develop a product. In other words, institutions produce a workforce with very low skills in producing products. This weakness in the education institutions has forced foreign firms to employ high-skilled labour from abroad.

Currently, there is a lack of research related to MSC and economic development. Most of the studies conducted produced a report rather-than empirical data. Two of the main crucial issues with respect to MDC development are the market demand for ICT graduates and the ICT course curriculum in public and private universities and colleges. The role played by foreign MSC-status firms in helping and developing the ICT industry in the country remains very much unclear. These issues should be explored further to gauge relevant indicators for future development.

REFERENCES

Government of Malaysia. (1996). *Seventh Malaysia plan 1996-2000.* Kuala Lumpur, Malaysia: Percetakan Nasional Malaysia.

Government of Malaysia. (2001). *Eighth Malaysia plan 2001-2005.* Kuala Lumpur, Malaysia: Percetakan Nasional Malaysia.

Government of Malaysia. (2006). *Ninth Malaysia plan 2006-2010.* Kuala Lumpur, Malaysia: Percetakan Nasional Malaysia.

Malaysian Industrial Development Authority (MIDA). (2005). *Performance of the manufacturing & related services sectors 2004.* Kuala Lumpur, Malaysia: Author.

Minges, M., & Gray, V. (2002). *Multimedia Malaysia: Internet case study.* International Telecommunication Union (ITU).

Ministry of Finance. (2001). *Economic report 2001/2002.* Kuala Lumpur, Malaysia: Percetakan Nasional Malaysia.

Ministry of Finance. (2002). *Economic report 2002/2003.* Kuala Lumpur, Malaysia: Percetakan Nasional Malaysia.

Ministry of Finance. (2006). *Economic report 2006/2007.* Kuala Lumpur, Malaysia: Percetakan Nasional Malaysia.

Multimedia Development Corporation (MDC). (1996). *Investing in Malaysia's MSC: Policies, incentives & facilities.* Kuala Lumpur, Malaysia: Author.

Multimedia Development Corporation (MDC). (2003). *National report on the ICT sector in Malaysia.* Unpublished manuscript.

Yusuf, M., & Radzi, M. (2003). *A national initiative: Presenting a success story.* Unpublished manuscript, MSC Technology Center, Cyberjaya, Malaysia.

Chapter V
Macroeconomic Announcements, Asymmetric Volatility, and IT:
Evidence from JGB Futures

Takeo Minaki
Hokusei Gakuen University, Japan

Ichihiro Uchida
Aichi University, Japan

Hiroshi Kamae
Hitotsubashi University, Japan

ABSTRACT

This study analyzes the impact of macroeconomic announcements on the conditional volatility of Japanese government bond (JGB) futures returns. As information technology continues to develop, the arrival and the processing of new market-related information become more rapid. Using high-frequency data of JGB futures, we find that announcement shocks influence the dynamics of bond market volatility. Our results provide empirical evidence that the JGB futures market does not immediately incorporate implications of macroeconomic announcement news. The volatility of JGB futures returns persists for a while. Moreover, after distinguishing among types of shocks, volatility is asymmetric. Negative shocks have a stronger impact on subsequent volatility than do positive shocks.

INTRODUCTION

Recently, some event studies have used high-frequency data to investigate the efficient market hypothesis (EMH), which requires examination of announcement effects on volatility. For this chapter, we specifically examine scheduled news: macroeconomics announcements and asymmetric volatility.

Regarding volatility, precedent studies show that it is not constant through time. For example, Arshanapalli, d'Ouville, Fabozzi, and Switzer (2006), Wang, Wang, and Liu (2005), Ederington and Lee (2001), Bollerslev, Cai, and Song (2000), Jones, Lamont, and Lumsdaine (1998), Andersen and Bollerslev (1997), Glosten, Jagannathan, and Runkle (1993), and Nelson (1991) use volatility models such as the GARCH model to analyze market efficiency. Aside from those studies, many early investigations such as those of Fleming and Remolona (1999), Li and Engle (1998), and Ederington and Lee (1993) have similarly analyzed volatility.

Glosten et al. (1993), Nelson (1991), and Ederington and Lee (2001) also analyze the asymmetry of volatility. However, few studies have examined the government bond market; instead, they have investigated stock markets. The present study was intended to elucidate asymmetric volatility for a government bond market.

The asymmetric volatility effect refers to the tendency that good and bad news about returns differently affect the conditional volatility. Many studies have addressed the conditional volatility of stock returns. For example, Black (1976) argues that a drop in the value of a stock increases financial leverage, which renders the stock more risky and increases its volatility (the so-called leverage effect hypothesis). Recently, Goeij and Marquering (2006) report asymmetry in bond return volatility. Because financial leverage is inapplicable to government bonds, the leverage argument cannot explain asymmetry in bond volatility.

In this chapter, we investigate the asymmetric volatility in the Tokyo Stock Exchange (TSE) for Japanese government bond (JGB) futures. First, it is examined whether macroeconomic announcements influence volatility. Next, after including announcement effects into the model of the asymmetry of volatility, market efficiency is analyzed.

Minaki (2006), using identical data to those used in this study, demonstrates that the JGB futures market in TSE is not efficient. However, that study did not address asymmetric volatility. Therefore, we devote attention to the asymmetry of volatility and verify market efficiency.

We follow Glosten et al. (1993) and Ederington and Lee (2001), and examine whether the dynamics of volatility is different after positive and negative shocks.

Moreover, we use the surprise to estimate the model. That difference is calculated using the expected value that the Bloomberg is reporting and the actual value. To investigate the influence of the announcement effects, we must consider the importance of the difference between the actual data and the expectations of macroeconomic announcements: the surprise caused by the announcement, that is, market participants' unpredicted components of data. The difference between the actual value of macroeconomic announcements and their expected value is important, as described by Balduzzi, Elton, and Green (2001) and Fleming and Remolona (1999), when the influence of public information is estimated. Therefore, we also use surprise variables. For this study, we presume that unpredicted information, the so-called surprise, is important for measuring announcement effects.

Results show that the asymmetry of volatility is apparent in the JGB futures market. When a price falls unexpectedly rather than increasing, volatility is higher in the subsequent interval. In addition, the effects of macroeconomic announcements are considerable. Moreover, the JGB futures market is inefficient.

The remainder of this chapter is organized as follows. Next it presents the empirical framework used in this study. Then it describes the data used for analyses. In the section after that, we discuss the empirical results. Finally, we conclude this study.

VOLATILITY MODEL

A high- (low-) volatility period tends to continue for some time after volatility increases (decreases). Such a phenomenon is called volatility clustering. In securities markets, a large change of volatility concentrates and takes place in a certain period. In a recent study, Minaki (2005, 2006) and Kamae and Minaki (2004) examine JGB futures market efficiency. Using the GARCH model, the authors conclude that the JGB futures market is not efficient. In the present study, we examine the asymmetric volatility in the JGB futures market using the generalized GJR model.

First, we adopt the OLS method to distinguish which macroeconomic announcements influence volatility significantly. The purpose of using the OLS method here is merely to identify important macroeconomics variables that should be used in the GJR model. Then, to measure the influence of unpredictable information, we use surprise elements, not a macroeconomic announcements dummy (0,1).

We follow Balduzzi et al. (2001) and Fleming and Remolona (1999), and define the surprise as:

$$E_{i,t} = F_{i,t} - A_{i,t},$$ (1)

where $F_{i,t}$ denotes the expected value of macroeconomic news i in period t that the Bloomberg service is reporting; $A_{i,t}$ denotes the actual value of the macroeconomic news i. Then, $E_{i,t}$ denotes the difference between the expectation and the actual value.

Fleming and Remolona (1999) show that normalization is required to compare announcement effects because differences exist in each macroeconomic announcements unit.

$$S_{i,t} = {E_{i,t}}\big/{\bar{S}_{i,t}}, \bar{S}_{i,t} = \frac{1}{N_i}\sum |E_{i,t}|$$ (2)

In those equations, N_i denotes a number of the macroeconomic announcement i. We use the surprise variable $S_{i,t}$ to signify the announcement effects.

The OLS estimate equation is:

$$R_t - \bar{R}| = a_0 + \sum_{i=1}^{I} a_i S_{i,t} + u_t,$$ (3)

where $| R_t - \bar{R} |$ denotes volatility, R_t represents a return at period t, and $\bar{R}$ denotes the average of returns; i denotes a number of macroeconomic announcement ($i = 1, \ldots, 12$). This measurement was used by Jones et al. (1998), but it is only used with the OLS method.

The GARCH Model

For the OLS method, we adapt $| R_t - \bar{R} |$ as the volatility. To estimate it precisely, we use the GARCH (1,1) model and the GJR model for specification of the conditional volatility. As Bollerslev (1986) and Campbell, Lo, and MacKinlay (1997) show, the GARCH (1,1) model fulfills the principle of the saving and can catch the effect of ARCH of higher order. First, we use the AR (1) process to model returns as:

$$R_t = a_0 + a_1 R_{t-1} + e_t,$$ (4)

where e_t denotes unexpected returns (the error term), and:

$$h_{t+1} = w + \xi e_t^2 + \lambda h_t,$$ (5)

where h_t denotes the conditional variance of the error term. The coefficient ξ indicates the extent to which a volatility shock in this period feeds through to the next period's volatility. Furthermore, $\xi + \lambda$ measures the rate at which this effect subsides over time.

We use surprise variables to estimate announcement effects on volatility. As Ederington and Lee (2001) and Bollerslev et al. (2000) report, it is necessary to control the effects of macroeconomic announcements when using the GARCH model.

$$h_{t+1} = w + \xi e_t^2 + \lambda h_t + \sum_{i=1}^{I} V_i S_{i,t} \qquad (6)$$

A macroeconomic announcement i influences volatility significantly if a coefficient V_i is statistically significant. We can judge whether such an announcement's effect exists. The coefficient V_i is typically larger than zero: News arrivals are associated with higher risk. The risk used in this chapter means that a price of JGB futures becomes volatile when macroeconomic announcements are released. Consequently, V_i might be interpreted as a premium for bearing the macroeconomic announcements' arrival risk. In short, the shock will persist for some time by $\xi + \lambda$ of approximate unity. However, the shock will persist infinitely into the future for $\xi + \lambda = 1$.

The GJR Model (Generalized GJR Model)

Next, to model the conditional variance, we extend the GJR model of Glosten et al. (1993). This specification has some appealing features. First, it enables examination of the influence of macroeconomic announcements on the JGB futures market volatility. Second, it permits a certain level of asymmetry in conditional variance. It is said that volatility mainly responds asymmetrically after a large shock: either very good or very bad news (Black, 1976). Such large shocks in the bond market are usually related to macroeconomic announcements. For that reason, we use the extended specification to capture such a phenomenon.

In this specification, the conditional volatility is shown by v_t as follows:

$$v_t = \eta + \lambda v_{t-1} + \xi e_{t-1}^2 + \gamma D_{t-1}^- e_{t-1}^2 + \sum_{i=1}^{I} V_i S_{i,t} \qquad (7)$$

Therein, $D_{t-1}^- = 1$ if e_{t-1} is negative at time $t-1$ and zero; otherwise $E(e_t) = 0$, Var $(e_t) = v_t$. We allow for the possibility that negative announcements engender more persistent effects than positive news. Equation 7 incorporates a news effect. The model predicts that, on announcement days, the level of the conditional volatility differs from that of non-announcement days, which is measured using V_i. Important news might be released on those days. Therefore, we expect that the conditional volatility will be higher on announcement days.

If $\gamma > 0$, volatility rises in the subsequent interval to that of the interval in which the price drops unexpectedly rather than in intervals following an interval in which the price rises unexpectedly.

If asymmetric volatility is observed, market participants react more strongly to bad information (the error term residual is negative) than good information (the error term residual is positive). We infer that this phenomenon means that the market participants have a sentiment for the investment. In behavioral finance, this might be called investor sentiment.

DATA

Price Data

This section describes the data used for analyses: JGB futures. To examine the effects of macroeconomic announcements in the bond market, we use the high-frequency (tick-by-tick) returns on the JGB futures. The data were obtained from Nikkei NEEDS (Tick Saiken Sakimono Option). The returns were calculated for every interval: One interval is 1 minute. Our data cover the period

April 2, 2001, through June 28, 2001. They provide a total of 26,226 observations in TSE.

The contracted price data at every 1-minute interval delimits the interval as 9:00 to 9:01, 9:02 to 9:03, and so on until 17:59 to 18:00. If no contract is made at an interval, the average of the interval immediately before and the interval immediately after is used: We calculate an average value of the previous interval and next interval as the return.

We selected three months (April 2, 2001, through June 28, 2001) from our available data from October 2000 to March 2002. We selected the one contract month that was most active in trading in our available data. We judged that active dealings were done in the sample period because more quotes are updated than in any other period.

Because the surprises in announcements are arguably relevant, we are interested in testing whether large unexpected shocks cause different volatility persistence following major announcements. The data on macroeconomics announcements and median survey expectations are from Bloomberg Japan. We calculated announcement surprises according to the difference between the median survey and the actual data.

In recent event studies, high-frequency data are often used to analyze market efficiency. The intraday pattern of the return and volatility cannot be observed using daily data. It is thought that high-frequency data are necessary to analyze the influence caused by public information accurately. As information technology advances, the arrival and the processing of the new information to a market occurs more rapidly than before. Therefore, market participants can order more rapidly and easily than before by using the information. It is another problem whether market participants correctly interpret the information.

We calculated the absolute value of the difference between returns and the average return as volatility when we only use the OLS method.

In TSE, trading session hours are 9:00 to 11:00 a.m., 12:30 to 15:00 p.m., and 15:30 to 18:00 p.m. All JGB futures transactions are effected in accordance with the auction market principle, namely, price priority and time precedence. Two matching algorithms are visible. The first, the Itayose algorithm, is used mainly to determine the opening and closing prices of each trading session. The second, the Zaraba algorithm, is used during trading sessions to continuously match orders under price priority and time precedence principles. If an order imbalance is visible, TSE posts a special quote to induce opposite-side orders and ameliorate sudden price swings.

Table 1. Description of the announcement variables and their release time. Many are released at 8:50 a.m.

Variable	Release Time
Family Income and Expenditure Survey	8:00 a.m.
Unemployment Rate	8:00 a.m.
Consumer Price Index	8:00 a.m.
Money Supply	8:50 a.m.
Trade Statistic	8:50 a.m.
Trade Payment	8:50 a.m.
Corporate Goods Price Index	8:50 a.m.
Bank of Japan's Quarterly Economic Survey (Tankan)	8:50 a.m.
GDP	8:50 a.m.
Industrial Produce Index	8:50 a.m.
New Residence Starts	14:00 p.m.
Machinery Orders	14:00 p.m.

Macroeconomic Announcements

Data about actual macroeconomic announcements are reported by their related ministries. The data on macroeconomic news survey expectations are from Bloomberg Japan. The survey expectations serve as a measure of the market's expected valuation of the particular announcement. We calculated announcement surprises according to the difference between the median survey and the actual data.

We consider 12 different macroeconomic announcements that provide a fairly complete characterization of macroeconomic announcements. Macroeconomic announcements are the following: money supply, trade balance (trade statistic), trade payment, Corporate Goods Price Index (CGPI), Bank of Japan's Quarterly Economic Survey (Tankan), gross domestic product (GDP), Industrial Produce Index (IIP), new residence starts (new dwellings started), machinery orders, Family Income and Expenditure Survey, unemployment rate, and Consumer Price Index (CPI).

We must consider when macroeconomic news is released when we investigate the effects of mac-

Table 2. Statistics for TSE

	Price	Return	Volatility
Sample Mean	13964.4	-0.00003	0.00612
SE of Sample Mean	0.63149	0.00007	0.00006
Standard Error	102.27	0.0114	0.0097
Variance	10458.49	0.0001	0.0001
Kurtosis	-0.7379	27.7121	43.8637
Skewness	-0.6148	0.9585	4.3187
Observations	26226	26226	26226

Figure 1. TSE volatility

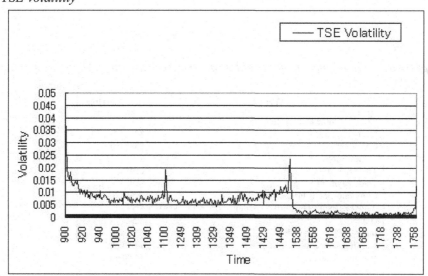

roeconomic announcements on volatility. Effects on volatility might last a short time or a long time in intraday. Therefore, it is assumed that the influence of macroeconomic announcements released at 8:00 a.m. and 8:50 a.m. appear in the first interval that JGB futures trading starts: 9:00 a.m. to 9:01 a.m.

Macroeconomic announcements are not published until the scheduled time to prevent information from leaking beforehand. At the scheduled time, market participants soon know important announcements online. Information technology has advanced rapidly in the last few years. As it advances, the arrival and the processing of new information to a market will be hastened increasingly. The number of private investors has also increased. Even private investors can receive information instantly. Even so, many participants to the JGB futures market are institutional investors who probably know the news soon. They do not need several hours to get the information.

Table 2 describes relevant statistics of JGB futures returns on the TSE.

EMPIRICAL RESULTS

We next examine in which way macroeconomic announcement shocks affect conditional variance in the bond market.

In Figure 1, to illustrate the dynamics of intraday volatility, the mean value at 1-minute intervals is shown. This figure shows *W*-shaped (two *U*-shaped) market patterns. Volatility shows two clear *U*-shaped patterns each day. That is, from 9:00 a.m. to 11:00 a.m. and from 12:30 p.m. to 15:00 p.m.

Figure 2 presents the dynamics of volatility on the announcement days of the macroeconomic index and on non-announcement days.

However, no difference of volatility is apparent between the announcement days and non-announcement days. Table 3 shows also that non-announcement days have higher volatility than that of the announcement days.

We had inferred that volatility of the announcement day would be higher than that of non-announcement days. This unexpected result might be attributable to the measurement of volatility by $|R_t - \bar{R}|$. These results indicate that we must use a model like GARCH or GJR even though we used them in the OLS method.

Next, we consider the announcement effect, the so-called news effect, in the OLS method. The results portrayed in Table 4 show that a surprise of 9 significantly explains the TSE volatility dynamics.

The OLS method identifies the significant macroeconomics variables to use in a volatility model

Figure 2. The dynamics of intraday volatility on news day and non-news day

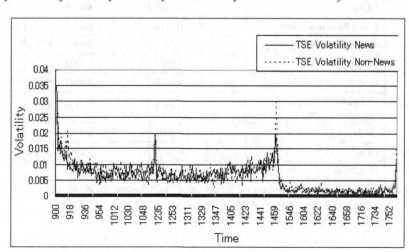

like GJR, but it cannot indicate the persistence of volatility. Therefore, we examine asymmetric volatility and announcement effects using the GJR model. To examine the impact of announcements on conditional volatility, we estimate the GJR specifications with and without announcement effects. The results are presented in Table 5.

Results of the GARCH Model

Using significant variables in the OLS model, we can make an estimate according to the GARCH model. The results of GARCH without announcement effects show that volatility is persistent in the TSE because $\xi + \lambda = 0.99$. In this case, $\xi + \lambda$ is nearly 1. Because we infer that volatility persists,

Table 3. Volatility on news day and non-news day

	TSE Volatility	
	News Day	**Non-News Day**
Sample Mean	0.00611	0.00614
SE of Sample Mean	0.00020	0.00023
Standard Error	0.00408	0.00482
Variance	0.00002	0.00002
Kurtosis	8.48339	24.75706
Skewness	1.70865	3.22784
Observations	423	423

Table 4. OLS surprise

Dependent Variable TSEVOLA			
Variable	**Coefficient**	**Standard Error**	
1. Constant	0.0061	0.0001	
2. Money Supply	-0.0210	0.0097	**
3. Trade Statistic	0.0181	0.0033	***
4. Trade Payment	-0.0148	0.0043	***
5. Unemployment	-0.0228	0.0102	**
6. CGPI	-0.0395	0.0156	**
7. CPI	0.0269	0.0076	***
8. New Residence Starts	0.0114	0.0060	*
9. Machinery Orders	0.0301	0.0091	***
10. Tankan	-0.0062	0.0062	
11. GDP	0.0975	0.0247	***
12. Family Income and Expenditure Survey	-0.0234	0.0129	*
13. IIP	0.0002	0.0100	
14. sp	0.0000	0.0000	
15. ABS sp	0.0233	0.0029	***

***, **, and * respectively indicate that the corresponding coefficients are statistically significant at the 1%, 5%, and 10% levels.
sp is the total value of the surprise of all macroeconomic indicators.
ABS {sp} is a total of the absolute value of the surprise

Table 5. GJR without announcement effects

GJR TSE			
Variable	Coefficient	Standard Error	
1. Constant	2.34E-05	1.80E-06	***
2. λ	0.8989	0.0064	***
3. ξ	0.0319	0.0026	***
4. γ	0.0374	0.0004	***
(λ+ξ+ γ)	0.97		

***, **, and * respectively indicate that corresponding coefficients are statistically significant at the 1%, 5%, and 10% levels.

Table 6.GJR with announcement effects

Variable	Coefficient	Standard Error	
1. Constant	-2.6237E-11	1.9918E-10	
2. λ	0.8938	0.0019	***
3. ξ	0.0166	0.0011	***
4. γ	0.0371	0.0004	***
5. V1	-0.0009	0.0075	
6. V2	-0.0024	0.0051	
7. V3	0.0007	0.0046	
8. V4	0.0081	0.0116	
9. V5	0.0168	0.0169	
10. V6	0.0032	0.0074	
11. V7	0.0055	0.0042	
12. V8	0.0025	0.0040	
13. V9	0.0022	0.0080	
14. V10	0.0083	0.0129	
15. V11	0.0165	0.0024	***
(λ+ξ+ γ)	0.95		

V1 through V10 respectively denote the surprise variables of money supply, trade statistics, trade payments, unemployment rate, CGPI, CPI, new residence starts, machinery orders, GDP, and the Family Income and Expenditure Survey. V11 is a total of those absolute values. ***, **, and * respectively indicate that corresponding coefficients are statistically significant at the 1%, 5%, and 10% levels.

as $\xi + \lambda$ approaches unity, volatility persists longer in JGB futures markets.

Here, although we describe the estimation result easily, the results of GARCH with the announcement effects, using the surprise variables estimated significantly using OLS, show that $\xi + \lambda = 0.90$ in TSE. The results of the GARCH model imply that high-volatility clustering pertains after macroeconomic announcements are released. A high- (low-) volatility period persists for some time after volatility increases (decreases) because of the effects of the announcement. As for the cause of volatility clustering, results show that the effect of the announcements is one factor. Next, we consider an asymmetric volatility model.

Results of the GJR Model

In this section, according to a price increase or decrease in the previous interval, we examine whether volatility is asymmetric or not. To elucidate the asymmetry of volatility, we use a model including a dummy that identifies positive shock and negative shock. Results shown in Tables 5 and 6 illustrate that, because of $\gamma > 0$, volatility is higher in intervals succeeding an unexpected price decrease than in intervals succeeding unexpected price increases.

Table 5 shows results obtained using the GJR model without announcement effects. Evidence of asymmetric volatility shows that volatility increases in intervals after an unexpected price decrease.

Is asymmetric volatility still observed after considering announcement effects in the GJR model? Table 6 shows the results of the GJR model with the announcement effects. As in the GJR model without the announcement effects, asymmetric volatility is significant. Even if we include announcement effects into the GJR model, evidence exists that, after an unexpected price decline, volatility increases in the immediately proceeding interval. Negative announcement

shocks typically have a stronger influence on the subsequent volatility than positive announcement shocks. Therefore, all asymmetry of volatility does not result solely from macroeconomic risk.

When the magnitude of the influence of each surprise variable on volatility is considered, Table 6 shows that macroeconomic announcements are important.

Moreover, results show that the JGB futures market is not efficient in the TSE. Consequently, volatility persists for some time after macroeconomic announcements. It may not be irrelevant that the JGB futures market is inefficient and the volatility is asymmetric. When all market participants are rational, the difference in market participants' reactions to new information should not be generated by whether the error term is positive or negative. Market participants should have same reaction to positive information and negative information. The residual becomes information in itself. Therefore, market participants interpret that information and determine their positions. However, after a price decreases unexpectedly in an interval, volatility is increased in the next interval, implying that market participants react more strongly to negative information than to positive information.

CONCLUSION

This chapter investigates asymmetric volatility and announcement effects, and the extent to which volatility persistence is explained by macroeconomic announcements in the JGB futures market of TSE. To that end, we accommodate the GJR model in such a way that macroeconomic announcements and their surprise are accounted for. We use high-frequency data of JGB futures for the period of April 2, 2001, through June 28, 2001.

Results show that volatility on announcement days persists in JGB futures markets, inconsistent with the immediate incorporation of information into prices. Moreover, negative announcement shocks typically have a greater impact on the subsequent volatility than positive announcement shocks. After introducing macroeconomic announcements into the model, estimates of asymmetric volatility are significant, indicating that after a price decreases unexpectedly in an interval, volatility is high in the next sequential interval. That characteristic of asymmetric volatility does not disappear, even if announcement effects are introduced. Such effects might not be the only factor causing asymmetric volatility, but they are factors causing volatility persistence.

Ederington and Lee (2001) and Bollerslev et al. (2000) report that it is important to introduce announcement effects into a model like GARCH because the announcement effect is one factor causing volatility persistence. Therefore, the JGB futures market in TSE is not efficient.

Finally, we refer to policy implications: Macroeconomic announcements affect volatility significantly. For that reason, it might be necessary to announce them during non-market hours. If such a policy were undertaken, volatility resulting from the macroeconomic announcements might be suppressed. As volatility is reduced, liquidity might rise.

ACKNOWLEDGMENT

We thank Professor Masayuki Susai and Hiroshi Moriyasu for their helpful comments. We are especially grateful to Professor Yutaka Kurihara. Minaki and Kamae also thank Postal Life Insurance Foundation of Japan for its financial support.

REFERENCES

Andersen, T., & Bollerslev, T. (1997). Intraday periodicity and volatility persistence in financial markets. *Journal of Empirical Finance*, 115-158.

Arshanapalli, B., d'Ouville, E., Fabozzi, F., & Switzer, L. (2006). Macroeconomic news effects on conditional volatilities in the bond and stock markets. *Applied Financial Economics, 16*, 377-384.

Balduzzi, P., Elton, E. J., & Green, T. C. (2001). Economic news and bond prices: Evidence from the U.S. treasury market. *Journal of Financial and Quantitative Analysis, 36*(4), 523-543.

Black, F. (1976). Studies of stock market volatility changes. *1976 Proceedings of the American Statistical Association, Business and Economics Statistic Section*, 177-181.

Bollerslev, T. (1986). Generalized autoregressive conditional heteroskedasticity. *Journal of Econometrics, 31*, 307-327.

Bollerslev, T., Cai, J., & Song, F. M. (2000). Intraday periodicity, long memory volatility, and macroeconomic announcement effects in the US treasury bond market. *Journal of Empirical Finance, 7*(1), 37-55.

Campbell, J., Lo, A., & MacKinlay, A. (1997). *The econometrics of financial markets*. Princeton University Press.

Ederington, L., & Lee, J. (1993). How markets process information: News releases and volatility. *Journal of Finance, 48*, 1161-1191.

Ederington, L., & Lee, J. (2001). Intraday volatility in interest-rate and foreign-exchange markets: ARCH, announcement, and seasonality effects. *The Journal of Futures Markets, 21*, 517-552.

Fleming, M. J., & Remolona, E. M. (1999). What moves bond prices? *Journal of Portfolio Management, 25*(4), 28-38.

Glosten, L., Jagannathan, R., & Runkle, D. (1993). On the relation between the expected value and the volatility of the nominal excess returns on stocks. *Journal of Finance*, 1779-1801.

Goeij, P., & Marquering, W. (2006). Macroeconomic announcements and asymmetric volatility in bond returns. *Journal of Banking & Finance, 30*, 2659-2680.

Jones, C. M., Lamont, O., & Lumsdaine, R. L. (1998). Macroeconomic news and bond market volatility. *Journal of Financial Economics, 47*(3), 315-337.

Kamae, H., & Minaki, T. (2004). Tests of efficiency in the JGB futures market in Japan. *Journal of Personal Finance and Economics, 20*, 21-45.

Li, L., & Engle, R. (1998). *Macroeconomic announcements and volatility of treasury futures* (Discussion Paper). San Diego, CA: University of California, San Diego.

Minaki, T. (2005). Volatility, spread, volume of JGB futures and macroeconomic announcements. *The Hitotsubashi Review, 134*(5), 231-255.

Minaki, T. (2006). The efficiency test of JGB futures market: Evidence from TSE and SGX. *Journal of Personal Finance and Economics, 22-23*, 177-193.

Nelson, D. B. (1991). Conditional heteroskedasticity in asset returns: A new approach. *Econometrica, 59*, 347-370.

Wang, P., Wang, P., & Liu, A. (2005). Stock return volatility and trading volume: Evidence from the Chinese stock market. *Journal of Chinese Economic and Business Studies, 3*(1), 39-54.

Chapter VI
The Macroeconomic Benefits of Intelligent Enterprise

Thomas F. Siems
Federal Reserve Bank of Dallas, USA

ABSTRACT

New information technologies, including e-commerce and the Internet, have brought fundamental changes to 21ˢᵗ century businesses by making more and better information available quickly and inexpensively. Intelligent enterprises are those firms that make the most from new information technologies and Internet business solutions to increase revenue and productivity, hold down costs, and expand markets and opportunities. In this chapter, the macroeconomic benefits that intelligent enterprises can have on the U.S. economy are explored. We find that the U.S. economy has become less volatile, with demand volatility nearly matching sales volatility, particularly in the durable goods sector. Evidence also suggests that firms are utilizing new information technologies to lower inventory levels relative to sales, leading to higher productivity growth, lower prices, and more competitive markets.

INTRODUCTION

Schumpeter (1939, 1950) presents arguments that innovation's transforming effects on economies is nothing new. In fact, because the macroeconomic benefits from the development and implementation of new technologies are positive and significant, the process he describes as "creative destruction" should be embraced. Railroads, steam power,

illumination, cable lines, electricity, air transportation, air conditioning … all these inventions, and many more, have contributed to "economic evolution." That is, free-market economies are in a process of continuous change, where new ideas and new technologies destroy old products and old ways of doing things. This evolutionary process has profound consequences for what is produced, where things are produced, and who will produce them. Intelligent enterprises of the 21st century know and understand this, and work to position themselves to take advantage of new opportunities and new markets in this rapidly changing environment.

Clearly, the process of creative destruction—also referred to as "the churn"—can be upsetting and turbulent, as old industries disappear, existing jobs are redefined, and new industries created. As Cox and Alm (1992) point out, "innovation has always had the direct effect of creating new businesses and industries and the indirect effect of destroying many of the jobs in the existing industries that they eclipsed." As a result, the job mix changes, but the total labor market expands and macroeconomic productivity increases, thereby raising incomes and overall living standards for individuals in the economy.

Today, the churn is at work in the so-called "New Economy"—a view adopted in the late 1990s that is characterized by a higher sustained level of productivity growth brought on primarily by the implementation of new technologies, enabling faster economic growth with less inflation. While some may argue that the New Economy was smoke and mirrors because of misguided claims that the business cycle would end and stock prices for Internet-related firms would rise forever, Formaini and Siems (2003) argue that the reality of the New Economy is a more resilient and flexible economy. Faster productivity growth has led to higher real wages, as well as lower unemployment and lower inflation.

A number of researchers have documented the productivity acceleration of the late 1990s. Oliner and Sichel (2000) calculate that information technology capital—computer hardware, software, and communications equipment—added 0.5 percent per year to economic growth in the 1980s. By the late 1990s, however, the contribution to economic growth from information technology capital grew to 1.4 percent per year. Moreover, the percentage of income earned in the economy from information technology capital more than doubled

over this time period, rising from 3.3 percent in the 1980s to 7.0 percent by the late 1990s.

In addition to Oliner and Sichel's research, studies by Jorgenson and Stiroh (2000) and the Council of Economic Advisers (2001) show a large pick-up in labor productivity growth in the non-farm business sector during the late 1990s. Consistent among the studies is the finding that shows the extent to which the rapid accumulation of new information technologies contributed to the rising rate of labor productivity growth. The main message here is that the development and implementation of new information technologies drove a large fraction of the recent productivity acceleration.[1]

While "New Economy companies" in the computer and semiconductor sectors contributed a great deal to the overall acceleration of productivity growth, "Old Economy" (traditional manufacturing) firms also largely contributed. Old Economy companies' demand for new information technologies increased as they found many efficiency-enhancing ways to use the new innovations. DeLong and Summers (2001) suggest that the principal effects of the New Economy are more likely to be "microeconomic" than "macroeconomic," although improvements at the firm level eventually produce macroeconomic gains. Competitive pressures require that successful firms employ information technologies effectively to reduce costs and improve profitability.

Such intelligent enterprises come in all sizes and shapes. They are Internet-related New Economy companies and Old Economy manufacturers. They are new start-ups and 100-year-old enterprises. Baily (2001) uses data from the Bureau of Economic Analysis to show labor productivity growth by industry over two periods: 1989-1995 and 1995-1999. Labor productivity growth is computed by dividing each industry's output as measured by the value added in that industry (gross product originating) by the number of full-time equivalent employees. The results reveal that service industries, particularly wholesale and retail trade, finance, and personal services, have the greatest increases in labor productivity growth from the early 1990s to the late 1990s. The durable goods manufacturing sector also saw a large pick-up in labor productivity growth between the two periods.

Labor productivity growth in wholesale trade increased nearly five percentage points; for retail trade the increase was 4.25 percentage points. Finance labor growth productivity increased more than 3.5 percentage points and the increase was about 2.5 percentage points for durable goods manufacturing.

Perhaps most interesting, the importance of new information technologies in managing industry supply chains and in promoting financial innovations cannot go unnoticed. Higher labor productivity growth can be linked to the implementation of information technologies. Baily (2001) ranks industries by information technology intensity and finds that the most-intense information technology users had more than a 50 percent larger acceleration in productivity growth than the less-intense users. The information-technol-

ogy-intensive firms increased labor productivity growth by 1.75 percentage points, whereas the less-intensive users increased by 1.15 percentage points. Research findings by Nordhaus (2002) and Stiroh (2002) are also consistent with these results.

In this chapter, this research is consolidated and extended to argue that there are significant macroeconomic benefits from the development and implementation of new information technologies. Specifically, over the past two decades, evidence suggests that firms developing and/or implementing New Economy technologies—operating in conjunction with a more innovative and deregulated financial market—have helped the U.S. economy become more stable. Also, because better information and its improved availability leads to lower transaction costs, it makes sense for intelligent enterprises to focus on specialization and the customization of products and services to an even greater extent than previously. In addition, evidence suggests that the Internet has not been over-hyped, but may, in fact, be under-hyped as new online business solutions like business-to-

Figure 1. U.S. Real GDP Growth has become more stable

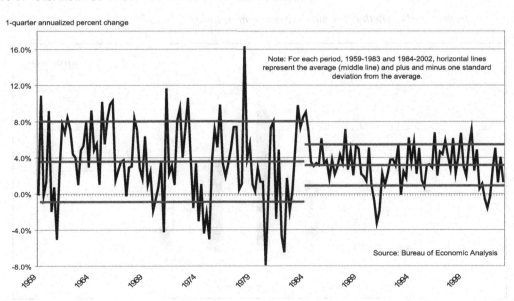

business (B2B) supply chain management systems and electronic marketplaces (e-marketplaces) greatly help boost productivity and keep prices low. Finally, the U.S. experience offers lessons for other countries. The greatest productivity improvements appear to come from the productive use of new information technologies, as intelligent enterprises seek new ways to deploy them. The competitive environment in the U.S. demands that firms find new ways of conducting business to lower costs, expand markets, and boost efficiency.

GREATER ECONOMIC STABILITY

As shown in Figure 1, U.S. real GDP growth has been less volatile in recent years than in the 1960s, 1970s, and early 1980s. Using the first quarter of 1984 (designated as 1984:1) as the break date, real GDP growth volatility has declined from 4.5 percentage points in the 1959:1-1983:4 period to just 2.3 percentage points in the 1984:1-2002:4 period.[2] This 2.2 percentage point reduction in volatility is statistically significant and is a powerful indicator

that the U.S. economy has become more stable. In particular, and as displayed in Figure 2, extreme movements in output—growth rates below -4 percent and more than +10 percent—are much less likely today than 20 or 30 years ago. As a result, outright declines in GDP dropped from 18 percent of the quarters in the earlier period to just 9 percent of the quarters since 1983.

Table 1 reports the standard deviation of GDP growth and its major components for the two sample periods. The table shows a reduction in growth volatility for all of the major components of GDP, but the greatest decline occurs in durable goods. Whereas aggregate GDP growth volatility falls by 49 percent from the pre-1984 period to the post-1983 period, volatility in durables drops by 51 percent, in non-durables by 36 percent, in services by 23 percent, and in structures by 42 percent. Thus, durables volatility is most closely associated with the volatility of aggregate GDP. But, because the durable goods sector accounts for only about 20 percent of total output in the economy, we must also take into consideration the sector's size and the correlation between its growth and GDP growth to determine more

Figure 2. Extreme GDP Growth rates much less common today

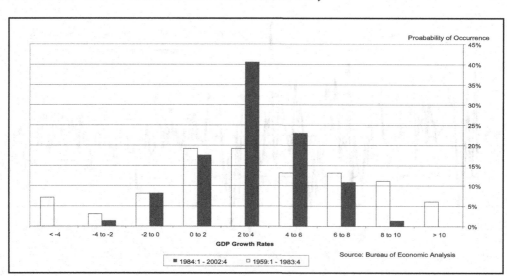

precisely the sector's overall contribution to the reduction in GDP volatility.

Koenig, Siems, and Wynne (2002) conduct such an analysis and find three GDP components that stand out as the largest contributors to reduced GDP volatility.[3] Figure 3 shows that inventory investment, consumer durables, and residential investment together make-up more than 83 percent of the total reduction in the volatility of GDP. Roughly 41 percent of the 2.2 percentage point reduction in GDP volatility since the 1959-1983 period comes from inventory investment, with about 25 percent of the reduction coming from durables and 17 percent from residential investment.

These three components, therefore, seem to be most responsible for the economy's greater stability and provide some clues about the likely underlying causes of improvement. Since the early-1980s, U.S. businesses have adopted improved inventory control and supply chain management systems that have increased operating efficiencies by making better use of more accurate information. In addition, financial deregulation and innovation since the mid-1980s have reduced the sensitivity of residential construction and consumer lending to swings in market interest rates. Households and businesses have greater access to credit and financial intermediaries have credit-scoring systems and more information available to make better

lending decisions. Thus, it appears that tighter inventory controls and financial deregulation and innovation have contributed a great deal to the economy's increased stability.[4]

This finding is reinforced in Kahn, McConnell, and Perez-Quiros (2002) who perform an experiment like the one presented in McConnell and Perez-Quiros (2000). Using a structural break of 1985:1 for durables growth, an artificial series for durable goods growth is generated under the counterfactual assumption that the residual variance post-1984 is equal to its average value in the pre-1985 period. From this, the authors find that the volatility reduction in the durable goods sector is large enough to account for more than two-thirds of the decline in aggregate volatility. Again, improved inventory management is a plausible answer to explain much of this decline.

New optimization techniques, production process improvements, and information technologies have combined to provide tremendous opportunities to streamline industry supply chains and reduce reliance on inventory buffers. At all points along industry supply chains, decision-makers (and artificial intelligence systems) can use real-time information to quickly limit imbalances between demand and production. Thus, better information should be associated with both a reduction in production volatility and tighter inventory levels as production decisions better match actual demand.

Table 1. Evidence of economic stability

	GDP Growth Volatility	
Sector	1959:1 - 1983:4	1984:1 - 2002:4
Durables	17.51%	8.62%
Nondurables	7.25%	4.67%
Services	1.79%	1.38%
Structures	11.81%	6.79%
Aggregate	4.46%	2.27%

Source: Bureau of Economic Analysis, author's calculations.

Figure 3. More than 83 percent of reduced GDP volatility from three sectors

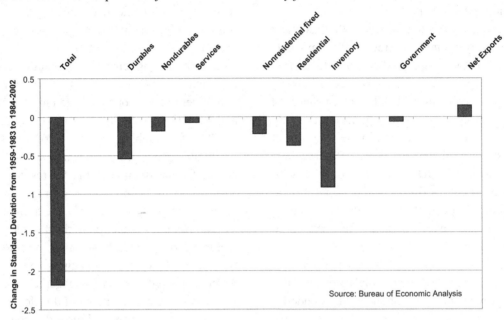

Table 2. Production growth volatility getting closer to sales growth volatility

	Growth Volatility	
Sector	1959:1 - 1983:4	1984:1 - 2002:4
Production	8.04%	4.77%
Sales	5.35%	4.35%
Ratio of Production to Sales Variability	1.50	1.10
Durables Production	17.51%	8.62%
Durables Sales	10.12%	8.73%
Ratio of Durables Production to Sales Variability	1.73	0.99

Source: Bureau of Economic Analysis, author's calculations

Lee and Amaral (2002) describe the effective deployment of a supply chain performance management system at DaimlerChrysler's Mopar Parts Group. As they say, supply chain performance management is more than a measurement process. It is a cycle of identifying performance exceptions, understanding issues and alternatives, responding to problems/opportunities, and

Figure 4. Durables inventory-to-shipments ratio fell dramatically in the 1990s

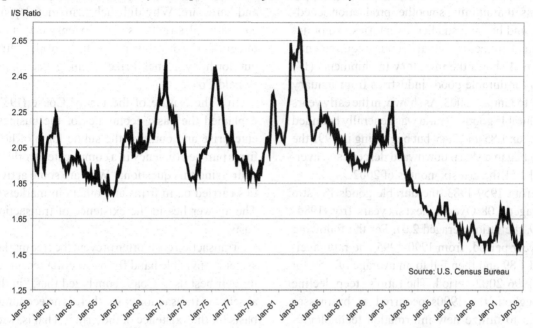

continuously validating the data, processes and actions. In the first year following implementation of this system, DaimlerChrysler shrunk their decision cycle time from months to days, reduced transportation costs, increased the percentage of orders completely filled, and reduced inventories by $15 million.

With better supply chain performance measurement and inventory management, we ought to see goods production becoming smoother relative to goods sales. As shown in Table 2, that is exactly what has happened. Before 1984, production growth volatility was 2.69 percentage points greater than sales growth volatility; after 1983, this difference declined to 0.42 percentage points. As a result, the ratio of production to sales variability dropped from 1.5 in the pre-1984 period to 1.1 in the post-1983 period. We see an even more dramatic story for durables: before 1984, production growth volatility for durables was 7.39 percentage points higher than durables sales growth volatility; after 1983, the difference disappears so that the ratio of durables production to sales variability drops from 1.7 to 1.0.

It is important to note that growth volatilities in both sales and production have fallen, but the volatility of production growth has fallen much more than the volatility of sales growth. While the volatility in sales growth improved by 19 percent from the pre-1984 period, production growth volatility improved by 41 percent. In the durable goods sector, the volatility in durables sales growth improved by 14 percent from the pre-1984 period, whereas durables production growth volatility improved by 51 percent.

Thus, the goods sector, and in particular the durable goods sector, has not only become more stable, but, as signified by the reduction in the ratio of production volatility to sales volatility, has also seen production volatility become more stable relative to sales volatility. This finding leads us to conclude that there has, indeed, been a change in the way that inventories are managed and that such changes have led, in turn, to a more stable economic environment in the United States.

The inventory-to-shipments ratio in the goods-producing sectors of the economy provides more evidence that firms are becoming increasingly more sophisticated in managing industry supply chains, maintaining smoother production schedules, and holding smaller inventories and/or accurately projecting actual demand requirements. Figure 4 shows the inventory-to-shipments (IS) ratio for durable goods industries from January 1959 to January 2003. As shown, in the early years the durable goods IS ratio was generally bounded between 1.85 and 2.45, but beginning in 1991 the ratio began a sharp downward descent and averaged 1.51 the last six months of 2002.

From 1959-1983, the durable goods IS ratio averaged 2.08. Over the next six years, from 1984-1989, the ratio averaged 2.07. For the following six-year period, from 1990-1995, the ratio averaged 1.89 and then fell to an average of 1.59 for the 1996-2002 period. The ratio's steep decline throughout the 1990s occurred as businesses began to utilize new information technologies that helped them squeeze greater efficiencies from their supply chains. Flexible manufacturing, "just-in-time" inventory management and material requirements planning systems, just to name a few ideas, became reality as they were implemented over the Internet (or secure intranets) and allowed manufacturers—particularly durable goods manufacturers—to boost productivity and reduce output volatility.

SPECIALIZATION AND CUSTOMIZATION

In a fundamental sense, the basic organizational structure of the business enterprise has changed as firms have become more intelligent and have better and quicker access to critical information. In the past, firms pursued efficiency by vertically integrating. According to Edmonds (1923), by 1920, General Motors had extended its scope so that its units or subsidiaries produced not only all engines used in cars, but a large proportion of other components—gears, axles, crankshafts, radiators, electrical equipment, roller bearings,

warning signals, spark plugs, bodies, plate glass, and hardware. Why did such firms develop organizational structures with extensive vertical integration? For answers, we turn to ideas first put forth by Nobel Prize-winning economist Ronald Coase.

In "The Nature of the Firm," Coase (1937) explained the basic economics of the business enterprise and outlined the subtle logic of how firms pursue efficiency in a complicated world by addressing this question: "Why are some activities carried on in firms and others in markets?" The answer lies in the existence of transaction costs.

Transaction costs often prevent the free market system's invisible hand from directing resources to their best use.[5] Coase concluded that, "in the absence of transaction costs, there is no economic basis for the existence of the firm."[6] That is, with transaction costs, it is often cheaper to carry on activities within firms. Thus, the desire to reduce transaction costs effectively led to the emergence of the vertically integrated enterprise.

Generally speaking, Coase argued that firms exist because information (transaction and coordination) costs are too high for each buyer to feasibly employ each production input and then coordinate the production of the desired good or service. But as these costs fall because of new information-sharing technologies, firms should specialize and trade to a greater extent than ever before. Such firms would be expected to have greater focus and more customized services, yet still create efficiencies through established business partnerships.

Is there any evidence that transaction costs are declining? And if so, what are the macroeconomic implications as businesses reorganize their organizational structures?

Turning first to the issue of transaction costs, Lucking-Reiley and Spulber (2001) argue that B2B e-commerce substitutes capital—in the form of computer data processing and Internet communications—for labor services, thereby increasing the speed and efficiency of economic transactions. They divide potential productivity gains from B2B e-commerce into four areas: automation of transactions, new market intermediaries, consolidation of demand and supply through organized exchanges, and changes in the extent of vertical integration. The authors' conclude that even small enhancements in the efficiency of transactions will eventually produce overall large savings.

Moreover, by reducing transaction costs, increasing management efficiency, and increasing competition, Litan and Rivlin (2001) estimate that the Internet will bring total annual cost savings to the U.S. economy of $100 billion to $230 billion. This translates into an annual contribution to productivity growth of 0.2 to 0.4 percent above what it would otherwise have been.

At a microeconomic level, Dell Inc. provides a quintessential example. Dell's Internet-based build-to-order system has allowed the firm to reduce the number of days' supply of inventory in parts and subassemblies from 31 days in 1996

to around four today. Using new information technologies, Dell has turned traditional manufacturing on its head by saying it will not build anything until it receives an order from a customer. Dell customizes product attributes to exactly what the customer demands, and in doing so, the firm has essentially eliminated all inventories from its supply chain.

At a macroeconomic level, lower transaction costs that lead to greater firm specialization and focus should yield higher productivity growth (more output per man-hour), a greater number of business establishments (locations), and fewer employees per establishment. The U.S. economy has, indeed, experienced higher (and less volatile) productivity growth, especially since 1995. As shown in Figure 5, during the six-year period from 1990-1995, productivity growth in the nonfarm business sector averaged 1.6 percent (with a standard deviation of 2.8 percentage points). But since 1995, productivity growth has increased by more than a full percentage point to an average 2.7 percent (with a standard deviation of 2.6 percentage points).

Figure 5. Productivity growth has generally increased in recent years

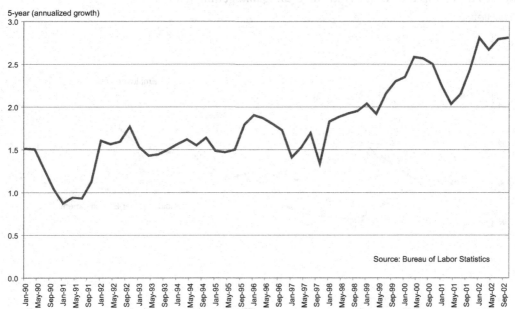

Statistics from the U.S. Census Bureau show that the total number of business firms has increased by 11.0 percent from 1991 to 1999 (the last year for which data are available). The total number of business establishments—defined as a physical location where business is conducted or where services or industrial operations are performed—has increased by 13.0 percent. Employment has increased 19.9 percent over this same time period.

But the distribution of the employment increases by the employment size of the enterprise has not been uniform. Smaller firms (those with less than 500 employees) have actually seen slower employment growth than larger firms (those with more than 500 employees). Small firms have seen employment increase 13.7 percent from 1991-1999, whereas large firms have seen employment grow at nearly twice that rate (27.0 percent). But the bigger increase for large firms may be due to the fact that large firms are establishing more physical locations in which to conduct business than small firms. Large firms have increased their total number of establishments from 1991 to 1999 by 29.2 percent, whereas small firms increased the number of establishments by 10.8 percent.

As shown in Figure 6, from 1991 to 1999, large firms increased the average number of employees per firm by 6.0 percent, but the number of employees per establishment declined by 1.7 percent. While this evidence is not overwhelming, it does suggest the possibility that large firms are breaking their businesses into smaller pieces and getting leaner with fewer employees per establishment.

Numerous examples abound from many industries where companies are vertically disintegrating and outsourcing more and more of what they once did, or could do, themselves. Henry Ford's first large manufacturing facility in Detroit used to employ 100,000 workers and make 1,200 cars a day. Today, that same plant produces 800 Mustangs a day and employs 3,000 workers. Such evidence is consistent with the view advocated by Coase that as transaction costs decline, firms will pursue their competitive advantage and focus more on specialization and trade.

Figure 6. Large firms are vertically disintegrating and getting leaner

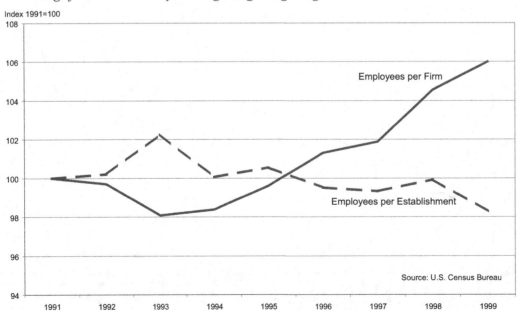

THE IMPACT OF THE INTERNET

The Internet's impact on the way business is conducted is undeniable, yet at the same time, it is not fully understood nor is the Internet's presence in business fully implemented. Internet business solutions such as B2B e-marketplaces and supply chain management systems hold great potential in boosting productivity and keeping prices low.[7] Intelligent enterprises of the 21st century will need to embrace such systems to stay competitive, increase operating efficiencies, improve services, and expand markets.

Varian et al. (2002) interviewed 2,065 companies to measure the economic benefits of the Internet in the U.S. The authors report that the deployment of Internet business solutions has thus far yielded cumulative cost savings of $155 billion to U.S. organizations, with another $373 billion expected once all current solutions have been fully implemented by 2010. The impact on productivity growth could be profound; Internet business solutions have the potential to drive 40 percent of the projected increase in U.S. productivity from 2001-2011.

How will the Internet drive such a large increase in productivity growth? Because the Internet's application to commercial business is relatively new, projecting the Internet's impact on productivity growth is really more of an art than a science. Sufficient data are not yet available to use standard statistical analyses for estimating the Internet's impact on economic growth. Nevertheless, Varian et al. (2002) put forth several reasons why the Internet will lead to higher productivity.

The Internet is a powerful communications medium that allows access for anyone to connect anywhere in the world instantaneously at little cost and with great flexibility. This increased information availability directly leads to *lower transaction costs*. That is, search and information costs are lower, bargaining and decision costs are lower and policing and enforcement costs are lower. Better

information that is available faster and cheaper also leads to *efficiency improvements* in the production and delivery of goods and services. That is, inventories can be maintained at lower levels, decision-makers at physically distant locations can communicate and cooperate more effectively, and supply chain performance measurement can be monitored and recalibrated in real-time. In addition, to the extent that the Internet *enhances transparency*, many markets will move closer to a market structure characterized by perfect competition and pressures will intensify for firms to adopt cost reducing and efficiency enhancing improvements facilitated by the Internet.[8]

Lee and Whang (2001) describe the Internet as an efficient electronic link between entities, creating an ideal platform for sharing information with those who need it. The effective integration of supply chains comes from "information hubs" that allow multiple organizations (or divisions within one organization) to interact and process information in real-time. The authors' report that a recent study by Stanford University and Accenture of 100 manufacturers and 100 retailers found that companies reporting higher than average profits were also the ones engaged in higher levels of information sharing.

The attempt to develop e-marketplaces presents tremendous opportunities to dramatically restructure industry supply chains. Thomas (2000) describes e-marketplaces as electronic, Internet-based commerce arenas for groups of buyers and suppliers within a specific industry, geographic region, or affinity group. The first e-marketplaces—FreeMarkets.com, VerticalNet.com, and Grainger.com—formed in 1995 and 1996 to essentially serve as middlemen between suppliers and buyers. The number of e-marketplaces grew rapidly in the late-1990s as venture capitalists envisioned fantastic efficiency enhancements and lower procurement costs for businesses participating in such markets.[9] While B2B e-commerce and e-marketplaces were among the hottest investment sectors, many e-marketplaces have failed to produce the desired results.

Despite the collapse of many dot-coms, the Internet has not been over-hyped and may, in fact, be under-hyped. Most efficiency improvements that lead to broad-based macroeconomic productivity gains will show up in so-called Old Economy businesses. For example, as shown in Table 3, Brooks and Wahhaj (2000) estimate that moving purchasing activities onto the Internet will provide various industries with input-cost savings of 2 percent to 39 percent, depending on the industry. Overall, such input cost savings have potentially large impacts on reducing aggregate prices in the economy, which, in turn, could ultimately boost productivity and GDP growth much higher than it would otherwise have been.

For businesses, the Internet allows firms to reorganize the way they process information flows. Put simply, the Internet helps firms reduce the paper trail (by putting it online), produce more output with less labor, and hold less inventory in the supply chain. All of these improvements generate higher levels of output with fewer resources, ultimately raising living standards and helping to contain inflationary pressures.

WORLDWIDE IMPLICATIONS

Since the Internet and many information technologies are available worldwide, one might expect any macroeconomic benefits—like rising labor productivity growth, lower unemployment, or lower inflation—to also occur in other world economies, particularly in the largest developed economies. While the U.S. economy is far and away the largest economy in the world, the fact is economic performance between the U.S. and other developed economies has widened further since the mid-1990s.

Table 3. The Internet's impact on purchasing activities

Industry		Cost Savings (percent)
Aerospace		11
Chemicals		10
Coal		2
Communications		5-15
Computing		11-20
Electronic Components	2	9-39
Food Ingredients		3-5
Forest Products		15-25
Freight Transport		15-20
Healthcare		5
Life Science		12-19
Metals		22
Media and Advertising		10-15
Maintenance, Repair, and Operating Supplies		10
Oil and Gas		5-15
Paper		10
Steel		11

Research by van Ark, Inklaar, and McGuckin (2002) present evidence that from 1995-2000, productivity growth in the U.S. was nearly double the rate experienced in the largest European Union economies, which includes Austria, Denmark, Finland, France, Germany, Ireland, Italy, Netherlands, Spain, and Sweden. Moreover, the largest differentials in productivity growth occurred in the information and communication technology (ICT) intensive industries. There was little difference in productivity growth rates in the non-ICT industries.

Their analysis suggests that ICT diffusion in Europe is following similar industry patterns to those observed in the U.S., but at a considerably slower pace. The authors' conclude that the key differences between Europe and the U.S. are in the intensive ICT-using services, where the U.S. has experienced much stronger productivity growth. Most of the overall gap in productivity growth between the U.S. and Europe can be found in the retail, wholesale trade, and securities (finance) sectors.[10]

Baily (2001) examines GDP per capita from 1995-2000 and concludes that the major European industrialized economies and Japan are all operating at a level of economic activity that is slightly less than three quarters of the level experienced in the United States. Since higher levels of GDP per capita can result from higher productivity or from more hours worked, Baily analyzes the interrelationship in 2000 between how many hours a country's residents work and productivity (output per hour). Against the major industrialized economies, the United States is an obvious outlier, with both high employment and high productivity. In other words, the U.S. has been the only economy, thus far, to combine full employment with high productivity.

Most researchers find (and speculate to a certain extent) that the U.S. experience is a result of good macroeconomic policies and a competitive economic environment. Policies that encourage the productive use of new information technolo-

gies in an environment that demands economic efficiency in order to maximize shareholder wealth tend to lead to rising productivity growth. The benefits from information technologies must be exploited. Highly competitive economies constantly force companies to search for better ways to conduct business or develop new products/ services. And the greatest improvements can be found in utilizing new technologies that increase a firm's efficiency and effectiveness.

CONCLUSION

The U.S. economy is evolving and changing at ever-increasing speed. New information technologies and Internet-enabled information-sharing systems provide 21st century businesses and individuals with more valuable information, allowing better decisions to be made faster and cheaper. As a result, the potential for the Internet and related information technologies to impact the economy is significant.

In this chapter, the macroeconomic benefits of implementing Internet business solutions has been demonstrated in a number of ways. The U.S. economy has become less volatile, with demand volatility nearly matching sales volatility, particularly in the durable goods sector. Evidence also suggests that firms are utilizing the Internet and related information technologies to lower inventory levels relative to sales, and to boost productivity. Finally, the greatest impact will likely occur among Old Economy firms, especially those with potentially large information flows.

REFERENCES

Andrews, D. (1993). Test for parameter instability and structural change with unknown change point. *Econometrica,* 61(July), 821-856.

Andrews, D. & Ploberger, W. (1994). Optimal tests when a nuisance parameter is present only under the alternative. *Econometrica,* 62(November), 1383-1414.

Baily, M. (2001). Macroeconomic implications of the new economy. *Proceedings of the Symposium on Economic Policy for the Information Economy*, Federal Reserve Bank of Kansas City (August 30-September 1), pp. 201-268.

Brooks, M. & Wahhaj, Z. (2000). The 'new' global economy—Part II: B2B and the Internet. *Global Economic Commentary*, Goldman Sachs, (February 9), 3-13.

Chen, A.H. & Siems, T.F. (2001). B2B emarketplace announcements and shareholder wealth. *Economic and Financial Review*, Federal Reserve Bank of Dallas, First Quarter, 12-22.

Coase, R.H. (1937). The nature of the firm. *Economica,* 4(November), 386-405.

Coase, R. H. (1988). *The Firm, The Market, and the Law* (chapter one). Chicago, IL: The University of Chicago Press.

Council of Economic Advisers. (2001). *Economic Report of the President*, Washington, D.C.: U.S. Government Printing Office, January.

Cox, W. M. & Alm, R. (1992). *The churn: The paradox of progress.* Federal Reserve Bank of Dallas Annual Report Essay.

DeLong, J. B. & Summers, L.H. (2001). The 'new economy': Background, historical perspective, questions, and speculations. *Economic Review*, Federal Reserve Bank of Kansas City, Fourth Quarter, 29-59.

Edmonds, C.C. (1923). Tendencies in the automobile industry. *American Economic Review,* 13, 422-441.

Formaini, R. L. & Siems, T.F. (2003). New economy: Myths and reality. *Southwest Economy*,

Federal Reserve Bank of Dallas, 3(May/June), 1-8.

Gordon, R. J. (2000). Does the 'new economy' measure up to the great inventions of the past? *Journal of Economic Perspectives,* 14(4), 49-74.

Jorgenson, D. W. & Stiroh, K.J. (2000). Raising the speed limit: U.S. economic growth in the information age. *Brookings Papers on Economic Activity*, 125-211.

Kahn, J. A., McConnell, M.M. & Perez-Quiros, G. (2002). On the causes of the increased stability of the U.S. economy. *Economic Policy Review*, Federal Reserve Bank of New York, (May), 183-202.

Koenig, E. F., Siems, T.F. & Wynne, M.A. (2002). New economy, new recession? *Southwest Economy*, Federal Reserve Bank of Dallas, 2(March/April), 11-16.

Lee, H. L. & Amaral, J. (2002). Continuous and sustainable improvement through supply chain performance management. Stanford Global Supply Chain Management Forum, SGSCMF-W1-2002 (October).

Lee, H. L. & Whang, S. (2001). E-business and supply chain integration. Stanford Global Supply Chain Management Forum, SGSCMF-W2-2001 (November).

Litan, R. E. & Rivlin, A.M. (2001). Projecting the economic impact of the Internet. *American Economic Review,* 91(May), 313-317.

Lucking-Reiley, D. & Spulber, D.F. (2001). Business-to-business electronic commerce. *Journal of Economic Perspectives,* 15(Winter), 55-68.

McConnell, M. M. & Perez-Quiros, G. (2000). Output fluctuations in the United States: What has changed since the early 1980s? *American Economic Review,* 90(December), 1464-1476.

Nordhaus, W.D. (2002). Productivity growth and the new economy. *Brookings Papers on Economic Activity*, 2, 211-266.

Oliner, S.D. & Sichel, D.E. (2000). The resurgence of growth in the late 1990s: Is information technology the story? *Journal of Economic Perspectives*, 14(4), 3-32.

Schumpeter, J.A. (1939). *Business Cycles: A Theoretical, Historical, and Statistical Analysis of the Capitalist Process*. New York: McGraw-Hill.

Schumpeter, J. A. (1950). *Capitalism, Socialism, and Democracy* (third ed.). New York: Harper and Brothers.

Siems, T.F. (2001a). B2B e-commerce: Why the new economy lives. *Southwest Economy*, Federal Reserve Bank of Dallas, 2(July/August), 1-5.

Siems, T. F. (2001b). B2B e-commerce and the search for the holy grail. *Journal of e-Business and Information Technology*, (Fall), 5-12.

Smith, A. (1776). *An Inquiry into the Nature and Causes of the Wealth of Nations*. Reprinted in 1937, edited by Edwin Cannan. New York: The Modern Library, 423.

Stiroh, K. J. (2002). Information technology and the U.S. productivity revival: What do the industry data say? *American Economic Review*, 92(5), 1559-1577.

Thomas, C. (2000). E-markets 2000. In G. Saloner & A.M. Spence (Eds.), *Creating and Capturing Value: Perspectives and Cases on Electronic Commerce* (pp. 253-285). New York: John Wiley & Sons.

van Ark, B. (2002) Measuring the new economy: An international comparative perspective. *Review of Income and Wealth,* 48(1), 1-14.

van Ark, B., Inklaar, R. & McGuckin, R. (2002). 'Changing gear' productivity, ICT and service industries: Europe and the United States. Groningen Growth and Development Centre, Research Memorandum GD-60 (December).

Varian, H., Litan, R.E., Elder, A. & Shutter, J. (2002). The net impact study. Retrieved in January at: http://www.netimpactstudy.com/Net-Impact_Study_Report.pdf.

ENDNOTES

[1] Gordon (2000) does not dispute the rise in productivity, but questions the magnitude and importance of New Economy technologies. He finds that the New Economy's effects on productivity growth are largely confined to the durable goods manufacturing sector and are mostly absent in the remaining 88 percent of the economy.

[2] McConnell and Perez-Quiros (2000) document the 1984:1 break date by testing for the type of structural change described in Andrews (1993) and Andrews and Ploberger (1994).

[3] The analysis presented in Koenig, Siems, and Wynne (2002) is updated here to include available GDP data through 2002:4.

[4] Of course, they are other possible explanations for the economy's increased stability that are not mutual exclusive, such as better monetary policies that have successfully created a low inflation environment, good luck induced stability in final demand, and smaller and fewer price shocks to the economy.

[5] Economist Adam Smith (1776) argued that private competition free from government regulations allows for the production and distribution of wealth better than government-regulated markets. As Smith said, private businesses organize the economy most efficiently as if "by an invisible hand."

[6] See Coase (1988).

[7] See Siems (2001a) for more on why the fundamentals behind B2B e-commerce and its impact on the economy remain strong. While most productivity gains and cost reductions will occur between businesses, the greatest long-term beneficiaries of Internet business solutions will be consumers, who will enjoy lower prices and higher living standards.

[8] As explained in Siems (2001b), B2B e-commerce and e-marketplaces move many markets closer to the textbook model of perfect competition that can be characterized by many well-informed buyers and sellers, low-cost access to information, extremely low transaction costs, and low barriers to entry.

[9] Chen and Siems (2001) find that investors reacted favorably to B2B e-marketplace announcements during the July 1999 – March 2000 period, with slightly higher abnormal returns associated with vertical (intra-industry) than horizontal (cross-industry) e-marketplaces.

[10] There are, of course, measurement issues on ICT's impact on economic growth. These issues are complicated further when making international comparisons and are discussed in van Ark (2002).

Section II
Domestic and Global Markets in the IT Age

Chapter VII
International Reserves Accumulation:
Some Lessons from Asia

Michael Gapen
International Monetary Fund, USA

Michael Papaioannou
International Monetary Fund, USA

ABSTRACT

This chapter examines the global implications from recent reserve accumulation in Asia. Advances in information technology and the closer integration of world markets have complicated economic policy making by increasing countries' vulnerability to capital account crises and introducing new channels of risk transmission. To safeguard against these developments, many countries accumulated unprecedented levels of international reserves. Current account deficits in some industrial countries have supported such reserve accumulation, in particular for Asian countries that have promoted export-led growth underpinned by competitive exchange rates. Asian economies have been willing to absorb the cost of reserve accumulation rather than adjusting their exchange rate levels. This strategy, however, has increased the likelihood of protectionist measures from abroad, which could lead to contractions in trade and output. Moreover, these dynamics may transition to a generalized real appreciation of the major Asian currencies, while mounting pressure for a reduction of the U.S. fiscal deficit to sustainable levels.

INTRODUCTION

The widespread application of new information technologies has revolutionized the way firms organize their activities, leading to a flattening of the corporate structure and dispersion of production activities worldwide. The unfolding of this process has facilitated the expansion in trade of goods and services, the creation of free trade zones like the North American Free Trade Area (NAFTA), common currency areas like the Eurozone countries, and the underpinning of the drive to liberalize capital accounts in order to aid the free flow of financial capital. In short, information technology has stimulated the process of globalization, increasing the connectedness and interdependence (i.e., integration) of global trade and financial markets.

The process of globalization is envisaged to aid economic development by allowing for specialization, the efficient allocation of productive resources, and reduced costs through competition. However, these positive aspects come with an increase in potential economic vulnerability. As economies have become more reliant on trade and private capital flows, they have also become more vulnerable to the volatility of such flows. The high degree of economic integration means that problems in any one country that appear isolated at first may trigger a widespread regional financial crisis, as seen in the Asian crisis of 1997 to 1998, or even a global one, as seen in the emerging market turmoil of 1998 to 2001. Therefore, the advance of information technology and its impact on the world economy has complicated the decisions of economic policy makers, with the increased vulnerability to capital account crises and new channels of risk transmission leading countries to seek innovative strategies for risk management and prevention.

One risk mitigation strategy that many countries have undertaken is to accumulate international reserves. The economic disruption caused by the Asian crisis of 1997 to 1998, for example, led policy makers to believe that additional reserve holdings should be acquired, regardless of acquisition or carry costs. In the 10 years following the crisis, total global reserves tripled to \$4,234 billion at the end of 2005. Developing countries hold 68.5% of global reserves and developing Asia alone accounts for 44% of global reserves, a level that surpasses that for all developed countries. The

crisis has also been a catalyst for proponents of the Asian Monetary Fund (AMF), which would aim at providing supplementary foreign exchange resources to members in crisis periods so as to avoid potential systemic regional implications from contagion effects.

The need for effective reserve management policies by governments is thus the indirect result of the widespread adoption of information technology and the integration of world markets. Several studies have examined the dynamics of the currency and financial crises, as well as their macroeconomic consequences (Corsetti, Pesenti, & Roubini, 1998a, 1998b). However, only a few studies have analyzed Asia's macroeconomic policies following the turbulent period in relation to reserve management and the resulting substantial accumulation of international reserves. The present chapter intends to fill this gap. Namely, it focuses on the implications of macroeconomic behavior and reserve management policies after the evolution of the crisis, and draws lessons that policy makers can take forward as the 21st century unfolds.

Following a brief overview of the economic setting, we first examine the theoretical underpinnings of reserve accumulation through the use of a buffer stock model of reserve demand and find that reserve levels should be, inter alia, dependent on the level of government expenditures and debt. We then add these two variables to a standard estimating equation for reserve holdings, which typically specifies reserves as being dependent on economic scale factors, international transactions and volatility, and measures of openness. Using annual data from 24 developing countries from 1990 to 2002, we find that government spending and debt are still highly significant, and conclude that further development of theoretical buffer stock models might prove useful. However, the process outlined above still underpredicts reserve demand for Asian countries when applied out of the sample in 2003 to 2005. Consequently, we examine other hypotheses for reserve demand including the desire to maintain competitiveness through export-led growth strategies, the creation of the Asian Monetary Fund, and a conducive international environment that has so far forestalled the anticipated economic adjustment process.

Finally, we discuss lessons learned from the accumulation of reserves in the Asian region. While the Asian economies have clearly benefited from the higher reserve balances through substantial reductions in country risk, the prolonged accumulation of reserves from persistent structural imbalances could also have important implications for the regional economies, as well as for the global financial system. The adjustment process is likely to be prolonged given the ability of the public sectors in Asia and the United States to enact mutually reinforcing policies largely beyond the reach of the private sector and market forces. We conclude that the international community will have to cope with the consequences of recent reserve accumulations since there are no enforceable adjustment policies or established practices on how to avoid large global imbalances.

THE ECONOMIC SETTING

At the end of 1995, 2 years prior to the Asian financial crisis of 1997 to 1998, total global reserves (minus gold) amounted to $1,474 billion. As shown in Figure 1, this amount was evenly split between industrial countries, which held 50.4% of total reserves minus gold, and developing countries, which held the remaining 49.6%. Within the developing-country universe, Asia led with 29.4% of global reserves, followed by the Western hemisphere (8.8%), Middle East (5.1%), and Africa (1.8%). Ten years later, total global reserves had tripled to $4,234 billion at the end of 2005, with reserve accumulation in developing countries far outpacing that in industrial countries. As shown in Figure 2, developing countries now hold 68.5% of global reserves. The increase in global reserves has mostly been concentrated in developed and

developing Asia, with many of today's largest holdings of reserves in this region. At the end of 2005, for example, China topped the list with $946 billion in reserves, followed by Japan ($834 billion), Taiwan ($253 billion), South Korea ($210 billion), India ($132 billion), and Singapore ($116 billion; Figure 3).

By any conventional standard of adequate reserve holdings, Asian countries far outpace their developing-country regional counterparts. Figures 4 to 6 plot reserves in months of imports, reserves to short-term external debt by remaining maturity, and reserves to total external debt, respectively. Asian countries have increased their import coverage ratio from below 6 months in 1995 to nearly 11 months by end the end of 2005. Along with Africa, this accounted for nearly all the increase in the developing-country sample since trends in remaining developing countries were relatively flat during the same time period. Reserves to short-term external debt for the Asian countries also increased markedly from 420% in 1995—an already high level relative to the average for developing countries as a whole—to a high of 1,300% by the end of 1999; before it had fallen to 840% by end the end 2005, more than 8 times the coverage and nearly twice as high as the developing-country sample of 477%. Finally, the ratio of reserves to total external debt also increased rapidly for Asian countries from 76% in 1995 to 229% in 2005. This compares favorably to the remaining developing-country counterparts, which ranged from a low of 34% for the Western hemisphere to a high of 55% for Africa in 2005.

The post-Asian-financial-crisis period appears to be a turning point in reserve management policies in these countries as each of the indicators in Figures 4 to 6 turned sharply upward from 1998 onward. Furthermore, by many traditional measures of reserve effectiveness or adequacy, the level of Asian reserves has grown substantially and appears adequate to insulate against possible negative economic shocks. Understanding the motivations behind the strategy of reserve accumulation are, therefore, important to understanding the current level of reserves held by Asian countries.

Several recent studies have examined key determinants of an optimal level of international reserves, while a significantly smaller number of studies examine issues relating to the accumulation of reserves beyond an optimum level. Among others, Flood and Marion (2002) provide a general overview of the literature on reserve accumulation and its determining factors. Bahmani-Oskooee and Brown (2002) and Aizenman and Marion (2002) explore econometrically the post-crisis high demand for reserves by Asian countries and the relatively low demand by some other developing countries. Using a sample of 125 developing countries, Aizenman and Marion show that traditional explanatory factors such as the size of international transactions, their volatility, the exchange rate regime (fixed vs. floating), and political considerations are good predictors of reserve holdings in Asia before the 1997 financial crisis. However, after the crisis, these factors tend to underpredict Asia's reserve demand as higher perceived sovereign risk and higher fiscal liabilities, both funded and unfunded, appear to lead to relatively large precautionary demand for international reserves. In contrast, other developing countries with high discount rates, political instability, or political corruption seem to find it optimal to hold smaller precautionary balances.

A related topic that has drawn considerable attention concerns optimal reserve management policies and practices once an optimal level of reserves has been achieved. Through its effort to help members set appropriate objectives and principles and build adequate institutional and operational foundations for good reserve management, the International Monetary Fund (IMF, 2004) provides summary guidelines for foreign exchange reserve management. Also, Keeley (2002) offers best practices on reserve management that could lead to an optimal performance of reserves. With regard to employed practices, Beschloss and Mendes (1999-2000) report on survey results of 40 central banks, representing both developed and emerging markets. They note that main trends on reserve management policies include greater emphasis on the determination of appropriate strategic asset allocation to meet the multiple objectives of maintaining liquidity, preserving capital, immunizing external liabilities, and maximizing return. An earlier survey of 48 central banks had also revealed that central bankers believe that larger reserves are needed to provide a cushion against external shocks and crises, and that there is strong pressure to enhance the performance of reserve portfolios (Pringle & Weller, 1999).

Numerous other studies deal with individual countries' policies of reserve accumulation and their implications. For example, Sidaoui (2004) provides a detailed account of Mexico's policies that led to the relatively fast accumulation of international reserves between 1996 and 2002 under the present floating exchange rate regime, the cost considerations relating to this accumulation, and the rationale for the authorities' decision to eventually take measures to ease the pace of the accumulation. For Asian countries, Dooley, Folkerts-Landau, and Garber (2003) consider the issue of reserve accumulation as a normal evolution of the international monetary system. They argue that this evolution involves the emergence of a fixed exchange rate periphery in Asia with a development strategy based on export-led growth supported by undervalued exchange rates, capital controls, and official capital outflows in the form of accumulation of reserve asset claims on the United States. This development de facto reestablishes the United States as the center country in a new Breton Woods international monetary order. The authors argue that this strategy will further foster Asia's economic growth and allow for its movement to the center. Then, as financial liberalization requires floating rates among the countries of the center, Asia would move toward a more flexible exchange rate regime.

THEORETICAL UNDERPINNINGS OF RESERVE ACCUMULATION IN ASIA: A BUFFER STOCK APPROACH

We first examine a theoretical buffer stock model of reserve holdings to identify factors that may be contributors to the reserve accumulation strategies of developing Asia after the financial crisis of 1997 to 1998. These factors are then used along with some traditional explanatory variables to estimate equations of reserve holdings. Finally, we investigate the significance of other factors in determining the level of reserves in Asia, including the high competitiveness of Asian countries following the Asian financial crisis and the conducive international environment for reserve accumulation.

A Buffer Stock Model of Reserve Demand

This section outlines the demand for international reserves in the simple buffer stock model of Aizenman and Marion (2002) to investigate how governments should optimally target a level of reserves when faced with conditional access to capital markets and adjustment costs. The presence of intertemporal distortions, costly adjustment, and intermittent access to markets is an appropriate framework for describing reserve demand in Asia following the crisis. The model is a two-period economy with two possible states of nature in the second period characterized by uncertainty based on random productivity. The government finances its inelastic spending though taxation, which includes a nonlinear loss function directly related to the level of taxes. The government is also able to borrow in capital markets, but may default in the second period depending on the revealed state.

Output in the current period is certain, but is dependent on the realized productivity shock in the second period. Therefore, output in period t and $t+1$ is:

$$Y_t = 1, \quad Y_{t+1} = \begin{cases} 1+\theta_h & with \ \Pr(1/2), \\ 1-\theta_l & with \ \Pr(1/2), \end{cases} \quad (1)$$

where θ_h refers to the high productivity state and θ_l refers to the low productivity state in Period 2. If the low productivity state is revealed in Period 2, the government defaults on its external debt. While the event of default eliminates the need to pay principal and interest, we assume that there is some penalty related to default equal to a share of output, γY_{t+1}. If productivity is high in the second period, the government has sufficient resources to pay its bondholders and returns $(1 + r_t)B_t$, where r_t is the contracted interest rate and B_t is the stock of bonds issued in the first period.

Government expenditures, which are fixed at the level $\overline{G}$, are financed by taxes, bonds, or international reserves. As in Barro (1979), we assume that taxation is costly in that collection results in deadweight loss through distortions. In particular, net tax revenue to the government is equal to:

$$T_t = Y_t \left(\tau_t - \frac{1}{2}\lambda \ \tau_t^2 \right), \quad (2)$$

where $1/2\lambda \ \tau_t^2$ is the deadweight loss associated with the tax rate, τ_t. Rearranging equation (2) to solve for the tax rate as a function of the ratio of tax revenue to output yields:

$$\tau_t = \frac{1 - \sqrt{1 - 2\lambda(T_t/Y_t)}}{\lambda}. \quad (3)$$

International reserves acquired in period t, through additional taxation or bond issuance, can also be used to finance expenditures, including debt payments, in period $t+1$. We assume that reserves earn the risk-free rate, r_f. Taken together, the government budget constraints across periods is defined by:

$$T_t = \overline{G} + Res_t + B_t,$$

$$T_{t+1,h} + (1+r_f)Res_t = \overline{G} + B_t(1+r_t),$$

$$T_{t+1,l} + (1+r_f)Res_t = \overline{G} + \gamma(1-\theta_l), \qquad (4)$$

where $T_{t+1,h}$ and $T_{t+1,l}$ are the level of net taxes in the second period when productivity is high and low, respectively.

In the simple two-period economy, the government chooses the amount of debt and reserves in period *1* subject to the government budget constraints in equation (4), the tax function in equation (3), and productivity in equation (1) to maximize the utility of consumers according to: (see equation (5)), where β is the discount rate and consumers are assumed to have risk-neutral preferences. The first-order conditions for bonds and reserves yield the following conditions[1]: (see equation (6)), where,

$$\eta_1 = \overline{G} + Res_1 - B_1,$$

$$\eta_{2,h} = \frac{\overline{G} + B_1(1+r_1) - (1+r_f)Res_1}{1+\theta_h},$$

$$\eta_{2,l} = \frac{\overline{G} + \gamma(1-\theta_l) - (1+r_f)Res_1}{1-\theta_l}. \qquad (7)$$

In equation (6), note that bonds are insufficient to smooth against intertemporal shocks due to the possibility of defaults. Without sufficient reserves, a default in Period *2* requires that additional taxes be raised to cover the loss-given default. In contrast, the level of international reserves is chosen to equate the marginal cost of taxation across periods. The loss in utility from the acquisition of reserves in the first period is set equal to the discounted value of the gain from lower taxes in the second period.

Equation (6) implies $\eta_{2,h} = \eta_{2,l}$. Using this in the condition for reserves in equation (6) and assuming that $1/(1+r_f) = \beta$, we derive an optimal decision rule for reserves:

$$Res_1 = f(\overline{G}, B, \theta, \gamma, \beta) \qquad (8)$$

The optimal level of reserves is linearly dependent on the level of government expenditures, the level of issued bonds, and the loss-given default. Reserve levels are positively related to fiscal expenditures while helping to smooth taxes across periods to protect against default. In contrast, reserve levels are negatively related to the level of bonds since both play a role in smoothing intertemporal shocks in equations (6) and (7). Finally, the level of reserves is nonlinearly dependent on the variability of productivity shocks. As the variability of the economy increases, so does the variability of taxes and the associated deadweight

Equation 5.

$$\underset{B,Res}{Max}\left\{(1-\tau_1) + \frac{1}{2}\beta\left[(1+\theta_h)(1-\tau_{2,h}) + (1-\theta_l)(1-\tau_{2,l})\right]\right\}$$

Equation 6.

$$B_1: \quad \frac{1}{\sqrt{1-2\lambda\eta_1}} = \beta(1+r_f)\frac{1}{\sqrt{1-2\lambda\eta_{2,h}}},$$

$$Res_1: \quad \frac{1}{\sqrt{1-2\lambda\eta_1}} = \beta\frac{1}{2}(1+r_f)\frac{1}{\sqrt{1-2\lambda\eta_{2,h}}} + \frac{1}{\sqrt{1-2\lambda\eta_{2,l}}},$$

loss. The optimal response is to acquire additional reserves.

Estimating Reserve Holdings from the Buffer Stock Model: Some Preliminary Results

In order to test the implications of the buffer stock model above, we add government spending and bonds to a standard estimating equation for reserve holdings. Standard estimating equations for reserve holdings usually specify reserves as dependent on economic scale factors, international transactions and volatility, and some measure of openness. We use population, real gross domestic product (GDP) per capita, the ratio of imports to GDP, and the volatility of the nominal effective exchange rate to account for these standard estimating variables.[2] To this we added the ratios of government spending and total public-sector debt to GDP as suggested by the buffer stock model above.[3] Thus, our estimating equation is, (see equation (9)), where *res* is the level of reserves minus gold in U.S. dollars deflated by the U.S. GDP

Equation 9.

$$\ln(res_{it}) = \alpha + \beta_1 \ln(pop_{it}) + \beta_2 \ln(cap_{it}) + \beta_3 \ln(imp_{it}) + \beta_4 \ln(gov_{it}) + \beta_5 \ln(vol_{it}) + \beta_6 \ln(debt_{it}) + \varepsilon_t,$$

Table 1. Regression output of reserve holdings 1990-2002

	Countries	24	
	Number of obs.	250	
	R-squared	0.59	
	Adj. R-squared	0.58	
	S.E. of regression	0.81	
	Sum squared resid.	160.84	
	Coefficient	Std. Error	t-Statistic
constant	2.68**	0.30	8.99
pop	0.81**	0.05	17.07
cap	0.07	0.05	1.48
imp	0.81**	0.11	7.15
gov	0.79**	0.15	5.10
vol	-0.01	0.02	-0.64
debt	-1.15**	0.11	-10.55

** Indicates statistical significance at 5 percent. Standard errors are corrected for heteroskedasticity and autocorrelation.

Source: IMF International Financial Statistics database and IMF estimates. Sample based on annual data from 1990-2002 for 24 developing countries. Limitations in country data and number of observations are due to lack of sufficient data availability. Dependent variable is *res*, the level of reserves minus gold in US dollars deflated by the U.S. GDP deflator. Explanatory variables are total population (*pop*), real GDP per capita in US dollars (*cap*); the standard deviation of the nominal effective exchange rate (*vol*); and the ratios of imports of goods and services (*imp*), government spending (*gov*), and total public sector debt (*debt*) to GDP. All variables are in logged form.

Table 2. Regression output of reserve holdings: Subperiods from 1990-1997 and 1998-2002

Sub-period I: 1990-1997			
Countries	24		
Number of obs.	152		
R-squared	0.60		
Adj. R-squared	0.58		
S.E. of regression	0.81		
Sum squared resid.	94.27		
	Coefficient	Std. Error	t-Statistic
constant	2.90**	0.35	8.21
pop	0.72**	0.07	10.93
cap	0.07	0.05	1.45
imp	0.75**	0.14	5.40
gov	0.85**	0.20	4.29
vol	-0.03	0.02	-1.25
debt	-1.12**	0.12	-9.16

Sub-period II: 1998-2002			
Countries	24		
Number of obs.	98		
R-squared	0.83		
Adj. R-squared	0.81		
S.E. of regression	0.53		
Sum squared resid.	26.03		
	Coefficient	Std. Error	t-Statistic
constant	-0.75	0.52	-1.43
pop	1.13**	0.07	16.83
cap	0.75**	0.13	5.77
imp	0.67**	0.14	4.90
gov	0.43**	0.18	2.44
vol	-0.02	0.02	-0.69
debt	-0.90**	0.26	-3.47

** Indicates statistical significance at 5 percent. Standard errors
are corrected for heteroskedasticity and autocorrelation.

Source: IMF International Financial Statistics database and IMF estimates.
Sample based on annual data from 1990-2002 for 24 developing countries.
Limitations in country data and number of observations are due to lack
of sufficient data availability. Dependent variable is *res*, the level of reserves
minus gold in US dollars deflated by the U.S. GDP deflator.
Explanatory variables are total population (*pop*), real GDP per capita in US dollars (*cap*)
the standard deviation of the nominal effective exchange rate (*vol*); and
the ratios of imports of goods and services (*imp*), government spending (*gov*),
and total public sector debt (*debt*) to GDP. All variables are in logged form.

deflator, *pop* is the total population, *cap* is real GDP per capita in U.S. dollars, *vol* is the standard deviation of the nominal effective exchange rate, and *imp*, *gov*, and *debt* are the ratios of imports of goods and services, government spending, and total public-sector debt to GDP.

Table 1 presents the results from the above regressions using annual data from 24 developing countries from 1990 to 2002. The regression results confirm the findings from other standard estimating equations while fully confirming the implications from the buffer stock model.[4] The coefficients on population and the ratio of imports of goods and services to GDP are both positive and highly significant. Furthermore, the coefficient on the ratio of government expenditures to GDP is positive while the coefficient on total public-sector debt to GDP is negative. Both are highly significant and the coefficients match that suggested in the buffer stock model of reserve holdings.[5] The results of this regression suggest that buffer stock models of reserve holdings may

Figure 1. Share of total reserves: 1995

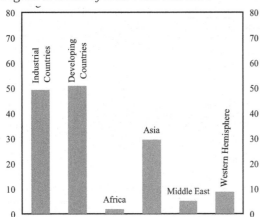

Figure 2. Share of total reserves: 2005

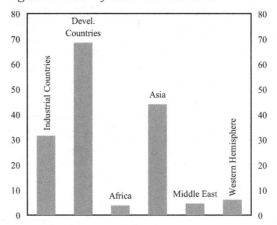

Figure 3. Largest holdings of reserves: 2005

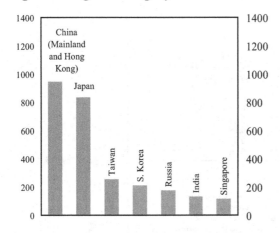

Figure 4. Reserves in months of imports

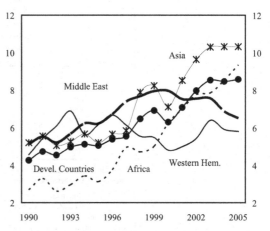

Figure 5. Reserves to short-term external debt[1]

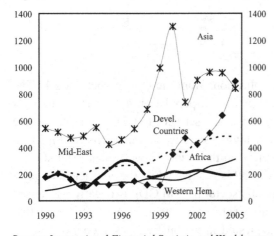

Figure 6. Reserves to total external debt.

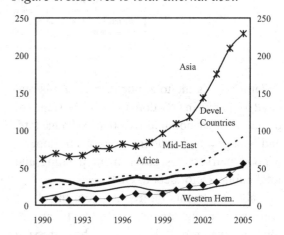

Source: International Financial Statistic and World economic Outlook, IML

*   In Figure 1-6, reserves are defined as reserves minus gold

[2]   Short-term by remaining maturity

hold important clues to reserve accumulation behavior of governments. Nevertheless, further study in this area could prove useful.

In order to examine the hypothesis that the behavior of reserve holding by governments fundamentally changed after the Asian financial crisis, two additional regressions were performed to test whether the estimated relationship remained stable across two subperiods: from 1990 to 1997 and from 1998 to 2002. The results of these regressions are displayed in Table 2 and reject the hypothesis that the estimated relationship remains unchanged across the two subperiods. The results of this test suggest that the motivation for holding reserves may indeed have changed in the years following the Asian financial crisis. The increased precautionary demand from a buffer stock model may be one explanation for the structural shift in reserve demand evidenced in the data.

However, despite the relative goodness of fit of the above estimating equation when including government spending and debt ratios, the estimating equation still underpredicts reserve holdings by Asian countries when applied out of sample. Specifically, applying the estimated equation from Table 1 to selected Asian countries in the out-of-sample period of 2003 to 2004 results in consistent underprediction of the actual reserve holdings. Therefore, we conjecture that reserve demand in Asia is driven by additional factors to the buffer stock models of reserve demand. We then examine some other factors that might underpin reserve demand in the next sections.

OTHER POSSIBLE UNDERPINNINGS OF RESERVE DEMAND IN ASIA

High Competitiveness, Terms of Trade, and Export Promotion

In the years following the Asian financial crisis, many of the affected economies incurred sub-

stantial real exchange rate depreciations. The resulting improved competitiveness and terms of trade eventually resulted in improved trade balances for most Asian countries, which drove the economic recovery across the region. In many cases, however, the real exchange rate depreciation has persisted or even widened against the major world currencies despite persistent trade surpluses. Figure 7, for example, plots the real effective exchange rate for three selected crisis-affected countries vs. that of the U.S. dollar and euro for the period 1996 to 2004. For each of the three selected countries—Malaysia, Philippines, and Singapore—the real effective exchange rate at the end of 2004 was below or substantially below that found immediately after the crisis in 1998. This trend has remained in place despite the fact that the real trade balance for Malaysia increased from $41 million in 1996 to $242 million by 2003, or a five-fold increase in 7 years.[6] The real trade balance for Singapore rose from $77 million to $277 million during the same time period.

One explanation for the persistently competitive Asian economies has been the belief that governments in the region have tried to facilitate their export promotion policies through managing their U.S. dollar exchange rates. As such, their exchange rate regime and policies were often effected by a system of controls and taxes on capital inflows and exchange market interventions (buying dollars for local currencies) to limit exchange rate appreciations. The limited exchange rate changes against the dollar led to the Asian currencies' significant undervaluation, which fed their export growth. China often features as the most prominent Asian country with an overvalued currency, allegedly giving Chinese exporters an unfair advantage over their competitors. Its trading partners, especially the United States and European Union, charge that the Chinese yuan is overvalued by about 40%, and have repeatedly called for the yuan's immediate revaluation or a potential tariff (Schumer & Graham, 2005). China resists such claims and, instead, has adopted a

Figure 7. Real effective exchange rates: Selected crisis-affected countries vs. major currencies (Source: IMF International Financial Statistics database)

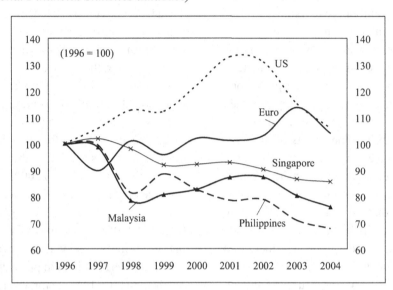

Note: U.S. and Euro real effective exchange rates based on real unit labor costs while selected Asian-economy real effective exchange rates based on relative Consumer Price Index

gradual loosening of its tight controls over foreign exchange dealings. This has included an opening of its onshore foreign exchange market and a small revaluation of the yuan against the U.S. dollar. (The value of the yuan was set at 8.28 per U.S. dollar from 1994 until about a year ago.)

The Asian Monetary Fund

A second explanation for reserve accumulation is related to the creation of the Asian Monetary Fund.[7] The economic dislocation that resulted from the financial crisis may also have convinced regional policy makers that a country's foreign exchange reserves alone may not be enough to stifle speculative attacks during a crisis period. This belief has been one of the main catalysts in the Asian region behind the push to develop the AMF (Lipscy, 2003), which aims at providing supplementary foreign exchange resources to members in crisis so as to avoid potential systemic regional implications from contagion effects. The

effect that the creation of the AMF will have on demand for reserves, however, has yet to be fully understood. The creation of the AMF will require substantial contributions from member countries, involving the acquisition of sufficient amounts of the principal reserve currency, leading to an increase in reserve demand. However, the creation of the AMF may dampen or eliminate the need for massive accumulation of reserves by individual member countries over the medium term since the AMF intends to swiftly dispatch funds to members in need. Consequently, its resources may be viewed as a substitute to domestic foreign exchange reserves, reducing the demand for reserves throughout the region.

A Conducive International Environment

Finally, the international environment has been supportive of the current arrangement and has so far forestalled the anticipated normal economic adjustment process. Asia's predisposition to maintain export-led growth has resulted in dramatic current account surpluses throughout the region, which have been traditionally channeled toward financing the historically large and persistent U.S. current account deficit. Asia's investments in U.S. Treasury securities originate primarily in the official sector of these countries, which had so far paid less attention to risk and return characteristics of these securities. However, the official sector has recently started to increasingly behave according to portfolio diversification theories and, in turn, appears to have started reducing its historical preference for the U.S. dollar as a reserve currency. Table 3, reproduced from IMF (2005), shows that developing countries held about

Table 3. Share of national currencies in total identified official holdings of foreign exchange at the end of the year in (percent)

	1995	1996	1997	1998	1999	2000	2001	2002	2003	2004
All countries										
U.S. dollar	59.0	62.1	65.2	69.4	71.0	70.5	70.7	66.5	65.8	65.9
Japanese yen	6.8	6.7	5.8	6.2	6.4	6.3	5.2	4.5	4.1	3.9
Pound sterling	2.1	2.7	2.6	2.7	2.9	2.8	2.7	2.9	2.6	3.3
Swiss franc	0.3	0.3	0.3	0.3	0.2	0.3	0.3	0.4	0.2	0.2
Euro 2/	-	-	-	-	17.9	18.8	19.8	24.2	25.3	24.9
Deutsche mark	15.8	14.7	14.5	13.8	-	-	-	-	-	-
French franc	2.4	1.8	1.4	1.6	-	-	-	-	-	-
Netherlands guilder	0.3	0.2	0.4	0.3	-	-	-	-	-	-
ECU 3/	8.5	7.1	6.0	1.2	-	-	-	-	-	-
Other currencies 4/	4.8	4.3	3.8	4.5	1.6	1.4	1.2	1.4	1.9	1.8
Industrial Countries										
U.S. dollar	52.3	57.4	59.1	67.6	73.5	72.5	72.7	68.9	70.5	71.5
Japanese yen	6.7	5.7	5.9	6.9	6.7	6.5	5.6	4.4	3.8	3.6
Pound sterling	2.1	2.1	2.0	2.1	2.2	2.0	1.9	2.1	1.5	1.9
Swiss franc	0.1	0.1	0.1	0.2	0.1	0.2	0.3	0.6	0.2	0.1
Euro 2/	-	-	-	-	16.1	17.1	18.0	22.4	22.1	20.9
Deutsche mark	16.6	15.9	16.2	13.4	-	-	-	-	-	-
French franc	2.3	1.7	0.9	1.2	-	-	-	-	-	-
Netherlands guilder	0.2	0.2	0.2	0.2	-	-	-	-	-	-
ECU 3/	13.6	12.3	11.2	2.3	-	-	-	-	-	-
Other currencies 4/	6.0	4.7	4.4	6.2	1.4	1.6	1.5	1.7	1.9	2.0
Developing Countries										
U.S. dollar	70.3	68.5	72.4	71.2	68.2	68.2	68.6	64.0	60.7	59.9
Japanese yen	7.0	8.1	5.7	5.6	6.0	6.0	4.9	4.7	4.4	4.3
Pound sterling	2.2	3.5	3.3	3.3	3.7	3.6	3.6	3.8	3.9	4.8
Swiss franc	0.7	0.6	0.6	0.5	0.4	0.3	0.3	0.2	0.2	0.2
Euro 2/	-	-	-	-	19.9	20.6	21.8	26.1	28.9	29.2
Deutsche mark	14.4	13.0	12.5	14.3	-	-	-	-	-	-
French franc	2.4	2.0	2.1	2.1	-	-	-	-	-	-
Netherlands guilder	0.5	0.3	0.5	0.4	-	-	-	-	-	-
ECU 3/	0.0	0.0	0.0	0.0	-	-	-	-	-	-
Other currencies 4/	2.6	3.9	3.0	2.7	1.7	1.3	0.9	1.2	1.9	1.6

1/ Table is reproduced from the IMF Annual Report 2005 (IMF 2005a), p. 109. Only IMF member countries that report their official holdings of foreign exchange are included in this table.

2/ Not comparable with the combined share of euro legacy currencies in previous years because amounts exclude the euros received by euro area members when their previous holdings of other euro area members' legacy currencies were converted into euros on January 1, 1999.

3/ In the calculation of currency shares, the ECU is treated as a separate currency. ECU reserves held by the monetary authorities existed in the form of claims on both the private sector and the European Monetary Institute (EMI), which issued official ECUs to European Union central banks through revolving swaps against the contribution of 20 percent of their gross gold holdings and U.S. dollar reserves. On December 31, 1998, the official ECUs were unwound into gold and U.S. dollars; hence, the share of ECUs at the end of 1998 was sharply lower than a year earlier. The remaining ECU holdings reported for 1998 consisted of ECUs issued by the private sector, usually in the form of ECU deposits and bonds. On January 1, 1999, these holdings were automatically converted into euros.

4/ Foreign exchange reserves that are reported to be held in currencies other than those listed above.

60% of their reserve holdings in U.S. dollars in 2004, which is below the 68% recorded in 1999 and 70% in 1995. This decline in the U.S. dollar's position has been rebalanced to the euro, which now makes up 29% of developing-country reserve holdings, up from 20% in 1999. However, while developing countries have displayed a tendency to rebalance away from the U.S. dollar at a relatively fast pace, the dollar's position has fallen less in the total country sample, comprising 66% of total reserve holdings in 2004, down from 71% in 1999, but up from 59% in 1995. As a result, the accelerated accumulation of international reserves by the Asian countries seems to have been achieved with some rebalancing away from the dollar, but without altering to any significant degree their dollar exchange rates.

LESSONS FROM ASIA'S RESERVE ACCUMULATION

As described in the previous section, the present situation of a significant reserve accumulation by Asian countries is the result of a confluence of events. These include traditional factors of reserve accumulation like liquidity, facilitation of trade and debt transactions, insulation from economic shocks, and consumption smoothing. More recently, however, these factors have been augmented by two main global trends: (a) the export-led growth strategy in place throughout Asia in the post-crisis period, and (b) the accommodative fiscal and balance-of-payments situation in the United States. Nevertheless, the reserve accumulation has both positive and potentially important negative implications for the regional and global financial system.

The Asian economies have especially benefited from the higher reserve balances through a substantial reduction in country risk. Spreads on public-sector external debt in the crisis-affected countries have fallen in the years following the crisis, and credit ratings awarded by the major rating agencies have improved markedly. The private sector has also benefited as reduced sovereign credit risk and the improved liquidity position of the public sector has led to higher access to international capital markets by private-sector issuers. The higher reserve levels have also made it less likely that an unforeseen credit event, for example, stemming from "too-important-to-fail" entities, will severely disrupt domestic financial conditions and lead to spillover effects throughout the region.

The increased demand for reserves immediately following the crisis was largely viewed as a rational response to the need to restore confidence in financial systems, enhance public-sector credibility, and protect against sudden stops in capital flows. The increase in demand for reserves was met by an increase in the supply of reserves as devalued real exchange rates precipitated nascent trade surpluses. In this regard, the active accumulation of reserves by Asian countries may constitute a good practice and, thus, could serve as a model for other developing countries in similar circumstances.

Nevertheless, the prolonged accumulation of reserves from persistent structural imbalances could have important implications for the regional economies as well as the global financial system. In a freely floating system, prolonged accumulation may make the eventual exchange rate adjustment process more painful and difficult than would otherwise be the case. Macroeconomic imbalances that persist for an extended period of time may eventually exacerbate financial market volatility and, therefore, the reserve accumulation strategy in a conducive international environment could threaten the stability of the international financial system. Meanwhile, there is little consensus over how long the present arrangement can persist without a substantial adjustment. For example, Dooley et al. (2003) believe that the current economic relationship between China and the United States may represent a new stable Bretton Woods system that could persist for the foreseeable future.

Among the factors that may prolong the adjustment process is the ability of the public sectors in Asia and the United States to enact mutually reinforcing policies, namely Asia's reliance on export-led growth and the U.S. current account deficit, largely beyond the reach of the private sector and market forces. In the short term, the United States has been largely able to finance its annual deficit without marginal increases in long-term interest rates due to the channeling of Asian current account surpluses into U.S. Treasury securities. In contrast, the Asian economies have been willing to absorb the carry costs of marginal reserve accumulation in order to maintain the favorable exchange rate levels. Additional dollar inflows have been absorbed, for example, by a combination of open market operations, additional public-sector saving, higher reserve requirements, and bank deposits at the central bank, without generating domestic inflation and higher interest rates that may restrict growth. The export-led growth strategy, however, has increased the likelihood that protectionist measures may surface from outside the region, which could have substantial economic costs.

These short-term dynamics are likely to transition to a generalized real appreciation of the major Asian currencies and efforts to reduce the U.S. fiscal deficit over the longer term. Market participants are expecting that, if enacted, the real appreciation of the Asian currencies would proceed through a series of realignments in the official nominal dollar exchange rates. In this way, exchange rates would be more reflective of economic fundamentals, which are widely perceived to contribute to a well-functioning world financial system. Concurrently, market

expectations are for an eventual consolidation in U.S. fiscal policy as dependence on foreign financing becomes excessive and payments on debt become overly burdensome. This, in turn, would reduce the supply of dollar-denominated assets in international financial markets, including Asian markets, and diminish pressures for a U.S. dollar depreciation and/or the existence of currency misalignments. However, it should be noted that external shocks, such as the ongoing increase in world oil prices, may play a catalytic role in redistributing and possibly recycling stocks of international reserves.

CONCLUSION

A consequence of the widespread application of information technology and the integration of global markets has been the desire by many developing countries to hold ample international reserves, a policy that may have regional or even global implications. The logic of the high accumulation of reserves is to adequately secure a country from adverse external shocks and thus prevent it from possible financial crises. The post-Asian-crisis period has attested to that logic as Asian countries have benefited from a credit risk perspective through reserve accumulation. The regression analysis conducted in this chapter also supports this conclusion and suggests that further work is warranted on buffer stock and other economic models of optimal reserve accumulation. However, it is evident that these traditional reserve demand models have not fully captured recent reserve accumulation by Asian countries.

Current account deficits in some major industrial countries have been conducive to reserve accumulation by Asian countries as these countries have often sought to promote an export-led growth strategy underpinned by competitive exchange rates. Since there are no enforceable adjustment policies or established practices on how to avoid large reserve accumulations, the international community will have to cope with the consequences. The main implications of high reserve accumulation for the international financial system relate to overall world financial stability and potential exchange rate fluctuations. The concentration of reserves creates a potential financing risk for the debtor country, in this case the United States, with probable adverse effects on world exchange rates.

The accumulation of reserves by a particular country or region creates the need for sensible reserve management practices, including the estimation of an optimal level of reserves, the establishment of good practices in terms of managing liquidity and risk-adjusted returns, and the development of policies for a gradual recycling of reserves. In order to avoid currency misalignments and protectionist tendencies, strategies for reserve accumulation would be better set within a flexible exchange rate system that properly internalizes the costs and benefits of various actions. In lieu of pursuing consistently undervalued exchange rates to promote export growth, the use of productivity-enhancing policies could actively be pursued to compensate for the eventual real exchange rate appreciation.

The creation of the AMF may indeed eliminate the need for the massive accumulation of reserves for member countries, and its existence could lead to closer regional ties and to the de facto formation of the Asian block of countries. If its formation leads to similar arrangements as in other parts of the world, this development could push forward the regionalization of the world economy, with well-known consequences for global trade, finance, and exchange rate relations. For a quantitative estimation of the impact of a possible formation of an Asian block on the international economy, a further investigation would be warranted.

ACKNOWLEDGMENT

The authors thank Christopher Decker for helpful comments and suggestions. The views expressed in this chapter are those of the authors and do not necessarily represent those of the IMF or IMF policy.

REFERENCES

Aizenman, J., & Marion, N. (2002). *The high demand for international reserves in the Far East: What's going on* (NBER Working Paper No. 9266)? Cambridge: National Bureau of Economic Research.

Bahmani-Oskooee, M., & Brown, F. (2002). Demand for international reserves: A review article. *Applied Economics, 34*, 1209-1226.

Barro, R. (1979). On the determination of the public debt. *Journal of Political Economy, 87*, 940-971.

Ben-Bassat, A., & Gottlieb, D. (1992). Optimal international reserves and sovereign risk. *Journal of International Economics, 33*, 345-362.

Beschloss, A., & Mendess, W. (1999-2000). Reserve management policies and practices. *Central Banking, 10*(4), 88-96.

Corsetti, G., Pesenti, P., & Roubini, N. (1998a). *What caused the Asian currency and financial crisis? Part I: A macroeconomic overview* (NBER Working Paper No. 6833). Cambridge: National Bureau of Economic Research.

Corsetti, G., Pesenti, P., & Roubini, N. (1998b). *What caused the Asian currency and financial crisis? Part II: The policy debate* (NBER Working Paper No. 6834). Cambridge: National Bureau of Economic Research.

Dooley, M., Folkerts-Landau, D., & Garber, P. (2003). *An essay on the revived Breton Woods system* (NBER Working Paper No. 9971). Cambridge: National Bureau of Economic Research.

Flood, R., & Marion, N. (2002). Holding international reserves in an era of high capital mobility. *Brookings Trade Forum 2001.*

Huang, K. (1995). Modeling China's demand for international reserves. *Applied Financial Economics, 5*, 357-366.

International Monetary Fund. (2004). *Guidelines for foreign exchange reserve management.* Washington, DC: Author.

International Monetary Fund. (2005). *Annual report.* Washington, DC: Author.

Islam, A. M., Khan, M., & Islam, M. M. (1994). An empirical test of the demand for international reserves. In D. K. Ghosh & E. Ortiz (Eds.), *The changing environment of international financial markets.* New York: St. Martins Press.

Keeley, T. (2002). Reserve management: A new era. *Central Banking, 12*(3), 71-77.

Lipscy, P. (2003). Japan's Asian Monetary Fund proposal. *Stanford Journal of East Asian Affairs, 3*(1), 93-104.

New momentum for an Asian Monetary Fund. (2005, May 13). *Asia Pacific Bulletin.*

Pringle, R., & Weller, B. (1999). *Reserve management and the international financial system.* London: Central Banking Publications.

Schumer, C. E., & Graham, L. O. (2005, June 8). Will it take a tariff to free the yuan? *The New York Times.*

Sidaoui, J. J. (2005). *Policies for international reserve accumulation under a floating exchange rate regime: The experience of Mexico (1995-2003). Globalization and monetary policy in emerging markets* (BIS Paper No. 23). Basle: Bank of International Settlements.

ENDNOTES

[1] Derivation of the condition on bonds in equation (6) is based on the condition that the expected return on bonds is equal to the risk-free rate. See Aizenman and Marion (2002) for additional details.

[2] If the nominal effective exchange rate was not available, we used the official nominal exchange rate as a substitute.

[3] We also used the ratio of external debt to GDP in place of total public-sector debt. This did not alter the thrust of the results.

[4] See Ben-Bassat and Gottlieb (1992), Islam, Khan, and Islam (1994), Huang (1995), Aizenman and Marion (2002), and Bahmani-Oskooee and Brown (2002).

[5] The results indicate that GDP per capita and the volatility of the nominal effective exchange rate are not significant. This is primarily due to the lack of sufficient data on total public-sector debt, which limits the overall number of observations. In a separate regression, we dropped the measure of total debt to GDP while maintaining the remaining variables, including the ratio of government spending to GDP. Eliminating the debt data allows us to greatly expand the data set to over 80 countries from 1980 to 2004. This data set was examined with and without fixed country effects. Population, real GDP per capita, government spending to GDP, and the volatility of the nominal ef-

fective exchange rate are found to be highly significant, confirming results from other studies (e.g., Aizenman & Marion 2002) including the negative coefficient on the volatility of the nominal effective exchange rate. The only insignificant variable is the ratio of imports of goods and services to GDP.

6   The real trade balance was calculated by deflating the U.S. dollar's value of the trade balance by the U.S. GDP deflator.

7   In May 2005, the members of the Association of Southeast Asian Nations (ASEAN) plus China, Japan, and South Korea announced their intention to strengthen the Chiang Mai Initiative (CMI), reestablishing momentum toward the creation of the Asian Monetary Fund. Proposals included doubling the size of the CMI to nearly $80 billion and increasing emergency access by members without IMF conditionality. See "New Momentum for an Asian Monetary Fund" (2005).

Chapter VIII
IT and Thai Stock Market Development

Chollada Luangpituksa
Kasetsart University, Thailand

ABSTRACT

This chapter describes the development of the stock market in Thailand since it was established in 1975. During these 30 years, the stock market in Thailand has introduced computer systems to facilitate investors and listed companies both in financial data and administrative work. Particularly, the Internet trading system has been introduced to enhance market growth. This can be traced from the increasing volume of trade each day. The growth of the Thai stock market has changed the structure of Thai economy and affects the economic development of Thailand.

INTRODUCTION

The stock market is one of the most important sources for companies to raise money to increase business investment. Many profitable investments require a long-term commitment of capital, but investors might not want to tie up their savings for such a long period. A liquid equity market allows savers to sell their shares easily if they so desire, thereby making shares relatively more attractive investments. As savers become comfortable with investing for the long term in equities, they are likely to rebalance their portfolios toward equities and away from shorter term financial investments. For firms, this rebalancing lowers the cost of shifting to more profitable—that is, more productive—longer term projects. Higher productivity capital, in turn, boosts economic growth. It also increases returns on investments in equity, which may prompt individuals to save more, adding further to investment in physical capital and thus fueling economic growth (Levine, 1997). Filer, Hanousek, and Campos (1999) found a strong relationship between stock market activity and future economic growth for the low- and lower-middle-income countries. A more developed equity market might provide liquidity that lowers the cost of the foreign capital that is essential for development, especially in low-income countries that cannot generate sufficient domestic savings. The liquidity of the stock market is measured by the total value of shares traded as a share of the gross domestic product (GDP), which is likely to vary with the ease of trading. The second measure of liquidity is the value of trade shares as a percentage of total market capitalization. This ratio indicates that greater turnover predicts faster growth (Levine, 1996). Furthermore, a well-developed stock market can foster economic growth in the long run and well-functioning stock markets can promote economic development by fueling the engine of growth through faster capital accumulation and by tuning it through better resource allocation (Caporale, Howells, & Soliman, 2004). Granger-causality tests were used to provide evidence of a positive and significant causal relationship going from stock market development to economic growth, particularly for less developed countries. Stock market development is measured by three variables: (a) market capitalization over GDP, (b) turnover velocity (the ratio of turnover to market capitalization), and (c) the change in the number of domestic shares listed (Filer et al.). Lee also conceded that a network was important for automated trading, and the number of exchanges might proliferate simply because automated exchanges were so cheap to operate (as cited in Herring & Litan, 2002). However, Hobijn and Jovanovic (2000) argued that the capitalization-GDP ratio was likely to decline and then rise after any major technological shift. Paul Mahoney believes that technology will continue to increase the size and decrease the costs of trading in secondary securities markets and lead even more financial transactions to take place through securities markets (as cited in Herring & Litan). Furthermore,

technological progress explains 37% of the 3.9% annual growth in the stock market over the 1885 to 1998 period (Jovanovic & Rousseau, 2000). As for the number of domestic shares listed, a new technology or product is often developed by the single entrepreneur who initially finds it hard to get funds, develop the product, and find customers. If the product is good, customers eventually line up and investors flock in (Greenwood & Jovanovic, 1999). Stijn Clasessens, Daniela Klingebiel, and Sergio Schmukler of the World Bank Group identified that the more successful a country is in strengthening its financial infrastructure, the more likely are its firms to list on larger, more liquid foreign markets (as cited in Herring & Litan, 2002), and a distribution network may facilitate fundraising at a lower cost (Herring & Litan). Maru (1997) also found that economic growth is accompanied by expansion of the stock market. In Asia, economic growth fosters growth of the stock market. From the above literature, stock market development and liquidity with technological support fosters economic growth. The Thai stock market is not an exception; since its establishment, the Thai stock market has developed its structural organization and rules and regulations to enhance a transparent and fair trading system with information disclosure and dissemination for domestic and foreign investors. Advanced computer technology has been introduced and developed to facilitate the trading system and post-trade system accurately and efficiently, and it fosters economic growth. This chapter aims to describe the Thai stock market both in terms of its institutional and technological development since it was established in 1975. The implementation of advanced technology and its effects on the Thai stock market will be discussed in the second part. Finally, the relation between Thai stock market development and its economic growth will be analyzed.

THE DEVELOPMENT OF THE THAI STOCK MARKET

The Establishment of the Thai Stock Market

Since 1950, the Thai government has aimed to develop Thailand to be an industrialized country. The private sector has been promoted to invest in the manufacturing sector, particularly in the import substitution industry. To mobilize capital to support Thailand's industrialization and economic development, the creation of Thailand's first officially sanctioned and regulated securities market was initially proposed as part of the Second National Economic and Social Development Plan (1967-1971). However, before an official capital market was formulated, Houseman & Co. Ltd., Siamerican Securities Ltd., and Z & R Investment and Consultants had started their businesses as middlemen for trading securities between the leading Thai companies and foreigners in 1953, although the volume was very small. Until 1962, an unofficial stock exchange, the Bangkok Stock Exchange, had been in existence but rather inactive. There were only five companies listed on the stock exchange on the first day of the trade, and annual average volume of trade during 1964 to 1973 was about 90 million baht (Bank of Thailand [BOT], 1986). In May 1974, the Securities Exchange of Thailand Act was promulgated to establish a new stock exchange and to place it under the general supervision of the Ministry of Finance. The law also required the Bangkok Stock Exchange to cease operations as a stock exchange within 9 months. On April 30, 1975, the Securities Exchange of Thailand was officially set up as a juristic entity to (a) serve as a center for the trading of listed securities and to provide the essential systems needed to facilitate securities trading without distributing any profits to members, (b) undertake any business relating to the securities exchange, such as a clearinghouse, securities depository center (SDC), securities

registrar, or similar activities, and (c) encourage the general public to become shareholders in a variety of local industries.

On January 1, 1991, its name was formally changed to the Stock Exchange of Thailand (SET). It operates under the legal framework laid down in the Securities and Exchange Act (or the SEC [Securities and Exchange Commission] Act; *Section 14 of Securities and Exchange Act B.E. 2535*, 1992). Its main operations include securities listing, the supervision of listed companies and information disclosure, trading, market surveillance and member supervision, information dissemination, and investor education (*SET Group*, n.d.).

The Development of the Thai Stock Market

SET's development for 30 years can be divided into three periods: the beginning period (1975-1985), the internationalization period (1986-1996), and the modern-technology period (1997-2005). The details for its development in each period were focused on trading, rules and regulations, institutions, and technology, as follows:

- **The Beginning Period (1975-1985):** This period was the time for good foundation construction to develop the stock market in Thailand. SET issued rules and regulations to prevent stock manipulation and ensure transparent and fair trading, established related organizations to facilitate trading, educated investors and entrepreneurs about the capital market, and promoted the supply in the market via tax incentives under the government policies.

- **Rules and Regulations:** To prevent short-term manipulation, SET has improved regulations, disclosed information to the public, and introduced tax reduction for listed companies. The Act on the Undertaking of Finance Business, Securities Business and

Credit Foncier Business, B.E. 2522 (1979), was legitimated to supervise and control the securities business, the securities exchange and related businesses, and organizations related to the securities business, and was amended in 1984. At the same time, the second Securities Exchange of Thailand Act, B.E. 2527 (1984), was enacted. To disclose information to the public, SET has requested all listed companies to submit audited quarterly financial statements. SET also posted a "notice pending" (NP) sign on a stock to inform investors that at this particular time, SET is awaiting clarification or additional information from the company that issued the stock, or SET is awaiting disclosure of the company's financial statements or other reports that must be filed at specified intervals. When the listed company as requested and required by SET has made sufficient clarification of certain additional information, the NR (notice received) sign is posted on the stock to replace the NP sign.

- **Institutions:** During this period, trading on SET was conducted on all bank business days, normally from Monday through Friday during 10:30 to 12:30 a.m.; in 1981, it changed to 9:30 to 11:30 a.m. All transactions were auctioned by post on a board system and were cleared and settled within the third consecutive business day following the trading day (T+3).

The securities depository was set up to facilitate the clearing and settlement of transactions of the SET members who have share accounts with the depository. It also provides a securities depository, securities transfer, and securities registration. In 1985, it was developed to be the securities depository center to do post-trading and registration processes more accurately and efficiently.

In 1980, the Thai stock market price index, the SET Index, was introduced. Previously, the TISCO Index and the Book Club Index, which were developed by the TISCO and Book Club finances and securities companies, were used as the stock market price indexes. The SET Index is a composition index calculated based on stock prices on the main board of SET. It is a market capitalization weighted index that compares the current market value of all listed common stocks with the value on the base date of April 30, 1975, when the SET Index was first calculated and set at 100 points. Its calculation is adjusted in line with new listings, delistings, and capitalization changes (*Glossary*, n.d.). The members of the stock exchange formulated the Assembly of the Members of Stock Exchange of Thailand to collaborate in solving the securities business problems and to provide information among each other. It joined with SET to set the rules and ethics in doing securities business to be standards in the future. It changed its name to the Association of Members of Stock Exchange in 1981, and in 1992, its name was changed to the Association of Securities Companies.

- **Trading:** The stock market had started to be active in 1977. Increasing stock prices in the market by Thai investors' stock manipulation induced companies to finance its funds with SET. The listed companies were increased about 3 times from 1975, up to 61 companies. The market capitalization also rose more than 6 times in 1975, with the value of 33 billion baht. During 1979 to 1985, the volume of trade in SET slowed down due to the world recession. At the end of 1985, the SET Index closed at 134.95 with a total turnover value of 15,333.99 million baht because foreign investors started to invest in the Thai stock market.
- **Technology:** Due to the trade volume increased drastically in 1978, SET introduced a computer system for securities registration work. In December 1981, SET changed the paying system to the Net Payment System

Figure 1. SET Index during 1975 to 1985

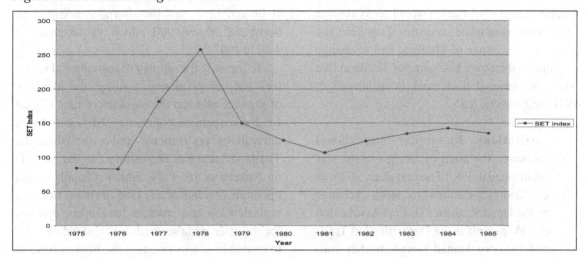

instead for the payment for each transaction.

- **The Internationalization Period (1986-1996):** The world and domestic economic recovery since 1986 as well as high liquidity, high performance of the listed companies, and low interest rates induced investors to come back to SET. Moreover, the Thai government restructured the tax system for investors, and amended the legislation for foreign investors who need to send their returns back home. SET introduced the fully computerized trading system, and set rules and regulations to develop the market to enhance competitiveness over the regional stock market.

- **Rules and Regulations:** SET amended the act to let small enterprises and state enterprises list on the second board in the market and introduced new financial instruments such as warrants and convertible debentures to be traded in the market. SET posted the XD, XR, XI, and XA signs on a stock 3 days before the stock's book closing date in order to warn investors that on that day,

buyers of the stock are not entitled to the particular rights to be given to investors in the forthcoming book closing. Those signs' meanings are the following: XD or excluding dividends, meaning buyers are not entitled to dividend payment; XI or excluding interests, which means buyers are not entitled to interest payment; XR or excluding rights, meaning buyers are not entitled to preemptive rights in subscribing to new share issues; and XA or excluding all, meaning buyers are not entitled to any rights prescribed at the time (*Glossary*, n.d.).

To initiate a new legal framework and mark a new era for the Thai capital market, on March 16, 1992, the Securities and Exchange Act, B.E. 2535 (*Section 14*, 1992), was promulgated to reinforce the unity, consistency, and efficiency in the supervision and development of the market. The enactment of the SEC Act empowered the Securities and Exchange Commission to be established as an independent state agency with responsibility for the supervision and development of the capital market under the direction and guidance of the board of the SEC. According to this new **act,** the stock market and the supervision office should be separated. The stock market would act as a center for the trading of listed securities. Therefore, the Securities Exchange of Thailand had to change its name to the Stock Exchange of Thailand like other international stock markets on January 1, 1991 (*SET Group*, n.d.).

- **Institutions:** To support international investors, the alien or foreign board was established in 1987. The year after, SET was certified as the authorized stock exchange by the Japan Securities Dealers Association (JSDA) as well as the Department of Trade and Industry, United Kingdom; they confirmed SET as an approved market to allow investment by unit trusts. Furthermore, the market became a member of the Federation International des Bourses de Valeurs (FIBV) or the World Federation of Exchange and the International Organization of Securities Commission (IOSCO) to cooperate in market development to meet international standards.

To develop the market to be more international, the Center for Capital Market Studies (CCMS) was founded in 1988 as a research center for SET development. The Listed Companies Association was formulated by SET's listed companies to represent their views regarding the activities and development of the Thai capital market and to collaborate with other organizations in promoting capital market investment. To promote and to develop standards in securities and financial analysis, SET and the securities companies jointly set up the Securities Analysis Association (SAA).

In 1992, SET introduced the Scripless System to be the clearing and settlement system in order to reduce risks to the clearinghouse. It acts as a guarantor of the system, boosts confidence in the system, enhances liquidity in the market, supports cross-border trading, and shortens the settlement cycle. The trading time was divided into

two sessions: The morning session was between 10:00 and 12:30, and the afternoon session was between 2:30 and 4:00, which was extended to 4:30 in 1993.

To increase the number of institutional investors and competition in trading, the Ministry of Finance allowed the issuance of new mutual fund management companies. SET introduced derivatives instruments and established the Thailand Securities Depository Co. Ltd. or TSD on November 16, 1994, which officially began operations on January 1, 1995. Its main function is to develop and promote back-office systems for the after-trade services in Thailand in order to enable investors to attain the highest level of efficiency and meet international standards (*SET Group*, n.d.). It is the central securities depository and the only clearinghouse and SDC in Thailand, implementing an internationally accepted multilateral netting system for the clearing and settlement of securities traded on the market by the delivery-vs.-payment (DvP) method. TSD has achieved the G-30 recommendations, the international standards for a securities after-trade organization (TSD, 2006).

The 74 finance and securities companies agreed to set up the Bangkok Stock Dealing Center (BSDC) in 1995. The BSDC was the over-the-counter (OTC) securities market for the medium and small companies that could not be listed in SET. However, the number of listed companies and trade volume were rather small because those listed companies could not get tax reduction as those in SET. Hence, its operation was terminated in 1999 after the financial crisis in 1997.

On June 17, 1996, the SET 50 Index, a market capitalization weighted price index, was first launched. The index is computed from the share prices of the top 50 listed companies on SET with large market capitalization and high liquidity on the base date of August 16, 1995. The list of constituent stocks in the SET 50 Index is revised every 6 months.

- **Trading:** Since 1986, SET has become one of the fastest growing markets in Asia. Though during this period the unstable world money market caused the Thai stock market to fluctuate sometimes, the SET Index's daily average turnover and market capitalization had rising trends. The Thai economy was bustled by exports and an influx of foreign capital after financial liberalization boosted the stock market to have market capitalization of over 1 trillion baht in 1992. The SET Index closed at 1,753.73 on January 4, 1994, which was the highest point since the market first operated. The SET market capitalization reached 3.3 trillion baht at the end of 1994, a tremendous success when considering that the market capitalization in 1985 was only 49.5 billion Baht, an effective growth rate of 59% per year. However, due to the Mexico crisis and rumour of Thai financial institutions' stability problems in the following years, the market slowed down and market capitalization was 2,559.58 million baht with negative growth. Figure 2 represents the SET Index during this period.

- **Technology:** To develop the computer system for trading in the market, SET signed a

contract with the Midwest Stock Exchange of the USA. In the first stage, SET introduced the computer system for market surveillance by monitoring securities trading activities, analyzing any unusual trading, and facilitating any investigation of suspicious cases. The system was introduced to the following:

1. The SDC for handling the tasks of securities deposit, withdrawal, and transfer. The system enables the SDC to provide fast and convenient services to its members, custodians, and investors, and greatly enhances clearing and settlement efficiency.

2. The share registrar (SRG) for the securities registration process, which applies to all new securities; any transfer of ownership; the maintenance of a shareholder book; and any dividend and benefit payments. It is handled via the Scripless System, or by issuance of physical share certificates.

3. The price reporting system (PRS) to display real-time trading information on both individual stocks and sectors for data vendors, brokerage firms, and institutions that need to use the mar-

Figure 2. SET Index during 1986 to 1996

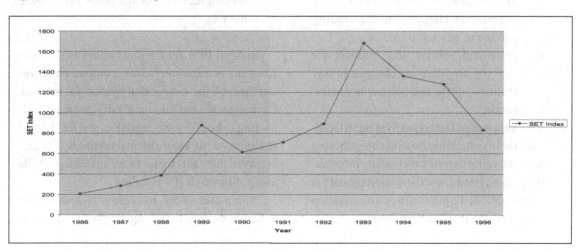

ket data for their day-to-day business operations, externally redistributing such data to their clients with their company-developed software, and updating market movements for investment decision.

To enhance the effectiveness and efficiency of market surveillance functions, the system was developed to be the Automated Tools for Market Surveillance or ATOMS in 1992. ATOMS consists of three systems, as follows:

- **The Automated Alert System:** It is the tool for monitoring real-time trading activities. The alert system compares the movements of price and trading volume for each security with parameters based on its past transactions. If there is an unusual change in terms of price and/or trading volume for any security, the alert system will alert the stock watch staff with an audio signal. The staff will be able to promptly investigate the reason for that unusual change and notice any security with unusual changes in its trading pattern. The current alert system comprises three alert modules, as follows.
  a. Price alert module for noticing any extraordinary changes in the price of any security.
  b. Volume alert module for noticing any uncommon changes in the trading volume of any security.
  c. Price and volume alert module for noticing any unusual changes in any security's price and volume in combination.
- **The Automated Detection System:** It facilitates the investigating function by gathering and analyzing the relevant trading information. This system is used in both stages of the investigation: the preliminary investigation stage and the investigation stage.

- **The Documentation System:** It is the information management system that supports the operations of the alert and detection systems. It links directly to the alert system, detection system, securities trading system, and listed-company disclosure system. Hence, the staff in any surveillance stage can access the information promptly and easily.
- **Investigation Process:** When there is an alert, the stock watch staff will trace out the cause of that alert. They check if there are any factors causing the unusual trading change, such as any public disclosure of material information or any significant news. If there are no sufficient factors to explain the case, it will be sent for preliminary investigation. In this stage, the detection system is used to trace and analyze the trading activities causing the case based on information in the report, the company profile, and the trading record. If there are any evidence indicating malpractices, the case will be sent to the investigation stage. The investigation stage is conducted by the investigation division in order to prevent bias. The detection system also facilitates the work at this stage; the staff can promptly access the relevant information from the documentation system. If they find any solid evidence for malpractice, the case will be sent to the related authority for enforcement consideration (*SET Group*, n.d.).

In April 1991, the trading system was changed from an open auction to fully computerized trading through the Automated System for the Stock Exchange of Thailand or ASSET, which enables trading to be efficient, equitable, and fluid. In this trading system, two principal methods of trading are available: automatic order matching (AOM) and put-through (PT) trading.

Automatic order matching is a computerized screen-based trading method as provided by ASSET that allows brokers to electronically send buy or sell orders from their offices to the SET trading computer. ASSET implements an order queuing process and arranges the orders according to price and time priority. Orders are first grouped according to price with the best price taking precedence. Then, within each price group, orders are arranged according to the earliest time. In terms of the matching process, there are two methods: continuous order matching and the call market method.

Continuous order matching procedures operate during the regular trading sessions. ASSET continuously matches the first buy and sell orders in the queue, and at the same time, confirms each executed transaction via the member's (broker's) terminal.

Call market matching is utilized by calculating the opening and closing prices of a security at the opening and closing of the trading hours. This method allows brokers to enter their orders to be queued for matching at a specified time at a single price that generates the greatest trading volumes for that particular stock.

Simultaneously, ASSET begins to automatically match the first buy and sell orders in the queue while at the same time confirming each executed transaction via the brokers' terminals.

In put-through trading, ASSET allows brokers to advertise their buy or sell interests by announcing bid or offer prices. Members may then deal directly with each other, either on behalf of their clients or for themselves. Prices may be adjusted during the negotiation; hence, the effective executed price may not be the same as that advertised and may not follow the price spread rules. After concluding negotiations, dealers must send details of the result(s) to ASSET for recording purposes.

The computer system was adjusted to facilitate trading settlement and share delivery to be within 3 working days after trading (T+3) as is the international standard. After this change, the volume of daily average turnover jumped from 233.821 billion baht on April 29 to 361.861 billion baht on April 30. Total market capitalization rose to 897.181 billion baht at the end of the year while the SET Index declined 91.52 points, which was still 98.5 points higher than the previous year. Furthermore, all information about the Thai stock market such as historical securities trading, listed company profiles and their financial statements, and market information were stored in the database named SIMS (SET Information Management System).

In 1996, TSD became a member of BAHT-NET (Bank of Thailand Automatic High Volume Transaction Network). BAHTNET is an electronic network that is used for transmitting and receiving messages between BOT and financial institutions or other organizations maintaining deposit accounts at BOT for settling large-value funds transfer on a real-time gross-settlement basis (online RTGS; Bank of Thailand, 2006). With this new development, the payment method was changed from the use of cheques to electronic fund transfers through settlement banks and the BAHTNET system in order to reduce risk and transaction costs, and to make the process more speedy.

- **The Modern-Technology Period (1997-2005):** Though the Thai economy was depressed by the financial crisis in 1997, measures to strengthen the financial sector and to revive the economy had been implemented. Since 2000, the Thai economy had a sign of recovery and SET focused on the quality of listed companies, advanced technological services, and product variety. Many subsidiaries were established to provide information and services to investors.

- **Rules and Regulations:** To increase liquidity in the market and to reduce finance and securities companies' risk on margin accounts or securities trading accounts, SET suggested that those companies use the credit balance method. On July 1, 1998, SET requested that listed companies file disclosure information both in Thai and English via electronics or the Electronic Listed Company Information Disclosure (ELCID) system to ensure greater effectiveness and efficiency in information disclosure. SET changed its regulations on the trading of property funds' investment units so that they could be traded similar to common stocks in the property development sector. The trading regulations on transferable subscription rights were also modified.

- **Institutions:** To create new fundraising opportunities for innovative businesses with high potential growth as well as to provide a greater range of investment alternatives, the Market for Alternative Investment (MAI) was established under the Securities Exchange of Thailand Act. It officially commenced operations on June 21, 1999. On September 3, 2002, the MAI Index, which is based on the same calculation method that the SET Index uses and includes all MAI listed common stocks, was launched. The index base date is September 2, 2002, with an index value of 100. At the end of 2002, there were six listed companies and the index closed at 127.49 with the average daily value of 57.96 million baht. The number of listed companies reached 36 with a market capitalization of 14.310 billion baht and an average daily value of 146.70 million baht at the end of 2005. SET recognized the importance of promoting collaboration and good relationships with both overseas exchanges and related organizations. It signed the MOU with the Hong Kong Exchanges and Clearing Co., Ltd., for the exchange of information. SET also adjusted its organization and administrative structures to enhance efficiency in providing services to related parties in the securities industry.

To support the implementation of business and marketing strategies, the Capital Market Opportunity Center (CMOC) was established to support businesses in raising funds through capital markets efficiently, as well as to expand the investor base, promote understanding about capital markets and investment, raise the industry's professional standards, and conduct marketing activities and related services (*The Stock Exchange of Thailand Annual Report 2003*, 2004). The Capital Market Master Plan was formulated by brainstorming ideas from various organizations to establish measures to help revitalize and develop the Thai capital market.

SET also introduced nonvoting depository receipts (NVDRs), which are issued by the Thai NVDR Co., Ltd., one of the SET subsidiaries. This new product will help facilitate investment by foreigners who otherwise face constraints in investing in Thai stocks, as well as help increase trading liquidity in the market (*The Stock Exchange of Thailand Annual Report 2001*, 2002). SET promoted good corporate governance (GC) and improved the strength of listed companies by establishing a set of practical guidelines for listed companies to implement GC.

To develop Thailand's capital market by facilitating an Internet trading system and disseminating market information widely, accurately, timely, comprehensively, and efficiently, Settrade.com Co., Ltd., was established by SET on October 13, 2000; its operation began on November 13, 2000, to provide Internet trading platforms and leverage investment technology for brokerage houses in order to accommodate retail investors with increasing trading channels.

On August 6, 2002, SET established Family Know-How Co. Ltd. (FKH). The company aims to encourage the development of an investment culture in Thai society to promote and develop knowledge about finance and investment that can be delivered to individual investors, thereby creating a large pool of quality investors as part of the plan to develop both SET and MAI, to publicize the development of Thai financial institutions and the investment environment, as well as to burnish the image of Thai investment at the international level, to engage in a campaign to promote the concepts associated with good governance, and to generate interest in and promote an understanding of the merits of privatization as well as the progress of such privatizations (*The Stock Exchange of Thailand Annual Report 2002*, 2003).

The Bond Electronic Exchange (BEX) started trading in November 2003 and has been consistently growing. There were 37 new issues listed on BEX in 2005, bringing the total up to 73 as of December 2005. The total outstanding value of BEX listings dramatically jumped from 194.850 billion baht at the end of 2004 to 770.460 billion baht at the end of 2005, a 295% increase. In addition, BEX launched its trading system, the Fixed Income and Related Securities Trading System (FIRSTS), exclusively designed for direct trading among institutions, to be operational in this year.

To support the trading and hedging of Thai derivative products and to introduce a new risk management tool for all parties in the Thai capital market, SET established a new subsidiary, the Thailand Futures Exchange Public Company

(TFEX) on May 17, 2004, as a derivatives exchange. Aside from preparing integrated trading and clearing via a reliable electronic trading platform, TFEX has been promoting a better understanding of derivative products to clients and investors. It is ready to begin operations in 2006, starting with trading SET 50 Index futures. Starting from 2004, SET calculated the Industry Group Index in order to clearly reflect the changes in stock prices in each industry group.

SET, in collaboration with its member companies, established the Securities Investor Protection Fund (SIPF) to help improve investors' confidence in securities trading. Investors will be automatically protected by the SIPF when they open trading accounts with any SIPF member. With the joined hands of SET and the Thai Investor Association, the Investor Club was created to develop the status of investors and protect their rights, making it an important engine to effectively increase the investor base. In further efforts to create a quality investor base, SET coordinated with securities companies to establish the Quality Service Association. This organization provides quality services aimed at retail investors in the stock market. Apart from this, SET has actively supported the implementation of TSD's Scripless System. The securities deposit system has been expanded to listed companies so more investors will add their shares to it. TSD also expanded its back office and fund registrar services to asset

Figure 3. SET Index during 1997 to 2005

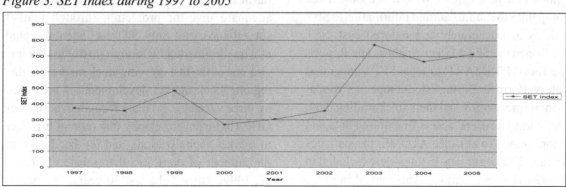

management companies, thereby supporting the growth of the provident fund business.

- **Trading:** The economy recession and unfavorable investment climate made the Thai capital market unattractive. Therefore, the average daily turnover during 1997 to 2000 declined except in 1999. Since 2000, the SET Index has continued increasing and reached 772.15 points in 2003 with the highest record of market capitalization at 4.789 trillion baht since the stock exchange started operating as shown in Figure 3. Thai investors have rallied as the first-rank investors in the market instead of foreign investors.

- **Technology:** To enhance the efficiency of the capital market's infrastructure, SET has developed new practical measures to be in line with technological advancements and to cope with any possible transaction expansion. SET reduced the recovery time as well as enhanced the performance and reliability of the securities trading systems, and increased the mobility of member companies' linkage systems with SET. SET also has developed its trading systems to cope with debentures trading.

The effectiveness and efficiency of the post-trading systems of the Thailand Securities Depository Co., Ltd. were also improved by fully integrating them to ready the systems to better cope with multimarket clearing needs. SET developed the new ELCID system to enable listed companies to submit data and information to SET quickly and accurately at a reduced cost. SET developed the SET Market Analysis and Reporting Tool (SETSMART) to act as SET's integrated data platform for storing listed companies' fundamental information and their stock trading data, facilitating its users' access to required data and information. To enhance ATOMS, the statistics and stock prices of new listings were included in its statistical calculations. This helped improve

the efficiency of the organization's regulatory functions. In addition, SET regrouped all listed companies under eight new industry groups to better reflect related business trends as well as the country's economic outlook. Settrade.com has developed its own Web site (http://www.settrade.com) to be both an investment portal and a free service to provide information to the public, in support of SET's policy of increasing the number of investors in the Thai capital markets. For example, Settrade.com also joined hands with 17 brokers and the Securities Analysts Association to launch the analyst consensus service on its Web site. In terms of the other services, Settrade.com has collaborated with related businesses and institutions to develop the following innovative services to support the investment and securities business: e-payment and Internet banking, mobile alerts (via AIS and DTAC, mobile phone companies), the Trading Simulation Game, and initial public offering (IPO) via the Internet. To expand the investor base, SET held seminars, fairs, and education events to promote greater understanding of investment in securities for both local and foreign investors.

THE THAI STOCK MARKET DEVELOPMENT AND TECHNOLOGY

As aforementioned, SET has implemented advanced technology to facilitate both the trading system and post-trading system, to enhance the fairness of securities trading, and to provide adequate investor protection through market surveillance. Not only SET has been accepted as a quality market by foreign institutes, but it is also one of the fast growing stock markets in this region. Stock market development is measured by three variables: (a) market capitalization over GDP, (b) turnover velocity (the ratio of turnover to market capitalization), and (c) the change in the number of domestic shares listed (Filer et al., 1999). During the last 30 years, the market capitalization over GDP of the Thai stock market was at a low level during 1975 to 1985 (Figure 4). Advanced technology increased dramatically in 1991 and 1992 after ASSET and ATOMS were introduced. The openness of the financial sector since 1993 was also a significant factor for the growth of the market's size. After the economy recovered from the 1997 crisis and starting Internet trading in 2000, the ratio began to rise again. In Figure 6, the number of domestic shares listed is used instead of the change in the number of domestic shares since it can confirm that the financial infrastructure has been strengthened with more firms listed, as the World Bank Group has studied. Though the turnover velocity in Figure 5 did not follow the same pattern as the two ratios, its fluctuation can be traced as an increasing trend during the three periods: the beginning period, the internationalization period, and the modern-technology period. During the beginning period, the ratio fluctuated because of stock manipulation, while in both later periods, the fluctuation was caused by external factors.

THE THAI STOCK MARKET DEVELOPMENT AND ECONOMIC GROWTH

The causal link between stock market development and economic growth was tested by Caporale et al. (2004). The evidence suggested that a well-developed stock market could foster economic growth in the long run, and that the stock market plays a key role in allocating capital to the corporate sector, which will have a real effect on the economy in the aggregate. In addition, well-developed and active stock markets alter the pattern of demand for money, and boosting stock markets creates liquidity and hence spurs economic growth (Caporale et al.). Levine used the total value of shares traded as a share of GDP to measure market liquidity. This ratio is likely to vary with the ease of trading. The second measure of liquidity is the value of trade shares as a percentage of total market capitalization. This ratio indicates that greater turnover predicts faster growth. Figure 7 shows the movement of the total value of shares traded as a share of GDP, the value of trade shares as

Figure 4. Market capitalization/GDP

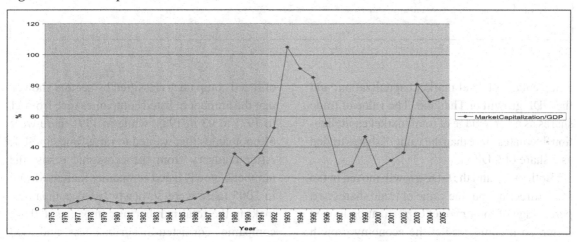

Figure 5. Turnover velocity

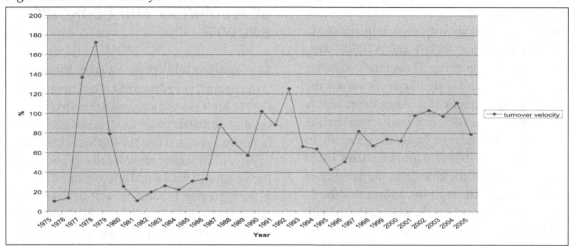

Figure 6. Number of listed shares

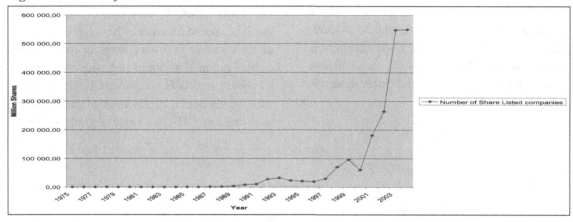

a percentage of total market capitalization, and the GDP growth of Thailand. The value of trade shares as a percentage of total market capitalization fluctuates more than the value of shares traded as a share of GDP.

Both ratios and the GDP growth moved in the same direction, but the value of trade shares as a percentage of total market capitalization moved faster, so it could predict the economy growth and it can be said that market liquidity fosters economic growth.

Moreover, stock market development has changed the Thai economic structure. The data

of listed companies classified by sectors showed that the number of listed companies rose from 21 in 1975 to 93 in 1985, while in 1991 there were 61 companies that wanted to raise funds in SET. After recovery from the economic crisis, the number of newly listed companies increased, and in 2005 there were 36 newly listed companies, making the total number of companies 470. 42 companies consisted of agribusiness, and food and beverage companies; 18 were resources companies; 37 were consumer products companies; 68 were financial companies; 52 were industrial companies; 89 were property and construction

Figure 7. Stock market liquidity and GDP growth

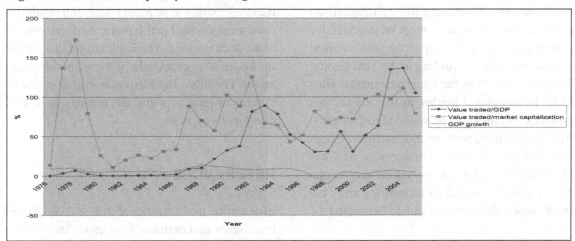

Figure 8. Percentage of manufacturing sector and agricultural sector to GDP

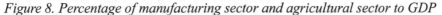

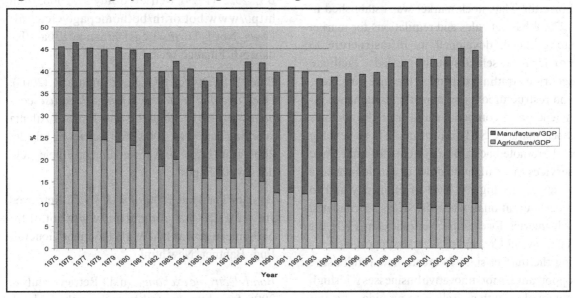

companies; 80 were services companies; and 45 were technology companies. These numbers are evidence that the Thai economic structure has changed from one with an agricultural base to one based on manufacturing and services, as can be seen in Figure 8. The percentage of the agricultural sector to GDP declined from 25% in 1975 to 10% in 2004, while the percentage of the manufacturing sector to GDP rose from 18% in 1975 to 35% in 2004.

FUTURE TRENDS

The Thai stock market will expand its operations to more product varieties, particularly derivates.

In 2006, TFEX, a subsidiary of SET, will start its operations. To accomplish its mission, an efficient computer system must be provided for market participants to easily access the network at a reasonable cost. According to the Thai Capital Market Master Plan, the Thai stock market aims to be an integrated market in this region that provides various types of financial instruments, well-equipped and well-functioning through high technology for investors. Furthermore, SET has planned to be a public company in the near future. The empirical research on technology and Thai stock market development should be studied.

CONCLUSION

Since the Thai stock market was established in 1975, it has set rules and regulations for market surveillance, developed its infrastructure to provide the essential systems needed to facilitate securities trading, expanded the investors base, and restructured its organization to enhance efficiency and competitiveness over the region's stock markets. SET has set up TSD to develop and promote back-office systems for after-trade services in Thailand in order to enable investors to attain the highest level of efficiency and to meet international standards. SET has formulated subsidiaries, for example, Settrade.com, FKH, the Thai NVDR Co., and so forth, to support increasing the market size. To create new fundraising opportunities for innovative businesses with high potential growth as well as to provide a greater range of investment alternatives for investors, MAI was established. The ATOMS computerized system was introduced to monitor securities trading activities as well as to detect and investigate abnormal trading activities promptly. In April 1991, ASSET was created to enable trading to be efficient, equitable, and fluid. Internet trading, which enables investors to send buy or sell orders directly from anywhere, is a significant factor to accelerate the growth of trade volume per month.

The ease of accessing the trading system can foster the stock market to be more liquid, and results in economic growth. Furthermore, the development of the stock market in Thailand can mobilize funds for businesses, especially in the manufacturing sector. Therefore, the Thai economic structure is moving toward an industrial economy as that of developed countries.

REFERENCES

About MAI. (n.d.). Retrieved July 8, 2006, from http://www.mai.or.th/en/about/about.html

Act on the undertaking of finance business, securities business and credit foncier business, B.E. 2522. (1979). Retrieved July 27, 2006, from http://www.bot.or.th/bothomepage/General/ Laws_Notif_Forms/Legal/Finance%20act/Finance-E/FinanceAct-E.htm

Baier, L. S., Dwyer, P. G., Jr., & Tamura, R. (2003). *Does opening a stock exchange increase economic growth* (Federal Reserve Bank of Atlanta Working Paper No. 2003-36)? Retrieved July 26, 2006, from http://www.frbatlanta.org/filelegacy-docs/wp0336.pdf

Bank of Thailand. (2006). *BAHTNET.* Retrieved July 28, 2006, from http://www.bot.or.th/ bothomepage/BankAtWork/Payment/General/ Eng_Bahtnet_New.html

Bond electronic exchange. (n.d.). Retrieved July 8, 2006, from http://www.bex.or.th/en/about/about.html

Caporale, M. G., Howells, G. A. P., & Soliman, M. A. (2004). Stock market development and economic growth. *Journal of Economic Development, 29*(1), 33-50. Retrieved July 26, 2006, from http://jed.econ.cau.ac.kr/newjed/full-text/29-1/02_J665_.PDF#search=%22economic%20development%20and%20stock%20market%20%22

Filer, K. R., Hanousek, J., & Campos, F. N. (1999). *Do stock markets promote economic growth* (Brooking Institute Working Paper No. 267)*?* Retrieved July 26, 2006, from http://www.brook. edu/comm/conferencereport/cr10.pdf#search=% 22herring%20and%20litan%22

Glossary. (n.d.). Retrieved July 10, 2006, from http://www.set.or.th/en/education/glossary/glos-sary_pa.html

Greenwood, J., & Jovanovic, B. (1999). *The information technology revolution and the stock market* (NBER Working Papers No. 6931). Retrieved July 26, 2006, from http://www.nber. org/papers/w6931.pdf

Herring, R., & Litan, R. (2002). *The future of securities markets* (Conference Report No. 10). Retrieved July 26, 2006, from http://www.brook. edu/comm/conferencereport/cr10.pdf#search=% 22herring%20and%20litan%22

History of the Association of Securities Companies. (n.d.). Retrieved July 27, 2006, from http:// www.asco.or.th/history.asp

History of the stock exchange of Thailand. (n.d.). Retrieved July 13, 2006, from http://www.set. or.th/en/about/history/history_p1.html#history

Hobijn, B., & Jovanovic, B. (2000). *The information technology revolution and the stock market: Evidence* (NBER Working Paper No. 7684). Retrieved July 26, 2006, from http://www.nber. org/papers/w7684.pdf

Jovanovic, B., & Rousseau, L. P. (2000). *Technology and the stock market: 1885-1998* (Working Paper No. 0042). Retrieved July 26, 2006, from http://www.vanderbilt.edu/Econ/wparchive/ workpaper/vu00-w42.pdf

Levine, R. (1996). Stock markets: A spur to economic growth. *Finance & Development.* Retrieved July 26, 2006, from http://www.imf. org/external/pubs/ft/fandd/1996/03/pdf/levine. pdf#search=%22stock%20market%20and%20e conomic%20development%22 & http://jed.econ. cau.ac.kr/newjed/full-text/29-1/02_J665_.PDF#s earch=%22stock%20market%20and%20econom ic%20development%22

Levine, R. (1997). Stock market, economic development, and capital control liberalization. *Perspective, 3*(5), 1-8.

Market surveillance. (n.d.). Retrieved July 4, 2006, from http://www.set.or.th/en/operation/supervi-sion/surveillance_p1.html

Maru, J. (1997). The role of institutional investors in the development of Asian stock markets: Singapore, Malaysia, and Thailand (Part 1). *Newsletter, 7,* 1-4. Retrieved August 2, 2006, from http://www/ier.hit-u.ac.jp/COE/japanese/ Newsletter/No.7.english/junko.html

Money and Financial Section Department of Economic Research Bank of Thailand. (1980). Financial institutions in Thailand. *Bank of Thailand Quarterly Bulletin, 3,* 22.

Rules & regulation. (n.d.). Retrieved July 6, 2006, from http://www.set.or.th/en/rules/rules.html

Section 14 of Securities and Exchange Act B.E. 2535. (1992). Retrieved July 27, 2006, from http://www.sec.or.th/en/enforce/regulate/se-cact1_e.shtml#sect8

SET Group. (n.d.). Retrieved July 1, 2006, from http://www.set.or.th/en/about/setgroup/set-group_p1.html

The Stock Exchange of Thailand annual report 1999. (2000). Retrieved July 13, 2006, from http:// www.set.or.th/en/about/about.html

The Stock Exchange of Thailand annual report 2000. (2001). Retrieved July 13, 2006, from http:// www.set.or.th/en/about/about.html

The Stock Exchange of Thailand annual report 2001. (2002). Retrieved July 13, 2006, from http:// www.set.or.th/en/about/about.html

The Stock Exchange of Thailand annual report 2002. (2003). Retrieved July 13, 2006, from http://www.set.or.th/en/about/about.html

The Stock Exchange of Thailand annual report 2003. (2004). Retrieved July 13, 2006, from http://www.set.or.th/en/about/about.html

The Stock Exchange of Thailand annual report 2004. (2005). Retrieved July 13, 2006, from http://www.set.or.th/en/about/about.html

The Stock Exchange of Thailand annual report 2005. (2006). Retrieved July 13, 2006, from http://www.set.or.th/en/about/about.html

The Thailand Securities Depository. (n.d.). Retrieved July 27, 2006, from http://www.tsd.co.th/

Trading system. (n.d.). Retrieved July 4, 2006, from http://www.set.or.th/en/operation/operation.html

Chapter IX
Key Drivers of Internet Banking Adoption:
The Case of Spanish Internet Users

Carlos Lassala Navarré
University of Valencia, Spain

Carla Ruiz Mafé
University of Valencia, Spain

Silvia Sanz Blas
University of Valencia, Spain

ABSTRACT

The objective of this chapter is to provide students and managers with a holistic view into the different factors that influence online banking adoption and to use the study's findings to develop strategies for managers on how to maximize the rate of Internet banking adoption. Research done with a sample size of 450 Spanish Internet users has highlighted that Internet banking adoption is more likely in young, highly educated, and high-income consumers. Internet affinity, online use experience, and some perceived benefits are also key drivers of online financial-services-purchase decision making. Perceived financial, social, and psychological risk negatively influences the use of online banking services.

INTRODUCTION

Information technologies are encouraging the use of new shopping methods such as online and mobile shopping that are favouring economic growth and providing companies and consumers with additional benefits with respect to traditional shopping channels. In the world of banking, IT has led to significant improvements in terms of more flexible payment methods and more user-friendly systems. The development of online banking and electronic payment systems by financial institutions will result in a more efficient banking system.

The indicators used to measure banking system efficiency include the cost-income ratio. Increased competition in the sector requires the search for new sources of income and/or cost contention (Otto, 2003). In this respect, the use of e-banking as an alternative distribution channel for banking services makes it possible to save on costs and will undoubtedly contribute toward improving the bank efficiency ratio.

The properties of the Internet (time and cost savings, error-free service, etc.) make it an ideal medium for delivering banking services (Howcroft, Hamilton, & Hewer, 2002). Sundarraj and Wu (2005) looked at other distribution channels such as mobile banking services and interactive TV sets, and argued they would greatly expand the market for personal financial services.

Several studies report that online banking is the most profitable division in banking (Mols, 1998; Pikkarainen, Pikkarainen, Karjaluoto, & Pahnila, 2004). Banks get notable cost savings as they can operate in a more efficient way, reduce their branch networks, and downsize the number of service staff. The success of online banking in Spain is evidenced by the number of current and potential users of these services, with 45% of Internet users frequenting financial Web sites (Nielsen/Netratings, 2006), and also by the fact that e-commerce with credit cards reached the figure of €1.2 billion (4.8 million operations) in 2005, an increase of 74% over the previous year (Comisión del Mercado de las Telecomunicaciones [CMT], 2006).

Despite the growing importance of online banking, there are still not enough studies that provide a holistic view of factors influencing Internet banking adoption. It is also crucial for managers to understand which aspects customers of financial services value the most and the barriers to adoption in order to assign resources effectively to obtain competitive advantages and increase efficiency in the banking system.

Previous research into Internet banking has mainly focused on its adoption in the context of high e-commerce adoption rates in regions such as North America, Denmark, the United Kingdom, or Finland (Daniel, 1999; Mols, 2000; Pikkarainen et al., 2004) and to a lesser extent in developing regions such as Malaysia, Taiwan, and Turkey (Jaruwachirathanakul & Fink, 2005; Polatoglu & Ekin, 2001; Suganthi, Balachandher, & Balachandran, 2001). This study offers an insight into online banking in Spain, which has not previously been investigated. Distinct differences and common trends between Spain and other countries were observed with clear indication of marketing strategy to be deployed by the service providers.

In this chapter, we define online banking as "an Internet portal, through which customers can use different kinds of banking services ranging from bill payment to making investments" (Pikkarainen et al., 2004).

The chapter aims to present an in-depth study of the factors influencing online banking adoption. The chapter's specific goals are the following:

1. Provide a holistic view of factors influencing online banking adoption.
2. Identify consumer segments more likely to adopt online financial services.
3. Analyse the perceived benefits and barriers that encourage and discourage the adoption of Internet banking services.
4. Provide empirical research on the Spanish market that analyses the influence of demographics, online experience, attitudes toward the Internet, and perceived benefits and risks in the decision to use online financial services rather than traditional ones.
5. Provide future trends in the Internet banking industry and use the study's findings to develop strategies for managers on how to maximize the rate of Internet banking adoption.

CONSUMER ADOPTION OF ONLINE BANKING SERVICES

Consumer adoption of Internet banking has been researched from several perspectives: (a) consumer perceptions and expectations of service quality (Jun & Cai, 2001), (b) consumer motives and acceptance of techno-based banking services (Al-Ashban & Burney, 2001; Filotto, Tanzi, & Saita, 1997), and (c) consumer usage, demographics, attitudes, and behaviours toward online and mobile banking (Akinci, Aksoy, & Atilgan, 2004; Jayawardhena & Foley, 2000). This chapter focuses on the last of these three perspectives. It analyses the impact of demographics, online experience, Internet attitude, and perceived benefits and barriers on Internet banking adoption.

Demographics

Previous studies describe users of electronic banking services in countries with high e-commerce adoption rates as young (Karjaluoto, Mattila, & Pento, 2002; Marshall & Heslop, 1988), highly educated (Jayawardhena & Foley, 2000; Kolodinsky, Hogarth, & Hilgert, 2004; Leblanc, 1990; Marshall & Heslop), and with a medium-high to high income (Kolodinsky et al.; Lockett & Litter, 1997; Mattila, Karjaluoto, & Pento, 2003). In contrast to electronic bank users in the West, Chinese online bank users are predominantly males, not necessarily young or highly educated (Laforet & Lin, 2005).

Men and women seem to differ in their shopping orientations and shopping behaviour. Men are goal-oriented shoppers while social motives are more important for women, so men value more shopping benefits provided by e-banking. Moreover, men are more familiar with the medium and are less influenced by the perceived shopping risk (Marshall & Heslop, 1988).

The new technological advances in some direct shopping methods like Internet banking need to take into account the individual's capacity to understand the changes and complexities in the new technologies. Consumer needs, interests, and attitudes vary with age, and younger consumers are more predisposed to adopt innovations such as online banking. Research done by Filotto et al. (1997) in Italy showed younger consumers more than older consumers like to use automatic teller machines (ATMs). Al-Ashban and Burney (2001) analysed telebanking adoption in Saudi Arabia and found that it is negatively associated with age and positively associated with income and education level. Mattila et al. (2003) added that household income and education have a significant effect on the adoption of Internet banking among mature consumers in Finland.

A high education level also correlates positively with online experience. In contrast, lack of experience with the Internet prevents low-educated mature consumers from evaluating the benefits of online banking; they tend to prefer brick-and-mortar bank branches (Mattila et al., 2003).

Online Experience

The response of Internet users to marketing actions changes as their use and experience of the Internet grows (Dahlen, 2002). Karjaluoto et al. (2002) showed that the use of ATMs and the Internet had a significant impact on attitudes toward online banking and usage. Polatoglu and Ekin (2001) maintain that people who are familiar with the Internet and e-mail do not find Internet banking to be complex. Black, Lockett, Winklhofer, and Ennew (2001) found that complexity in conducting financial transactions over the Internet was inversely related to a consumer's experience. Research by Gerrard and Cunningham (2003) concluded that where a population has a reasonable level of personal computer (PC) proficiency and includes frequent Internet users, the procedures for using Internet banking are not perceived to be complex. Lee, Kwon, and Schumann (2005) indicated that lack of experience with technology-based services, the Internet, and new technologies significantly decreases a consumer's likelihood of adopting technology-based services, and that persistent nonadopters generally lack experiences that are compatible with the skills needed to use Internet banking. Online experience also decreases consumers' perceived risk and increases confidence in online banking transactions (Ba, 2001; Mukherjee & Nath, 2003).

Internet Attitude

A positive attitude to innovation, and in particular to the benefits provided by the Internet, influences the decision to purchase online. In the literature, we find a set of studies that relate individuals' attitudes to online banking with their financial-services online purchase decisions. In the study by Gerrard and Cunningham (2003), a positive attitude to financial innovations is related to Internet banking adoption. Pikkarainen et al. (2004) applied the technology acceptance model (TAM; Davis, 1989) in Finland and found that perceived usefulness and information on Internet banking on a Web site can be used to predict online banking consumer acceptance.

On the other hand, Mattila et al. (2003) show perceived difficulty in using computers as an inhibitor of online banking adoption among senior consumers in Finland. Suganthi et al. (2001) report technophobia can also be a factor affecting customer reluctance to opt for Internet banking.

Perceived Benefits

Consumers use online banking for the benefits it provides in comparison to other delivery channels. Online financial services offer consumers a set of benefits that favour adoption, including the opportunity for the user to control bank accounts at any time and place, access to useful information for making investment and financing decisions, and savings on time and cost (Ainin, Lim, & Wee,

2005; Gerrard & Cunningham, 2003; Polatoglu & Ekin, 2001; Suganthi et al., 2001).

Lower Fees

Internet delivery is cheaper than physical channels. A simple transaction for a noncash payment at a branch is likely to cost the bank as much as 11 times more than over the Internet. Using the Internet, financial service providers can pass on their operating cost savings to consumers either through lower prices or higher interest-rate earnings (Lee et al., 2005). Moreover, the Internet eliminates any physical barrier and makes it possible to carry out financial transactions from the part of the world where the cost is lower. Consumers will also have access to online search engines that will allow them to compare financial services for the best terms and conditions worldwide.

Price is an important choice criteria used by most consumers in deciding where to shop online. Economically motivated shoppers see price as an important cost component and compare prices between different alternatives. Consumers are often conscious of the expenses associated with banking and are better informed about alternative options. As Jayawardhena and Foley (2000) pointed out, any financial service provided must be at minimal cost or competitive cost, and preferably no cost. Consumers seek to carry out complex transactions at minimal cost and without expensive paid advice.

Help with Financial Decision Making

Banking technological developments make it much easier and cheaper for customers to compare and contrast products and to establish multiple banking connections. Better communications technology help consumers with financial decision making due to the fact that they can obtain fast, transparent, and updated information (Bradley & Stewart, 2002).

Time Savings

Most consumers are becoming busier, so they are trying to save time in order to improve their quality of life. This is confirmed by the increase in telephone-assisted banking and also the widespread use of the now ubiquitous ATMs. The convenience and ease of carrying out financial transactions from home attracts increasing numbers of consumers who value their free time.

Bank location and transport costs are also decisive in the decision to adopt Internet banking. Electronic channels eliminate all displacement problems. This is particularly positive for consumers whose age or physical disabilities prevent them from going to the brick-and-mortar bank branch and also for users with time restrictions due to work and family obligations.

Ability to Control Bank Accounts at Any Time and Any Place

Internet-enabled consumers will be able to change banks at the press of a button in the comfort of their homes. Lockett and Litter's (1997) study of the adoption of direct banking services in the United Kingdom evidenced that the most important perceived positive attribute of direct banking was its 24-hour-a-day availability. Consumers like to have a private, quick, and efficient bank account service at any time.

Consumers feel the need to have bank balances in check because customer accounts are more active and users feel the need to reconcile frequently. All banks offer at least view-only functions, and most of them offer action functions because it reduces the workload for bank staff at both branch and call centres and relieves congestion for ATMs.

Personalised Information

Currently, consumers expect banks to know who they are, what type of services they ordered in

the past, and how they prefer to be contacted, demanding ever more personalised attention. The provision of personalised customer service to assist consumers in performing transactions via the Internet as well as providing specific value-added services, which are currently not provided through traditional banking channels, can also help to reduce customer reluctance to change from traditional ways of operating (Suganthi et al., 2001). The key to achieving user loyalty is to be found in the bank's capacity to personalise its supply, adapting it to the customer's needs. In this sense, banks can use multiple distribution channels enabling different products to be targeted at different demographic segments.

Bank managers can try out new financial services and advertising on the Internet and obtain an immediate response. The Internet offers a perfect combination of standardised campaigns and personalisation, with the capacity to reach thousands of consumers and give them individualised treatment, thus increasing their loyalty.

Perceived Shopping Risk

According to Forsythe and Shi (2003), the perceived risk of online shopping is the Internet user's expectation of loss in a given electronic transaction. The different types of perceived shopping risk (financial, psychological, social, product ans wate of time risk) have a significant influence on the choice of the shopping channel as they become a barrier to performing Internet banking transactions (Gerrard & Cunningham, 2003; Hewer & Howcroft, 1999; Polatoglu & Ekin, 2001; Suganthi et al., 2001).

Financial Risk

Financial risk is associated with the loss of money (in cash or through the credit card) by the consumer. Previous research focused on countries with different levels of e-commerce adoption showed that the perceived financial risk is an important predictor of Internet banking adoption. Sathye (1999) investigated the adoption of Internet banking by Australian consumers and identified security concerns and lack of awareness as the main obstacles to adoption. Gerrard and Cunningham (2003) found security concerns over Internet banking high in both adopters and nonadopters in Singapore. Research by Lee et al. (2005) focused on U.S. consumers shows that prospective adopters are more concerned than current adopters with transaction security and monetary benefits when choosing an Internet-based banking service.

Psychological Risk

Another important barrier to the consolidation of electronic transactions is consumers' disappointment and frustration generated by the violation of consumers' privacy, that is, perceived psychological risk. Gerrard and Cunningham (2003) found that consumers were concerned that the bank may pass customer profiles over to other companies in the banking group, resulting in the information being used to try and sell additional products. Users want to control what kind of data are collected and for what purposes, and how long data are recorded (Pikkarainen et al., 2004).

Social Risk

The perceived social risk is caused by the lack of face-to-face contact. The physical separation between the bank advisor and the consumer makes it all the more important to generate trust and thus achieve greater loyalty toward the bank's Web site (Flavián, Guinaliu, & Torres, 2005; Mukherjee & Nath, 2003). Consumers' attitudes to the different methods of purchasing depend on their characteristics, with those who most value social relationships being the most reluctant to develop a positive attitude to Internet banking. In the Malaysian context, research by Suganthi et al. (2001) shows that personal relationships

between customers and bankers transcend many boundaries, especially so in rural areas.

Product Risk

Many consumers do not purchase online because they fear that the product received will not meet their expectations, that is, because of the perceived product risk. Asymmetry in online banking information and the lack of personal contact prevent the consumer from correctly evaluating the characteristics of the product, decreasing confidence (Ba, 2001). One of the problems of e-shopping is that customers are unable to try out Internet services beforehand in the same way they can try out a jacket before purchasing. Some banks in the West have responded to this need by developing Web sites that allow potential users to try out Internet banking (Gerrard & Cunningham, 2003). The ability to conduct a trial may confirm how easy it is to use Internet banking and provides the necessary confidence to consumers with high perceived shopping risk.

Time-Loss Risk

The Internet provides a lot of information on the products and services offered, and a variety of financial Web sites where the Web user can carry out their transactions. Despite the fact that the Internet lowers the cost of acquiring information, consumers also incur costs from using online banking: the time of learning how to buy on a certain Web site, the time to wait for it to respond, and the additional cognitive effort expended in this expanded search process. Furthermore, Web site download speed is another factor influencing online banking adoption (Jayawardhena & Foley, 2000). The use of extensive high-resolution graphics and an inefficient host server can also increase the perceived risk of waste of time for the current and future users of Internet banking. Moreover, speed is also dependent on the user's computing hardware and method of connection.

THE CASE OF SPANISH INTERNET USERS

After identifying the key drivers of e-banking adoption, the second part of the chapter presents an empirical study of the Spanish market.

It should be noted that 4,512,902 Spanish Internet users have used some of the services offered by financial entities on the Internet in 2005, which represents 29.82% of all Spanish Internet users and 10.23% of the total population (Instituto Nacional de Estadística [INE], 2005). Growth in the e-banking adoption rate over recent years is due to the penetration and consolidation of online banking and a general increase in the number of Internet users. According to Nielsen/Netratings (2006), 5.8 million Internet users have visited financial Web sites or portals between the months of November 2005 and January 2006 (106.4% over the previous year), and average surfing time has been an hour and a half per person.

The conceptual model of online banking adoption, which will be contrasted in the Spanish market (see Figure 1), is an outcome of the literature review presented above.

The quantitative analysis provides answers to the following research questions:

a.   How do demographics influence e-banking adoption?

b.   What are the main perceived benefits and barriers to online financial services purchasing for Spanish consumers?

c.   How does online experience influence Internet banking adoption?

d.   What are the effects of Internet affinity on the decision to use online financial services?

Methodology

We examined data from 450 personal interviews with Internet users aged 18 years and over, of which 243 use online financial services. The study collected information using quota sampling on the basis of gender and age determined by the AECE study[2] (Asociación Española de Comercio Electrónico, 2005; see sample distribution in Table 1). The field work was done from September to October 2005.

The questionnaire was developed and tested with nine focus groups to examine the dynamics of bank services users (company managers, customers, and banking professionals) with different levels of familiarity with financial Web sites. The qualitative research, as with previous studies, focused on Internet banking in cultural environments different to that in Spain (Black et al., 2001; Gerrard & Cunningham, 2003) and helped us to identify Spanish consumer standards of behaviour attitudes in the adoption of this type

Figure 1. Conceptual model

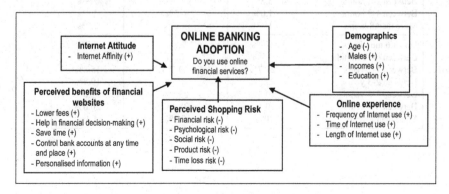

of services. Based on the information provided by focus-group meetings, the questionnaire was modified and finalized.

In the quantitative analysis, we first tested for significant differences between the demographics and behavioural profiles of online banking adopters (consumers who have used online financial services) and non-online-banking adopters (consumers who have never used online financial services) using the chi-square technique (see Table 1). Second, we used logistic regression to empirically contrast the model proposed in Figure 1.

Results

Table 1 shows the description of the sample. 56% of Spanish consumers have adopted Internet banking (they use both traditional and online financial services), while the rest only use traditional banking services.

Table 1. Profile of respondents

Characteristic		Nonadopters (N=207)	E-Banking Adopters (N=243)	Total N=450	Chi-Square
Gender	Female	45.4%	40.3%	57.3%	χ2 = 2.150; p = 0.341
	Male	54.6%	59.7%	42.7%	
Age	18-24	41.1%	25.1%	32.4%	χ2 = 15.630; p = 0.004
	25-34	22.2%	32.9%	28.0%	
	35-44	16.4%	22.6%	19.8%	
	45-54	11.6%	11.5%	11.6%	
	55 or more	8.7%	7.9%	8.2%	
Education	School-leaving certificate	6.2%	0.8%	1.6%	χ2 = 17.712; p = 0.001
	Primary studies	25.7%	8.6%	12.4%	
	Secondary education	32.6%	32.1%	36.0%	
	University graduates	35.5%	58.4%	50.0%	
Income	Below average	41.7%	29.2%	34.8%	χ2 = 10.440; p = 0.015
	Around average	22.4%	19.2%	21.0%	
	Above average	28.6%	41.5%	35.7%	
	Well above average	7.3%	9.3%	8.4%	
Internet Use Frequency	Several times a day	25.1%	44.0%	35.3%	χ2 = 9.218; p = 0.423
	Once a day	23.0%	18.1%	15.8%	
	Several times a week	24.8%	24.3%	29.1%	
	Once a week	9.2%	5.3%	7.1%	
	Twice a month	8.2%	2.4%	5.1%	
	Less than once a month	9.7%	5.7%	7.6%	
Internet Use Time (per week)	Less than 15 minutes	14.5%	10.7%	12.4%	χ2 = 7.654; p = 0.766
	Between 15-30 minutes	30.8%	22.6%	21.8%	
	Between 30 mins.-1 hour	34.3%	27.6%	30.7%	
	Between 1-2 hours	12.7%	18.9%	20.7%	
	Between 2-4 hours	5.3%	9.9%	7.8%	
	Between 4-8 hours	1.0%	6.2%	3.8%	
	More than 8 hours	1.4%	4.1%	2.9%	
Length of Internet Use	Under 6 months	9.7%	7.8%	8.7%	χ2 = 60.565; p = 0.000
	Between 6-12 months	15%	4.5%	9.3%	
	Between 1-2 years	21.7%	10.7%	15.8%	
	Between 2-3 years	23.2%	16.9%	19.8%	
	Between 3-5 years	20.3%	23.5%	22.0%	
	Between 5-8 years	10.1%	28.4%	20.0%	
	More than 8 years	0%	8.2%	4.4%	

The descriptive analysis of the sample shows that consumers who use online banking services are both men (59.7%) and women (40.3%), with most of them aged below 44 (80.6%), highly educated (58.4% have had university studies), and with a high level of income (50.8% above average). A high percentage of the Internet banking adopters are heavy Internet users (62.1% access the Internet everyday and 66.7% access it more than 30 minutes per week). 60.1% of Internet users have over 3 years of online use experience.

A comparison of the e-banking adopter profile with that of the nonadopter reveals significant differences with respect to age (X2=15.630; p=0.004), education (X2=17.712; p=0.001), income (X2=10.440; p=0.015), and length of Internet use (X2=60.585; p=0.000).

A variable that captures the importance of a medium for the individual is affinity. A five-item scale from previous studies was used to measure affinity (Rubin & Perse, 1988) as shown in Table 2. Evaluation for each item ranged from 1, *totally disagree*, to 5, *totally agree*.

The Internet affinity scale was subjected to statistical analysis, verifying its multidimensionality and compliance with the psychometric properties established by the literature. Cronbach's alpha had a value of 0.80. Scale content validity was verified from the literature review (Rubin & Perse, 1988). Convergent validity was verified by the fact that in the confirmatory model, all the standardised factorial loads were above 0.5 and were all significant (t>3.291). Finally, discriminant

validity was confirmed by the fact that variable correlation in the confirmatory model did not exceed 0.8. The Internet affinity scale was applied to Spanish Internet users.

Table 2 shows that the non-e-banking adopter attaches less importance (affinity=2.35) than the e-banking adopter (affinity=2.66) to the Internet. The total mean of the Internet affinity scale was 2.52.

Perceived benefits and perceived shopping risks were also measured on a five-point scale. The ability to control bank accounts and help in financial decision making are the most valued benefits to both the e-banking adopter and the nonadopters, and the financial and social risks are the main obstacles to using online financial services. In general, the non-e-banking adopter perceives lower benefits with Internet banking and a greater perceived purchase risk (see Table 3).

A logistic regression (N=450 Internet users) was used to test the proposed model. For the regression, online banking adopters were coded as a dichotomous variable including consumers who have used online financial services (n=243) against those who said they had never used online financial services (n=207). Independent variables included demographics (gender, age, education, and income), online experience (Internet exposure, time and length of use), Internet affinity, perceived benefits, and perceived shopping risk (financial, product, time-wasting, psychological, and social risk; see Table 4).

Table 2. Affinity scale

Affinity	**Nonadopters (N=207)**	**E-Banking Adopters (N=243)**	**Total N=450**
Connecting to the Internet is one of my main daily activities.	2.16	2.63	2.42
If the Internet is down, I really miss it.	2.11	2.53	2.34
The Internet is important in my life.	2.05	2.56	2.34
I can go for several days without connecting to the Internet.	3.58	3.57	3.57
I would be lost without the Internet.	1.83	2.02	1.93
Mean	2.35	2.66	2.52

Table 3. Perceived benefits and perceived shopping risk of online banking services

Perceived Benefits	Nonadopters	Adopters	Total	Perceived Shopping Risk	Nonadopters	Adopters	Total
Lower fees	3.67	3.90	3.79	Financial risk: Nonsecurity of data transfer	4.72	4.05	4.39
Saved time	2.66	3.03	2.86	Social risk: Lack of face-to-face contact	4.49	4.02	4.26
Information for decision making	3.68	4.13	3.92	Psychological risk: Reluctance to give private information	3.62	3.03	3.33
Personalised information	2.91	3.36	3.15	Product risk: Mistakes made during data entry	3.11	2.51	2.81
Ability to control bank accounts at any time and place	3.86	4.32	4.11	Time-loss risk: Slow data transfer	3.04	2.30	2.61

Hypothesis testing of the significance of the regression coefficients (β) gave the following results (see Table 4).

- There are six variables with nonsignificant coefficients ($p > 0.05$) according to the Wald statistic. Therefore, the gender of the Internet user together with the frequency and time of Internet use are variables that do not significantly influence the decision to use online financial services. Some perceived benefits and barriers of online banking services such as personalised information, and product and time-loss risk do not appear to influence online banking adoption, either.

- The results show that it is 0.499 times less likely that Internet users adopt e-banking if they are seniors, and it is 2.457 and 2.009 times more likely in users with high education levels and income.

- The greater the online experience, the more likely it is that e-banking adoption will occur. Online banking adoption is 3.654 times more likely if the consumer's online use experience is more than 3 years than if it is less than 6 months.

- Affinity is another significant variable in the model. Thus, it is 1.557 times more likely that the interviewee will use online financial services if he or she feels affinity with the Internet than if less importance is attached to it.

- In terms of the perceived benefits and barriers, the results show that it is 1.807 times more likely that e-users will use online financial services if they save time, it is 1.724 times more likely if they find help in financial decision making, it is 1.501 times more likely if they can control bank accounts at any time and place, and it is 1.469 times more likely if they perceive cost savings. On the other hand, it is 0.633 times less likely they will use online financial services if they perceive financial risk, 0.648 times less likely if they perceive social risk, and 0.576 times less likely if they perceive psychological risk.

Having checked the statistical significance of the estimated logistic regression coefficients, we proceed to verify the overall significance of the model. The chi-square value of the empirical model shows a value of 148.976, with 39 degrees

Table 4. Logistic regression for predicting online banking adoption

Variable[3]	B	SE	Wald	Sig.	Exp(B)
G1	0.012	0.014	0.709	0.400	1.012
A2	-0.695	0.202	11.837	0.000	0.499
E3			11.478	0.075	
E3(1)	0.179	1.195	0.022	0.874	1.196
E3(2)	0.911	0.525	3.011	0.079	2.486
E3(3)	0.899	0.329	7.466	0.005	2.457
I4			10.232	0.081	
I4 (1)	0.181	1.205	0.022	0.881	1.196
I4 (2)	0.425	0.244	3.033	0.085	1.529
I4 (3)	0.698	0.319	4.787	0.031	2.009
IUF			3.801	0.799	
IUF(1)	0.355	1.182	0.090	0.759	1.426
IUF(2)	0.739	1.202	0.377	0.526	2.093
IUF(3)	0.501	1.241	0.162	0.688	1.650
IUF(4)	1.339	1.645	0.662	0.399	3.815
IUF(5)	0.292	1.037	0.079	0.778	1.339
IUT			5.059	0.536	
IUT(1)	0.089	1.047	0.007	0.932	1.093
IUT(2)	0.334	0.995	1.112	0.737	1.396
IUT(3)	0.190	0.975	0.038	0.845	1.209
IUT(4)	0.123	0.990	0.015	0.901	1.130
IUT(5)	0.106	1.035	0.010	0.919	1.111
IUT(6)	1.735	1.448	1.436	0.231	5.668
OSE			21.032	0.000	
OSE(1)	0.427	0.246	3.012	0.079	1.532
OSE(2)	0.697	0.318	4.804	0.025	2.007
OSE(3)	1.019	0.261	15.242	0.000	2.770
OSE(4)	1.296	0.392	10.930	0.000	3.654
AFF	0.443	0.135	10.723	0.001	1.557
LF	0.385	0.211	3.329	0.041	1.469
ST	0.592	0.228	6.741	0.008	1.807
HFDM	0.545	0.194	7.892	0.005	1.724
CBA	0.406	0.105	15.045	0.000	1.501
PI	0.152	0.402	0.142	0.696	1.164
FRISK	-0.457	0.152	9.039	0.002	0.633
SRISK	-0.433	0.128	11.443	0.000	0.648
PSYRISK	-0.551	0.207	7.085	0.006	0.576
PRORISK	-0.239	0.196	1.486	0.251	0.787
TLRISK	-0.431	0.704	0.374	0.525	0.649
Intercept	-1.682	1.329	1.601	0.197	0.186

of freedom and a significance of 0.000. This value is greater than the value of the corresponding theoretical model in level of significance of both 0.05 and of 0.01 (chi-square value equals 55.76 and 63.69, respectively), and is therefore statistically significant. In addition, the value -2LL has reduced (-2LL0=571.325 and -2LL1=432.243), which verifies the fact that this model provides a better fit than the model that only contains the constant.

Given the high sample size, we have also obtained a good fit of the chi-square test with Hosmer and Lemeshow. The chi-square value is equal to 9.116, with 8 degrees of freedom (significance=0.333), an empirical value that is below the theoretical value for a significance level of 0.05 (X2=15.51). It may be stated, therefore, that the model fit is good.

Furthermore, the model presents very good predictive capacity: 74.6% of the cases are correctly classified given a cut-off value of 0.5. We also have been able to calculate the Z* statistic, which is distributed as a normal. Since we have obtained a value of Z* (9.98> 1.96) valid for a significance level of 0.05, this leads us to reject the null hypothesis that the number of cases correctly classified by the model does not differ from the expected classification only due to random effects.

FUTURE TRENDS

According to Bradley and Stewart (2002), by 2011, 85% of retail banks will have adopted Internet banking. Those retail banks that decide not to adopt Internet banking as part of their distribution strategy must either operate as niche players or reevaluate their strategy.

Four future trends can be observed in the current financial markets, which are undoubtedly favoured by the introduction of the Internet in the financial sphere.

1. The existence of a disintermediation process with a growing trend toward a more direct relation between the savers and the issuers of financial assets.

2. The phenomenon of globalisation, which favours a broader supply of financial services, greater cooperation between the different institutions, and greater transparency in the information systems for international markets.

3. The elimination of legal restrictions on financial activity. In addition to the new business opportunities created and banks' greater freedom in decision making, there is also a threat of new competitors due to the elimination of the barriers imposed by regulation. Governments will aim to focus regulation on solvency guarantees and customer protection.

4. Financial innovation will give rise to new instruments that will increase bank efficiency in three main areas: (a) procedures (both internal bank management techniques [back office] and external customer relations [front office]), (b) markets (changes in the structures and mechanisms in the already existing markets and the creation of new organised markets), and (c) products (new investment, financing, and risk-transfer products).

CONCLUSION

The main academic contribution of this chapter is that it will give managers and students insight into the Internet banking industry, its impact on economic development, and the different factors that influence online banking adoption. In addition, these factors can be applied to the specific context of the Spanish market. Specifically, this study will improve managers' understanding of consumer demographics, online experience, Internet attitude, and perceived benefits and barriers and their relation to the use of online financial services.

Developments in technology in recent years have meant a radical change in financial systems, through which we have seen how the geographical barriers of time and communication can be totally overcome. Internet banking encourages online shopping in a country because as banks modernise in order to offer their customers online financial services, they facilitate the development of secure and efficient e-commerce. Access to banking services by either the Internet or mobile phone boosts investment in the economy, thus favouring economic growth.

The behaviour of private investors (customers of financial intermediaries) has also changed significantly, especially in terms of relations with financial institutions. Interactive services offer a new type of relationship between the customer and the financial institution. These services can adopt different forms, depending on the area in which they are linked, and include money withdrawal, payments, money transfers, credit card services, loans, foreign currency, stocks, opening an account, cheques, investment funds, and so forth.

E-banking technologies provide customers the following benefits: (a) transparent, updated information that responds accurately to the orders given by the customer, (b) the ability of customers to choose how they wish to manage their finances, (c) personalised products and services (i.e., bank Web sites with confidential pages and personal log-ins for the customers who contract them), (d) financial innovation, and (e) savings on costs due to increased competition between banks.

The logistic regression analysis on the set of variables analysed has highlighted the fact that online banking adoption is more likely in young, highly educated, and high-income consumers. These results confirm previous research (Daniel, 1999; Karjaluoto et al., 2002; Sathye, 1999) that shows a clear-cut division between the rich, who would use online banking, and the poor, who would possibly prefer traditional banking services.

Internet users with higher education levels are more predisposed toward online banking adoption, possibly because of the characteristics of financial products (complex and specialised). The literature review has linked age and adoption of technologies, with younger persons being more likely to adopt. Internet banking services probably do not fit in with the banking behaviour of senior consumers and the way they have historically managed their finances (i.e., there is not a bank branch to visit or they do not receive bank statements by post).

Gender has no significant influence on the decision to use online financial services. It can be explained because the influence of gender on Internet banking adoption is moderated by other variables such as marital status. As Kolodinsky et al. (2004) pointed out, married couples may have jointly held accounts and are more likely to adopt e-banking services than either single males or single females.

Online use experience, Internet affinity, and most of the perceived benefits are also key drivers of online financial services purchase decision-making because consumers with longer Internet use, with high Internet affinity, and who perceive higher benefits from financial Web sites use more online financial services, while novice Web users prefer using only traditional branches. However, frequency and time of Internet use are not significantly influential variables. One explanation of this result may be that novice Internet consumers use the Internet for amusement, for work, or to obtain financial information, but do not perceive the utility of carrying out financial transactions online. In this case, it is necessary first for them to assimilate the advantages offered by Internet banking (lower fees, help on financial decision making, time savings, the control of bank accounts, etc.) because this will encourage future online banking adoption. Previous research shows that greater online experience leads to improved relations with the medium as the individual is more familiar with it and values its benefits more

(Gerrard & Cunningham, 2003; Lee et al., 2005; Polatoglu & Ekin, 2001).

The influence of perceived shopping risk on Internet banking adoption depends on the type of impediments that we are considering, with the perceived shopping risk of the financial, social, and psychological types being those with significant influence. The influence of perceived financial risk is corroborated in previous studies, according to which security is an important impediment increasing the perceived shopping risk in virtual environments (Laforet & Lin, 2005; Sathye, 1999). We can, therefore, conclude that the Internet user's lack of trust in the system of payment on the Web may hinder the consolidation of e-banking adoption. Also, the impossibility of controlling access by third parties to the personal data provided during the process of surfing the financial Web site can explain the influence of the refusal to provide personal data (psychological risk) on Internet banking adoption.

Although consumers are developing more positive attitudes toward purchasing online, a vast majority of bank customers would still like to opt for personal interaction when doing their bank transactions and feel that the personal touch of officers and managers adds value to each transaction. Social motives increase satisfaction with the traditional way of operating and induce consumers to keep visiting bank branches and, therefore, explain the influence of perceived social risk on Internet banking adoption.

The risks associated with the product and wasted time did not significantly influence the decision to carry out financial transactions online, possibly because these impediments are not yet important for Internet users.

This chapter can help managers to develop effective strategies to attract online consumers and, therefore, to gain competitive advantages.

Internet banking adoption is greater among young, highly educated, and wealthy Internet users, so we recommend that marketers interested in the Spanish market make this segment a priority. However, holding demonstrations to test new technologies, providing opportunities for simplified financial management, adapting financial products and prices for users in relation to their profiles, and creating user-friendly Web sites can help companies to widen their target market to senior, low-income, and low-educated consumers.

We also recommend that managers inform consumers of the confidentiality with which their personal details are treated and the security of payments made on the Web site, and use discussion forums and recommender systems so consumers can share with others their opinions and interests and raise any doubts, and therefore, reduce the perceived social shopping risk.

There are still many users who, although they visit financial Web sites for information, prefer to carry out bank transactions in brick-and-mortar branches. Thus, with the aim of generating trust, we recommend that banks integrate commercial channels. For example, an attractive, reliable Web site would help to increase the transactions generated in traditional branches while good positioning in the physical world would reduce consumer feelings of mistrust of online banking transactions.

In terms of the limitations of this study, there are complementary aspects not included in the questionnaire that we think would be interesting to analyse. As a future line of research, we are considering complementing this study with the development and validation of a scale to measure shopping orientations and perceived shopping risk in online banking. The consumer's cultural background is one of the aspects that can influence the creation of a favourable climate for developing and consolidating electronic transactions worldwide (Van Birgelen, De Ruyter, De Jong, & Wetzels, 2002). For this reason, we consider that another interesting line of research would be to contrast the validity of the proposed behavioural model with samples of consumers from other cultures and compare the results obtained.

REFERENCES

Ainin, S., Lim, C. H., & Wee, A. (2005). Prospects and challenges of e-banking in Malaysia. *The Electronic Journal of Information Systems in Developing Countries, 22,* 1-11.

Akinci, S., Aksoy, S., & Atilgan, E. (2004). Adoption of Internet banking among sophisticated consumer segments in an advanced developing country. *The International Journal of Bank Marketing, 22*(3), 212-232.

Al-Ashban, A., & Burney, M. (2001). Customer adoption of tele-banking technology: The case of Saudi Arabia. *International Journal of Bank Marketing, 21*(3), 191-200.

Asociación Española de Comercio Electrónico (AECE). (2005). *Estudio sobre comercio electrónico B2C.* Retrieved July 12, 2006, from http://www.aece.es

Ba, S. (2001). Establishing online trust through a community responsibility system. *Decision Supporting Systems, 31*(3), 323-336.

Black, N., Lockett, A., Winklhofer, H., & Ennew, C. (2001). The adoption of Internet financial services: A qualitative study. *International Journal of Retail & Distribution Management, 29*(8), 390-398.

Bradley, L., & Stewart, K. (2002). A delphi study of the drivers and inhibitors of Internet banking. *International Journal of Bank Marketing, 20*(6), 250-260.

Comisión del Mercado de las Telecomunicaciones (CMT). (2006). *Informe sobre comercio electrónico en España a través de entidades de medios de pago 2005.* Retrieved Juny 23, 2006, from http://www.cmt.es

Dahlen, M. (2002). Learning the Web: Internet user experience and response to Web marketing in Sweden. *Journal of Interactive Advertising, 3*(1),

1-3. Retrieved September 2, 2006, from http://jiad.org/vol3/no1/dahlen/index.htm

Daniel, E. (1999). Provision of e-banking in the UK and the Republic of Ireland. *International Journal of Bank Marketing, 17*(2), 72-82.

Davis, F. D. (1989). Perceived usefulness, perceived ease of use, and user acceptance of information technology. *MIS Quarterly, 13*(3), 319-340.

Filotto, U., Tanzi, P., & Saita, F. (1997). Customer needs and front office technology adoption. *International Journal of Bank Marketing, 15*(1), 13-21.

Flavián, C., Guinaliu, M., & Torres, E. (2005). The influence of corporate image on consumer trust: A comparative analysis in traditional versus Internet banking. *Internet Research: Electronic Networking Applications and Policy, 15*(4), 447-470.

Forsythe, S., & Shi, B. (2003). Consumer patronage and risk perceptions in Internet shopping. *Journal of Business Research, 56,* 867-875.

Gerrard, P., & Cunningham, J. B. (2003). The diffusion of Internet banking among Singapore consumers. *The International Journal of Bank Marketing, 21*(1), 16-28.

Hewer, P., & Howcroft, B. (1999). Consumers distribution channel adoption and usage in the financial services industry: A review of existing approaches. *Journal of Financial Services Marketing, 3*(4), 344-358.

Howcroft, B., Hamilton, R., & Hewer, P. (2002). Consumer attitude and the usage and adoption of home-based banking in the United Kingdom. *International Journal of Bank Marketing, 20*(3), 111-121.

Instituto Nacional de Estadística (INE). (2005). *Encuesta sobre equipamiento y uso de tecnologías de la información y comunicación en los hogares.* Retrieved February 10, 2006, from http://www.ine.es/inebase/cgi

Jaruwachirathanakul, B., & Fink, D. (2005). Internet banking adoption strategies for a developing country: The case of Thailand. *Internet Research: Electronic Networking Applications and Policy, 15*(3), 295-311.

Jayawardhena, C., & Foley, P. (2000). Changes in the banking sector: The case of Internet banking in the UK. *Internet Research: Electronic Networking Applications and Policy, 10*(1), 19-30.

Jun, M., & Cai, S. (2001). The key determinants of Internet banking service quality: A content analysis. *The International Journal of Bank Marketing, 19*(7), 276-291.

Karjaluoto, H., Mattila, M., & Pento, T. (2002). Factors underlying attitude formation towards online banking in Finland. *International Journal of Banking Marketing, 20*(6), 261-272.

Kolodinsky, J. M., Hogarth, J. M., & Hilgert, M. A. (2004). The adoption of electronic banking technologies by US consumers. *International Journal of Bank Marketing, 22*(4), 238-259.

Laforet, S., & Lin, X. (2005). Consumers' attitudes towards online and mobile banking in China. *International Journal of Bank Marketing, 23*(5), 362-380.

Leblanc, G. (1990). Customer motivations: Use and non-use of automated banking. *International Journal of Bank Marketing, 8*(4), 36-40.

Lee, E., Kwon, K., & Schumann, D. (2005). Segmenting the non-adopter category in the diffusion of Internet banking. *International Journal of Bank Marketing, 23*(5), 414-437.

Lockett, A., & Litter, D. (1997). The adoption of direct banking services. *Journal of Marketing Management, 13*, 791-811.

Marshall, J. J., & Heslop, L. A. (1988). Technology acceptance in Canadian retail banking: A study of consumer motivations and the use of ATMs. *International Journal of Bank Marketing, 6*(4), 31-41.

Mattila, M., Karjaluoto, H., & Pento, T. (2003). Internet banking adoption among mature customers: Early majority or laggards? *Journal of Service Marketing, 17*(5), 514-528.

Mols, N. P. (1998). The behavioural consequences of PC banking. *International Journal of Bank Marketing, 16*(5), 195-201.

Mols, N. P. (2000). The Internet and services marketing: The case of Danish retail banking. *Internet Research: Electronic Networking Applications and Policy, 10*(1), 7-18.

Mukherjee, A., & Nath, P. (2003). A model of trust in online relationship banking. *International Journal of Bank Marketing, 21*(1), 5-15.

Nielsen/Netratings. (2006). *Global Internet trends*. Retrieved July 26, 2006, from http://www.nielsen-netratings.com

Otto, A. (2003). *Handbook of international banking*. MA: Edward Elgar Publishing.

Pikkarainen, T., Pikkarainen, K., Karjaluoto, H., & Pahnila, S. (2004). Consumer acceptance of online banking: An extension of the technology acceptance model. *Internet Research: Electronic Networking Applications and Policy, 14*(3), 224-235.

Polatoglu, V. N., & Ekin, S. (2001). An empirical investigation of the Turkish consumers' acceptance of Internet banking services. *International Journal of Bank Marketing, 19*(4), 156-165.

Rubin, A. M., & Perse, E. M. (1988). Audience activity and soap opera involvement. *Human Communication Research, 14*(2), 246-268.

Sathye, M. (1999). Adoption of Internet banking by Australian consumers: An empirical investigation. *International Journal of Bank Marketing, 17*(7), 324-334.

Suganthi, B., Balachandher, K., & Balachandran, K. (2001). Internet banking patronage: An empirical investigation of Malaysia. *Journal of*

Banking and Commerce, 6(1). Retrieved May 22, 2001, from http://www.arraydev.com/commerce/jibc/0103_01.htm

Sundarraj, R., & Wu, J. (2005). Using information-systems constructs to study online and telephone-banking technologies. *Electronic Commerce Research and Applications, 4,* 427-443.

Van Birgelen, M., De Ruyter, K., De Jong, A., & Wetzels, M. (2002). Customer evaluations of alter-sales service contact modes: An empirical analysis of national culture's consequences. *International Journal of Research in Marketing, 19,* 43-64.

Chapter X
E–Commerce Contribution to Economic Growth:
The Case of Thailand

Ing-wei Huang
Assumption University, Thailand

Songsak Vanichviroon
Assumption University, Thailand

ABSTRACT

As the trend of ICT development is gaining larger influence over countries' development and growth, e-commerce plays an important role in enhancing the growth of several developed and developing economies over the 21st century. This chapter aims to build the analytical base to support the importance of the development of e-commerce by investigating the role and contribution of e-commerce to economic growth and development. The chapter first investigates past contributions of e-commerce to economic growth in developed countries. Second, past research findings and frameworks are utilized to investigate the contribution of e-commerce toward economic growth, focusing on the case of e-commerce in Thailand. The study found that e-commerce plays an important role in enhancing the economic growth of Thailand. Two important findings supported the growth of e-commerce. First is the increase in sales generated by the use of e-commerce. Second, e-commerce induces the productivity development of firms through higher competition and innovation.

INTRODUCTION

Today the trend of ICT development is gaining larger influence over countries' development and growth. It would not be surprising to see the elements that evolved from the developments of ICT (such as e-commerce, e-marketing, e-business, and e-learning) have increasingly provided support toward enhancing countries' growth and development, especially in highly sophisticated industries. The introduction of e-commerce and e-business seems to create a tremendous contribution to the growth of many developed nations and is continuing its increasing impact on the developments of many developing economies over the 21st century.

Some recent literature pointed out the increasing contribution of e-commerce toward economic development in several developed countries such as the United States, Canada, Australia, and the United Kingdom (Adam, Mulye, Deans, & Palihawadana, 2002). It was found that from 1997 to 2000, the value of sales from e-commerce increased from less than $20 billion to nearly $300 billion. Moreover, some researchers expect that the contribution of e-commerce will grow faster than the contribution from traditional sales. Especially in the United States in the year 2000, e-commerce represented more than 80% of the worldwide e-commerce that took place, having a significant effect on the large economic sectors such as communications, finance, and retail where it accounts for 15% of the global gross domestic product (GDP).[1]

In Thailand, the idea of e-commerce utilized in business sectors and other electronic support systems in businesses have just started to gain attention from several government and private sectors during the past few years.[2] Major support went to the promotion of e-commerce for small and medium-sized enterprises (SMEs) and other businesses that wish to engage in online services. Moreover, an e-commerce resource center was established in 1999 to provide additional research and development in the field under the supervision of NECTEC (National Electronics Computer and Technology Center; ECRC, 2006). Although there seems to be increasing support for the development of e-commerce in Thailand, very limited findings and research have focused on the significance of e-commerce development and how such developments can contribute positively to the growth of the Thai economy.

RESEARCH OBJECTIVE

As the study of the importance of e-commerce in Thailand is still in the initial stage and research in this field is quite limited, this chapter aims to build the analytical base to support the importance of the development of e-commerce. This will be done by investigating the role and contribution of e-commerce to economic growth and development.

The predominant concept of economic development has been broadly applied to four major areas including growth development, human development, social development, and other development aspects. To make the investigation of the contribution of e-commerce less complex, this chapter will emphasize only on the growth development perspective. This is because the growth element tends to be a universally accepted factor in evaluating a country's economic well-being as can be seen from the utilization of GDP, industrial output, and exports and imports figures as indicators of development in several research papers (Fraumeni, 2001; Steven & Session, 2002).

To find the role of e-commerce in economic development, first it is important to investigate the past contribution of e-commerce to economic growth in developed countries as opposed to developing countries. This is because experiences in developed countries can provide a sound base for supporting e-commerce in developing countries.

Second, the chapter will study the linkage between e-commerce and economic development to provide a framework for the significance of e-commerce in enhancing growth. Much research pointed out the benefits of e-commerce where it contributes to the increase of sales and output (Adam et al., 2002; Chuang & Shaw, 2005; Hanson, 2000; Ruengsrichaiya, 2004; Saeed, Grover, & Hwang, 2005). This chapter will adopt the research findings and framework utilized by past research as a base for developing the analysis on the contribution of e-commerce toward economic development and growth, focusing on the case of e-commerce in Thailand. Third, an empirical analysis of the contribution of e-commerce toward economic growth in Thailand will be conducted. Combinations of both quantitative and qualitative analysis are utilized to evaluate the significance of e-commerce's contribution to economic growth with respect to the framework built in the previous section. The results will provide an answer toward the significance of e-commerce in affecting the economic growth and development in Thailand.

Scope of Research

The study will look at the overall picture of the business activity conducted through e-commerce considering both business-to-business (B2B) and business-to-consumer (B2C) types of models.[3] More specifically, the study will consider in particular the benefits and contribution of e-commerce from the brick-and-click business model as opposed to the brick-and-mortar model.[4]

The empirical analysis investigates businesses and manufacturers that acquired e-commerce registration and are registered with the Department of Business Development, Ministry of Commerce, Thailand.[5] From a total of 2,600 companies registered, 140 companies are sampled[6] and surveyed; 57 companies are found to be of the brick-and-click type of business and the rest are of the pure click type of businesses.

Research Methodology

The study will utilize both primary and secondary data to support the analysis for the contribution of e-commerce to Thai economy. Primary data are taken from surveys distributed to producers registered with the Department of Business Development. Data from the producers will be focused on the contribution of e-commerce to overall output sales, which will provide information for the analysis on e-commerce contribution

to growth. Secondary data on Thailand's Internet and e-commerce contributions will be collected from recognized institutions working in ICT such as NECTEC, the Ministry of ICT, the Ministry of Commerce, the National Statistics Office, and other public and private sectors that provide resources on ICT basis.[7]

CONTRIBUTIONS OF E-COMMERCE IN DEVELOPED COUNTRIES

Looking at the overview of e-commerce, statistics show the increasing trend of e-commerce influence on economies of developed nations. Strauss, El-Ansary, and Frost (2006) provided information about Internet penetration[8] worldwide in 2004. Internet penetration in Australia accounted for 66.14%, in Germany 50.81%, in the United Kingdom 56.76%, in Japan 61.28%, and in the United States 64.03%. This showed the importance of Internet utilization in many developed countries, which can represent a potential backing of e-commerce as a support for business development. In addition, Internet Software and Tehan (as cited in Laudon & Traver, 2004) showed the growth of Internet use in over 245 countries in 2003, which accounts for over 170 million Internet hosts, an increase from 70 million in the year 2000. These studies supported the finding that with the large base of potential buyers worldwide connected through the Internet, sellers find the Internet as an existing market that is expanding rapidly.[9]

As the usage of e-commerce significantly increases with the fall in price of personal computers and technology equipment, and the improvement of ICT that further supports the quality of infrastructure for e-commerce, growth through utilizing e-commerce in several developed countries became more prominent. The rapid growth of Internet use is an evidence for the contribution of e-commerce to a country's growth, which can be observed from the increasing use of e-commerce in several developed countries. The following provides a few examples of the substantial role and contribution of e-commerce in the United States, the United Kingdom, and Australia.

E-Commerce in the United States

Today, the U.S. economy is overwhelmed by the dependency on Internet utilization. Margherio (1998) pointed out that the IT share of the U.S. economy had increased from 6.4 to 8.2% from 1993 to 1998 due to the increasing use of the Internet technology in business activities. Internet technology is found to be changing the way people are doing business, facilitating higher price competition in the market.[10] Wind and Mahajan (2001) indicated that many U.S. companies found e-commerce to be a potential market and several firms have shifted their selling processes to e-commerce. For instance, Intel had reported an increase in sales of $2 billion in 1998 during the later half of the year after utilizing e-commerce. In addition, IBM in 2001 benefited from initiating online purchasing for $12 billion but enhanced sales to $15 billion online.

The U.S. Census Bureau (2006) estimated that the U.S. retail e-commerce sales for the second quarter of 2006 were $26.3 billion, which is an increase of 4.6% from the first quarter in the same year. This is higher than the increase in total retail sales for the same period, which increased by 0.9%. Comparing between 2005 and 2006, retail e-commerce sales had increased by 23% while total retail sales increased by only 6.6% in the same period. These figures show that e-commerce sales in the United States in 2006 contributed more than the normal traditional sale of goods.

E-Commerce in United Kingdom

Adam et al. (2002) showed the intercountry comparison of household personal computer adoption, Internet connection, and online purchasing in the United Kingdom compared to those of the United States, Canada, and Australia. In the United Kingdom, the number of households with personal computers accounted for 41%, households online 29%, and households that have shopped online 10%. This showed that the United Kingdom represents another major country where ICT plays an important role in the country. AC Nielsen (2006) showed that more than 55% of people in the United Kingdom have Internet access at home, with the percentage increasing to 80% if including Internet access from the workplace, schools, and Internet cafes. In addition, the Economist Intelligence Unit (EIU, 2006) showed an increase in the number of broadband subscribers from around 3.2 million in 2003 to around 6.1 million in 2004. AC Nielsen also reported that U.K. households utilize the Internet mainly to visit commercial Web sites, and an increasing amount of research illustrates a growing number of shoppers, annual expenditure, purchase frequency, and average expenditure online during the past 3 years.

E-Commerce in Australia

Strauss et al. (2003, 2006) showed a strong growth of Internet usage in Australia, where the population using the Internet accounted for 25.8% in 2002 and increased to 66.14% in 2004. It was reported that household usage of Internet access at the end of the year 2000 was 37% of all households and was predicted to increase to 50% by the end of 2001. Strauss et al. (2003) also showed a strong growth of the use of e-commerce, which approximately doubled each year since 1998. The research showed that approximately 20% of household Internet users from nearly all age groups utilize the Internet for goods purchases. The most common purchased items include books or magazines, which accounted for 36% of items; music at 20%; computer software at 18%; and computer hardware at 10%.

LITERATURE REVIEW

With the different experiences of the contribution of e-commerce found in several developed nations discussed above, an investigation into the basic explanation as to how e-commerce can contribute to economic growth in each country is conducted. E-commerce is increasingly playing an important role in the economies of the 21st century. It is a result of improvements in information technology and communication networks endorsed by the continuous decrease in price of IT equipment. Several research works in ICT assisted in reducing costs, increasing the transparency of prices of goods, and improving sales processes in B2B, B2C, and C2C (consumer-to-consumer) types of businesses.[11] In addition, the openness of network communication through the Internet facilitated real-time communication within firms, among firms, and between firms and consumers, which reduces significantly the time for transactions and the space needed for store fronts. It created a new type of business network through the utilization of the Internet and represents a new marketing channel for products.[12] With these positive implications of e-commerce toward business transactions and improved efficiency, a linkage from e-commerce contribution to economic growth can be formalized from theoretical models proposed by Ruengsrichaiya (2004), Hanson (2000), and Adam et al. (2002).

Framework of the Linkage of E-Commerce to Economic Growth

Looking at the contribution of e-commerce to economics growth, there are two major perspectives that have been conducted and analyzed. First is the perspective of e-commerce contribution to increase in sales. Second is a more general description of the benefit of e-commerce in inducing productivity and revenue for firms.

Contribution of E-Commerce to Sales

Ruengsrichaiya (2004) provided a theoretical model that supports the market to have e-commerce as the additional channel that will increase the overall output of firms. The model considers the market of products in two different situations with and without e-commerce as a base to compare contribution from the e-commerce market with the traditional market. The model proposed that e-commerce represents a substitution to the original markets. However, e-commerce might not only substitute the original market, but can further expand the existing market as well. E-commerce can increase additional sales through inducing impulse buying, providing different product options, and processing buyer evaluation while shoppers surf on the Net.[13]

Ruengsrichaiya's (2004) framework in explaining the role of e-commerce in contributing to sales output is given in the following. He proposed that e-commerce plays a role in substituting normal shopping. In the framework, values from 0 to 1 represent the total purchase of customers, with 0 to θ being the share of sales through normal shopping and θ to 1 representing the rest of the sales from cyber shopping or e-commerce.

Parameter of Substitution Between Normal and E-Commerce Markets

If e-commerce substitutes the traditional market, from the perspective of output growth seen in Ruengsrichaiya's (2004) framework, this will not contribute to changes in the gross output of the economy. However, when e-commerce contributes to more than substitutes the existing sales in the traditional market, the increase in output generated from e-commerce will represent an increase in production, which leads to the increase in overall economic output. Such an increase in output generated from different industries will contribute positively toward the country's gross output, which can lead to economic growth.

Figure 1.

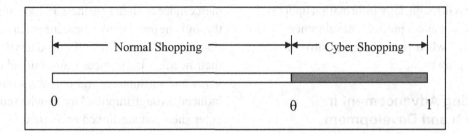

Contribution of E-Commerce from Productivity and Revenue Base Growth

Another framework commonly cited is the contribution of e-commerce in enhancing productivity and revenue for the firm. Hanson (2000) pointed out the importance of e-commerce today and presented e-commerce as a tool that combines economics, marketing, and technology together, assisting individuals in accomplishing several means in the globalizing world. He proposed major benefits from the use of the Internet, which could be divided into two major perspectives: (a) productivity growth base benefits and (b) revenue growth base benefits. Adam et al. (2002), who studied the diffusion of Internet usage in e-commerce, summarized Hanson and other research work, and categorized the major Internet benefits into five areas of benefits, which are (a) enhancing global presence, (b) establishing and maintaining a competitive edge, (c) shortening or eradicating components of the supply chain, (d) inducing cost savings, and (e) enhancing advantage in research and development. These benefits are found to bring productivity and sales growth, which will contribute toward overall output of the firm, leading to economic growth.

The following provides a brief description of the five characteristics and how each enhances economic growth and development.

Productivity Growth Base Benefits

The productivity growth base benefits are features that increase the productivity of a firm's performance as a result of e-commerce. This includes the enhancement of global presence, the establishment and maintenance of a competitive edge for products, and the advancement in research and development from utilizing e-commerce.

Enhancing Global Presence

E-commerce creates global presence of the product through enhancing online branding development. It provides a wider market perspective than the normal business based on the brick-and-mortar business model. This means that e-commerce provides an additional channel of marketing products other than the traditional channel. Such will enhance an increase in revenue to the firm, generating income and the development of the business sector, leading to an increase in gross domestic output.[14]

Establishing and Maintaining a Competitive Edge

The Internet is a means of updating product technology that gives producers information about a product's innovation and development through online category building and online quality enhancement. E-commerce producers can utilize the benefit of e-commerce and the Internet in establishing and maintaining the firm's competitiveness through daily information updates.[15] This will enhance product development and productivity, which will bring a positive impact on output growth.

Enhancing Advancement in Research and Development

As the Internet provides benefits in establishing and maintaining the competitiveness of firms, this enforces firms to continuously engage in research and development to come up with newer innovations and product upgrades.

Revenue Growth Base Benefit

The revenue growth base benefits are features that induce more sales and revenue for the firm as a result of e-commerce. This includes shortening or eradicating components of the supply chain and inducing cost savings.

Shortening or Eradicating Components of Supply Chain

The revenue-based benefits could be divided into the benefits that accrue to the provider (producer) and to the user (consumer). Regarding the provider-based benefit, e-commerce provides producers with a means to increase revenue through administrative processes in advertising and sales of the product. New possibilities like content sponsorship, retail alliances, banner advertising, prospect fees, sales commissions, and an appropriate payment structure are being utilized to support higher sales of e-commerce systems.[16] Producers who provide these services can earn revenues in the form of fees paid for advertising from other firms. On the contrary, producers who utilize these services can benefit from the wider and more conspicuous market channel in advertising the product utilizing lower expenditure. This reduces cost in finding potential customers.

As for the consumer-based benefit, e-commerce induces higher business and consumer sales through the provision of more information, which eases customer search for the products that match their needs. This reduces transactional costs for firms and customers, and enhances more sales induced through impulse buying when customers enter sites that are linked or related.

Inducing Cost Savings

E-commerce also provides a means to saving on costs for the firm through the provision of customer support documents, product manuals, and low-cost samples. These can lead to valuable contact information for future sales and upgrades for customers, which will reduce producers' costs for finding the information of prospective customers and for posting documents and samples to nontarget groups. Overall, such cost savings will bring back more efficiency and revenue to the firm, which will enhance growth and development.

EMPIRICAL INVESTIGATION OF E-COMMERCE CONTRIBUTION IN THAILAND

With the proposed framework and benefits from e-commerce discussed above, the study will adopt these frameworks and create an assessment of these factors for analyzing the contribution of e-commerce in Thailand. First, a brief overview of e-commerce in Thailand will be provided from an analysis of secondary data from different private and public sources in Thailand.

Overview of E-Commerce in Thailand

With the large contribution in sales and output generated from e-commerce seen in many developed nations, it should be depicted that this growth in ICT and e-commerce represents a potential growth in developing countries as well. As increasing support for ICT and e-commerce development has been pushed by the Thai government during the past few years, it is important that the analysis of e-commerce contribution first considers the development of the basic infrastructure in Thailand.

Observing the trends of e-commerce in Thailand compared to developed countries, the rate of Internet penetration in Thailand was found to be 13.1% in 2004,[17] which is 3 times lower than in many developed nations. Although the penetration rate is still low, new statistics show a continuous rise in the utilization of the Internet in Thailand. The Internet Information Research Center (2006) indicated that the total number of Thai domains utilizing *dot.th* is continuously increasing from 6,766 in 2001 to 21,083 domains in 2006. Moreover, the total domestic Internet traffic in Thailand has rapidly increased from 15,167 GB per day at the beginning of 2005 to 42,154 GB per day by the end of 2005. NECTEC (2006) further indicated that the number of Internet users in Thailand increased from 3,500,000 in 2001 to 6,970,000 in 2004.

From a survey conducted by the National Statistics Office (2006) in 2004 and 2005, the number of companies utilizing computers had increased from 139,113 in 2004 to 170,744 in 2005, which represents an increase of 22.7%. The number of firms that utilize the Internet increased from 67,643 in 2004 to 89,157 in 2005, increase in percentage from 48.6% to 52.2%. As for firms that utilize Web sites for business, the number of firms increased from 8,989 firms (1.1% of total

surveyed firms) in 2004 to 30,206 firms (4%) in 2005. Of these firms, the number of firms that utilized e-commerce in business increased from about 2,300 firms in 2004 to 9,300 firms in 2005, an increase from 0.3% to 1.3% of all surveyed firms. In most of the e-commerce transactions surveyed in 2005, 21.6% of the firms that utilized e-commerce have online payment services. Moreover, the number of firms that provide e-commerce services is higher for larger enterprises.

Sales Contribution from E-Commerce

As the information provided by different organizations in Thailand have limitations in the scope of the study and cannot provide conclusions upon the sales contribution of e-commerce, an additional survey was conducted. 140 firms from 13 categories of industries[18] are surveyed. Within these companies, 57 firms are of the brick-and-click type of business model.

With respect to the analysis of the contribution of e-commerce to a firm's share of sales output, it was found that e-commerce increased sales for 82% of the firms surveyed. Table 1 provides the summary of the number of firms that are found to have increased sales after using e-commerce.

In addition, it was found that among the firms that had an increase in total sales after using e-commerce, over 40% of the firms are found to have had an increase in total sales between 1 to 20%, and over 50% had an increase in total sales between 21 and 60% after utilizing e-commerce. This implies that e-commerce adds to the existing sales in these firms and contributed to more than

Table 1. Sales contribution from e-commerce in brick-and-click firms

Sales Contribution from E-Commerce		
	No. of Firms	%
Total Brick-and-Click Firms	57	100%
- With Increase in Sales	47	82.5%
- With No Increase in Sales	10	17.5%

just substitutes the existing sales in the brick-and-mortar business model. Table 2 provides the number of brick-and-click firms that had an increase in total sales categorized according to five percentage ranges.

It is also interesting to point out that around 6% of firms had an increase in total sales of over 60 to 100% after using e-commerce. This implies that e-commerce can represent a major sales enhancement for producers, which would increase production and generate output growth to the economy.

As e-commerce is found to be significant in generating growth, the source of the growth needs to be investigated. Factors that contribute to the increase in sales from e-commerce has been investigated from firms that responded with an increase in sales after utilizing e-commerce. Table 3 summarizes the factors that producers perceive

as contributing to sales, which are classified into seven categories.

It is obvious that the factor that contributes most to the increase in sales is the provision and availability of information. Around 30% of the responses pointed out that the increase in sales was due to information availability from e-commerce, which creates more awareness and understanding of the product and triggers an increase in customer purchases.

Apart from information availability, producers also responded that e-commerce increases convenience for customers and producers in terms of contacting each other and reducing transaction and transportation costs to purchase products compared to the store front. A few respondents also mentioned that e-commerce provides 24-hour service and a cheap way to compare product costs.

Table 2. Increase in total sales from e-commerce in brick-and-click firms

Brick-and-Click Firms with Increase in Sales Categorized by % Increase in Sales from E-Commerce		
Percentage Range	**No. of Firms**	**%**
1%-20 %	20	42.6%
21%-40%	12	25.5%
41%-60%	12	25.5%
61%-80%	2	4.3%
81%-100%	1	2.1%

Table 3. Factors that induce sales from e-commerce

Factors that Induce Sales from E-Commerce	
	%
Information Availability	30.4%
Convenience	25.3%
Product Features	15.2%
Services	8.9%
Promotional Marketing	7.6%
Market Channels	6.3%
Reliability	3.8%
Others	2.5%

Another important factor contributing to increased sales from e-commerce is the increase in the variety of products and new products, which represent a product feature factor accounting for 15% of the respondents. The increase in the variety of products has a direct effect on stimulating consumer purchases. E-commerce makes the introduction of new products and development easier and faster, which facilitates rapid change in product features that better suit consumer needs and create new product developments.

Factors that Induce Sales from E-Commerce	
	%
Information Availability	30.4%
Convenience	25.3%
Product Features	15.2%
Services	8.9%
Promotional Marketing	7.6%
Market Channels	6.3%
Reliability	3.8%
Others	2.5%

Moreover, e-commerce reduces the need for inventories, providing producers with a benefit in putting more variety of products for consumers to choose from, resulting in increased sales. The fourth factor is service. E-commerce provides an improvement in service with increasing Internet options that can clarify questions for the customer about the product, such as the provision of a Web board, frequently asked questions (FAQs), and other additional services that induce customer purchases.[20] Around 8% of the respondents implied that the improved services and provision of Web boards and FAQ services had induced their sales. In addition, 7% found that promotional campaigns posted on the Internet are easily depicted and contributed to increasing sales. Strauss et al. (2003) explained that many online retailers utilize promotional pricing to encourage purchases.[21]

E-commerce also supports a wider market channel, whereby 6% of the producers perceived that e-commerce provided more channels to distribute products, contributing to the increase in sales. Producers explained that e-commerce makes it easier to reach and find target groups, supporting an expanding customer base. In addition, e-commerce creates more channels to market products to potential customers and reduces the need to stock inventories; firms can contact suppliers to send products directly to customers.[22]

The last factor, which represents about 3% of the producers' responses, is the reliability of the Web e-commerce system. A few producers pointed out that the utilization of e-commerce registration licenses provides an acceptance from the customers, which induces sales to the firms.

These factors represent important benchmarks for the development of e-commerce that would support continuous developments in ICT infrastructures to contribute to economic development and growth.

Productivity and Revenue Growth Benefits from E-Commerce

Due to the perceived increase in sales from the use of e-commerce and factors found to affect the increase in sales from e-commerce, further investigations have been taken to analyze the reasons toward the use of e-commerce. This is to see whether the benefits expected from e-commerce from previous studies are seen in the developments of e-commerce in Thailand.

With respect to the e-commerce benefit framework proposed by Hanson (2000) and Adam et al. (2002), a similar approach is taken through investigating the reasons for the producer's use of e-commerce. From a total of 28 reasons provided by the respondents, the reasons can be classified into six categories of benefits from e-commerce, which matched the framework of Hanson and Adam et al. in the productivity and revenue growth benefits framework. Table 4 shows the percentage of firms that provide the reasons for using e-commerce with respect to the five benefits that were proposed in the literature review.

With respect to the first reason of the eradication of components of the supply chain, it is found that 35% of the firms perceived that e-commerce provides the benefit in enhancing convenience for both producers and consumers in coordinating and supporting sales. From the consumer benefit perspective, 72 firms surveyed expressed that e-commerce makes it more convenient and fast for their customers in selecting products. As many as 11 firms from the 72 firms expressed that e-commerce is beneficial in providing a 24-hour service to customers, which tends to save time and costs for customers, inducing sales to the company. From the producer benefit perspective, some producers pointed out that e-commerce enhance higher efficiency in firm management, inducing marketing and sales as well as providing an easy way for exporting products, which reduces large transaction costs for the firm. In addition, several producers found that e-commerce supported a wide range of new market channels for their product at a much lower cost and reduced unnecessary processes and inventories for the firm.

The second most important reason for using e-commerce is cost savings. About 59 firms surveyed reveal that e-commerce reduces the costs in marketing and advertising products. It provides a way to market products utilizing less staff and lower cost in sending samples and brochures to customers since customers can view products online before purchasing. In addition, additional information can be sent to customers through electronic mail, which is faster and incurs a lower cost.

The third important reason for using e-commerce is the enhancement of firms' global presence. From the surveyed firms, 46 firms expressed that e-commerce provides global reach. Firms are widely recognized through the use of the Internet. Moreover, utilizing e-commerce eases firms in finding and targeting customers because it provides additional channels that make it easier for customers to access information about the firm and for firms to find information on potential customers.

The fourth and fifth reasons for using e-commerce are relatively connected as they deal with technology and product development. They represent around 11% of the firms' responses, which pointed out that e-commerce is a means of providing information on the product worldwide, making it possible for producers and consumers to compare product features with other firms and enhancing competition, product variety, and new innovations. Several firms responded that e-commerce is a way to present a variety of products and a cheaper means to introduce new products.

These are reasons that producers provide for utilizing e-commerce. It is quite evident that the benefits investigated somehow matched those

Table 4. Reasons for the use of e-commerce by Thai firms

Reasons for Using E-Commerce	
	%
Eradicate Components of Supply Chain	35.1%
Induce Cost Savings	28.8%
Enhance Global Presence	22.4%
Establish and Maintain Competitive Edge	7.3%
Enforce Research and Development	3.9%
Others	2.4%

proposed by previous studies and highly support the increasing contribution of e-commerce toward enhancing the sales of firms.

CONCLUSION

From the overall analysis, it is clear that e-commerce plays an important role in enhancing the economic growth of Thailand in the 21st century. Two important findings support the growth of e-commerce. First is the increase in sales generated by the use of e-commerce. Higher sales growth is also supported by cost reductions and cost savings found in e-commerce systems. Second, e-commerce induces the productivity development of firms through higher competition and innovation from the provision of more transparency in information availability across countries, which supports continuous output growth. As the trend in Thailand's ICT development continues to grow, it becomes evident that e-commerce supports and induces higher output growth facilitated by improved productivity, creating sustainable economic growth.

FUTURE TRENDS

As Thailand is still at the verge of expanding the e-commerce market, it has the potential to expand into additional markets by exploiting improvement in technology. With continuous improvement in technology, newer forms of product offerings can be created such as mobile commerce, which will serve as another means of enhancing sales. Thus, the evaluation of newer methods should be conducted to compare the efficiencies and benefits to that of existing methods.

In addition, the study undertaken is comprised of a broad analysis observing the contribution of e-commerce from all industries as a whole. However, e-commerce tends to be highly dependent on

technology-related industries. As a result, future studies focusing on the contribution of e-commerce to economic growth in specific industries can be conducted.

ACKNOWLEDGMENT

The authors would like to acknowledge the assistance of the ABAC Poll of Assumption University, Thailand, in compiling the data for the analysis in the chapter.

REFERENCES

AC Nielsen. (2006). *Online shopping is here to stay*. Retrieved August 20, 2006, from http://uk.acnielsen.com/insights/OnlineShopping.shtml

Adam, S., Mulye, R., Deans, K., & Palihawadana, D. (2002). E-marketing in perspective: A three country comparison of business use of the Internet. *Marketing Intelligence and Planning, 20*(4), 243-251.

Chuang, M. L., & Shaw, W. H. (2005). A roadmap for e-business implementation. *Engineering Management Journal, 17*(2), 3-13.

Darby, R., Jones, J., & Madani, G. A. (2003). E-commerce marketing: Fad or fiction? Management competency in mastering emerging technology: An international case analysis in the UAE. *Logistics Information Management, 16*(2), 106-113.

E-Commerce Resource Center (ECRC). (2006). *E-commerce for sustainable economic development*. Retrieved May 22, 2006, from http://www.ecommerce.or.th/about.html

Economist Intelligence Unit (EIU). (2006). *Industry briefing: Latest telecoms and technology data*. Retrieved August 20, 2006, from http://www.viewswire.com/index.asp?layout=homePubTypeEB

Fillis, I., Johannson, U., & Wagner, B. (2004). Factors impacting on e-business adoption and development in the smaller firm. *International Journal of Entrepreneurial Behavior and Research, 10*(3), 178-191.

Fraumeni, B. M. (2001). E-commerce: Measurement and measurement issues. *American Economic Review, 91*(2), 318-322.

Garicano, L., & Kaplan, S. N. (2001). *The effect of business-to-business e-commerce on transaction cost* (NBER Working Paper No. 8017).

Hanson, W. (2000). *Principles of Internet marketing.* South-Western, Thomson Learning.

Internet Information Research Center. (2006). *Total number of Thai domains under .TH.* Retrieved July 28, 2006, from http://iir.ngi.nectec.or.th/domain/domainths.html

Javorski, M. (2005). ICT use in small and medium business in Poland growth factors and inhibitors. In *Information society technologies in the European research area.* Academia Romana.

Keretho, S., & Limstit, P. (2002). *E-commerce the way of business in Thailand.* National Electronics and Computer Technology Center (NECTEC).

Krishnamurthy, S. (2003). *E-commerce management: Text and cases.* South-Western, Thomson Learning.

Laudon, K. C., & Traver, C. G. (2004). *E-commerce: Business, technology, society* (2nd ed.). Pearson, Addison Wesley.

Margherio, L. (1998). *An abridgement of "The Emerging Digital Economy."* Retrieved August 13, 2006, from https://www.esa.doc.gov/Reports/EmergingDig.pdf

Napier, A., Rivers, O., Wager, S., & Napier, J. B. (2006). *Creating a winning e-business* (2nd ed.). Thomson, Course Technology.

National Electronics Computer and Technology Center (NECTEC). (2006). *The number of Internet users in Thailand.* Retrieved July 28, 2006, from http://www.nectec.or.th/Internet/#iu

Ruengsrichaiya, K. (2004). On the effects of e-commerce: Equilibrium and existence of markets. *Thammasat Economic Journal, 22*(2), 139-181.

Saeed, K. A., Grover, V., & Hwang, Y. (2005). The relationship of e-commerce competence to customer value and firm performance: An empirical investigation. *Journal of Management Information Systems, 22*(1), 223-256.

Salvatore, D. (2004). *Managerial economics in a global economy* (5th ed.). South-Western, Thomson Learning.

Steven, L. K., & Session, D. N. (2005). *The relationship between poverty, economic growth, and inequality revisited* (ewp-ge/0502002). Retrieved March 15, 2006, from http://econwpa.wustl.edu/eprints/ge/papers/0502/0502002.abs#viewing

Strauss, J., El-Ansary, A., & Frost, R. (2003). *E-marketing* (3rd ed.). Prentice Hall.

Strauss, J., El-Ansary, A., & Frost, R. (2006). *E-marketing* (4th ed.). Pearson Prentice Hall.

U.S. Census Bureau. (2006). *Quarterly retail e-commerce sales 2nd quarter 2006.* Retrieved July 28, 2006, from http://www.census.gov/mrts/www/data/html/06Q2.html

Wind, J., & Mahajan, V. (2001). *Digital marketing: Global strategies from the world's leading experts.* John Wiley and Sons, Inc.

ENDNOTES

[1] See Salvatore (2004, pp. 118-125).

[2] Increasing support for e-commerce development started shortly after the Asian

economic crisis as a means to enhance SME development and the promotion of products under the OTOP (One Tambon One Product) program.

[3] B2B is an e-business model in which the e-business sells its products or services to other businesses or brings multiple buyers and sellers together. B2C is an e-business model in which the e-business sells its products or services directly to the consumer (Napier, Rivers, Wager, & Napier, 2006).

[4] Brick-and-click firms represent companies that combine brick-and-mortar business facilities with e-business operations. Brick-and-mortar firms represent businesses that conduct their transactions from a physical location or businesses with a store front (Napier et al., 2006).

[5] Data sources for the questionnaire come from the registered companies with the Department of Business Development; information on the companies is provided on the Department of Business Development Web site at http://www.dbd.go.th/edirectory (retrieved June-August 2006).

[6] Although the number of companies registered with the Department of Business Development is 2,600 companies, some companies by the time of the investigation no longer existed and some Web sites are no longer operating, which reduced the number of observations by a large amount. As a result, the study utilizes major producers in different industrial categories as samples for the survey, collecting a total of 140 surveys from 13 industrial categories.

[7] Additional information about world Internet and e-commerce trends is collected from Web site statistics, e-commerce textbooks, and other IT-related academic journals.

[8] Internet penetration represents the number of Internet users divided by the country's population. This represents the share of the population that uses the Internet.

[9] Barua, Desai, and Srivastava (as cited in Wind & Mahajan, 2001, p.102)

[10] Barua et al. (as cited in Wind & Mahajan, 2001, p.103)

[11] Garicano and Kaplan (2001) studied the changes in transaction costs as a result of B2B e-commerce and found that it reduces coordination costs and increases efficiency. Ruengsrichaiya (2004) further added that e-commerce makes markets more transparent; consumers can find products with lower transaction costs and are able to easily compare prices from different manufacturers.

[12] See Ruengsrichaiya (2004) and Garicano and Kaplan (2001).

[13] Impulse buying is purchasing with little or no advanced planning as shoppers surf the Net. The provision of options represents additional alternatives for shoppers. The buyer evaluation process represents the comparison and evaluation of product features available on the Internet, which induces purchasing.

[14] See Hanson (2000, p. 127).

[15] See Hanson (2000, pp. 128-129).

[16] See Hanson (2000, pp. 132-136).

[17] See Strauss et al. (2006, p. 412).

[18] Includes the automotive, jewelry, chemical and drug, office-appliance, computer and accessories, entertainment, food and beverage, furniture, tourism, apparel, industrial equipment, gift, and other industries. These categories are assigned with respect to the categorization of industries from the Department of Business Development.

[19] Hanson (2000) also pointed out that the Internet induces the speed of product innovation; producers are forced to continuously find new ways in discovering user needs and rapidly launch new products to support the change in consumer needs. Such methods tend to rely on high flexibility and speed in processing market feedback.

[20] Strauss et al. (2003) reflect that customer service is enhanced by the ability to receive customer feedback. The use of e-mail 24 hours a day provides the ability to respond more rapidly to customer concerns even if the telephone operator and customer service personnel are not available.

[21] Strauss et al. (2003) mentioned that promotional pricing encourages a first purchase, encourages repeat business, and closes sales. It provides an expiration date that helps create a sense of urgency for the consumer.

[22] Strauss et al. (2003) discussed the use of e-commerce as a channel to shift sales to manufacturers directly.

Chapter XI
IT and Software Industry in Vietnam

Yuko Iwasaki
Yokkaichi University, Japan

ABSTRACT

Vietnam has been advancing toward a market economy since 1986. Industrialization has progressed with a high rate of growth. One of the factors of the economic growth of Vietnam has been FDI. Japanese companies are among those that have a strong interest in Vietnam. Japanese companies are recently taking note of Vietnam's IT and software industries. Now, however, interest is increasing in offshoring as a means for developing in this sector.

INTRODUCTION

Vietnam has been advancing toward a market economy since 1986. After the Asian currency crisis in 1997, foreign direct investment (FDI) decreased and the growth rate slowed down, but since then, the country has followed a trend of recovery and industrialization has progressed with a high rate of growth.

One of the factors of the economic growth of Vietnam has been FDI. Japanese companies are among those that have a strong interest in Vietnam. Up until now, the manufacturing industry has been at the center of Japanese companies' investment in Vietnam. However, Japanese companies are recently taking note of Vietnam's IT and software industries. Now, interest is increasing in offshoring as a means for developing in this sector.

In this chapter, the Vietnamese IT and software industries are surveyed, and the relations between Japan and Vietnam that have led to offshoring are considered.

RECENT ECONOMIC DEVELOPMENT

Since its adoption of the Doi Moi policy in 1986, Vietnam has promoted a market economy while also maintaining a socialist system. Due to the effort of the Doi Moi policy, FDI increased up to the first half of the 1990s, and high growth was recorded. However, after the Asian currency crisis of 1997, FDI decreased again, and the growth rate became slow. Since then, the present tendency has been maintained and the growth rate in 2005 showed a high 8.4% rate of growth with the progress of industrialization. Domestic demand was strong, and exports also remained strong.

While the manufacturing and service sectors expanded, the share of agriculture in the economy continued to decline (although it is still a major sector in terms of employment). Exports of electric goods continued to drive growth. Good performance was recorded.

FDI has been one of the factors of economic growth since 2000. Recently, with the increasing risks posed by the worsening business environment in China, Vietnam, with its low labor costs and stable political climate, is highly appreciated by investors anxious to spread their risks. Investment is increasing mainly in the manufacturing industry. Major investors are Japanese companies related to computers, electrical parts, automobile parts, motorbikes, and printers. Also, the Vietnamese government has improved businesses conditions for foreign firms.

Vietnam enjoys an especially high estimate among Japanese companies, whose direct investment in the country is increasing. In a medium-term survey conducted by the Japan Bank for International Cooperation (JBIC, 2005), Vietnam was ranked fourth in the world as a promising site for enterprise development (in approximately the next 3 years). For the longer term (approximately 10 years), it was ranked third by Japanese companies (Table 1).

Among the reasons given for this were the cheap labor force, the country's attractiveness as a catcher for the risk, and its outstanding human resources. On the other hand, problems still to overcome include the insufficient infrastructure and the inadequacies and lack of transparency in the legal system.

As for its external economic relations, Vietnam participates in such organizations of regional integration as the Association of Southeast Asian Nations (ASEAN), the ASEAN Free Trade Area (AFTA), and the Asia Pacific Economic Cooperation (APEC). Its affiliation with the World Trade Organization (WTO) is expected to come about in 2006. Once Vietnam is affiliated with WTO, trade liberalization and the opening of the domestic market to foreign companies will be pursued.

Table 1. Promising countries and regions for overseas business operations over the medium and long terms (Source: JBIC, 2005)

Rank	Medium Term (next 3 years or so)	Long Term (next 10 years or so)
1	China	China
2	India	India
3	Thailand	**Vietnam**
4	**Vietnam**	Russia
5	U.S.A.	Thailand
6	Russia	U.S.A.
7	South Korea	Brazil
8	Indonesia	Indonesia
9	Brazil	South Korea
10	Taiwan	Malaysia

In Vietnam, state-owned enterprises have so far borne an important role in achieving national prosperity through industrial development. However, with the current trend toward trade liberalization seen in economic globalization, the affiliation with WTO, and so on, competition with other countries has become very severe. For Vietnam, it is now vital to press on with the reform of state enterprises and to strengthen its competitiveness in the international market.

THE LEVEL OF IT IN VIETNAM

Vietnam is behind in its IT progress by any world standard. For example, in *The 2006 E-Readiness Rankings* (Economist Intelligence Unit), which

Table 2. IT indicators in Vietnam and Asian countries (Source: International Telecommunication Union [ITU])

	Main Telephone Lines per 100 Inhabitants		Cellular Mobile Subscribers per 100 Inhabitants	
	2000	2005	2000	2005
Vietnam	3.23	18.81	1.00	9.54
China	11.18	26.63	0.35	29.90
India	3.20	4.51	6.58	8.16
Asia	9.73	15.77	6.63	23.22

	Internet Users per 100 Inhabitants		PCs per 100 Inhabitants	
	2000	2005	2000	2005
Vietnam	0.25	12.72	0.76	1.26
China	1.74	8.44	1.59	4.08
India	0.25	5.44	0.76	1.54
Asia	3.10	9.78	3.24	6.51

	Main Telephone Lines per 100 Inhabitants		Cellular Mobile Subscribers per 100 Inhabitants	
ASEAN4	2000	2005	2000	2005
Indonesia	3.23	5.73	1.78	21.06
Malaysia	19.92	16.79	22.01	75.17
Philippines	4.00	4.16	8.44	39.5
Thailand	9.10	10.95	4.97	42.98

	Internet Users per 100 Inhabitants		PCs per 100 Inhabitants	
ASEAN4	2000	2005	2000	2005
Indonesia	0.92	7.18	1.02	1.36
Malaysia	21.39	42.37	9.45	19.16
Philippines	2.01	5.32	1.93	4.46
Thailand	3.74	11.03	2.79	5.58

investigated the diffusion of IT and the state of the fulfillment of businesses based on digital environments in countries around the world, Vietnam is placed at the very low level of 15th out of the 16 Asian nations surveyed, and 66th among 68 nations worldwide. (In 2005, it was ranked 15th out of 16 Asian nations and 61st among 65 nations worldwide.) This is a report that summarizes statistics on the diffusion of PCs (personal computers) and the Internet, the use of IT by firms and consumers, the digital response level of legal facilities and educational organizations, and so forth in various countries.

However, the diffusion of main and cellular phones and the Internet is now picking up in pace. Table 2 gives the diffusion of phones, the Internet, and PCs in Vietnam and other Asian countries. The data show the IT diffusion on an upward trend for Asian countries. In Vietnam, the diffusion of main phone lines was 18.8% and that of mobile phones was 9.54% (in 2005). The Internet user data of Vietnam and China was behind ASEAN4 countries in 2000, but are picking up. Vietnamese IT infrastructures have improved rapidly, especially for main phones and the Internet. However, most Internet users are concentrated in Hanoi and Ho Chi Minh City (approximately 70%). The Ministry of Posts and Telecomatics continues to lower charges for Internet and telecommunications services to expand the number of Internet users.

IT DEVELOPMENT IN ASIA

Asian countries have played an important and active role in IT development, especially in the PC industry. The newly industrialized economies (NIEs) and ASEAN countries showed rapid growth in IT manufacturing and trading since 1980s. These economies have made significant contributions to the global supply of IT products and components. As products matured, their production was relocated to low-cost areas.

During the last 10 years, China and India have joined in IT development. China has become a major production hub for IT products, and now the IT software industry has developed in both India and China. China's software exports have expanded rapidly. In 2005, China's software exports were valued at $3.6 billion, up from $7 million in 2001. Major export partners are Japan (approximately 60%) and the Unites States and Europe (20%).

India is now a major IT software producer and exporter in the world. IT development in India has differed from that in the other Asian countries. Highly trained scientific and technical personnel from India have been migrating to the United States since the 1960s, and many of them were engaged in the development of computers and the communications industry. The high-level skills of India supplied qualified personnel to do jobs on site (in the United States) at first. After that, major IT producers set up subsidiary software centers in India (Braum, 2001).

As mentioned, India has highly skilled IT workers, and the business form of India is converting from that of onshore to offshore. While operating onshore means doing business in the customer's country (for example, in the United States or Europe), offshoring means producing software in India by Indian personnel. Lower prices and high-level skills have made the Indian software industry very competitive.

THE MARKET SCALE OF THE VIETNAMESE IT INDUSTRY

The market volume of the IT industry in Vietnam in 2005 was $828 million ($630 million in hardware and $190 million in software), an increase of 20.9% compared with the year before. In 1996, the market had only been worth $150 million, rising to $300 million in 2000 (Table 3).

IT-RELATED POLICY

The 2005 Plan for IT Use and Development was announced as a national policy in 2001. This plan proposed the following basic targets in order to bring the country's IT level up to the global standard by 2005:

- The diffusion of IT across the whole of Vietnam.
- 4 to 5% of the population as Internet users.
- An annual growth rate of 20 to 25% in the IT industry.
- The training of 50,000 IT specialists.

The putting in place of a telecom infrastructure was achieved ahead of the target. However, the training of competent personnel fell short of the target, not going above 20,000 employees. IT specialists are in short supply in Vietnam.

The announcement followed in 2005 of the Development Strategy for Information Communication Technology up to 2010 and of the Policy Plan up to 2020. This strategy and plan will serve as the foundation of Vietnam's future IT policy. In them, the most effective tool for national information development and modernization, and the importance of utilizing IT in economics and industry were brought out (e-citizenship, e-government, e-enterprises, e-transactions, and e-commerce). Moreover, high priority was given to the nurturing of an IT industry, especially the software and information-content industries, as a means of encouraging the creation and development of an information society. The policy also attaches importance to the laying of an IT infrastructure and the training of component specialists. The targets up to 2010 and 2015 for the promotion of IT use in economics and industry are as follows:

- By 2010, the IT industry will be promoted to the country's top industry, with a year-to-year growth rate of 20 to 25% and gross annual earnings of $6 to 7 billion.
- Through promotion of the IT infrastructure, the target for 2010 is to ensure 30 to 42 telephones per 100 people, 8 to 12 Internet service accounts (30% of them broadband), an Internet diffusion rate of 25 to 30%, and personal computer ownership of 10 per 100 people.
- By 2015, the diffusion of fixed telephones will be lowered to 20 per 100 people, while that of cellular phones will be raised to 30.

To ensure that the targets for 2010 and 2015 are attained, a range of definite measures have been specified:

Table 3. Trends of the market scale (millions USD; Source: Ho Chi Minh City Computer Association, 2006)

Year	Total	Hardware	Software
2000	300	250	50
2001	340	250	60
2002	400	325	75
2003	515	410	105
2004	685	545	140
2005	828	630	178

- Diffusion of IT knowledge.
- Promotion of practical uses for IT.
- Reinforcement of state's IT administration capacity.
- Ensuring of attractive conditions for foreign capital.
- Increasing of quantity and quality of IT labor.
- Strengthening of research and development system.
- Enhancement of legal environment in support of IT.
- Domestic and international cooperation.
- Integration with international IT market, especially for software and contents.

THE SOFTWARE INDUSTRY AND OFFSHORING

Within the industry, one of the fields that the government sees as very important is the software industry. The value of the software industry market in Vietnam in 2004 was $140 million. This marked a spectacular increase from $75million in 2002 and $105 million in 2003. 25% of the profits in the software industry are obtained from exports overseas. Vietnam started exports of software in 1997.

OFFSHORING

Behind the recent market expansion in Vietnam, one factor that can be mentioned is an increase in outsourcing (offshoring) for overseas products.

Offshoring is the entrusting of part of a system development to a firm in another country (Figure 1). It has the advantage when using cheap and plentiful workforces.

Inspired by the example of India, which achieved rapid growth through offshoring from America and Europe, moves have been made by Vietnam to make use of its trained labor force to build up a software industry. Firms have also increased to about 600 by the end of 2005. Looking at them regionally, about 30% of these firms are located in Ho Chi Minh City or Hanoi. Corporate competition is intensifying with the increase in the number of companies. The following are some examples of the main software companies.

- FTP Software (Hanoi)
- TMA Software (Ho Chi Minh City
- Paragon Solutions Vietnam (PSV; Ho Chi Minh City)
- Silk Road (Ho Chi Minh City)
- Global Cybersoft (Ho Chi Minh City)

These companies have earned a name for reliable quality by acquiring CMM (capability maturity model) and CMMI (capability maturity model integration) under a quality-control standard code that objectively shows their capacity in developing software. Vietnam enjoys the following advantages in its software industry. First, its labor costs are cheap (about 60 to 70% of the cost in China), and the proportion of young people in the population is high. Second, the will to study is high and levels are excellent in the scientific and math fields. The potential for competitiveness in the software industry is ample.

Figure 1. An example of offshoring (Source: Ministry of Economy, Trade, and Industry [MEIT], 2006)

□ → Proposal	□ → System planning	□ → System design	□ → System manufacture	□ Operations and maintenance
Firm placing original order	Firm placing original order	Partly entrusted to overseas firm	Partly entrusted to overseas firm	Firm placing original order

However, there are few software companies of a scale exceeding 100 employees, and a lot of small and medium-sized enterprises exist. This poses the problem of a shortage of outstanding human resources in the industry as a whole. The training of competent personnel will be a challenge for the future. The government is setting preferential measures of taxation for the promotion of the software industry.

The market value of offshoring in 2005 was $70 million. In 2002 the market had only been worth $20 million.

OFFSHORING BY JAPANESE COMPANIES

Offshoring by Japanese companies can be seen to have increased rapidly in the past several years. The scale of Japanese offshoring, which was ¥20 billion in 2002, rose to ¥48.9 billion and then ¥52.7 billion in 2004 (Table 4). The background cause for this increase is that while the scale of software development is growing, the shortage of

trained labor in Japan is serious, and in order to cope with shortening development times and the need for cost cutting, firms are therefore seeking a cheep and abundant labor force overseas.

With their cheap and plentiful workforces, India and China both make attractive offshoring sites, but for firms in Japan, China is the country most usually chosen on account of the geographical nearness and the fact there is a high level of aptitude for mastering Japanese.

The technical levels of companies in China and India are improving with the increase in the offshoring from Japan and the West. Points particularly attended to by Japanese companies when choosing an offshoring partner are the quality and quantity of technical workers available, whether Japanese can be understood, and whether the dealing prices are right. Although the volume of business with Vietnam is still small, Japanese companies are considering it as a new offshoring site. The scale of offshoring in Vietnam in 2004 showed a rapid seven-fold increase compared with the year before. Behind this growth lies the fact that the Vietnamese software industry

Table 4. The scale of offshoring by Japanese companies (millions of Yen; Source: Japan Information Technology Services Industry Association [JISA], 2005)

	2004	Share (%)	Compared with 2003 (%)
China	33,241	63.1	+26.5
U.S.A.	5,147	9.8	+3.2
India	4,255	8.1	-32.6
Australia	3,133	5.9	+19.3
U.K.	2,126	4.0	+16.4
Philippines	2,117	4.0	-15.1
South Korea	1,415	2.7	-24.4
France	548	1.0	-34.3
Canada	262	0.5	-57.5
Vietnam	216	0.4	+620.0
Others	237	0.4	-78.1
Total	52,697	100.0	+28.1

recognizes Japan as an important market and has expanded its business in that direction. In 2005, the software association of Vietnam (Vietnam Software Association, VINASA) announced its 5-year plan for the development of the software industry (2006 to 2010). This plan sets a target of $1 billion in annual sales for software by 2010, with $400 million heading for Japan. Japanese companies are keenly observing Vietnam as a country where they can rely on finding excellently skilled workers at low cost.

As we have seen, Vietnam's purpose is changing to a market economy and introducing foreign capital to promote the IT industry with the aim of rapidly catching up with its nearby neighbors. With affiliation with WTO scheduled for 2006, this trend toward open markets and economic reform will progress further. Furthermore, there will also no doubt be improvement in the investment climate for foreign companies. For relations between Japan and Vietnam with regard to IT, while it is important to continue with the economic relations built up in the past through official development assistance (ODA) and FDI, it is also especially vital that the Japanese government and private firms should cooperate in the training of Vietnamese personnel.

CONCLUSION

For the ordering company, offshoring has merits, such as a reduction in development costs and the shortening of development times. On the other hand, for the country receiving orders, the government and private firms put more importance on policies for the fostering of information technology industries, both for the sake of economic growth and secure employment, and also for the furtherance of the information society. The proof of the effectiveness of this approach has already been seen in India.

In offshoring activities of Japanese companies, the values recognized with regard to China and India are well-established, and the time is now ripe to move on to the next stage. As a new location for offshoring, firms are taking close note of Vietnam, although many challenges exist in the present development of Vietnamese enterprises. One of the problems is a shortage of outstanding human resources in the industry as a whole. The training of competent personnel will be a challenge for the future. This will create a pool of highly skilled personnel that will be a foundation for the industry.

For Japan and Vietnam, which is still a developing country, it is important on both sides to work for an expansion of business by building a partnership for such aims as the training of IT personnel.

REFERENCES

Asia Development Bank (ADB). (2000). *Asian development outlook 2000 update.* Retrieved August 1, 2006, from http://www.adb.org/

Asia Development Bank (ADB). (2006a). *Asian development outlook 2006.* Retrieved August 1, 2006, from http://www.adb.org/

Asia Development Bank (ADB). (2006b). *Asian development outlook 2006 update.* Retrieved August 31, 2006, from http://www.adb.org/

Asia Development Bank (ADB). (2006c). *Key indicators 2006.* Retrieved August 1, 2006, from http://www.adb.org/

Braum, P. (2001). *Information and communication technology in developing countries of Asia.* Retrieved August 1, 2006, from http://www.adb.org/

Center of the International Cooperation for Computerization (CICC). (2005). *Asia computerization report (Vietnam).* Tokyo.

Center of the International Cooperation for Computerization (CICC). (2006). *Asia computerization report (Vietnam)*. Tokyo.

Erran, C., & Paul, T. (2005). *Offshoring information technology*. Cambridge: Cambridge University Press.

Ho Chi Minh City Computer Association. (2006). *Vietnam ICT outlook 2006*. Retrieved August 1, 2006, from http://www.hca,org.vn/

Japan Bank for International Cooperation (JBIC). (2005). Survey report on overseas business operations by Japanese manufacturing companies. *JBICI Review, 13*. Retrieved August 1, 2006, from http://www.jbic.go.jp/english/research/report/review/

Japan Information Technology Services Industry Association (JISA). (2005). *Survey of overseas dealings in the computer software field 2005*. Retrieved August 1, 2006, from http://www.jisa.or.jp/

Ministry of Economy, Trade, and Industry (MEIT). (2006). *2006 white paper on international economy and trade*. Retrieved August 31, 2006, from http://www.meti.go.jp/

Ministry of Internal Affairs and Telecommunication. (2006). *2006 White paper on information and communications in Japan*. Retrieved August 31, 2006, from http://www.soumu.go.jp/menu_05/hakusyo/index.html

Section III
Innovative Engineering in IT

Chapter XII
The Influence of New Information and Communication Technologies on Transaction Costs of Micro-, Small- and, Medium-Sized Enterprises

Utz Dornberger
University of Leipzig, Germany

Luis E. Bernal Vera
University of Leipzig, Germany

Alejandro Sosa Noreña
University of Leipzig, Germany

ABSTRACT

This chapter discusses the relationship between the use of information and communication technologies and transaction costs within micro, small, and medium-sized enterprises (MSMEs). The fundamental problem in this relationship is the asymmetric distribution of information. This asymmetry leads to problems such as adverse selection and moral hazards. Thus, the links between ICTs and the improvement of economic performance can be explained based on the capability of these technologies in reducing information asymmetries and therefore increasing firms' competitiveness. In the case of MSMEs, implementing new ICTs help diminish their frequent lack of information. However, the reduction of transaction costs and their better performance depend not only on the use of ICTs, but also on the integration of these technologies in the strategies and day-to-day activities of the MSMEs. For this reason, the training of the personnel and management is crucial when implementing ICTs in these firms.

INTRODUCTION

The links between new information and communication technologies and the improvement of the economic performance of enterprises can be explained based on the capability of these technologies in reducing information asymmetries. Due to the reduction of information asymmetries, it is possible to reduce transaction costs of the respective companies, which is reflected in their economic performance. Furthermore, the new ICTs increase the entrepreneur's negotiating power with his or her customers and suppliers as well as foster the creation of new business connections. From this, there is a contribution to the optimization of the competitive position of companies, which influences their commercial and economic performance.

All these benefits are derived from the adaptation of new technologies in the day-to-day activities of the firm and are perfectly applicable to micro, small, and medium-sized enterprises (MSMEs). In fact, it is within this economic sector where companies can profit most from the implementation of these new technologies. Implementing new ICTs enables companies to diminish the problematic lack of information they often face. In this way, these firms get stronger due to their inherent flexibility (owing to their own small-sized nature), and this in the end represents a differential advantage in the competitive world of business.

However, there is still a debate regarding whether and how the adoption of ICTs reduces transaction costs and improves firm competitiveness. Several empirical studies could not establish a clear correlation between the adoption of ICTs and performance indicators of the respective MSMEs.

This chapter provides the theoretical background and empirical evidence to discuss the relationship between the use of ICTs and transaction costs within MSMEs. It also analyzes different factors that could help interpret the controversial results of empirical investigations, makes recommendations on how ICTs could be better utilized, and provides insight into future research trends.

THEORETICAL BACKGROUND

Transaction Costs, Economic Development, and ICTs

The transaction costs theory defined by Ronald Coase (1937) in his article "The Nature of the Firm" suggests that the main reason for establishing a firm was the existence of costs for using the price mechanism of the market. As opposed to the principles of Neoclassicism, Coase establishes that market information is not complete and that limited human mental capacity exists for its processing (North, 1995). However, the amount of information is limited mainly because the information spreads asymmetrically. This asymmetry constitutes one of the main reasons for high transaction costs, uncertainty, and therefore deficits in approaching the market. The proper use of ICTs reduces this distribution of inequality by producing the contrary effect, hence leading to the reduction of transaction costs and uncertainty as well as the increase of market efficiency.

Leff (1984) and Norton (1992) establish a clear correlation between transactional costs and development, and telecommunications.[1] Norton bases this relation on two facts. First, in many underdeveloped economies, there exists a lack of information due to its high access costs. Hence, these economies possess poor information markets, leading, as a result, to inefficient decisions. Second, when using telecommunication facilities, the information can flow easier, increasing the market efficiencies by improving the decision-making process and reducing transactional costs.

In an attempt to give a more detailed explanation of the relationship between telecommunications, the reduction of transaction costs, and economic growth, Leff (1984) affirms that telecommunications allow for a reduction in the fixed costs of acquiring information as well as the variable costs of participating in the market, thus promoting economic improvement of these organizations using the market.

The increased costs of information transmission lead to a reduction in the quantity and quality of the available information. At this point, the influence of using ICTs increases in importance because it should reduce the cost of acquiring information. This cost reduction illustrates benefits in both the quality and quantity of acquired information, which in turn improve the decision-making processes of the firms. The consequence is an overall increase in efficiency of public and private organizations, finally reflecting generalized economic growth.

In short, the expansion of better telecommunication technologies consequently leads to the reduction of costs in the acquisition of new information. This effect produces a decrease of uncertainty, promoting an increase in arbitrage,[2] market efficiency, and participation in the market. All these factors also have a direct influence on economic growth.

These affirmations were demonstrated empirically by Norton (1992). In his empirical analysis, which was made by using an equation for determining the level of a country's development and the influence of the telecommunications factor on it, he observed the following:

- There is a strong and positive correlation between the indicators of the telecommunications infrastructure and the respective economic growth.
- Telecommunications increase growth by reducing macroeconomic uncertainty. This issue is demonstrated by the fact that the average number of telephones shows a strong negative effect on the monetary instability of a country.

Thanks to the reduction of transaction costs caused by the use of telecommunications, the efficiency of capital markets and investment channels increased. Norton (1992) finally concludes that, although these data have to be considered with caution, his analyses show that the communication infrastructure is crucial for economic growth. Thus, the communication infrastructure becomes an aid for activities that improve the development and promotion of investments. Nevertheless, this factor is less important than other conventional macroeconomic forces like, for example, stable monetary growth, low inflation rates, or the level of market openness.

Influence of ICT on Business Transactions of MSMEs

As mentioned above, one of the fundamental problems faced when talking about the relationship between transaction costs, ICTs, and economic development is the asymmetric distribution of information on the market. This asymmetry consequently leads to new problems such as adverse selection and moral risks in economic relationships.

Adverse selection occurs when, due to the information inequalities between the buyer and seller, bad products or customers have a higher probability of being chosen. A clear example of choosing bad products due to a lack of information is the case of used-cars sales. In this case, the seller of used cars knows which cars are good and which are bad. The seller looks for chances to take advantage of this information, intending to sell the bad cars by hiding important information to the buyer. The opposite case is the health insurance business. Here, the insurance holder is the one possessing more information about his or her habits and customs, which might endanger his or her health. The insurance holder can hide this information from the insurance company in order to get a lower premium. In this case, the insurance company bears the risk of choosing a bad insurance holder.

The moral risk is the risk of one contracting party changing his or her behavior and causing damage to the other party after signing a contract. Insurance companies can once again illustrate an example of this problem. After signing an insurance agreement against theft, if the insurance holder suffers an assault, the insurance company, due to a lack of information, has to verify that the robbery really happened.

Information asymmetry leads to problems closely connected to three kinds of transaction costs:

- Transaction costs ex ante, that is, previous to concluding a contract. These are the costs of searching for information about business partners and products or services. These costs are related to the adverse-selection issue.
- Negotiation and decision costs that occur during the process of signing a contract.
- Transaction costs ex post, that is, costs appearing after signing a contract. These costs are related to the moral-risk problem.

Normally, MSMEs are hardly affected by the information asymmetries mainly caused by the lack of knowledge of the market. However, this problem often cannot be avoided due to the high transaction costs arising by trying to increase the amount of information close to the market where MSMEs are participating. A way to reduce this information asymmetry and to reach positive effects in reducing transaction costs is the use of ICTs. Applying ICTs, MSMEs can reduce the costs of searching for information, negotiating, and controlling. This reduction of costs reduces the information asymmetry and allows small businesses to participate in the market in a more active way. This improved participation leads to a reduced risk of making wrong decisions due to a lack of information.

Flexibility is an important competitive characteristic of the MSMEs that enables them to adapt to fast-changing market environments. Adaptability to market fluctuations is considered to be strongly influenced by the quantity of information MSMEs obtain from their competitive surroundings. In this aspect, ICT's capacity to improve information flowing between companies becomes a promoting factor of the flexibility in this economic sector.

The capacity of a company to acquire customers and suppliers is closely tied to its competitiveness. This is also influenced by the information that flows through the enterprise. The relationship between competitiveness and information is deeply discussed by McFarlan (1984) and Porter and Millar (1985). While McFarlan determines in which way information technology has changed competition in markets, Porter and Millar gives a deeper insight into the role information plays as part of a company's competitiveness. The improved access to market information by using ICTs favors the company's negotiating power with its customers and suppliers. Furthermore, ICTs help strengthen already existing business relations with customers and/or suppliers.

CONTROVERSIAL EMPIRICAL EVIDENCE

Despite the potential benefits of ICTs, there is a debate on whether and how the adoption of ICTs improves the performance of enterprises. While many empirical studies provide evidence of the positive effects of ICT adoption on the performance of the firm (Brynjolfsson & Hitt, 2000; Matambalaya & Wolf, 2001; Müller-Falcke, 2002; Organization for Economic Cooperation and Development [OECD], 2004) Others have shown no relation between computer use and firms' performance (Bitler, 2001). A large statistical survey prepared in 13 OECD countries provides evidence that the use of ICTs has contributed to improve firm performance in terms of increased market share, expanded product range, customized products, and better response to clients' demand. In developing countries, studies in East Africa (Matambalaya & Wolf) and India (Müller-Falcke) show that ICTs have a positive impact on the productivity of MSMEs.

On the other hand, a study carried out in 1998 by the U.S. Survey of Small Business Finances (SSBF), which focused on firms with fewer than 500 employees, suggests that firm performance, as measured by profit or sales, is not associated with computer use (Bitler, 2001).

Controversial results were also obtained by empirical investigations focusing on the impact of ICTs on transaction costs as well as customer development in MSMEs. Lohrke, McClure Franklin, and Frownfelter-Lohrke (2006) highlighted that MSMEs can apply ICTs to establish direct customer contact, thereby reducing reliance on channel intermediaries for customer support. MSMEs facing high asset specificity in product information transmitted to and received from customers employed the Internet to a greater degree than those facing lower information specificity. These findings highlight the important benefit that Internet use can provide in reducing the transaction costs of MSMEs (Lohrke et al.). The fact that ICTs increase business relations is substantiated by another empirical study published by the United States Agency for International Development (USAID, 2000) regarding projects promoting the use of ICTs in Croatia. One of the study's conclusions indicated that the application of ICTs caused the creation of 285 new business relations on a local, regional, and national level in the participating countries.

In contrast, a large empirical study of 1,915 micro and small-sized enterprises analyzing the impact of ICTs on transaction costs as well as the capability to gain new clients and suppliers shows different results (Bernal Vera, 2005). Based on the research data, the author found it was neither possible to reject nor to corroborate the influence of new ICTs on transaction costs. Furthermore, a significant correlation between the use of new ICTs and access to new clients and suppliers could not be observed. The main reasons are as follows:

- Despite the high perception regarding the importance of the use of the new ICTs (e.g., the Internet) in managerial activities, these technologies still do not have the usage level of traditional technologies like the telephone. This means that Peruvian MSMEs are still not taking full advantage of the benefits of the new ICTs.
- Even though most of the firms in this survey agreed that the importance of using computer programs for controlling their internal activities was very high, its implementation inside the evaluated enterprises is still at an intermediary stage.
- Regarding the use of the Internet, indicators show a very advanced stage of connectivity of the investigated MSMEs. Furthermore, the great importance of "Internet cabins" as Web connectivity promoters for small enterprises could be proved. However, in spite of the high connectivity indexes, the number of MSMEs that have an active presence on the Internet was very low. This situation shows that these MSMEs are not able to take full advantage of the benefits regarding their commercial contacts that are possible to achieve using this technology.
- It is important to note the low level of investment in new ICTs that is revealed by this study. Although the usage index of these kinds of technologies among the studied firms is high, the lack of investment in both updated equipment and training in the use of new ICTs may limit the future benefits derived from the utilization of these technologies.

The main conclusion of this study is that a high level of ICT infrastructure does not represent a competitive factor per se. ICTs offer tools that, if used in a proper way, increase the enterprise's competitiveness. For this reason, the demonstration of better economic performance depends not only on the use of these technologies, but also on the integration of these technologies in the entrepreneurial strategies of the MSMEs.

SOLUTIONS AND RECOMMENDATIONS

The claims that the high acquisition costs of the new technologies impede the access of micro and small businesses to them have been losing importance over time. The constant reduction in the prices of hardware, software, and telecommunications has brought along higher accessibility for all current and potential users, including the MSMEs. An excellent example of this matter is Peru, where public access points play a very important role as connectivity promoters for MSMEs. Regarding Internet penetration, Peru is one of the most advanced countries in South America. This is manly because at the end of the 1990s, there was a rapid expansion of so-called public Internet cabins. According to the Organismo Supervisor de Inversión Privada en Telecomunicaciones (OSIPTEL, 2005), the Peruvian agency for the supervision of private investment in the telecommunications sector, at the end of the year 2005, there were more than 33,600 public Internet cabins all around the country. Due to their quantity and diffusion, these kinds of business units are nowadays the main access point to the Internet in the micro- and small-business sector.

One of the crucial factors that must be taken into account when dealing with the implementation of ICTs in MSMEs is the human factor, especially the capacity of the people inside the organization to assimilate the new technologies and ways of doing things. For these reasons, it is important to develop programs directed toward the acquisition of skills for maximizing the usage of information technologies within MSMEs. In

this way, internal barriers and resistance when it comes to the implementation of a new way of working and interacting with the clients and suppliers is not traumatic and is even proactive. Employees could be trained in such a way that they, by their own initiative, request changes and demand new implementations. Therefore, investment in new ICTs must be accompanied by training programs in the areas of strategy and entrepreneurial planning directed toward these specific kinds of enterprises. This will allow the MSMEs to clearly define both their goals as an enterprise as well as the ways they could benefit from the new ICTs when reaching these objectives. Training programs need to be more focused on managerial understanding and skills for the successful application of ICTs in order to get them integrated (formally) in the business strategy of the firm. The effective integration of e-business approaches in the marketing strategies of enterprises could be a typical example.

Recent studies in countries that are members of OECD (2004) show that most governments provide ICT training or training support. Financial support to cover part of the training costs is a common strategy in governmental training programs. Interestingly, several programs provide training and business consultation services dedicated to enhancing the integration of ICT and business strategies in enterprises. The U.K. Online for Business initiative is an example of such a program combining online training resources with off-line business support services. On the other hand, governments should also develop a favorable business environment that supports private ICT training and consulting providers offering more specialized services at reasonable prices. In fast-changing environments, governmental training programs can transfer basic ICT knowledge to MSMEs, whereas commercial training services may be more sensitive to the more specific needs of their clients.

It is very important to make the MSMEs aware of the strategic importance of using ICTs for their own businesses in terms of the diminution of transaction costs as well as the differentiation that could be achieved over the competitors by implementing these technologies in an agile way and pressuring the utilization of these features inside their industry. In doing this, active MSMEs can force the exit of weak competitors that are not able to catch up and compete within the new market condition. Being the first in using a certain type of technology can easily develop into the denomination and recognition of being the company setting the standards in the market (or at least in the niche), which is very valuable in developing a successful strategy. As highlighted by Lohrke et al. (2006), MSMEs can use the Internet for establishing direct contacts with customers. MSMEs must take into account the range of possibilities of becoming integrated with their suppliers and clients by offering special services such as inventory administration, logistics coordination, demand forecast, and so forth based on ICT applications.

FUTURE TRENDS

International organizations have cited a myriad of benefits to MSMEs that can be gained from the adoption of new ICTs. Despite these benefits, MSMEs in developing countries as well as in OECD countries have shown different levels of ICT investment and use. The following trends will influence the adoption of ICTs in MSMEs in the near future, and will ultimately lead to a stronger division of ICT and non-ICT users in every economic sector.

- As in the case of Peru, the role played by the state is crucial in promoting the use and importance of new ICTs. In developing countries, the trend will be, from the side of the state, to move a large part of the information flow to the Internet. In this way, the calls and new contracts of the governments will grow in transparency and accessibility for smaller firms, and enterprises will transfer other contact possibilities to authorities and agencies. Additionally, governments will also choose this information channel for providing information and receiving reports, like tax declarations and license applications. This situation will contribute to increase the motivation of formal registered MSMEs to obtain access to the Internet.

- Another important trend in the role played by the ICTs inside the MSMEs is the new generation's takeover. Young people are more likely to be familiarized with the new ICTs and apply them actively in several situations of their lives. Since a large part of the MSMEs are family businesses, there is a clear trend that the more influence the younger generation of the family clan has over their firms, the more intense the use of ICTs inside of them will be.

- Since the portion of MSMEs in developing countries using ICTs actively is relatively low, those enterprises utilizing them still possess a special feature that gives them a certain advantage when compared to their competitors. The trend in the developing countries will be the gradual recognition of the advantages that the use of ICTs produces, leading to the implementation of ICTs in more and more companies. Simultaneously, the rest of the companies will realize the danger of not taking the adoption of ICTs seriously, for without them, it will be difficult to survive.

- It is expected that those enterprises that are increasing their business activities in foreign countries will reinforce their own presence on the Internet due to strategic reasons; however, for the rest of the enterprises, the motivation of appearing online will remain low since this tool is still not perceived as an advantage and is relatively demanding in terms of time.

Future research can be built on the present findings by investigating the impact of ICT adoption on business performance in different sectors. Small traders or service firms may employ ICTs in different ways as in manufacturing firms. Distributors and retailers will especially benefit from the increasing connectivity of society in developing countries, resulting in new business-to-client interfaces that will be easily applicable for MSMEs.

CONCLUSION

As reviewed in the theoretical discussion, many investigations have tried to demonstrate a relationship between the use of ICTs and economic development. This chapter especially discusses the influence of the ICTs in diminishing transaction costs. There is still an ongoing debate about whether and how the adoption of ICTs helps reduce transaction costs and improves firms' general performance. The demonstration of the reduction in transaction costs and the better performance of firms depend not only on the use of ICTs, but also on the integration of these technologies in the entrepreneurial strategies of the MSMEs. Therefore, training programs in the areas of strategy and entrepreneurial planning must accompany investment in new ICTs. This will allow MSMEs to clearly define both their goals as an enterprise as well as the ways they could benefit from the new ICTs by reaching these objectives. These training programs need to be more focused on managerial understanding and skills for applying ICTs in order to implement business strategies successfully.

REFERENCES

Bernal Vera, L. E. (2005). *Influencia de las nuevas TIC en el desempeño comercial de las PYMEs del Perú*. Unpublished master's thesis, University of Leipzig, Saxony, Germany.

Bitler, M. P. (2001). *Small businesses and computers: Adoption and performance* (Working Paper No. 2001-15). San Francisco: Federal Reserve Bank of San Francisco.

Brynjolfsson, E., & Hitt, L. (2000). Beyond computation: Information technology, organizational transformation and business performance. *Journal of Economic Perspectives, 14*(4), 23-48.

Coase, R. (1937). The nature of the firm. *Economica, 4*(16), 386-405.

Leff, N. (1984). Externalities, information cost, and social benefit-cost analysis for economic development: An example from telecommunications. *Economic Development and Cultural Change, 32*(2), 255-276.

Lohrke, F. T., McClure Franklin, G., & Frownfelter-Lohrke, C. (2006). The Internet as an information conduit: A transaction cost analysis model of US SME Internet use. *International Small Business Journal, 24*(2), 159-178.

Matambalaya, F., & Wolf, S. (2001). The role of ICT for the performance of SMEs in East Africa: Empirical evidence from Kenya and Tanzania. *ZEF Discussion Papers on Development Policy, 42*. Retrieved September 8, 2006, from http://www.zef.de/711.0.html

McFarlan, F. (1984). Information technology changes the way you compete. *Harvard Business Review, 62*(3), 98-103.

Müller-Falcke, D. (2002). Use and impact of information and communication technologies in developing countries' small businesses: Evidence from Indian small scale industry. In *Development economics and policy*. Frankfurt am Main, Germany: Peter Lang Pub.

North, D. (1995). The new institutional economics and third world development. In J. Harriss, J. Hunter, & C. Lewis (Eds.), *The new institutional economics and third world development*. London: Routledge.

Norton, S. (1992). Transaction cost, telecommunications, and the microeconomic growth. *Economic Development and Cultural Change, 41*(1), 175-196.

Organization for Economic Cooperation and Development (OECD). (2004). *ICT, e-business and SMEs.* Retrieved September 8, 2006, from http://www.oecd.org/dataoecd/32/28/34228733.pdf

Organismo Supervisor de Inversión Privada en Telecomunicaciones (OSIPTEL). (2005). Cabinas públicas de acceso a Internet por modalidad de acceso. *OSIPTEL Statistics.* Retrieved September 8, 2006, from http://www.osiptel.gob.pe/InfoEstadistica/Internet%(6)_C6.7.xls

Porter, M., & Millar, V. (1985). How information gives you competitive advantage. *Harvard Business Review, 63*(4), 149-160.

United States Agency for International Development (USAID). (2000). *Croatia ICT assessment.* Retrieved September 8, 2006, from http://unpan1.un.org/intradoc/groups/public/documents/UNTC/UNPAN013159.pdf

NOTES

[1]   Although in these paragraphs we use the term *telecommunication*, the concepts can be applied perfectly to the new ICTs.
[2]   Arbitrage is the practice of obtaining the advantage of an unbalanced state between two or more markets: a combination of business operations exploding this disequilibrium with the price differences in the different markets as profit.

ABBREVIATIONS

ICT: Information and communication technology

MSME: Micro, small, and medium-sized enterprises

OECD: Organization for Economic Cooperation and Development

OSIPTEL: Organismo Supervisor de Inversión Privada en Telecomunicaciones (Peruvian Agency for the Supervision of Private Investment in the Telecommunications Sector)

SME: Small and medium-sized enterprise

SSBF: Survey of Small Business Finances

UK: United Kingdom (of Great Britain and North Ireland)

U.S.: United States (of America)

USAID: United States Agency for International Development

Chapter XIII
Information Technology Industry Development and the Knowledge Economy:
A Four Country Study

Phillip Ein Dor
Tel-Aviv University, Israel

Michael Myers
University of Auckland, New Zealand

K.S. Raman
National University of Singapore, Singapore

ABSTRACT

It is generally accepted that knowledge has become a third major factor of production, in addition to the traditional factors—labor and capital. Information technology production is a significant factor in the knowledge economy both because it is a major enabler of that economy and because it is itself highly knowledge intensive. Many countries around the world are looking for ways to promote the development of the knowledge economy, and information technology industries in particular. An important question is to what extent—and how—small developed countries might succeed in this endeavor. This study suggests a modified and more comprehensive version of the Ein-Dor et al. (1997) model of IT (information technology) industry success in small developed countries. Whereas the earlier model of IT industry success was based solely on the macro-economic theory of Grossman and Helpman (1991), the revised model suggested here incorporates Romer's (1990) work in New Growth economics. A significant advance over earlier work in this area is the use of both longitudinal and time slice data. This article provides an in-depth analysis of the IT industry in four countries over a five-year period: Finland, Israel, New Zealand and Singapore. It analyses some changes that occurred over the period 1994 through 1998 and thus provides a reasonably comprehensive picture of the factors affecting the production of IT in these small developed countries. Our study reveals that four of the five endogenous variables studied have a close relationship to the development of IT industries in small developed countries. These variables are research and development, technological infrastructure, firm strategies, and capital availability. On the other hand, domestic IT use does not seem to be a major factor in IT industry development. Our analysis thus largely supports the more comprehensive model of IT industry success. These findings should be of interest to both researchers and policy makers seeking to develop the knowledge economy and information technology industries in particular.

INTRODUCTION

For countries in the vanguard of the world economy, the balance between knowledge and resources has shifted so far towards the former that knowledge has become perhaps the most important factor determining the standard of living—more than land, than tools, than labor. Today's most technologically advanced economies are truly knowledge-based. (World Bank, 1999)

Some contemporary economists have suggested that knowledge has become a third factor of production in leading economies. Paul Romer, in particular, has proposed his "New Growth Theory" as an alternative to the neo-classical model of economics (Romer, 1990). Whereas neo-classical economics recognised just two factors of production (labor and capital), Romer has suggested that technology (and the knowledge on which it is based) is an intrinsic part of today's economic system.

Consequently, many governments around the world are looking for ways to promote the development of the knowledge economy, and information technology industries in particular. According to many New Growth economists, information technology is best regarded as the facilitator of knowledge creation in innovative societies (OECD, 1996). Information technologies do not by themselves create transformations in society, but they are the enablers of change. New information technologies are tools for releasing the creative potential and knowledge embodied in people. Particularly important from the perspective of this study is the fact that IT industries are themselves knowledge industries in the sense that they employ knowledge intensive research, design, and production processes.

Using the macro-economic work of Grossman and Helpman (1991) and Romer (1990) as a base, this study attempts to provide a comprehensive picture of the factors affecting the production of IT in small developed countries. It does so by providing an in-depth analysis of the IT industry in four countries—Finland, Israel, New Zealand and Singapore—the last three over a five-year period. These four countries were chosen because they are comparable in many ways, making it easier to identify the factors leading to differential development of their IT industries. Given that IT industries provide a technical platform for innovation and are a key component in fostering the development of the knowledge economy, we believe it is important to identify the key drivers in fostering IT industry success. The primary purpose of this article is to identify what these drivers might be.

This study analyses the relative changes that occurred over the period 1994 through 1998. We believe that our use of both longitudinal and time slice data represents a considerable advance over earlier studies of a similar nature. Furthermore, an effort has been made to identify and employ consistent bodies of data wherever possible.

Earlier studies (Dedrick et al., 1995; Ein-Dor et al., 1997) were based mainly on 1993 and 1994 data. However, developments in IT industries were extremely rapid in the period between the two studies and it was assumed that this would help in identifying the relevant factors. This study revisited the earlier studies in order to determine whether their conclusions still held five years later and whether changes may have occurred in the explanatory factors. Admittedly, the data are not particularly recent, but it should be remembered that the objective of this study is to identify IT industry success factors; as these factors do not change rapidly, the particular time period studied is of little consequence, as long as it is one in which development has occurred and the factors can be identified.

The article is organised as follows. It begins by exhibiting some background data of the four countries. As the dependent variable in our study is IT industry success, it then develops a measure of such success and determines the level of success of the countries studied. Next, it presents the macro-economic model underlying this study. Attention then shifts to a presentation of the data regarding the respective countries' IT industries and an attempt is made to relate the changes in performance over time to the variables in our model. In the final concluding section, directions for future research and implications for policy makers are suggested.

BACKGROUND DATA

Previous studies have suggested a number of exogenous variables over which countries have little control. There are two main groups of exogenous variables; the first relates to ethnic and quality of life factors, while the second encompasses economic factors. The current values of these items for the four countries are exhibited in Table 1. Some obvious facts arising from the table are:

1. The ethnic composition of the four countries is very different, the predominant groups being Semitic for Israel, European for New Zealand and Finland, and Asian in Singapore.
2. The religious affiliations of the four countries differ widely.
3. The predominant languages of all four are different, although English plays a major role in all of them: as the mother tongue in New Zealand, as the official language of administration and most public activity in Singapore, and as a widely used second language in Finland and Israel.

Of the four countries, only New Zealand is well endowed with raw materials. The countries differ widely in their proximity to market regions and their trade patterns might be expected to be markedly different.

Given that any changes in the exogenous variables tend to be very slow, we believe that it is highly unlikely that any changes that may have occurred in the IT industries are attributable to them.

Table 2 exhibits some data that will be frequently used in the following analyses, particularly population and GDP data. (Note: Data are generally presented by development rank where that emphasizes relevant relationships; otherwise they are presented by alphabetical order of country names.)

The data show some quite significant demographic and economic changes in the countries under consideration during the period studied. The populations of New Zealand and Singapore grew by about 6% over five years and that of Israel by about 10%; only the population of Finland remained unchanged during the period considered. In Israel and Singapore, these changes were due to natural growth and, especially, to significant levels of immigration. In New Zealand, immigration was less dominant and the growth is attributable to natural increase. No matter what

Table 1. Summary of exogenous variables – 1997

Exogenous variables	Finland	Israel	New Zealand	Singapore
People:				
Ethnic groups	Finn 93% Swede 6% Lapp 0.11% Gypsy 0.12% Other 0.02%	Jewish 82% Non Jewish (mostly Arab)18%	European, mostly British 88% Polynesian 9%.	Chinese 76% Malay 15% Indian 6%
Official languages	Finnish, Swedish	Hebrew, Arabic	English, Maori	Chinese, English, Malay, Tamil,
Religions	Evangelical Lutheran 89% Greek Orthodox 1% None 9% Other 1%	Jewish 82% Muslim 14% Other 4%	Anglican 24% Presbyterian 18% Roman Catholic 15%	Buddhist Taoist Muslim Christian Hindu
Human development:				
UNDP Human Development Index (1999 rank of 174 countries)[3]	13	23	18	22
Life expectancy	Male 74 Female 81	male 76 female 80	male 74 female 80	male 75 female 81
Infant mortality/1000 live births	3.8	9	7	5
Literacy	100%	95%	100%	(1993) 91%
Newspaper circulation	455 per 1000 pop.[2]	242 per 1000 pop.	304 per 100 pop.	350 per 1000 pop.
Leading export partners[4]	Germany 11.0% UK 10.0% Sweden 9.8% Russia 7.3%	USA 32.1% UK 6.2% Hong Kong 5.3% Belgium/Luxembourg 5.0% Japan 4.6% Netherlands 4.4%	Australia 20.2% Japan 14.5% USA 10.4% UK 6.2%	USA 18.4% Malaysia 17.5% Hong Kong 9.6% Japan 7.1% Thailand 4.6% Taiwan 4.5
raw materials	few	few	many	none

Sources. (1) Unless otherwise stated: K-III Reference Corporation (1997). (2) Finnish Newspapers Association (2000). (3) United Nations Development Program (1999). (4) The Economist. Pocket World in Figures (1999).

Table 2. Population and economic indicators and changes therein

Country	Population (millions) 1994/1998 [1]	Population Rank 1994/1998 [1]	GDP (US$bn) [2]	Per Capita GDP (US$) [3]	Per Capita GDP Rank of 53 countries [3]	Area km^2
Finland – 1994	5.1	103		$19,221	16	337,030
Finland – 1998	5.1	105	125.1	$24,292	14	
Change	0	-2		+26%	+2	
NZ – 1994	3.5	122		13,006	22	267,800
NZ –1998	3.6	121	52.7	15,470	24	
Change	+2.8%	+1		+19%	-2	
Israel – 1994	5.1	104		13,727	23	21,950
Israel – 1998	5.6	100	98.8	16,330	22	
Change	+9.8%	+4		+19%	+1	
Singapore – 1994	3.3	124		24,187	9	625
Singapore – 1998	3.5	118	84.4	21,789	17	
Change	+6%	+6		-10%	-8	

the causes, the growth that occurred moved the three countries up one to six places in the world population rankings. Only Finland receded in the population rankings as a consequence of its zero population growth.

The changes in per capita gross domestic product (GDP) are more dramatic. The increase in this datum varied from 19% in New Zealand and Israel to a remarkable 26% in Finland; Singapore alone exhibited negative growth resulting from the Asian economic crisis of the late 1990s. The positions of the countries in the international ranking by GDP were little changed, except for the 8-place decline of Singapore for the reason given. In the context of the present article, the interesting question, of course, is to what extent the per capita GDP changes can be linked to IT industries.

RESEARCH METHOD

In most earlier studies of this type, a major weakness has been the inadequacy and limited availability of good statistical data. Some of the most serious problems have been as follows:

- Lack of availability of consistent data from a single source. For example, reported data concerning domestic IT expenditure may have been gathered from various national sources. The inconsistent definitions of data make accurate comparisons impossible.

- Data from a single source may not convey exactly the meaning that is desired. Whereas the statistical categories for traditional industries may have been provided in great detail, those for IT are more likely to have been defined less precisely. The standard statistical classifications suffer from low granularity in the IT context. Thus, for example, it may be difficult to differentiate between different kinds of communication costs; software might be considered a service, and the data not related to that on hardware; computers may be lumped together with office machines.

Our solution to these problems has been to use *single sources* wherever possible, and to use sources with good quality reporting of IT usage. We are fortunate that such sources have become available in recent years. These sources include *The Economist Pocket World in Figures, The Global Competitiveness Report, UNESCO Statistical Yearbook,* and *The World Competitiveness Yearbook.* Our use of these global sources strengthens the article and, we believe, represents a significant advance over much of the earlier work in this area, which generally relied on inconsistent national sources.

In those instances where data from single sources are not available, an attempt has been made to use official national sources such as the US Census Bureau and the Singapore National Computer Board. As a last resort, journal and newspaper data were occasionally utilized. In some cases, where it was not possible to obtain a data item for all four countries from a single source, multiple sources were used that may relate to proximate years rather than to a single year.

Considerable use has been made here of survey data published by the World Economic Forum in *The Global Competitiveness Yearbook 1999.* "The survey questions were selected to provide a reasonably comprehensive view of what leading businessmen perceive to be happening in their countries, with special emphasis on questions for which alternative quantitative data are not available." Responses were obtained from about 4,000 executives in the 59 countries reported.

The data points in the surveys are much closer for the different countries than for the objective data. Apparently, most managers surveyed tend to see the situation in their own countries in a relatively favorable light. In order to compensate for this and to make the differences more obvious, we have normalized the survey data in some of the charts. The same has been done for other data where necessary. In each case, the normalization is explained for the specific chart displayed.

THEORETICAL MODEL

The relationship between production and use of information technology (IT) and economic development of countries has received increasing attention in recent years. The role of IT in the rapid economic growth of some Asia-Pacific countries has received particular attention (Blanning et al., 1997; Dedrick & Kraemer, 1995, 1998; Kraemer

et al., 1992). These studies show that Hong Kong, New Zealand, and Singapore are economically developed and advanced in IT production and use even though they are small countries with less than 10 million population. Beyond the Asia-Pacific region, Ireland, Israel, and Nordic countries with populations of less than 10 million are major IT producers and/or sophisticated users (Dedrick et al., 1995). Production and use of IT in these countries are out of proportion to their size and natural resources.

Of the numerous country level studies on IT production and use, three focus on small developed countries with populations of less than 10 million. In a descriptive study of nine geographically and culturally diverse small developed countries, Dedrick et al. (1995) suggest that the likely success factors are the level of economic development, a basic education system, sophistication in IT use, telecommunications infrastructure, and government policies towards trade, investment, and IT. In a detailed study of Israel, New Zealand, and Singapore, Ein-Dor et al. (1997) built on the macroeconomic theoretical framework provided by Grossman and Helpman (1989, 1991). They concluded that although the three countries are very similar in terms of the level of economic development, the IT industry seemed most developed in Israel, followed by Singapore and New Zealand. Exogenous variables such as geographical location, availability of raw materials, and national culture did not seem to provide explanations for the different levels of IT industry development. Of the endogenous variables, local IT use and firm strategies did not seem to explain the differential levels of IT industry development. The dominant factor, which seemed to provide some explanation, was government policy towards promoting IT industries directly, in supporting IT industry R&D, and in education policies providing appropriately trained labor pools. More recently, Watson and Myers (2001) used the Ein-Dor et al. (1997) model to study the IT industry and IT use in Finland and

New Zealand based on 1998 data. They found that Finland and New Zealand are very similar in terms of economic development and country size. Despite this similarity, Finland's IT industry is more developed than New Zealand's, particularly in the hardware sector. Their research suggests that government promotion of IT, high levels of private sector R&D investment, and an education system that produces IT-literate graduates are the most important factors in IT industry success.

The theoretical basis of this article is a modified and more comprehensive version of the model suggested earlier by Ein-Dor et al. (1997). It is a more general version of the Grossman and Helpman (1991) model but now incorporates Romer's (1990) work.

Grossman and Helpman analyse how governments can help in promoting technology and knowledge via research and development (R&D) subsidies. Romer suggests that technology and knowledge are a third factor of production together with labor and capital. He adds human capital, defined as the cumulative effect of formal education and on-the-job training, as an important factor that affects growth. In addition to the variables

suggested by Grossman and Helpman's model and Romer, our model includes national culture and firm strategies.

The elements of the model are as follows:

1. *Control variables:* those which define country size
2. *Dependent variables:* those which define IT industry success
3. *Independent variables:*
   (a) Exogenous variables — those over which countries have little or no control:
   i.   Resources,
   ii. Proximity to markets,
   iii. National culture
   (b) Endogenous mediating factors:
   i.   Domestic IT use
   ii. Human capital development
   iii. Research & development; technological sophistication
   iv. Firm strategies
   v.   Availability of capital

In this model, government policies are not considered as a separate variable but are discussed

Figure 1. Model of IT industry success factors

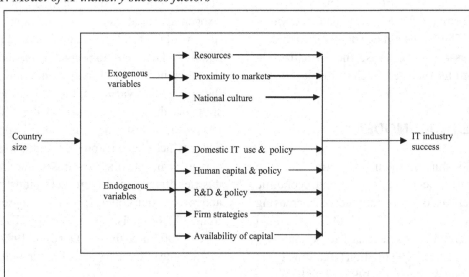

within the context of the other factors. Graphically, our model may be represented as in Figure 1.

DATA

IT Industry Development Measures

As the countries under consideration are small, one cannot expect to find in them broad coverage of the spectrum of IT products. Furthermore, being as small as they are, their internal IT markets are also necessarily small. Thus, IT product exports have been chosen as a measure of the development of IT industries for those countries. Since they have only limited product lines and small internal markets, exports are a good indicator of total IT production. This measure does not specify the quality of the exports, whether locally designed and manufactured products, vertical production, or products assembled from imported components and re-exported. Unfortunately, such data are not available.

The second measure is the number of firms engaged in the IT industry and their size relative to firms in other industries. While there are no consistent data on this item, it does provide some indication of industry development.

The third measure chosen was the number of IT firms listed on local and foreign stock exchanges. This measure is somewhat more problematic, for at least three reasons:

1. It reflects financing strategies chosen by entrepreneurs and firms. These strategies are influenced by factors such as availability and attractiveness of other types of funding, interest rates, exchange rates and so forth. Thus, they do not directly reflect the condition of a country's IT industry.

2. It reflects investor perceptions of the country in question and of its IT industry and is not necessarily an objective measure, especially in the short run until markets have learned the attributes of the industries involved.

3. The question arises whether the ability of an IT industry to raise capital on stock markets is an indicator of development, or perhaps rather a reason for success. At the very least, there is something of a reinforcing effect in which successful IPOs breed an industry that, if successful, in turn encourages the market.

In spite of these shortcomings, we nevertheless feel that this is a useful indicator of industry development, or at least the degree to which it is perceived to be a success.

The data for 1998 on the three measures for the four countries studied are exhibited in Table 3.

From Table 3 we see that IT exports relative to GDP vary from 0.87% for New Zealand up to 9.5 % for Israel with Finland at 6.19%, and Singapore with 4.14%. This ranking is repeated for IT exports per capita which range from $133 for New Zealand to $1,756 for Israel with Finland and Singapore at $1,518 and $1,191 respectively.

An additional measure in Table 3 is stock market listings. In spite of the reservations mentioned above, this measure is some indication of the level of activity in the IT industries and the number of firms active in them. Again, the data indicate Israel in the top ranking followed by Finland, Singapore, and New Zealand, in that order.

The final measure in Table 3 is the number of IT firms among the largest firms in the country. Here, again, the same rankings are evident as in the previous two measures. Israel and Finland rank first and second; New Zealand and Singapore have nearly the same ranking. Table 4 summarises the rank orders of the four countries on the measures used.

The consistency of the results would seem to support the conclusion that in terms of success in developing IT industries, the overall ranking is Israel, Finland, Singapore, and New Zealand, in that order.

In conclusion, it seems that all four countries in the study have developed indigenous IT industries, albeit with varying levels of prominence. The remainder of this article attempts to tease out the causes of the differences in level of IT industry development.

The model presented in Figure 1 has much in common with that of the Global Competitiveness Yearbook (IMD, 1999). Because of this similarity, it is of interest to consider whether the global competitiveness factors can explain the observed differences in IT industry success in the countries studied. The comparison in Table 5 of the global competitiveness rankings with the IT industry development rankings defined previously indicates little correlation. This is true of the overall rankings and holds by and large for the detailed competitiveness factors. Thus, Israel and New Zealand have about the same competitiveness rankings (24 and 20 respectively) but are at opposite ends of the IT industry development ranking. We can only conclude that the global competitiveness factors, while making sense at the level of the total economy, are probably too coarse to capture the specific items which contribute to IT industry development as defined above. It is the objective of the rest of this paper to identify these specific items.

Next we compare the development data from 1994 with the current data. Unfortunately, the 1994 data for Finland were not available in the earlier study (Ein-Dor et al., 1997). Data for the three countries for which data are available for both 1994 and 1998 (Table 6) indicate rapid growth during that period. Total IT exports grew by 250% for Israel, 310% for New Zealand, and a remarkable 744% for Singapore. It is true that the total world IT market expanded rapidly during this period, but it would seem that these three countries expanded their roles within it more than proportionately.

Control Variable — Country Size

Country size is the control variable in this study. By country size, we are referring mostly to population and economic development figures, rather than land area. We believe that land area is unlikely to be significant with regard to the IT industry. The data for 1998 for all four countries are summarized in Table 7 (more detail is provided in Table 2).

It can be seen that all four countries are quite alike in terms of population and all fall within European levels of per capita GDP.

Exogenous Variables

Resources

Of the countries studied, only New Zealand has significant quantities of natural resources. However, as was found in previous studies, natural resources are not a significant requirement for IT industry development. In fact, many of the countries with successful IT industries tend to be resource-poor. Examples not in our study are Taiwan, Hong Kong, and Ireland. Thus, this is a factor that may be dropped from future considerations of IT industry development.

Proximity to Markets

For bulky goods, proximity to markets is still an important factor determining trade patterns. Even with the advent of the global economy, it appears that most countries still trade mainly with others in their own region. This is reflected in Table 8, which exhibits the trading patterns for the countries in this study.

The foreign trade patterns of the four countries are very different. The USA is the major export market for Israel and Singapore and an important one for New Zealand, but not for Finland. Beyond that, two of the countries trade mainly with their

Table 3. IT industry development and success measures

IT Industry Development	Finland	Israel	New Zealand	Singapore
Number and size of IT firms Firms in IT: IT firms/largest firms	4200[1] 4/50 = 8%[2]	n.a. 40/150 = 27%	2529[4] 12/200[5] = 6%	5500[1] 25/400 = 6%[2]
IT industry employment	5.5%[3]	4.0%[2,6]	2.6% (1996)[1]	6.1%
locally developed products		H/W & S/W	SW/HW	H/W & S/W
IT exports: Hardware	7,255m[4]	$7,784m[1]	$281m[1]	$3,710m[3]
Software Total	$488[1] $7,743	$1,601m[5] $9,385m	$198m[1] $479m	$0.46bn[3] $4.17bn[3]
IT exports per capita	$1518	$1756.3	$133.1	$1191.4
IT exports/GDP	6.19%	9.50%	0.87%	4.94%
IT stock market listings Domestic Foreign	27[5] 1	ca. 80[3] ca. 80[4]	3[2]	35[4] 2[5]

Sources. Finland (1) Nygard, Ann Marie and Kunnas, Tarja. (1998). Computer Networking Hardware/Software. Finland: International Trade Administration. (2) Finnfacts. (12/11/1999). 50 Largest Finnish Companies. www.finnfacts.com/ Ffeng0399/ record_profits.htm (3) Statistics Finland. (1999a). On the Road to the Finnish Information Society - Summary. www.stat. fi/tk/yr/tttietoti_en.html (4) Statistics Finland. (1999b). Production and Foreign Trade of High-Technology Products. www. stat.fi/tk/yr/tthuippu1_en.html. (5) Helsinki Stock Exchange. (1999). Listed Companies. www.hex.fi/eng/listed_companies/

Israel *(1) Central Bureau of Statistics. (August 1999). (2) Central Bureau of Statistics. (October1999). (3) Tel-Aviv Stock Exchange (1999). (4) NASDAQ lists 96 Israeli companies (http://www.nasdaq.com/reference/israel_companies.stm). A quick scan of the list indicates that 76 of these are in IT. A few Israeli companies are listed on other exchanges, so 80 is probably a good estimate of the current total number of Israeli IT companies listed abroad. (5) Koren. (January 25, 2000), Keren, Tsuriel . (Jan 25, 2000). (6) Breakdown of IT industry employees (7) Dun & Bradstreet Israel Ltd.*

New Zealand *(1) Ministry of Commerce. Statistics on Information Technology in New Zealand. Wellington (April, 1999). (2) The New Zealand Company Registrar 1996-97 – 35th Edition (April 1999), Prepared by Headliner Publishing Co. Published by Mercantile Gazette Marketing Ltd., Christchurch. (3) Government web page. www.govt.nz. Stats from Statistics NZ. (4) NZ Computer Industry Directory 1999. A Computerworld publication. Published by IDG Communications (5) 1998 Top 200 New Zealand Companies. Deloitte & Touche Consulting Group. Management Magazine (1999), 45(11), 74-87.*

Singapore *(1) IDC Singapore. The classification covers computer and telecommunication hardware and software; IT and telecommunication services; and high-tech office equipment. Nearly 87% are small enterprises that employ less than 25 people. (2) Several large IT firms are subsidiaries of large multinationals. (3) National Computer Board, Singapore. IT Focus, (1998). This gives 1997 figures. Flat growth for 1998 is assumed due to the Asian economic crisis. (4) This figure was obtained by studying the background and activities of companies in the Stock Exchange of Singapore database. (5) Two more Singapore companies, Chartered Semiconductors and Pacific Internet, were listed on NASDAQ in 1999.*

Table 4. IT development rankings for four countries

	IT exports/ GDP	IT exports per capita	Stock market listings	IT firms/ largest firms
Finland	2	2	2	2
Israel	1	1	1	1
New Zealand	4	4	4	3
Singapore	3	3	3	3

Table 5. Global competitiveness rankings versus IT industry development rank

	IT industry development rank	Overall competitiveness	Domestic economy	Internationalization	Government	Finance	Infrastructure	Management	Science & technology	People	Mean (columns 3-10)
Israel	1	24	22	23	29	24	25	14	15	19	21.375
Finland	2	3	4	11	10	8	2	3	6	1	12.500
Singapore	3	2	18	2	1	9	13	4	12	4	6.750
New Zealand	4	20	31	33	9	18	14	10	24	16	20.375

Table 6. Changes in IT industry development measures

IT Industry Development	Israel 1994	Israel 1998	New Zealand 1994	New Zealand 1998	Singapore 1994	Singapore 1998
IT product sales: IT industry sales IT sales/GDP	$4.15bn 6% of GDP	$7.78bn 9.5%	$1.5bn 3.5% of GDP	$3.46bn 3.5%	$1.56bn 3.8% of GDP	$4.17bn 4.9%
Number and size of IT firms firms in IT: IT firms/largest firms	350 34/200=17%	40/150=27%	300 15/200=7.5%	2529 12/200=6%	600 6/400=1.5%	5500 25/400=6%
IT industry employment	3.3%	4.0%[2.6]	2.8%	2.6%	10%	6.1%
IT exports: Hardware Software Total	$2.50bn $0.17bn $2.67bn	$7.78bn[1] $1.60bn[5] $9.38bn	$58m $59m $117m*	$281m $198m $479m	n.a. n.a. $494	$3.71bn $0.46bn $4.17bn
stock market listings domestic foreign	35 30	ca. 80[3] ca. 80[4]	2 -	3	7 2	35 2

Table 7. Population and economic development

Country	Population (millions)	Per Capita GDP	Land area km^2
Finland	5.1	22,121	337,030
Israel	5.6	17,276	21,950
NZ	3.6	15,470	267,800
Singapore	3.5	25,059	625

Table 8. Leading export partners—1999 (Source: The Economist. Pocket World in Figures, 1999)

Finland		Israel		New Zealand		Singapore	
Germany	11.0%	USA	32.1%	Australia	20.2%	USA	18.4%
UK	10.0%	UK	6.2%	Japan	14.5%	Malaysia	17.5%
Sweden	9.8%	Hong Kong	5.3%	USA	10.4%	Hong Kong	9.6%
Russia	7.3%	Belgium/Lux.	5.0%	UK	6.2%	Japan	7.1%
		Japan	4.6%			Thailand	4.6%
		Netherlands	4.4%			Taiwan	4.5%

Table 9. Hofstede scores for countries studied (Source: Hofstede, 1980).

	Finland	Israel	New Zealand	Singapore
power distance (PDI)	33	13	22	74
uncertainty avoidance (UAI)	59	81	49	8
individuality (IDV)	63	54	79	20
masculinity (MAS)	26	47	58	48

nearest neighbours—Europe for Finland, the Pacific area for New Zealand. Israel and Singapore differ from this pattern in that their main trading partner is the USA; beyond that, Singapore trades mainly with neighboring Asian countries while Israel trades further afield because of political tensions between Israel and its nearest neighbors. In general, the pattern is one of countries trading with their nearest neighbours, despite the current rhetoric associated with globalisation.

In the context of this article, the question is whether proximity to markets has any effect on the development of IT industries. From the above data, it would appear not. Finland is the only country in the study close to all its major markets. The other three countries trade with a mix of countries near and far. This is the case for

total exports. Given the ease with which almost all IT products can be rapidly delivered anywhere in the world, the conclusion would seem to apply even more forcibly to IT products.

Culture

In most previous papers, researchers have concluded that culture is not a major factor explaining differences in IT industry development. However, the evidence provided has been largely circumstantial and so we decided to examine this conclusion further. Hofstede (1980) has frequently been to the basis for studies of the effect of cultural differences in the IS setting. Table 9 and Figure 2 exhibit Hofstede's scores for the four countries in this study on the four factors he examined—power distance, uncertainty avoidance, individualism, and masculinity.

Figure 2 exhibits the scores by IT industry development ranking. The most striking feature of these data is the almost total lack of consistency. Individuality and masculinity show no relationship to our development ranking. Power distance and uncertainty avoidance suggest a relationship to the success ranking for ranks 1 to 3. However, fourth ranked New Zealand controverts that suggestion by being the closest to first ranked Israel on those two factors. We conclude that these particular measures of culture are not closely related to IT industry success.

Given the considerable cultural differences between the countries and the fact that all four have substantial IT industries, this supports previous studies showing the relatively unimportant role of culture (Ein-Dor et al., 1997). It should be noted, however, that Hofstede did find some correlations between his dimensions and levels of economic activity. For example "the one consistent correlate (of UAI with economic activity)

is faster economic growth with higher UAI" (p. 154). The UAI curve does not support this with respect to IT industry development.

Other studies have begun to question the importance of culture in economic development. Thus, a recent article argues that what are frequently known as "Asian" or "Confucian" values are not the dominant force in Asia's recent economic success that they are often held out to be (*The Economist,* 2000). Rather, cultural values of the type quoted may be a result of a level of economic development, not its determinant. Thus, personal and family connections (*guanxi*), frequently identified with Asian entrepreneurship, were equally representative of earlier stages of European economic development; the Rothschild, Thyssen, Siemens, and Wallenberg families are just a few examples that come to mind. It is argued that, with their development, Asian economies are now beginning to emulate the modern capitalist structures of the West, thereby emulating its historical development.

However, the seeming lack of connection between Hofstede's four dimensions of culture

Figure 2. Hofstede's international differences in work-related values (Hofstede, 1980)

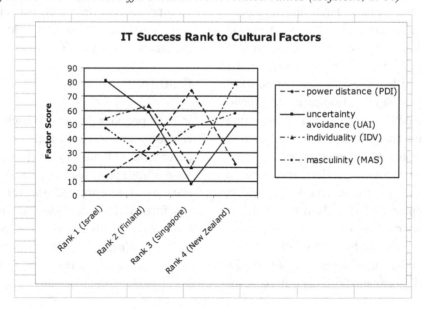

and IT industry development does not necessarily mean that culture is unimportant. There may be other cultural dimensions that come into play or cultural factors that are mediated by other variables such as the role of government. At the very least, there is a need to consider the interplay between culture and government policies that attempt to change it. However, a consideration of culture at this level of analysis is outside the scope of this article.

Summary of Exogenous Variables

In summarising our discussion of exogenous variables, we can conclude that the existence of natural resources and proximity to major markets has little effect on IT industry success. The effects of national culture are less clear-cut. However, given the variety of cultures exhibited by the countries studied, it seems that there is no obvious relationship between cultural factors and IT industry development. If this is so, then exogenous factors play a minor role in IT industry success and we must look for endogenous factors to explain some of the findings on IT industry success.

Endogenous Variables

Domestic IT Use

High levels of domestic IT use might be assumed to be a factor promoting the domestic IT industry. In fact, the government of Singapore has for many

years now encouraged IT use for precisely that reason. However, the data do not seem to support this assumption very strongly.

Our analysis is based on two objective items and two opinion survey items. The objective data are the number of PCs and number of Internet servers relative to population; these are generally considered good measures of levels of IT use. The opinion data are from surveys of managers reported in The Global Competitiveness Report 1999 and refer to diffusion of computer use and management use of computers.

Addressing first the objective data, these are exhibited in Table 10 and Figure 3 (which is a graphic representation of the levels of IT use relative to IT industry development rankings); there seems to be no consistent relationship between the two. Israel, with the highest IT industry development ranking, has the lowest domestic use of IT. Finland, second in the success rankings is first in domestic IT use.

The subjective data provide some insight into the perceptions of managers concerning the use of IT in their countries. These data are exhibited in Table 11.

Table 12 combines the objective and subjective data. These data have been normalised to permit simultaneous presentation of different dimensions and scaling. In every case in which data have been normalised, the normalisations are specified after the table. The normalised data are exhibited in Figure 4. The figure shows that Finland completely dominates the other three countries in terms of domestic IT use. On every

Table 10. Measures of domestic IT use by IT industry development rankings (Source: World Economic Forum, 1999)

	Israel	Finland	Singapore	New Zealand
Development ranking	1	2	3	4
Internet hosts/1M[1]	14692.3	94581.5	18561.3	44676.0
PCs/1000 pop.[1]	219.3	354.0	315.5	319.6

Figure 3. Domestic IT use to IT success ranking

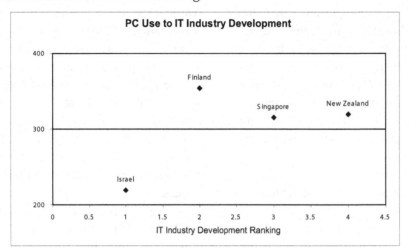

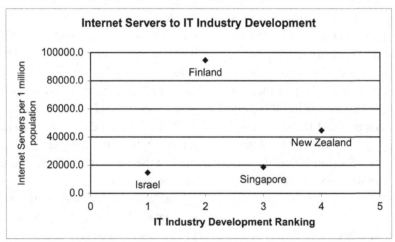

Table 11. Perceptions of IT use by IT industry development rankings

	Israel	Finland	Singapore	New Zealand
Development ranking	1	2	3	4
Diffusion of IT use[1]	6.61	6.84	6.58	6.51
Management use[2]	5.87	6.21	6.02	6.52

Source. World Economic Forum (1999). (1) The use of computers is highly sophisticated and widespread (2) Managers person-ally use computers and information technology extensively.

Table 12. Computer use

	Development rank	Diffusion[1] - actual	Diffusion[1] – normalized	Management use[2] – actual	Management use[2] – normalized	Internet hosts per 1 million population	PCs per 1000 population
Israel	1	6.61	5.56	5.87	5.51	1.09	3.41
Finland	2	6.84	6.84	6.21	6.21	7.00	5.50
Singapore	3	6.58	5.39	6.02	5.82	1.37	4.91
New Zealand	4	6.51	5.00	5.62	5.00	3.31	4.97

Source. World Economic Forum (1999). (1) The use of computers is highly sophisticated and widespread (2) Managers personally use computers and information technology extensively.

Normalization: Diffusion and Management Use extended to the range 5 to the maximum value for the item. Internet hosts and PCs per 1000 population proportionately normalized to the range 0 to 7.

Figure 4. Dimensions of domestic IT use

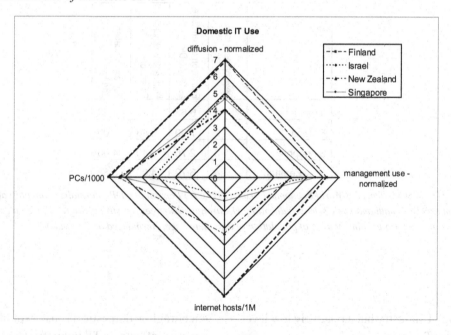

dimension except diffusion, Israel is dominated by at least two other countries.

These results merit some thought. It is quite possible that domestic IT use plays an important role in promoting IT industries in large countries; this is almost certainly the case with respect to the U.S., and probably also applies to China. However, when the local market is small, firms wishing to play a role in the IT industries must perforce look for markets elsewhere and the level of domestic use may be irrelevant. Further evidence for this argument may be supplied by India, which has a

Table 13. Education data

	Development rank	Education expenditure as % of GDP[1]	Math and Science Education - score[2]	Math and Science Education - rank	Tertiary education Enrolment – rank[3]
Israel	1	7.2	5.10	12	23
Finland	2	7.6	6.48	12	4
Singapore	3	3.0	5.49	1	26
New Zealand	4	7.3	4.00	35	7

Source. Item 1. UNESCO, Items 2-3.World Economic Forum (1999). (1) Percent of GDP. (2) "The school system excels in math and basic science education. (1=strongly disagree, 7 = strongly agree)". (3) Enrolment as % of population of designated age.

Table 14. Education data — Normalized

	Development rank	Education expenditure as % of GDP[1]	Math and Science Education[2]	Tertiary education Enrolment[3]
Israel	1	6.63	5.10	4.28
Finland	2	7.00	6.48	7.00
Singapore	3	2.76	5.49	4.00
New Zealand	4	6.72	4.00	5.88

Source. Item 1. UNESCO, Items 2-3.World Economic Forum (1999). (1) Percent of GDP - normalized on interval 0-7. (2) The school system excels in math and basic science education. (1=strongly disagree, 7 = strongly agree) Given a top score close to 7, left unnormalized. (3) Enrolment as % of population of designated age. Normalized on interval 4-7.

burgeoning IT industry but a relatively low level of domestic IT use.

This is not to imply that encouragement of domestic use is wasted effort. While encouraging domestic IT use of itself may not directly encourage IT industries, it may play an important role in preparing cadres of people with the requisite skills to permit development of such an industry. In any case, it is hardly likely that a policy of encouraging domestic IT use would have any negative effects on IT industry development; in the worst case, it may not be quite as beneficial as supposed.

Human Capital

As defined earlier, human capital is a set of skills a population can acquire by education and training.

Figure 5. Education system dimensions

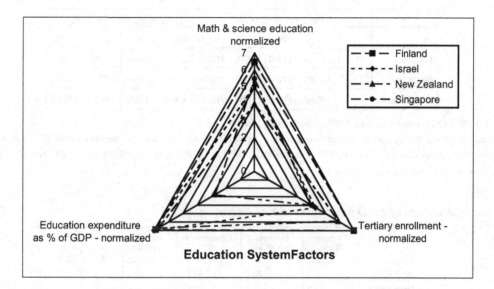

The data presented here on education are from the World Economic Forum's (1999) rankings and survey of managers and from UNESCO's data on education budgets. The data are exhibited in Tables 13 and 14 and in Figure 5. Please note that the math and science education ranks represent managers' subjective feelings about the state of education in their countries, whereas the education expenditure and tertiary enrolment data are objective findings. The data in Table 14 and Figure 5 have been normalised as specified following the table.

According to Figure 5, Finland leads in all three dimensions, although the education expenditures of Israel and New Zealand are, in percentage, very close. These data contain some surprising elements.

First is the very low percentage of GDP spent by Singapore on education. (It should be noted, however, that education accounts for 23% of the total government budget.) This is even more surprising when taken together with the high score on math and science education. One can only conclude that Singapore's education system must

be remarkably efficient compared to the others.

A second surprise is that New Zealand's high rate of tertiary enrolment does not seem to have had a great impact on its IT industries. This might be explained by the way tertiary students are distributed across the various disciplines.

A third surprise is that Israel scores third on math and science education and yet has managed to lead the four countries studied in IT industry development. One plausible explanation is the large number of well-trained scientists and engineers who immigrated to Israel in the 1990s and may have compensated for deficiencies in the education system. Thus, Israel may be living on borrowed time unless it can upgrade its educational system. On the other hand, it should be noted that much of Israel's IT industry is in the hands of start-up ventures with young managers, many of them graduates of ICT training in the Israel Defence Forces (Ariav & Goodman, 1994). Thus, relevant military training and experience are probably also factors compensating for the less developed public education system.

Table 15. National R&D outlays and numbers of researchers

	Rank	Research as % of GNP				Researchers/1M inhabitants			
Israel	1	2.23	(1989)	2.35	(1997)	4,828	(1984)	5087	(1997)
Finland	2	1.20	(1987)	2.70	(1997)	2,146	(1987)	2,799	(1995)
Singapore	3	0.91	(1984)	2.32	(1995)	930	(1984)	2,318	(1995)
New Zealand	4	0.95	(1989)	1.04	(1995)	1,450	(1989)	1,663	(1995)

Source. UNESCO Statistical Yearbook 1999. Selected R&D Indicators.
Note: Data for the number of researchers in Israel are not available for recent years. The number for 1997 was computed by multiplying the number of researchers in 1984 by the increase in % of GDP devoted to R&D between 1989 and 1997 (5.4%); this is clearly a very conservative estimate

Table 16. Distribution of R&D funds by sector of origin

	IT Industry Rank	Business enterprise	Government	Higher education	Private non-profit	Funds from abroad
Israel 1995	1	35.7	40.7	10.2	7.0	6.5
Finland 1995	2	57.7	37.4	0.4	—	4.5
Singapore 1995	3	62.5	31.4	2.4	—	3.7
New Zealand 1993	4	33.9	54.7	8.9	—	2.4

R&D and Technological Infrastructure

Research and development are usually acknowledged as important underpinnings of high tech industry success. This is often buttressed by evidence that "Silicon Valley" type development is at least partly due to the proximity of high standard academic institutions. Data on percent of GNP devoted to research and number of researchers relative to population are exhibited in Table 15. Table 16 exhibits sources of R&D funds.

Table 15 indicates that the development rankings closely reflect the number of researchers per million population. Table 16 shows that Israel has a higher percentage of its R&D outlay originating in universities and that it also has a higher percentage of its research funded from abroad than do the other countries. This presumably has a twofold effect; foreign funded R&D is frequently

also channelled to universities from bi-national funds (e.g., joint Israel-German and Israel-US funds) and international organisations such as the European Union research programs. On the basis of the perception that high-tech industries develop in proximity to clusters of universities, we speculate that university R&D provides the greatest spur to IT industrial development. It should also be noted that in 1989, Israel spent a much larger portion of its GNP on R&D than did the other countries at that time, so there may well be a cumulative effect which was still being felt. It is also quite possible that the substantial growth in the R&D expenditures of Finland and Singapore will be reflected in their industries when more recent data become available.

In the other two dimensions—research institutions and scientists and engineers—Finland is second to Israel. While it is intuitively obvious that these dimensions promote IT industry develop-

Figure 6. IT industry development relative to government R&D funding

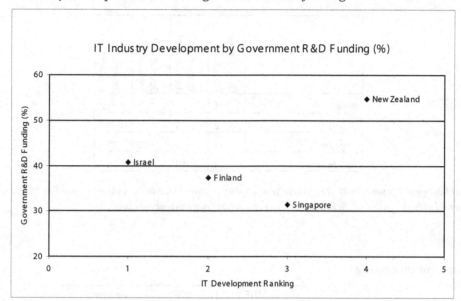

Table 17. Technology infrastructure scores

	Development Ranking	Technological Sophistication[1]	Scientists and Engineers[2]	Research Institutions[3]	Technological Sophistication[1] Normalized	Scientists and Engineers[2] Normalized	Research Institutions[3] Normalized
Israel	1	5.82	6.32	6.32	5.58	6.32	6.32
Finland	2	5.95	5.89	5.79	5.95	5.77	5.51
Singapore	3	5.65	5.62	4.80	5.10	5.42	4.00
New Zealand	4	5.26	4.52	5.10	4.00	4.00	4.46

Source. World Economic Forum (1999). (1) Overall, your country is a world leader in technology. (2) Scientists and engineers are prevalent and of high quality. (3) Scientific research institutions are truly world class.
Normalization. All data normalized on the interval 4-7.

ment, the data underscore this perception. It is not clear why Finland's lead in the educational factors and technological sophistication does not translate into a lead in the other two dimensions. One plausible explanation is, again, the large number of scientists and engineers who immigrated to Israel in the 1990s, many of whom gravitated to research institutions and so may have compensated for its less developed education sector.

These data do not accord very well with the model of Grossman and Helpman (1989, 1991). Their analysis found that the first-best growth path "can be attained with subsidies to both R&D and the production of intermediates". The second-

Table 18. Technology infrastructure rankings

	Development Ranking	Technological Sophistication[1]	Scientists and Engineers[2]	Research Institutions[3]
Israel	1	7	1	2
Finland	2	5	9	7
Singapore	3	9	13	21
New Zealand	4	16	44	17

Source. World Economic Forum (1999). (1) Overall, your country is a world leader in technology. (2) Scientists and engineers are prevalent and of high quality. (3) Scientific research institutions are truly world class.

Table 19. Innovation rankings

	UIF[1]	DIF[2]	Innovation Factor
Finland	2	5	3
Israel	4	19	16
New Zealand	20	16	18
Singapore	10	17	16

Source. World Economic Forum (1999). (1) Upstream Innovation Factor rank. (2) Downstream Innovation Factor Rank

Figure 7. R&D and technological sophistication

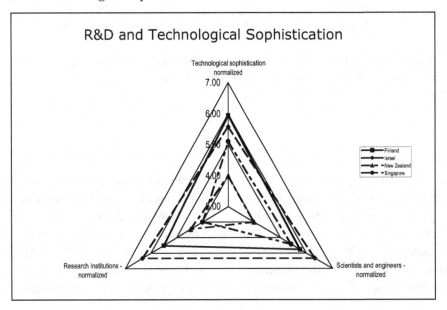

best growth path can be achieved with subsidies to R&D alone. However, the success rankings developed here bear only a tenuous relationship to the portion of R&D funding provided by the government; this is highlighted by the fact that New Zealand has the highest proportion of government R&D funding, as exhibited in Figure 6. Another point of interest in the data is that the highest business and lowest government contributions to R&D are in Singapore.

In addition to R&D outlays, an important factor in developing high-tech industries is the nature of the technological infrastructure, the environment within which R&D take place. Table 17 exhibits survey data on managerial perceptions of three infrastructure items—national technological sophistication, availability and quality of scientists and engineers, and quality of research institutions. Table 18 exhibits country rankings on the same items. The data are displayed graphically in Figure 7.

The data on technological sophistication appear to paint a clear picture in which Israel leads in scientists and engineers and research institutions and is second on technological sophistication. As mentioned, Israel has been fortunate in the influx of trained personnel it experienced with the break up of the Soviet Union and also has highly regarded research institutions. Thus it would seem that there is a clear relationship between these items and IT industry development.

As a final element of technological infrastructure, Table 19 exhibits innovation rankings. These indicate that Israel, New Zealand and Singapore are ranked very closely on this factor while Finland is ranked much more highly. The case of Israel is rather interesting as its ranking is composed of a very high upstream innovation factor (UIF) and a rather low downstream innovation factor (DIF). This apparently reflects the nature of Israeli R&D, which is very innovative, but less successful in marketing the resulting innovations.

Table 20. Elements of firm strategies

	Development rank	MCI[1]	Obtaining Technology[2]	International Brands[3]	Absorbing new technology[4]	Competitive Advantage[5]	Exporting Companies[6]
Score							
Israel	1	20	5,74	4.66	5.79	5.86	5.59
Finland	2	2	5.74	5.84	6.16	5.84	5.58
Singapore	3	12	4.33	4.56	5.53	5.21	5.21
New Zealand	4	16	4.72	5.39	5.35	4.62	4.82
Rank							
Israel	1	20	3	22	6	7	11
Finland	2	2	3	7	2	10	13
Singapore	3	12	23	25	16	21	16
New Zealand	4	16	14	15	9	14	20

Source. World Economic Forum (1999). (1) Microeconomic Competitiveness Index rank. (2) Companies obtain technology by pioneering their own new products or processes. (3) Companies, which sell internationally, have developed their own international brands. (4) Companies are aggressive in absorbing new technology. (5) Competitive advantages of your nations companies in international markets are due to unique products and processes. (6) Exporting companies conduct not only production, but product development, distribution, and marketing.

Firm Strategies

Firm strategies are characterised here by five elements—the method by which technology is obtained, the development of international brands, absorption of new technology, the uniqueness of products, and the breadth of the value chain. These data, together with the questions asked are exhibited in Table 20. As a matter of interest, the microeconomic competitiveness index ranks are also exhibited. The data are displayed graphically in Figure 8.

The picture arising in this connection is rather an interesting one. Finnish firms clearly have the best-rounded strategy, scoring highly on all five dimensions. Singapore's strategy is concentrated on export companies managing a large portion of the value chains for their products. New Zealand's strategies are based on internationally known brand names and on unique products and processes. Israel is roughly equal to Finland on three of the dimensions—pioneering own technologies, unique products and processes, and coverage of the value chain, while scoring much lower than Finland on absorption of new technology and

brand names. Thus, it would seem that firms concentrating on the three dimensions common to Finland and Israel are best placed in terms of IT industry development.

Availability of Capital

The availability of capital to fund new start-ups and to maintain existing firms and their growth is clearly a major factor in IT industry development. This is not a purely endogenous factor as, in addition to local availability of capital, it also depends on exogenous factors such as the availability of foreign direct investment, ability to raise capital overseas, and so forth. However, foreign capital is most readily available when the internal situation is favorable and, in that sense, even foreign investment may be viewed, at least in part, as an endogenous factor. Data on some elements of capital availability are exhibited in Table 21 and charted in Figure 9. The elements listed are availability of venture capital, gross domestic investment, R&D spending, and IT stock market listings, both domestic and foreign. It should be noted that only the last of these relate

Figure 8. Firm strategy dimensions

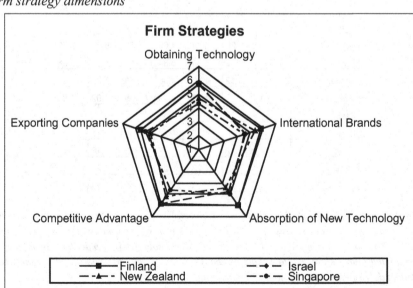

Table 21. Availability of capital rankings

	Development rank	Venture Capital Availability[1]	Gross domestic investment rank[2]	R&D Spending[3]	Domestic IT Stock Market Listings[4]	Foreign Stock Market Listings[4]
Israel	1	5.51	20.71	5.32	80	80
Finland	2	5.05	19.00	5.53	27	1
Singapore	3	3.77	32.10	4.59	35	2
New Zealand	4	4.59	20.12	3.85	3	0
normalized						
Israel	1	5.51	4.1	5.32	6.7	6.7
Finland	2	5.05	3.8	5.53	2.5	0.1
Singapore	3	3.77	6.4	4.59	3.2	0.1
New Zealand	4	4.59	4.0	3.85	0.3	0

directly to IT industries; however, in countries with important IT sectors, much of other sources are invested in IT.

Based on these data, it appears that, overall, capital is more readily available in Israel than elsewhere, especially by means of stock offerings. Singapore is clearly endowed with high domestic investment, but overall availability is about on a par with Finland. Capital seems to be least available in New Zealand.

As the capital availability data seem to follow the IT industry ranking quite closely, it would appear that this is indeed an important factor determining IT industry success.

CONCLUSION

In this chapter we have provided an in-depth analysis of the IT industry in four countries: Finland, Israel, New Zealand and Singapore. We have also presented the relative changes that occurred over the period 1994 through 1998. We believe that our use of both longitudinal and time slice data represents a considerable advance over earlier studies of a similar nature. As such,

this paper represents one of the first attempts to provide a comprehensive picture of the factors affecting IT production in small developed countries over time. The findings are probably also more broadly applicable to knowledge use and knowledge based industries in general and to small countries in particular.

The primary purpose of this article has been to identify the key drivers in fostering IT industry success in these countries. Given that IT industries provide a technical platform for innovation and are a key component in fostering the development of the knowledge economy, we believe that such a quest is well justified.

Our study has revealed that four of the six endogenous variables have a close relationship to the success of IT industries in small developed countries. Our analysis thus largely supports the model of IT industry success developed earlier (Figure 1). Research and development, technological infrastructure, firm strategies, and capital availability all appear to have significant impacts on the development of IT industries.

Rather surprising are our findings that domestic IT use and education seem to have little impact. In the case of domestic use we surmise

Figure 9. Availability of capital

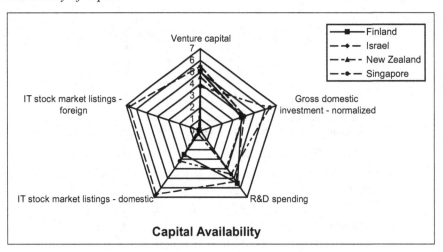

that this is because of the nature of IT industries in small countries, in which the local market is not a dominant factor. In the case of education, the finding may be an artefact of the small sample size and of the special case of Israel with massive immigration of scientists and engineers within that small sample. It may also indicate that education is a necessary but not a sufficient factor in IT industry success.

We believe our findings have important implications for researchers and policy makers interested in the relationship between the production and use of information technology (IT) and economic development. Many countries around the world are looking for ways to promote the development of the knowledge economy, and information technology industries in particular. Our article suggests that policy makers need to concentrate on fostering research and development, the technological infrastructure, firm strategies and capital availability if they wish to promote the development of indigenous IT industries.

Finally, we recommend that our findings should be treated with caution. The constructs that we have developed need further refinement and additional efforts need to be made to develop universal and consistent data sources. Much addi-

tional research is required, and especially research which looks at a broader range of countries, both small and large. Given a large enough sample, it should be possible to apply statistical testing, thus lending greater credibility to any relationships found. We do believe, however, that our present findings represent one step towards understanding the factors that affect the development of IT industries in small developed countries, and may be relevant to other countries as well.

REFERENCES

Ariav, G., & Goodman, S.E. (1994). Israel: Of swords and software plowshares. *Communications of the ACM, 37*(6), 17-21.

Blanning, R.W., Bui, T.X., & Tan, M. (1997). National information infrastructure in Pacific Asia. *Decision Support Systems, 21,* 215-227.

Central Bureau of Statistics (Israel). (1999, August). Exports by economic branch. *Monthly Bulletin of Statistics, 50*(8).

Central Bureau of Statistics (Israel). (1999, October). K. labour and wages. *Monthly Bulletin of Statistics, 50*(10).

Dedrick, J.L., Goodman, S.E., & Kraemer, K.L. (1995). Little engines that could: Computing in small energetic countries. *Comm. of the ACM, 38*(5), 21-26.

Dedrick, J.L., & Kraemer, K.L. (1995). National technology policy and computer production in Asia-Pacific countries. *Information Society, 11,* 29-58.

Dedrick, J.L., & Kraemer, K.L. (1998). *Asia's computer challenge: Threat or opportunity for the United States and the world?* New York: Oxford University Press.

Deloitte & Touche Consulting Group. (1998). 1998 top 200 New Zealand companies. *Management Magazine, 45*(11), 74-87.

Dun & Bradstreet Israel Ltd. (n.d.). *Leading industrial companies by sales revenue: 150 Companies.*

The Economist. (1999). *Pocket world in figures.* London: Profile Books.

The Economist. (2000, April 29-May 5). *Asian capitalism: The end of tycoons.*

Ein-Dor, P., Myers, M.D., & Raman, K.S. (1997). IT in three small developed countries. *Journal of Management Information Systems, 13*(4), 61-89.

Finnfacts. (1999). *50 largest Finnish companies.* Retrieved November 11, 1999: *www.finnfacts. com/Ffeng0399/record_profits.htm*

Finnish Newspapers Association. (2000). Facts about the Finnish press. Retrieved May 17, 2000: *http://www.sanoma lehdet.fi/en/tietoa/graafi1. shtml#3*

Grossman, G., & Helpman, E. (1989). Growth and welfare in a small open economy. Working paper no. 2970. National Bureau of Economic Research. Cambridge, MA.

Grossman, G., & Helpman, E. (1991). *Innovation and growth in the global economy.* Cambridge, MA: MIT Press.

Hofstede, G. (1980). *Culture's consequences: International differences in work-related values.* Beverly Hills, CA: Sage Publications.

IMD. (1999). *The world competitiveness yearbook 1999.* Lausanne.

K-III Reference Corporation. (1997). *The world almanac and book of facts 1997.*

Keren, T. (2000, January 25). 99 software exports up 33% to $2 Bln. *Globes.*

Koren, O. (1999, November 22). The export institute: 2000 will be a turning point in exports; will grow by 6% - to 17 billion dollars. *Ha'aretz.*

Kraemer, K.L., King, J.L., & Gurbaxani, V. (1992). Economic development, government policy, and the diffusion of computing in Asia-Pacific countries. *Public Administration Review, 52*(2), 146-156.

Ministry of Commerce. (1999, April). *Statistics on information technology in New Zealand.* Wellington.

National Computer Board, Singapore. (1998). *IT Focus.*

New Zealand Company Registrar 1996-97 (35th ed.). (1999, April). Prepared by Headliner Publishing Co. Published by Mercantile Gazette Marketing Ltd., Christchurch.

Nygard, A.M., & Kunnas, T. (1998). *Computer networking hardware/software.* Finland: Int. Trade Administration.

NZ Computer Industry Directory 1999. (1999) A Computerworld publication. Published by IDG Communications.

Romer, P.M. (1990). Endogenous technological change. *The Journal of Political Economy, 98*(5), Part 2, S71-S102.

Statistics Finland. (1999a). *On the road to the Finnish information society - Summary.* Retrieved from http://www.stat.fi/tk/yr/tttietoti_ en.html

Statistics Finland. (1999b). *Production and foreign trade of high-technology products.* Retrieved from http://www.stat.fi/tk/yr/tthuippu1_ en.html

Statistics New Zealand. (1998). *New Zealand official yearbook* (101st ed.). Wellington, NZ: Department of Statistics.

Tel-Aviv Stock Exchange. *Electronics and computer listings.* Retrieved November 17, 1999, from http://www.tase.co.il/qsystem/index. cgi?subsection

UNESCO Institute for Statistics. *Public expenditure on education as percentage of gross national product and as percentage of government expenditure.* Retrieved September 28, 2000, from http://unescostat.unesco.org/i_pages/IndPGNP. asp

UNESCO Institute for Statistics. *UNESCO statistical yearbook 1999.* Science and technology: III.1 Selected R&D indicators. Retrieved from http://unescostat.unesco.org/statsen/statistics/ yearbook/tables/

UNESCO Institute for Statistics. *UNESCO statistical yearbook 1999. Science and technology: III.3 Percentage distribution of gross domestic expenditure on R&D by source of funds.* Retrieved from http://unescostat. unesco.org/statsen/statistics/yearbook/tables\SandTec\

United Nations Development Program. (1999). Human Development Index (HDI). *Human development report 1999.* Retrieved July 7, 2000, from http://www.undp.org/hdro/HDI.html

U.S. Bureau of the Census. (1999). Report WP/98. *World population profile, 1998.* Washington, D.C.: U.S. Government Printing Office. Retrieved from http://www.census.gov/ftp/pub/ipc/www

Watson, R., & Myers, M.D. (2001). IT industry success in small countries: The case of Finland and New Zealand. *Journal of Global Information Management, 9*(2), 4-14.

World Bank. (1999). *World development report 1998/99: Knowledge for development.* Washington: World Bank. Retrieved from http://www. worldbank.org/wdr/wdr98/

World Economic Forum. (1999). *The global competitiveness report 1999.* Geneva, Switzerland.

This work was previously published in the Journal of Global Information Management, Vol. 12, No. 4, , pp. 23-49, copyright 2004 by Idea Group Publishing (an imprint of IGI Global).

Chapter XIV
Information Technology and Environment

Zhao Meng
Kunming University of Science and Technology, China

Zheng Fahong
Kunming University of Science and Technology, China

Lu Lei
Kunming University of Science and Technology, China

ABSTRACT

The development of science and technology enhances the economy. However, it also involves many environmental problems. In China, as a developing country, the concentration of the population in cities causes several things. The first is an ecological crisis caused by the environmental problems. On the other hand, with the help of IT, we can monitor the environment in real time online. IT provides so many methods to analyze the data and to control the pollution. So many environmental information systems for environmental impact assessment and environment management have been developed. Making mathematic models to simulate the environment's change, such as to simulate the diffusion of gas in the air, is very helpful for environment impact assessment and environment protection. Information technology is very helpful in handling environmental information.

INTRODUCTION

With the development of the economy, environmental problems become more and more serious all over the world. In developing countries, environmental pollution even restricts economic development. In the science sector, a rapidly growing community conceived new computer applications making and exchanging information in the field of environmental protection. Many information technologies, such as database management systems, real-time computing, geographic information systems (GISs), remote sensing (RS), and multimedia, have been used in dealing with environmental problems. During the past two decades, environmental informatics has been established as an interdisciplinary subject (a combination and integration of computer science, environmental science, and approaches to sustainable development; Werner, Werner, & Kristina, 2006).

Environmental pollution is very serious. The situation of the environment is considerably severe. National SO_2 and COD exhaust exceeds the environment's capacity at 60% and 70%, respectively, 70% of seven water systems are subjected to pollution in different degrees, 75% of lakes have become eutrophic, the air quality of two thirds of cities does not reach environmental standards, one third of the national territories are polluted by acid rain, 50% of city residents are living with noise over the environmental standard, and groundwater in 90% of larger cities is subject to pollution in different degrees. These data well-explain that the environmental situation we face is rigorous. Environmental problems become the most concerning (Wu, 2005).

Information technology permeates extensively in every trade, changing economic and social features deeply. In the environment realm, information technology mainly applies to environmental quality monitoring and management, pollution-source supervision and management, environmental statistics, environmental assessment, ecosystem construction and management, nuclear safety and management, environmental information release, and so forth. It provides technical support and service to environmental management workers and assistance in decision making. It has an important function to raise synthesized decision ability regarding the environment, and to develop and promote environmental supervision

to a modern level, strengthen governmental public service ability, set up a resource economy friendly to the environment, and carry out the strategic target of environmental protection.

In this chapter, the application of information technologies in the environmental realm (environmental data collection, data processing, and information systems establishment) are discussed. Automonitoring is widely used in environment quality monitoring and pollution-source monitoring. It uses many information technologies, such as online data collection equipment, data delivering technologies, and data processing technology. Databases, data warehouses, and mathematic models are used in data processing and management. Many information technologies must be integrated in establishing environmental information systems. The most useful and helpful information technology is space technology. IT can also be used to help construct decision support systems.

BACKGROUND

Information technology's development in the environmental protection realm can be divided into three stages: the early part of the 1990s to mid-1990s, the preparation period; 1996 to 2001, the foundation period; and from 2002 to the present, the growth period (Xu, 2005).

In the preparation period, the main content of environmental informatization was the construction of simple management information systems (MISs) and the development of databases.

In the foundation period, all levels of environmental protection bureaus took to transaction automation, and the construction of a network system for environmental information was core. With the construction of environmental information organizations and network development as the foundation, information technology was mainly used in transacting governmental management affairs and providing technical support and service; the system structure regarded C/S as principle.

In the growth period, a series of typical application systems flowed out with comprehensive platforms being representative; the system structure regards the B/S or multilayer system structure as principle. With government Web site construction, application development, data sharing, networks, and standards, information technologies began extensively being applied in various environmental management businesses, and they pushed the development of environmental protection businesses vigorously.

Currently, environment informatization is in the standard construction and scientific management stage. Through the continuous exploration and effort by environment management groups, environmental protection gained plentiful and substantial results and proud achievements. The environmental protection work acquired substantial benefits. Environment-information-based work becomes necessary for environmental protection, and environment informatization has begun to grow, with steps taken into development gradually.

INFORMATION TECHNOLOGIES IN THE FIELD OF THE ENVIRONMENT

Environment Data Collection

Environment Data

Environment data include environment metadata, environment laws and standards data, environment literature and communication data, environment quality data, environment statistics data, environment background data, ecosystem environmental protection data, biodiversity protection data, radiation environment data, and other environment-management-related data (social economic information and planning, programming, etc.). However, according to the data characteristics, the environment data can be divided into four kinds of forms: spatial data, attribute data, relation data, and temporal data (Nie, 2005). In the environment businesses, the core of environment data is the monitoring information of environment quality and pollution sources (Zeng, Chen, & Li, 2005).

Collection of Environment Quality Monitoring Data

In China, environmental monitoring mainly includes automatic monitoring and handicraft monitoring, and along with information technical progress, it develops toward intelligent monitoring gradually. The content of the environmental quality automonitoring system mainly includes the monitoring of air, water, noise, and biology factors.

The national environmental protection system currently has 2,389 total environmental monitoring stations at different levels. There is one national central station, 41 provincial stations, 401 prefecture-level stations, 1,914 county-class stations, and 32 radiation monitoring stations. Nationwide, the environmental monitoring network system has already been founded.

The air automonitoring technique was made widely available quickly; by the first half of 2003, the whole country had constructed 631 sets of air automonitoring systems. In the meantime, the central station started to develop the hookup of the air automonitoring stations in the main cities and checked the quality of the air automonitoring systems. Several provincial stations developed the hookup of air automonitoring systems in the whole province, such as Jiangsu Province, Zhejiang Province, and Liaoning Province (National Environmental Monitoring Center, 2006).

From September 1999 to December 2003, the National Environmental Protection Bureau constructed 82 water quality automonitoring stations on basins of the Songhua River, Liao River, Hai River, Yellow River, Huai River, Yangtze

River, Zhu River, Tai Lake, Chao Lake, Dianchi Lake, and so on. Monitoring items are the water temperature, pH level, DO (dissolved oxygen), TB (turbidity), EC (electronic conductivity), hypermanganate exponent, ammonia nitrogen level, and TOC (total organic carbon; National Environmental Monitoring Center, 2006).

In addition to the above automonitoring systems, we also have a water monitoring network, inshore sea monitoring network, sandstorm monitoring network, East Asia acid sedimentation monitoring network, and so forth to provide related data for the environmental protection bureaus. Also there are many local environmental automonitoring networks that have been constructed in some provinces.

Collection of Pollution-Source Autosupervising Data

In is important to push forward the construction of pollution-source autosupervising systems that can carry out valid supervision of polluting enterprises, can acquire related data expediently, and can be advantageous to adopting prevention and emergency measures in time to react to important pollution accidents. It can also lower the cost of environment protection to enforce laws in the meantime, and to improve the efficiency of enforcing the laws.

The construction and management of pollution-source autosupervising systems rely on several realms, such as environmental monitoring, automatic control, computers, electronics correspondence, and so forth. It is a complicated system to engineer.

A pollution-source autosupervising system can be divided into two sections: a data collection subsystem and information integration subsystem.

The data collection subsystem is a part of the pollution control facilities, and includes the pollutant exhaust supervising instruments installed at the scene of the pollution source (online monitoring and analysis instruments for COD, TOC, pH, water pollution, sulfur dioxide, smoke, dust, and air pollutants), flowmeters and kinemometers, running recording instruments at pollution control facilities (black box), and instruments for data collection and delivery (used for data saving, encrypting, displacement, and receiving, and for sounding alarms).

The information integration subsystem includes computer information terminal equipment and a supervision center system (pollution-source autosupervising center's information management software and databases, etc.).

Pollution-source autosupervising systems have already had history for more than 10 years, and have already carried out COD, NH_3-N, SO_2, and NO_x pollution automonitoring analysis automatically on the scene, wireless delivery, long-range controlling, and real-time alarming. According to the inquisitions of 113 main environmental protection cities, 3,225 pollutant-outlet automatic supervision projects have already been carried out in 3,006 enterprises; online monitor is close to 7,000 setups. The different-level environmental protection bureaus have already built 84 supervision centers of different scales. Some cities invest a great deal of funds and manpower to construct autosupervision systems and have already started producing results. Jinan City has set up fume autosupervision systems in companies that own over 90% of coal consumption, carried out the automatic supervision of pollutants such as sulfur dioxide, nitrogen oxide, and carbon monoxide, and so forth. Xiamen City has carried out the automatic supervision of the whole city's wastewater treatment factory and the main pollutants of the important water pollution sources in the city, and has already used online monitoring data in the pollutant discharge fee's expropriation. Rugao City, in Jiangsu Province, monitors the water quality and the quantity of the wastewater treatment plant's discharge automatically every day. The wastewater treatment plant can draw money from the construction department, relying on the proof-of-treatment amount from the environmental bureau. Pollution-source autosupervision has already become an indispensable part in the city's environmental supervising system (Wu, 2005).

Criterions and Standards about Environmental Automonitoring

In order to promote the development of automatic monitoring, strengthen data share, expand the data's applying scope, deepen the application of data resource excavation, and let the automatic monitoring data develop a larger function in environmental protection, a series of criteria and standards have been issued successively. The environmental monitoring central station began to authenticate enterprises and their products. Related norms and standards are the data delivering standard of online pollution-source autosupervising systems, the management means of pollution-source autosupervising, the environmental air quality automonitoring technical specification, the rainfall automonitoring technical request and examination method, and so on.

Environmental Data Management

Environmental Data Primary Handling

Only after the necessary sorting and processing, monitoring data and diagrams can become meaningful to users and valuable decision makers. Environmental data processing mainly includes data reorganizing, statistics analysis and pollution evaluation, estimating and forecasting, environmental quality report compilation, and the establishment of pollution treatment counterplans, and also includes data delivering, saving, indexing, and output.

The whole reorganizing method of the original data includes an initial sorting and categorizing phase with simple statistical work. Through auditing original record forms and examining data when categorizing, the data is reorganized. The whole reorganizing process includes collecting related data and resources; calculating using daily, monthly, or annual statistics forms of monitoring results; and carrying put certain analysis and inductions.

Table 1. The situation of data transmission of main business data in the central station

Monitoring Business	Units who report to the leadership	Contents of Transmission	Method of Transmission
Air quality daily	118 cities	Daily average value of monitoring spot	Through FTP
Air quality forecast	90 cities	Daily average forecast value of monitoring spot	Through FTP
Surface water monthly	Provincial bureaus	Monthly average value of nation control cross-section or spot	Through FTP
Portable water sources monthly	113 cities	Water quantity and standard data at intake spot	Through FTP
Environmental quality annually	Provincial bureaus	Monitoring data at spots of national systems (water, air, noise, acid rain)	Through FTP
Environmental statistics annually	Provincial bureaus	Basic data of 70,000 companies and all pollution sources' statistic data all over the country	E-mail
Water quality automonitoring and water quality weekly	82 automonitoring stations	Real-time data and weekly data	Through FTP or satellite
Sandstorm emergency monitoring	Sandstorm monitoring stations	Wind speed, wind direction, horizontal visibility, TSP, PM_{10}	Fax and e-mail
Seawater bathing place weekly	19 seawater bathing places	Seawater quality and swimming suitability	Fax and e-mail

Further data processing and management relate closely to database and environmental information system work, and will be mentioned in the next part.

Environmental Data Transmission

The environmental data transmission method is through FTP (file transfer protocol) or e-mail. Some business data can be transferred through satellite or fax, as in Table 1 (Wen, Liang, & Wen, 2005).

Database

The database is the sill of information system and one of the most valid means of managing the information system's mass of complex data. A database system constitutes a database, software for data managing, a database management system, the database application, the system terrace, and database administrators.

The data are saved according to the pattern provided by database system. The database management system is a kind of software for managing the database; it is the core of the database system. The database management system deals mainly with the definition, handling, controlling, and service of data. Database management systems in common use are VFP, DB2, INGRE5, UNIFY, IN-FORMIX, ORACLE, SYBASE, SQLSERVER, and so forth.

The database application can support various application programs and build up applying logic. The tool languages in common use are C, COBOL, FORTRAN, and PowerBuilder, among others. The system terrace includes the operating system, and computer and network system.

The administrator of the database mainly carries on with the database design, maintenance, and surveillance, making the system keep the best appearance with the most high efficiency.

The state's environmental monitoring central station and each station in every province and city has built up an environment monitoring database. The central station databases include an environmental quality annual report database, major-city daily air quality and forecasting database, monthly surface water database, and environmental statistics annual report database. A national space database has also already been initially established, and mainly includes a 1:400,000 map of the country's cities, a 1:50,000 city area database, national remote sensing videos, and a land-covering database (Wen et al., 2005). Others have environmental databases of Chinese resources, environmental databases of Xinjiang resources in the ecosystem, atmospheric environment and science databases, macroscopic environmental databases, space environmental databases, environmental chemistry databases, the Earth's environment and weather-variety database, synthesized databases of the national ecosystem environment, environmental databases of the South China Sea's physics and chemistry, ecosystem environmental databases, the tropical gulf ecosystem's environmental databases, database of the Zhujing River's estuary ecosystem, database of China's middle-east region's ecosystem, and so forth.

The construction of the databases laid a good foundation for the environmental information system. For excavating further information from the data and providing support for decisions, we have to develop related environmental information systems.

Data Warehouse

For strengthening the decision supporting system, we must build an environmental data warehouse. The data warehouse is a data aggregate that faces the topics, is integrated, is stable, and verifies according to the time. The relationship hidden in the data, uncared-for factors, and other information helpful to forecast trends and aid decision making can be found through online analysis technology and data excavation (Zhang & Tian, 2005).

Environment Mathematics Model

The environmental system is a complex and huge miscellaneous system. It is constructed by many subsystems with different characteristics that cross one another. Each characteristic of the subsystems can be illustrated using a mathematical model, so the mathematical models in the environment system are various. An environment mathematical model is divided into the simulation model and the management model. The simulation model is mainly used for environmental system behavior emulation, estimation, and evaluation, but the management model is used for the environmental system's programming and management decisions; the simulation model is the foundation of the management model (Zheng & Chen, 2003).

The amount of calculation according to the mathematical model is very huge, so the computer's technical development applies software to construct and use models more quickly and efficiently. Extensively applied in the environment realm currently are the river water quality model, estuary water quality model, lake and reservoir water quality model, surface water quality management model, groundwater quality model, air quality basic model, air pollution prediction model, multimedia environment ecology mathematics model, and so forth. There are many kinds of software on the surface water quality model in general use, such as QUAL2.E, QUAL2.E UNCAS, STEADY, Streeter Phelps, WASP, WQRRS, HEC5 Q, and so on. The ISC3, CALPUFF, UAM-V model, and others are software related to the air environment that are in use. Customers can choose related software to use according to their needs.

Earth-Space Technology

Earth-space technology is a combination of all GISs, RS systems, and global positioning systems (GPSs), and is called the 3S technique. These are the essential foundation tools for making the modern environmental information system and enhancing its efficiency. GISs with a geographic space database is the foundation of a computer system, carrying out the collection, management, analysis, imitation, and display of space-related data under the support of the computer software and hardware, adopting the analysis method of the geography model. GIM can provide variously spatial and dynamic geographic information in good time, and is built to service geological research and decision making. Geographic information systems and remote sensing are two techniques that develop independently, but have a close relation. On one hand, the remote-sensing information is the important information source of geographic information systems; on the other hand, remote-sensing inquisition needs to make use of the assistance data (including various maps, data measurement and statistics data, etc.) within the geography information system to improve data classification accuracy and graphics accuracy. Navigation satellite timing and GPS have shown to be well-suited applications in geodetic survey, engineering survey, city planning, lithosphere movement monitoring and earthquake forecasting, oceanography, glaciology, and meteorology, and have been recognized in many nations.

GPS's application in remote-sensing inquisition mainly includes two aspects: (a) first, to identify things that can be used as control points such as bridges, joints of rivers, and villages, and then to arrive on the spot, make use of GPS assurance at each actual position (longitude and latitude degrees), and carry out geometry rectification and projection transformation on the picture, and (b) according to the space's coordinates, locate the sample pixels on the picture, making sure of the sample pixels' corresponding earth style and using it to classify (GPS World, n.d.).

ENVIRONMENTAL INFORMATION SYSTEM

Definition of Environmental Information System

In order to promote the valid exploitation of environmental data and to contribute efforts to the environmental protection work efficiently, comprehensively making use of the various information technologies and developing the environmental information system was subjected to more and more values. The environmental information system is a comprehensive system with a decision assistance function, which combines actual investigation results and analysis of customer need and the environment's own scientific role with dynamic online environment monitoring data as the main data source; it inosculates the database,

data warehouse, 3S technique, model technique and multimedia technique, artificial intelligence technique, imitation technique, and the Internet. The main functions of the environmental information system include the following.

The system carries out the efficient and accurate online monitoring, obtaining, saving, analysis, management, and expression of data related to the environment's main factors, such as water, air, noise, and ecosystems, at a large multidimensional, multisource scope.

The system also inosculates high-resolution remote-sensing monitoring information, imitates environmental evolvement using multitime sequence pictures, and instructs environmental programming and management work.

Another function is to carry out the integration of the 3S technique with online monitoring, the environment model, the Internet, office

Figure 1. The structure of a typical environmental information system (Cui & Sun, 2003)

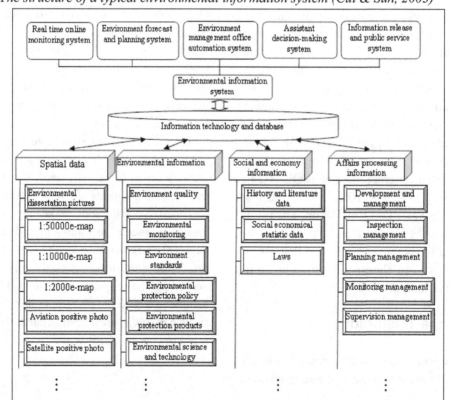

automation, and policy-making support to keep the view clear.

The system also studies and develops special-subject environmental subsystems based on information technology. These include pollution-source and environment quality online monitoring subsystems, environment capacity allotment subsystems, dynamic environment programming subsystems, environment quality estimating and forecasting subsystems, early-warning subsystems for environment pollution accidents, decision-making assistance subsystems, comprehensive management and office automation subsystems, environment information release and public service subsystems, and so on.

Finally, the system researches and develops the environment decision-support system under the support of the information technologies.

Cui and Sun (2003) put forward the structure of an environmental information system. It shows the environmental information system's various functions.

Environmental Information System Developing Foundation

An environmental information management organization has been built up that has three grades: the national level, province level, and city level. With the help of the Asian Development Bank, World Bank, and Japanese government, the National Central Bureau Information Center, 32 province-class environment information centers, and 110 city environment information centers have been constructed and provided with advanced computer software, hardware, and network equipments.

Each province-class environmental protection bureau and a majority of prefecture environmental protection bureaus have constructed government Web sites and local area network (LAN) official business systems. In the meantime, the national government's Web site of the central bureau's overall publicity and governmental affairs has outstanding characteristics and acquired the award of Chinese Excellent Government Gate Web Site. The National Environmental Protection Bureau's comprehensive terrace of governmental affairs was set up in June 2004. That terrace gathers the network management, system application, data sharing, and information service as a whole, becoming a technical forerunner that is applied extensively with perfect function, safe credibility, and an efficient information infrastructure. It provides an integrated environment and system for environment application systems, providing an all-direction information technology support for governmental affairs transactions, information sharing, decision management, and the unfurling of governmental affairs of the State Environmental Protection Administration.

In order to raise environment data to the management level completely and to strengthen the shared service of the environmental data, the State Environmental Protection Administration of China has started to construct a national center at the end of 2004. Building a commonwealth, fundamental, strategic condition terrace with a science and technology foundation can improve science and technology's innovation environment effectively, strengthen science and technology's development ability, and provide powerful support for science and technology's farsighted development and breakthrough.

In order to guarantee environment informatization's positive development, a series of laws and standards have been drawn up. The national environmental information center of the State Environmental Protection Administration has already released the "the Ninth Five-Plan on Environmenta Imformatiozation and Long-Range Objective through the year 2010," "the Administration for Environment Information" (Temporary), "the Guideline of national Environment Informatization Construction of the Tenth Five-Year Plan." "the State Environmental Protection Administration e-governmental affairs responsibility division" tentative method for application software development in the

State Environmental Protection Administration, the environmental information standardization manual, and so forth.

Relying on study items with the help of Japan, more than 1,000 people in the environment information center have been organized to learn about environment informatization. A talented troop with stronger business ability and management levels has been built up.

A satellite communications network, the national province-class environmental protection bureau, and 121 city environmental protection bureaus have already been set up. They are linked to the whole 87 water quality automonitoring stations, and carry out no paper-file delivery between the central bureau and the provincial bureaus (Wang, 2005).

We release environmental information to society through Web sites, newspapers, and TV, including information on the daily air quality of 84 major cities, the air quality forecasting of 68 major cities, the weekly water quality of 82 major sections of the main national water systems, and the weekly water quality of 28 bathing beaches in 16 cities in the summer that are subject to widespread social concern (Li, 2005).

Environmental Information System's Actual Development

The State Environmental Protection Administration contraposes the actual need for environment quality management, environment statistics management, construction items examination and approval management, drainage declaration management, effluent fees management, scale breed aquatics factory management, and other environment management businesses. They developed many application systems, such as the national environmental statistics MIS, the national environment quality monitoring management system, the national pollutant discharge declaration information management system, the national ecosystem investigation information

management system, the national environment superintendence information system, the accident response information management system, and so forth. Environment management work efficiency and standardization have been raised, obtaining well-applied results.

FUTURE TRENDS

Information technology has gotten extensive application of various and national scope in the environmental protection realm. However, there are still some problems that exist. To aim at later environment informatization, we have to accomplish the following tasks:

1. To push forward e-governmental affairs to elevate the environment supervision and service level. Related software and hardware facilities and personnel training must be completed as soon as possible, especially in poor regions.

2. To strengthen network integrating work, perfect environment information terrace construction, push forward environment information to standardize and connect networks with each other, construct with "gold circle engineering," organize the research and development strategy of environment information, improve independent creative ability, push environmental information management system reform, and make great efforts to carry out numerical environmental protection

3. To complete the setting up of a national environment data center as soon as possible and construct a nationwide unifying terrace to carry out data sharing

4. To perfect systems in existence and make them exert their biggest function, pay attention to the establishment of the enterprise-class application system, and overcome low-level development that can result in funds

waste, low-efficiency use, and difficulty in integration

5. To strengthen the application of GIS and other earth-space technologies, combining them together with the environmental data's spatial and temporal features, so they can be more available for decision-making personnel.

In recent years, information technology has developed very quickly and has produced many new techniques and methods. The development of computer processing and the distributive data system has made sharing information resources in the larger scope probable, but the establishment of a unifying standard is still the biggest problem when carrying out different systems' integration. Information multimedia can extend to the environmental information system's application realm and raise its service quality. The environmental information system will turn to network usage with the intelligence function and software development industrialization. Various information technologies' combined use is also a development direction.

CONCLUSION

Information technical development can promote the establishment of an environmental monitoring information system, pollution-source supervision information system, ecosystem protection information system, and nuclear safety and radiation information system, and can be advantageous in collecting great quantities of accurate data and carrying out qualitative and quantitative analysis. It can also provide scientific decision support for environment management. Through the establishment of information systems, time and region restrictions of environment management can be broken through, and environmental information objectivity and reliability can be guaranteed to the highest degree. This is advantageous in break-

ing regional protectionism, and strengthening environmental laws enforcement ability. Through building up environmental real-time monitoring and the environment abrupt affairs emergency conductor system, we are ably to quickly respond to the environmental emergencies, estimate the influence and bane of the affairs correctly, and then carry out the conductor to process and guarantee national environmental safety. Through the establishment of environment Web sites and electronic governmental affairs, people can make use of the modern information network to collect and unfurl environmental protection information. It is advantageous to open an efficient way for government and public interaction, to guarantee the public knows what has happened, to inspect or to participate in environmental protection, to better guarantee public rights, and to mobilize and exert the enthusiasm of the public to participate in environmental protection public affairs. Information technology application enhances the efficiency of handling official business and doing management work, and can help environmental protection bureaus get environment quality information and dynamic data on pollution sources in time. Through environmental protection information unfurled to the public and open governmental affairs that make environmental protection work clear, we can strengthen the drumbeating of environmental protection and education, raise all people's environmental protection consciousness, and push forward environmental protection management efficiently.

By actively applying information technology, we can enhance the efficiency of environment protection work, save a great deal in costs, reform and innovate new work patterns, promote scientific policy making, prevent misplay and hazard production, and really show the environmental protection principle of prevention coming first. In the meantime, resources and information technology can provide essential technical support for important pollution accidents and ecosystem tragedy (Liu, 2005).

REFERENCES

Cui, X., & Sun, Q. (2003). IT's application in environmental protection information systems. *Environmental Technology, 2*, 31-34.

GPS World. (n.d.). *The combination of GIS, GPS and RS.* Retrieved July 20, 2006, from http://www.51gps.com/Article/ShowArticle.asp?ArticleID=1070

Li, Z. l. (2005). *Promote e-government, service to environmental management, construct harmonious society.* Paper presented at the Second Meeting of the National Environmental Information Management and Technology's Application, Beijing, China.

Liu, H. Z. (2005). *Motif address of deputy director-general of Department of Science and Technology in the State Environmental Protection Administration of China.* Paper presented at the Second Meeting of the National Environmental Information Management and Technology's Application, Beijing, China.

National Environmental Monitoring Center of China. (n.d.-a). *Brief introduction of water quality auto-monitoring weekly report.* Retrieved from http://www.cnemc.cn/emc/indexs.asp?id=2&cid=26

National Environmental Monitoring Center of China. (n.d.-b). *Construction of urban air quality auto-monitoring system.* Retrieved from http://www.cnemc.cn/country/index.asp?id=1&cid=6

National Environmental Monitoring Center of China. (2006). *Data delivering and interface standard technological criterion of pollution sources on line automatic monitoring systems (exposure draft).* Retrieved July 20, 2006, from http://www.zhb.gov.cn/epi-sepa/zcfg/w3/download/banhan2005-344-2.doc

Nie, Q. H. (Ed.). (2005). *Digital environment.* Beijing, China: Science Press.

Wang, Y. Q. (2006). *The discussion of environment informatization task by deputy director general of the State Environmental Protection Administration of China.* Retrieved July 20, 2006, from http://www.gov.cn/zfjs/2006-06/01/content_297619.htm

Werner, P., Werner, G., & Kristina, V. (2006). Survey of environmental informatics in Europe. *Environmental Modelling & Software, 20*, 1-9. Retrieved June 30, 2006, from http://www.ses-evier.com/locate/envsoft

Wen, X. C., Liang, N., & Wen, X. M. (2005). Informatization thinking and target of environmental monitoring. In F. C. Xu (Ed.), *The application and management of environmental information technology* (pp. 30-34). Beijing, China: Chemical Industry Press.

Wu, X. Q. (2005, November). *Enhancing pollution sources auto-monitoring work improving the efficiency of executing the environmental laws.* Paper presented at the Meeting on the Spot of National Pollution Sources Auto-Monitoring Work. Retrieved from http://www.sepa.gov.cn/hjjc/jcxx/200601/t20060116_73517.htm

Xu, F. C. (2005). *Environment informatization and innovation.* Paper presented at the Second Meeting of the National Environmental Information Management and Technology's Application, Beijing, China.

Zeng, X. Y., Chen, K. A., & Li, H. Y. (2005). *Environmental information systems.* Beijing, China: Science Press.

Zhang, Q. Y., & Tian, W. L. (2005). *Environmental management information system.* Beijing, China: Chemical Industry Press.

Zheng, T., & Chen, C. Y. (2003). *Mathematical models of environmental system.* Beijing, China: Chemical Industry Press.

Section IV
Socioeconomic Development in the IT Age

Chapter XV
International Institute for Knowledge Management

Jayanth Paraki
Telemedicine Research Laboratory, India

ABSTRACT

The statements, "Life educates," and, "Education is life," are correct in general, but when a formal system of education is organized, society selects from all those cultural experiences to which the child is exposed those aspects of its culture that it regards as most valuable for its own coherence and survival. The power of information technology should be harnessed to plan, design, and execute projects that address the United Nations Millennium Development Goals, especially poverty reduction and the reduction of child mortality, and to promote sustainable development to improve the quality of life in the developing world. The rest of the chapter highlights some of the global problems, issues, and ongoing efforts to solve some of the problems and justify the need for an International Institute for Knowledge Management to specifically focus on the UN Millennium Development Goals.

INTRODUCTION

The statements, "Life educates," and "Education is life," are correct in general, but when a formal system of education is organized, society selects from all those cultural experiences to which the child is exposed those aspects of its culture that it regards as most valuable for its own coherence and survival. The power of information technol-

ogy should be harnessed to plan, design, and execute projects that address the United Nations Millennium Development Goals (UN MDGs), especially poverty reduction and the reduction of child mortality, and to promote sustainable development to improve the quality of life in the developing world. The rest of the chapter will highlight some of the global problems, issues, and ongoing efforts to solve some of the problems and justify the need for an International Institute for Knowledge Management (IIKM; Collison & Parcell, 2004) to specifically focus on the UN Millennium Development Goals.

BACKGROUND

UN Millennium Development Goals

The eight MDGs, which range from halving extreme poverty to halting the spread of HIV and AIDS and providing universal primary education all by the target date of 2015, form a blueprint agreed to by all the world's countries and all the world's leading development institutions. They have galvanized unprecedented efforts to meet the needs of the world's poorest.

United Nations Secretary-General Kofi A. Annan

"We will have time to reach the Millennium Development Goals—worldwide and in most, or even all, individual countries—but only if we break with business as usual. We cannot win overnight. Success will require sustained action across the entire decade between now and the deadline. It takes time to train the teachers, nurses and engineers; to build the roads, schools and hospitals; to grow the small and large businesses able to create the jobs and income needed. So we must start now. And we must more than double global development assistance over the next few years. Nothing less will help to achieve the Goals."

The millennium goals represent a global partnership for development. The deal makes clear that it is the primary responsibility of poor countries to work toward achieving the first seven goals. They must do their part to ensure greater accountability to citizens and the efficient use of resources. However, for poor countries to achieve the first seven goals, it is absolutely critical that rich countries deliver on their end of the bargain with more and more effective aid, more sustainable debt relief, and fairer trade rules well in advance of 2015. Can the IIKM be erected on a solid foundation, perform satisfactorily, and garner the support of the rich countries? Where should the IIKM be located? Time alone will answer these questions.

Goal 8 of the Millennium Development Goals sets out by the year 2015 to do the following:

1. Develop further an open trading and financial system that is rule based, predictable, and nondiscriminatory. It includes a commitment to good governance, development, and poverty reduction—nationally and internationally.

2. Address the least developed countries' special needs. This includes tariff- and quota-free access for their exports, enhanced debt relief for heavily indebted poor countries, the cancellation of official bilateral debt, and more generous official development as-

Table 1. UN Millennium Development Goals

1. Eradicate extreme poverty and hunger	2. Achieve universal primary education	3. Promote gender equality and empower women	4. Reduce child mortality
5. Improve maternal health	6. Combat HIV/ AIDS, malaria, and other diseases	7. Ensure environmental sustainability	8. Develop a global partnership for development

sistance for countries committed to poverty reduction.

3. Address the special needs of landlocked and small-island developing states.

4. Deal comprehensively with developing countries' debt problems through national and international measures to make debt sustainable in the long term.

5. Develop decent and productive work for youth in cooperation with the developing countries.

6. Provide access to affordable essential drugs in developing countries in cooperation with pharmaceutical companies.

7. Make available the benefits of new technologies, especially information and communications technologies, in cooperation with the private sector.

INFORMATION TECHNOLOGY

Japanese Conclusion: Mitsuhiro Kagami, Masatsugu Tsuji

The IT revolution during the 1990s brought about lots of merits as well as demerits for mankind. It dramatically changed people's lives and ways of thinking due to its extraordinary nature, especially the transcendence of time, place, and social status. We are now facing the third industrial revolution. First was the industrial revolution of the late 18th century when the steam engine and other machines dramatically changed production methods as well as people's lives. The second was the invention of electricity at the end of the 19th century, which brought forth mass-production techniques and lit up the world. The third started with the application of artificial intelligence pioneered during the "space race" in the 1960s, moved on to the use of easy, cheap, and reliable computers in the 1980s, and has finally reached the Internet or information revolution through IT-related technologies. In

the IT revolution, some salient characteristics can be observed as follows. First, individuals can participate in cyberspace. This implies individuals can easily surpass national boundaries, and the concept of national sovereignty must be reconsidered in many ways. Second, the Internet allows one to step over time and location, and thus 24-hour working is possible by imposing each assignment on people at different locations around the globe. It enormously increases the efficiency of business activities, particularly in software industries. Third, traditional business hierarchies are disappearing when faced with the reality of electronic data interchange (EDI), and existing industries such as intermediaries and vertically integrated parts procurements are vanishing. Moreover, from the enterprise point of view, objective changes from cost minimization to consumer satisfaction in the entire supply chain are occurring. Fourth, a great volume of information can be instantaneously transmitted through the Internet such as computer-aided design (CAD) and computer-aided manufacturing (CAM) information, and hence industrial efficiency is greatly improved. At the same time, consumers can enjoy accessing the World Wide Web content (entertainment, fashion, education, culture, etc.) and change their lifestyles as well as their way of thinking. This can be further augmented by adopting broadband facilities in the near future. Fifth, the process of deregulation and privatization is strongly correlated with the IT revolution. Since infrastructure such as telecommunications and electricity supply tend to be run by state-owned enterprises in many developing countries, progress in deregulation and privatization in developing countries crucially affects the process of the IT revolution in those countries. Finally, the implementation of IT can work to bypass certain traditional development stages of industrialization. India and Israel, for example, have now enjoyed a leapfrogging pattern of industrialization by supplying software services and skilled technicians. The IT revolution, therefore, has given rise to serious impacts on society: positive as well as negative.

Merits

Because of e-mail facilities, worldwide one-to-one communication is possible. It saves time and money and increases efficiency in many fields. The Internet connects us with instant information exchanges and makes us rich in such domains as education, academia, medical treatments, industry, culture, mass media, and entertainment. On the economy side, productivity (multifactor productivity) has increased by the use of IT, especially since the latter half of the 1990s. The IT industry itself has created many jobs and functioned as an engine of growth for the world economy. IT applications such as EDI and electronic fund transfer (EFT) have made business easier, quicker, cheaper, and more efficient.

New types of businesses and new IT utilizations have emerged such as e-commerce (business to business [B2B] and business to consumer [B2C]), e-government, e-education, and e-medicine. Leapfrogging patterns based on technological development may help certain developing countries, such as India, grasp momentum for growth and enable them to bypass traditional developmental stages (a "digital jump"). Individual participation has made people happier and has resulted in more decentralization at every level of social institution, and thus, has enhanced democracy.

Demerits

- **Digital Divide:** Those who can have access to the Internet can enjoy the benefits of the IT revolution, but those who cannot are left behind. This gap takes place within one country but also between advanced and developing countries.

- **Unemployment:** New models such as B2B and B2C skip existing intermediaries and result in redundancies in related sectors, albeit the IT industry job creation counters this to some degree.

- **Supporting Industries:** Because EDI multinational corporations can purchase their parts and components worldwide, domestic supporting industries (small and medium enterprises) do not grow in developing countries.

- **Monopoly:** Idea-based industries are apt to occupy the whole market due to the knowledge intensity and network externalities. Microsoft is a good example. At the same time, access charges play a very important role and thus incumbent large firms tend to stay in a monopolistic position by maintaining high access charges due to their huge sunk costs.

- **Online Crimes:** It is easy to violate laws in cyberspace relating to copyrights, taxation, fraud, money laundering, hazardous information, and cyber terrorism.

- **Privacy:** Infringement on privacy is also easy, such as wire and wireless tapping, hacker activities, and so forth, especially by public authorities.

- **Human Resource Bottleneck:** Computer literacy becomes very important, and the IT industry faces a lack of trained people. This also applies worldwide. Given this, advanced countries further become "brain magnets" while developing countries such as India and China face "brain drains."

- **Mass Hysteria:** Individual participation sometimes gives rise to Web-misguided movements such as the NPO's and NGO's protest against globalization at world conferences such as those of International Monetary Fund (IMF) and World Trade Organization (WTO). We definitely need international measures and cooperation to prevent these negative aspects, especially digital-divide and computer-related crimes. Further progress is expected to continue in the IT revolution, and its influence will bring about unprecedented but irresistible transformation in our society in this new century. However, the recent U.S. economic slowdown at the beginning of 2001 and the supply shortage in California's electricity supply industry highlight the fact that the IT revolution is not always going to be a bed of roses and does not guarantee a recession-free future economy. Furthermore, we have to be mindful that deregulation and excessive reliance on competition may lead us to ignore the long-term stable supply of deregulated products. Therefore, we have to carefully examine the present progress of the IT revolution and globalization for each economy, and chart our own right way in searching for the correct policy mix garnered from forerunners' experiences in order to utilize fully the latecomers' advantage.

Education is the pivot around which centers of excellence thrive and flourish. International cooperation is urgently required to nurture the merits of the Japanese conclusion while stringent counteroperations are equally important to prevent the demerits from raising an ugly hood of dissent, insurgency, noncooperation, and stalemates in dialogue and discussions. We need the International Institute for Knowledge Management to actualize the profits through a network of global business leaders who unanimously support all the UN Millennium Development Goals. Goal 8 requires priority consideration, and to achieve all the other goals, global partnership for development is most critical.

CURRENT GLOBAL SCENARIO AND SOME OF THE PROBLEMS: CAN INFORMATION TECHNOLOGY PROVIDE THE SOLUTIONS?

Water and Sanitation

The world is in danger of missing global targets for providing clean water and sanitation unless there is a dramatic increase in the pace of work and investment between now and 2015, according to a new report from the World Health Organization (WHO) and UNICEF. The situation is becoming particularly acute in rapidly growing urban areas. WHO estimates that in 2005, 1.6 million children under age 5 (an average of 4,500 every day) died from the consequences of unsafe water and inadequate hygiene. Can better supply-delivery chain models improve the situation for children and reduce mortality? What is the role of IT in this situation? Can we detect patterns (Suresh & Mahesh, 2006) of child mortality in different countries and launch a global assault to reduce child mortality?

Causes of Blindness and Visual Impairment

In spite of the progress made in surgical techniques in many countries during the last 10 years, cataracts (47.9%) remain the leading cause of visual impairment in all areas of the world, except for developed countries. Other main causes of visual impairment in 2002 are glaucoma (12.3%), age-related macular degeneration (AMD; 8.7%), corneal opacities (5.1%), diabetic retinopathy (4.8%), childhood blindness (3.9%), trachoma (3.6%), and onchocerciasis (0.8%). The causes of avoidable visual impairment worldwide are all of the above except for AMD. In the least developed countries, and in particular Sub-Saharan Africa, the causes of avoidable blindness are primarily cataracts (50%), glaucoma (15%), corneal opacities (10%), trachoma (6.8%), childhood blindness (5.3%), and onchocerciasis (4%). Looking at the global distribution of avoidable blindness based on the population in each of the WHO regions, we see the following: Southeast Asia at 28%, the Western Pacific at 26%, Africa at 16.6%, the Eastern Mediterranean at 10%, America at 9.6%, and Europe at 9.6%. In addition to uncorrected refractive errors, these six diseases or groups of diseases, for which there are effective known strategies to eliminate them, make up the targets of the WHO Global Initiative to Eliminate Avoidable Blindness, VISION 2020: The Right to Sight, which aims to eliminate these causes as a public health problems by the year 2020. Cataracts, onchocerciasis, and trachoma are the principal diseases for which world strategies and programmes have been developed. For glaucoma, diabetic retinopathy, uncorrected refractive errors, and childhood blindness (except for xerophthalmia), the development of screening and management strategies (Wilson, 2002) for use at the primary care level is ongoing at WHO.

Facts About Cancer: Diet and Physical Activity's Impact

Cancer is becoming an increasingly important factor in the global burden of disease. It accounts for 7.1 million deaths annually (12.5% of the global total). Dietary factors account for about 30% of all cancers in Western countries and approximately up to 20% in developing countries; diet is second only to tobacco as a preventable cause. Approximately 20 million people suffer from cancer, a figure projected to rise to 30 million within 20 years. The number of new cases annually is estimated to rise from 10 million to 15 million by 2020. In addition, some 60% of all cases will occur in the less developed parts of the world. Yet, with the existing knowledge, at least one third of cancer cases that occur annually

throughout the world could be prevented. While tobacco use is the single largest causative factor, accounting for about 30% of all cancer deaths in developed countries and an increasing number in the developing world, dietary modification and regular physical activity are significant elements in cancer prevention and control. Overweight and obesity are both serious risk factors for cancer. Diets high in fruit and vegetables may reduce the risk for various types of cancer, while high levels of preserved and/or red meat consumption are associated with increased cancer risk.

GLOBAL EMPLOYMENT TRENDS

Despite robust gross domestic product (GDP) growth in 2005, labour market performance worldwide was mixed, with more people in work than in 2004 but at the same time more people unemployed than the year before. Overall, the global unemployment rate remained unchanged at 6.3% after 2 successive years of decline. At the end of 2005, 2.85 billion people aged 15 and older were in work, up 1.5% over the previous year, and up 16.5% since 1995.

Given that unemployment is just the tip of the iceberg, the focus in developing economies should not be solely based on unemployment alone, but also on the conditions of the work of those who are employed. In 2005, of the over 2.8 billion workers in the world, nearly 1.4 billion still did not earn enough to lift themselves and their families above the $2-a-day poverty line—just as many as 10 years ago. Among these working poor, 520 million lived with their families in extreme poverty on less than $1 a day. Even though this number is less than 10 years ago, it still means that nearly every fifth worker in the world has to face the almost impossible situation of surviving with less than $1 a day for each family member. There are around 534 million persons who can be classified as the working poor in developing countries (in 1997). Around 95% of these working poor of the developing world live in low-income countries. The working poor constitute around 25% of the employed labour force in all developing countries (http://www.ilo.org). In other words, one in every four employed persons in the developing world belongs to a poor household.

HOW DO WE ENABLE KNOWLEDGE SHARING AND DIFFUSION AMONG INTERNATIONAL ORGANIZATIONS?

WHO

The World Health Organization (http://www.who.int) is the United Nations specialized agency for health. It was established on April 7, 1948. WHO's objective, as set out in its constitution, is the attainment by all peoples of the highest possible level of health. Health is defined in WHO's constitution as a state of complete physical, mental, and social well-being and not merely the absence of disease or infirmity. WHO is governed by 192 member states through the World Health Assembly. The health assembly is composed of representatives from WHO's member states. The main tasks of the World Health Assembly are to approve the WHO programme and budget for the following biennium and to decide on major policy questions.

The Civil Society Initiative

The Civil Society Initiative (CSI) fosters relations between WHO and nongovernmental and civil society organizations and is responsible for the administration of formal relations as set out in the principles governing relations between WHO and nongovernmental organizations (NGOs). Counterparts at each WHO regional office serve in the same capacity. WHO country offices may also work with NGOs at the national level. The objectives of WHO's relations with NGOs are to

promote the policies, strategies, and activities of WHO and, where appropriate, collaborate with NGOs in jointly agreed activities to implement them. WHO may also seek to harmonize intersectoral interests among various sectoral bodies concerned in a country, regional, or global setting.

NGOs and Health

Evolving concepts about health and the articulation of its links to poverty, equity, and development have recently widened the range of WHO's partners. No longer the domain of medical specialists, health work now involves politicians, economists, lawyers, communicators, social scientists, and ordinary people everywhere. The involvement of civil society has profoundly affected not only the concepts underpinning public health, but the formulation and implementation of public health programmes and policies as well. Nongovernmental organizations and other civil society actors have engaged with WHO to implement health programmes at the country level, made outreach to remote areas and populations possible, advocated public health issues to a broad audience, addressed sensitive issues, and worked in alliance with WHO to raise funds more effectively.

The United Nations

The United Nations is central to global efforts to solve problems that challenge humanity. Cooperating in this effort are more than 30 affiliated organizations, known together as the UN system. Day in and day out, the UN and its family of organizations work to promote respect for human rights, protect the environment, fight disease, and reduce poverty.

As the UN's development agency, the United Nations Development Programme (UNDP) uses its global network to help the UN system and its partners to raise awareness and track progress of the UN MDGs while it connects countries to the knowledge and resources needed to achieve these goals.

The Food and Agriculture Organization of the United Nations

The Food and Agriculture Organization (FAO) was founded in 1945 with a mandate to raise levels of nutrition and standards of living, to improve agricultural productivity, and to better the condition of rural populations.

NGO Section of the Department of Public Information at the United Nations

The NGO Section of the Department of Public Information (DPI-NGO) at the United Nations headquarters serves as the liaison between the department and NGOs associated with DPI. These NGOs disseminate information about the UN, thereby building knowledge of and support for the organization at the grassroots level. Currently, close to 1,600 NGOs from all regions of the world are associated with DPI.

United Nations Environment Programme

The United Nations Environment Programme (UNEP) provides leadership and encourages partnership in caring for the environment by inspiring, informing, and enabling nations and peoples to improve their quality of life without compromising that of future generations.

UNITED NATIONS EDUCATIONAL, SCIENTIFIC, AND CULTURAL ORGANIZATION

The United Nations Educational, Scientific, and Cultural Organization (UNESCO) contributes to peace and security in the world by promoting collaboration among nations through education, science, culture, and communication in order to further universal respect for justice, the rule of law, and human rights and fundamental freedoms without the distinction of race, sex, language, or religion.

The Office of the United Nations High Commissioner for Refugees

The Office of the United Nations High Commissioner for Refugees (UNHCR) is mandated to lead and coordinate international action to protect refugees and resolve refugee problems worldwide. Its primary purpose is to safeguard the rights and well-being of refugees.

World Bank

The World Bank is one of the world's largest sources of development assistance. Its primary focus is on helping the poorest people and the poorest countries.

World Food Programme

The World Food Programme (WFP) is the United Nations' frontline agency in the fight against global hunger. It has emergency and development projects in 82 countries worldwide.

The World Trade Organization

The WTO is the only global international organization dealing with the rules of trade between nations. At its heart are the WTO agreements, negotiated and signed by the bulk of the world's trading nations and ratified in their parliaments. The goal is to help producers of goods and services, exporters, and importers conduct their business.

IS THERE A WAY FORWARD?

The IIKM built on the basis of the Deming System of Profound Knowledge (http://www.deming.org) is ideal to realize the UN Millennium Development Goals. Technology infrastructure is not very complicated and comprises data centers, network bridges, and Internet connectivity. Security is of paramount importance, and all information in the data centers should be protected against data loss and theft. The use of videoconferencing facilitates discussions and deliberations, maintains the continuity of processes, and aids decision making. In a recent experiment (August 2006), the author attempted a videoconferencing session with Peru using the Skype technology in an office in Bangalore, India. The Telemedicine Initiative in Peru is an attempt to use ICT in sustainable development and connect various rural telecenters (approximately 33,000) through a data center. Data centers are the key to successful knowledge sharing and diffusion among the various international organizations that are listed in this chapter. Positioning the data centers in critical locations requires ingenuity, experience, insight, and zeal for travel and cultural interaction.

APPLICATION OF DEMING CHARTER POINTS

- **Point 1:** Strive toward One World. The one-world paradigm stresses the need for the peaceful coexistence of all the people on this planet. The United Nations is central to global efforts to solve problems that challenge humanity. Cooperating in this effort are more than 30 affiliated organizations, known together as the UN system. Day in and day out, the UN and its family of organizations work to promote respect for human rights, protect the environment, fight disease, and reduce poverty. The IIKM would cooperate with UN in its global ef-

forts while striving to disseminate quality services globally.
- **Point 2:** View Education and Culture as Instruments of Global Peace and Cooperation. UNESCO contributes to peace and security in the world by promoting collaboration among nations through education, science, culture, and communication in order to further universal respect for justice, the rule of law, and human rights and fundamental freedoms without the distinction of race, sex, language, or religion. The IIKM would involve the private sector and UNESCO through a series of short films, documentaries, and mass-media campaigns to create public awareness about HIV and AIDS, preventable blindness, and other diseases posing a threat to mankind.
- **Point 3:** Begin Small and Grow. UNESCO-sponsored educational films would begin to be screened in all schools and colleges across the world, without underestimating minority institutions.
- **Point 4:** Develop a Win-Win Economic Model by Promoting Private-Public NGO Partnerships.
- **Point 5:** Select and Apply a Working Example to Prove the Efficiency of the Model. The IIKM would improve constantly and forever the system of knowledge management. If there is no suitable working model, a working model would be generated through a pilot project. WHO's TYP (Three-Year Performance Improvement Programme) would be studied to ascertain current opportunities for planning global KM projects (Malhotra, 2000).

TYP

TYP is a far-reaching WHO-wide effort to optimize the organization's contribution to Health Action in Crises. TYP is strengthening WHO's capacity to support member states and others in preparing for and responding to crises. Crisis preparedness, and response mechanisms and expertise are being strengthened at WHO country and suboffices, with back-up at regional offices and Geneva. TYP is an outcome of a broad consultative process with partners. More than 400 key experts from UN agencies, NGOs, WHO, and other health stakeholders contributed to its formulation. With the encouragement of regional directors and the director general, representatives from all levels of WHO came together under the TYP to create a unified WHO plan for enhanced performance in crises. This includes both a global framework for WHO's contribution in this area, and a unified work plan. The plan incorporates inputs from WHO's six regional offices. TYP focuses on achieving agreed standards of performance. Processes are being streamlined, capacity is being built up, and performance benchmarks are being set. The rigorous monitoring of progress and performance against benchmarks yields critical information for management. This guides progress in implementing WHO's contribution to better health outcomes for people in crises.

TYP focuses on WHO's four core functions in emergencies:

- Assessing health priorities in crises and emergency settings.
- Coordinating health stakeholders and interventions.
- Ensuring that gaps are identified and filled in.
- Supporting local capacity and systems strengthening.

- **Point 6:** Institute Training.
- **Point 7:** Adopt and Institute Leadership. Leadership in some ways means identifying areas for action and enabling resources to reach a destination. What resources are needed for TYP? WHO needs financial and human resources to take forward the TYP in a way that contributes to sustainable development

of the capacity of the organization. This is to help all health stakeholders deliver effective action and, when essential, to provide direct public health support in crises. A proposal was developed in May 2004 estimating that $24 million in funding would be needed to initiate this capacity-building programme over 3 years. Several member states came forward with funds for Year 1 and Year 2, and current funding partners are the following.

Canadian International Development Agency (CIDA)

Department for International Development (DFID) European Commission Humanitarian Aid (ECHO) Swedish International Development Cooperation Agency (SIDA)

However, estimated funding needs remain unmet. Implementing TYP is clearly a challenge. We predict that we need at least 3 years to put needed systems in place, demonstrate their utility and viability, and ensure that those yielding the best health outcomes are sustainable. Enhancing WHO's contribution and, in turn, health actors' performance in crises requires the support and commitment of all stakeholders. We expect TYP to catalyze lasting change in the way WHO and others prepare for and respond to the needs of people in crises.

- **Point 8:** Drive Out Fear Among Workers and Employees by Providing a Profitable Working Environment (Suresh & Mahesh, 2006).
- **Point 9:** Break Down Barriers between Staff Areas. Unique work spaces will be created employing the Internet as a major communication tool.
- **Point 10:** Eliminate Slogans, Exhortations, and Targets for the Workforce.
- **Point 11:** Eliminate Numerical Controls for the Workforce.
- **Point 12:** Remove Barriers that Rob People of Pride of Workmanship.

- **Point 13:** Encourage Education and Self-Improvement. Education that is unrelated to an employee's job may be the most critical of all.
- **Point 14:** Take Action to Accomplish the Transformation.

STATISTICS

Deming (http://www.deming.org) stressed the need for statistical validation in any problem-solving situation. How do we employ statistics to counter a growing problem like population explosion? What does India's population indicate? In the year 2005, it was 1,103,371,000. Table 2 compares it with other South Asian countries.

Reflecting on Deming Charter Point 11 and setting numerical targets for population control in India, one would have to discover a new process, and to do that it is necessary to possess a working knowledge (Davenport & Prusak, 1997) of the

existing population control programmes. Can we borrow and apply best practices from the business reengineering processes to population control? Are there any lessons to be learned from industry? Is the economic development of a country linked to its population? It is evident that several tough questions need equally tough answers. There is ample scope for research in this area.

FUTURE TRENDS

The Internet Research Task Force's (http://www.irtf.org/index) mission is to *promote research into the evolution of the future of the Internet by creating focused, long-term, and small research groups working on topics related to Internet protocols, applications, architecture, and technology. Research in life sciences, too, is urgently required, and some of the problems mentioned require a great deal of thinking and tenacity to come up with practical solutions* (http://www.wm-forum.

Table 2. Population statistics

Country	Population Total (in thousands), 2005
India	1,103,371
Indonesia	222,781
Bangladesh	141,822
Thailand	64,233
Myanmar	50,519
Nepal	27,133
Korea	22,488
Sri Lanka	20,743
Bhutan	2,163
Timor-Leste	947
Maldives	329

org). The dramatic increase in wireless and mobile devices coupled with the desire to connect them to the ever-growing Internet is leading to a mobile Internet, where support for terminal mobility will soon be taken for granted. However, terminal mobility must not be taken for granted, and more research is required to provide suitable devices for the physically challenged and terminally ill. For instance, a paraplegic or a terminally ill person would benefit from communicating with similarly affected individuals through a worldwide network of support groups. Since these support groups could exist practically all over the world in different countries, it is imperative to standardize protocols, equipment, devices, and wireless communication (Becerra-Fernandez, González, & Sabherwal, 2004).

CONCLUSION

Information technology must be advanced to promote economic growth, which translates into the creation of decent jobs and encourages investment and entrepreneurship, skills development, proper labour standards, and sustainable livelihoods. Facilitating enterprise creation is key (Edvinsson & Malone, 1997). The International Institute for Knowledge Management will stand out as a pioneering global enterprise and facilitate the realization of the UN Millennium Development Goals. Internet research must be favored and supported to create new knowledge discovery and dissemination.

REFERENCES

Becerra-Fernandez, I., González, A., & Sabherwal, R. (2004). *Knowledge management: Challenges, solutions and technologies.*

Collison, C., & Parcell, G. (2004). *Learning to fly: Practical knowledge management from leading and learning organizations.* New York: Capstone Publishing.

Davenport, T., & Prusak, L. (1997). *Working knowledge.* Harvard.

Edvinsson, L., & Malone, M. (1997). *Intellectual capital: Realising your company's true value by finding its hidden brainpower.* New York: HarperBusiness.

Malhotra, Y. (2000). *Knowledge management and virtual organizations.* Hershey, PA: Idea Group Publishing.

Suresh, J. K., & Mahesh, K. (2006). *Ten steps to maturity in knowledge management: Lessons in economy.* Oxford: Chandos.

Wilson, T. D. (2002). The nonsense of "knowledge management." *Information Research, 8*(1). Retrieved from http://InformationR.net/ir/8-1/paper144.html

ADDITIONAL READINGS

Bhagat, P. M. (2005). *Pattern recognition in industry.* New York: Elsevier.

Graz. (2002). Retrieved from http://www.wm-forum.org

IP Mobility Optimizations (Mob Opts) Research Group, Internet Research Task Force. (n.d.). Retrieved from http://www.irtf.org/

International Labour Organisation (n.d.) Retrieved from http://www.ilo.org/public/english/index.htm

Schwartz, D. (Ed.). (2005). *Encyclopedia of knowledge management.* Hershey, PA: Idea Group Publishing.

World Health Organization. (n.d.). An illustrated guide to knowledge management. *Wissensmanagement Forum (Hg.).* Retrieved from http://www.who.int

Chapter XVI
Application of Computer Technology in Mechanical Industry of China

Jian-Xiong Liu
Kunming University of Science and Technology, China

Zheng-Ming Xiao
Kunming University of Science and Technology, China

Cha-Biao You
Kunming University of Science and Technology, China

Yu-Fei Wu
Yunnan Telecommunication Co., Ltd., China

ABSTRACT

With its constant development and completion of function, and its fast popularization in the world, the impact of computer technology on the mechanical industry of China is more and more far reaching. CAD, CAM, CAE, CIMS, computer controlling, and network information play a very important role in the rapid development and promotion of the quality of the mechanical industry in China. The application of computer technology has made enormous contributions to the improvement of the manufacturing industry and economic development of China. In this chapter, the application situation of CAD, CAM, CAE, CIMS, computer controlling, and network information technology in the mechanical industry of China is analyzed.

INTRODUCTION

With the constant development and perfection of computer technology, the computer has already gotten deeply into modern industrial production and all aspects of people's daily lives, playing more and more extensive and important functions. Meanwhile, the computer has had more and more extensive and deep application in Chinese industry, and the capability of industrial enterprises in China has being strengthened constantly and powerfully.

In order to get rid of traditional dependence on experience and coarse mechanical design and machine methods, namely, simple turning, milling, planing, grinding, manual drawing, and so forth, which have prevailed for decades in China, the introduction of computer technology into the mechanical industry has great and far-reaching meaning in accelerating the development of mechanical design, manufacturing, and quality promotion in China. Since its reform and opening, the mechanical industry of China has seen rapid development, especially as we entered the 21st century and after the country's formal accession into World Trade Organization (WTO). China's mechanical design and manufacturing industry integrated with the world progressively; as various new technologies, especially computer technologies, are introduced and applied constantly, China's mechanical industry has realized a qualitative leap.

The mechanical industry is an important industry in China's economic construction. China is paying more and more attention to revitalizing and developing its mechanical industry. At present, through participating in the keen competition of the world product market, the demand for mechanical products runs up and up while the requirement for product quality becomes higher and higher. Mechanical design and manufacturing technology directly influence the development of the manufacturing industry, product update, and competitive power. Whether the mechanical industry is developed or not, it has already become a most important sign to weigh the comprehensive strength of a nation. A combination of computer technology and mechanical industry is the only way to rapidly improve the level of the mechanical industry of China.

CAD, CAM, and CAE Technology

CAD Technology

Computer-aided design (CAD) is widely applied in industry. It has become what people are familiar with and a new technology that contributes to production. As we entered the 21st century, with the rapid development of the network application technology of the computer, CAD technology has been used widely in enterprises and has already become practical for productivity.

Study on CAD technology in China began in 1960s, but at that time, the study and application range was very narrow, mainly concentrated on a few universities and institutes. In the early 1980s, China began to relatively broaden its CAD technological studies and technology import, and began to develop domestic CAD software. Since the middle of the 1980s, the Chinese government began to popularize CAD application technology in relevant industries. In the 1990s, many study institutions in China carried out a large amount of studies on the basic theory and software development of CAD technology and got great achievement. Through the efforts over the past 20 years (X. Song, 2000), China has already preliminarily set up a CAD software industry with a certain market scale and independent copyright. It also set up an application training network and consulting service system for CAD nationwide, and made a set of CAD technical standards for China, combining the needs of CAD application projects. The country launched scientific studies fruitfully, and established a set of management systems, measures, and methods in CAD application projects. At present, China has already adopted CAD technology extensively in every field related to products and engineering design, and it is playing an important role there (Li & Chen, 2006). China is becoming the important base of the world manufacturing industry.

China has reached the goal of the actualized development, demonstration, and popularization of CAD application technology (DUAN, 2005). By 2000, in 600 demonstrating enterprises organized and actualized by China's government in 29 provinces and cities, the average application popularity rate of CAD was 95%, the coverage rate was 92.8%, and the average occupation rate of the PC (personal computer) was 84%.

Nowadays, prevailing CAD software that China has introduced from other countries and applied in mechanical industry are mainly as follows (Zhang, 2003):

1. Unigraphics (UG) and SolidEdge developed by the Unigraphics Solutions Company.
2. Pro/Engineer developed by the U.S. Parameter Technological Company (PTC).
3. I-DEAS developed by U.S. SDRC Company.
4. CATIA developed by the DassaultSystems engineering department of the France Dassault Company.
5. SolidWorks developed by the U.S. SolidWorks Company.
6. AutoCAD and MDT (Three-Dimension Mechanical CAD System) developed by the U.S. Autodesk Company for the PC.

With constant deepening in CAD studies in China, numerous good domestic CAD software have been independently developed.

Gaohua CAD

Gaohua CAD is a serial of CAD products developed by TsingHua University, including ghdrafting, supporting computer-aided drawing; ghmds, a mechanical design and drawing system; ghcapp, a craft design system; ghgems, a modeling system of three-dimensional geometry; ghpdms, a products data management system, and ghcam, an automatic NC programming system.

CAXA

CAXA is a complicated three-dimensional CAD and CAM (computer-aided manufacturing) software with a Chinese interface, developed by the Beijing Beihang-Haier Software Co., Ltd., independently to face the industry of China.

Kaimu CAD

Kaimu CAD is drawing management software with an independent copyright based on the PC platform. Developed by the Huazhong University of Science and Technology, it faces project practice, simulates people's thinking of design and drawing, and is easily and simply handled.

Daheng CAD

The Daheng mechanical CAD system (HMCAD) was developed in 1991 and aims at the mechanical manufacturing and design industry.

CAM Technology

CAM was developed to meet NC manufacturing applications. The CAM system is closely related to the CAD system. CAM generally means all activities of the manufacturing process, from a blank slate to the manufacturing and assembling of products, being aided by computer, including craft preparation, production work plans, the control of material circulation operations, production control, quality control, NC machine tools, robots, and other production units. CAD and CAM technology applied to the mechanical manufacturing industry has obvious superiority.

In China, most mechanical processes employ CAM systems; even quite small enterprises have NC manufacturing equipment (Chu & Dong, 2003). At present, CAD and CAM technology are widely used in the mechanical manufacturing industry and bring prominent economic efficiency. According to preliminary statistics, in 67% of mechanical manufacturing departments, 95% of their product design patterns were made using CAD. In addition, every product design cycle was shortened to 30% of the original on average, which greatly reduces the time that a product takes from being designed to being put into production and the product design cost by about 15% to 30%. In 7% of mechanical manufacturing departments, CAD/CAM technology is applied to every step of product design and manufacturing, reducing the costs of product design, promoting the quality of products, reducing the processing course by 20% to 40%, and reducing manpower costs by 10% to 25%. Employing CAD/CAM-integrated technology in product design and manufacturing can improve the quality of products effectively, shorten the production cycle, and solve the difficult problems of modeling complicated parts and programming. CAD/CAM-integrated technology is a technological revolution in the field of contemporary engineering design, analysis, and manufacturing.

In the field of mechanical manufacturing, CAM is bringing revolutionary change. In China, prevailing CAM software are MasterCAM, Cimatron, and the NC module of UG.

CAE Technology

Computer-aided engineering (CAE) technology is an emerging technology that is based on the combination of computer technology and engineering analysis technology. CAE software is a comprehensive and knowledge-intensive product, which formed through a mix of calculated mechanics, computational mathematics, structural dynamics, digital simulation technology, engineering management science, and computer technology (Hu, 2005).

Applying CAE technology to computer simulation can contribute to finding a machining mechanism and offers theoretical support for improving

machinability (Yang, 2005). Professors of many universities in China and relevant experts have carried out a lot of beneficial studies and made certain achievement. In mechanical operation, the fatigue problem is unavoidable. In order to study the fatigue problem, a large number of fatigue experiments are engaged, which is time consuming and money consuming and needs a large amount of manpower and material resources; furthermore, some complicated problems are still unable to be solved with testing machines at present. Computer simulation techniques have offered a new way for solving this problem.

CIMS Technology

Computer-integrated manufacturing system (CIMSs) are one of the main branch technologies that employ computer application technology in the field of industrial production. This concept was first put forward in 1973 by Harrington (U.S.A.) but was not approved by people until the 1980s.

A popular definition of CIMS is "employing computers to realize the modern production through information integration, in order to get the overall benefits of enterprises." The whole study and development of CIMS, that is, with respect to goals, structure, composition, constraints, the optimization and realization of a system, and so forth, have reflected the integrity and consistency of a system.

Compositions of CIMS

CIMS can generally be divided into four functional subsystems and two supporting subsystems. The functional subsystems mainly include the management information subsystem, product design subsystem, manufacturing automation or flexible manufacturing subsystem, and quality-guarantee subsystem. Two auxiliary subsystems are the computer network subsystem and database subsystem.

Process of CIMS Application Demonstration Project in China

Since 1989, 20 enterprises have been successively selected to be CIMS demonstration plants. More than 40 enterprises have launched the application of CIMS in more than 10 provinces (municipal). These enterprises cover many types of mechanical manufacturing industries, for example, airplanes, vehicles, electronics, household appliances, costumes, communications, the petrochemicals, metallurgy, coal, chemicals, and so forth.

China has been employing the demonstration project since 1989. According to the depth and scope that the project has implemented, we can divide it into three steps:

1. **1989-1992:** The selection of typical application plants, feasible demonstration, preliminary design, and detailed design
2. **1993-1995:** The breakthrough process phase of implementing typical application enterprises. Typical application plants, especially the Beijing No.1 machine tool plant, Shenyang air-blower plant, Company of Airplane Industry of Chengdu, and so forth, made breakthroughs, obtained obvious economic and social benefits, and contributed to the popularization and application of CIMS. In 1994, CIMS application began to be popularized in many small areas.
3. **1997-present:** The government is determined to accelerate applying CIMS to promote China's manufacturing industry and realize the industrialization of relevant high-technology related to CIMS.

It is proved by practice that the implementation of CIMS has strengthened the competitive power of enterprises, promoted the development of China's CIMS technology industry, and offered an effective way for Chinese enterprises to realize essential transformation to a socialist market mechanism and intensive production.

CAPP Technology

Computer-aided process planning (CAPP), through entering the geometric information (graphic) and craft information (material, heat treatment, output, etc.) of parts into a computer, outputs craft files such as the craft route, craft course, and so forth. CAPP is the indispensable composition of the CIMS system. With the application of computers in manufacturing enterprises, executing the auxiliary design of crafts by computer has been available. The application of CAPP will provide a practical, feasible way to improve the quality of the craft files, shorten production preparing cycles, and liberate craft workers from masses of tedious, repeated work. At present, systems adopted by China's enterprises are mostly atypical CAPP and comprehensive CAPP systems developed based on the created type, atypical type, interchangeable type, and intelligent type systems.

PDM Technology

Product data management (PDM) is a technology that is based on computer software techniques, is product centered, and realizes the integrated management of data, processes, and resources related to products. PDM technology is the important component of a CIMS system. PDM products that China developed have already entered domestic PDM markets, but they are mostly used in book and document management; though it is still poor in function, performance, and stability compared to that in developed countries, PDM has already shown its advantages in meeting enterprises' demands, giving price advantage, providing technical support, and so forth.

At present, the application of Chinese-developed PDM products in enterprises includes the following aspects:

1. Achievement of enterprise product data.
2. Enterprise unified coding.

3. Management of enterprise product structure.
4. Process management of the engineering department.
5. Treatment of enterprise product data.
6. Integration of engineering and production fields.
7. Abstraction of enterprise engineering information.

Industrial Computer Control Technology

The high-speed development of communication and network technology and micro-electric techniques has brought enormous revolutions to computer control technology (CCT). Resorting to the technology, the task that cannot be finished by conventional control technology can be finished; also, performance indexes that could not be reached can be achieved by CCT now. With the development of computer technology, network technology, advanced control strategies, and intelligence instruments of the field bus, the level of the control technology of computers will be improved greatly.

In the 1990s, the development of the control technology of computers was more obvious. Computer control systems were further improved, employment was more popular, and the price was dropping constantly; meanwhile, its functions were more abundant and performance was also more reliable. With the rapid development of data communication technology, network technology, and computer software, the extension and intension of computer control systems both far exceeded those in the past. In the field of mechanical industry, the application of computer control technology is becoming more and more extensive. Adopting computers to control the manufacturing process of products and accurately control the process of the production line can achieve the production purposes efficiently and with high quality.

Computer control in the mechanical industry of China saw considerable development in the middle and later 1990s, having been adopted in many manufacturing fields for realizing automation. For example, in the auto industry, it completed car assembly production lines. The adoption of computer control technology by most producers in China helped improve production efficiency, control the production procedure, and improve assembling crafts. In 1983, industrial computer control was listed in the national popularization and development plan, which developed industrial computer control under the great support of the country and joint efforts of computer control industries nationwide.

It can be foreseen that computer control technology will gain rapid development following the development of computer technology and automatic control technology, which will bring enormous economic benefit to the national economy.

Network Information Technology

Global competition makes the situation of enterprises more and more difficult. The market's requirement for individualized products is higher and higher, and users are further critical of listing times, quality, price, and service. Enterprises are forced to turn from extensive manufacturing models to extensive customization (Y. Song & Gao, 2005). For a long time, product development mostly used the traditional design; it went through the processes of concept design, detailed design, procedure design, processing design, testing and verification, and the modification of design. Many subsequent factors cannot be well-considered in the early stages of design, such as manufacturability, assembly performance, quality guarantees, and so forth, which will unavoidably cause large changes in product design and the development cycle, high cost, and difficulty in meeting the requirements of market competition. Productive enterprises can win users and the market with the help of the constant development and functional completion of IT and the appearance of various product design methods that are rapid, are highly efficient, and can meet consumers' individualized requirements.

At present, standing on the strategies of "revitalizing the nation through science and education," "industrialization following informatization," and the "informatization of manufacturing industry," all levels of government in China attach great importance to the manufacturing industry network, which has played a very good role in network implementation. The manufacturing industry network needs a good environment; in it, there should be information and resource bases, cooperative enterprise-to-enterprise environments, cooperative enterprise-to-customer environments, talent resources, technological service environments, and material circulation information mainly offered in the form of a combination of online and off-line material through the region network.

The rapid prototyping information network of China (http://www.crpm.org.cn), managed by Xi'an Jiaotong University for vast and scattered medium- and small-sized enterprises, offers long-range RP&M manufacturing services. On the one hand, it improves the utilization rate of domestic RP&M equipment, and on the other hand, it extends the application coverage (industry range and geographical area) of RP&M technology, which improves the rapid development of new products for medium- and small-sized enterprises.

The Chinese manufacturing industry network has already run from distributing and inquiring about information online in the past to setting up and sharing information and knowledge, cooperatively designing and manufacturing products, setting up professional services for supply chain management and customer relationship management, and so forth. The Chinese manufacturing industry network assumes heavy responsibility and needs further improvement; it is in need of efforts and cooperation from various fields from top to bottom if China hopes that networking will really contribute to its industrialization.

CONCLUSION AND PROSPECT

It can be seen that the constant development of computer technology greatly contributes to the rapid development and quality promotion of the mechanical industry in China; the level of China's mechanical industry is catching up with the developed countries that are advanced in mechanical design and manufacturing, and has been close to even surpassing some of those countries in some fields. CAD/CAM/CAE/CIMS; computer control technology, network information technology, computer-relevant mechanical design, manufacturing, management, and information sharing technology will contribute greater and greater to the development of the mechanical industry of China. In order to speed up the development of China's mechanical industry, we should continue to insist and expand on opening to the outside world; introduce and absorb the advanced equipment and methods of mechanical design, manufacturing, and management from developed countries, especially computer-aided technology; accelerate talent acculturation by ourselves; set up a knowledge innovation system; develop equipment and software with independent intellectual property rights actively; melt computer technology into China's mechanical industry thoroughly; and reinforce the integration of design, manufacturing, management, intelligence, informatization, and networking in China's mechanical industry. These are the most important aspects in work in the long run in China.

REFERENCES

Chu, X., & Dong, M. (2003). Manufacture information engineering and its implementation in enterprise. *Journal of Kunming University of Science and Technology, 3*, 49-52.

Duan, Q. (2005). The development and application of CAD technology in the mechanical engineering design. *Shanxi Science and Technology, 3*, 59-60.

Hu, X. (2005). Current situation of the development and trend of mechanical design technology. *Light Industry Machinery, 3*, 4-6.

Li, Y., & Chen, D. (2006). The development and trend of mechanical CAD technology in China.

Journal of Wuhan University of Technology, 3, 73-76.

Song, Y., & Gao, S. (2005). Networked in manufacturing technology and application in metalforming machinery. *China Metalforming Equipment Manufacturing Technology, 6*, 19–22.

Song, X. (2000). Comprehensive introduction of CAD for machine. *Metallurgical Collection, 6*, 43-45.

Yang, T. (2005). Using computer simulation technology for mechanical design. *Mechanical Research Application, 4*, 14.

Zhang, Y. (2003). CAD/CAM/CNC technologies for machining. *Coal Mine Machinery, 12*, 49-51.

Chapter XVII

A Study of the Relationships between Economic Climates, National Culture, and E-Government Readiness:
A Global Perspective

Princely Ifinedo
Cape Breton University, Canada

ABSTRACT

As ICT-enabled services such as e-government initiatives diffuse globally, it is becoming clear that some nations are not faring as well as others. Yet, the notion of e-government stands to benefit the sorts of countries that are lagging behind the most. Here, we examine the relationships between economic climates and national cultural factors on the one hand, and e-government readiness on the other. Our results showed significant relationships between nations' economic climates, some cultural dimensions, and e-government readiness. We discussed our findings in the context of three relevant socioeconomic theories. We also highlighted the study's implications for researchers, policy makers, and governments.

INTRODUCTION

In the past few years, the world has witnessed the advent of e-government (Accenture, 2004; Moon, 2002). Development reports, surveys, and studies indicated that almost all the governments in the world have embraced one form of e-government or another (Breen, 2000; InfoDev, 2003; Moon, 2002; InfoDev, 2003; UNPAN, 2005). E-government can be described as an emerging model involving both the citizenry and the state, where the importance of citizen input in policy formulation and implementation is recognized and valued (Breen; InfoDev; Moon;). Governments around the world are finding it appealing to use ICT-enabled initiatives that are cost effective to bring governance to their populations (InfoDev; Moon; UNPAN). The trend is noticeable in all countries, be they rich or poor. According to UN-PAN (p. 45), "Steady progress in ICT diffusion, human capital development and Member States' e-government websites in the last 3 years led to an improvement in the e-government readiness world average to 0.4267 in 2005 compared to 0.4130 in 2004." The foregoing scores come from an index known as E-Government Readiness, which provides information on the diffusion of e-government globally. The index clearly shows that some countries and regions have better rankings and scores than others. For example, the index for the year 2005 puts the average for Africa and other developing societies at around 0.253, which is obviously below the world's average; high-ranking countries include several European countries and the United States, and this group of countries has consistently obtained scores around 0.8000 and above since the inception of the index (see UNPAN). We ask the following questions. What could be the reasons why some countries or regions have better rankings or scores than others? Could the differing socioeconomic climates and cultural factors existing among nations be responsible for this disparity?

While several studies (e.g., Ford, Conelly, & Meister, 2003; Nath & Murthy, 2004; Robinson & Crenshaw, 1999) have investigated the diffusion of ICT products such as the Internet globally, very few have studied the diffusion of e-government (Kovačić, 2005) or its relationship with contextual factors such as economy type and culture as we intend to do in this chapter. In similar past studies focusing on e-government, other researchers have dealt with its diffusion within single nations or regions (e.g., Altman, 2002; West, 2003). In contrast to those efforts, this study takes a global look at e-government readiness among nations. Again, the work of Kovačić only looked at the impact of national culture on e-government readi-

ness, and the author did not consider the impact of other contextual influences such as economic climates. Even though Kovačić did not model economic variables in his study, he underscores their relevance by noting:

When the effect of other hard variables (economic variables, for example) are significant, then the cultural variables are redundant. If the cultural variables are still significant in spite of included economic variables, then the effect of culture on observed phenomenon, i.e. e-government readiness and its components could be confirmed. (p. 149)

It is our view that by explicitly modeling the relationship between economic variables as well as cultural factors on e-government readiness, our knowledge in this area will be enhanced. Conclusions from Robinson and Crenshaw (1999), Cronin (2002), Nath and Murthy (2003, 2004), Gregorio, Kassicieh, and Neto (2005), and UNPAN (2005) have all shown that the differing economic climates are positively related to the diffusion of the adoption and use of ICT-related products and services such as e-government. Here, we will begin by investigating the relationships between national culture and economic climates (economy types) of nations on the one hand, and e-government readiness on the other. Then we will draw from relevant theories to interpret our results. The conclusion of this work will benefit researchers, governments, and other policy makers.

LITERATURE REVIEW

Theories

With regard to the disparities in the global diffusion of e-government, we believe that the modernization theory, human development theory, and human capital theory may enable us to understand such differences. We briefly define each below as follows:

- **Modernization Theory:** We define modernization using the definition provided in the *Oxford Advanced Learner's Dictionary*: "to make a system, methods, etc., more modern and more suitable for use at the present time" (Hornby, 2000, p. 855). In essence, e-government is meant to modernize governance. That said, the modernization theory goes back a long way, that is, a few years after the Second World War. However, interest in the theory was attributed to the works of McClelland (1961) and others (e.g., Goldthorpe, Lockwood, Bechhofer, & Platt, 1968). McClelland offers explanations as to the nature of the relationship between societies and technological advancement (see So, 1991; Udogu, 2004). He was of the view that some societies were more advanced than others because of the cultural and personality traits of their citizens and political actors. From a similar line of reasoning, other researchers have also shown that modernization is related to national development (Payne & Nassar, 2003). That is, relatively modernized societies have a higher tendency to adopt, use, and benefit from emerging technologies and services than do societies that are yet to reach such levels of sophistication (Goldthorpe et al.; Harrison, 1988; McClelland; So).

- **Human Development Theory:** This is a relatively new economic theory that emerged in the 1980s. The proponents of this theory include Ul-Haq (1972), Streeten (1982), and Amartya (1999). The theory was proposed to counter the dominant thinking in the economic development theory (see Prugh, Costanza, Daly, & Goodland, 1999). The latter focuses on the maximization of economic growth while the former aims to provide insights as to how human well-being can

be improved (Amartya; Costanza, 1991; Streeten). Essentially, the theory draws from ecological economics, sustainable development, welfare economics, and feminist economics (Amartya; Costanza; Prugh et al.). Central to the human development theory is the capacity approach (see Amartya), which suggests that all human societies can transform in a functional manner. One identified constraint to this order is a lack of resources, which is seen as capability deprivation. In a nutshell, the proponents of this theory imply that when there are no deprivations, the well-being of all societies can be attained; more significantly, they do not limit developmental discourse to growth of national products, technological advance, or social modernization.

- **Human Capacity Theory:** The underlying thinking of this theory is, in some respects, related to the preceding theory in that it focuses on developmental issues in societies. Basically, the human capacity theory suggests that societies with highly educated populations will have higher levels of development (Becker 1964; Schultz, 1961). Proponents of this theory claim that "employees acquire the skills for the use of technology through formal education [and when societies invest in education, they do so to increase their productivity...and improve the chances for development]" (Agbo, 2003, p. 3).

E-Government and its Index

E-government, as described by the World Bank, is the use of ICT to transform government by making it more accessible, effective, and accountable to its citizenry (InfoDev, 2003). E-government involves the utilization of technologies such as the Internet to improve the services, functions, and processes of governance (Cottrill, 2001; Moon, 2002). It involves more than establishing a Web server and hosting government sites. However, the Internet plays a vital role in establishing e-government initiatives (Breen, 2002; Sharma & Gupta, 2003). Due to the spread of ICT products such as the Internet and other relevant technologies, many governments—both in developing and developed nations—have started adopting e-government (Accenture, 2004; UNPAN, 2005). Wimmer and Traunmuller (2001) contend that the main objectives of e-government should include the following: (a) restructuring administrative functions and processes, (b) reducing and overcoming barriers to coordination and cooperation within the public administration, and (c) monitoring government performance. According to UNPAN (p. 30), the "e-government Readiness Index is a composite index comprising the Web measure index, the Telecommunication Infrastructure index and the Human Capital index." The Web Measure Index measures the sophistication of a state's online presence, including its interactive, transactional, and networked presence. The Telecommunication Infrastructure Index measures the availability of ICT-related products for countries while the Human Capital Index measures the levels of skills, educational opportunities, and literacy levels among countries; please see UNPAN for more detailed information as it encompasses the economic and social development contexts of countries.

Economic Environments or Wealth of Nations

Clearly, the economic climates or economies around the world differ and can be assessed in various ways (World Bank, 2005). The use of gross domestic product (GDP) per capita is widely used in comparing the wealth of nations. It refers to the value of the total goods and services produced within a nation in a given year, divided by the average population for the same year. The World Bank produces this indicator annually. This

indicator also permits the classification of nations into three main groupings. At the top of the echelon is a group of countries that have very high GDP per capita; examples include most European countries, the USA, Canada, and Japan. Emerging economies (sometimes called transiting economies) occupy the middle ground (International Monetary Fund [IMF], 2000; World Bank). This group of countries has liberalized environments and a relatively high GDP per capita that is usually lower than those of the developed economies. Countries in this group include Russia, Poland, and China. The last grouping consists of countries with very low per capita GDP. Examples in the third category include all the countries in Africa and some in Latin America and Asia. Please see Table 1 for illustrations of countries in each category. Finally, national wealth or standards of living across countries can also be gauged using GDP purchasing-power parity (GDP-PPP). This measure is used to adjust for differences in the cost of living in different countries (World Bank).

National Culture

Hofstede (1984, p. 21) defines culture as, "the collective programming of the mind which distinguishes the members of one group from another." Culture has been researched by several authors (e.g., Hall, 1976; Hofstede; Trompenaars, 1994), but the work of Hofstede has been widely recognized as the most dominant framework for theory development and validation in cross-cultural studies, and several studies in IS and other areas have used it (Ford et al., 2003; Myers & Tan, 2002; Nath & Murthy, 2004). According to Ford et al., the cultural dimensions developed by Hofstede provide a lens to develop a priori as well as compare different national cultural contexts vis-à-vis technologies use and adoption. The four main cultural dimensions in Hofstede's typology are briefly described below. We summarize each dimension using explanations taken from a page dedicated to the works of Hofstede online at http://www.geert-hofstede.com/geert_hofstede_resources.shtml (ITIM, 2006).

- **Power Distance Index (PDI):** "focuses on the degree of equality, or inequality, between people in the country's society. A high Power Distance ranking indicates that inequalities of power and wealth have been allowed to grow within the society." (ITIM, 2006)
- **Individualism (IDV):** "focuses on the degree the society reinforces individual or collective achievement and interpersonal relationships. A high Individualism ranking indicates that individuality and individual rights are paramount within the society. Individuals in these societies may tend to form a larger number of looser relationships. A low Individualism ranking typifies societies of a more collectivist nature with close ties between individuals." (ITIM, 2006)
- **Masculinity (MAS):** "focuses on the degree the society reinforces, or does not reinforce, the traditional masculine work role model of male achievement, control, and power. A high Masculinity ranking indicates the country experiences a high degree of gender differentiation. A low Masculinity ranking indicates the country has a low level of differentiation and discrimination between genders." (ITIM, 2006)
- **Uncertainty Avoidance Index (UAI):** "focuses on the level of tolerance for uncertainty and ambiguity within the society—i.e. unstructured situations. A high Uncertainty Avoidance ranking indicates the country has a low tolerance for uncertainty and ambiguity. A low Uncertainty Avoidance ranking indicates the country has less concern about ambiguity and uncertainty and has more tolerance for a variety of opinions." (ITIM, 2006)

RESEARCH FRAMEWORK AND HYPOTHESES

The research model or framework of this study is shown in Figure 1. The outer part of the model shows the three theories that we intend to draw upon in interpreting the relationships between our variables. At the heart of the framework is the representation showing the influences that economic climates and national culture have on

Figure 1. The research framework

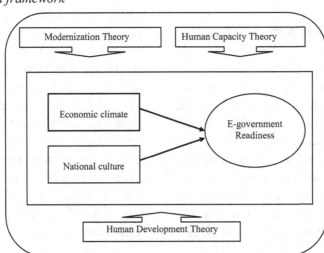

238

e-government readiness. At this level, we are suggesting that the economic and cultural factors will exert significant influence upon e-government readiness. We are suggesting causality, though researchers such as Sørnes, Stephens, Sætre, and Browning (2004) and Kovačić (2005) have implied that the relationships between culture and ICT-enabled services such as e-government are by no means causal.

The UNPAN (2005) survey indicated that several high- and middle-income countries show the most readiness for e-government. Other the studies (e.g., Gregorio et al., 2005; Nath & Murthy, 2003, 2004; Robinson & Crenshaw, 1999) have also shown that wealthier countries tend to have more access to resources to build on the potential of ICT-enabled services such as e-business and e-government. The foregoing information permits us to predict that economic climates of nations will be significantly related to their e-government readiness. That is, wealthier countries will have higher scores on the E-Government Readiness Index than those with lesser economic resources. We frame the three following hypotheses, taking into account the three different ways by which countries around the world can be classified economically.

H1a: There will be a significant positive relationship between economic climate, as represented by GDP (purchasing-power parity of nations), and e-government readiness.

H1b: There will a significant positive relationship between economic climate, as represented by GDP per capita of nations, and e-government readiness.

H1c: There will a significant positive relationship between economic climate, as represented by economy type, and e-government readiness.

Comparison of E-Readiness Assessment Models (2001) suggests that "the unique cultural and historical environment of a region must be taken into account as part of a national ICT policy to truly gauge the country's e-readiness for the future." In this regard, recent studies (Ford et al., 2003; Gregorio et al., 2005; Kovačić, 2005; Nath & Murthy, 2003) have established significant relationships between the rate of diffusion of ICT-enabled services and products such as e-business and e-government on the one hand, and national culture on the other. Ford et al. and Nath and Murthy (2004) found negative relationships between the diffusion of the Internet—a key tool for e-government—and UAI and MAS. Kovačić found that e-government readiness is significantly correlated with the cultural dimensions of IDV and PDI; his findings indicated that e-government readiness is negatively related to PDI and positively related to IDV. This might be interpreted to mean that e-government tends to be lower in countries having high PDI and higher in countries with higher IDV. Furthermore, the regression model developed by Kovačić also showed that the other cultural dimensions are in fact pertinent in explaining the unevenness in e-government readiness for the selected countries in his sample. Following the findings and conclusions in Kovačić, Ford et al., and Nath and Murthy (2004), it is logical to suggest that national culture has strong influence on the e-government readiness of nations. To investigate the pertinence of each of the four cross-national dimensions used in this study, we formulate a separate hypothesis for each as follows.

H2a: There will be a significantly positive relationship between IDV and e-government readiness.

H2b: There will be a significantly negative relationship between PDI and e-government readiness.

H2c: There will be a significantly negative relationship between UAI and e-government readiness.

Table 1. Economy climates, cultural dimensions, and E-Government Readiness Index

Country	Economic Climate Variables			National Cultural Dimensions				EGOV
	ECO	Per Capita GDP (US$; 2005 estimate)	GDP-PPP (US$; 2005 estimate)	PDI	IDV	MAS	UAI	
Thailand	1	$8,300	$560.7 billion	64	20	34	64	0.5518
Panama	1	$7,200	$22.76 billion	95	11	44	86	0.4822
India	1	$3,300	$3.611 trillion	77	48	56	40	0.4001
Colombia	1	$7,900	$337.5 billion	67	13	64	80	0.5221
Saudi Arabia	1	$12,800	$338 billion	80	38	52	68	0.4105
Jamaica	1	$4,400	$12.17 billion	45	39	68	13	0.5064
Nigeria	1	$1,400	$174.1 billion	77	20	46	54	0.2758
Kenya	1	$1,100	$37.15 billion	64	27	41	52	0.3298
South Africa	1	$12,000	$533.2 billion	49	65	63	49	0.5075
Morocco	1	$4,200	$138.3 billion	70	46	53	68	0.2774
UAE	1	$43,400	$111.3 billion	80	38	52	68	0.5718
Philippines	1	$5,100	$451.3 billion	94	32	64	44	0.5721
Malaysia	1	$12,100	$290.2 billion	104	26	50	36	0.5706
Indonesia	1	$3,600	$865.6 billion	78	14	46	48	0.3819
Iran	1	$8,300	$561.6 billion	58	41	43	59	0.3813
Mexico	2	$10,000	$1.067 trillion	81	30	69	82	0.6061
Brazil	2	$8,400	$1.556 trillion	69	38	49	76	0.5981
Bulgaria	2	$9,600	$71.54 billion	70	30	70	85	0.5605
Czech Rep.	2	$19,500	$199.4 billion	57	58	57	74	0.6396
China	2	$6,800	$8.859 trillion	80	20	66	30	0.5078
Vietnam	2	$2,800	$232.2 billion	70	20	40	30	0.3640
Russia	2	$11,100	$1.589 trillion	93	39	36	95	0.5329
Estonia	2	$16,700	$22.29 billion	40	60	30	60	0.7347
Poland	2	$13,300	$514 billion	68	60	64	93	0.5872
Hungary	2	$16,300	$162.6 billion	46	80	88	82	0.6536
Belarus*	2	$6,900	$70.68 billion	93	39	36	95	0.5318
Chile	2	$11,300	$187.1 billion	63	23	28	86	0.6936
Slovakia	2	$16,100	$87.32 billion	104	52	110	51	0.5887
Lithuania*	2	$13,700	$49.21 billion	45	50	65	67	0.5786
Romania	2	$8,200	$183.6 billion	90	30	42	90	0.5704
Australia	3	$31,900	$640.1 billion	36	90	61	51	0.8679
Austria	3	$32,700	$267.6 billion	11	55	79	70	0.7602
Belgium	3	$31,400	$325 billion	65	75	54	94	0.7381
Canada	3	$34,000	$1.114 trillion	39	80	52	48	0.8425
USA	3	$41,800	$12.36 trillion	40	91	62	46	0.9062
Finland	3	$30,900	$161.5 billion	33	63	26	59	0.8231

continued on following page

Table 1. continued

Sweden	3	$29,800	$268 billion	31	71	5	29	0.8983
Singapore	3	$28,100	$124.3 billion	74	20	48	8	0.8503
Japan	3	$31,500	$4.018 trillion	54	46	95	9	0.7801
France	3	$29,900	$1.816 trillion	68	71	43	86	0.6925
United Kingdom	3	$30,300	$1.83 trillion	35	89	66	35	0.8777
Malta	3	$19,900	$7.926 billion	56	59	47	96	0.7012
Germany	3	$30,400	$2.504 trillion	35	67	66	65	0.8050
South Korea	3	$20,400	$965.3 billion	60	18	39	85	0.8727
Switzerland	3	$32,300	$241.8 billion	34	68	70	58	0.7548

Legend: ECO is the economy type, and EGOV is the E-Government Readiness Index
* estimates from ITIM (2006) and Mockaitis (2002)

H2d: There will be a significantly negative relationship between MAS and e-government readiness.

METHODOLOGY

As indicated, the purpose of this chapter is to examine the relationships between contextual factors such as economic climates and culture on the one hand, and e-government readiness on the other. To that end, we obtained data for 45 countries from different sources. One criterion that informed the choice of the selected countries was the availability of their cultural dimension scores from Hofstede's (1984) cross-cultural typology; we also ensured that countries from different geographical regions of the world are included in our analysis. Using guidelines from IMF (2000) and the World Bank (2005), we painstakingly collected data from the countries that can broadly be classified as developing, emerging, and developed economies (please see Table 1); we represented the countries with 1, 2, and 3, respectively. The selected countries in this study account for more than 90% of the world population and 95% of global economic output. For the economic climate variables, we used GDP per capita, GDP-PPP, and

a classification of world's economies as discussed here. We obtained the cultural dimensions of each country from the work of Hofstede, which is also kept online at ITIM (2006). E-Government Readiness Index scores were obtained from UNPAN (2005). We used correlation and regression analysis for the data using the SPPS 13.0 software. It is worth mentioning that in the bid to normalize the GDP and GDP-PPP variables, we transformed both variables using a logarithmic function, that is, *In*.

RESULTS

We present the descriptive statistics, that is, the means (m), standard deviations (SD), minimum, and maximum of the variables in Table 2. The range of the used variables seems adequately representative with the exception of the economic variables. For example, the mean of the variable of per capita GDP is $16,913.33, which is clearly greater than the average for the developing countries (m = 9,000.67, SD = 10,222.67); however, we noticed that the country with the highest per capita GDP in our sample is United Arab Emirates (UAE), which is incidentally a developing country. Thus, we are confident in our data distribution.

Table 3 provides the correlation matrix; the intercorrelations among the eight variables are shown. We see a positive relationship between the economy-type variable and e-government readiness ($r = 0.859$, $p < 0.01$). Also, the GDP per capita is positively related to e-government readiness ($r = 0.862$, $p < 0.01$), but GDP-PPP did not yield any significant result, perhaps due to the fact that some of the sampled countries, both emerging and developed economies, in our data have relatively high GDP-PPPs comparable to those of developed economies. For example, the GDP-PPP of China, India, Mexico, and Brazil compare reasonably well with those of highly developed economies.

This information regarding the GDP-PPP variable suggests that comparing nations by that variable may not permit much insight. Thus, we will focus our analysis using both the GDP per capita and the economy type.

Regarding the cultural variables, we can see that there is a highly significant relationship between PDI and e-government readiness ($r = -0.565$, $p < 0.01$). Also, there is a positive significant relationship between IDV and e-government readiness ($r = 0.589$, $p < 0.01$). The results did not show any significant relationships between MAS and UAI on the one hand, and e-government readiness, on the other. Overall, four out of

Table 2. Descriptive statistics

Variable	Minimum	Maximum	Mean	Standard Deviation
PDI	11.00	104.00	63.16	21.74
IDV	11.00	91.00	46.00	22.74
MAS	5.00	110.00	54.20	18.72
UAI	8.00	96.00	61.42	23.97
EGOV	0.2758	0.9062	0.6147	0.1741
Per Capita GDP	$1,100.00	$43,400.00	$16,913.33	$11,899.99
GDP-PPP	$7.93 billion	$12.36 trillion	$1.1 trillion	$2,289.04
ECO	1	3	2	0.83

Table 3. Correlation matrix

Variable	ECO	*In*(Per Capita GDP)	*In*(GDP-PPP)	PDI	IDV	MAS	UAI	EGOV
PDI	-.546**	-.476**	-.059	1	-.633**	-.020	.175	-.565**
IDV	.587**	.637**	.198	-.633**	1	.204	-.010	.589**
MAS	.054	.153	.150	-.020	.204	1	-.152	.032
UAI	.011	.056	-.191	.175	-.010	-.152	1	-.076
EGOV	.859**	.862**	.224	-.565**	.589**	.032	-.076	1
ECO	1	.736**	.241	-.546**	.587**	.054	.011	.859**
In(Per Capita GDP)	.736**	1	.210	-.476**	.637**	.153	.056	.862**
In(GDP-PPP)	.241	.210	1	-.059	.198	.150	-.191	.224

** Correlation is significant at the 0.01 level (two-tailed).

the seven hypotheses were confirmed. It is worth mentioning that the results in this work mirror those of Kovačić (2005). Accordingly, the findings of this study benefit from external validity.

In order to understand the effect of the contextual factors, that is, economic climates and national culture on the e-government readiness of nations, we performed ordinary least squares (OLS) regression analysis. First, we regressed all the variables, seven of them, on the e-government readiness variables. Our result ($R^2 = 0.86$, $F = 38$, $p = 0.000$) shows that all the variables account for up to 85% variation in e-government readiness. We checked for multicollinearity problems using the variance inflation factor (VIF) in SPSS 13.0; the test statistics for each of the variables was not greater than 10, which is accepted as a threshold (see Kleinbaum, Kupper, & Muller, 1988). Second, we entered only the four variables that yielded a significant relationship with the dependent variable: e-government readiness. The results at this stage are $R^2 = 0.85$, $F = 62$, and $p = 0.000$. Just as in the preceding analysis, we did not notice the presence of any multicollinearity problems. Above all, the two models—the one with seven variables and the other with four variables—compare reasonably well with only slight differences in squared R and F values. In brief, the two models provide results that statistically affirm the relevance of economic climates and cultural factors in explaining e-government readiness among countries.

DISCUSSION AND CONCLUSION

In this chapter we asked the question: Could the differing socioeconomic climates and cultural factors between countries explain their differences on the E-Government Readiness Index? We found a significant relationship between the economic resources available to nations and their ranking on the E-Government Readiness Index. This finding is not new and has in fact been reported elsewhere. For example, the UNPAN (2005, p. 43) survey states, "The preponderance of high and middle-income countries in the top 50 indicates that e-government readiness in a country is related to income. As expected high income countries have the resources and the platform of infrastructure to build on the potential of information technologies." The modernization, human capacity, and human development theories underscore the relationships between resource availability and progressive development on a variety of fronts, including the nexus between societal progress and technological achievement. Therefore, it comes as no surprise that the more endowed a nation is, the more likely it is to accept and subsequently benefit from e-government services. We briefly noted that e-government offers an opportunity for governments to use ICT to restructure their functions and processes, reduce barriers to coordination, and integrate their citizenry into governance. Regarding the relationships between economic climates and e-government readiness, our results affirm the dire states of affairs in poorer nations.

With respect to the influence of culture on e-government readiness, our data showed that not all the dimensions of national culture impact e-government readiness. We were unable to confirm that MAS and UAI have significant relationships with e-government readiness. In brief, it can be argued that the extent to which a society tolerates uncertainty and ambiguity within its society and the degree to which a society reinforces the traditional masculine work role model associated with achievement, control, and power have no significant correlations with government readiness. This result lends credence to the findings in the work of Kovačić (2005). The significant details indicate that e-government readiness is lower in societies or cultures where inequalities between its people or between its government and its citizenry are higher. In such societies, the governed and those in positions of power see each other as being different; thus, e-government initiatives have thrived and may continue to do so. Furthermore, it is not surprising that the data analysis suggested that societies that value individual or interpersonal relationships highly have better scores on the E-Government Readiness Index; e-government is all about inclusion and focuses on meeting the needs of the diverse entities in a society (InfoDev, 2003; Wimmer & Traunmuller, 2001). Kovačić's study also supported the view that governments in countries with strong individualistic cultures are more positive about increasing their level of e-government readiness. Implicit in the modernization theory is the view that a society's cultural orientation (we have attempted to highlight the significant ones in this study) may have a bearing on the way that society fares on technological-related matters. Put simply, societies with conducive cultural orientations tend to fare better than those lacking such technological innovations and use. The developed economies of Europe, Japan, and the USA will continue to occupy good positions on such indices perhaps due to this reasoning.

There are implications from this study for researchers, governments, and other international policy makers. First, this study has shown that global information technology researchers need not downplay the importance of wide-ranging contextual factors when researching the digital divide among nations. Existing socioeconomic theories like the ones discussed here may also be enriching. This endeavor provides support for related studies. In particular, policy makers are made aware of the pertinence of differing economic climates and national culture in planning and managing the adoption and diffusion of ICT-enabled services globally. What the human capacity and human development theories are suggesting is that when nations with less favorable economic, social, and cultural conditions have the sorts of capacities needed to enable them to make positive changes to their well-being, it is possible that progress on developmental fronts or issues such as e-government can be better harnessed.

We believe the right steps have already begun in this regard. For example, policy makers around the globe are increasingly coming to the realization that in order to attenuate the ever-increasing digital divide gap among nations, poorer nations have to be assisted in building their capacities. In general, studies have suggested that the existing unequal ICT diffusion patterns, which contribute to what is widely referred to as the digital divide, are "the result of market or social failures and are leading to negative economic, social and political consequences [among nations of the world]" (UNPAN, 2005, p. 20). The recently concluded World Summit on the Information Society (WSIS-2005) in Tunisia raised similar concerns. While international efforts can be marshaled toward providing resources to developing societies, we believe it is the onus of each country's people and governments to make concerted efforts in smoothing out aspects of its culture that may need modifications or improvements. Future studies are needed on this before it can be achieved.

There are limitations to this study. We have not suggested that Hofstede's (1984) cross-cultural typology used for our analysis is not without its limitations. We concur with criticism leveled at Hofstede's framework that his approach overlooks the fact that there are often several ethnic and cultural groupings within a single country and that culture may not be a static phenomenon (Myers & Tan, 2002). Future studies could use other cross-cultural typologies to increase our knowledge of how cultural factors impact e-government readiness. Although the segmentation of countries that we used follows the guidelines from the IMF (2000) and the World Bank (2005), we are hard-pressed to say that the approach is without criticism; it is likely that other classifications will offer different results. Finally, studies using more than 15 countries for each economy type may be more enlightening than this present effort.

REFERENCES

Accenture. (2004). *High performance government.* Retrieved August 28, 2005, from http://www.accenture.com

Agbo, S. (2003, July). *Myths and realities of higher education as a vehicle for nation building in developing countries: The culture of the University and the new African Diaspora.* Paper presented at the Second Global Conference, Oxford, United Kingdom.

Altman, D. (2002). Prospects for e-government in Latin America: Satisfaction with democracy, social accountability, and direct democracy. *International Review of Public Administration, 7*(2), 5-20.

Amartya, S. (Ed.) (1999). *Development as freedom.* New York: Oxford University Press.

Becker, G. S. (1964). *Human and capital: A theoretical and empirical analysis, with special reference to education.* New York: Columbia University Press.

Breen, J. (2000). At the dawn of e-government: The citizen as customer. *Government Finance Review, 16*(5), 15-20.

Comparison of e-readiness assessment models. (2001). Retrieved September 10, 2006, from http://www.bridges.org/e_readiness_assessment

Costanza, R. (1991). *Ecological economics: The science and management of sustainability.* New York: Columbia University Press.

Cottrill, K. (2001). E-government grows. *Traffic World, 265*(10), 19.

Cronin, B. (2002). The digital divide. *Library Journal, 127*(3), 48.

Ford, D. P., Conelly, C. E., & Meister, D. B. (2003). Information systems research and Hofstede's culture consequences: An uneasy and incomplete partnership. *IEEE Transactions on Engineering Management, 50*(1), 8-25.

Goldthorpe, J. H., Lockwood, D., Bechhofer, F., & Platt, J. (1968). *The affluent worker: Industrial attitudes and behaviour.* Cambridge: Cambridge University Press.

Gregorio, D. D., Kassicieh, S. K., & Neto, R. D. (2005). Drivers of e-business activity in developed and emerging markets. *IEEE Transactions on Engineering Management, 52*(2), 155-166.

Hall, E. T. (1976). *Beyond culture.* New York: Anchor Press.

Harrison, D. (1988). *The sociology of modernization and development.* London: Unwin Hyman Publishers.

Hofstede, G. (1984). *Culture's consequences.* London: Sage Publications.

Hornby, A. S. (2000). *Oxford advanced learner's dictionary of current English.* Oxford: Oxford University Press.

InfoDev. (2003). *E-government handbook for developing countries.* Retrieved November 6, 2004, from http://unpan1.un.org/intradoc/groups/public/documents/APCITY/UNPAN007462.pdf

International Monetary Fund (IMF). (2000). *Transition economies: An IMF perspective on progress and prospects.* Retrieved July 27, 2005, from http://www.imf.org/external/np/exr/ib/2000/110300.htm#I

ITIM. (2006). *Geert Hofstede cultural dimensions.* Retrieved September 6, 2006, from http://www.geert-hofstede.com/hofstede_dimensions.php

Kleinbaum, D. G., Kupper, L. L., & Muller, K. E (1988). *Applied regression analysis and other multivariable methods.* Boston: PWS-Kent.

Kovačić, Z. J. (2005). The impact of national culture on worldwide e-government readiness.

Informing Science: International Journal of an Emerging Discipline, 8, 143-158.

McClelland, D. C. (1961). *The achieving society.* New York: van Nostrand Publishers.

Mockaitis, A. (2002). *The influence of national cultural values on management attitudes: A comparative study across three countries.* Unpublished doctoral dissertation, Management and Administration, Vilnius University, Vilnius, Lithuania.

Moon, J. M. (2002). The evolution of e-government among municipalities: Rhetoric or reality? *Public Administration Review, 62*(4), 424-433.

Myers, M. D., & Tan, F. B. (2002). Beyond models of national culture in information systems research. *Journal of Global Information Management, 10*(1), 24-32.

Nath, R., & Murthy, V. N. R. (2003). An examination of the relationship between digital divide and economic freedom: An international perspective. *Journal of International Technology and Information Management, 12*(1), 15-23.

Nath, R., & Murthy, V. N. R. (2004). A study of the relationship between Internet diffusion and culture. *Journal of International Technology and Information Management, 13*(2), 123-132.

Payne, R. J., & Nassar, J. R. (2003). *Politics and culture in the developing world: The impact of globalization.* New York: Longman Publishers.

Prugh, T., Costanza, R., Daly, H., & Goodland, R. (1999). *Natural capital and human economic survival.* Boca Raton, FL: CRC Press-Lewis Publishers.

Robinson, K. K., & Crenshaw, E. M. (1999). *Cyber-space and post-industrial transformations: A cross-national analysis of Internet development.* Retrieved May 10, 2004, from http://www.soc.sbs.ohio-state.edu/emc/RobisonCrenshawCyberla.pdf

Schultz, T. W. (1961). Education and economic growth. In N. B. Henry (Ed.), *Social forces influencing American education.* Chicago: University of Chicago Press.

Sharma, S. K., & Gupta, J. D. N. (2003). Building blocks of an e-government: A framework. *Journal of Electronic Commerce in Organizations, 1*(4), 1-15.

So, A. (1991). *Social change and development.* Newbury Park, CA: Sage Publications.

Sørnes, J.-O., Stephens, K. K., Sætre, A. S., & Browning, L. D. (2004). The reflexivity between ICTs and business culture: Applying Hofstede's theory to compare Norway and the United States. *Informing Science: International Journal of an Emerging Discipline, 7*, 1-30.

Streeten, P. (1982). Approaches to a new international economic order. In *World development report.* New York: Oxford University Press.

Trompenaars, F. (1994). *Riding the waves of culture.* London: Nicholas Brealey.

Udogu, I. E. (2004). African development and the immigration of its intelligentsia: An overview. *A Journal of African Migration, 3.* Retrieved September 2, 2006, from http://www.africamigration.com/

Ul-Haq, M. (1972). Employment and income distribution in the 1970s: A new perspective. *Development Digest, 9*(4), 3-8.

UNPAN. (2005). *UN global e-government readiness report 2004.* Retrieved July 25, 2005, from http://www.unpan.org/egovernment4.asp

West, D. M. (2000). *Assessing e-government: The Internet, democracy and service delivery by state and federal governments.* The World Bank. Retrieved September 10, 2006, from http://www.Worldbank.org/publicsector/egov/EgovReportUS00.htm

Wimmer, M., & Traunmuller, R. (2001). Trends in electronic government: Managing distributed knowledge. *Proceedings of the 11th International Workshop on Database Expert Systems Applications.*

World Bank. (2005). *Development data and statistics.* Retrieved December 10, 2005, from http://web.worldbank.org/

Chapter XVIII
Society and World Wide Web in Developing Countries:
The Case of Turkey

Mustafa Zihni Tunca
Suleyman Demirel University, Turkey

Isa Ipcioglu
Dumlupinar University, Turkey

ABSTRACT

Information and communication technologies (ICTs) have become ever more prevalent in the last decade. ICTs profoundly affect both global and national economies. Nevertheless, the common view in the literature is that the development of ICTs has been mostly limited to developed countries and has been relatively slower in the rest of the world. There are many factors affecting the acceptance and use of ICTs in developing countries. Although one of the most appealing research areas in recent years is the technology acceptance of consumers, there is a little evidence that the findings of the majority of the technology acceptance studies carried out in developed countries could be generalized to developing countries. In this study, it is aimed to investigate why Turkish people use the Internet. After summarizing the recent household ICT usage statistics, the most popular online activities offered by the top 100 Turkish Web sites are analyzed.

INTRODUCTION

Information and communication technologies have become ever more prevalent in the last decade. The Internet and e-commerce have especially received great interest from researchers. Nowadays, studies on ICTs are no longer limited to the understanding of the development of digital economies. While scholars from different disciplines investigate various perspectives of the digital economy, practitioners and commercial research companies also work heavily on the strategies to successfully integrate the virtual and physical environments.

One of the most appealing research areas in recent years is the technology acceptance of consumers. Not only scholars in marketing and management fields work on this area, but also others in psychology and sociology disciplines make important contributions to the literature. However, academic research on this area is fragmented and narrowly focused on the characteristics of online consumers, and lacks a global structured framework.

Although dramatically increasing access to ICTs would provide several benefits to developing countries, in reality, there are many factors affecting the acceptance and use of information and communication technologies. First of all, there is an obvious digital divide between upper and lower income groups, and urban and rural areas. Secondly, the diffusion of ICTs primarily depends on the existence of necessary logistics, financial, and communication infrastructures, which are not entirely established in developing countries. Third, the SMEs (small and medium-sized enterprises) in developing nations lag far behind developed-country markets in the availability of the technical prerequisites for conducting electronic commerce. Finally, in addition to the difficulties with communicating in English, which is the common language of the Internet, some countries such as Saudi Arabia and China also come upon the problem of adopting the use of Latin letters. Hence, there is a little evidence that the findings of the majority of the technology acceptance studies that are carried out in developed countries could be generalized to developing countries.

In this chapter, it is aimed to investigate the existing status of e-commerce and the factors affecting online shopping in Turkey. This investigation is very important to clarify why electronic commerce is still not considered a significant market driving force in developing countries. In the following sections, after a brief introduction to the ICTs in developing countries, statistics about the present use of ICTs in Turkey is given. Then, using the Web statistics of the top 100 Turkish Web sites, a detailed investigation of Internet usage is presented. Finally, implications of the findings and the future expectations are discussed.

INFORMATION AND COMMUNICATION TECHNOLOGIES IN DEVELOPING COUNTRIES

The importance of ICTs has been widely documented in the literature. Various studies have been conducted to identify the global use of ICTs (Efendioglu & Yip, 2004). The common belief is ICTs profoundly affect both global and national economies (Ho, Kauffman, & Liang, in press). The Economist Intelligence Unit (2003) highlighted that ICTs had changed the nature of global relationships, sources of competitive advantage, and opportunities for economic and social development.

In recent years, the concept of e-readiness is widely investigated by development agencies, research organizations, academia, and business enterprises as a result of the rapid Internet penetration rate all over the world and the remarkable advances in uses of ICTs in business and industry (Mutula & van Brakel, 2006). A country's e-readiness is a measure of its e-business environment, a collection of factors that indicate how amenable a market is to Internet-based opportunities (Economist Intelligence Unit, 2003). E-readiness assessment tools attempt to measure IT use and its impact on developed and developing countries (Indjikian & Siegel, 2005). For instance, The Economist Intelligence Unit (2005) has been publishing an annual e-readiness ranking of the world's 65 largest economies to assess their ability to promote and support digital business and ICT services since 2000.

The majority of the e-readiness research aims to measure the level of infrastructure development, connectivity, Internet access, applications and services, network speed, quality of network access, ICT policy, ICT training programs, human resources, computer literacy, and relevant content (Mutula & van Brakel, 2006).

The common view in the literature is that the development of ICTs has been mostly limited to developed countries and has been relatively slower in the rest of the world (Dewan, Ganley, & Kraemer, 2005; Gruber & Verbove, 2001). While countries with a high level of e-readiness can use the Internet to improve services and create new opportunities (Mutula & van Brakel, 2006), a lower level of e-readiness limits the advancement of such improvements in developing countries (Ho et al., in press). Hence, the digital divide between developed and developing countries still exists.

The digital divide can be at the national level, between different demographic groups, and internationally between different countries (Andonova, 2006). Internet access in many developing countries hardly spreads beyond the urban areas. Furthermore, there is a gap between upper and lower social groups in terms of Internet access. This is essentially due to the cost of two main requirements: the Internet and computers. Finally,

some countries such as Saudi Arabia and China also encounter a problem with using Latin letters on the Internet. A detailed review of barriers to the ICTs in developing countries can be found in Tunca et al. (2003).

USE OF INFORMATION AND COMMUNICATION TECHNOLOGIES IN TURKEY

Although e-readiness studies intend to provide a unified framework to evaluate the extent of the digital divide between developed and developing countries, the existing e-readiness tools fail to adequately address the issue of information access (Mutula & van Brakel, 2006). Indeed, different dimensions of the digital divide such as the economic level of individuals, economic prosperity of nations, ethnicity, age (young or old), rural or urban location, gender, geographic location, quantitative and qualitative aspects, and dial-up and broadband access must also be clarified for the investigated countries (Rao, 2005).

Hence, despite the fact that Turkey's 2005 e-readiness rank is 43 out of 65 largest economies (Economist Intelligence Unit, 2005), it is important to understand the effects of the aforementioned demographic and technical dimensions of the digital divide over Turkey. The *Annual*

Table 1. Distribution of computer and Internet users by age groups (Source: Adapted from 2005 Household IT Usage Research, http://www.tuik.gov.tr)

Age Groups	Percentage of Computer Users	Percentage of Internet Users
16-24	7.69	6.27
25-34	5.60	4.47
35-44	2.67	1.97
45-54	1.33	0.95
55-64	0.29	0.22
65-74	0.07	0.05
Total	17.65	13.93

Household IT Usage Research (http://www.tuik. gov.tr) of the National Statistics Institute of Turkey provides useful insights about the e-readiness of the country. In this section, three critical findings of the *2005 Household IT Usage Research* will be summarized.

Table 1 depicts the distribution of computer and Internet users by age groups. According to the *2005 Household IT Usage Research*, only 17.65% of the active population (aged between 16 and 74) uses the computer, while the rate of Internet usage is 13.93%.

There are two emerging facts in Table 1 about the use of ICTs in Turkey. First, the diffusion of

ICTs in the country is still slow as computer and Internet usage are limited to less than 20% of the active population. Second, the majority of the computer and Internet users are in the age rage of 16 to 34. Hence, the most popular activities on the Internet are expected to be suitable to young Internet users. The nature of the online activities in Table 2 confirms these findings. While the most popular activities (i.e., reading or writing e-mail, reading magazines, downloading music files, online chat, etc.) are typically preferred by young Internet users, e-commerce activities, such as online banking and online shopping, are less popular in the country.

Table 2. Activities on the Internet (Source: 2005 Household IT Usage Research, http://www.tuik.gov.tr)

Online Activities	%
Writing/reading e-mail	66.84
Reading newspaper or magazine	55.77
Downloading (or playing) games, photographs, or music	43.58
Gathering information about products/services	43.31
Online chat	40.39
Gathering information from public Web services	37.64
Accessing online radio and TV broadcasting	28.18
Online educational activities	26.83
Downloading software	22.81
Gathering information about health	22.38
Gathering information about travel/accommodation	14.25
Internet banking	12.90
Videoconference	11.36
Downloading legal forms/documents	10.65
Job search	10.57
Online courses (foreign language, computing, etc.)	7.22
Uploading filled legal forms/documents	6.02
Buying or ordering goods/services	5.59
Other educational activities	4.37
Other financial services	2.95
Getting online advice from a doctor	1.86
Selling goods/services in auctions	1.07
Online appointments with doctors	0.50
Requesting online prescriptions	0.02

The final statistics from *2005 Household IT Usage Research* display the reasons for not shopping online in Table 3. The findings can be grouped under preferences, perception, trust, or infrastructure. The most important reason for not shopping online is about the lack of tradition in remote shopping. Internet users often search for products and prices online, but they prefer purchasing in physical stores (Ho et al., in press). Turkish consumers still behave emotionally and would like to see and touch goods on shelves in physical stores (Tunca, Ipcioglu, & Zairi, 2004).

The findings in Tables 1 to 3 can be summarized as follows:

- Computer and Internet usage is limited to a small number of Turkish people.
- The majority of the Internet users are young generations.
- E-commerce is not sufficiently adopted in the country.
- The Internet is mainly used for entertaining activities.

Although these findings provide important insights about the use of ICTs in Turkey, more details about online activities cannot be acquired from the results. Furthermore, the findings are mostly based on empirical studies. In fact, it has been suggested in the literature that the judgment of online consumers depend heavily upon individual preferences and environmental factors (Nysween & Pedersen, 2002). For instance, while requesting online prescriptions is stated by 0.02% of the interviewers as an online activity in Table 2, online prescriptions are not presently allowed in Turkey. One possible explanation for this statement can be the misunderstanding of some interviewers about the online services.

AN INVESTIGATION OF ONLINE ACTIVITIES USING WEB STATISTICS OF TOP 100 TURKISH WEB SITES

One of the useful data collection methods to understand online activities is gathering the required information directly from Web statistics, such as server log files (Tunca & Sutcu, 2006). In this method, accurate data are directly obtained from Web sites, and potential disadvantages of the bias

Table 3. Reasons for not shopping online (Source: 2005 Household IT Usage Research, http://www.tuik.gov.tr)

Reasons	%
No need to shop online	75.37
Not willing to give credit card details due to security reasons	22.56
Preferring physical stores because of loyalty or habits	20.01
Not willing to give personal information through the Internet	10.42
Finding online merchants more expensive	4.88
Insufficient knowledge to shop online	4.52
Having difficulties to stay at home to receive orders on the delivery time	1.91
Receiving orders very late	1.44
Lack of trust about product deliveries, returns, and services after sales	1.14
Having no credit card	0.96
Problems with Internet access	0.04
Other reasons	1.56

factor are significantly reduced. Other benefits of using Web statistics include the following:

- More recent data could be obtained.
- The data collection, preparation, and analyses stages could be quicker and easier.
- The cost of data collection could be reduced dramatically.

It is assumed that the top 100 Turkish Web sites would provide insightful information about online activities in Turkey. Therefore, the top 100 Turkish Web sites have been determined and the necessary data about those Web sites was collected from the Alexa.com Web site. Alexa.com ranks among the most popular Web sites around the world based on specific criteria such as the average number of visits. The investigated 100 Turkish Web sites were collected under 12 groups, which are education, entertainment, finance, IT, media, directories and search engines, public services, shopping, sports, telecom, travel and holiday, and miscellaneous services.

Table 4 presents the distribution of the Web sites by the year that they launched. As seen in Table 4, most of the investigated Web sites were established during the 1999 to 2001 period, whereas only a few Web sites were established in

Table 4. Distribution of the Web sites by launch year

Year	Number of Web Sites
1985 to 1995	3
1996	5
1997	2
1998	2
1999	13
2000	18
2001	11
2002	6
2003	9
2004	4
2005	3

recent years. Therefore, it is expected that most of Web sites should have enough online experience to fulfill online visitors' expectations.

Another important statistic about the Web sites is the download speed of the first page. It was cited by Gann (1999) that if a Web site cannot be accessed within 7 seconds, approximately 10% of visitors will leave the site; if the delay exceeds 8 seconds, 30% of visitors will leave; and if the delay lasts for more than 12 seconds,

Figure 1. Download speed frequencies

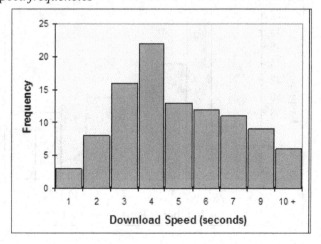

at least 70% of visitors will look elsewhere for their goods or services. However, it is important to note that those figures are not recent enough to use as benchmarks because of the fast Internet connection facilities, such as asymmetric digitial subscriber line (ADSL), cable, and integrated services digital network (ISDN) in present days. Indeed, it is possible to state that currently Internet users expect Web sites to download quicker than the figures given above. Figure 1 illustrates the histogram chart for the download speeds of top 100 Turkish Web sites. It is apparent in Figure 1 that the average download speed of the first pages of the top 100 Web sites is about 4 seconds, which is reasonable.

Another important metric is the number of visits per million users. This metric basically demonstrates the proportion of all Internet users who visit a given Web site throughout a day. The histogram chart given in Figure 2 illustrates that most of the investigated Web sites have been visited by 200 or 300 out of 1 million Internet

Figure 2. Frequencies of average number of visits per million users

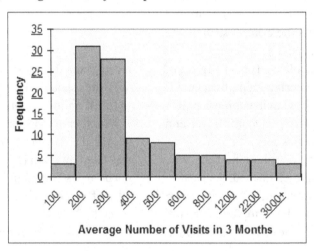

Figure 3. Frequencies of average number of page views

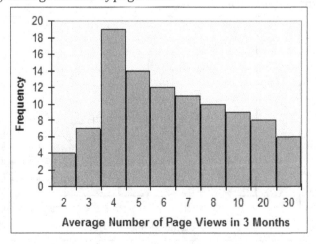

users. Since this metric considers all Internet users around the world, an average number of 250 Turkish visitors out of 1 million worldwide Internet users can be accepted as satisfactory.

The chart in Figure 3 illustrates the average number of pages visited on a particular Web site. This data is important as it primarily provides a general understanding of how many different pages are being visited on different types of Web sites. It is expected that a popular Web site would convince its visitors to see more pages during the visit. Figure 3 depicts that approximately four pages are being visited on the investigated Web sites.

Table 5 presents the summary statistics of the top 100 Turkish Web sites in 12 groups. As seen in the second column of Table 5, online media (newspapers, magazines, etc.), entertainment (online games, chat rooms, etc.), and directories and search engines (including Web mail and SMS Web sites) represent 64% of the most popular Web sites. The rest of the Web sites in the other nine groups stand for only 36% of the top 100 Web sites.

Unsurprisingly, telecom operators are the most experienced organizations on the Web. Interest-

ingly, although e-tailers have been in service since 1999, online shopping is not as popular as newer online activities such as online games. Information about the Internet presence of the public institutions' Web sites (educational institutions and other public services) was not available.

Figure 4 illustrates the trend lines of download speed and average number of page views, depending on the changes in reach per million users. As seen in Figure 4, while the number of visits (i.e., reach per million users) increases, download times of the first pages of the Web sites also slightly increase. This is simply because of the insufficient capacities of the Web servers that cannot supply web services quickly when overloaded. While the Web sites in the telecom, public, and travel and holiday groups could be easily accessed, IT, entertainment, media, and sport Web sites are relatively slower.

The average number of page views in Figure 4 follows a concave trend line. While the average number of visited pages is higher on less popular Web sites, a sharp decreasing trend is seen as the sites become more popular. A close investigation of Figure 4 highlights that the web sites causing the bowl-shaped trend line are in the group of

Table 5. Summary statistics of the top 100 Turkish Web sites in 12 groups

Categories	No. of Web sites	Online Since	Download Speed	Reach per Million Users	Average No. of Page Views
Directories & Search Engines	12	1997	4.78	1,469	10
Education	2	n/a	4.00	188	3
Entertainment	19	2002	5.29	240	11
Finance	4	1999	3.03	608	2
IT	1	2001	8.70	422	6
Media	33	2001	5.37	495	6
Misc. Services	7	2001	3.16	358	4
Public	4	n/a	1.65	355	5
Shopping	5	1999	4.28	294	9
Sports	9	2001	5.37	230	5
Telecom	3	1996	1.97	306	7
Travel & Holiday	1	2000	1.10	81	27

directories and search engines as they are visited by a large number of Internet users to seek various information throughout the day. In order to reduce the excessive effect of the Web sites in this group, the group of directories and search engines was removed from the chart in Figure 5. As a result, a decreasing trend line has been obtained for the average number of pages.

It is important to note that the reach per million users does not always individually provide useful information as to the popularity of a Web site. For instance, as seen in Table 5, while the Web sites

in the finance group are visited by 608 out of 1 million Internet users, the average number of page views is only two. On the other hand, 81 out of 1 million Internet users visited 27 pages on travel and holiday Web sites, presumably to seek for a cheaper flight ticket or a bargain holiday deal. Besides this, it is necessary to consider the total number of Web sites in each group to achieve more reliable information about the popularity of Web site groups.

In order to make precise predictions about the most popular online activities, the following equations have been utilized:

Figure 4. Trend lines of download speed and average number of page views

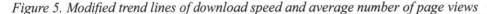

Figure 5. Modified trend lines of download speed and average number of page views

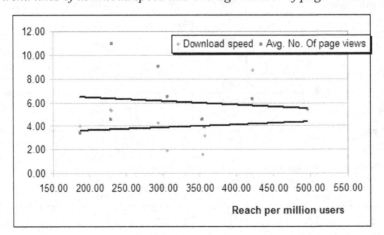

$$P_i = \frac{T_i}{\sum T} \qquad (1)$$

and

$$T_i = W_i * R_i * V_i \qquad (2)$$

where

P_i is the popularity of online activity group i,

T_i is the total number of pages visited in group i,

W_i is the total number of Web sites in group i,

R_i is the reach per million users of group i, and

V_i is the average number of page views in group i.

As seen in Table 6, the most popular online activities offered by the top 100 Turkish Web sites represent similarities to the activities that have been found in the *2005 Household IT Usage Research* of the National Statistics Institute of Turkey given in Table 2. Approximately 85% of

the total pages on the top 100 Turkish Web sites have been visited for the benefits of communication, search, news, and entertainment services. Ho et al. (in press) indicate that the tremendous increase in worldwide Internet usage does not necessarily correlate directly with the increase of online transactions. Evidently, e-commerce, e-government, and e-banking, which are three essential activities of the digital economy, receive quite little interest from Turkish Internet users. Less than 7% of the pages have been visited to access such services.

CONCLUSION

This study identifies and analyzes the details of the Internet usage statistics of the top 100 Turkish Web sites in order to understand the details of online activities. The findings in this chapter confirm the general conclusions of the earlier investigations of the National Statistics Institute of Turkey. Indeed, the results of this study provide

Table 6. The most popular online activities in Turkey

Groups	Online Activities	%
Directories and Search	Information search, job search, communication (e-mail, SMS)	47.28
Media	News, articles, television and radio programs	24.38
Entertainment	Confession, dating, erotic contents, fortune telling, forums, horoscopes, chat, online games	13.20
Shopping	Shopping, bidding	3.65
Miscellaneous Services	Dictionaries, free downloads, Web site hosting	2.68
Sports	Football league news, general sports events	2.57
Public	Public services	1.76
Telecom	Communication services	1.64
Finance	Online banking, miscellaneous financial services	1.17
IT	Software downloads, online help	0.73
Travel and Holiday	Travel and holiday search, online booking	0.60
Education	Academic information about universities	0.34

additional useful information about Internet usage based on actual Web statistics.

There are some emerging questions about the use of ICTs in Turkey. The first question is how to make ICTs available to more people. As given in Table 1, computer and Internet usage is limited to the young generation in Turkey. In order to attract more people to benefit from ICTs, the cost of computer ownership and Internet access should be reduced by the government, which could be accomplished by decreasing the taxes. Free computer and Internet usage courses should also be provided. Such actions can increase the utilization of ICTs in the country.

The second question is how to make online shopping more popular. Government can support e-commerce by reducing the taxes for online transactions and assuring the security of online shopping with registered e-tailers. Online merchants should also offer lower prices and better values than in physical stores. It is also important to offer more goods and services for young Internet users.

Finally, it is important to take necessary actions to prevent the illegal transmission of copyrighted materials. Young Internet users especially tend to share music and video files through the Internet and violate laws on intellectual property rights. This problem requires special efforts from the government, Internet service providers, and organizations, as well as other related corporations.

The major limitation of this study is the difficulties in obtaining the necessary information about the demographic details of the visitors of the top 100 Turkish Web sites. This is primarily due to the most important drawback of utilizing secondary data. The major data in this study were limited to those published by Alexa.com due to the difficulties of obtaining confidential information from the Web sites. Hence, the findings of the *2005 Household IT Usage Research* of the National Statistics Institute of Turkey have been used as the primary source for background information.

However, more demographic details such as the gender, education, location, and occupation of the Internet users would be more enlightening to understand online behaviors.

Another drawback is the impossibility of identifying the Web sites in other languages that Turkish Internet users frequently visit. For instance, while the Turkish domain of the Google search engine (http://Google.com.tr) is the most popular search engine in the country, it is very difficult to identify what percentage of Turkish Internet users prefer the Google.com Web site for searches unless we get relevant data directly from the Web site.

In the future, more detailed investigations would be very useful. However, special attention has to be given to a complementary empirical study. While appropriate data can be collected directly from the Web site administrators, a survey can also be conducted with visitors during the same period.

REFERENCES

Andonova, V. (2006). Mobile phones, the Internet and the institutional environment. *Telecommunications Policy, 30*, 29-45.

Dewan, S., Ganley, D., & Kraemer, K. L. (2005). Across the digital divide: A cross-country multi-technology analysis of the determinants of IT penetration. *Journal of the Association for Information Systems, 6*(12), 409-432.

Economist Intelligence Unit. (2003). *The 2003 e-readiness rankings* (White paper). London: The Economist Group.

Economist Intelligence Unit. (2005). *The 2005 e-readiness rankings* (White paper). London: The Economist Group.

Efendioglu, A. M., & Yip, V. F. (2004). Chinese culture and e-commerce: An exploratory study. *Interacting with Computers, 16*, 45-62.

Gann, R. (1999). Every second counts. *Computing, 28*, 38-40.

Gruber, H., & Verbove, F. (2001). The diffusion of mobile telecommunications services in the European Union. *European Economic Review, 45*(3), 577-589.

Ho, S.-C., Kauffman, R. J., & Liang, T.-P. (in press). A growth theory perspective on B2C e-commerce growth in Europe: An exploratory study. *Electronic Commerce Research and Applications*.

Indjikian, R., & Siegel, D. S. (2005). The impact of investment in IT on economic performance: Implications for developing countries. *World Development, 33*(5), 681-700.

Mutula, S. M., & van Brakel, P. (2006). An evaluation of e-readiness assessment tools with respect to information access: Towards an integrated information rich tool. *International Journal of Information Management, 26*, 212–223.

Nysween, H., & Pedersen, P. E. (2002). An exploratory study of customers' perception of company Websites offering various interactive applications: Moderating effects of customers' Internet experience. *Decision Support Systems, 10*(46), 1-14.

Rao, S. S. (2005). Bridging digital divide: Efforts in India. *Telematics and Informatics, 22*, 361-375.

Tunca, M. Z., Ipcioglu, I., & Zairi, M. (2004). Barriers to online retail activities in emerging economies: The case of Turkey. *International Journal of Applied Marketing, 1*(1), 1-10.

Tunca, M. Z., & Sutcu, A. (2006). Use of statistical process control charts to assess Web quality: An investigation of online furniture stores. *International Journal of Electronic Business, 4*(1), 40-55.

Chapter XIX
E–Learning Implementation and Its Diverse Effects

Biju Issac
Swinburne University of Technology (Sarawak Campus), Malaysia

Jasmine Mering
Swinburne University of Technology (Sarawak Campus), Malaysia

Raymond Chiong
Swinburne University of Technology (Sarawak Campus), Malaysia

Seibu Mary Jacob
Swinburne University of Technology (Sarawak Campus), Malaysia

Patrick Then
Swinburne University of Technology (Sarawak Campus), Malaysia

ABSTRACT

The rapid growth of technological advances in recent years has opened a completely new dimension to progress in education and training. The emergence of e-learning has created not only business and educational opportunities, but also significantly improved the standard of the society. This chapter explores the implementation of e-learning and its impact on a community, similar to a university or corporate setup. To this aim, a brief introduction into e-learning technology and an example of using the Blackboard Learning System are brought forth, along with some critical success factors. Projecting the e-learning advantages along with the digital library concepts, the economic benefits of such implementation are highlighted. The discussion then moves to the perspective of students and teachers on e-learning. As the trend in the technological world is moving toward mobility, the wireless e-learning perception is also conferred. In the concluding remarks, e-learning implementation is noted as a positive endeavor to boost economic growth.

INTRODUCTION

E-learning is a generic and concise term commonly used to describe technology-driven instruction in the fields of online learning, Web-based training, and software-based learning. The benefits of e-learning are no longer in dispute. As such, more and more educational institutions have included e-learning programs as part of their business model. As e-learning programs become the norm, the corollary effects of such adoption are not only felt at the level of the learner and the institution, but also at the societal level. To date, the proliferation of academic literature on the study of educational technology has yet to address the causal effects of e-learning programs and economic growth. The lack of study in this area does not in any way indicate the absence of this notion, but reflects a new consciousness that has just emerged.

This chapter investigates how e-learning programs contribute to the society. It also includes an analysis of a survey performed on a Malaysian university to explore the general attitudes toward e-learning, and analyze the relation between these attitudes and attitudes toward new technologies. The overall experience of the university in relation to the e-learning initiative is considered, and by doing so, the authors hope to substantiate the contention that e-learning augments economic growth. Quoting Mrs. Viviane Reding, European Commissioner for Information Society and Media (as cited by European eLearning Industry Group [eLIG], 2006), "If Europe is to be a dominant economic and social force on the global stage it must act as a cohesive unit wherever possible. E-learning is an opportunity for Europe to utilize the power of technology for real social and educational change, bringing benefits to academia and to business…" Mrs. Reding's reference to Europe can be extended to any other nation in the world, and her words resonate the belief that e-learning is a powerful tool that can bring about economic growth.

The organization of the chapter is as follows. Initially, the concepts of e-learning are introduced, followed by the core elements and technology in e-learning. Then, an example of an e-learning initiative based on a university scenario along with its implementation and critical success factors are presented. Subsequently, the benefits of e-learning with emphasis on the digital library are discussed in length. Later on, a statistical analysis of students' perception on e-learning is done. Immediately after is a brief account on the teachers' perception. As a future trend in e-learning style, the university network setup through secure wireless access is described, and eventually the chapter concludes with a positive note on e-learning and its overall effect on economic growth.

E-LEARNING CONCEPTS

The rapid growth of information technology has opened up the possibilities of corporate learning and a completely new dimension to progress in education and training. Educational and training programs that were once delivered only through a face-to-face setting can now be done electronically due to the advancement of technologies. As a result, the advent of e-learning has enabled not just flexible learning that is independent of time and space, but also significantly reduced the cost in acquiring necessary educational or professional training. E-learning is thus being considered by many to be the next revolution in the marketplace, with an estimated potential growth of 23.7 billion worldwide in 2006 according to a study conducted by the International Data Corporation (Downes, 2003).

Before going into further details of the e-learning concepts, it is necessary to look at some of the definitions of e-learning that have been proposed by various parties. Waller and Wilson (2001) from the Open and Distance Learning Quality Council in the United Kingdom defined e-learning as "the effective learning process created by combining digitally delivered content with (learning) support and services." This brief but concise definition shows that e-learning is in digital form. In a more lengthy definition, Broadbent (2002) refers to e-learning as training, education, coaching, and information that are delivered digitally, be it synchronous or asynchronous, through a network via the Internet, CD-ROM, satellite, and even supported by the telephone. From this more elaborated definition, we see that e-learning can be synchronous, where the learning process is carried out in real time and led by an instructor, or asynchronous, where the learners can self-pace their progress. Zhang, Zhao, Zhou, and Nunamaker (2004) in their paper described e-learning as "technology-based learning in which learning materials are delivered electronically to remote learners via a computer network." This definition further supplements that there is a shift in the trend from old-fashioned classroom learning to more mobile learning where remote learners everywhere can learn.

As e-learning is still a relatively new discipline, the term tends to evolve from time to time based on the technological advancements. As such, the above-mentioned definitions are by no means definitive, but are more of a suggestive basis. Generally, the emergence of e-learning concepts since a decade ago can be reasoned from two factors: the needs of corporations and the availability of technological advances (Faherty, 2002; Urdan & Weggen, 2000). From the corporation aspect, one must cope with the fact that knowledge plays an important role in delivering immediate skills and just-in-time information the industries need nowadays. As knowledge becomes obsolete swiftly, it is essential for corporations to find a cost-effective way of delivering state-of-the-art training to their workers. From the technological aspect, global network access has become widely available with increased Internet bandwidth, a broad selection of available software packages, and a wide range of standardized e-learning products. This has made it possible for everybody with a computer and an Internet connection to learn in a way that is most convenient and comfortable. Learners are able to customize their learning activities based on their own styles and needs, and decide for themselves when to study in the midst of busy schedules.

Nevertheless, many corporations still hold doubts toward the effectiveness of e-learning. Deficiencies in support, content, and quality of teaching, and cultural and motivational problems are some of the main concerns that have been raised (Rosenberg, 2001). For individuals, especially the older generations, fear of technology is something to overcome (Nisar, 2002). This somehow confines the prospect of e-learning to just a limited number of age groups. Meanwhile, the flexibility of self-paced learning also leads to the possibility of spending less time in study when workload in other areas increases, which could be quite destructive to the learning process.

Although some obstacles do exist in the adoption and implementation of e-learning, the benefits of e-learning can be tremendous if the design and delivery are well catered for. A few core elements that are deemed to be essential for the successful implementation of e-learning systems have thus been identified. The following section describes these core elements of e-learning.

Core Elements of E-Learning

E-learning has been a much-talked-about revolution in recent years. Whether it is simply another method of delivering training, or a major strategic initiative that will notably aid the industry and academia depends strongly on the design of its core elements. Based on a basic structure for e-learning proposed by Broadbent (2002), the following elements have been derived as critical to the success of e-learning.

- The Learner
- The Content
- The Technology

- The Instructor
- The Environment

Many people believe that the learner should be the centre of all efforts in an e-learning system. However, it is undeniable that the content of e-learning is as important since the aim of e-learning is to transfer knowledge to the learner based on the content. In order to transfer content to a specific group of learners effectively, the technology that supports the e-learning system plays a critical role. Different sorts of audio or visual realization of the content relies on different kinds of technologies to do the job. As such, the content and technology are very much indivisible.

Equally indivisible are the learner and environment. Different learners from different backgrounds, cultures, and workplaces learn differently. In order for the learners to learn effectively, the delivery of e-learning should be able to accommodate the different environments the learners live in.

Last but not the least, the instructor sits as a mediator in between the learner and the content as well as the environment the learner comes from and the technology used for delivering the content. The role of the instructor is, on one hand, to validate the content and ensure that the technology available is sufficient for transferring the content to the learner, and on the other hand, to support the learner and ensure that the needs and expectations of the learner are met based on the environment. The correlation of the five core elements in e-learning can be depicted as in Figure 1.

Technology in E-Learning

In its broadest terms, technology could basically mean everything. A search on the Web shows that technology could be a study, a process, an application, a mechanism, a technique, a computer, a projector, a CD-ROM, or even a pen and paper. In the context of e-learning, however, it is generally understood that technology here refers to those associated with computers and the Internet. Even though the learner and content are the focus that shapes the design of e-learning, technology determines its nature. This section describes the four principal e-learning technologies according to Faherty (2002), namely, the CD-ROM, Web-based training, learning management system (LMS), and learning objects.

Before computers were widely available in the 1970s, instructor-led classroom learning was the primary, if not the only, method of training. In the 1980s, the development of e-learning started with some stand-alone software packages that

Figure 1. Core elements in e-learning

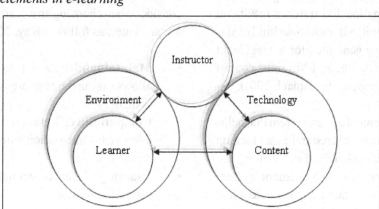

were run solely on personal computers (PCs), and CD-ROMs are one of the typical examples of these stand-alone e-learning software packages. CD-ROM is a high-density storage medium for digital files and data. It is used to store the content of training courses and distributes the learning materials to learners, often with the inclusion of some multimedia files like audio or video clips. The use of CD-ROM for e-learning was initially very expensive due to the difficulty in technicality and the customization needed. The price soon became more affordable when prepackaged software were being sold on a large scale. The problem with CD-ROM, however, is that it can be used only in asynchronous learning.

When the corporate intranets became common in the 1990s, Web-based training arose, offering flexibility in the deployment and maintenance of e-learning. With the connection of an intranet, the content of e-learning that could only be stored on CD-ROMs previously was made available on a host server. Learners were able to access the training materials through the intranet and even interact with other learners or the instructors in a synchronized environment where they could share and support one another.

The wide coverage of the Internet throughout the world soon allowed a more extensive Web-based e-learning system called the *learning management system* to emerge. The LMS is an online software package that enables the management and delivery of content and learning materials to learners. Information and training results on learners can be monitored with some kind of statistical reports being generated for management purposes. At a minimum, an LMS must consist of the following components (Ismael, 2001):

- A learning-content design system that helps to design well-structured training based on the needs and background of learners.
- A learning-content management system that creates and maintains the content and learning materials.

- A learning support system that allows for student registration, delivery of the learning content, online assessment, tracking of learner achievements, collaboration through virtual classrooms, and so forth.

With the LMS, it is generally believed that an anytime and anywhere learning environment could be established. However, the amount of learners must be substantial for a worthwhile effort to be invested on LMS.

Since the concept of object-oriented software development rose to the horizon in the middle of the 1990s, different fields in the industries have been trying hard to create software or programs that are reusable. As a result, learning objects have been introduced to make it possible for content reuse in e-learning. It is common for a corporation to have employees with overlapping learning needs or for a university to have several degrees with overlapping subjects. For this reason, learning objects play an important role to minimize the customization required by allowing the content of some overlapping subjects to be easily loaded into the LMS for reuse purposes.

Nowadays, the use of those technologies mentioned above in e-learning is widespread. It is necessary to highlight that among all the technologies available, the latest is not always the best. As such, the selection of these technologies is very much dependent on the needs of a certain e-learning system. To round up this section, five factors to consider when choosing an e-learning technology are presented as follows (Kay, 2002):

- **Maintainability:** Refers to technology that allows easy update and adjustment of course content.
- **Compatibility:** Refers to technology that allows easy integration with other packages on the market.
- **Usability:** Refers to technology that allows user friendliness.

- **Modularity:** Refers to technology that allows reusable components to reduce development time.
- **Accessibility:** Refers to technology that allows usability by any learner irrespective of software platform used or personal disabilities

E-LEARNING INITIATIVE IN A UNIVERSITY SETUP

Most of the research and implementation conducted in the field of e-learning are spearheaded by academia of higher learning institutions. This shows the importance of e-learning in the delivery of the academic programs amongst the universities. This section explores the learning continuum that can be adopted by universities based on the e-learning approach that is preferred.

Implementation through Blackboard Learning System

The implementation of e-learning can greatly help students, staff, universities, and the society as a whole. The Blackboard Learning System (BBLS) is a Web-based learning management system that helps the teaching faculty to distribute course materials and enables intercommunication between teachers and students. Blackboard is a powerful and easy-to-use tool to build and manage a Web component for the courses someone is teaching. Both the faculty members and the students can access the Blackboard sites anytime, anywhere from any Web browser (*Blackboard*, 2006).

The BBLS consists of options to post announcements and place learning materials such as lecture slides and other related teaching aids along with the discussion forum threads. Facilities to maintain internal assessment records are available in the online grade book, and students can make soft-copy submission through the digital drop box. BBLS is thus an excellent tool to provide students with some promptly updated information on a subject matter through Web technology, which can be greatly beneficial. A sample BBLS screen shot is shown in Figure 2.

From the lecturer point of view, the e-learning implementation of assessments can be effectively done through BBLS. The online test option on Blackboard was explored and found

Figure 2. Blackboard Web page layout for a subject with navigation buttons that students can use

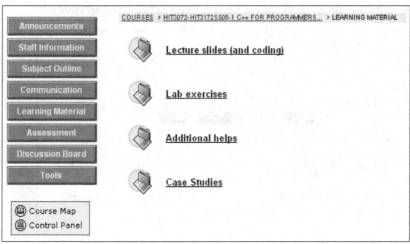

to be a great way to do formative assessments as a series of online assessments. Any online test can be easily created on the system. The online test or assessment can be created using the options in the Blackboard Test Canvas. The tests can be made of questions involving multiple choices, true or false answers, multiple answers, ordering, matching, filling in the blanks, and essays, as shown in Figure 3. Questions could be arranged in a random order, imported from an existing question pool, or uploaded separately. Once a student decides to take the test, a screen to preview the assessment and to select the right answer appears. Once the online test is taken, the review of the assessment is presented to the students with detailed feedback. It may be noted that in the review of the assessment, the students can see their score, and immediate feedback is given with detailed explanations.

There are also some other advantages that the e-learning implementation of assessments can offer. For example, it gives immediate feedback to students so that the learning process happens without delay as compared to the traditional classroom-based approach. The options to create detailed feedback help the students to get to the root of a mistake with sufficient explanation. It also makes the learning aspect quite attractive to the students as they have to take the assessment online and the scores are shown to the students so that proper evaluation on one's standing in terms of subject knowledge is made clear. To enhance the feedback or online correspondence expected from the lecturer, other Blackboard tools like the discussion forum and virtual classroom can be used (Jacob & Issac, 2005). In the discussion forum, the discussion thread can be initiated by any student asking questions of the peers or the lecturer. The series of discussion threads that would follow is visible to all the members in a class. If the bandwidth of the network is high, the virtual classroom can be a good option for students to interact with their lecturer and get any doubts clarified.

Critical Success Factors

As with any project undertaking, there are critical success factors that need to be addressed to ensure that the undertaking is successful and meets its objective. This section discusses the critical success factors that need to be addressed by educational

Figure 3. The Test Canvas gives the option to create tests as multiple choice, true or false, multiple answer, ordering, matching, or fill in the blank (Jacob, Issac, & Sebastian, 2006)

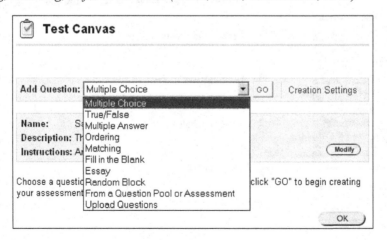

institutions when devising and deploying their e-learning initiatives. Three general categories are discussed, namely, the organizational and societal factors, the technological factors, and the pedagogical factors.

Organizational and Societal Factors

The presence of a policy governing an e-learning initiative reflects the commitment from the top management to create a conducive environment for the e-learning programs. However, in reality, only a handful of educational institutions have implemented such policy. This is due to the fact that up until recently, e-learning has always been an afterthought, and the move to offer e-learning is merely to hop on the bandwagon. Needless to say, such action has adverse effects and indirectly contributes to the high attrition rates that the e-learning programs are plagued with. A major e-learning initiative will affect everything from faculty workload to tuition. Thus, it is essential that the management of a university devises and develops a policy that is executable with their e-learning initiative. This change in policy must address a variety of issues such as cultural background, skill level, and off-line support. Having a policy alone does not ensure the success of e-learning programs. The other crucial factor is the acceptance amongst the instructor and the learner. The fact is that e-learning programs, like any other e-business initiative, require a shift from the traditional paradigm to a new one. Bates noted (as cited in Fein & Logan, 2003) that transitioning from face-to-face instruction to online learning can be a difficult change to make and requires making a paradigm shift. For some academics and students alike, working with technology is not second nature, and the cyber world is an uncharted territory.

Academic institutions have to make the effort in understanding the source of this problem in order to manage the problems successfully and convert the skeptics to become advocates of e-

learning programs. Another crucial contention that needs to be addressed is the monetary investment in the initiative. Undoubtedly, e-learning programs require high up-front cost and a considerable amount of funds to maintain. Although in most cases e-learning programs are expected to be a revenue builder for the educational institution, the fact of the matter is that the majority of distance learning programs either lose money or just break even. Thus, the governing policy has to formulate an appropriate tuition model so that there will be adequate funding that can be used for staff development and the maintenance of the programs.

Technological Factors

E-learning programs are usually facilitated by LMS, which is essentially an electronic platform that is used to assist the virtual interaction between the instructor and the learner and also between the learners themselves. Selecting the right LMS for the program is a huge undertaking as it simulates the environment where learning will take place. An LMS such as Blackboard offers a variety of tools that generally supports content management and collaborative learning. Siemens (2004) asserts that the LMS must create a learning environment that is a place for learner expression and content interaction, a place to connect with other learners and to the thoughts of other learners in a personal and meaningful way, and a place to conduct dialogues with the instructors. It acts as a repository for learning materials and should be modularized so that additional functionality and tools can be added based on what learners want or need. A good LMS supports collaborative learning and also different modes of learning.

LMS has taken the centre stage in any e-learning program. As such, it is crucial that the LMS environment can achieve the objectives of the subject and the program as a whole. To achieve this, the LMS environment must be perceived as usable. As with all other applications, usability requirements and functional requirements of an application are a matter of importance, although the earlier takes precedence for a user with low computing skills. Usability and user experience goals must be addressed by the identified platform. It should ideally be efficient and effective to use, safe, easy to learn, and easy to remember, and should have good utility. The LMS must give the user total control over the environment to reduce the level of frustration, which will ultimately motivate the user to interact more with it.

An equally important issue to address is the learner's and instructor's accessibility to the hardware and software required for the e-learning program. The unavailability of these resources can be the major inhibiting factor that will contribute to the success of e-learning programs. The LMS should also be supported across multiple platforms, and it should ideally be Web based so that it can be accessed by computers that have browsers.

User support must be available. Sufficient effort should be put into training the instructors and the participants so that they are equipped with the acceptable level of skills necessary to use the LMS competently.

Pedagogical Factors

Having the right technology in place is not enough to determine the success of an e-learning program. It is also important that the programs be learner focused, bearing in mind that the pedagogy that suits the classroom environment does not necessarily suit the online environment. Clear learning objectives must be communicated to the instructors and the learners prior to the commencement of the course so that all the participants know what is expected of them. Measures must be put in place throughout the duration of the program to gauge the performance of the participants and the effectiveness of the delivery method. This relates to the aspect of instructional design, which involves the content of the materials, the format

of the materials, the suitability and delivery of the assessments, and ultimately the tools used to support collaborative learning.

GENERAL BENEFITS OF E-LEARNING

If an academic institution is able to address the above issues, they are on their way to the full realization of the benefits associated with e-learning programs. The paramount benefit of any e-learning program is the ability to extend the learning process beyond the four walls of the classroom, thus allowing participants to engage in learning anytime and anywhere. This increase in the learner's convenience opens more doors to working individuals who are unable to commit themselves to a fixed lecture schedule due to their work commitments. The following points highlight the major benefits of e-learning in a corporate or business as well as academic environment.

Just-in-Time Training

Knowledge is delivered on demand with up-to-the-minute information. In a corporate environment, learners can access training instantly at the office, at home, or on the road 24 hours a day and seven days a week. Education is available when and where the user wants and needs it. Training may be done in bite-sized chunks as per convenience. Learners receive a consistent message regardless of when or where they access training. In a university or academic environment, the use of BBLS can augment the classroom learning and teaching as explained before with instant access to learning materials.

Cost Effectiveness

According to the findings of Horton (2000), in a corporate environment, the elimination of traveling expenses helps organizations save up to 40 to 60% by running e-learning. Learners can learn at their own computer without leaving the work site. E-learning satisfies the training needs of a geographically dispersed workforce without large investments in travel and living expenses. Since there is no travel involved for the student or instructor, the cost of e-learning courses is substantially less than learning similar material in a traditional classroom environment. The detailed savings are depicted in Table 1.

In a university environment, the use of e-learning helps students to acquire online study materials from Web sites, which can form a collection of study or reference notes, thus saving them from buying books and reducing printing costs.

Self-Study

In a corporate environment, some e-learning programs are designed to allow participants to learn at their own pace and thus cater to participants from different backgrounds. Learners can skim over materials already mastered and concentrate their efforts on the state-of-the-art knowledge and skills. They can focus on the topics that are related to their latest job description and technological trends. Remarkably, quicker productivity can be yielded from the individual learner that leads to the growth of the organization. Since participants can learn at their own time and pace, the amount of information retained from the training is often greater, which results in increased information retention. By making academic courses more accessible, this will generate a more skilled workforce that can contribute to the economic growth of a country. In a university scenario, e-learning can supplement traditional classroom learning, thus allowing the students to study more independently.

Content and Delivery Cycle

Generally, learning materials with uniform standards can be maintained for all learners. This standard is particularly useful for e-learning providers to study learners' acceptance of the materials, especially if the learners are from different cultural backgrounds. The learning environment has minimum errors and consistent delivery. The delivery cycle time of the content is also reduced significantly, which in turn enables companies using e-learning to deliver training to many people quickly (Welsh, Wanberg, Brown, & Simmering, 2003). In a university environment, exporting the content of an existing course and importing it into a similar new course with some modifications allows not only content reuse, but also requires little time.

Measurement and Timely Feedback

A myriad of tools can be incorporated into the e-learning packages to monitor students' progress and produce detailed usage reports. This can be given as feedback to students or learners. With the ability to create assessments, it is trivial to find what users have learned, when they have completed courses, how they performed, and their levels of improvement. Automated reporting and statistical analysis of the learning process can be produced in order to quantify the e-learning benefits to organizations and universities.

Table 1. Costing savings of e-learning (Horton, 2000)

Company	Original Cost of Training	Cost of E-Learning	E-Learning Savings
Hewlett-Packard	$7 million	$1.5 million	$5.5 million
Cisco	$1,200-$1,800 per learner	$120 per learner	$1,080-$1,680 per learner
Novell	$1,800 per learner	$700-$900 per learner	$900-$1,100 per learner

Repository and Easy Access

The e-learning system can be a place for lecturers and students to interact frequently. This can enhance the ease of learning with easy-to-access lecture slides, discussion forums, extra notes, and quizzes. In addition, learners can access a host of other online digital libraries for assignments and exams. This concept of easy access to a stored repository of knowledge and information makes student learning faster and efficient.

Increased Effectiveness of Classroom Training

When combined with a classroom learning strategy, e-learning can increase the value of classroom learning. By using e-learning to educate team members on basic topics, classroom learning can focus on team building that can only effectively be taught in a face-to-face environment.

We should keep in mind that e-learning supports traditional learning in a great way, though it is never meant to replace traditional learning with books. Once the student community enjoys the benefits of e-learning, it would bring in more local and foreign students into an academic organization, which eventually can bring in more capital. From the corporate point of view, the concept of e-learning definitely lifts the face of any organization and would make it a better place to be in. This can have a ripple effect in spreading the news through word of mouth or other forms of advertisement about the organization. From the academy point of view, a university that has an e-learning system to complement the existing learning structure would definitely attract more students.

DIGITAL LIBRARY

One of the learning access breakthroughs that have happened in the recent past (mostly from the early 1990s) with the advent of the Internet is the proliferation of digital data that are distributed throughout the world. Years back, access to most of the information was quite manual, involving one to order a book or get it from a library. Now, that is a bygone history, a pitiful stone age in this information technology era. Today, for an active learner, whether a researcher or student, there exists unlimited access to digital library contents. Generally, digital library access can be of two types: subscribed digital library access and free digital library access.

In a subscribed digital library, the subscribed access can be made through an organization's or university's subscription or through a personal subscription. For example, one can electronically access the digital information from any of the following Web sites: IEEE (IEEE Xplore), which gives full-text access to the world's highest quality technical literature in electrical engineering, computer science, and electronics; ACM (ACM Digital Library), which gives a vast collection of citations and full text from ACM journal and newsletter articles and conference proceedings; SpringerLink, which gives premiere electronic data sources from Springer for researchers in biomedicine, life science, clinical medicine, physics, engineering, mathematics, computer science, humanities, and economics; Blackwell Synergy, which gives details on many subjects like business, economics, finance and accounting, engineering, computing and technology, health sciences, humanities, law, mathematics and statistics, and medicine; and a host of other digital banks like Business & Industry, Ebscohost, Emerald Fulltext, InfoTrac, ProQuest, Taylor & Francis, and Wiley Interscience, which are all available to the user at the click of a mouse. This bursting overflow of high-quality digital content access was inconceivable many years ago. Thus, e-learning can change the pace at which a learner can access and use the needed information, which eventually makes the learning process more efficient.

In a free digital library, the access to quality learning materials is given free of charge. A classic example of this is OpenCourseWare (OCW) introduced by the Massachusetts Institute of Technology (MIT) in 2001. MIT's initiative on OCW was innovative. Their Web site can be found at http://ocw.mit.edu/. The OCW is a project aiming to provide basic course materials for around 2,000 subjects for use by anyone, absolutely free of charge. At present, around 1,400 courses are already online. It provides free and searchable access to MIT's course materials for teachers, students, and self-learners around the world. It is up to any learner to make use of such quality online facilities. In total, 2.3 million unique visitors came to the site from November 1, 2003, to October 31, 2004, generating nearly 4.2 million visits. 36% of OCW visitors come from North America, 16% each from East Asia and Western Europe, 11% each from Latin America and Eastern Europe, and the remaining 9% from the Middle East, Africa, the Pacific, Central Asia, and the Caribbean combined (MIT, 2005).

STUDENT PERCEPTIONS ON E-LEARNING AND ANALYSIS

As discussions on the use of e-learning in university education focus on ways for teachers to incorporate e-learning into their mode of delivery, this section incorporates a discussion on e-learning from the student perspective (Keller & Cernerud, 2002). The scenario presented here is a university setup where e-learning is practiced through BBLS as a supplement to the regular classroom-based delivery style. Figure 4 shows the Blackboard usage for one subject over a 14-week period.

This analysis was aimed to explore and analyze factors crucial to overcome the possible hindrances of implementation e-learning in university education. Three specific objectives were: (a) to explore students' general attitudes to e-learning, (b) to analyze the relationship between the attitudes of students toward e-learning and factors like attitudes to new technologies and learning styles, and (c) to explore the most important advantages

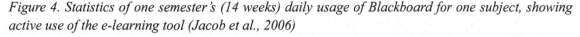

Figure 4. Statistics of one semester's (14 weeks) daily usage of Blackboard for one subject, showing active use of the e-learning tool (Jacob et al., 2006)

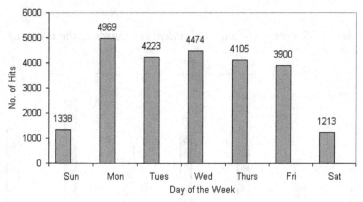

and disadvantages that the students experienced in the context of e-learning.

The scope of the study included students who have used e-learning in at least two main subjects during the previous year. The questionnaire was distributed to a large sample of 165 students across business and engineering streams in a university. The instrument measured the first objective using seven closed questions designed using the Likert scaling on a scale of 1 to 5, where 1 represents *I agree totally* and 5 represents *I disagree totally*. It also had one question to check on the extent of disruption by technical problems (coded on a scale of 1 to 5 representing *never* to *very often*).

The second objective was measured using five other closed-ended questions. Two open-ended and closed-ended questions checked on the advantages and disadvantages of the e-learning platform. As depicted in Figure 5, the majority of the responses for the questions on the use of the BBLS platform have shown a mean close to 1 (*I agree totally*) or 2 (*I agree to a large extent*). The best mean was close to 1.5 and the worst mean close to 3.5. The implication was that the students agreed to a large extent to the easiness, flexibility, assistance, and improved communication offered by the BBLS platform.

The survey revealed marginal differences concerning the attitudes to the usage of the BBLS between the two streams of the university, namely, engineering and business. 68% of engineering students and 90% of business students responded in positive agreement to the ease of use of the Web platform. 56% of engineering students and 90% of business students responded that the Web platform assisted them quite a lot in their studies. 66% and 89% respectively of engineering and business students confirmed that the platform has offered flexibility concerning their studies. 46% of engineering students and 62% of business students responded in favour of the fact that the use of the BBLS platform has improved the pedagogic value of the courses. 40% of engineering students and 55% of business students have agreed that the usage has improved their possibilities to solve problems related to their courses. Regarding the disruption of the BBLS usage by technical problems, only 4% of the students responded that this occurs very often, as compared to 62% who said sometimes and 18% who said never.

A factor analysis performed on the closed-ended questions showed a close interrelationship (factor score of 0.71) between the questions. Then, a multiple regression analysis was attempted us-

Figure 5. The mean Likert scale rating (1-5) of the student responses to the usage of BBLS in the university

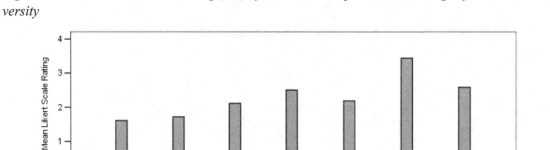

ing the dependent variable of attitude measured as a total index for each individual. The four independent variables used were gender, area of specialization (engineering or business), attitudes to new technology (measured in five levels, innovator, early adopter, early majority, late majority, and laggard), and learning style (measured in two categories, abstract or concrete and active or reflective). No significant statistical relationships were seen between attitudes and learning styles or attitudes to new technology, but there was a significant relationship ($p<0.1$) between attitude and gender at a 10% significance level.

Through the open-ended questions, information was gathered on the most important advantage and disadvantage based on the students' experience with the e-learning system in the university. The qualitative information was content analyzed and classified into main categories. The main advantage highlighted was that there was easy access to learning materials and resources, followed by the next favoured advantage of being able to view test results. The system was praised as a tool that made university life less time consuming. A quarter of the students felt that the platform made them feel overdependent on the computer for help. A minority commented on the inconsistent usage of the platform across different courses. Students still insisted that such a Web platform should not be seen as a substitute for personal teaching. Some expressed concern that the BBLS can bring in a machine-oriented perspective to the teacher-student and student-student relationships. In general, nevertheless, students felt that the BBLS boosts efficiency and effectiveness on both sides (the student and the lecturer) of the learning endeavor.

TEACHERS' GENERAL PERCEPTIONS ON E-LEARNING

E-learning has become a reality from a technological point of view, but how about from the teachers'

point of view? There is a customary belief that classroom learning is the best way to maintain a learning process. So how do the teachers perceive e-learning as a new paradigm of learning? How ready are they? This section aims to determine the motivations for teachers to design and implement e-learning in their teaching.

Based on a survey conducted by White, Tastle, and Fox (2003), many teachers feel that the preparation time for e-learning is significantly longer as compared to classroom learning. This is due to the fact that converting classroom materials to e-learning materials is not just as simple as converting a Word document into hypertext markup language (HTML) format. To some extent, teachers are required to learn some scripting languages such as ASP, JavaScript, Perl, CGI interfaces, and so forth for developing electronic versions of tests and marking schemes. Nevertheless, many LMSs nowadays like the BBLS and WebCT have eased the tasks of teachers by providing numerous automated functions. With the aid of these LMSs, most of the teachers think that the effort spent on developing e-learning materials is worth it as the prospect of reusing the materials saves much of the blues in the future.

Meanwhile, a majority of the teachers who were involved in e-learning before believe that some kind of real-time interactions are necessary in an e-learning environment. Internet relay chat, an online system that allows users to chat live using text or audio Internet telephony, is an appealing choice. Besides that, videoconferencing is also useful for geographically distanced teachers and students to hold discussions in real time. Also, teachers generally believe that technical skills can only be developed when students are involved in some kind of hands-on practices. In view of this, they have suggested that e-learning should work closely with the industries in order to produce students with technical competency.

At the present time, the use of e-learning is still limited in education as many universities are hesitant in using e-learning as their major learning method. A survey conducted by Nisar (2002) showed that those under the age of 40 have been receiving the notion of e-learning quite well from a technological point of view. Finally, cultural acceptance is another issue that has been raised by some teachers as they are afraid that differences in demographics and psychographics may predispose students against e-learning (Kamsin, 2005). Conversely, however, a significant number of teachers think that e-learning has actually allowed students, especially foreign students, to maintain a better sense of community. Some students who are introverted or cannot speak a local language well will often feel isolated within a campus environment. These people may feel more comfortable communicating with others through the e-learning setting.

FUTURE TRENDS: E-LEARNING THROUGH WIRELESS ACCESS

Wireless technology has brought along with it mobile and seamless access to digital information, giving rise to a new paradigm called mobile learning. Access to a host of digital information is good enough, but when that is added to mobility, learning styles could be improved furthermore. Generally, many universities have 802.11 wireless networks that help the students access e-learning tools like BBLS and other digital libraries. Various wireless access points can be placed in common areas like cafeterias, libraries, reading rooms, and so forth to facilitate online data access in a wireless fashion.

A sample university network with wireless access is shown in Figure 6 with some basic security

Figure 6. The wireless network in a university showing mobile laptops (Chan, Ang, & Issac, 2005)

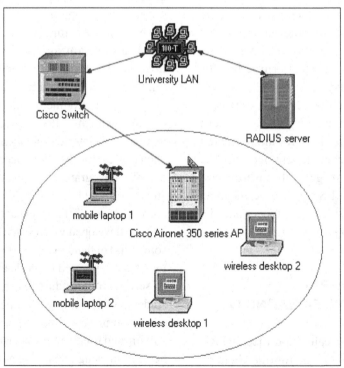

features. Students can opt for laptops and move into the wireless access range to get connected to the university network for access to their student files and other e-learning resources. This liberates them from the need for being stationed at a lab or library setup, where things can be rigid and mobility may not be that possible. For basic security, the wireless node needs to be authenticated with a RADIUS authentication server.

As in any wireless network implementation, security is a major concern when an intruder mimics an e-learning user. In the secure network design shown in Figure 7, the firewall between the Internet cloud and enterprise network weeds out unauthorized access. The firewall between the wireless local area network (WLAN) and the enterprise network stops or filters attacks from the WLAN side. Virtual private network (VPN) provides secure tunneling through the use of the IPSec protocol by using a separate VPN server. A cheaper option, though, would be to have a firewall that is VPN enabled and has the VPN server features inbuilt into one box. Nevertheless, a VPN server for a large enterprise or university is a better option. Lastly, a RADIUS authentication server that provides the 802.1x authentication and

wi-fi (wireless fidelity) protected access (WPA) with an advanced encryption protocol can be used for secure WLAN communications (Issac, Chee, & Mohammed, 2005). This could help to keep the e-learning resources and other network resources in good safety.

To add to that, mobile learning (m-learning) uses hardware that is commonly used by students nowadays, like laptops with integrated wireless cards, personal digital assistants (PDAs), tablet PCs, and Bluetooth devices. Instead of planned and purpose-built computer labs, multifunction rooms are being used to support a range of learning goals. These rooms make use of mobile chairs and desks, wireless projectors, and interactive whiteboards to create an interactive learning environment. The decision to move to a wireless or mobile environment rests on a number of factors like cost effectiveness in building the system, security aspects, and the reliability of bandwidth service in that area. As per some estimates, the cost of developing or expanding a wired network is around twice as expensive as that of wireless systems (Thomas, 2005).

Figure 7. Secure university network with wireless access using IPSec-based VPN over WLAN (Issac et al., 2005)

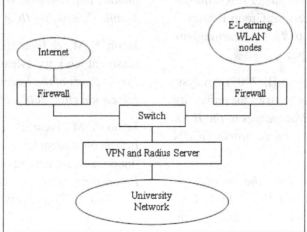

CONCLUSION

This chapter illustrated the implementation of e-learning and its effects on the society as a whole. Generally, successful implementation of e-learning can be beneficial to three parties, namely, the learner or student community, the teaching community, and educational institutions or organizations. As the formation of economic growth comes from the way a country generates its wealth based on investment capital and labour through education and training, the benefits of e-learning on the three communities mentioned would in turn have a positive impact on the country and thus boost its economy. Today, traditional classroom learning alone is no longer able to provide students with adequate knowledge and skills necessary for the increasingly sophisticated global world. E-learning can thus provide an alternative solution that is cost effective and efficient to fill the gap (Flynn, Concannon, & Bheachain, 2005). As a final remark, e-learning is the future that could improve lives and bring the economy to new heights if it is harnessed well.

REFERENCES

Blackboard. (2006). Retrieved from http://www.blackboard.com/us/index.aspx

Broadbent, B. (2002). *E-learning: Present and future.* Ottawa Distance Learning Group. Retrieved October 11, 2005, from http://www.elearninghub.com/docs/ODLG_2002.pdf

Chan, F., Ang, H. H., & Issac, B. (2005). Analysis of IEEE 802.11b wireless security for university wireless LAN design. *Proceedings of the IEEE International Conference on Networks* (ICON 2005), 1137-1142.

Downes, S. (2003). *Where the market is: IDC on e-learning.* International Data Corporation. Retrieved February 10, 2006, from http://www.downes.ca/cgi-bin/website/show.cgi?format=full&id=12

European eLearning Industry Group (eLIG). (2006). *The European eLearning Industry Group: Promoting eLearning in Europe.* Retrieved April 21, 2006, from http://www.elig.org/

Faherty, R. (2002). *Corporate e-learning.* Dublin, Ireland: Dublin Institute of Technology.

Fein, A. D., & Logan, M. C. (2003). Preparing instructors for online instruction. *New Directions for Adult and Continuing Education, 100*, 45-55. Retrieved April 23, 2006, from Wiley InterScience database.

Flynn, A., Concannon, F., & Bheachain, C. N. (2005). Undergraduate students' perceptions of technology-supported learning: The case of an accounting class. *International Journal on E-Learning, 4*(4), 427-445.

Horton, W. (2000). *Designing Web-based training: How to teach anyone anything anywhere anytime.* New York: John Wiley and Sons, Inc.

Ismael, J. (2001). The design of an e-learning system beyond the hype. *The Internet and Higher Education, 4*(3-4), 329-336.

Issac, B., Chee, V. K. M., & Mohammed, L. A. (2005). Security considerations in the design of wireless networks. *Proceedings of the International Conference on Wireless Networking and Mobile Computing (ICWNMC '05)*, 136-141.

Jacob, S. M., & Issac, B. (2005). Formative assessment and its e-learning implementation. *Proceedings of the International Conference on Education (ICE 2005)*, 258-263.

Jacob, S. M., Issac, B., & Sebastian, Y. (2006). Impact on student learning from traditional continuous assessment and an e-assessment proposal. *Proceedings of the 10th Pacific Asia Conference on Information Systems (PACIS 2006)*, 1482-1496.

Kamsin, A. (2005). Is e-learning the solution and substitute for conventional learning? *International Journal of the Computer, the Internet and Management, 13*(3), 79-89.

Kay, D. (2002). *E-learning market insight report: Drivers, developments, decisions.* United Kingdom: FD Learning Ltd.

Keller, C., & Cernerud, L. (2002). Students' perceptions of e-learning in university education. *Journal of Educational Media, 27,* 56-67.

Massachusetts Institute of Technology (MIT). (2005). *2004 Program Evaluation Findings Report.* MIT OpenCourseWare. Retrieved July 28 from http://ocw.mit.edu/OcwWeb/Global/AboutOCW/evaluation.htm

Metros, S. (2003). *E-learning implementation strategy and plan.* Retrieved April 21, 2006, from http://telr.osu.edu/resources/ITelearning.pdf

Nisar, T. (2002). Organizational determinants of e-learning. *Industrial and Commercial Training, 34*(7), 256-262.

Rosenberg, M. J. (2001). *E-learning: Strategies for delivering knowledge in the digital age.* New York: McGraw-Hill.

Simens, G. (2004). *Learning management systems: The wrong place to start learning.* Retrieved June 20, 2006, from http://www.elearnspace.org/Articles/lms.htm

Thomas, M. (2005). *E-learning on the move, May 2005.* Retrieved April 25, 2006, from http://education.guardian.co.uk/elearning/comment/0,10577,1490476,00.html

Urdan, T., & Weggen, C. (2000). *Corporate e-learning: Exploring a new frontier.* Equity Research. Retrieved November 15, 2005, from http://www.spectrainteractive.com/pdfs/CorporateELearingHamrecht.pdf

Waller, V., & Wilson, J. (2001). *A definition for e-learning.* Open and Distance Learning Quality Council. Retrieved October 11, 2005, from http://www.odlqc.org.uk/odlqc/n19-e.htm

Welsh, E. T., Wanberg, C. R., Brown, K. G., & Simmering, M. J. (2003). E-learning: Emerging uses, empirical results, and future directions. *International Journal of Training and Development, 7*(4), 245-258. Retrieved April 21, 2006, from Blackwell Synergy database.

White, B. A., Tastle, W. J., & Fox, D. (2003). Barriers to e-learning in information systems. *Proceedings of the Information Systems Education Conference (ISECON 2003).* Retrieved February 10, 2006, from http://isedj.org/isecon/2003/3523/

Zhang, D., Zhao, J. L., Zhou, L., & Nunamaker, J. F., Jr. (2004). Can e-learning replace classroom training? *Communications of the ACM, 47*(5), 75-79.

Chapter XX
The Significance of the Existence of Women's Colleges and Their Entry into Science–Related Fields

Akiko Nishio
Mukogawa Women's University, Japan

ABSTRACT

This chapter discusses the importance of increasing the number of women who are active in science-related fields, especially in science and technology, because of the microlevel profit that will be derived by individual women and the macrolevel benefit stemming from the effective use of human resources in society. Furthermore, it considers whether women's colleges could play a key role in training and educating capable women in these fields. The chapter also stipulates the significance of women's colleges and their entry into science-related fields and investigates the educational practices adopted by such colleges. The conclusion drawn from the discussion is that it is essential for women's colleges that have entered into these fields to ensure that the significance of their existence is recognized, that their educational practices are based on this recognition, and that such a coherent and meaningful practice will enable these colleges to produce capable women who will play an active role in and contribute to society.

INTRODUCTION

Why is it important to increase the number of female students who major in science-related fields[1]—particularly, science and technology—in higher education? Is it possible for women's colleges to play a role in educating and training female students in science-related fields? These two questions are addressed in this chapter.

Today, it is a well-known fact that the proportion of women in developed countries who are active in science-related fields—particularly in science and technology—is extremely low, and the clear gender difference that this situation reflects is considered an important issue in these countries for the following two reasons.

The first reason for paying close attention to gender differences in educational fields is that in today's globalizing world, it is essential for individual countries to retain citizens who are knowledgeable about and skilled in the fields related to science and technology in order to compete and cooperate with other countries. However, in many countries, there is a dearth of people with such capabilities. Therefore, some countries have taken measures to address this serious concern. For example, during the 1990s in the United States, under the Clinton administration, the improvement of mathematics and science education was considered a national project. Former U.S. President Bill Clinton regarded mathematics and science as extremely important subjects for retaining human resources and national power. The measures taken by the Clinton administration showed that the president considered that permitting a situation wherein many people are illiterate in the science-related fields, particularly in science and technology, would be a fatal loss for the country. Indeed, some studies suggest that training more women in these fields is essential for the empowerment of individual countries (Darke, Beatriz, & Ruta, 2002; Epstein, Elwood, Hey, & Maw, 1998; Kimura, 2005; Muramatsu, 1996; Ogawa, 2001). Moreover, in some countries, such as in the United States, United Kingdom, Canada, Australia, and Japan, various educational programs have been established to encourage women to enter the fields of science and technology. Girls into Science and Technology (GIST) in the United Kingdom, Women in Science and Technology in Australia (WISTA), and Creating

Cultures of Success for Women Engineers (WomEng) 2002-2005 in the European Union (EU) are some examples of such programs.

The second reason for focusing on this issue is related to the first one: Many women in particular appear to be excluded from or sidelined in the labor market while only a handful of people, often men, are at an advantage, for example, in terms of employment, promotion, and income (Kress, 1998). The problem of the digital divide among people has been a serious global as well as domestic concern (Antonelli, 2003; Kimura, 2001), and the digital divide between genders is also a part of the problem. The main reason why women have not yet advanced considerably in science-related fields is that the proportion of female students majoring in such fields is significantly low in higher education. In fact, a number of studies have already pointed out the existence of this situation in higher education (Forgasz, 1998; Graetz, 1991; Kay, Lublin, Poiner, & Proser, 1989; Kimura, 2005; Nelson & Rogers, 2004; Organization for Economic Cooperation and Development [OECD], 2004). For example, OECD (2004) states the following, based on a study that surveyed 30 signatories:

....major differences remain among fields of study. In humanities, arts, education, health and welfare, more than two-thirds of the tertiary-type A graduates are females, on average in OECD countries, whereas less than one-third of mathematics and computer science graduates and less than one-fifth of engineering, manufacturing and construction graduates are females. (pp. 81-82)

Moreover, according to the same report by OECD (2004), the proportion of females obtaining a first tertiary type-A qualification in mathematics and computer science is 30% on average in OECD countries, whereas it is only 9% in Japan, which has the lowest rate along with Switzerland. The low proportion indicates that the delay in the entrance of Japanese women into science-related fields is extremely serious not only when compared with the position of Japanese men, but also when compared with that of women in other countries.

Clearly, it is crucial for Japan to increase the number of women who are active in science, technology, and related fields because of the microlevel profit that will be derived by individual women and the macrolevel benefit stemming from the effective use of human resources in society.

In order to increase the number of women who are active in science-related fields, it may be advantageous to entrust women's colleges with the role of educating and training female students in such fields for the following two reasons. First, numerous studies have reported that female students in science-related fields, especially those at coeducational colleges, tend to encounter various problems due to their gender. Second, long-term discussion on the significance of the existence of women's colleges has highlighted many advantages for female students studying at these colleges, which indicates the possibility that women's colleges are more appropriate for female students than are coeducational institutions. Tracing a link between these two reasons, this chapter attempts to clarify the implications of women's colleges entering into science-related fields and its accompanying problems.

PROBLEMS FEMALE STUDENTS ENCOUNTER WHILE MAJORING IN SCIENCE-RELATED FIELDS

As mentioned earlier, many studies have reported that female students majoring in science-related fields, especially those at coeducational colleges, are likely to face various problems. Here, we shall review some of the problems reported in these studies. First of all, some studies (Betzs & Hackett, 1983; Hackett, 1985) suggest that female students tend to have significantly lower self-efficacy than male students regarding mathematics-related subjects including computer science. Seymour (1995b) also reports that there is a tendency for more female than male students to switch from a science, mathematics, and engineering (SME) major to a non-SME major. According to Seymour (1995a), the four main reasons for this tendency are "the loss of interest in science; belief that a non-SME major holds more interest or offers a better education; poor teaching by SME faculty; feeling overwhelmed by the pace and load of curriculum demands" (p. 199). Other studies (Gray, 1996; Niddiffer & Bashaw, 2001) also suggest that female students have difficulty in finding role models due to the lack of female faculty. Moreover, Maeda (1996) states that female students in science-related fields reported with relatively higher frequency than those in the humanities that they felt a sense of danger in returning home at night because of the necessity of staying behind in laboratories for research, and also found it inconvenient to use several facilities and equipment—which are often designed for male students. Moreover, they found it difficult to join male peer groups.

As we have seen here, science-related fields appear to be traditionally male dominated (Muramatsu, 1996); therefore, it seems inevitable that female students would encounter various problems in the process of continuing their studies. Moreover, often, the majority of the faculty members and peers at coeducational colleges are men. In such a situation, female students are more likely to be required to adapt to the male culture and/or endure a sense of isolation because they belong to the minority group.

Table 1. The significance of the existence of women's colleges: Aspects, concrete claims, and criticisms

Aspects of the significances of existence	Concrete claims	Criticisms
(a) A Women's college has an environment in which female students are respected.	• An environment in which women's rights and capabilities are respected helps female students gain confidence, develop self-respect, and be progressive (Kim, 2002; Makino, 2004; Yamamoto & fujimura, 2000)	• The gender exclusivity of women's colleges resulted in the lack of regular contact with male students/men and the experience of working only with women poses a problem (Kawakami, 1986). • Students are women's colleges are less satisfied with the quality of social life experienced on campus than are those at coeducational colleges (Astin, 1993; Smith, 1990).
(b) There are advantages for female students due to the absence of male students.	• Since there are many opportunities to act without relying on the opposite sex, female students can become autonomous and progressive, develop a sense of responsibility, leadership, critical-thinking abilities, and problem-solving skills (Aso, 1987; Heianjogakuin ed., 2000; Kim, 2002; Kim & Alvarez, 1995; Matsuzawa, 2000; Sugita, 1996; Whitt, 1994; Yamamoto & Fujimura, 2000). • They develop the ability to act without gender bias (Manning, 1994, 2000). • They become women who are not confined by 'a glass ceiling' (Heianjogakuin ed., 2000).	• If female students or graduates are given the opportunity of exercising their leadership skills only among groups of women, the leadership abilities that they gain at college would therefore not be useful in groups comprising or including men (Kawakami, 1986).
(c) There are a variety of programs related to women's and gender studies and programs, especially for female students, which help women become independent.	• There are various programs related to women's studies/gender studies and such programs discuss the experiences of successful women; this fosters independence in female students (Heianjogakuin ed., 2000; Kameda et. al., 2000; Kim, 2001, 2002).	
(d) The proportion of female faculty members and that of female executives to male executives is often higher at women's colleges than at coeducational colleges, with various educational effects.	• The higher proportion of female faculty members and of female executives to male executives in women's colleges can help female students find role models and mentors (Heianjogakuin ed., 2000; Kameda et al., 2000; Miyake, 2003; Tidball, 1973; Yamamoto & Fujimura, 2000). • An environment in which a majority of the faculty as well as students is female predisposes women-only colleges to be more liberal and progressive, and that a liberal faculty and environment promote students' critical-thinking abilities and analytical and problem-solving skills (Kim, 2002). • Regular interaction between students and the faculty members has positive educational effects; for example, it motivates students to take greater interest in studies and increases the percentage of those who obtain baccalaureates (Kim & Alvarez, 1995).	• The faculty members can rarely act as a role model in colleges due to the lack of interaction with students(Kim, 2002; Nihonjoshidaigaku Sogokenkyosho, 1999). • A higher proportion of female faculty members is not necessarily a predictor of the several dimensions of female students' development (Kim, 2001; Kim & Alvarez, 1995).
(e) Many successfully women and academically outstanding students have graduated from women's colleges.	• A large proportion of women executives and female students who go on to study in medical schools and law schools have graduated from women's colleges (Heianjogakuin ed., 2000; Oates & Williamson, 1978; Tidball 1973, 1985, 1986; Wolf-Wendel, 1998; Yamamoto & Fujimura, 2000). • In response to the criticisms made by Kim and Alverez (1995), and Stoecker and Pascarella (1991), demonstrative studies which controlled the influence of the characteristics of educational institutions, students' academic preparations, and the socioeconomic status of students' families were conducted (e.g., Smith, Wolf, & Morrison, 1999; Wolf-Wendel, 1998). These studies support Tidball's and other's findings–a high proportion of female executives and students who go on to study in medical schools and law schools have graduated from women's colleges.	• The influence of students' academic preparations and that of the socioeconomic status of students' families is unclear (Kim & Alvarez, 1995). • The influence of characteristics of educational institutions is unclear (Stoecker & Pascarella, 1991).

THE IMPLICATIONS OF WOMEN'S COLLEGES ENTERING INTO SCIENCE-RELATED FIELDS: A DISCUSSION THROUGH THE PERSPECTIVE OF THE SIGNIFICANCE OF WOMEN'S COLLEGES

A Review of the Debate on the Significance of the Existence of Women's Colleges

This section will attempt to clarify the implications of women's colleges entering into science-related fields. In order to do so, we will first review the debate about the significance of the existence of women's colleges and confirm that this significance does indeed exist. Table 1 lists the main aspects of significance for the existence of women's colleges cited by previous studies.

As shown in Table 1, the significance of the existence of women's colleges can be categorized into five aspects: (a) A women's college has an environment in which female students are respected, (b) there are advantages available for female students due to the absence of male students, (c) there are a variety of programs related to women's and gender studies designed especially for female students, which help women become independent, (d) the proportion of female faculty members to male faculty members and that of female executives to male executives is often higher at women's colleges than at coeducational colleges, with various educational effects, and (e) many successful women and academically outstanding students have graduated from women's colleges. As indicated in Table 1, these five aspects of the significance of women's colleges have been substantiated by demonstrative studies that were often conducted in the United States.

However, there are criticisms against most of these aspects, namely, a respectful environment, advantages in the absence of male students, a higher proportion of female faculty, and the num-

ber of successful women who have graduated from these colleges. We shall review these criticisms and deliberate upon their appropriateness.

First, Kawakami (1986) criticizes the first aspect by pointing out the gender exclusivity of women's colleges; the study implies that an educational environment without male students is unnatural and that the lives of female students in such an environment are unhealthy. However, female students seem to acquire abilities such as assertiveness and autonomy more quickly under such a circumstance, namely, in an environment with no male students. Societies and educational systems are still often male oriented and there exist various types of discriminations against women. Considering the negative aspects of society and the educational system, it may be advantageous for female students to be separated from their male counterparts for some time and be trained while being free from gender discrimination to the greatest extent possible in order that they become able to enter society with assertiveness, autonomy, confidence, and self-respect.

Regarding Kawakami's (1986) criticism against the significance of the second aspect, if indeed, as the criticism claims, female students or graduates of women's colleges can exhibit their leadership skills only among women, and therefore these skills are not useful when dealing with men, then it would be impossible for women's colleges to produce many competent graduates who could function as executives in the labor market. However, in reality, there seem to be many women in leadership roles (Heianjogakuin, (ed.) 2000; Yamamoto & Fujimura, 2000). It is still a reality that only a handful of women can become presidents of listed companies in Japan. Nevertheless, 7 out of the 20 high-ranking colleges that produce women presidents are exclusively women's colleges (Toyokeizaishimpo-Sha as cited in President-Sha, 2006).

Various studies, such as Nihonjoshidaigaku Sogokenkyusho (1999) and Kim (2002), criticize the aspect of the high proportion of female faculty on the grounds that the belief that a high propor-tion of female to male faculty members would encourage female students to easily find role models is naïve. However, these studies do not necessarily criticize all of the concrete examples shown in Table 1.

Moreover, as shown in Table 1, the aspect regarding the many successful women who have graduated from women's colleges was severely criticized once. However, various demonstrative studies that reviewed institutions' characteristics, women's academic preparation, and/or their family's socioeconomic status later substantiated this aspect of significance.

The review of criticisms outlined here leads us to be convinced that the significance of the existence of women's colleges is indeed valid.

The Significance of Women's Colleges Entering into Science-Related Fields

First, taking into account the fourth significant aspect, which indicates that the proportion of female to male faculty members is often higher at women's colleges than at coeducational colleges, it may be possible that the proportion of female to male faculty members is higher at women's

Table 2. Women's colleges that have entered into science-related fields including computer and informa-tion science in Japan, the United States, and Korea

Country	Name of College (Year of Establishment)	Faculties, Departments, Majors, and Colleges related to Computer and Information Science and other Science-Related Fields
Japan	Ochanomizu University (1875)	Faculty of Science: Mathematics, Physics, Chemistry, Biology, Information Science
	Tsuda College (1900)	Department of Mathematics Department of Computer Science
	Nara Women's University (1908)	Faculty of Science: Department of Mathematics, Department of Physics, Department of Chemistry, Department of Biological Sciences, Department of Information and Computer Science
USA	Mount Holyoke College (1837)	Science and Mathematics: Astronomy, Biochemistry, Biological Sciences, Chemistry, Computer Science, Environmental Studies, Geography, Mathematics, Neuroscience and Behavior, Physics, Statistics
	Mills College (1852)	Biochemistry, Biochemistry and Molecular Biology, Biology, Biopsychology, Chemistry, Computer Science, Engineering, Environmental Science, Mathematics, Physics, Psychology
	Wellesley College (1870)	Mathematics and Science Majors: Biological Chemistry, Biological Sciences, Computer Science, Mathematics, Neuroscience
	Smith College (1871)	Science Majors: Astronomy, Biochemistry, Biological Sciences, Chemistry, Computer Science, Engineering, Geology, Mathematics, Neuroscience, Physics, Psychology
	Trinity College (1894)	College of Arts and Sciences: Applied Statistics, Biochemistry, Biology, Chemistry, Engineering, Environmental Science, Information Systems and Technology, Mathematics, Physical Science, Physics
Korea	Ewha Womans University (1886)	College of Natural Sciences: Division of Mathematical and Physical Sciences, Division of Molecular and Life Sciences College of Engineering: Division of Computer-Information Communication Engineering, Division of Architecture, Division of Environmental and Food Technology
	Sookmyng Women's University (1906)	College of Science: Division of Natural Science, Division of Mathematics and Statistics, Division of Computer and Information Science

colleges even in science-related fields. This proportion has traditionally been low in these fields, and therefore science and technology have remained male-dominated spheres. In addition, at women's colleges, female students do not have to worry about loneliness or isolation due to their gender. Furthermore, the multiplier effect of all the aspects of significance cited in Table 1 may work effectively to educate and train female students in science-related fields to be future pioneers. If this is the case, the implications of women's colleges entering into science-related fields are the education, training, and producing of women who will play an active role in these fields in society and contribute to it by recognizing the significance of the existence of women's colleges and providing female students studying there the appropriate education and educational environment based on such a recognition.

EDUCATIONAL PRACTICES OF WOMEN'S COLLEGES THAT HAVE ENTERED INTO SCIENCE-RELATED FIELDS

Women's Colleges that have Entered into Science-Related Fields

In many developed countries, higher education is no longer the exclusive domain of certain elite people but is accessible to the public as well, as Trow (1991) suggests. The greater the number of people studying in higher education and the greater the diversity in students' ages, genders, races, and socioeconomic status, the more sensitive do institutions of higher education become toward the educational expectations of these students. Simultaneously, those institutions are required to keep pace with changes in the labor market and modify their educational programs in order to adapt to the changes in the purpose of higher education. For many students, higher education is no longer merely a means of achieving pure sophistication but also a means of seeking better jobs and social status. Many colleges, including women's colleges, therefore, cannot overlook the changes in the labor market.

There are women's colleges in various countries, such as Japan, the United States, Korea, China, and Israel. There are 86 women's colleges in Japan (National Women's Education Center [NWEC], 2006)—the highest number—followed by 58 in the United States in 2006 (Women's University Coalition, 2006). Some of these colleges have already begun offering courses in science-related fields including computer and information science. Table 2 gives examples of those women's colleges that have entered into science-related fields.

The list of colleges presented in Table 2 are limited to colleges that are (a) traditionally well-known, (b) academically sound to fulfill seating capacities and to compete with coeducational colleges that already have science-related schools and faculties, and (c) financially strong to invest in and maintain educational facilities as well as academic faculties. The entry into science-related fields is considered to have stemmed from individual colleges' response to the demand of a section of society, especially women who were active in science-related fields. At the same time, it is speculated that these colleges were also eager to enter into other fields that are expected to attract new entrants. Due to the overall unpopularity of single-sex colleges among young people (Kawashima, 2004), and despite being traditionally and academically well-known, colleges face a risk of becoming coeducational or, at worse, of closure to some extent.

Recognition of the Aspects of Significance of Women's Colleges and the Educational Practices Followed: Studies of Women's Colleges in Japan, the United States, and Korea

This section focuses on women's colleges in Japan, The United States, and Korea as shown in Table 2 and examines the recognition of the aspects of significance of these colleges. For this purpose, we should discuss the following five aspects of significance of women's colleges: (a) A women's college has an environment in which female students are respected, (b) there advantages available for female students due to the absence of male students, (c) there are a variety of programs related to women's and gender studies designed especially for female students, which help women become independent, (d) the proportion of female faculty members to male faculty members and that of female executives to male executives is often higher at women's colleges than at coeducational colleges, with various educational effects, and (e) many successful women and academically outstanding students have graduated from women's colleges.

The home pages of these colleges were reviewed. Special attention was paid to the introduction of the colleges, particularly the presidents' remarks (or messages) and those of science-related faculties, departments, and colleges. These home pages were considered as being a useful means to obtain the latest information these colleges were providing and to understand the degree of the recognition of the aspects of significance of women's colleges. We will also occasionally review literature on educational practices followed in these colleges. In other words, we will examine the sensitivity of individuals to the aspects of the significance of these colleges in following their educational practices. The following summarizes the recognition of the five significant aspects of

women's colleges, which can be found on each of their home pages.

A women's college has an environment in which female students are respected.

Regardless of which country they belong to, many women's colleges seem to have a common understanding of the first aspect. They use words and phrases such as "respect" or "rights" of individual students (Ochanomizu), "women-centered education" (Mills), and "gender equality" (Ewha). In particular, some American women's colleges, such as, Wellesley and Smith understand this and at the same time accept the reality that there will be criticism against the exclusivity of women's colleges. The acceptance of the criticism seems to urge the colleges to assert that their students come from diverse age groups, family backgrounds, and so forth, and that some students are from other colleges. Furthermore, Smith College appears to be making every effort to facilitate a more respectful environment for female students and women by introducing the "gender mind" and women's studies throughout its campus (Kameda, Hashimoto, & Matsumoto, 2000).

There are advantages available for female students due to the absence of male students.

Regardless of which country they belong to, some colleges subscribe to this aspect. Nara Women's University, for example, subscribes to this aspect by stating that a women's college provides an environment where women can easily display their abilities. Smith College does not directly subscribe to this second aspect; however, it acknowledges the positive effects of leadership experiences gained during college on students' futures. The college seems to be aware of the advantage that female students can enjoy leadership experiences in the absence of male students.

There are a variety of programs related to women's and gender studies designed especially

for female students, which help women become independent.

Many women's colleges design programs related to women's and gender studies especially for female students. However, surprisingly, only a few of these colleges directly subscribe to this aspect. It is not certain as to whether many other women's colleges consider it necessary to bear this aspect in mind, or whether they are unaware of the aspect, even while they set various programs for female students. In contrast, Wellesley College spreads the college mission to their students, which is unique and effective in motivating their students to study hard and become independent women. Smith College indirectly refers to the positive educational effects of such programs by mentioning the effectiveness of the overall educational practices followed in women's colleges; a study result reported by Indiana University was used for this purpose.

The proportion of female faculty members to male faculty members and that of female executives to male executives is often higher at women's colleges than at coeducational colleges, with various educational effects.

This fourth aspect may be the one that brings out the difference among Japanese, American, and probably Korean women's colleges the most. The ratio of women presidents, for example, is more than 90% in American women's colleges (Kameda et al., 2000), while it is still not high among Japanese women's colleges. It is therefore not surprising that all of the Japanese women's colleges do not (or cannot) subscribe to this fourth aspect. Nonetheless, the proportion of female faculty members to male faculty members and that of female executives to male executives is often higher in women's colleges than in coeducational colleges, even in Japan, mainly because majors, for example, those related to human sciences, home economics, and education, offered in women's colleges are often aimed at female students rather than male students and are taught

by a relatively high proportion of female faculty than male faculty members. Moreover, it may be possible that the proportion of female faculty members to male faculty members is higher in women's colleges even in science-related fields where the proportion of female faculty members to male faculty members has traditionally been low and therefore male dominated. Considering these possibilities, it would have been possible for many more women's colleges to subscribe to this aspect if they were aware of the educational effectiveness for female students.

Many successful women and academically outstanding students have graduated from women's colleges.

Many women's colleges assert that they have produced successful women and academically outstanding students, and that their alumnae have been successful in gathering information for employment. Moreover, many colleges in Western countries such as the United States and Britain seem to be aware of the effectiveness of alumnae in obtaining endowments and new entrants regardless of whether the colleges are single sex or coeducational. The women's colleges in America are no exception to this awareness. Yet, Smith College emphasizes the vastness and strength of their alumnae, comparing it with the Ivies, a group of prestigious coeducational colleges in the United States. This attitude reflects their confidence as a women's college that produces successful graduates and maintains strong alumnae.

In reviewing women's colleges' recognition of the five aspects of significance of women's colleges, it can be said that many women's colleges are aware of at least one or two of these aspects. However, there is a considerable difference in the degree of the recognition of the significance among these colleges. Of all the colleges, Smith College appears to have by far recognized the significance in the widest and deepest manner. The college seems to be studying the significance from various studies including the one by Indiana University and trying to apply them to its educational practices. As other interesting examples mentioned earlier, Smith College tries to facilitate a more respectful environment for female students by introducing the gender mind and women's studies throughout its campus. Ewha Womans University frequently uses words such as "gender" as well as "globalization" and "information technology", although it does not necessarily refer to the five aspects of significance of women's colleges. Considering these cases, "gender" certainly appears to be a key word that empowers not only students, but also the women's colleges themselves that have entered into science-related fields.

To be successful in producing competent women in science-related fields and in playing a role in contributing to the society, it is essential for women's colleges to be aware of the significance of the existence of women's colleges, hopefully with the knowledge of gender, and to manage the college based on this recognition.

CONCLUSION

This chapter discussed the importance of increasing the number of women who play an active role in science-related fields, especially in science and technology, because of the microlevel profit that will be derived by individual women and the macrolevel benefits stemming from the effective use of human resources in society. The chapter then proceeded to consider whether women's colleges could play a role in training competent women in the science-related fields, thus overcoming the problems that female students in these fields tend to encounter in higher education, particularly while studying in coeducational colleges. An insight into this was found in the five aspects of the significance of the existence of women's colleges, and the chapter applied those aspects to the implications of women's colleges entering into science-related fields. Then, the chapter stipulated

that the implications of women's colleges entering into science-related fields is as follows: to educate, train, and produce women who will play an active role in such fields in society and contribute to it by recognizing the significance of women's colleges and subsequently providing female students with the appropriate education and educational environment on the basis of such a recognition. This chapter then performed a survey of the educational practices adopted by some major women's colleges in Japan, the United States, and Korea that had already entered into science-related fields, and attempted to discern whether their educational practices were conducted based on the recognition of the five aspects of significance. Consequently, it became evident that several of them were aware of at least one or two aspects, but at the same time, there were considerable differences in the degree of the recognition.

It is essential for every women's college that has entered into science-related fields to recognize the significance of women's colleges, and conduct educational practices based on that recognition. Adopting such a coherent and meaningful practice will certainly lead these colleges to produce competent women who will play an active role in society and be able to contribute to it.

REFERENCES

Antonelli, C. (2003). The digital divide: Understanding the economics of new information and communication technology in the global economy. *Information Economics and Policy, 15*, 173-199.

Aso, M. (1987). Joshi no kotokyoiku nitsuiteno mittsu no teigen. In Nihonjoshidaigaku Joshi-kyoiku-Kenkyu-Sho (Ed.), *Joshidaigakuron* (pp. 10-25). Tokyo: Domesu-Shuppan.

Astin, A. W. (1993). *What matters in college?* San Francisco: Josey-Bass.

Betz, N. E., & Hackett, G. (1983). The relationship of mathematics self-efficacy expectations to the selections of science-based college majors. *Journal of Vocational Behavior, 23*, 329-345.

Darke, K., Beatriz, C., & Ruta, S. (2002). Meeting the challenge: The impact of the National Science Foundation's program for women and girls. *Journal of Women and Minorities in Science and Engineering, 8*, 285-303.

Epstein, D., Elwood, J., Hey, V., & Maw, J. (Eds.). (1998). *Failing boys? Issues in gender and achievement.* Buckingham, United Kingdom: Open University Press.

Ewha Womans University. (2004). *Ewha Womans University.* Retrieved September 14, 2006, from http://www.Ewha.ac.kr/

Forgasz, H. (1998). The typical Australian university mathematics student: Challenging myths and stereotypes? *Higher Education, 36*, 87-108.

Graetz, B. (1991). Gender, equity and participation in Australian education. *New Education, 13*(1), 3-11.

Gray, M. W. (1996). Recruiting and retaining graduate students in mathematical sciences and improving their chances for subsequent success. In B. Grevholm & G. Hanna (Eds.), *Gender and mathematics education* (pp. 39-44). Lund, Sweden: Lund University Press.

Hackett, G. (1985). The role of mathematics self-efficacy in the choice of math-related majors of college women and men: A path analysis. *Journal of Counseling Psychology, 32*, 47-56.

Heianjogakuin. (Ed.). (2000). *Kokusai-shimpoziumu no kiroku: Ima naze joshidaigaku ka? Joshikotokyoiku no atarashii yakuwari.* Kyoto, Japan: Heianjogakuin.

Kameda, A., Hashimoto, H., & Matsumoto, Y. (2000). Joshidaigaku no hatten wo saguru:

America joshidaigaku shitsu hokoku. Jumonjigakuendaigaku Shakaijoho-gakubu. *Shakaijoho-So*, 129-153.

Kawakami, F. (1986). Joshidaigaku: Sonzoku no hoko wo saguru. In A. Amano (Ed.), *Joshikotokyoiku no zahyo* (pp. 140-150). Tokyo: Kakiuchi-Shuppan.

Kawashima, Y. H. (2004). *Daigakukyoiku to gender: Jenda wa America no daigaku wo dou kaikakushiaka.* Tokyo: Toshin-Do.

Kay, J., Lublin, J., Poiner, G., & Proser, M. (1989). Not even well begun: Women in computing courses. *Higher Education, 18*, 511-527.

Kim, M. (2001). Institutional effectiveness of women-only college: Cultivating students' desire to influence social conditions. *Journal of Higher Education, 72*(3), 287-321.

Kim, M. (2002). Cultivating intellectual development: Comparing women-only colleges and coeducational colleges for educational effectiveness. *Research into Higher Education, 43*(4), 447-481.

Kim, M., & Alvarez, R. (1995). Women-only colleges: Some unanticipated consequences. *The Journal of Higher Education, 66*, 641-648.

Kimura, R. (2005). Onna wa rikei ni mukanainoka: Kagakugijutsu-bunya to jenda. In R. Kimura & R. Kodama (Eds.), *Kyoiku/kazoku wo jenda de katareba* (pp. 151-174). Tokyo: Hakutaku-Sha.

Kimura, T. (2001). *Dejitaru-debaido towa nanika.* Tokyo: Iwanami-Shoten.

Kress, G. (1998, June 11). The future still belongs to boys. *The Independent (Education)*, pp. 4-5.

Maeda, T. (1996). Daigaku no rikei-kyoiku to joshigakusei. In Y. Muramatsu (Ed.), *Josei no rikei-noryoku wo ikasu: Senko-bunya no jenda-bunseki to teigen* (pp. 125-147). Tokyo: Nihon-hyoron-Sha.

Makino, N. (2004). Joshidaigaku no saikin no doko nikansuru kenkyu: Amerikagasshukoku to Chugoku wo chushinni, Nihon joshidaigaku kyoiku gakka-no-kai. *Nigen-Kenkyu, 40*, 71-81.

Manning, K. (1994). Metaphorical analysis in a constructivist study of college rituals. *Review of Higher Education, 18*(1), 45-60.

Manning, K. (2000). *Rituals, ceremonies, and cultural meaning in higher education.* Westport, CT: Bergin & Garvey.

Matsuzawa, K. (2000). Ima naze joshidaigaku ka? Joshidaigaku no sonzoku-igi. In Heianjo-gakuin (Ed.), *Kokusai-shimpoziumu no kiroku: Ima naze joshidaigaku ka? Joshikotokyoiku no atarashii yakuwari* (pp. 18-27). Kyoto, Japan: Heianjogakuin.

Mills College. (2006). *Mills College.* Retrieved September 14, 2006, from http://www.mills.edu/

Miyake, E. (2003). Josei-kotokyoiku to empowament no kanosei: Doshishajoshidaigaku-sotsu-gosei nimiru joseizo, doshishajoshidaigaku. *Doshishajoshidaigaku Gakujutsukenkyu Nempo, 54*(2), 21-57.

Mount Holyoke College. (2006). *Mount Holyoke College.* Retrieved September 15, 2006, from http://ww.mtholyoke.edu/

Muramatsu, Y. (1996). Preface: Senko-bunya no jenda-bunseki no igi to kenkyu no gaiyo. In Y. Muramatsu (Ed.), *Josei no rikei-noryoku wo ikasu: Senko-bunya no jenda-bunseki to teigen* (pp. 1-16). Tokyo: Nihonhyoron-Sha.

Nara Women's University. (2004). *Nara Women's University.* Retrieved September 14, 2006, from http://www.nara-wu.ac.jp/

National Women's Education Center (NWEC). (2006). *Number of universities and junior college.* Retrieved September 25, 2006, from http://www.nwec.jp/

Nelson, D. J., & Rogers, D. C. (2004). *A national analysis of diversity in science and engineering faculties at research universities.* Retrieved September 5, 2006, from http://www.org/issues/diverse/diversity_report.pdf

Niddifer, J., & Bashaw, C. T. (2001). *Women administrators in higher education.* Albany, NY: Sate University of New York Press.

Nihonjoshidaigakau Sogokenkyusho. (1999). *Daigakusotsugyo 20 nengo no josei no seikatu/seikatsuishiki/daigakuhyoka nikansuru chosa-hokokusho: Joshidaigakaushusshin/kyogaku-daigakushusshinbetsu-bunsekikekka.* Tokyo: Nihonjoshidaigkau.

Oates, M. J., & Wiliamson, S. (1978). Women's colleges and women achievers. *Signs: Journal of Women in Culture and Society, 3*, 795-806.

Ochanomizu University. (2006). *Ochanomizu University.* Retrieved September 14, 2006, from http://www.ocha.ac.jp/

Ogawa, M. (2001). *Feminizumu to kagaku/gijutsu.* Tokyo: Iwanami-Shoten.

Organization for Economic Cooperation and Development (OECD). (2004). *Education at a glance: OECD indicators 2004.* Paris: Author.

President-Sha. (2006). *President.* Tokyo: Author.

Seymour, E. (1995a). Guest comment: Why undergraduates leave the sciences. *American Journal of Physics, 63*(3), 199-202.

Seymour, E. (1995b). The loss of women from science, mathematics, and engineering undergraduate majors: An explanatory account. *Science Education, 79*(4), 437-473.

Smith College. (2006) *Smith College.* Retrieved September 14, 2006, from http://www.smith.edu/

Smiths, D. G. (1990). Women's colleges and coed colleges: Is there a difference for women? *Journal of Higher Education, 61*(2), 181-195.

Sookmyng Women's University. (2004). *Sookmyng Women's University*. Retrieved September 14, 2006, from http://e. sookmyng.ac.kr/

Sugita, T. (1996). Nihonshakai to joshigakusei. In N. Toshitani, Y. Yuzawa, T. Sodei, & E. Shinozuka (Eds.), *Kogakurekijidai no josei: Joshidaigaku karano messeji* (pp. 22-39). Tokyo: Yuhikaku.

Tidball, M. E. (1973). Perspective on academic women and affirmative action. *Educational Record, 54*(2), 130-135.

Tidball, M. E. (1985). Baccalaureate origins of entrants into American medical schools. *Journal of Higher Education, 56*, 385-402.

Tidball, M. E. (1986). Baccalaureate origins of recent natural science doctorates. *Journal of Higher Education, 57*, 660-620.

Toyokeizaishimpo-Sha. (2006). *Yakuin shikiho data text*. Tokyo: Toyokeizaishimpo-Sha.

Trinity College. (2006) *Trinity College: Education for global leadership*. Retrieved September 24, 2006, from http://www.trinitydc.edu/

Trow, M. (1991). *University and society: Essays on the social role of research and higher education*. London: Jessica Kingsley Publishers.

Tsuda College. (2006). *Tsuda College*. Retrieved September 24, 2006, from http://www.tsuda. ac.jp/

Wellesley College. (2005). *Wellesley College*. Retrieved September 14, 2006, from http://www. wellesley.edu/

Whitt, E. J. (1994). "I can be anything": Student leadership in three women's colleges. *Journal of College Student Development, 35*(3), 198-207.

Wolf-Wendel, L. E. (1998). Models of successful African-American, European American and Hispanic women. *Journal of Higher Education, 69*(2), 144-172.

Women's University Coalition. (2006). *Members of the Women's College Coalition*. Retrieved September 25, 2006, from http://www.women-scolleges.org/members.html

Yamamoto, K., & Fujimura, K. (2000). Joshidaigaku no sonzaiigi nikansuru hikaku-kenkyu: America/Igirisu/Kankoku/Nippon. Toyoeiwa-jogakuindaigaku. *Jimbun/Shakaikagaku-Ronshu, 18*, 121-189.

ENDNOTE

[1] Science-related fields in this paper means engineering, manufacturing and construction, life science, natural science and agriculture, mathematics, and computer science, excluding health, in accordance with the categorization of OECD (2004).

Chapter XXI
Potential Challenges and Benefits of Information Technology and Economic Development in Sri Lanka

Kennedy D. Gunawardana
University of Sri Jayewardenepura, Sri Lanka

ABSTRACT

This chapter discusses the potential challenges and benefits of information technology and economic development in Sri Lanka by reviewing the awareness and readiness of the selected opportunities. This chapter also identifies the enabling factors and bottlenecks, and forecasts the future growth of ICT developments in Sri Lanka as a host in Asia. Furthermore, developing ICT, professional services, and offshoring opportunities should be a high priority for the development strategy of the country. This chapter presents the findings from the survey that assessed the potential for ICT in Sri Lanka. Sri Lanka is an island state of contrasts in terms of its economic development and ICT capability. Research on a Web survey of government institutes revealed that 30% of ministries in the country do not have Web sites or may not have Web access since they are inactive. 38% of the ministries are still in the infant stage, and information available on Web pages is often little in content and limited to a few pages. Only about 17% of ministries offer interactive Web content, where users have access to regularly updated information, can communicate through e-mail, and can download government documents through the Internet. 15% of the ministries provide some online services to the citizens. Public- and private-sector economic entities do not develop Web sites in the local language; all Web sites are in English even though 80% of the population depend on their own local language. The majority in Sri Lanka do not speak English.

INTRODUCTION

The software and telecom sectors of Sri Lanka's ICT industry, despite many problems and a rela- tively small size, are thriving. There are nonethe- less a number of significant problems facing the industry. They include the lack of transparency in government acquisitions (the largest prospective client), lack of moderately priced international bandwidth, lack of trained ICT professionals and a management class knowledgeable about ICT, and the existence of a tax structure that does not reward local sales. In recent years, the United States Agency for International Development (USAID) has funded a number of projects aimed at increasing the competitiveness of various industries in Sri Lanka, and ICT is one of its prime focal points. Its ICT-sector studies are well done, and their recommendations, if followed, will help guide the industry. There is some danger that it may widen its scope to include the application of ICT in peripheral areas, and as a result dilute its resources and no longer focus on the original crucial targets. The use of ICT in the commercial sector in general is irregular. Some financial institutions have invested heavily in ICT, and as a result are country leaders in the use of technology.

Other sectors are far behind, and their use of ICT is spotty at best. Even those companies that have invested in ICT often do so in restricted ways that are poorly integrated into their businesses. The same is true of the use of the Internet. In part, this is related to the small percentage of Sri Lankans with access to the Internet, but the prime reason is, no doubt, the low level of managerial knowledge about the ICT capabilities in the business area.

At all levels of aggregation, statistics about any aspect of ICT in Sri Lanka are highly misleading and can be deceptive when used for policy purposes. Virtually all ICT activity is centered in Colombo, with small pockets in the Galle and Kandy areas. There is clearly a desire to spread ICT development over a wider geographic area than just Colombo, but it appears that it is not going to be an easy task.

The regions outside of the urban areas are particularly poorly served with respect to electricity and telecommunications. Moreover, the rural areas do not provide the level of comforts and conveniences often (but not always) expected by people with the high-end technical and manage-

rial skills needed to drive this sector. Lastly, the supply of lower level technical skills is substantially lower in these regions. The shortage of knowledgeable teachers and trainers willing to work in rural areas compounds and propagates the problem. The regions currently under Liberation Tigers of Tamil Eelam (LTTE) control or in dispute are a special case. They are subject to the above problems, but there are also opportunities should the peace process be successful. The areas will need massive rebuilding of infrastructure. If this rebuilding is done intelligently, the new 21st century infrastructure will be a model to which other areas, and in fact countries, will aspire. The telecenter movement is in its infancy in Sri Lanka. Telecenters are community-based points of access to telecom and digital services. In many countries, telecenters have provided the focal point for introducing technology into rural areas, and in fact to disadvantaged groups in urban settings. The concept shows up in many reports and plans, but despite this, there are very few active telecenters. Of more concern is that the groups that are developing telecenter plans are doing this in isolation from each other and from the worldwide community, which has a rich body of knowledge on what works and what does not.

Sri Lanka is a country that depends on the support of developed countries and international agencies. Although this support is greatly appreciated, at times the donor agencies invest in ways that are, at best, uncoordinated and a poor use of scarce foreign funding and scarce domestic human and organizational resources. The support needs to be better integrated within national planning and priority setting exercises.

Sri Lanka tends to look exclusively toward countries such as India and Singapore for its models and alliances. Cooperative opportunities from other areas, and particularly those related to the British Commonwealth or the United Nations, seem to be particularly ignored, despite their potentially beneficial nature.

Underlying most issues in Sri Lanka is the 21-year civil unrest and conflict between the government of Sri Lanka and the Liberation Tigers of Tamil Eelam, which has controlled various territories in the northern and eastern parts of the island and have been the source of various disruptions in the south. Although the impact is far wider than just ICT, there is no doubt that ICT development has suffered greatly. When it comes to socioeconomic development and the uses of technology, Sri Lanka is a country of achievements and contrasts.

It has achieved levels of life expectancy, education, and health on par with countries having twice Sri Lanka's real gross domestic product (GDP) per capita. It has maintained and improved that performance while having to deal with domestic political problems, including a major increase in military expenditures during the 1990s and an over five-fold increase in persons in the military between 1985 and 1995. With the current promise of peace in the northeast, there is potential for a substantial peace dividend to be devoted to socioeconomic development, as well as renewed interest by overseas development assistance agencies.

Sri Lanka remains a mainly rural country while facing increasing urbanisation, with an expected one third of its population residing in urban areas by the year 2015.

Nowhere are the achievements, contrasts, and challenges more apparent than in the deployment of technology across the regions of Sri Lanka and the sectors of Sri Lanka's economy. The country has achieved a United Nations Development Program Human Development Index that is impressive relative to its GDP per capita. Its health care system includes the latest technologies, open-heart surgery, and computerized tomography (CT) and magnetic resonance imaging (MRI) scans (although access to some of these in public hospitals is limited), while at the same time relying on patient record systems from the 1800s or no patient records at all. The

southwest, and the Colombo area in particular, has fibre-optic networks running along roads where carts are pulled by bullocks. Universities teach advanced computer science programs, but the entire administration of the university, including students' academic records, is based on paper and manual operations.

ICT Environment

Overall, Sri Lanka has maintained impressive progress in terms of its human and socioeconomic development given its resource constraints and the unfortunate challenges of civil unrest, the associated diversion of government resources for military purposes, and the resulting human and economic dislocations. Likewise, Sri Lanka has a marvelous potential for using ICT to help the country with its overall development and help it to thrive in all respects. In many cases, the bits and pieces of the foundations have been laid, and substantial chunks of the necessary technical and institutional infrastructure are already in place.

There are several crucial areas that must be addressed. On many fronts, the ICT picture that emerges for Sri Lanka is that of a patchwork quilt, or a crossword puzzle, with many of the squares blank and unconnected. Significant and state-of-the-art bits and pieces of the technology are in place. Bits and pieces of the necessary organizational structures in the public, private, academic, government, and nongovernmental sectors are in place. Bits and pieces of policy and regulatory processes are in place. What appears lacking is how these pieces are knitted together through collaboration and the application of appropriate overall policies, political will, and market signals. To do this will take significant political determination on the part of the central government and a significant buy-in by domestic stakeholders. This cannot be achieved solely by the marketing of good ideas nor can it be imposed by fiat from above by the central government. Domestic stakeholder buy-in is, of course, the outcome of a domestic process of consultation and consensus building. There also appears to be a risk of excess reliance on the belief that ICT development in Sri Lanka can be driven by external forces, be they software export markets, the export of ICT services (e.g., call centers), or the import of foreign capital. In the following sections, this survey will focus on those particular aspects of the ICT environment that present both challenges and opportunities for ICT development in Sri Lanka.

Human Resource Development

Education has been a priority in Sri Lanka since ancient times, and continues to be to this day, resulting in one of the highest literacy rates in the area. However, for ICT development and growth, general literacy is not sufficient. An adequate supply of skilled ICT professionals and a population literate in the uses of computers and telecommunications are clearly required in Sri Lanka. They are required both for Sri Lanka's success in the development and application of an ICT sector, and for enlisting ICT in Sri Lanka's overall development. At the moment, adequate supplies of ICT-literate human resources are problematic. There are serious supply constraints in the provision of skilled ICT professionals. The level of worker and citizen training in computer use is low. General ICT literacy is low, particularly in the rural sector. It is notably low or spotty in many areas of government, a sector that in many countries leads the others in the use of ICT.

The educational sector has multiple and special roles to play in assisting ICT in the development of the nation. Consider the postsecondary (university) sector. It is a producer of ICT inputs in the forms of skilled ICT workers and, where successful, a producer of new inventions and ideas. It is a major source of skilled labor and leadership material for the other sectors in the economy. It thus has a duty to equip graduates with the tools and knowledge to use ICTs in their daily work.

It also has a duty to help both students and the community understand the social, economic, and organizational issues surrounding ICT policy and deployment at all levels in society. It is (or should be) a consumer of ICTs in the execution of its duties as an educational sector. In developed countries, along with the health sector and social services (pensions, welfare, etc.), the educational sector has a major demand for information management systems (MISs) to track products (transcripts, courses, facilities, staff, etc.). In reality, in Sri Lanka, the entire operation of most universities (with the possible exception of payroll) is performed manually. The Norwegian Agency for Development Cooperation (NORAD) is currently working with several universities to install automated student record systems.

Beyond its MIS demands, education is expected to experience major benefits from the use of ICT for technology-enhanced learning (TEL). TEL includes everything from electronic and digital support for distance education to technology-enhanced classrooms and virtual laboratories. Networked access is also seen as an efficient response to binding constraints in terms of trained instructors and classroom facilities. For example, at the moment, instructors from Colombo have to journey to Ruhuna to teach courses that could be taught at considerable savings in time and travel costs by using a digital video link between Colombo and Ruhuna. Moreover, with such a link, instructors that cannot be convinced to make the trip could still teach at Ruhuna. Unfortunately, all too often, the mentioned expectations are not met. Where this has been attempted elsewhere without some degree of planning and forethought, the costs have been high and the benefits low. There is a considerable body of lessons learned and evidence about what works and what does not. However, despite the evidence, ICT educational initiatives are frequently rushed forward because of supplier pressure (companies or donor agencies eager to close the deal or start the project). They are frequently started without planning because of internal competition for IT resources (groups will take what they can get with little concern for an implementation strategy or the costs associated with the one-time grant of equipment).

The necessary planning processes here are neither difficult nor unique to the sector. There needs to be a planning process that identifies priorities through stakeholder participation since the stakeholders will have to execute the plan. There has to be, as always, senior-level buy-in, best in the form of identified champions responsible for keeping the process moving. There needs to be a wise blend of central policy and local autonomy so that implementation can respond to local conditions. None of this has happened elsewhere without some degree of coordinated planning. Specific care has to be taken when the process includes resources provided by external donors. That creates the risk of rushed and poorly thought out project formation as stakeholders compete for funding within the education profession. As we confirmed, among stakeholders in Sri Lanka, there is general agreement that ICTs have a role to play in primary and secondary education. There is less agreement as to how to implement a strategy to achieve the objectives of computers in education at these levels. Given the current state of education in Sri Lanka, and the budget constraints facing any deployment of computers in the classroom, careful thought has to be given for where to start and what to do first.

There is considerable scope for learning from others on this front. The education world is littered with successes and failures, large and small. There is evidence that the existing efforts are taking place in near isolation. One lesson learned, and relearned all too often, is that simply placing computers in classrooms is a recipe for failure. Another lesson learned, and not imitated widely enough, is that using computers to train and upgrade teachers can have a high payoff. It not only increases the supply and quality of teachers, but it produces teachers able to introduce computers into the curriculum in ways that work.

This is an area where the ministry responsible for primary and secondary education can take the lead, not only in setting policy and implementation, but also in drawing together that consortium of stakeholders whose wisdom and support will be necessary to make things work. Formulating where to start this process should be one result of ministry participation in a national ICT planning process. Recent reports indicate that the Ministry of Education will be seriously addressing the issue of technology in schools. One hopes that this will be done both with due haste and with due caution. As the final draft of this report is being completed, a video link is now operational and is beginning to be used.

The lack of sufficient, trained ICT professionals has been a recurring focus in ICT studies and reports in Sri Lanka. There seems to be four main drivers for this shortage.

1. Sri Lanka produces only a small number of ICT-trained university graduates (albeit high quality) each year. The number of positions in the state-funded universities is severely limited. This is part of a bigger problem. Sri Lanka has a good record for primary and secondary education, but only about 6% of successful secondary school graduates attend university (12,000 out of 200,000).

2. Sri Lanka loses many ICT graduates soon after graduating. Their ICT skills demand far higher salaries abroad. In addition, the ongoing civil unrest has been a contributing factor.

3. Sri Lanka has a number of state-supported, commercial, and quasiprivate technical training institutes. However, the quality of training is highly variable.

4. Sri Lanka faces a serious shortage of experienced ICT professionals, that is, senior people with 6 to 10 years of experience in
    *   Software design
    *   Project management
    *   Network design and management

This shortage is felt both in industry and education as there is a shortage of qualified teachers of higher level ICT curricula.

University Education

The problem of insufficient ICT graduates has several dimensions, some of which are being addressed on multiple fronts.

1. All 14 state-funded universities provide some measure of ICT education. However, in the majority of them, it is just some computer science or information management courses within a general BS degree. Humanities students may not even benefit from this level of training.
2. Several fee-levying institutes (arms of foreign universities) offer computer science programs, but the prices tend to be above what most of the population can afford.
3. State-funded university ICT training is being increased, a recent example being the new Faculty of Information Technology at the University of Moratuwa. However, this effort is tightly constrained by the limited supply of senior instructors.
4. The University of Colombo has recently begun an innovative 3-year program called the External Degree of Bachelor of Information Technology, called BIT for short.
5. The Sri Lanka Institute of Information Technology (SLIIT) was recently created under the auspices of the government of Sri Lanka as a joint venture between the Ministries of Education and Higher Education, Internal and International Commerce and Food, and Finance and Planning. It comes under the Ministry of Technology, and its operation is funded primarily from student fees. As it only started operations less than 2 years ago, it is premature to gauge its potential impact. Many of its instructors come from existing universities, and one can assume

its curriculum will be appropriate to meet industry needs.

Discussions with Sri Lankan software companies and educational institutions indicate that a typical salary for an ICT university graduate is approximately $200 to $300 month. In private industry, this may typically rise to as high as $1,000 a month after several years, depending on individual skills and business conditions. These salaries do not compete with overseas salaries if the person has an interest in leaving Sri Lanka. While there are nonpecuniary attractions for individuals to remain in Sri Lanka (family, lifestyle), the salary differential is a factor that cannot easily be changed. Some leading software firms pay as high as $1,750 per month for their best staff. At that level, retention rates rise significantly. The promise of an end to the civil conflict is another positive factor currently at play.

There are some attempts to repatriate overseas Sri Lankan ICT professionals back to Sri Lanka. This has been more successful in recent times with the end of the overheated overseas market for ICT skills during the so-called dot-com period.

The combination of ICT skills demand and limited access to postsecondary education in Sri Lanka has fuelled the growth of a large number of ICT-related technical training facilities in the country. This rapid and unregulated growth has led to virtual repatriation, meaning to use the skills of expatriates even though they are still living outside of Sri Lanka. Often this means subcontracting work to them, or using them to market products or services on behalf of Sri Lankan companies. There are a few companies that are starting to do this now, but in general, it is an untapped resource.

Rapid growth has also produced serious problems of quality assurance. There are stories of parents investing their life savings to pay for training for a child, only to find out that the graduate had not received sufficient training to make him or her employable. The twin problems of how to increase both the supply and the quality of training across a number of skill areas and skill levels are problems that should be addressed in collaboration across the relevant stakeholders, including the training institutes. Sri Lanka is not in a position to simply institute various levels of formal certification of ICT training facilities. There can be schemes such as the University of Colombo's external BIT plan that certifies skills. There are discussions going on at a number of levels to institute the formal certification of ICT professionals. Certification not only labels the prospective employee, but the type of certification will provide guidance to employers who do not themselves have the skills to identify good employees. In addition, publishing student performance by training institutes will allow students, and their families, to identify quality and influence training quality. Publishing statistics on how many graduates obtain employment by utilizing their new skills will also provide a measure of success, but one must be careful that these statistics are honestly presented. That is, one should not only provide negative feedback in the case of noncompliance with rules or standards, but should work with the stakeholders to improve quality. There is a perhaps apocryphal story that some Canadian schools surveyed their students to see how many were employed. 10% said they were employed, 10% said they were not, and 80% did not reply. The schools assumed that the 80% who did not reply were too busy working to reply, and published that 90% of their students found employment.

There remains a serious obstacle to a rapid ramp up of ICT activity in the software sector and the large-scale application of ICT to organizations. While it is possible to quickly expand the supply of entry-level ICT personnel, it is not possible to immediately produce high-level professionals, especially when that includes 6 to 10 years of proven experience in software design, project and implementation management, and network management. Some of this demand could be met

by the virtual repatriation of the senior skills of expatriate Sri Lankans abroad. Again, an end to the civil unrest will also help, both in the potential for full-time repatriation of ICT skills and for the short-term return work stints of expatriates whose ICT skills are being repatriated online the rest of the time. It remains to be seen as to who might organize such efforts. One interesting and successful way to circumvent this problem has been to subcontract high-end tasks to the Computing Services Center (CSC), a group within the Institute of Computer Technology (ICT) of the University of Colombo. ICT is one of the few really concentrated centers of technological expertise in the country, and the CSC has been involved in many successful projects. These have included feasibility studies, project specification and design, tender evaluation, and network design and implementation, as well as overall system development. This group has been involved in some of the most strategic projects involving both government and private enterprises. As a side benefit, this also serves to give staff members an additional source of income, partially alleviating the low academic salaries. To a large extent, the shortage of experts is one of the real constraints to rapid growth in the Sri Lankan ICT industry and to rapid deployment of ICT to sectors in the Sri Lankan economy.

For the application of ICT across the non-ICT sectors of Sri Lanka (government, health, primary and secondary education, small and medium enterprises [SMEs], the rural sector), far more people will need to be computer literate and computer trained. There are many user-training programs in place, but as in the case of more technical training, the quality of the training programs is uneven and erratic. The institution of the so-called Computer Driver's License will be effective in helping to manage and measure the growth in computer literacy, and to give employers a measure of confidence in hiring staff. A strategy of ranking training facilities in terms of testing results, as used by the BIT program, would also help here.

An important focus is teaching computer literacy in primary and secondary schools.

As ICT becomes more a part of everyday life, it will be increasingly necessary for all citizens to have some basic familiarity with computers. Technology revolutions are complete when such skills are taken for granted and the technology seems to have disappeared into the background. It is easy to say that using them in primary and secondary schools will help. It is more difficult to say what this means in actual practice. It can mean using computers to increase the efficiency of the administration and management of the schools. It can mean using them to produce more and better teachers. It can mean using them to deliver better curriculum and a better learning experience. It can mean teaching students basic computer skills as the first step toward either Computer Driver's License proficiency, or as a start toward an ICT career. For any of these to work, it is necessary to (a) be clear as to what the actual goals are, (b) have an evidence-supported strategy for getting there, and (c) engage in a planning process in which both stakeholders and champions are brought on side. A recent draft plan produced by the Ministry of Education seems be making aggressive moves in this direction. At this time, the aggressive moves should be seen as a declaration of intent and a willingness to champion efforts. It is essential that the other steps take place, steps that wed strategy to resources, or Sri Lanka will run the risk of reproducing the shortcomings of similar efforts elsewhere.

The main shortcoming is the tendency to substitute the provision of technology for a proper implementation strategy. It is better to deploy one half, or one quarter, the number of computers to successful uses, both for the deliverables and the transferable lessons learned, than it is to engage in a technology-intense rollout of more computers met by failure. One challenge is helping donor agencies understand the issues here, both with regard to computers in the school and computers in the community. A method that has been suc-cessful elsewhere is to only provide technology to a school if there is a local champion and if school management really wants this project to succeed. A champion could be a staff member at the school, or a local company that will provide help and guidance. The essential characteristic of a champion is that he or she passionately cares that the computers will be used, and will do what-ever is necessary to ensure that outcome. When coupled with local management that wants success (and will thus not arbitrarily get in the way), the outcome is invariably good. A success in a school with a local champion tends to spread to nearby schools with a ripple effect. It is also noteworthy that, to date, the technology has not been used in support of other educational goals, specifically those related to English and other language train-ing. It has been found that exposure to the still largely English-dominated computer and Internet world does wonders to increase functional Eng-lish language skills. The poor quality of English language education, particularly in rural areas, was highlighted as a major problem by several interviewees. The prognosis for entry-level ICT professional training at the tertiary level is promis-ing, as described in preceding sections. However, there has been too little progress in introducing computers, computer skills, and computer-based tools to university students who are not enrolled in technology-related disciplines. It is common for an arts graduate to never use a computer in his or her studies. This handicaps both the student and the organization where that student will work. The graduate has neither the computer skills nor an overview of how computers fit into the orga-nizational structure and processes surrounding the work. This issue needs to be addressed. For starters, all university students should receive, or have the opportunity to acquire, basic computer literacy training. Some universities are already doing this, but it is not universal. In some cases, this involves formal classes or short-term training programs. In other cases, this can be accomplished by giving students e-mail accounts and access to a computer drop-in center. Twenty-five years ago, students in industrial countries took formal courses to learn to type.

Sri Lankans have proved themselves eminently educable, and this has been duly recognized in global comparisons. So, the prognosis for the outcomes of future effort in this area is good. To ensure this, there will have to be a deliberate focus not only on tertiary education, but the use of computers in primary and secondary schools, and on the introduction of computer training for instructors at all levels. In recent years, the education budget has been compromised by the military demands of the civil unrest. There is the possibility of deploying a peace dividend and of renewed foreign donor assistance to an expanded program of ICT-supported education and curriculum reform.

Other countries with much lower GDP per capita than Sri Lanka have managed to ramp up their production of ICT professionals and in parallel ensured that all university graduates are ICT literate. Sri Lanka must do the same.

There are many Internet service providers (ISPs) in Sri Lanka, with Sri Lanka Telecom Corporation (SLT) being the largest. At last count, there were 17 active providers, with an additional 10 licenses issued. Most of these players are quite small. The vast majority of subscribers are in the Colombo area, but there are points of presence in several other urban centers. SLT offers access to its ISP service as a local call from anywhere on the island. However, this service is only available to those who use SLT local loops for their voice telephone. As noted in Attachment A, there are cases where the SLT loops cannot sustain a data connection. All ISPs (or their downstream supplier) interconnect at the Sri Lanka Domestic Interchange, so in theory, intracountry traffic will never go offshore. The cost of Internet ISP access is comparable to similar services elsewhere in the world. Many non-SLT providers only offer

dial service of 28.8 to 33.6 kbps, and access from many non-SLT local loops is limited to 28.8 kbps (presumably due to the use of compressed 32kb voice services). A typical price (from SLT) is $11 per month for 150 hours. The actual per-minute cost of dial-up Internet access is normally high because of the additional per-minute cost of voice service in Sri Lanka. The base cost of a telephone line is low (about $3 to $4 per month). However, the cost per minute, particularly during weekday daylight hours, is abnormally high (for SLT, it is $1.80 per hour after the first 8 hours). Attachment A recounts experiences of attempting to access the Internet from hotels in Colombo and in other areas. It also provides more details on telephone usage costs from the three providers as well as from several major hotels. The overall conclusion is that the ability to access the Internet is not quite as bulletproof as the suppliers claim. Discussions with both SLT and TRC employees said that moderate to heavy Internet users would have more economical access with a leased line (at about $200 per month), a solution that is not economical in its own right nor feasible for the vast majority of Internet users in Sri Lanka.

Most observers believe that the industry must be completely opened up, with a level playing field for all players and a competitive market for ICT services, including VoIP (voice over Internet protocol). Both safeguards and new initiatives are needed to ensure that rural areas are well-served. Of particular importance is competitive market access to undersea external connectivity. With the emergence of wireless competitors, SLT has demonstrated that it can adapt and could successfully compete in a competitive environment. In some ways, SLT has followed the market in a sector where strategic leadership involves leading the market. In a more competitive environment, new and enhanced products and services will be offered, attracting business that would otherwise bypass Sri Lanka altogether.

ICT and Economy

The use of the Internet is just a particular ICT application, but nevertheless, a cornerstone application. Moreover, the problems here are symptomatic of the more general ICT issues in Sri Lanka. As mentioned above, various industries in Sri Lanka are making use of e-mail and the Web. However, it is notable that virtually none of them have truly integrated it into their business. It was difficult to find examples where the use of either e-mail or the Web was a crucial link to business success. More likely, it was ancillary, and not highly viewed. As an example mentioned earlier, some hotels have Web sites and even allow booking over the Web. However, they do not actually expect people to use it and set prices online to virtually ensure that it is not used. Web sites are typically very incomplete and generally lack sufficient information (such as prices) to be used as a practical selling medium. Certainly part of the reluctance of businesses to use the Internet is the relatively small number of Internet users within the country. Even the bank that has instituted Internet banking has done so for the visibility it provides, not because it is a major path for customer activity. This will not likely change without some economic motive, which will not be there until there is far wider use of the Internet in general. That will not happen without lowered price barriers, enhanced rural access, and increased ICT literacy.

As a small island economy, Sri Lanka has no alternative but to develop its export markets. When the governments of the past have realized this truth and sought to promote export-oriented trade, rapid economic growth followed. Thus, the economy took off in the late 1970s when government enacted a series of trade reforms. Again, in the 1990s, the privatization of the plantations led to a remarkable rise in the volume of tea exported.

The key success factors of Sri Lanka's future economic growth are no different. "Export or perish" remains a truism for the island. It is what can be exported that has changed in a 21st century economy. In the past, goods and capital could be exported relatively easily while services and labor could not. In those days, successful economic strategies attempted to attract capital to the economy in order to produce more goods that could be exported and traded for other goods that could not be produced at home. However, the technological advances of the late 20th and early 21st centuries mean that it is no longer true that goods are tradable and services are not. In fact more and more services are easily tradable. Countries that are realizing this are reaping great benefits from adapting their economies to be able to better compete in services trade.

The advances that have made this possible include cheap mobile connectivity, high-speed Internet access, and digital convergence. These advances have created a truly global marketplace for services, especially those that are labor intensive and can be commoditized and digitized: services such as legal advice, accounting and management consulting, ICT and software development, IT training, and call centers. In the industrial era, such services were delivered domestically and were often produced very close to the point of demand. Increasingly, such services are being produced in locations that are able to deliver the lowest cost and the highest quality product. As demonstrated in this chapter, this trend is just beginning and will continue to grow exponentially for the foreseeable future. Like an incoming tide, this trend cannot be rolled back. It offers tremendous opportunities for developing countries as well as considerable risks.

In the past, governments that shied away from this economic logic and chose autarky (self-sufficiency) over trade paid a heavy price in terms of decades of muted economic growth. In the future, governments that ignore the technological advances and their implications will also be left behind, unable to compete in a global economy where protectionism is no longer a viable option.

The Link to the Global Economy

What can Sri Lanka do to take advantage of the potential benefits of the newly established global trade in services? How can the island brand itself as an offshoring destination of choice for international investors? What government policies are required to ensure that Sri Lanka can play its role on the world stage? This part of the chapter sets out to answer these questions, providing simple policy prescriptions and practical advice for policy makers, enterprises, and other stakeholders.

Offshoring, or the process whereby one company delegates responsibility for performing a function or series of tasks to another company based in another country, now represents a $100 billion market that is growing at more than 30% per annum. In India, a global leader in this area, IT exports account for close to $20 billion and almost half of total export revenues. The total number of jobs created in the Indian IT industry is close to 1 million, many of them filled by women.

Developing ICT and professional-service offshoring opportunities should be a high priority for development-oriented countries such as Sri Lanka. Not only will the development of this industry segment create job and export opportunities, it will also create positive spillovers such as enhanced incentives for education, technology, and knowledge transfer; environmental protection; and an improvement in the quality of locally provided services.

Almost all the current demand for offshored services comes from developed countries. On the supply side, India is by far the largest player in the offshore services industry, closely followed by China, Mexico, and Brazil. At the moment, the services trade remains geographically segmented with Latin American companies serving North America and Eastern European countries serving Western Europe.

Services that will be offshored in the future will go far beyond the traditional call centers and back-office functions and will include investment and financial services, human resources, health services, retail functions, logistics, and customer support functions. It is estimated that this will result in 18 million jobs being offshored with a multiplier effect that could in turn create a further 60 million jobs in developing countries.

Firms move parts of their operations to offshore locations to reduce operating costs and capital requirements, and to increase productivity, global competitiveness, and operational efficiency. Countries wishing to attract offshore investments must therefore offer a politically and economically stable climate that also exhibits a low-cost structure, educated workforce, and sound infrastructure.

Sri Lanka boasts some of the cheapest labor and office rental costs in the region, but it remains hampered by high telephone and electricity charges as well as rigid labor legislation. Due to its population size, the island cannot offer the sheer numbers of ICT and professional employees that India and China can. It cannot compete easily to develop call centers or R&D (research and development) facilities. The most promising strategy for Sri Lanka lies in developing the niche market area of common corporate functions including human resources, legal services, finance and accounting services, and IT services.

A successful strategy to promote offshore services would include completing the unfinished telecom reform agenda, improving regulatory quality and competition to reduce prices, expanding Internet access and usage by rolling out a reliable fibre-optic network (as India has done), increasing electricity generation and reducing tariffs and in the long term, and expanding access to scientific and technical tertiary education (as both India and China have managed to do).

Government can also consider mobilizing the Sri Lankan diaspora interested in investing on the island, providing tax incentives to the industry, providing incentives for training, and supporting the branding and marketing efforts of the local industry.

Outsourcing occurs when one company delegates responsibility for performing a function or series of tasks to another company. When the second company is based in another country, outsourcing becomes offshoring. Offshoring was previously concentrated in the manufacturing sector as firms in developed countries offshored production tasks to developing countries in an effort to reduce costs and minimize expensive capital asset investments. The recent dramatic improvements in information technology and decreasing costs of data transmission have extended this concept to the tradability of services and have popularized professional-service offshoring as an alternative for firms looking to streamline costs, improve customer service, and focus their resources on enhancing their core competencies. Services offshoring now encompasses a wide array of export-oriented services spanning the entire value chain.

Economic Development and ICT

Economic growth is a critical factor in poverty reduction, and services provide a key engine for this type of growth. In countries that have grown quickly and have been able to sustain high growth rates over long periods, services have been responsible for much of that growth, generally growing much faster than other sectors of the economy. Even in countries that experienced a rapid growth of manufactured exports, there was also a parallel and rapid growth in services. The service sectors, from finance and accounting to IT and advertising, also provide valuable inputs that the manufacturing sector needs to be able to compete with effectively in global markets in terms of quality, flexibility, and reliability.

The services trade enables developing countries to potentially leapfrog the industrial development stage. The economic models of the past assumed that countries grew by creating an agricultural surplus and borrowing to invest in manufacturing capital. Only when countries went through the industrial stage of development could they consider a focus on services, as domestic demand for such services was still hopeful and the services trade was nonexistent. The communications revolution of the last decade now permits lower income countries to leapfrog that stage of development and directly focus on expanding the service sectors of their economies. The technology itself does not depend on first building a solid industrial base: Mobile telephones do not rely on an extensive network of landlines. Also, countries that have not yet invested heavily in old technologies can simply choose to bypass it. Sri Lanka now has more mobile phone subscribers than those with landlines.

The global market for offshoring is growing at 30%. While world trade has been expanding at a rate of 6.9% annually for both services and manufacturing over the last 20 years, the offshoring of services to developing countries, although still small in absolute terms, has been growing at a much faster rate.

Women are considerably advantaged by offshoring opportunities. The ability to complete more responsibilities from remote locations that might be located in or closer to their homes has allowed more women to enter the offshoring workforce. For instance, 49% of Wipro's (a large Indian offshoring company) workforce is female, while ICICI OneSource's workforce is 60% female. With female education and literacy on par with that of males in Sri Lanka, the country is well-positioned to take advantage of this potential.

Offshoring, especially captive offshoring, provides a significant contribution to FDI (foreign direct investment). In turn, FDI is often directly linked to economic growth because of the increased income sources and jobs generated, which subsequently reduces poverty. FDI also generates several indirect benefits that increase the productivity of the recipient economy through the adoption of managerial and technical best practices from foreign countries. In recent years, there has been a documented shift of FDI toward the services sector. The world's inward stock of FDI in services quadrupled between 1990 and 2002 while the share of services in the world's total FDI stock rose from 25% in the 1970s to about 60% in 2002.

Services accounted for about 85% of outward FDI stock for developing countries in 2001. FDI flows in services between developing countries themselves are growing even more rapidly than those between developed and developing countries: "By 2010, more than one-third of the FDI in developing countries will originate in other developing countries with India, China, Brazil, and South Africa being among the main players."

While FDI stimulates productivity improvements in general, service outsourcing has several specific characteristics that create unique spillover benefits and positive externalities for developing economies. These defining features differentiate service outsourcing from the traditional fields of manufacturing and goods outsourcing.

Incentives are created for education. While outsourced manufacturing relies on a cheap, low-skilled workforce, services outsourcing relies on a well-educated and highly skilled workforce. The employment of a relatively skilled labor force in services trade increases the return to education and thus the incentives to acquire skills that are marketable in the global economy. This is likely to become one of the crucial issues for long-term growth. Services offshoring has the potential to mitigate Sri Lanka's perennial problem of educated but unemployed youth. The quality of exported services improves, which benefits domestic consumers, especially manufactured-goods exporters, of the same services as well. For instance, call centers in developing countries that are established to cater for the U.S. market are also being operated around the clock to provide services to local customers. The same is happening in Sri Lanka with the recently established HSBC call center providing local services to the whole of Sri Lanka.

Technology and knowledge transfer results as services exports and outsourcing requires technical sophistication. For example, it is necessary to have dependable and cheap communication links with the rest of the world. Repeated and frequent interactions with foreign firms, and especially their direct presence, also increase knowledge transfer. This is not limited to technical knowledge but includes business standards and know-how, which are critical for the integration of national economies into the global economy and factor prominently in the long-run growth implications for any developing country.

Export-oriented zones have been shown to improve the quality of human capital and the productivity of the local workforce in domestic economies if foreign investors engage in substantial training and if the workplace encourages learning by doing, as in Singapore and the Philippines. Furthermore, learning can also occur at the managerial and supervisory level, thus potentially fostering local entrepreneurship. This is important since firms in developing countries often lack the production and marketing know-how required to enter world markets.

The processes tend to be more environmentally friendly. Services exports and outsourcing do not create many of the negative externalities associated with manufactured goods, such as environmental pollution and lower labor standards. The effects of this type of environmental degradation are usually ignored since it is hard to quantify these negative externalities and the actual consequences are only revealed over a long period of time.

Developed countries provide a large proportion of the demand for business services. The United States alone accounts for 13.3% of worldwide commercial services imports. The planned use of offshore outsourcing among corporate decision makers in the United States rose by a factor of six between 2001 and 2003. A similar trend appeared in the data from a 2004 survey of the top 500 European firms, according to which the responding companies had already offshored about 20,000 jobs and 44% of all those surveyed said that they intended to increase this number in the near future.

The offshoring market can also be segmented by function. In general, back-office functions that require a decreased amount of customer contact have the most potential to be performed in a remote location. The popularity of call centers, IT service, and back-office functions as outsourcing opportunities further supports this data. Most professional-services offshoring clients require university degrees, but the skill level still varies across the range of functions that are typically outsourced. While R&D responsibilities require an extremely highly skilled pool of labor, common corporate functions require less specialized industry knowledge

Future Strategies for the Development of the ICT Economy

The primary reason firms engage in offshore processing is to reduce labor costs. Due to increased competitive pressures, companies are constantly seeking ways to minimize costs: "With revenues largely stagnant since 2000, firms are under intense pressure to cut costs while retaining service levels." Since salaries comprise a significant portion of variable costs, the offshoring of business processes can provide sizeable savings to firms in developed countries. The findings of a technology research firm indicate that organizations that offshore accounting and customer service functions to China can possibly save 30% to 50% in labor costs when compared to executing those same processes in Tokyo, London, or Chicago. To give a specific industry example, a leading e-business software company in the United States was reportedly able to achieve 40 to 45% lower costs per overseas employee by outsourcing to programmers in India who earn as little as one

third of what their counterparts receive in the United States.

Firms can increase productivity and competitiveness through various channels. Outsourcing generic business processes allows firms to focus on their core competencies and increase innovation initiatives. This often enables firms to expand their operations and broaden their customer base: "For instance, tax authorities in high-cost countries can at present afford to check only a small number of tax declarations every year; by shifting some work to lower cost locations, they could raise the audit ratio significantly and improve their intake." Firms can also offer a wider range of services offered at a faster rate than if they managed all operations in house. By offshoring certain business processes, multinational companies can operate on a round-the-clock schedule, which can accelerate the delivery of work products, improve customer satisfaction, and reduce costs.

Organizational restructuring to achieve greater operational efficiencies is another consideration when resorting to outsourcing as a business strategy. Process performance is often improved because the service providers in developing countries often have very specialized experience in performing the unique operations that they are hired to execute. In some instances, outsourcing also presents an opportunity for better risk management and diversification, which can reduce firm liabilities and direct responsibilities.

While benefiting from the advantages offered by outsourcing, companies must also be able to manage the inherent risks. A strong internal governance system is a necessity in order to ensure effective monitoring of the deployment of resources between the offshore and local provision of services. Additionally, this is crucial to maintaining high-quality standards despite the geographical barriers that are a reality of offshoring. Companies that feature highly unionized work forces must also be careful to balance the political opposition that might accompany any decision to offshore certain service functions. Aside from handling this domestic risk, the outsourcing firm must also consider the geopolitical risk in the chosen offshore location.

Sri Lanka boasts some of the cheapest labor costs in the region. Since worker compensation constitutes a large portion of the variable costs borne by offshoring firms, this is a key determinant of an offshoring location's attractiveness. A comparison of labor costs per hour against some of Sri Lanka's competitors in the provision of offshoring services indicates Sri Lanka's relative attractiveness in this area. Labor costs per hour are significantly lower than those in other developing countries. Apart from looking at general labor costs, it is particularly important to study the wage rates for the respective occupations and functional responsibilities that might be outsourced.

The island continues to suffer from relatively high telephone charges. Although wages comprise the bulk of variable costs incurred by foreign firms, other infrastructure and business startup costs must also be considered. In the area of telecommunications costs, Sri Lanka does not appear to have a distinct advantage. The cost of a three-minute fixed-line phone call in Sri Lanka is almost double the cost in India, a country that specializes in call center services. Mobile costs are also significantly higher than those in India, but competitive when compared with other countries in the region.

Sri Lankan businesses pay some of the highest electricity costs in the world. High electricity prices are charged to industries and businesses in order to cross-subsidize residential customers, resulting in electricity tariffs that are high in comparison with most other countries. In addition to this, because of unreliable supply, additional costs are incurred to acquire and operate expensive generators. This often inhibits firms from investing productively in their core businesses.

Office rents in Colombo are low, on average, when compared with other major Asian cities. While the average monthly cost per square meter

is only $11.60 in Colombo, comparable costs in New Delhi range between $15.45 and $26.15. Office space in Shanghai, another major offshoring destination, costs nearly three times as much compared to Colombo.

Sri Lanka shows a pronounced weakness in the area of regulatory costs. The corporate income tax rate in the country is on the high end in relation to other countries in the region. However, in many cases, this comparison is not particularly significant since several governments offer substantial tax breaks to specific firms engaged in export service providing.

Perhaps the most significant cost arises from rigid labor regulations. South Asia has the highest firing costs in comparison with other countries in the region. Only in Sierra Leone are companies forced to pay higher severance payments to dismiss redundant workers, and lengthy court battles in Sri Lanka can often result in substantive legal expenses and inefficient use of resources. The Sri Lankan system also places undue discretionary powers in the hands of the labor commissioner, who has traditionally been prone to base severance payments on the ability of the employer to pay, thus effectively penalizing multinationals with deep pockets, the very firms that the country is trying to attract with an outsourcing strategy.

Offshoring companies are looking for large numbers of highly skilled and educated workers, particularly those trained in technical fields. It is not enough to have a low-cost wage structure. Several studies assess the attractiveness of a particular country as an outsourcing location by comparing the relative cost against the quality and size of the labor force. The strong presence of these two factors is primarily what contributes to India's and China's positions as the leading outsourcing destinations.

Due to its small size, Sri Lanka does not have the population size that China and India benefit from. While China and India have labor force sizes of 778.1 million and 472 million respectively, Sri Lanka's total population itself is below 19 million people, and the country's labor force stands at 7 million. The large pool of Indian workers in various densely populated cities allows foreign companies to attain greater savings by taking advantage of the economies of scale that result from concentrating activities in fewer locations. While the operations of certain processing or call centers in developed nations might be scattered in a number of places due to shallow local labor pools, large cities in developing nations provide large workforces that allow for significant expansion in a single area. Mumbai, Delhi, and Bangalore, for example, have 5 million inhabitants while other cities like Chennai, Hyderabad, and Kolkota feature similarly large pools of workers. From a quantitative standpoint, while the median size of a call center is 1,000 employees in India, the average size of a similar center in the United States is under 400, with many centers housing only between 150 and 300 employees.

India leads all markets in the number of university graduates that are produced each year (more than 2 million) because of its large population and numerous educational institutions. Additionally, it ranks on the low end of the average salary spectrum, which is why it has become a particularly attractive offshoring location. In comparison, Sri Lanka has a much smaller number of annual graduates who work at a relatively low wage despite their high skill level.

Sri Lanka's comparative advantage is in the quality and not the quantity of its labor force. Since professional-services provision requires educated workers with English-speaking ability and often technical skills as well, it focuses on a specific section of the labor force rather than including a country's total working population. A successful outsourcing strategy for Sri Lanka would therefore focus on niche markets rather than trying to compete directly with generic services that are being offered in India and elsewhere.

Despite high literacy rates, English has been neglected as a medium of instruction. In terms of literacy, the country ranks far ahead of many

countries competing for a share of the offshore services market in the area of adult literacy. Sri Lanka's colonial past has also endowed the country with a large English-speaking middle class, as well as a strong legal and accounting profession based on the British system and a cultural affinity for all things English. Unfortunately, the use of English as a medium of instruction was gradually dropped during the 1970s and 1980s as a rising tide of nationalism swept the country, and the younger generation is struggling to catch up. The government must address this issue when considering education policy reforms.

Tertiary education remains limited in Sri Lanka. The types of higher education opportunities available are a key factor in developing a skilled workforce. One of the fundamental policy objectives of the Sri Lankan government is to provide universal access to primary and secondary education. From an offshoring standpoint, however, firms will be particularly interested in the percentage of the population that has pursued studies beyond secondary schooling. Sri Lanka's tertiary education system includes universities, professional and other courses, and technical education, with the overall tertiary education enrollment rate at 11%. This number slightly exceeds the South Asian average of 10% and grew from an average of 8% in 1997, largely due to the expansion of public universities and an increase in private tertiary institutions and courses.

Government continues to underinvest in the education system compared to some of its neighbors. The country's education sector was initially given a high priority in the 1930s and 1940s with policy makers recognizing the positive social returns from a heavy investment in human capital. Nevertheless, in recent years, other Asian countries have surpassed Sri Lanka in their support of the education sector. Government spending on education as a percentage of overall government spending and as a percentage of national income is relatively low and is even less than the South Asian regional average in both cases. Additionally, the amount of resources devoted specifically to university education in Sri Lanka is extremely low, at only 1.58% of total government expenditure and 0.42% of GNP (gross national product) in 2003.

Technical education has been neglected. Despite Sri Lanka's early recognition of the contribution of education to economic and social development, the country now lags behind several of its regional competitors. In China, for example, radio and television universities have been created alongside traditional schools in order to meet the huge demand for technical education. Likewise, India "has one of the most developed educational systems in the world. Sri Lanka has taken a few steps in the correct direction, albeit on a much smaller scale. Although the 16 universities in the country might not yield an extremely high output of graduates, other institutions in the tertiary sector are providing a boost in the available number of Sri Lankan skilled workers. For example, the Department of Technical Education and Training oversees programs in 36 technical colleges, offering vocational training programs for 54,000 young people in 2004. There are also various other apprenticeship and training authorities that have been created under the direction of the Tertiary and Vocational Education Commission. Other institutions churning out large numbers of qualified workers annually include the Sri Lanka Institute of Information Technology, the Institute of Chartered Accountants in Sri Lanka, and the Sri Lanka branch of the Chartered Institute of Management Accountants, the National Institute of Business Management, and the Institute of Bankers of Sri Lanka.

In addition to possessing the required technical skills, a workforce with cultural familiarity is another critical requirement for a country attempting to provide outsourcing services. In addition to being able to speak the required language, however, knowledge of various idioms and colloquialisms will also be essential for tasks that involve customer interaction and customer

relationship management. This is why neighboring markets sometimes provide a greater potential for developing offshoring relationships since cultural similarities might be more prevalent within closer geographical regions.

In selecting potential investment locations, entrepreneurs look for a stable political and macroeconomic environment. Providing such an environment remains challenging in the Sri Lankan context. Such issues are, however, beyond the scope of this chapter

Increased offshoring depends on cheap and reliable telecommunications and IT infrastructure. Deregulation of these industries catalyzes their development and competitiveness at an early stage. Some cite the reform and deregulation of the communications infrastructure in India as the most significant policy reform for the IT-enabled services sector:

Beginning in the early 1990's, India liberalized its public monopoly telecommunications system and permitted Indian private providers to begin offshoring services. They could select their specializations, which ranged from providing niche services such as backbone and network management to full-service integrated voice and data operations. For larger cities, the result has been the creation of a telecommunications network with quality and cost levels approaching that of developed countries. Recently this service is being extended to second-tier cities, i.e., those with a population in excess of one million persons.

Telecommunications remains one of the fastest growing sectors in Sri Lanka, largely due to privatization of the industry. Sri Lanka began reforming this sector several years ahead of neighboring countries and started privatizing the sector in 1996. Since then, teledensity in the fixed-line sector has grown rapidly while the mobile sector, subject to private competition from Day 1, has experienced even more rapid growth.

Unfortunately, telecom regulation has not kept pace with privatization. The unfinished telecom reform agenda has left the country with a poorly regulated sector that has not been able to promote rapid expansion of a high-bandwidth data network. Sri Lanka should extend growth of the telecoms industry to the use of the Internet since this is one area where Sri Lanka lags behind some of its competitors. In 2002, Sri Lanka had 123 Internet hosts per million people while the comparable figures for Malaysia and the Philippines were 3,550 and 480 respectively.

Since high-speed data transmission is also a regular requirement for offshore service providing, countries aiming to succeed in this should have developed Internet facilities. Access to broadband is also highly desirable, although widespread broadband penetration is not common in several of Asia's developing countries. Sri Lanka lags behind many of its competitors in the availability of Internet hosts and as a result, does not boast as many Internet users as many other Asian countries. A notable step in the right direction is the recent establishment of the national ICT Agency, which is committed to expanding Internet access and is spearheading the roll out of a high-speed network on a least-cost subsidy basis to the island's underserved areas.

Electricity supply and availability is also a key challenge for Sri Lanka. Since the Ceylon Electricity Board sells electricity below the cost of supply, there is little incentive to expand access to the national grid: "Moreover, delays in implementing the plan for expanding least-cost generation capacity, and reliance on ad hoc purchases of emergency power, have resulted in the rapidly growing demand outstripping supply." Rolling blackouts were a common occurrence in the early 2000s and resulted in many independent businesses resorting to expensive private generators.

A well-developed physical infrastructure system is also desirable, but while certain utility and transportation infrastructure deficiencies in India have presented problems, several corporations have developed private solutions to these problems. For example, some companies operating out of India resort to multiple backup power supplies and use private buses to shuttle employees to work and avoid the absenteeism that often arises due to the poor transportation alternatives available. While these added outlays do add up, these costs appear to be manageable in the context of the overall savings generated.

The Sri Lanka transportation system is an area of pronounced weakness in the country's business environment. Despite the island's large network relative to both its population and its land area, the majority of the roads are in poor condition and an insufficient amount of funding is devoted to the upkeep of existing roads and road rehabilitation. Although this might be a greater problem for manufacturing firms where a large number of goods have to be transported on a daily basis, it can also have a substantial impact on service firms due to the resulting absenteeism among employees. The unreliability of public transportation also contributes to this problem. Since reliability and promptness are key requirements for a firm providing offshoring services, this might prove to be a serious constraint for Sri Lanka if resources are not devoted toward improving the road network.

Government policies regarding the security of intellectual property will also affect a country's potential to attract outsourcing clients. The IT industry in countries with advanced IT developments is extremely protective of intellectual property rights and will want to operate in an environment where workers are taught to respect such rights. Most countries in the Asian region face significant challenges in establishing strong intellectual property protection to fight rampant piracy, and several commentaries on the Sri Lankan IT sector also cite this as a problem.

There are several risks that companies take when outsourcing to foreign countries. Therefore, the overall investment climate should be one that mitigates these risks. Since political and macroeconomic risk factors into the decision-making process, countries with a greater degree of stability in these arenas will be more attractive investment prospects. As demonstrated in a recent investment climate survey of Sri Lanka, the country performs quite well in comparison with other South Asian countries on the measure of governance. Aside from more pronounced political instability due to the ongoing civil unrest, Sri Lanka ranks higher in the other areas of governance. The country also outperforms other lower middle income countries.

Providing incentives in order to promote the win-win nature of offshoring agreements is also an integral part of the process. While service providers offer low costs and high quality, which are desirable features, governments in countries exporting offshore services also play a role in creating a supportive environment for this industry through their approach to taxation and their encouragement of foreign investment. There are several regulatory barriers to conducting business that must be addressed if the country is to become a thriving offshore location. The Commissioner of Labor has ultimate discretion regarding the termination of employment and to date has never consented to nonvoluntary dismissal. Moreover, the size of mandated severance payments are often made on the basis of ability to pay, which penalizes the wealthiest multinationals, the very companies that Sri Lankan governments would like to attract. This situation results in labor market rigidity, which is a deterrent to FDI. Other hindrances to companies trying to do business in Sri Lanka include the exceptionally long time it takes to enforce contracts in the country along with the lengthy process required to register property in the country.

Sri Lanka's main strengths as a potential offshoring destination lie in the relatively low wage and cost structure. Even highly skilled and well-qualified workers are paid low salaries relative to other Asian countries. Despite its small size, the country turns out a significant number of technically qualified individuals, especially in IT, accounting, and business management.

There are some weaknesses that the island can never overcome, most importantly its size. However, other weakness such as the neglect of English and science, the limited number of graduates, and rigid labor practices can and must be overcome by concerted government and private-sector action. There is tremendous scope for improving the business environment, improving contract enforcement, and promoting a modern streamlined government-to-business interface as well as improving the state of the country's basic infrastructure.

Reputation is also an important factor in attracting offshoring investments since the quality of work that is produced and the resulting client satisfaction are extremely important. Firms need to know that service providers will function with flexibility, reliability, and promptness. Indian service providers, for example, substantiate their claims of producing high-quality work by pointing to their Capability Maturity Model (CMM) Level 5, Six Sigma, ISO 9000, and BS 7799 certifications.

With regard to reputation and worldwide recognition, some of Sri Lanka's neighboring competitors have already developed brand names and broadly marketed their strong comparative advantages in certain sectors of the global offshoring services market. For example, India has established its position as a leader in software development based on an early start and extensive IT experience, while the Philippines has leveraged its large American-style-speaking population and rapid telecommunication and technological advances to develop a prominent call center industry. Sri Lanka, on the other hand, has yet to establish itself as a high-caliber services offshoring location. The existing offshore market size is relatively small, and extensive quality rankings have not been conducted as in India.

However, offshore manufacturing already exists in Sri Lanka and has been particularly successful within the garments industry, which has developed as a response to quota protection.

Although the export of professional services features several characteristics that are quite different from those involved in manufacturing offshoring, the existence of this market could potentially provide insight when considering the relevant policy reforms to address in order to spur industry growth. This existing market might help in terms of establishing a reputation as a popular offshoring destination even though Sri Lanka's export service-providing market is still in a relatively infant stage.

CONCLUSION

At a general level, local enterprises wanting to provide services to foreign firms must make a concerted effort to market their unique strengths and develop focused business plans with clearly set goals for long-term growth. Firms should take a proactive approach toward finding partners locally as well as internationally to expand both their funding resources and client base. Sri Lankan companies should also try to achieve this goal through establishing strong links with overseas networks and foreign universities, particularly those with large Sri Lankan communities. Other issues to tackle include the following:

- **Financial Structure:** Since costs are a critical factor in a foreign firm's choice of offshoring location, it is extremely important that Sri Lanka firms provide services at rates that are comparable to or more attractive than those in competing markets. Firms should research the cost structures of competitors along with the menu of services provided and constantly aim to provide higher quality services at the lowest cost possible. Regular innovation and tailoring of services to specific client needs is necessary to ensure client satisfaction, but it is important to achieve this as efficiently as possible so as to retain a noticeable cost advantage.

- **People Skills and Availability:** In order to ensure that employees can meet customer service demands and keep up with new techniques and innovations, firms should initiate in-house or on-site training programs with a continuous focus on improving performance and the quality of services provided to ensure sustained customer satisfaction.

- **Business Environment:** Since communication with clients in remote areas is a defining feature of offshore service providing, local firms must ensure that they have well-developed information and communications technology systems. Unreliable ICT infrastructure hinders the ability of firms to provide services promptly, reliably, and efficiently. Companies should make detailed assessments of ICT requirements and address any resulting gaps as quickly as possible. Firms should also engage in conversations with public authorities in relevant sectors to highlight key areas where they need government support and ensure that there is an ongoing dialogue regarding the promotion of this sector.

The Sri Lankan government could play a useful role in creating awareness for both locals and potential international clients regarding the opportunities within the country's professional services industry. The Board of Investment is well-placed to play such a role. Government can also work to promote the benefits of working for a captive offshoring firm or for a Sri Lankan firm providing offshore services and overcome the traditional bias for public-sector employment. Likewise, awareness must be extended internationally since Sri Lanka has not yet established itself as an offshore service-providing powerhouse. Although this initiative must be led by the private sector, government can work with private companies using the BOI and its network of embassies overseas to promote a Sri Lankan role in international service provision. Maintaining a constant dialogue with the relevant stakeholders will play a key role in developing the Sri Lankan offshore services market. Other possible policy initiatives could include the following:

- **Tax Incentives:** Several governments aiming to support export-providing industries have provided extensive tax breaks to firms engaged in the export industry or have suspended the collection of various types of license fees. For example, India's Ministry of Finance exempted IT-enabled services from income taxes in September of 2000. Many export processing zones in various countries in Asia also offer similar financial incentives to encourage increased FDI.

- **People Skills and Availability:** The Sri Lankan government must refocus efforts on education with resources specifically devoted to developing the shared service skills and IT abilities of graduating students. The curricula of universities and schools should be revised to endow students with the specific skills that offshoring firms demand. Several Indian universities have been developed through strong government support in recent years in order to achieve this objective, while educational reforms in several countries now promote studies in technical fields.

- **Incentives for Training:** This is critical for achieving success in services exporting because of the constant innovation that is required. However, individual firms might not have enough motivation to invest the necessary resources into such programs, and therefore the government should create incentives for these firms to provide workers with suitable training programs that enhance the quality of the services provided by the country.

- **Improved Telecommunication and Information Technology Infrastructure:** This is a prerequisite to developing a professional services outsourcing market. Clients will be more likely to offshore services to areas where they maintain a high level of confidence in the local infrastructure since this will have a dominant effect on the quality of service that is ultimately provided. Fostering the development of ICT infrastructure in areas outside of major cities will also yield eventual benefits to Sri Lanka in the long run as it will allow ICT and professional services to be delivered from remote locations across the island. Governments should encourage computerization and automation in enterprises and should provide regulatory support for the development of cost-effective technologies such as VoIP that lower communications costs.

- **Improved Labor-Market Flexibility:** From a regulatory standpoint, the Sri Lankan government must also address several aspects of prevailing labor laws that create a rigid labor environment and deter FDI. The legal framework should cater to emerging industries and enable business to start up without presenting an array of administrative barriers. Firms should also have more freedom in their hiring and firing policies in order to prevent Sri Lanka from appearing as a less attractive place to do business than some of its neighboring countries that compete for offshoring business.

REFERENCES

Amiti, M., & Wei, S.-J. (2004a). Demystifying outsourcing. *Finance & Development, 12,* 36-39.

Amiti, M., & Wei, S.-J. (2004b). *Fear of service outsourcing: Is it justified* (IMF Working Paper No. 04,186)? International Monetary Fund.

Antonio, E. T., & Padojinog, W. C. (2003). IT-enabled services in the Philippines: Prospects and issues. *AT10 Research Conference, 2,* 20-21.

Chudnovsky, D., & López, A. (1999). *Globalization and developing countries: Foreign direct investment and growth and sustainable human development.* UNCTAD/UNDP Publisher.

Dossani, R., & Kenney, M. (2005). The next wave of globalization: Exploring the relocation of service provision to India. *Berkeley Roundtable on the International Economy Working Papers, 156,* 1-41.

Furniss, T. (2003). China: The next big wave in offshore outsourcing. *BPO Outsourcing Journal.* Retrieved July 15, 2006, from http://www.outsourcing-asia.com/china.html

Furniss, T., & Janssen, M. (2005). Offshore outsourcing. Part 1: The brand of India. *BPO Outsourcing Journal.* Retrieved July 2006 from http://www.outsourcing-asia.com/india.html

Graham, E. M., & Wada, E. (2001). Foreign direct investment in China: Effects on growth and economic performance. *SSRN.* Retrieved June 2006 from http://papers.ssrn.com/sol3/papers.cfm?abstract_id=300884

Hagel, J., III, & Ho, J. P. (2004). Capturing the real value of offshoring in Asia. *Crimson John Hagel Working Papers, 12,* 1-18.

International Labour Office (ILO). (2003). *Employment and social policy in respect of export processing zones (EPZs).* Retrieved July 13, 2006, from http://www.ilo.org/public/english/standards/relm/gb/docs/gb285/pdf/

International Trade Center. (2000). *Offshore back office operations: Supplying support services to global markets.* Geneva, Switzerland: Author & UNCTAD/WTO.

International Trade Center. (2001). *Innovating for success in the export of services: A handbook.* Geneva, Switzerland: Author & UNCTAD/WTO.

Jones, L. L. (2004). *Deciding where to offshore.* Retrieved June 2006 from http://www.joneslanglasalle.com/en-GB/research/

Kearney, A. T. (2003). *Selecting a country for offshore business processing: Where to locate.* Global Management Consulting Firm. Retrieved June 2006 from http://www.atkearney.com/shared_res/pdf

Kearney, A. T. (2004). *The changing face of China: China as an offshore destination for IT and business process outsourcing.* Global Management Consulting Firm. Retrieved July 10, 2006, from http://www.atkearney.com/main.taf?/pdf

Kim, W. (2004). On the offshore outsourcing of IT projects: Status and issues. *Journal of Object Technology, 3*(3), 1-6.

Klein, M., Aaron, C., & Hadjimichael, B. (2001). *Foreign direct investment and poverty reduction* (World Bank Policy Research Working Paper No. 2613). World Bank.

McKinsey Global Institute. (2003). *Offshoring: Is it a win-win game?* Retrieved June 25, 2006, from http://www.mckinsey.com/mgi/publications/win_win_game.asp

McKinsey Global Institute. (2005a). *The emerging global labor market. Part I: The demand for offshore talent in services.* Retrieved June 2006 from http://www.mckinsey.com/mgi/publications/emerginggloballabormarket/index.asp

McKinsey Global Institute. (2005b). *The emerging global labor market. Part II: The supply of offshore talent in services.* Retrieved June 2006 from http://www.mckinsey.com/mgi/publications/emerginggloballabormarket/index.asp

McKinsey Global Institute (2005c). *The emerging global labor market. Part III: How supply and demand for offshore talent meet.* Retrieved August 2006 from http://www.mckinsey.com/mgi/publications/emerginggloballabormarket/index.asp

Shirhattikar, G. (2005). Future winners and losers in global outsourcing. *Journal of International Business*. Retrieved June 2006 from http://www2. gsb.columbia.edu/journals/files/chazen/Global_ Outsourcing_CWJ_Final

UNCTAD. (2003). *E-commerce and development*. New York.

UNCTAD. (2004). Handbook of statistics. New York.

United States Government Accountability Office. (2004). *International trade: Current government data provide limited insight into offshoring of services*.

World Bank. (2005a). *Sri Lanka: Improving the rural and urban investment climate*. Retrieved June 28, 2006, from http://www.worldbank.lk/

World Bank. (2005b). *Treasures of the education system in Sri Lanka: Restoring performance, expanding opportunities and enhancing prospects*.

World Bank & MIGA. (2003). *Benchmarking FDI competitiveness in Asia*. Retrieved June 2005 from http://www.miga.org/miga_documents/asiareport.pdf

Chapter XXII
Socio Economic Influence on Information Technology:
The Case of California

Rasool Azari
University of Redlands, USA

James Pick
University of Redlands, USA

ABSTRACT

This chapter examines the influence of socio-economic factors on the employment, payroll, and number of enterprises of three technology sectors for counties in California. Based on correlation and regression analyses, the results reveal that factors that are important correlates of technology sectors are professional/scientific/technical services, other services, and educational services, ethnicity, and college education. As a whole, the findings emphasize the importance of the association of socio-economic factors with the per capita magnitude of the technology sectors. This chapter suggests steps that can be taken by the state of California and its county and local governments to foster technology and reduce the digital divide.

INTRODUCTION

During recent years the rapid change in information technology (IT) and its impact on society have been the concern of academia, industry leaders, government officials and policy makers. There is no doubt that the impact of technology on society is profound and that it has long lasting effects financially, politically, and culturally. But the growing abundance of literature and projects concerning the social consequences of the IT and the Internet underscore the need for a better understanding of the forces at work.

Technological change has been central to the U.S. economic growth and is the major force in raising the nation's factor productivity at an accelerated rate. Information technologies (IT) are reshaping every aspect of organizations and business enterprises, such as work processes, decision-making, workforce, employment structures, teamwork, and products. "Indeed, the potential of the ICT revolution to transform the global economy has been at the centre stage in international forums and discussions..." (ILO, 2001, p. v). For companies to stay viable and competitive, adjusting to an ever-increasing pace of change is a must. The rapid development of new technologies in the information age and the unequal ability of societies across various segments to adjust to and assimilate these constant changes has been recognized as a source of problems for the old socio-economic structures because it creates potentially disruptive frictions.

This information gap is expressed by the term "digital divide," which is generally defined as "unequal access to information technology" (Light, 2001, p. 709). The effective utilization and accessibility of IT is the subject that some of the recent studies are trying to address. As Katz (2002, p. 4) puts it: "Having knowledge of what is there with no means of obtaining it or having technology but no knowledge of how to use it does not constitute access."

The continued existence of the "digital divide" and the increasing inequality of wages in the U.S. during the last two decades pose considerable challenges to policy makers. California, with its talented and diverse workforce, has a unique role in this equation. The long-term expansion of California's high tech, even with its recent slowdown, has and will depend on its skilled workforce (CCST, 2002). It has been recognized as the leading high-tech state in the U.S. (AEA, 2001). In the year 2000, among all states, it ranked first in high-tech employment, number of high-tech industry establishments, high-tech exports, R&D expenditures, and venture capital investment (AEA, 2001). It led the nation in all high-tech industry segments except photonics, and was second in high-tech per capita wage

(AEA, 2001). Furthermore, 77 of its 1,000 private sector workers were employed by high-tech firms (AEA, 2001). Its R&D expenditure in 1998 was $43.9 billion, which was 19% of the nation's (AEA, 2001). California's leadership position in the technology sector justifies the importance of studies that analyze its sectoral growth in more detail and at smaller geographical scale, such as for counties in this chapter.

California slowed down in 2001; in particular the high-tech industry grew in California only by one percent, down sharply from 1999 and 2000, although this rate of growth varied from county to county (AEA, 2002). The slowdown is exacerbated by a large state government budgetary shortfall, which came to a head in 2002 and 2003, requiring stringent cutbacks and other actions. However, it is likely the state will recover from this problem in several years, and that it will not take away its technology leadership.

At the same time, there is a long-term weakness in its educational capability and readiness. "California is lagging behind other states in workforce readiness. Therefore its economic activities and slowdown, which include the Silicon Valley, much of the entertainment industry, and 48 federal government research labs, have repercussions on a global basis. If California cannot meet industry's demand for skilled labor, it could lose science and technology jobs to other states" (CCST, 2001; Conrad, 1999, p.1).

A recent study by CCST (2002) examined the reasons why California, even before the budget crisis, has fallen short in providing the requisite science and technology education to fulfill the high demand. This report points to substantial gaps in supply of skilled labor. For instance, the report points to a gap of 14,000 science and engineering works at the bachelor's degree level, out of 20,000 such degrees (CCST, 2001). Demographic growth has led to a huge increase in K-12 enrollments in the state, surging with a large proportion of immigrant students, while the education being provided is problematic (CCST, 2001). The report offers a flow diagram of production of high-tech workforce that centers on the public education system as well as workplace education and immigration to make up the deficits (CCST, 2001). The report finishes up with policy recommendations to increase the science and technology workforce that include strengthening educational programs at all levels, strengthening data-gathering and planning, and providing more marketing and funding for science and technology tracks (CCST, 2001). The report underscores a serious problem that in recent years has been solved by workforce immigration through special visas, although that is somewhat curtailed post 9/11.

Our study differs from other nationwide "divide" studies by emphasizing socio-economic correlates of information technology intensity for counties in California. It seeks to determine what social and economic factors are significant in distinguishing intensity of technology in three different industrial sectors in different counties in California. We consider the digital divide as a broad concept that includes economic, educational, and social aspects. For instance, a rich county economy is better able to afford technology and a highly educated county can better use it. Furthermore, social issues may also stimulate technology use. Since economic gains come, among others, from the adoption and adaptation of technology by individual users and by firms in business sectors, we use a framework that relates the socio-economic factors to the sizes of per capita employment, payroll, and enterprise prevalence in four different high-tech sectors in California. Among other things, we test whether or not education levels, community literacy in technology and presence of scientific/technical workforce are related to the size of county high- tech sectors. The aim here is to examine the associations between socio-economic factors and information technology for the counties in California. We are hoping that the results of this study will shed some light on the complex issues created by the emerging information technology

by identifying some of the problems and thereby clarifying the ongoing dialogue among different stakeholders. This may help policy makers and experts to resolve California's already developing social and economic problems brought on because of the recent changes in IT and possibly avoid or prepare for potential others.

Following this introduction, we first review the literature on the digital divide and wage inequality and proceed with the research questions. We continue with the methodology used, the findings, discussion of the results, a section on policy implications and chapter limitations, and a conclusion.

BACKGROUND

The term "digital divide" entered the American vocabulary in the mid-1990s and refers to the unequal access to information technology (Light, 2001). There are slight differences among the various definitions of digital divide. Castells (2001) and Katz's (2002) definition of the digital divide refers to inequality of individual and household access to the Internet. OECD's definition (2000) is not limited to consumer (household) access to technology but also defines and distinguishes the level of penetration and diffusion of ICT in various sized enterprises.

The uneven distribution of IT benefits across the U.S. is frequently pointed out. Major reports from the National Telecommunications and Information Administration, a unit of the Department of Commerce (NTIA, 1999, 2000, 2002) utilized the Current Population Survey of the U.S. Census to examine household distribution of access to technology including computers, phones, and the Internet. It defined "digital divide" as the divide between those with access to new technologies and those without. A key finding is that overall the nation "is moving toward full digital inclusion. The number of Americans utilizing electronic tools in every aspect of their lives is rapidly increasing" (NTIA, 2000, p. 4). By September 2001, 143 million Americans (ca. 54% of population) used the Internet and 174 million Americans used computers. The use of computers and the Internet is the highest among children and teenagers (NTIA, 2002). This rapid growth is among "most groups of Americans, regardless of income, education, race or ethnicity, location, age, or gender, suggesting that digital inclusion is a realizable goal" (NTIA, 2000, p. 4). Results of the NTIA data also show that ownership of a computer will increase the use of the Internet. So, access to computer is an important factor for the effective use of information technology and according to the NTIA data this ownership is growing rapidly.

Those Americans with high-income households enjoy much greater connectivity; other highly connected groups (holding income constant) are Asians, whites, and middle-aged, highly-educated, employed married couples with children. These are often found in urban areas and the West. On the other hand, low-income, Blacks, Hispanics, or Native Americans, seniors in age, not employed, single-parent (especially female) households, those with little education, and those residing in central cities or especially rural areas are the least connected (NTIA, 1999).

However, "a digital divide still remains" (NTIA, 2000, p. 15). Even though the utilization of computers expanded dramatically over a 15-year period for all groups in the U.S., a digital divide persisted and in some cases grew (NTIA as discussed in Noll et al., 2001). For instance in 1989, the percent of U.S. households that owned a computer, by educational level—elementary education and bachelor's or more education—was 1.9% and 30.6% respectively. In the year 2000, these numbers have changed to 12.8% for elementary and 75.7% for bachelor's or more education. The Hispanic-white ethnicity differences widened from 7.1 versus 16.0% in 1989 to 33.7 versus 55.7% in 2000 (NTIS data cited in Noll et al., 2001).

Furthermore, Lentz (2000) argues that the concept of the digital divide should be used in broader terms than merely describing end user problems and should extend also to community development. Other researchers apply the term to business, economy, and/or society levels, rather than the individual level (Baker, 2001; OECD, 2000). Baker points out that the policy problem of the digital divide is best addressed through multiple dimensions, that is, policies that address disparities in information technology diffusion at different geographic, economic, social, and organizational levels. In their book, *Social Consequences of Internet Use,* Katz and Rice (2002) analyzed the impact of the Internet on American society from three different perspectives—access, involvement, and interaction. "The book's three sections correspond to these three vital issues concerning Internet and human communication—access, civic, and community involvement, and social interaction and expression" (Katz, 2002, p. 4).

Florida and Gates (2001) examined the correlations of diversity indices with a high-tech index in the 50 largest metropolitan areas in the U.S. in 1990. The authors conclude that cultural, ethnic, and social diversity are linked to high tech. They do not prove causality, but speculate about the reasons for this. Among the explanations are that high-tech thrives in a creative atmosphere, which comes from community members (i.e., human capital) who are not mainstream or traditional but differ in their perspective, and are often new arrivals. Governments in metropolitan areas can foster community atmospheres that attract such diversity. College education was also shown to be linked to high tech as strongly as the composite diversity index (Florida & Gates, 2001).

Another issue that widens this digital gap is the phenomenon of wage divergence and inequality related to technological change. This issue has received the attention of many labor and trade economists (Feenstra, 1997) and it is widely believed that the development of the new technology increases the demand for skilled workers, thereby increasing the wage differential between skilled and unskilled workers. Even though empirical evidence from the literature on wage inequality is inconclusive and fragmented (Deardorff, 1998, p. 371), there is still a general consensus among many economists that technological change is the primary explanation for the widening gap in inequality of wages in the United States.

In addition, geography plays an important part in studies such as this one. Nations, states, counties, and cities have diverse features and characteristics that leave their particular marks. At the city level in the U.S., a wealth of high-tech data appeared in *California Cybercities,* published by the American Electronic Association (AEA, 2002). This study supports the large extent of the digital divide. Presenting data rather than analyzing them, this volume is useful as a data source, some of which is included in the present paper. It provides an overview of California's high-technology industry in the eight major metropolitan areas—Los Angeles, Oakland, Orange County, Sacramento, San Diego, San Francisco, San Jose, and Ventura.

The economy of California and its large technology sector started slowing in 2001. Many high-tech companies announced layoffs in 2001 and 2002 (AEA, 2002). San Jose, the leading high-tech city in California, experienced a dramatic decline in technology employment in 2001; of the eight metropolitan areas examined in 2002, Los Angeles, Oakland, and Sacramento had some high-tech employment growth in 2001 but a much lower growth rate than in 2000; the slowdown in the San Francisco and San Jose area was particularly high and many companies from there moved to the Oakland and Sacramento areas because of increases in business costs, particularly for land and labor. In 2002, San Jose ranked first in the concentration of high-tech workers, San Francisco second, followed by Oakland (AEA, 2002).

From the industry sector employment perspective the AEA reports that San Jose led in nine out of 13 technology industry sectors in 2000; San Diego led in consumer electronics manufacturing, Los Angeles led in defense electronics manufacturing, communication services, and data processing and information services; Orange County ranked second in six of the 13 electronic sectors. These technology sectoral differences stem from particular and often complex aspects of the development of California's metro areas in the mid to late 20th century (see Kling, Olin, & Poster, 1991, for an explanation of such phenomena in Orange County).

San Jose ranked first and San Francisco second in the compensation in the high-tech industry. Even in the slowed economy of 2001, the high-tech workforce for this industry was still paid significantly higher than average private sector workers; for example, in San Diego the earning of high-tech workers was 132% more than for the private sector workers, and in Sacramento there was a 126% differential. A point of interest here is the wage inequality. This supports the earlier contention of a widening wage inequality in the U.S.

Nationwide studies of socio-economic correlates of the sizes of technology sectors at the county level point to the importance of highly skilled professional/scientific/technical labor force (PST), ethnicity, and college education, and to a lesser extent support services, income, and federal funds grants (Azari & Pick, 2003a, 2003b). The primary finding of the association of PST with technology emphasizes the key factor of highly skilled workforce both to perform technology tasks and provide highly skilled support functions. The secondary finding of positive links to particular ethnicities supports the point that community diversity is positively tied to technology. These studies utilized methods and data somewhat similar to the present study. However, they differ by not separating out the nation's highest tech state of California and considering its particular technology, economic, and social attributes, and how that informs its policy options.

The many findings emerging from these and comparable studies support that socio-economic factors impact the use of IT. Furthermore, they suggest the causality depends on the unit of analysis, region, and choice of dependent variable, such as IS utilization impact, application area, or IT investment. As stated before, we consider the digital divide as a broad concept that includes economic, educational, and social aspects. For instance, a rich economy is better able to afford technology and a highly educated community can better utilize technology. Furthermore, social issues may also stimulate technology use. For example, socio-economic characteristics influence consumer uses of technology. In turn, consumers with scientific and technology skills provide technology employees for businesses. Those employees contribute to corporate receipts and payrolls. Cumulative corporate results constitute technology sectors in counties.

We believe that socio-economic factors and technological development are interrelated. "Technology is deeply affected by the context in which it is developed and used. Every stage in the generation and implementation of new technology involves a set of choices between different options. A range of interrelated factors—economic, social, cultural, political, organizational—affect which options are selected. Thus, a field of research has emerged where scholars from a wide variety of backgrounds seek to increase the understanding of technological development as a social process"

(Dierkes & Hoffman, 1992). Today technology has become so intertwined with our everyday life that a broad understanding of its utilization and distribution requires a thorough examination of the socio-economic environment. Paying attention to the relationship between socio-economic factors and the changes in the high-tech sectors may further shed some light on the problem and help to alleviate the digital divide.

RESEARCH QUESTIONS

This chapter has two research questions:

1. What are the most important socio-economic factors overall that influence the per capita economic sizes of the information, information services/data processing, telecommunications/broadcasting, and motion picture/sound recording technology sectors for counties in California?
2. How do these sectors differ with respect to the most important socio-economic factors that influence their economic sizes?

METHODOLOGY

This chapter investigates the association of technological development with socio-economic factors for counties in California. The data, all for year 2000, were from the U.S. Census of 2000, City and County Databook, and County Business Patterns detailed North American Industry Classifica-

Figure 1.

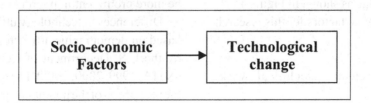

tion System (NAICS) data (U.S. Census, 2001, 2003a, 2003b). For each regression or correlation sample, all of California's 58 counties were initially included. However, in the correlation and regression samples, counties with missing data were excluded.

The basic assumption is that socio-economic factors, such as education, income, service sector composition, ethnicity, federal funding, and population growth, are associated with the size of technology receipts and payroll. It is evident that socio-economic factors and technology are frequently intertwined and interrelated. For instance, in a county, the presence of a wealthy population, a highly educated labor force, colleges/universities, and high R&D expenditures will likely increase the technology level by attracting capital investment and stimulating productive enterprises. At the same time, a county with a high technology level may attract highly educated people; may create prosperity and wealth in its citizenry; and may foster R&D.

Our research framework is based on the unidirectional relationship between the socio-economic factors and technological change as depicted in the figure. These factors are one of the most important variables in social and economic development studies. A study of bi-directional effects would require more sophisticated data collection and intermediate variables than are undertaken in this study.

It is clear that this framework may also flow in a feedback way in the opposite direction, in that larger county technology sectors may attract populations with certain socio-economic characteristics. We are not ready to present a comprehensive framework of these different dimensions and their linkages. Rather, this chapter focuses on unidirectional linkage as shown in Figure 1.

The socio-economic factors for this research are:

- professional/scientific/technical workforce,

- educational services workforce,
- other services workforce,
- median household income,
- college graduates,
- federal funds and grants,
- change in population 1990-2000, and
- proportions of Black, Asian, Latino, white, and female.

The unit of analysis is the county, because it is the smallest geographical unit for which a wide range of statistical data can be obtained. Its unit applies across the entire state, has accurate and extensive variables collected through the U.S. Census and other sources, and is stable geographically over time. It also represents a governmental and policy unit, so policy suggestions from research can inform governmental decision-making.

The selection of independent variables is based on prior studies. For example, counties with higher service components will also have higher levels of technology. We justify this variable by the substantial proportion of high-tech employees who work in services versus other sectors, and the growth in this proportion over time. For instance, in 2000, 63% of high-tech workers were in services, a proportion 11% higher than in 1994 (AEA, 2001). Hence, we reason that more service-oriented counties will have higher levels of technology workers, and the technology sectors will be more ample. We also reason that technology sectors will have lower levels in counties that receive higher levels overall of federal funding on a per capita basis. The federal grants include a large proportion of grants for social services, welfare, and community improvements. On a per capita basis, we reason that federal grants would be more prominent in poorer counties.

Differences in technology utilization are also based on demographic attributes as highlighted by the U.S. Department of Commerce studies (NTIA, 1999, 2000, 2002). For instance, in 1998 the proportion of the population using the Internet varied between 8% for very low income households (under $20,000) to 60% for high income ones (over $75,000) (NTIA, 1999). At the level of developing nations, per capita income was one of the most important influences on Internet and cell phone use (Dasgupta et al., 2001). Likewise, 47% of white households had a computer, versus 23 and 25% respectively for Blacks and Hispanics. In a recent publication, Lentz (2000) emphasizes that race and ethnicity should not be excluded from studies of high-tech jobs. Slowinski (2000) points to large differences between the ethnic groups as a cause of differences in the high-tech workforce. Crandall (2001) identifies ethnicity and income as important variables for access to computers and technology. Florida and Gates (2001) and Florida (2002) demonstrate a positive association between diversity and technology. They also show a strong relationship between college education and technology.

The U.S. Department of Commerce identified a gender gap, with about 3% more utilization of the Internet by surveyed males versus females (NTIA, 1999). We included change in county population based on our own reasoning that growing counties draw in workforce and capital investment, and tend to have growing educational institutions that encourage technology use. This attribute was included in two prior studies (Azari & Pick, 2003a, 2003b), although it was shown to be of minor significance.

Because socio-economic variables have proven to be of importance, we feel justified in including them, even though the units of analysis (i.e., individuals, firms, and nations) have varied in much of the prior research. We reiterate that although the directionality of effect may be in two directions, we emphasize in this study how socio-economic attributes influence technology level. Multicollinearity (Neter, 1996) is a minor issue because of the use of stepwise regression

technique with mostly only one or two independent variables entered.

To measure technological change, the dependent variables are employees per capita, payroll per capita, and number of enterprises per capita. The information sectors selected are:

- Information (broad sector),
- Information Services/Data Processing (IS/DP) — subsector of information,
- Broadcasting/Telecomm (B/T) — subsector of Information, and
- Motion Picture/Sound Recording (MP/SR) — subsector of Information.

For the Information Sector, only number of enterprises per capita is included, due to very high inter-correlations with the other dependent variables.

The following are several reasons why we selected these information sectors:

1) they utilize computers and modern information communication technologies;
2) they increase the productivity of institutions, shorten product life cycle, and reverse the composition of our labor force from mainly blue collar workers to predominantly service providers and knowledge workers;
3) they diminish the importance of distance and contribute to globalized markets and economies; and
4) they contribute nearly 60% to the American gross national product.

In summary, we explore the association of 12 independent socio-economic factors with three dependent variables, for four industry sectors. Correlation and stepwise linear regression analyses were conducted to test our models. The software utilized was SPSS version 11.

FINDINGS

The dependent variables are inter-correlated with the exception that MP-SR variables are not associated with those for IS-DP and B-T (see Table 1). The entertainment industry (movies, recording) does not correspond to the geographic patterns of information services and communications. This is not surprising on a common sense basis, since for instance computers and information technologies are centered in the Silicon Valley, while entertainment is centered in greater LA.

The regression findings for technology employment and payroll are all significant and demonstrate that the most important factor is PST employment, followed by education (see Table 2). PST is the most important in estimating IS-DP and B-T employment and payroll. The secondary factors are educational services (in one regression each for IS-DP and B-T) and percent Black for B-T payroll. On the other hand MP-SR is correlated with educational services and college graduates, as well as with percent change in population for MP-SR payroll.

Regressions for the number of technology enterprises are likewise all significant. PST and education are again the most significant, but education assumes a greater role than for employment and payroll. As seen in Table 3, PST is the most important predictive factor for the information sector as a whole, and for IS-DP, but it is not significant for B-T and MP-SR. Education is important for each regression—college graduates for the information, IS-DP, and B-T sectors, and educational services for the MP-SR sector. Federal grants are positively significant for IS-DP and B-T. Finally two ethnic variables, percent Asian for information sector and percent Latino for IS-DP, significantly reduce the number of enterprises.

DISCUSSION

The dominance of PST as a predictive factor of California's county technology sectors, as seen in Tables 1 and 2, corresponds to other nationwide county studies (Azari & Pick, 2003a, 2003b). In the case of California, it is the most prominent state in its PST human resource (AEA, 2001). However, the state's PST workforce per capita is varied in its distribution, and corresponds to county technology sectors. At one extreme, San Jose County has one of the greatest concentrations of PST workers in the nation, since it includes Silicon Valley's R&D establishment, famous scientific universities such as Stanford and U.C. Berkeley, and advanced government research centers such as NASA-Ames. The environment of discovery and science also is associated with a high concentration of technology sectors in computers, information systems, communications, the Internet, and Web entertainment. On the other hand, an opposite example is Stanislaus County in the far north, which has among the lowest levels in the sample of both PST per capita and technology sector sizes per capita. The full extent of this range, extending to rural, agricultural California, needs to be recognized.

The secondary yet very important educational factors are also key to fostering technology. These factors influenced the number of technology enterprises for the information, IS-DP, and B-T sectors (see Table 1) and affected payroll per capita for MP-SR (Table 2). CCST and other reports have pointed to a severe shortage of science and technology graduates, relative to the high demand of the nation's leading technology state (CCST, 2002). CCST ascribes this shortage to a number of structural weaknesses in K-12 and college education. Not enough science and technology opportunities are present in K-12, and there is reduced incentive and resultant low

Table 1. Correlation matrix of dependent variables, California sample, 2000

Table 1. Correlation Matrix of Dependent Variables, California Sample, 2000

	No. enterprises/ capita INF	No. employees/ capita IS-DP	Payrolls/ capita IS-DP	No. enterprises/ capita IS-DP	No. employees/ capita B-T	Payrolls/ capita B-T	No. enterprises/ capita B-T	No. employees/ capita MP-SR	Payrolls/ capita MP-SR
No. enterprises/capita INF	1.000								
No. employees/capita IS-DP	0.679*** (n=31)	1.000							
Payrolls/capita IS-DP	0.640*** (n=31)	0.859*** (n=31)	1.000						
No. enterprises/capita IS-DP	0.898*** (n=47)	0.814*** (n=31)	0.798*** (n=31)	1.000					
No. employees/capita B-T	0.678*** (n=44)	0.8575** (n=31)	0.543** (n=31)	0.731*** (n=42)	1.000				
Payrolls/capita B-T	0.713*** (n=44)	0.612*** (n=31)	0.582*** (n=31)	0.791*** (n=42)	0.960*** (n=44)	1.000			
No. enterprises/capita B-T	0.617*** (n=57)	0.544** (n=31)	0.511** (n=31)	0.613*** (n=47)	0.754*** (n=44)	0.737*** (n=44)	1.000		
No. employees/capita MP-SR	0.732*** (n=30)	0.283 (n=30)	0.177 (n=30)	0.478** (n=30)	0.243 (n=30)	0.266 (n=30)	0.273 (n=30)	1.000	
Payrolls/capita MP-SR	0.617*** (n=30)	0.150 (n=30)	0.067 (n=30)	0.350 (n=30)	0.108 (n=30)	0.134 (n=30)	0.161 (n=30)	0.967*** (n=30)	1.000
No. enterprises/capita MP-SR	0.719*** (n=54)	0.321 (n=31)	0.179 (n=31)	0.464*** (n=46)	0.319* (n=43)	0.338* (n=43)	0.248 (n=54)	0.929*** (n=30)	0.829*** (n=30)

Note: the top of each cell gives the Pearson correlation and the bottom sample size

Note: INF = Information Sector
IS-DP = Information Services-Data Processing Subsector
B-T = Broadcasting-Telecommunications Subsector
MP-SR = Motion Picture, Sound Recording Subsector

* correlation significant at 0.05 level
** correlation significant at 0.01 level
*** correlation significant at 0.001 level

Table 2. Standardized regression results for dependent variables, no. of employees and payroll, per capita, California sample, 2000

Table 2. Standardized Regression Results for Dependent Variables No. of Employees and Payroll, Per Capita, California Sample, 2000

	Employees per Capita for IS-DP Beta Value	signif.	Payroll per Capita for IS-DP Beta Value	signif.	Employees per Capita for B-T Beta Value	signif.	Payroll per Capita for B-T Beta Value	signif.	Employees per Capita for MP-SR Beta Value	signif.	Payroll per Capita for MP-SR Beta Value	signif.
Professional/ Scientific/ Technical Employees per capita	0.824	0.000***	0.457	0.020*	0.665	0.000***	0.763	0.000***				
Educational Services Employees per capita			0.446	0.023*	0.252	0.027*			0.552	0.002**		
Other-Services Employees per capita												
Median Household Income (in dollars)												
Federal Grants and Funds (in 1000's of dolllars)												
College graduates per capita											0.531	0.003**
Percent Change in Population 1990-2000											0.334	0.046*
Proportion of Population 65+												
Percent Black							0.216	0.029*				
Percent Asian												
Percent Latino												
Percent Female												
Regression adjusted R sqaure	0.669		0.704		0.601		0.667		0.280		0.329	
significance level		0.000***		0.000***		0.000***		0.000***		0.002**		0.005**
sample size (N)		31		31		31		31		31		31

* signif. at 0.05
** signif. at 0.01
*** signif at 0.001

Note: INF = Information Sector
IS-DP = Information Systems-Data Processing Subsector
B-T = Broadcasting-Telecommunications Subsector
MP-SR = Motion Picture, Sound Recording Subsector

numbers of science and engineering majors and the college level (CCST, 2002). Since California cannot produce sufficient skilled workers, and it is not currently receiving large domestic migration, the gap is being filled by highly skilled workforce immigrating from overseas, many of whom are being admitted to the U.S. on temporary visas for special needs (CCST, 2002). Getting back to our finding of the importance of education, this points to an increasingly dysfunctional state educational

system and the need for policy changes that are discussed later.

The lack of PST affects MP-SR seen for both number of technology enterprises (Table 1), and employees per capita and payroll per capita (Table 2). It may be ascribed to lack of connection between a general scientific/R&D climate and growth in the movie/recording industries. They may derive less benefit from basic science, engineering, or R&D, since they are not as dependent on a science

Table 3. Standardized regression results for dependent variable of number of technology enterprises, per capita, California sample, 2000

Table 3. Standardized Regression Results for Dependent Variable of Number of Tecbnology Enterprises, Per Capita, California Sample, 2000

	No. Enterprises per Capita for INF Beta Value	signif.	No. Enterprises per Capita for IS-DP Beta Value	signif.	No. Enterprises per Capita for B-T Beta Value	signif.	No. Enterprises per Capita for MP-SR Beta Value	signif.
Professional/ Scientific/ Technical Employees per capita	1.042	0.000***	0.934	0.000***				
Educational Services Employees per capita							0.580	0.000***
Other-Services Employees per capita								
Median Household Income (in dollars)								
Federal Grants and Funds (in 1000's of dolllars)			0.584	0.000***	0.584	0.000***		
College graduates per capita	0.267	0.004**	0.346	0.005**	0.346	0.005**		
Percent Change in Population 1990-2000								
Proportion of Population 65+								
Percent Black								
Percent Asian	-0.439	0.000***						
Percent Latino			-0.124	0.011*				
Percent Female								
Regression adjusted R sqaure		0.776		0.905		0.439		0.336
significance level		0.000***		0.000***		0.000***		0.000***
sample size (N)		42		40		42		42

```
*   signif. at 0.05        Note: INF = Information Sector
**  signif. at 0.01              IS-DP = Information Systems-Data Processing Subsector
*** signif at 0.001             B-T = Broadcasting-Telecommunications Subsector
                                MP-SR = Motion Picture, Sound Recording Subsector
```

climate. For instance, many aspects of movie making are not taught widely in universities, studied in government labs, or dependent on scientists. On the other hand, movies and recording industries do benefit by good education and abundant college graduates. The correlation analysis in Table 1 had detected that the values for MP-SR's independent variables were predominantly unrelated to those for IS-DP and B-T, so these different regression findings are not surprising.

Among the lesser factors in the findings, ethnicity effects only appear for three out of ten regressions, more strongly as an inverse effect of percent Asian on the number of technology enterprises for the information sector (see Table 3), and more weakly for the Latino and Black percentages in two other cases, seen in Table 2. They were also opposite from the hypothesized positive direction in two of three cases. The strong Asian effect is surprising and unexplained, given the major involvement of Asians in many technology fields in California. Further research is needed to determine the robustness of this finding and to determine its cause. Ethnicity's two weaker findings and absence in the remaining regressions do not lend backing, for California, to a recent framework linking diversity to technology (Florida, 2002; Florida & Gates, 2001). The explanation may be that this is due to the high level of diversity in the entire state. According to the U.S. Census (2003), its non-white percentage in 2000 was 40.5%. This means that diversity is reduced in prominence and overwhelmed by PST and education. Translating this into an everyday explanation, it implies that for a highly diverse state, there is an overall creative contribution stemming from the diversity, but that the *differences* in technology levels between counties are much more due to PST and education. The single positive association between Black population and payroll per capita for B-T is consistent with the diversity theories and several prior studies. We do not have an explanation for this specific

effect, especially since it applies to B-T payroll and not to B-T employment.

There are similarities and differences between the California and nationwide county findings with somewhat similar regression design, variables, and data (Azari & Pick, 2003a, 2003b). The current study's dominant importance for PST corresponds to the national findings. However, other positive factors appear for the nation, namely other services and household income, while ethnicity factors were more prevalent but inverse. At the same time, education was less prominent nationally (Azari & Pick, 2003a, 2003b). It would appear that California's educational deficit for technology workers pushes this factor to greater importance, while its high base level of diversity reduces that factor's importance. Those far-reaching ideas can be analyzed with more detailed future studies that, for instance, include data on state or county science/technology educational deficits and on perceptions of diversity.

It is worth mentioning several limitations of this study. Due to the geographical proximity of counties and the problem of urban sprawl in California, especially in metropolitan areas, there is a likelihood of daily workforce inter-county commuting. This limitation can be addressed in a future study that includes commuting flows and characteristics of commuters. Another limitation is the application of the stepwise multiple regression method. Regression results are estimates of the changes that would occur if the variables were entirely independent of one another. In complex social phenomena, such as those addressed in this study, single factor changes are rare. For example, income, education, and occupation are unlikely to change separately without inducing changes in the other components. Such cross-dependencies highlight the dangers of interpreting results as estimates of causal changes.

A further study limitation is that there may be extraneous factors that affect the analysis, such as laws and regulations; profit-making versus societal interests of technology firms; high-tech employment trends; venture capital investment; public and private technology education; and cultural, sociological and behavioral factors that influence businesses and their workers. Many are not available consistently for counties from the U.S. Census, but may be from other sources. Also, the study is limited by the model's unidirectionality, which goes from socio-economic factors to technology sector sizes. An expanded study could be based on a bidirectional feedback model, mediated by intermediate factors.

POLICY IMPLICATIONS AND FUTURE RESEARCH

The results of this study have various implications for different stakeholders—individuals, organizations, the government, and society as a whole. The following section addresses some of these concerns.

Since the debate on the digital divide ranges across individual consumers, businesses, technology sectors, counties and states, and whole economies, it is appropriate to indicate that these levels are inter-connected. As noted before, socioeconomic characteristics influence consumer uses of technology. In turn, consumers with scientific and technology skills provide technology employees for businesses. Those employees contribute to corporate receipts and payrolls. Corporate results add up to constitute technology sectors in counties. This framework may also flow in a feedback way in the opposite direction, in that larger county technology sectors may attract populations with certain socio-economic characteristics. Changes in technology demand continuous skill upgrading in the work force. Even though much remains to be done, the computer and ICT intensive industries are showing the greatest increase in the skill upgrading of their work force in California. This trend, though, bypasses many talented individuals and leaves a major part of the population behind

by limiting their chance to participate in and gain from the economic growth.

The importance and advantages for technology development of scientists, professionals, and college-educated workforce are stressed in this chapter. A college educated environment leads to improved skills and the ability to educate and retrain broad parts of the community. All this fosters technology industries and enterprise. This impact may be limited to technologically-skilled employees and hence the potential gains associated with this transformation are likely to be limited, which in turn means the digital divide is deepening. This dynamic needs to be adjusted by appropriate institutions and policy choices. The extent of the success of technological change depends also very much on the socio-economic context. Policy intervention must be targeted towards reducing the gap in social and economic factors since this study has shown that a direct influence exists between specific socio-economic factors and the dependent variables.

Preventing the divide from increasing, though, is no easy task. A big problem with technology arises from its inadequate distribution to society, and consequently, its unequal access to, and use by some members of society. But focusing solely on the more equal distribution of technologies will not solve the problem of the digital divide. Baker (2001) points to the additional influences of education, geography, race and income as indicated by studies conducted by the U.S. Department of Commerce (NTIA, 1999, 2000, 2002) and other studies (Benton, 1998; CCST, 2001; Hoffman, 1998). The technology gap existing in the U.S. was the subject of investigation by the Benton Foundation (1998), which arrived at "the conviction that the design of the communication system through which we will talk to one another, learn from one another, and participate in political and economic life together is too important to be left to the free market alone" (Lentz, 2000, p. 362).

California historically has been the leader of many social and political movements. Its policy implementations have repercussion worldwide. Being also a leader in high-tech sectors, California has the potential for influencing the problem of the digital divide and wage inequality. Part of the planning focus in California for technology needs to be on improving the general social, educational, and economic levels of counties.

Overall, the findings of this paper reinforce the notion that the digital divide exists and its causes are complex. To alleviate this problem the following policies are suggested for California and its counties:

- Promote and support science and high-end professions by investing in these segments of higher education and in R&D.
- Invest in broadly-based education, training, and lifelong learning.
- Develop policies to market science and high-end professional career paths to K-12 and college students.
- Create educational incentives for students to enter those career paths.
- Shift the dependence on reducing the high-tech educational gap from foreign immigration to the state's education system and its outflows.
- Shift the focus of unemployment protection to skills upgrading and lifelong education.
- Increase awareness of the negative and exclusionary effects the digital divide has on individuals and society in general and its possible subsequent results—unemployment, social unrest, and crime.
- Establish a comprehensive dialogue between different stakeholders in communities—government, businesses, educational, institutions, citizens—to foster a unified approach to encourage science and educational development and its benefit to all.
- Allocate resources more efficiently.

The current research project can be expanded in a number of ways. Other high-tech states and regions can be studied and compared, such as Washington D.C. and Boston. A multi-nation study of socio-economic factors and technology levels with counties or states as units of analysis could be conducted in order to establish if there are cultural and international differences. That study should include similar variables such as age, gender, ethnicity, education, high-tech employment trends, venture capital investments, international trade, high-tech average wage, R&D per capita, and technology transfer.

CONCLUSION

This chapter's focus is on two research questions. In conclusion, the study's statistical results, which have been described and discussed, support both of the questions and provide the following answers to them.

1. *What are the most important socio-economic factors overall that influence the per capita economic sizes of the information, information services/data processing, telecommunications/broadcasting, and motion picture/sound recording technology sectors for counties in California?*

   The most important factor is professional/scientific/technical workforce. The next factors in importance are college graduates and educational services. Of minor importance are ethnicity (with inconsistent directionality), federal grants and funds, and the very minor percent change in population.

2. *How do these sectors differ with respect to the most important socio-economic factors that influence their economic sizes?*

   By sectors, the information sector is influenced by PST and education about equally. That sector shows some positive effect from federal funds and grants, and minor inverse ethnic effects. IS-DP and B-T are similar in having a dominant PST effect, followed by lesser educational effects. There are specific, minor Latino and Black ethnicity effects. For MP-SR, educational services and college graduates dominate, with a minor percent population change effect.

These conclusions suggest that to develop its technology sectors further, California counties need to plan for and invest in building up more their scientific and professional workforce and related educational and scientific institutions, and to encourage educational opportunities and services. In a time of governmental budget constraints, California county governments and community and business leadership groups should strive to not lower their support for these factors, in order to maintain the counties' technology edge.

REFERENCES

American Electronics Association. (2001). *Cyberstates 2001: A state-by-state overview of the high-technology industry.* Santa Clara, CA: American Electronics Association.

American Electronics Association. (2002). *California Cybercities 2002.* Santa Clara, CA: American Electronics Association.

Azari, R., & Pick, J.B. (2003a). The influence of socio-economic factors on technological change: The case of high-tech states in the U.S. In R. Azari (Ed.), *Current security management and ethical issues of information technology* (pp. 187-213). Hershey, PA: IRM Press.

Azari, R., & Pick, J.B. (2003b). Technology and society: Socio-economic influences on technological sectors for United States Counties. *International Journal of Information Management,* in press.

Baker, P.M.A. (2001). Policy bridges for the digital divide: Assessing the landscape and gauging the dimensions. *First Monday* [Online], *6*(5). Available: *www.firstmonday.org*

Benton Foundation. (1998). *Losing ground bit by bit: Low-income communities in the information age.* Report. Washington, DC: Benton Foundation.

CCST. (2001). *Bridging the digital divide.* Sacramento, CA: California Council on Science and Technology.

CCST. (2002). *Critical path analysis of California's science and technology education system.* Report. Sacramento, CA: California Council on Science and Technology.

Conrad, A.C. (1999). *Industry sector analysis of the supply and demand of skilled labor in California.* Report. Sacramento, CA: California Council on Science and Technology.

Crandall, R.W. (2001). The digital divide: Bridging the divide naturally. *Brookings Review, 19*(1), 38-41.

Dasgupta, S., Lall, S., & Wheeler, D. (2001). *Policy reform, economic growth, and the digital divide: An econometric analysis.* Research Paper, World Bank. Washington, D.C.: Development Research Group.

Deardorff, A.V. (1998). Technology, trade, and increasing inequality: Does the cause matter for the cure? *Journal of International Economic Law,* 353-376. Oxford University Press.

Dierkes, M. (1992). 21st century technologies: Promises and perils of a dynamic future. *OECD.*

Feenstra, R.C., & Hanson, G.H. (1997, June). *Productivity measurement, outsourcing, and its impact on wages: Estimates for the US, 1972-1990.* NBER Working Paper, No. 6052.

Florida, R. (2002). *The rise of the creative class.* New York: Basic Books.

Florida, R., & Gates, G. (2001). *Technology and tolerance: The importance of diversity to high-technology growth.* Washington, D.C.: The Brookings Institution.

Graham, S. (2002). Bridging urban digital divides? Urban polarisation and information and communications technologies (ICTs). *Urban Studies, 39*(1), 33-36.

Hoffman, D.T.N., & Venkatesh, V. (1998). Diversity on the Internet: The relationship of race to access in usage. In A. Garmer (Ed.), *Investing in diversity: Advancing opportunities for minorities and the media* (p. 130). Washington, D.C.: The Aspen Institute.

International Labor Office. (2001). *World employment report: Life at work in the information economy.* Geneva: ILO.

Katz, E. J., & Rice, R.E. (2002). *Social consequences of Internet use: Access, involvement, and interaction.* Cambridge, MA: MIT Press.

Kling, R., Olin, S., & Poster, M. (1991). *Postsuburban California: The transformation of Orange County since World War II.* Berkeley: University of California Press.

Lentz, R.G. (2000, August). The e-volution of the digital divide in the U.S.: A mayhem of competing metrics. *Info, 2*(4), 355-377.

Light, J. (2001). Rethinking the digital divide. *Harvard Educational Review, 71*(4), 709-733.

Miller, D.C. (1991). *Handbook of research design and social measurement* (5th ed.). Sage Publication.

National Telecommunication Information Administration (NTIA). (2000). *Falling through the Net: Towards digital inclusion.* Washington, D.C.: U.S. Department of Commerce.

National Telecommunication Information Administration (NTIA). (2002). *A nation on line: How Americans are expanding the use of Internet.* Washington, D.C.: U.S. Department of Commerce.

Neter, J., Kutner, M.H., Nachtsheim, C.J., & Wasserman, W. (1996). *Applied linear statistical models.* Boston: WCB/McGraw-Hill.

Noll, R.G., Older-Aguilar, D., Ross, R.R., & Rosston, G.L. (2001). The digital divide: Definitions, measurements, and policy issues. *Bridging the digital divide* (pp. 1-12). Sacramento, CA: California Council on Science and Technology.

OECD. (2000). *OECD small and medium enterprise outlook.* Paris.

Slowinski, J. (2000). Workforce literacy in an information age: Policy recommendations for developing an equitable high-tech skills workforce. *First Monday,* [Online], *5*(7). Available: www.firstmonday.org

U.S. Census. (2001). *City and county data book.* Washington, D.C.: U.S. Census.

U.S. Census. (2003a). *U.S. census of population, 2000.* Washington, D.C.: U.S. Census. Available: www.census.gov

U.S. Census. (2003b). *County business patterns. Detailed NAICS classified data.* Washington, D.C.: U.S. Census. Available: www.census.gov

Warf, B. (2001). Segueways into cyberspace: Multiple geographies of the digital divide. *Environment and Planning B: Planning and Design, 28,* 3-19.

This work was previously published in Information Security and Ethics: Social and Organization Issues, edited by M. Quigley, pp. 48-72, copyright 2005 by IRM Press (an imprint of IGI Global).

Chapter XXIII
Strategies for Cultural Economic Development in Kamakura:
Managing Digital Contents and Cultural Assets

Sachiko Kishino
Ochanomizu University, Japan

Frederic Andres
National Institute of Informatics, Japan

ABSTRACT

Over recent years, the circumstances surrounding regional cultural assets have been significantly changed. A series of IT promotion projects implemented by the national government since the early 2000s have intensified regional initiatives in managing digital content of cultural assets. Behind this, there has been a growing expectation toward regional development through wide dissemination and proactive use of cultural information resources. In reality, though, many challenges still remain to become a driving force of regional economy. This means, in practice, a more strategic approach should be taken in the management of human, financial, and information resources. Using Kamakura as a case study, we present an integrated model that develops the underlying value of cultural assets into regional economic strength.

INTRODUCTION

The innovation of digital technology has caused a paradigm shift in the field of heritage management. It is characterized by increasing consciousness toward the digital archiving of cultural assets as an integral part of an information infrastructure (Makiuchi, 2000). Japanese National government-led approaches such as the Cultural Heritage Online Plan (Ministry of Education, Culture, Sports, Science and Technology, 2003) and Local Culture Digitalization Project (Ministry of Internal Affairs and Communications, 2003) have played an underpinning role in facilitating the accumulation, dissemination, and utilization of cultural information resources as broadband content.

Thanks to these efforts, many local authorities have become highly committed to digitalizing a variety of tangible and intangible cultural assets that represent their regions. According to the survey on the implementation of digital archives, nearly 90% of prefectural governments and more than 80% of museums throughout the nation have built digital archives and made them available on the Internet (Japan Digital Archives Association, 2005). However, despite such a remarkable increase in digitalization and networking, there has been little or no progress in the utilization of digital contents, especially in terms of contributing to the regional economy.

In the most basic sense, the digitalization of regional cultural assets is a means of manifesting regional attractiveness and quality; moreover, it can be a catalyst for interactions with the outside world (Kasaba, 2004). The biggest challenge that many regions face is to establish a cooperative framework for the continued improvement and effective use of digitalized cultural assets. In this chapter, we argue for the need to create a strategic mechanism for managing human, financial, and information resources so that it can generate long-term economic vitality. In this context, digital technology must be a cornerstone for ensuring that resources become value-added outputs enabling further cultural and economic activity. The conservation of cultural assets should be integrated into this value-chain mechanism and operated in a sustainable way.

In this chapter, we review and analyze the complex relationship among cultural assets, regional economies, and the innovation of digital technology. We particularly focus on the economic value of cultural assets and the controversial aspects that this has, and clarify the aim of digitalization in the context of regional economic development. The issues of ownership and rights management

are also taken into consideration. In a case study of Kamakura, a city with rich and varied cultural assets from medieval times, we propose an integrated regional model for sustainable development in order to convert the inherent value of cultural assets into regional economic benefits. Finally, the directions for future management of cultural assets are discussed.

BACKGROUND

Economic Value of Cultural Assets

Economic value is undoubtedly one of the most controversial natures that cultural assets have. It receives a great deal of attention in the context of regional economic policies and activities. More often than not, the concept of economic value is explained by two elements: use and nonuse. Use value (including direct use, indirect use, and optional use) refers to current and future commercial activities and any multiplier effects derived from them. For instance, tourism, sales of products, exhibitions, publications, and advertising can be included in this category. In contrast, nonuse value (including existence and bequest) refers to the notion that people do not intend to use a cultural asset (or visit a cultural heritage site), but that they do expect its continuing existence because of the significance that it has (Cegielski & Janeczko, 2001; IUCN, 1998; Pagiola, 1996).

When focusing on use value, we inevitably face the trade-off between the conservation and the utilization of cultural assets. For many historic cities, tourism plays a central role in the regional economy. Also, cultural assets are often exploited for tourist attractions. Indeed, the income brought by visitors' spending on accommodations, admission fees, meals, shopping, transportation, and other expenditures can be a financial base of a community (Cegielski & Janeczko, 2001). Yet, on the other hand, a growing number of visitors cause physical damage to cultural assets. For instance, air pollutants, noise, and vibration caused by visitor traffic have wide-ranging impacts on cultural assets and the historic environments surrounding them. Other negative factors are flash photography, graffiti, and even deliberate acts of destruction and disfigurement of properties (Palumbo, 2002).

Use value, by its very nature, cannot be isolated from the issues of human and financial resources for the sake of securing an asset's existence, that is, conservation, maintenance, restoration, regeneration, and even monitoring (Macháček, 2001). As a matter of fact, the cost and human capital required for preserving cultural assets and safeguarding the surrounding environments weigh heavily on local authorities and other concerned organizations. Even if not directly affected by visitors, assets are constantly exposed to age-related deteriorations, natural threats, and other unavoidable forces. The relationship between cultural significance and economic value is paradoxical. Sustainable management requires us to ensure that visitors are satisfied with their cultural and historical experiences and that revenue from them is secured, while at the same time minimizing the degradation of the cultural assets for the sake of current and future use (Kishino, 2005). A major challenge in this context is to establish shared strategies for both cultural wealth and economic growth.

Role and Aim of Digitalization

The fundamental role of digitalization is, by and large, made up of two elements: long-term storage of various information resources and their related access (Hodge, 2000; Hodge & Frangakis, 2004). Digital storage is a primary function of modern computing technology, and it can ensure long-term preservation of the digital contents of cultural assets. The recent remarkable advances in digital technology have enabled cultural information resources to be preserved in high-quality and high-resolution digital format, although there is ongoing debate about the duration of digital data, which turns out to be highly dependent on the rapid pace of technological change and media compatibility (Brown, 2003; Flecker, 2003; Jantz & Giarlo, 2005). While further studies need to be undertaken on sustainable digital storage, at this moment, it is important to strengthen the cultural information resource base through continuous updating efforts.

Meanwhile, the concept of accessibility is of importance to the management of digital contents of cultural assets. It encompasses the ideas of an asset being approachable, comprehensible, and even visibly perceptible. Digital technology has opened up the possibility for improving public accessibility to cultural assets by enabling the display of properties (once digitalized) that have been unavailable because of conservation and ownership issues, and the visualization of the composition of things that are hard to see with the naked eye, revealing their complex composition. This capability can provide a better understanding about cultural assets to the visitors and will enable them to see each asset from various scopes.

Yet, what we have to keep in mind is that the aim of digitalization is neither to substitute the existence of cultural assets nor to exceed the authenticity and significance that they have. Rather, it can be used to complement something that is made inapproachable, incomprehensible, or invisible because of various constraints in the real world, and then to create additional value in the information to be disseminated and utilized where appropriate. For instance, digital content can be utilized in on-site presentation tools in order to enhance public awareness of cultural assets, and also produced on a commercial basis in the form of DVDs, books, and other products for developing off-site interpretations.

However, there are at least two practical issues involved in the digitalization of cultural assets: intellectual properties and rights management. Needless to say, ownership and rights issues must be considered before the digitalization of cultural assets (NINCH Working Group, 2002). Indeed, the necessity of improving legislation in the form of preferential treatment for cultural information resources has been recognized (Fukami & Hayashi, 2002; Yamada, 2005). On the one hand, the idea of public domain (i.e., information or property that is uncopyrighted or whose copyright is expired) has been highlighted since the city of Kyoto achieved commercial success through managing the digital content of its regional cultural assets (pictures of the partitions in Nijyo Castle, which are now in the public domain) and producing various popular products from existing content (Shimizu & Miyahara, 2003; Shimizu & Osada, 2003). Applicability to the public domain is quite helpful for encouraging the management of digitalized cultural assets. Regional-level efforts are now required to disseminate and promote the digitalization of assets among potential users and stakeholders for the benefit of the entire regional economy.

Regional Framework

Cultural assets and digital content have a symbiotic relationship, particularly in terms of conservation

and utilization. Regional human resources play a pivotal role in bringing a greater synergy between them. As shown in Figure 1, human resources should embrace regional identity and creativity as essential attributes. The former refers to the perception of regional attractiveness and quality, while the latter means the ability of producing new ideas based on regional culture and history. These are the key elements that maintain and develop a regional cultural and economic base. Obviously, fostering human resources with these attributes is very important for the effectiveness and sustainability of cultural information resources' management.

However, in a realistic sense, regional development, including cultural wealth and economic growth, does require a long-term strategy, particularly in terms of establishing a regional cooperative framework. As regards human capital, the outsourcing of labor, which can stimulate the regional economy through the use of information technology, might have a short-term benefit, yet it cannot become a regional economic strength in the true sense. Our emphasis is on the creation of a solid structure for developing and securing

Figure 1. Concept of cultural economic development

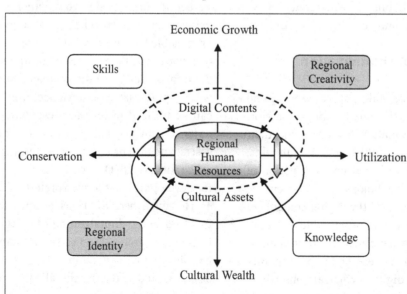

adequate human resources within a regional context.

CASE STUDY OF KAMAKURA

In the following case study, we will provide details of the close interaction between cultural assets, the regional economy, and digital technology. We will start with a brief summary of Kamakura's culture and history, and describe the current problems the city faces. After that, a practical model will be proposed in the context of regional development.

Brief Summary of Kamakura

Kamakura is located in the southeast of Kanagawa prefecture in the Kanto region of Japan. It is a satellite city of the Tokyo metropolitan area, which is about 50 km away. It became a political center in the 12th century when it was chosen by Minamoto Yoritomo, the founder and the first shogun of the Kamakura Shogunate, as the base of his new military government. The Kamakura government continued to rule Japan for over a century while the imperial court was left intact in Kyoto. After the decline of this government in the 14th century, Kamakura remained the political center of eastern Japan for some time (Shirai, 1999; Uesugi, 2003).

Kamakura has had a distinctive Buddhist culture, arising from exoteric-esoteric (Kenmitsu) Buddhism and other heretical sects. In particular, Zen Buddhism represents Kamakura Buddhist culture, and has left a great legacy. The city has important Zen-shu temples, including the five greatest Zen temples of Kencho-ji, Engaku-ji, Jyufuku-ji, Jyochi-ji, and Jyomyo-ji (Nuki & Ishii, 1997). A number of large and small temples, shrines, and other religious sites and monuments including a statue of a Great Buddha also exist within the city limits. Together, these cultural assets have created a distinctive cultural environ-

ment, and Kamakura is currently on a tentative list of World Cultural Heritage sites distinguished by the quality and quantity of its cultural assets.

Current Circumstances and Problems

Because of its unique cultural and historical background, Kamakura has become a popular tourist destination, attracting more than 17 million people every year. Approximately 4.5 million people, nearly one fourth of the total number of visitors, visit temples and shrines on a yearly basis (Chamber of Commerce and Industry of Kamakura, 2005). Kamakura's local industry and employment benefit from the spending of these visitors. The city has thus been considering various means and ways of attracting more visitors, and encouraging them to stay longer and spend more.

However, the city faces enormous challenges in preserving the significance of its cultural assets. The city spends a great deal every year on conservation, maintenance, monitoring, and acquisition of historic sites for safeguarding, and it heavily relies on financial assistance from the national and prefectural governments. Where possible, the costs and resources for conservation and promotion of regional cultural assets should be funded by visitors for the sake of sustainable management. To this end, it is necessary to create a value-chain mechanism and to capture economic benefits in a virtuous cycle.

Kyoto, for example, devised a successful market for digital content that takes full advantage of its regional cultural assets. Kyoto's business model is based on the use and reuse of existing content and systematic license management between local authorities, relevant industry, and the owners of cultural assets, such as temples and shrines (Shimizu, 2003). Indeed, it was good practice in that a certain proportion of royalties gained from business users have been spent on conservation and maintenance. However, in the context of regional development, the role of the community must be incorporated into a strategic framework. Here, we argue for the need to expand the opportunities for Kamakura's local businesses, universities, research institutes, NGOs (nongovernmental organizations), NPOs, and numerous other private entities to take part in the conservation and promotion of regional cultural assets by

making effective use of digital technology.

Strategies for Cultural Economic Development

In reality, the large majority of Kamakura's cultural assets are owned by individual organizations, mainly temples and shrines. This situation

Figure 2. Number of visitors and their spending in Kamakura

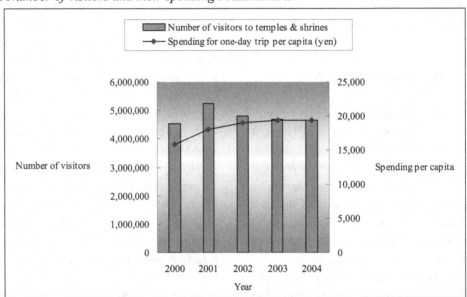

This graph is based on statistical surveys conducted by the Kamakura city government and the Chamber of Commerce and Industry of Kamakura from 2000 to 2004.

Figure 3. Cost for conservation of cultural assets in Kamakura (Yen)

	2000	**2001**	**2002**	**2003**	**2004**
Routine Maintenance	15,986,718	12,038,079	29,008,958	10,055,518	10,003,994
Repair/Restoration	94,765,050	159,388,203	35,290,290	141,986,600	156,280,070
Monitoring/Survey	85,938,413	8,725,715	97,788,583	105,091,748	86,888,197
Land Acquisition	193,820,018	256,060,327	269,698,743	323,088,110	169,702,403
Fostering/Training	1,462,702	1,554,854	1,467,661	1,961,916	0
Total	391,972,901	437,767,178	433,254,235	582,183,892	422,874,664

Note: This table is based on a statistical survey conducted by the Kamakura city government from 2000 to 2004. The figures include the amounts of financial assistance from the national and prefectural governments.

constitutes a structural impediment for the digital management of cultural assets. This problem is big enough that substantial measures need to be put in place so that Kamakura's wide-ranging cultural assets can be more effectively utilized for boosting the regional economy. In this respect, we recommend a community-based approach of collaborating to identify current needs and interests and taking action to generate regional benefits. We also recommend developing a problem-solving capacity so that the outcomes of the various efforts can be evaluated. This approach can help to promote intraregional confidence as well as establish an environment conducive to economic stability.

As shown in Figure 4, the city government must play a central role in the entire management, particularly in the phases of license contracts, digitalization, and the provision of goods and services, and it also must take the initiative in raising awareness in owners and regional community members about the conservation and promotion of regional cultural assets. The national and prefectural governments are also expected to make a large contribution through the provision of annual subsidies for the conservation and maintenance of national treasures and other important cultural assets, and yearly local allocation tax grants for improving the local infrastructure.

Action strategies for this purpose are, by and large, made up of three segments. In the phases of license contracts or agreements, which involve the most difficult and complex issues, the city ought to give legal advice and conduct mediations, negotiations, and audits. If necessary, it may arrange tripartite meetings among those concerned. Simultaneously, the city government should foster, train, and educate regional human resources so that they have adequate skills and knowledge about digital management. Where appropriate, the government should provide financial support to universities and research institutes for high value-added outcomes. Further efforts need to be made in the phase of the provision of

goods and services. The quality, effectiveness, and efficiency of the outcome should be assessed with criteria focusing on visitors' behavior and satisfaction. More importantly, the assessment should be reflected in current and future management improvements.

Digitalized information or content can be used for both profit and nonprofit purposes. The former purpose can be realized in the form of DVDs, books, and other products. For such commercial activities, users need to pay a certain proportion of royalties to the owner for conservation and maintenance of the cultural assets. The latter purpose can be realized as on-site interpretation and presentation tools to provide a better understanding of the cultural assets as well as to increase the quality of the visitors' on-site experiences. This can be instrumental as an alternate means of display, especially when cultural assets cannot be presented in public for conservation or other reasons. Furthermore, nonprofit activities using digital content can help to preserve the significance and quality of cultural assets from damage by visitors. Such activities do not require any royalty payment. In fact, nonprofit activities need a user-oriented information service assuming a diverse range of visitors since Kamakura's cultural assets exhibit tremendous diversity and complexity, and are a magnet for people of all ages and languages. For instance, elementary school children and elderly people may need different explanations about temples. That is, what is required is the effective use of digital content—text, sound, and images—according to the level of understanding and awareness of visitors. Moreover, visitors from abroad require multilingual interpretation materials as well as visual explanations without language barriers. The cultural backgrounds of visitors may present other challenges as well. For instance, Asians and Europeans may benefit from different explanations about Buddhist culture and history. It is important to compile suitable policies that account for the different needs and interests of the large variety of visitors to Kamakura. The diversification of on-site information provision methods can improve the satisfaction of visitors, and even affect their willingness to stay and visit Kamakura again.

DIRECTIONS FOR FUTURE MANAGEMENT

Cultural assets, by their very nature, can be best appreciated when they are on site or in close inter-action with places and people. Visitors to a site can contribute to the regional cultural and economic vitality, though they inevitably negatively affect cultural assets and the surrounding environment. As already mentioned, digital technology can be a cornerstone for the sustainable management of regional cultural assets when it is effectively used and managed through the cooperation of the regional community.

Yet, at the same time, there is an obvious necessity for opening up new fields of activity to complement traditional site-based management. For instance, it would be quite rewarding to set

Figure 4. Regional model for sustainable development

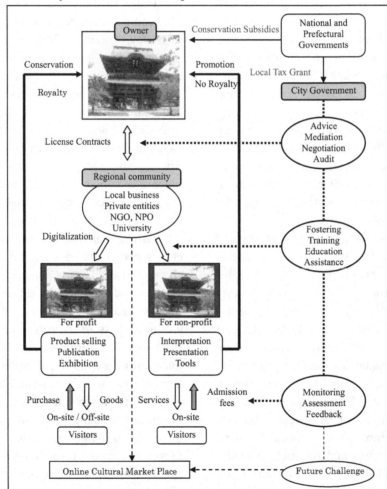

up an online cultural marketplace, connecting historic Kamakura to the outside world. Such a marketplace would be an active place in which regional community members can provide a variety of digital content representing Kamakura's culture and history to people around the world. This kind of cultural network should be a magnet that draws and holds together regional community members, especially the younger generation, who can become a leading force of regional economic growth.

In the modern world of information technology, even a small regional society can no longer exist in isolation from the rest of the world, and its unique culture will inevitably take its place on the world stage; hence, the task of developing its qualitative nature must be faced (Takemura, 2001). In such circumstances, continuous improvement of the cultural information infrastructure becomes crucial and the building of a regional capacity for global economic activities must be taken as a matter of priority.

CONCLUSION

Many historic cities, including Kamakura, are faced with difficulties in continuing their existence. Amidst the ongoing progress of digital technology and the remarkable improvement of broadband networks, many regions have begun establishing a cultural information resource base. However, they often lack tactical knowledge to be effective, and some have failed to develop the underlying value of their cultural assets into regional economic strengths. Culture, economy, and technology are all intricately related and should be managed in a strategic way so that they can become a regional dynamism. In the above case study of Kamakura, we introduced a comprehensive structure that converts digital innovation into economic value, thereby open-

ing the way for regional economic development. Yet, we still face many challenges as we seek sustainable solutions to the problems of cultural economic development.

REFERENCES

Brown, A. (2003). Preserving the digital heritage: Building a digital archive for UK government records. *Online Information 2003 Proceedings*, 65-68.

Cegielski, M., & Janeczko, B. (2001). *Economic value of tourism to places of cultural heritage significance: A case study of three towns with mining heritage.* University of Canberra, Tourism Program. Retrieved July 9, 2006, from http://www. ahc.gov.au/publications/generalpubs/economic-tourism/pubs/heritagetourism.pdf

Chamber of Commerce and Industry of Kamakura. (2005). *Regional report in 2005.* Retrieved August 18, 2006, from http://www.shokonet. or.jp/kamakura/chiiki_1.html

Flecker, D. (2003). Digital archiving: What is involved? *EDUCAUSE Review*, 10-11.

Fukami, T., & Hayashi, T. (2002). The digital archive of the cultural heritage and these applications. *Nihon Insatsu Gakkai-Shi, 39*(3), 19-22.

Hodge, G. (2000). Best practice for digital archiving: An information life cycle approach. *D-Lib Magazine, 6*(1). Retrieved June 24, 2006, from http://www.dlib.org/dlib/january00/01hodge. html

Hodge, G., & Frangakis, E. (2004). *Digital preservation and permanent to scientific information: The state of the practice.* International Council for Scientific and Technical Information & CENDI.

IUCN. (1998). *Economic values of protected areas: Guidelines for protected area managers.* Switzerland: World Commission on Protected Areas.

Jantz, R., & Giarlo, M. (2005). Digital preservation. *D-Lib Magazine, 11*(6). Retrieved June 24, 2006, from http://www.dlib.org/dlib/june05/jantz/06jantz.html

Japan Digital Archives Association. (Ed.). (2005). *Digital archives white paper 2005.* Tokyo: Transart Inc.

Kasaba, H. (2004). *Digital archive no kochiku to unyo* [The establishment and operation of digital archives from museums to regional development]. Tokyo: Suiyosha.

Kishino, S. (2005). *Accessibility and historic environment: Perspective on the heritage management in Kamakura.* Unpublished master's thesis, University College London, Institute of Archaeology, London.

Macháček, J. (2001, April). *Social and economic integration of Cultural Heritage Advanced Research Initiation assisting and developing networks in Europe.* Paper presented at Workshops ARIADNE, Praha, the Czech Republic.

Makiuchi, K. (2000, May). *Digital archive: The infrastructure for 5th contents segment. New technology for culture: MITI approach.* Paper presented at the Ninth International World Wide Web Conference. The Web: The next Generation, Amsterdam.

Ministry of Education, Culture, Sports, Science and Technology. (2003). *FY2003 white paper on education, culture, sports, science and technology.* Tokyo: Gyosei Corporation.

Ministry of Internal Affairs and Communications. (2003). *2003 white paper information and communications in Japan.* Tokyo: Gyosei Corporation.

NINCH Working Group. (2002). *The NINCH guide to good practice in the digital representation and management of cultural heritage materials.* Humanities Advanced Technology and Information Institute, University of Glasgow, & National Institute for a Networked Cultural Heritage. Retrieved July 9, 2006, from http://www.nyu.edu/its/humanities/ninchguide/III/

Nuki, T., & Ishii, S. (1999). *Kamakura Bukyo* [Kamakura Buddhism]. Yokohama, Japan: Yurindo.

Pagiola, S. (1996). *Economic analysis of investments in cultural heritage: Insights from environmental economics.* World Bank, Environment Department.

Palumbo, G. (2002). Threats and challenges to the archaeological heritage in the Mediterranean. In J. M. Teutonico & G. Palumbo (Eds.), *Management planning for archaeological sites: An international workshop organized by the Getty Conservation.* Los Angeles, CA: Getty Conservation Institute.

Shimizu, K. (2003a). Digital archives shinsenryaku [The New Strategies for Digital Archives].

Shimizu, K. (2003b). Digital Shisan Katsuyo Senryaku Kaigi [The Strategic Council on Digital Properties].

Shimizu, K., & Miyahara, N. (2003). *Cultural heritage online plan and regional digital archives* (Tech. Rep. No. 2003-EIP-21). Japan: Information Processing Society of Japan.

Shimizu, K., & Osada, Y. (2003). *Implementation of digital archives and challenges for the future* (Tech. Rep. No. 2003-CH-60). Japan: Information Processing Society of Japan.

Shirai, E. (1999). *Kamakura jiten* [The dictionary of Kamakura]. Tokyo: Kozaido.

Takemura, M. (2001). Digital archives and cultural memory. *The Technical Report on the Institute of Image Information and Television Engineers, 55*(1), 62-69.

Uesugi, K. (2003). *Minamoto Yoritomo to Kamakura Bakufu* [Minamoto Yoritomo and Kamakura Shogunate]. Tokyo: Shin-Nihon Press.

Yamada, S. (2005). *Conflicts between the cultural diffusion and the intellectual properties protection* (Tech. Rep. No. 2005-EIP-27). Information Processing Society of Japan.

342

Compilation of References

Abdulai, D. (2004). *Can Malaysia transit into the k-economy: Dynamic challenges, tough choices and the next phase.* Selangor, Malaysia: Pelanduk Publications.

About MAI. (n.d.). Retrieved July 8, 2006, from http://www.mai.or.th/en/about/about.html

AC Nielsen. (2006). *Online shopping is here to stay.* Retrieved August 20, 2006, from http://uk.acnielsen.com/insights/OnlineShopping.shtml

Acar, Y. (2002). *İktisadi büyüme ve büyüme modelleri.* Bursa, Turkey: Vipas, A.S. Uludag University Press.

Accenture. (2004). *High performance government.* Retrieved August 28, 2005, from http://www.accenture.com

Act on the undertaking of finance business, securities business and credit foncier business, B.E. 2522. (1979). Retrieved July 27, 2006, from http://www.bot.or.th/bothomepage/General/Laws_Notif_Forms/Legal/Finance%20act/Finance-E/FinanceAct-E.htm

Adam, S., Mulye, R., Deans, K., & Palihawadana, D. (2002). E-marketing in perspective: A three country comparison of business use of the Internet. *Marketing Intelligence and Planning, 20*(4), 243-251.

Agbo, S. (2003, July). *Myths and realities of higher education as a vehicle for nation building in developing countries: The culture of the University and the new African Diaspora.* Paper presented at the Second Global Conference, Oxford, United Kingdom.

Ainin, S., Lim, C. H., & Wee, A. (2005). Prospects and challenges of e-banking in Malaysia. *The Electronic Journal of Information Systems in Developing Countries, 22,* 1-11.

Aizenman, J., & Marion, N. (2002). *The high demand for international reserves in the Far East: What's going on* (NBER Working Paper No. 9266)? Cambridge: National Bureau of Economic Research.

Akinci, S., Aksoy, S., & Atilgan, E. (2004). Adoption of Internet banking among sophisticated consumer segments in an advanced developing country. *The International Journal of Bank Marketing, 22*(3), 212-232.

Al-Ashban, A., & Burney, M. (2001). Customer adoption of tele-banking technology: The case of Saudi Arabia. *International Journal of Bank Marketing, 21*(3), 191-200.

Altman, D. (2002). Prospects for e-government in Latin America: Satisfaction with democracy, social accountability, and direct democracy. *International Review of Public Administration, 7*(2), 5-20.

Amartya, S. (Ed.) (1999). *Development as freedom.* New York: Oxford University Press.

American Electronics Association. (2001). *Cyberstates 2001: A state-by-state overview of the high-technology industry.* Santa Clara, CA: American Electronics Association.

American Electronics Association. (2002). *California Cybercities 2002.* Santa Clara, CA: American Electronics Association.

Amiti, M., & Wei, S.-J. (2004a). Demystifying outsourcing. *Finance & Development, 12,* 36-39.

Amiti, M., & Wei, S.-J. (2004b). *Fear of service outsourcing: Is it justified* (IMF Working Paper No. 04,186)? International Monetary Fund.

Andersen, T., & Bollerslev, T. (1997). Intraday periodicity and volatility persistence in financial markets. *Journal of Empirical Finance*, 115-158.

Andonova, V. (2006). Mobile phones, the Internet and the institutional environment. *Telecommunications Policy, 30*, 29-45.

Andrews, D. & Ploberger, W. (1994). Optimal tests when a nuisance parameter is present only under the alternative. *Econometrica, 62*(November), 1383-1414.

Andrews, D. (1993). Test for parameter instability and structural change with unknown change point. *Econometrica,* 61(July), 821-856.

Antonelli, C. (2003). The digital divide: Understanding the economics of new information and communication technology in the global economy. *Information Economics and Policy, 15*, 173-199.

Antonio, E. T., & Padojinog, W. C. (2003). IT-enabled services in the Philippines: Prospects and issues. *AT10 Research Conference, 2*, 20-21.

Ariav, G., & Goodman, S.E. (1994). Israel: Of swords and software plowshares. *Communications of the ACM, 37*(6), 17-21.

Arısoy, E., & Demir, R. (2001). Eğitim, haberleşme ve ticari serbestliğin ekonomik büyümeye katkısı. *Dış Ticaret Dergisi, 23.*

Arshanapalli, B., d'Ouville, E., Fabozzi, F., & Switzer, L. (2006). Macroeconomic news effects on conditional volatilities in the bond and stock markets. *Applied Financial Economics, 16*, 377-384.

Asia Development Bank (ADB). (2000). *Asian development outlook 2000 update.* Retrieved August 1, 2006, from http://www.adb.org/

Asia Development Bank (ADB). (2006a). *Asian development outlook 2006.* Retrieved August 1, 2006, from http://www. adb.org/

Asia Development Bank (ADB). (2006b). *Asian development outlook 2006 update.* Retrieved August 31, 2006, from http://www.adb.org/

Asia Development Bank (ADB). (2006c). *Key indicators 2006.* Retrieved August 1, 2006, from http://www.adb. org/

Aso, M. (1987). Joshi no kotokyoiku nitsuiteno mittsu no teigen. In Nihonjoshidaigaku Joshikyoiku-Kenkyu-Sho (Ed.), *Joshidaigakuron* (pp. 10-25). Tokyo: Domesu-Shuppan.

Asociación Española de Comercio Electrónico (AECE). (2005). *Estudio sobre comercio electrónico B2C.* Retrieved July 12, 2006, from http://www.aece.es

Astin, A. W. (1993). *What matters in college?* San Francisco: Josey-Bass.

Azari, R., & Pick, J.B. (2003a). The influence of socio-economic factors on technological change: The case of high-tech states in the U.S. In R. Azari (Ed.), *Current security management and ethical issues of information technology* (pp. 187-213). Hershey, PA: IRM Press.

Azari, R., & Pick, J.B. (2003b). Technology and society: Socio-economic influences on technological sectors for United States Counties. *International Journal of Information Management,* in press.

Ba, S. (2001). Establishing online trust through a community responsibility system. *Decision Supporting Systems, 31*(3), 323-336.

Bahmani-Oskooee, M., & Brown, F. (2002). Demand for international reserves: A review article. *Applied Economics, 34*, 1209-1226.

Baier, L. S., Dwyer, P. G., Jr., & Tamura, R. (2003). *Does opening a stock exchange increase economic growth* (Federal Reserve Bank of Atlanta Working Paper No. 2003-36)? Retrieved July 26, 2006, from http://www.frbatlanta. org/filelegacydocs/wp0336.pdf

Bailey, M. H., & Lawrence, R. Z. (2001). Do we have a new economy? *American Economic Review, 91*, 308-312.

Baily, M. (2001). Macroeconomic implications of the new economy. *Proceedings of the Symposium on Economic Policy for the Information Economy*, Federal Reserve Bank of Kansas City (August 30-September 1), pp. 201-268.

Baily, M. N., & Gordon, R. J. (1988). The productivity slowdown, measurement issues, and the explosion of computer power. *Brookings Papers on Economic Activity, 2*, 347-431.

Baker, P.M.A. (2001). Policy bridges for the digital divide: Assessing the landscape and gauging the dimensions. *First Monday* [Online], *6*(5). Available: *www.firstmonday.org*

Balduzzi, P., Elton, E. J., & Green, T. C. (2001). Economic news and bond prices: Evidence from the U.S. treasury market. *Journal of Financial and Quantitative Analysis, 36*(4), 523-543.

Bank Negara Malaysia. (2006, March). *Monthly Statistical Bulletin.*

Bank of Thailand. (2006). *BAHTNET.* Retrieved July 28, 2006, from http://www.bot.or.th/bothomepage/BankAt-Work/Payment/General/Eng_Bahtnet_New.html

Barro, R. (1979). On the determination of the public debt. *Journal of Political Economy, 87*, 940-971.

Becerra-Fernandez, I., González, A., & Sabherwal, R. (2004). *Knowledge management: Challenges, solutions and technologies.*

Becker, G. S. (1964). *Human and capital: A theoretical and empirical analysis, with special reference to education.* New York: Columbia University Press.

Ben-Bassat, A., & Gottlieb, D. (1992). Optimal international reserves and sovereign risk. *Journal of International Economics, 33*, 345-362.

Benton Foundation. (1998). *Losing ground bit by bit: Low-income communities in the information age.* Report. Washington, DC: Benton Foundation.

Bernal Vera, L. E. (2005). *Influencia de las nuevas TIC en el desempeño comercial de las PYMEs del Perú.* Unpublished master's thesis, University of Leipzig, Saxony, Germany.

Beschloss, A., & Mendess, W. (1999-2000). Reserve management policies and practices. *Central Banking, 10*(4), 88-96.

Betz, N. E., & Hackett, G. (1983). The relationship of mathematics self-efficacy expectations to the selections of science-based college majors. *Journal of Vocational Behavior, 23*, 329-345.

Bitler, M. P. (2001). *Small businesses and computers: Adoption and performance* (Working Paper No. 2001-15). San Francisco: Federal Reserve Bank of San Francisco.

Black, F. (1976). Studies of stock market volatility changes. *1976 Proceedings of the American Statistical Association, Business and Economics Statistic Section*, 177-181.

Black, N., Lockett, A., Winklhofer, H., & Ennew, C. (2001). The adoption of Internet financial services: A qualitative study. *International Journal of Retail & Distribution Management, 29*(8), 390-398.

Blackboard. (2006). Retrieved from http://www.blackboard.com/us/index.aspx

Blanning, R.W., Bui, T.X., & Tan, M. (1997). National information infrastructure in Pacific Asia. *Decision Support Systems, 21*, 215-227.

Bollerslev, T. (1986). Generalized autoregressive conditional heteroskedasticity. *Journal of Econometrics, 31*, 307-327.

Bollerslev, T., Cai, J., & Song, F. M. (2000). Intraday periodicity, long memory volatility, and macroeconomic announcement effects in the US treasury bond market. *Journal of Empirical Finance, 7*(1), 37-55.

Bond electronic exchange. (n.d.). Retrieved July 8, 2006, from http://www.bex.or.th/en/about/about.html

Bozkurt, V. (1996). *Enformasyon toplumu ve Türkiye.* Istanbul, Turkey: Sistem Press.

Bradley, L., & Stewart, K. (2002). A delphi study of the drivers and inhibitors of Internet banking. *International Journal of Bank Marketing, 20*(6), 250-260.

Braum, P. (2001). *Information and communication technology in developing countries of Asia.* Retrieved August 1, 2006, from http://www.adb.org/

Breen, J. (2000). At the dawn of e-government: The citizen as customer. *Government Finance Review, 16*(5), 15-20.

Broadbent, B. (2002). *E-learning: Present and future.* Ottawa Distance Learning Group. Retrieved October 11, 2005, from http://www.elearninghub.com/docs/ODLG_2002.pdf

Brooks, M. & Wahhaj, Z. (2000). The 'new' global economy—Part II: B2B and the Internet. *Global Economic Commentary*, Goldman Sachs, (February 9), 3-13.

Brown, A. (2003). Preserving the digital heritage: Building a digital archive for UK government records. *Online Information 2003 Proceedings*, 65-68.

Brynjolfsson, E., & Hitt, L. (1996). Paradox lost? Firm-level evidence on the returns to information systems spending. *Management Science, 42*(4), 541-558.

Brynjolfsson, E., & Hitt, L. (2000). Beyond computation: Information technology, organizational transformation and business performance. *Journal of Economic Perspectives, 14*(4), 23-48.

Brynjolfsson, E., & Yang, S. (1996). Information technology and productivity: A review of the literature. *Advances in Computers, 43*, 179-214.

Campbell, J., Lo, A., & MacKinlay, A. (1997). *The econometrics of financial markets*. Princeton University Press.

Caporale, M. G., Howells, G. A. P., & Soliman, M. A. (2004). Stock market development and economic growth. *Journal of Economic Development, 29*(1), 33-50. Retrieved July 26, 2006, from http://jed.econ.cau.ac.kr/newjed/full-text/29-1/02_J665_.PDF#search=%22economic%20development%20and%20stock%20market%20%22

CCST. (2001). *Bridging the digital divide*. Sacramento, CA: California Council on Science and Technology.

CCST. (2002). *Critical path analysis of California's science and technology education system*. Report. Sacramento, CA: California Council on Science and Technology.

Cegielski, M., & Janeczko, B. (2001). *Economic value of tourism to places of cultural heritage significance: A case study of three towns with mining heritage*. University of Canberra, Tourism Program. Retrieved July 9, 2006, from http://www.ahc.gov.au/publications/generalpubs/economic-tourism/pubs/heritagetourism.pdf

Center of the International Cooperation for Computerization (CICC). (2005). *Asia computerization report (Vietnam)*. Tokyo.

Center of the International Cooperation for Computerization (CICC). (2006). *Asia computerization report (Vietnam)*. Tokyo.

Central Bureau of Statistics (Israel). (1999, August). Exports by economic branch. *Monthly Bulletin of Statistics, 50*(8).

Central Bureau of Statistics (Israel). (1999, October). K. labour and wages. *Monthly Bulletin of Statistics, 50*(10).

Chamber of Commerce and Industry of Kamakura. (2005). *Regional report in 2005*. Retrieved August 18, 2006, from http://www.shokonet.or.jp/kamakura/chiiki_1.html

Chan, F., Ang, H. H., & Issac, B. (2005). Analysis of IEEE 802.11b wireless security for university wireless LAN design. *Proceedings of the IEEE International Conference on Networks* (ICON 2005), 1137-1142.

Chen, A.H. & Siems, T.F. (2001). B2B emarketplace announcements and shareholder wealth. *Economic and Financial Review*, Federal Reserve Bank of Dallas, First Quarter, 12-22.

Chu, X., & Dong, M. (2003). Manufacture information engineering and its implementation in enterprise. *Journal of Kunming University of Science and Technology, 3*, 49-52.

Chuang, M. L., & Shaw, W. H. (2005). A roadmap for e-business implementation. *Engineering Management Journal, 17*(2), 3-13.

Chudnovsky, D., & López, A. (1999). *Globalization and developing countries: Foreign direct investment and growth and sustainable human development*. UNCTAD/UNDP Publisher.

Chun, H. (2003). Information technology and the demand for educated workers: Disentangling the impacts of adoption versus use. *The Review of Economics and Statistics, 85*(1).

Coase, R. (1937). The nature of the firm. *Economica, 4*(16), 386-405.

Coase, R. H. (1988). *The Firm, The Market, and the Law* (chapter one). Chicago, IL: The University of Chicago Press.

Collier, P. (1998). *Social capital and poverty: Social capital initiative* (Working paper No. 4). Washington, DC: The World Bank.

Collison, C., & Parcell, G. (2004). *Learning to fly: Practical knowledge management from leading and learning organizations.* New York: Capstone Publishing.

Comisión del Mercado de las Telecomunicaciones (CMT). (2006). *Informe sobre comercio electrónico en España a través de entidades de medios de pago 2005.* Retrieved Juny 23, 2006, from http://www.cmt.es

Comparison of e-readiness assessment models. (2001). Retrieved September 10, 2006, from http://www.bridges.org/e_readiness_assessment

Conrad, A.C. (1999). *Industry sector analysis of the supply and demand of skilled labor in California.* Report. Sacramento, CA: California Council on Science and Technology.

Corsetti, G., Pesenti, P., & Roubini, N. (1998a). *What caused the Asian currency and financial crisis? Part I: A macroeconomic overview* (NBER Working Paper No. 6833). Cambridge: National Bureau of Economic Research.

Corsetti, G., Pesenti, P., & Roubini, N. (1998b). *What caused the Asian currency and financial crisis? Part II: The policy debate* (NBER Working Paper No. 6834). Cambridge: National Bureau of Economic Research.

Costanza, R. (1991). *Ecological economics: The science and management of sustainability.* New York: Columbia University Press.

Cottrill, K. (2001). E-government grows. *Traffic World, 265*(10), 19.

Council of Economic Advisers. (2001). *Economic Report of the President*, Washington, D.C.: U.S. Government Printing Office, January.

Cox, W. M. & Alm, R. (1992). *The churn: The paradox of progress.* Federal Reserve Bank of Dallas Annual Report Essay.

Crandall, R.W. (2001). The digital divide: Bridging the divide naturally. *Brookings Review, 19*(1), 38-41.

Croix, D., & Doepke, M. (2004). Public versus private education when differential fertility matters. *Journal of Development Economics, 73*(2), 607-629.

Cronin, B. (2002). The digital divide. *Library Journal, 127*(3), 48.

Cui, X., & Sun, Q. (2003). IT's application in environmental protection information systems. *Environmental Technology, 2*, 31-34.

Dahlen, M. (2002). Learning the Web: Internet user experience and response to Web marketing in Sweden. *Journal of Interactive Advertising, 3*(1), 1-3. Retrieved September 2, 2006, from http://jiad.org/vol3/no1/dahlen/index.htm

Daniel, E. (1999). Provision of e-banking in the UK and the Republic of Ireland. *International Journal of Bank Marketing, 17*(2), 72-82.

Darby, R., Jones, J., & Madani, G. A. (2003). E-commerce marketing: Fad or fiction? Management competency in mastering emerging technology: An international case analysis in the UAE. *Logistics Information Management, 16*(2), 106-113.

Darke, K., Beatriz, C., & Ruta, S. (2002). Meeting the challenge: The impact of the National Science Foundation's program for women and girls. *Journal of Women and Minorities in Science and Engineering, 8*, 285-303.

Dasgupta, S., Lall, S., & Wheeler, D. (2001). *Policy reform, economic growth, and the digital divide: An econometric analysis.* Research Paper, World Bank. Washington, D.C.: Development Research Group.

Davenport, T., & Prusak, L. (1997). *Working knowledge.* Harvard.

Davis, F. D. (1989). Perceived usefulness, perceived ease of use, and user acceptance of information technology. *MIS Quarterly, 13*(3), 319-340.

Deardorff, A.V. (1998). Technology, trade, and increasing inequality: Does the cause matter for the cure? *Journal of International Economic Law,* 353-376. Oxford University Press.

Dedrick, J.L., & Kraemer, K.L. (1995). National technology policy and computer production in Asia-Pacific countries. *Information Society, 11,* 29-58.

Dedrick, J.L., & Kraemer, K.L. (1998). *Asia's computer challenge: Threat or opportunity for the United States and the world?* New York: Oxford University Press.

Dedrick, J.L., Goodman, S.E., & Kraemer, K.L. (1995). Little engines that could: Computing in small energetic countries. *Comm. of the ACM, 38*(5), 21-26.

Deloitte & Touche Consulting Group. (1998). 1998 top 200 New Zealand companies. *Management Magazine, 45*(11), 74-87.

DeLong, J. B. & Summers, L.H. (2001). The 'new economy': Background, historical perspective, questions, and speculations. *Economic Review,* Federal Reserve Bank of Kansas City, Fourth Quarter, 29-59.

Dewan, S., Ganley, D., & Kraemer, K. L. (2005). Across the digital divide: A cross-country multi-technology analysis of the determinants of IT penetration. *Journal of the Association for Information Systems, 6*(12), 409-432.

Dierkes, M. (1992). 21st century technologies: Promises and perils of a dynamic future. *OECD.*

Dooley, M., Folkerts-Landau, D., & Garber, P. (2003). *An essay on the revived Breton Woods system* (NBER Working Paper No. 9971). Cambridge: National Bureau of Economic Research.

Dossani, R., & Kenney, M. (2005). The next wave of globalization: Exploring the relocation of service provision to India. *Berkeley Roundtable on the International Economy Working Papers, 156,* 1-41.

Downes, S. (2003). *Where the market is: IDC on e-learning.* International Data Corporation. Retrieved February 10, 2006, from http://www.downes.ca/cgi-bin/website/show.cgi?format=full&id=12

Drucker, P. (1995). *Gelecek için yönetim* (F. Üçcan, Trans.). Ankara, Turkey: Türkiye İş Bankası Press.

Duan, Q. (2005). The development and application of CAD technology in the mechanical engineering design. *Shanxi Science and Technology, 3,* 59-60.

Dun & Bradstreet Israel Ltd. (n.d.). *Leading industrial companies by sales revenue: 150 Companies.*

E-Commerce Resource Center (ECRC). (2006). *E-commerce for sustainable economic development.* Retrieved May 22, 2006, from http://www.ecommerce.or.th/about.html

Economist Intelligence Unit (EIU). (2006). *Industry briefing: Latest telecoms and technology data.* Retrieved August 20, 2006, from http://www.viewswire.com/index.asp?layout=homePubTypeEB

Economist Intelligence Unit. (2003). *The 2003 e-readiness rankings* (White paper). London: The Economist Group.

Economist Intelligence Unit. (2005). *The 2005 e-readiness rankings* (White paper). London: The Economist Group.

Ederington, L., & Lee, J. (1993). How markets process information: News releases and volatility. *Journal of Finance, 48,* 1161-1191.

Ederington, L., & Lee, J. (2001). Intraday volatility in interest-rate and foreign-exchange markets: ARCH, announcement, and seasonality effects. *The Journal of Futures Markets, 21,* 517-552.

Edmonds, C.C. (1923). Tendencies in the automobile industry. *American Economic Review,* 13, 422-441.

Edvinsson, L., & Malone, M. (1997). *Intellectual capital: Realising your company's true value by finding its hidden brainpower.* New York: HarperBusiness.

Edvinsson, L., & Malone, M. M. (1997). *Intellectual capital: Realizing our company's true value by finding its hidden brainpower.* New York: Harper Collins Publishing.

Efendioglu, A. M., & Yip, V. F. (2004). Chinese culture and e-commerce: An exploratory study. *Interacting with Computers, 16,* 45-62.

Ein-Dor, P., Myers, M.D., & Raman, K.S. (1997). IT in three small developed countries. *Journal of Management Information Systems, 13*(4), 61-89.

Epstein, D., Elwood, J., Hey, V., & Maw, J. (Eds.). (1998). *Failing boys? Issues in gender and achievement.* Buckingham, United Kingdom: Open University Press.

Erkan, H. (1998). *Bilgi toplumu ve ekonomik gelişme.* Ankara, Turkey: Türkiye Is Bankasi Cultural Press.

Erkan, H. (2000). *Bilgi uygarlığı için yeniden yapılanma.* Ankara, Turkey: Imge Publishing.

Erran, C., & Paul, T. (2005). *Offshoring information technology.* Cambridge: Cambridge University Press.

Ertek, T. (2006). *Temel ekonomi.* Istanbul, Turkey: BETA Publishing Co.

Eser, U. (1993). *Türkiye'de sanayileşme.* Ankara, Turkey: Imge Publishing.

European eLearning Industry Group (eLIG). (2006). *The European eLearning Industry Group: Promoting eLearning in Europe.* Retrieved April 21, 2006, from http://www.elig.org/

Ewha Womans University. (2004). *Ewha Womans University.* Retrieved September 14, 2006, from http://www.Ewha.ac.kr/

Faherty, R. (2002). *Corporate e-learning.* Dublin, Ireland: Dublin Institute of Technology.

Feenstra, R.C., & Hanson, G.H. (1997, June). *Productivity measurement, outsourcing, and its impact on wages: Estimates for the US, 1972-1990.* NBER Working Paper, No. 6052.

Fein, A. D., & Logan, M. C. (2003). Preparing instructors for online instruction. *New Directions for Adult and Continuing Education, 100,* 45-55. Retrieved April 23, 2006, from Wiley InterScience database.

Filer, K. R., Hanousek, J., & Campos, F. N. (1999). *Do stock markets promote economic growth* (Brooking Institute Working Paper No. 267)*?* Retrieved July 26, 2006, from http://www.brook.edu/comm/conferencereport/cr10.pdf#search=%22herring%20and%20litan%22

Fillis, I., Johannson, U., & Wagner, B. (2004). Factors impacting on e-business adoption and development in the smaller firm. *International Journal of Entrepreneurial Behavior and Research, 10*(3), 178-191.

Filotto, U., Tanzi, P., & Saita, F. (1997). Customer needs and front office technology adoption. *International Journal of Bank Marketing, 15*(1), 13-21.

Finnfacts. (1999). *50 largest Finnish companies.* Retrieved November 11, 1999: *www.finnfacts.com/Ffeng0399/record_profits.htm*

Finnish Newspapers Association. (2000). Facts about the Finnish press. Retrieved May 17, 2000: *http://www.sanomalehdet.fi/en/tietoa/graafi1.shtml#3*

Fischer, S., Rudiger, D., & Richard, S. (1988). *Economics.* New York: McGraw-Hill Publishing Company.

Flavián, C., Guinaliu, M., & Torres, E. (2005). The influence of corporate image on consumer trust: A comparative analysis in traditional versus Internet banking. *Internet Research: Electronic Networking Applications and Policy, 15*(4), 447-470.

Flecker, D. (2003). Digital archiving: What is involved? *EDUCAUSE Review,* 10-11.

Fleming, M. J., & Remolona, E. M. (1999). What moves bond prices? *Journal of Portfolio Management, 25*(4), 28-38.

Flood, R., & Marion, N. (2002). Holding international reserves in an era of high capital mobility. *Brookings Trade Forum 2001.*

Florida, R. (2002). *The rise of the creative class.* New York: Basic Books.

Florida, R., & Gates, G. (2001). *Technology and tolerance: The importance of diversity to high-technology growth.* Washington, D.C.: The Brookings Institution.

Flynn, A., Concannon, F., & Bheachain, C. N. (2005). Undergraduate students' perceptions of technology-supported learning: The case of an accounting class. *International Journal on E-Learning, 4*(4), 427-445.

Ford, D. P., Conelly, C. E., & Meister, D. B. (2003). Information systems research and Hofstede's culture consequences: An uneasy and incomplete partnership. *IEEE Transactions on Engineering Management, 50*(1), 8-25.

Forgasz, H. (1998). The typical Australian university mathematics student: Challenging myths and stereotypes? *Higher Education, 36*, 87-108.

Formaini, R. L. & Siems, T.F. (2003). New economy: Myths and reality. *Southwest Economy*, Federal Reserve Bank of Dallas, 3(May/June), 1-8.

Forsythe, S., & Shi, B. (2003). Consumer patronage and risk perceptions in Internet shopping. *Journal of Business Research, 56*, 867-875.

Fraumeni, B. M. (2001). E-commerce: Measurement and measurement issues. *American Economic Review, 91*(2), 318-322.

Freeman, C. (1992). *The economics of hope: Essays on technical change, economic growth and the environment.* London: Printer Publishers.

Freeman, C., & Soete, L. (1997). *Yenilik ıktisadı* (E. Türkcan, Trans.). Ankara, Turkey: Tubitak Press.

Fukami, T., & Hayashi, T. (2002). The digital archive of the cultural heritage and these applications. *Nihon Insatsu Gakkai-Shi, 39*(3), 19-22.

Fukuda, Y., Sudo, O., & Hayami, H. (1997). *Economics of information.* Tokyo: Yuhikaku.

Furniss, T. (2003). China: The next big wave in offshore outsourcing. *BPO Outsourcing Journal.* Retrieved July 15, 2006, from http://www.outsourcing-asia.com/china.html

Furniss, T., & Janssen, M. (2005). Offshore outsourcing. Part 1: The brand of India. *BPO Outsourcing Journal.* Retrieved July 2006 from http://www.outsourcing-asia.com/india.html

Gann, R. (1999). Every second counts. *Computing, 28*, 38-40.

Garicano, L., & Kaplan, S. N. (2001). *The effect of business-to-business e-commerce on transaction cost* (NBER Working Paper No. 8017).

Gerrard, P., & Cunningham, J. B. (2003). The diffusion of Internet banking among Singapore consumers. *The International Journal of Bank Marketing, 21*(1), 16-28.

Glossary. (n.d.). Retrieved July 10, 2006, from http://www.set.or.th/en/education/glossary/glossary_pa.html

Glosten, L., Jagannathan, R., & Runkle, D. (1993). On the relation between the expected value and the volatility of the nominal excess returns on stocks. *Journal of Finance,* 1779-1801.

Goeij, P., & Marquering, W. (2006). Macroeconomic announcements and asymmetric volatility in bond returns. *Journal of Banking & Finance, 30*, 2659-2680.

Goldstein, H. A., & Luger, M. I. (1993). Theory and practice in high-tech economic development. In R. D. Bingham & R. Mier (Eds.), *Theories of local economic development* (pp.147-169). SAGE Publications.

Goldthorpe, J. H., Lockwood, D., Bechhofer, F., & Platt, J. (1968). *The affluent worker: Industrial attitudes and behaviour.* Cambridge: Cambridge University Press.

Gordon, R. J. (2000). Does the 'new economy' measure up to the great inventions of the past? *Journal of Economic Perspectives, 14*(4), 49-74.

Gordon, R. J. (2000). Does the "new economy" measure up to the great inventions of the past? *Journal of Economic Perspectives, 14*, 49-74.

Government of Malaysia. (1996). *Seventh Malaysia plan 1996-2000.* Kuala Lumpur, Malaysia: Percetakan Nasional Malaysia.

Government of Malaysia. (1996). *Seventh Malaysia plan 1996-2000.* Kuala Lumpur, Malaysia: Percetakan Nasional Malaysia.

Government of Malaysia. (2001). *Eighth Malaysia plan 2001-2005.* Kuala Lumpur, Malaysia: Percetakan Nasional Malaysia.

Government of Malaysia. (2001a). *Eighth Malaysia plan 2001-2005.* Kuala Lumpur, Malaysia: Percetakan Nasional Malaysia.

Government of Malaysia. (2001b). *The third outline perspective plan 2001-2010.* Kuala Lumpur, Malaysia: Percetakan Nasional Malaysia.

Government of Malaysia. (2006). *Ninth Malaysia plan 2006-2010.* Kuala Lumpur, Malaysia: Percetakan Nasional Malaysia.

Government of Malaysia. (2006). *Ninth Malaysia plan 2006-2010.* Kuala Lumpur, Malaysia: Percetakan Nasional Malaysia.

GPS World. (n.d.). *The combination of GIS, GPS and RS.* Retrieved July 20, 2006, from http://www.51gps.com/Article/ShowArticle.asp?ArticleID=1070

Graetz, B. (1991). Gender, equity and participation in Australian education. *New Education, 13*(1), 3-11.

Graham, E. M., & Wada, E. (2001). Foreign direct investment in China: Effects on growth and economic performance. *SSRN.* Retrieved June 2006 from http://papers.ssrn.com/sol3/papers.cfm?abstract_id=300884

Graham, S. (2002). Bridging urban digital divides? Urban polarisation and information and communications technologies (ICTs). *Urban Studies, 39*(1), 33-36.

Gray, M. W. (1996). Recruiting and retaining graduate students in mathematical sciences and improving their chances for subsequent success. In B. Grevholm & G. Hanna (Eds.), *Gender and mathematics education* (pp. 39-44). Lund, Sweden: Lund University Press.

Greenwood, J., & Jovanovic, B. (1999). *The information technology revolution and the stock market* (NBER Working Papers No. 6931). Retrieved July 26, 2006, from http://www.nber.org/papers/w6931.pdf

Gregorio, D. D., Kassicieh, S. K., & Neto, R. D. (2005). Drivers of e-business activity in developed and emerging markets. *IEEE Transactions on Engineering Management, 52*(2), 155-166.

Griliches, Z. (1988). Productivity puzzles and R&D: Another nonexplanation. *Journal of Economic Perspectives, 2*(4), 9-21.

Grossman, G. M. (1990). Promoting new industrial activities. *OECD Economic Studies, 14*, 87-125.

Grossman, G., & Helpman, E. (1989). Growth and welfare in a small open economy. Working paper no. 2970. National Bureau of Economic Research. Cambridge, MA.

Grossman, G., & Helpman, E. (1991). *Innovation and growth in the global economy.* Cambridge, MA: MIT Press.

Gruber, H., & Verbove, F. (2001). The diffusion of mobile telecommunications services in the European Union. *European Economic Review, 45*(3), 577-589.

Hackett, G. (1985). The role of mathematics self-efficacy in the choice of math-related majors of college women and men: A path analysis. *Journal of Counseling Psychology, 32*, 47-56.

Hagel, J., III, & Ho, J. P. (2004). Capturing the real value of offshoring in Asia. *Crimson John Hagel Working Papers, 12*, 1-18.

Hall, E. T. (1976). *Beyond culture.* New York: Anchor Press.

Han, E., & Kaya, A. A. (1999). *Kalkınma ekonomisi teori ve politika.* Eskişehir, Turkey: Etam Matbaası Press.

Hanson, W. (2000). *Principles of Internet marketing.* South-Western, Thomson Learning.

Harrison, D. (1988). *The sociology of modernization and development.* London: Unwin Hyman Publishers.

Heianjogakuin. (Ed.). (2000). *Kokusai-shimpoziumu no kiroku: Ima naze joshidaigaku ka? Joshikotokyoiku no atarashii yakuwari.* Kyoto, Japan: Heianjogakuin.

Helpman, E., & Trajtenberg, M. (1994). *A time to sow and a time to reap: Growth based on general purpose technologies* (NBER Working Paper Series No. 4854).

Herring, R., & Litan, R. (2002). *The future of securities markets* (Conference Report No. 10). Retrieved July 26, 2006, from http://www.brook.edu/comm/conferencereport/crl0.pdf#search=%22herring%20and%20litan%22

Hewer, P., & Howcroft, B. (1999). Consumers distribution channel adoption and usage in the financial services industry: A review of existing approaches. *Journal of Financial Services Marketing, 3*(4), 344-358.

History of the Association of Securities Companies. (n.d.). Retrieved July 27, 2006, from http://www.asco.or.th/history.asp

History of the stock exchange of Thailand. (n.d.). Retrieved July 13, 2006, from http://www.set.or.th/en/about/history/history_p1.html#history

Ho Chi Minh City Computer Association. (2006). *Vietnam ICT outlook 2006.* Retrieved August 1, 2006, from http://www.hca,org.vn/

Ho, S.-C., Kauffman, R. J., & Liang, T.-P. (in press). A growth theory perspective on B2C e-commerce growth in Europe: An exploratory study. *Electronic Commerce Research and Applications.*

Hobijn, B., & Jovanovic, B. (2000). *The information technology revolution and the stock market: Evidence* (NBER Working Paper No. 7684). Retrieved July 26, 2006, from http://www.nber.org/papers/w7684.pdf

Hodge, G. (2000). Best practice for digital archiving: An information life cycle approach. *D-Lib Magazine, 6*(1). Retrieved June 24, 2006, from http://www.dlib.org/dlib/january00/01hodge.html

Hodge, G., & Frangakis, E. (2004). *Digital preservation and permanent to scientific information: The state of the practice.* International Council for Scientific and Technical Information & CENDI.

Hoffman, D.T.N., & Venkatesh, V. (1998). Diversity on the Internet: The relationship of race to access in usage. In A. Garmer (Ed.), *Investing in diversity: Advancing opportunities for minorities and the media* (p. 130). Washington, D.C.: The Aspen Institute.

Hofstede, G. (1980). *Culture's consequences: International differences in work-related values.* Beverly Hills, CA: Sage Publications.

Hofstede, G. (1984). *Culture's consequences.* London: Sage Publications.

Hornby, A. S. (2000). *Oxford advanced learner's dictionary of current English.* Oxford: Oxford University Press.

Horrigan, J. (2002). Online communities: Networks that nurture long-distance relationships and local ties. *Pew Internet and American Life Project.* Retrieved September 1, 2006, from http://207.21.232.103/pdfs/PIP_Communities_Report.pdf

Horton, W. (2000). *Designing Web-based training: How to teach anyone anything anywhere anytime.* New York: John Wiley and Sons, Inc.

Howcroft, B., Hamilton, R., & Hewer, P. (2002). Consumer attitude and the usage and adoption of home-based banking in the United Kingdom. *International Journal of Bank Marketing, 20*(3), 111-121.

Hu, X. (2005). Current situation of the development and trend of mechanical design technology. *Light Industry Machinery, 3*, 4-6.

Huang, K. (1995). Modeling China's demand for international reserves. *Applied Financial Economics, 5*, 357-366.

Ibrahim, A., & Goh, C.C. (1998). *Multimedia super corridor.* Kuala Lumpur, Malaysia: Leeds Publications.

Ilyasoğlu, E. (1997). *Türk bilgi teknolojisi ve gümrük birliği.* Ankara, Turkey: Türkiye Is Bankası Press.

IMD. (1999). *The world competitiveness yearbook 1999.* Lausanne.

Indjikian, R., & Siegel, D. S. (2005). The impact of investment in IT on economic performance: Implications for developing countries. *World Development, 33*(5), 681-700.

InfoDev. (2003). *E-government handbook for developing countries.* Retrieved November 6, 2004, from http://unpan1.un.org/intradoc/groups/public/documents/APCITY/UNPAN007462.pdf

Instituto Nacional de Estadística (INE). (2005). *Encuesta sobre equipamiento y uso de tecnologías de la información y comunicación en los hogares.* Retrieved February 10, 2006, from http://www.ine.es/inebase/cgi

International Labor Office. (1999). *Yearbook of labor statistics.* Geneva, Switzerland: Author.

International Labor Office. (2001). *World employment report: Life at work in the information economy.* Geneva: ILO.

International Labor Office. (2004). *Yearbook of labor statistics.* Geneva, Switzerland: Author.

International Labour Office (ILO). (2003). *Employment and social policy in respect of export processing zones (EPZs).* Retrieved July 13, 2006, from http://www.ilo.org/public/english/standards/relm/gb/docs/gb285/pdf/

International Monetary Fund (IMF). (2000). *Transition economies: An IMF perspective on progress and prospects.* Retrieved July 27, 2005, from http://www.imf.org/external/np/exr/ib/2000/110300.htm#I

International Monetary Fund. (2004). *Guidelines for foreign exchange reserve management.* Washington, DC: Author.

International Monetary Fund. (2005). *Annual report.* Washington, DC: Author.

International Trade Center. (2000). *Offshore back office operations: Supplying support services to global markets.* Geneva, Switzerland: Author & UNCTAD/WTO.

International Trade Center. (2001). *Innovating for success in the export of services: A handbook.* Geneva, Switzerland: Author & UNCTAD/WTO.

Internet Information Research Center. (2006). *Total number of Thai domains under .TH.* Retrieved July 28, 2006, from http://iir.ngi.nectec.or.th/domain/domainths.html

Islam, A. M., Khan, M., & Islam, M. M. (1994). An empirical test of the demand for international reserves. In D. K. Ghosh & E. Ortiz (Eds.), *The changing environment of international financial markets.* New York: St. Martins Press.

Ismael, J. (2001). The design of an e-learning system beyond the hype. *The Internet and Higher Education, 4*(3-4), 329-336.

Ismail, A. (1999). Malaysia. In Asian Productivity Organization (Ed.), *Changing productivity movement in Asia and Pacific: Challenges and lessons* (pp. 170-191). Tokyo: Asian Productivity Organization.

Issac, B., Chee, V. K. M., & Mohammed, L. A. (2005). Security considerations in the design of wireless networks. *Proceedings of the International Conference on Wireless Networking and Mobile Computing (ICWNMC '05)*, 136-141.

ITIM. (2006). *Geert Hofstede cultural dimensions.* Retrieved September 6, 2006, from http://www.geert-hofstede.com/hofstede_dimensions.php

IUCN. (1998). *Economic values of protected areas: Guidelines for protected area managers.* Switzerland: World Commission on Protected Areas.

Jacob, S. M., & Issac, B. (2005). Formative assessment and its e-learning implementation. *Proceedings of the International Conference on Education (ICE 2005)*, 258-263.

Jacob, S. M., Issac, B., & Sebastian, Y. (2006). Impact on student learning from traditional continuous assessment and an e-assessment proposal. *Proceedings of the 10th Pacific Asia Conference on Information Systems (PACIS 2006)*, 1482-1496.

Jantz, R., & Giarlo, M. (2005). Digital preservation. *D-Lib Magazine, 11*(6). Retrieved June 24, 2006, from http://www.dlib.org/dlib/june05/jantz/06jantz.html

Japan Bank for International Cooperation (JBIC). (2005). Survey report on overseas business operations by Japanese manufacturing companies. *JBICI Review, 13.* Retrieved August 1, 2006, from http://www.jbic.go.jp/english/research/report/review/

Japan Digital Archives Association. (Ed.). (2005). *Digital archives white paper 2005.* Tokyo: Transart Inc.

Japan Information Technology Services Industry Association (JISA). (2005). *Survey of overseas dealings in the computer software field 2005.* Retrieved August 1, 2006, from http://www.jisa.or.jp/

Jaruwachirathanakul, B., & Fink, D. (2005). Internet banking adoption strategies for a developing country: The case of Thailand. *Internet Research: Electronic Networking Applications and Policy, 15*(3), 295-311.

Javorski, M. (2005). ICT use in small and medium business in Poland growth factors and inhibitors. In *Informa-*

tion society technologies in the European research area. Academia Romana.

Jayawardhena, C., & Foley, P. (2000). Changes in the banking sector: The case of Internet banking in the UK. *Internet Research: Electronic Networking Applications and Policy, 10*(1), 19-30.

Jones, C. I. (2001). *Iktisadi buyumeye giris* (A. Sanlı & T. Ismail, Trans.). Istanbul, Turkey: Literature Press.

Jones, C. M., Lamont, O., & Lumsdaine, R. L. (1998). Macroeconomic news and bond market volatility. *Journal of Financial Economics, 47*(3), 315-337.

Jones, L. L. (2004). *Deciding where to offshore.* Retrieved June 2006 from http://www.joneslanglasalle.com/en-GB/research/

Jorgenson, D. W. & Stiroh, K.J. (2000). Raising the speed limit: U.S. economic growth in the information age. *Brookings Papers on Economic Activity,* 125-211.

Jorgenson, D. W., & Stiroh, K. J. (2000). Raising the speed limit: US economic growth in the information age. *Brookings Papers on Economic Activity, 1,* 125-235.

Jovanovic, B., & Rousseau, L. P. (2000). *Technology and the stock market: 1885-1998* (Working Paper No. 0042). Retrieved July 26, 2006, from http://www.vanderbilt.edu/Econ/wparchive/workpaper/vu00-w42.pdf

Jun, M., & Cai, S. (2001). The key determinants of Internet banking service quality: A content analysis. *The International Journal of Bank Marketing, 19*(7), 276-291.

Kahn, J. A., McConnell, M.M. & Perez-Quiros, G. (2002). On the causes of the increased stability of the U.S. economy. *Economic Policy Review,* Federal Reserve Bank of New York, (May), 183-202.

Kamae, H., & Minaki, T. (2004). Tests of efficiency in the JGB futures market in Japan. *Journal of Personal Finance and Economics, 20,* 21-45.

Kameda, A., Hashimoto, H., & Matsumoto, Y. (2000). Joshidaigaku no hatten wo saguru: America joshidaigaku shitsu hokoku. Jumonjigakuendaigaku Shakaijoho-gakubu. *Shakaijoho-So,* 129-153.

Kamsin, A. (2005). Is e-learning the solution and substitute for conventional learning? *International Journal of the Computer, the Internet and Management, 13*(3), 79-89.

Kaplinsky, R. (1990). *The economies of small: Appropriate technology in a changing world.* London: Intermediate Technology Publications.

Karataş, M. (2003). Sosyo-ekonomik gelişmede yapısal değişim. *Stratejik Araştırmalar Dergisi, 1,* 169-190.

Karataş, M., & Bekmez, S. (2005). Türkiye'nin ıktisadi gelişmesinin dış ticaret ve teknolojik ılerleme açısından değerlendirilmesi. *Celal Bayar Üniversitesi İktisadi ve Idari Bilimler Fakultesi Yönetim ve Ekonomi Dergisi, 12*(2), 105-126.

Karataş, M., & Deviren, V. N. (2005). Türkiye'nin ıktisadi gelişmesinin beşeri sermaye ıçerikli solow modeli açısından bir değerlendirmesi. *İktisat İşletme ve Finans Dergisi, 233,* 68-87.

Karjaluoto, H., Mattila, M., & Pento, T. (2002). Factors underlying attitude formation towards online banking in Finland. *International Journal of Banking Marketing, 20*(6), 261-272.

Kasaba, H. (2004). *Digital archive no kochiku to unyo* [The establishment and operation of digital archives from museums to regional development]. Tokyo: Suiyosha.

Kaslıval, P. (1995). *Development economics.* Cincinnati, OH: Thomson Publishing.

Katz, E. J., & Rice, R.E. (2002). *Social consequences of Internet use: Access, involvement, and interaction.* Cambridge, MA: MIT Press.

Kawakami, F. (1986). Joshidaigaku: Sonzoku no hoko wo saguru. In A. Amano (Ed.), *Joshikotokyoiku no zahyo* (pp. 140-150). Tokyo: Kakiuchi-Shuppan.

Kawashima, Y. H. (2004). *Daigakukyoiku to gender: Jenda wa America no daigaku wo dou kaikakushiaka.* Tokyo: Toshin-Do.

Kay, D. (2002). *E-learning market insight report: Drivers, developments, decisions.* United Kingdom: FD Learning Ltd.

Kay, J., Lublin, J., Poiner, G., & Proser, M. (1989). Not even well begun: Women in computing courses. *Higher Education, 18*, 511-527.

Kaya, A. A. (2000). *Yeniliğe dayalı endüstriyel kalkınma ve Türkiye.* Unpublished manuscript, Ege University, Faculty of Economics and Administrative Science, Izmir, Turkey.

Kearney, A. T. (2003). *Selecting a country for offshore business processing: Where to locate.* Global Management Consulting Firm. Retrieved June 2006 from http://www.atkearney.com/shared_res/pdf

Kearney, A. T. (2004). *The changing face of China: China as an offshore destination for IT and business process outsourcing.* Global Management Consulting Firm. Retrieved July 10, 2006, from http://www.atkearney.com/main.taf?/pdf

Keeley, T. (2002). Reserve management: A new era. *Central Banking, 12*(3), 71-77.

Keller, C., & Cernerud, L. (2002). Students' perceptions of e-learning in university education. *Journal of Educational Media, 27*, 56-67.

Keren, T. (2000, January 25). 99 software exports up 33% to $2 Bln. *Globes.*

Keretho, S., & Limstit, P. (2002). *E-commerce the way of business in Thailand.* National Electronics and Computer Technology Center (NECTEC).

K-III Reference Corporation. (1997). *The world almanac and book of facts 1997.*

Kim, M. (2001). Institutional effectiveness of women-only college: Cultivating students' desire to influence social conditions. *Journal of Higher Education, 72*(3), 287-321.

Kim, M. (2002). Cultivating intellectual development: Comparing women-only colleges and coeducational colleges for educational effectiveness. *Research into Higher Education, 43*(4), 447-481.

Kim, M., & Alvarez, R. (1995). Women-only colleges: Some unanticipated consequences. *The Journal of Higher Education, 66*, 641-648.

Kim, W. (2004). On the offshore outsourcing of IT projects: Status and issues. *Journal of Object Technology, 3*(3), 1-6.

Kimura, R. (2005). Onna wa rikei ni mukanainoka: Kagakugijutsu-bunya to jenda. In R. Kimura & R. Kodama (Eds.), *Kyoiku/kazoku wo jenda de katareba* (pp. 151-174). Tokyo: Hakutaku-Sha.

Kimura, T. (2001). *Dejitaru-debaido towa nanika.* Tokyo: Iwanami-Shoten.

Kirmanoğlu, H. (2000). Beşeri kalkınma ve eğitim: Sağlık hizmetleri. *İktisat Dergisi, 397-398.*

Kishino, S. (2005). *Accessibility and historic environment: Perspective on the heritage management in Kamakura.* Unpublished master's thesis, University College London, Institute of Archaeology, London.

Klein, M., Aaron, C., & Hadjimichael, B. (2001). *Foreign direct investment and poverty reduction* (World Bank Policy Research Working Paper No. 2613). World Bank.

Kleinbaum, D. G., Kupper, L. L., & Muller, K. E (1988). *Applied regression analysis and other multivariable methods.* Boston: PWS-Kent.

Kling, R., Olin, S., & Poster, M. (1991). *Postsuburban California: The transformation of Orange County since World War II.* Berkeley: University of California Press.

Koenig, E. F., Siems, T.F. & Wynne, M.A. (2002). New economy, new recession? *Southwest Economy*, Federal Reserve Bank of Dallas, 2(March/April), 11-16.

Kolodinsky, J. M., Hogarth, J. M., & Hilgert, M. A. (2004). The adoption of electronic banking technologies by US consumers. *International Journal of Bank Marketing, 22*(4), 238-259.

Koren, O. (1999, November 22). The export institute: 2000 will be a turning point in exports; will grow by 6% - to 17 billion dollars. *Ha'aretz.*

Kovačić, Z. J. (2005). The impact of national culture on worldwide e-government readiness. *Informing Science: International Journal of an Emerging Discipline, 8*, 143-158.

Kraemer, K. L., Gurbazani, V., & King, J. L. (1992). Economic development, government policy, and the diffusion of computing in Asia Pacific countries. *Public Administration Review, 52*(2), 146-156.

Kress, G. (1998, June 11). The future still belongs to boys. *The Independent (Education)*, pp. 4-5.

Krishnamurthy, S. (2003). *E-commerce management: Text and cases.* South-Western, Thomson Learning.

Laforet, S., & Lin, X. (2005). Consumers' attitudes towards online and mobile banking in China. *International Journal of Bank Marketing, 23*(5), 362-380.

Lall, S. (1992). Technological capabilities and industrialization. *World Development, 20*(2), 86-165.

Laudon, K. C., & Traver, C. G. (2004). *E-commerce: Business, technology, society* (2nd ed.). Pearson, Addison Wesley.

Leblanc, G. (1990). Customer motivations: Use and non-use of automated banking. *International Journal of Bank Marketing, 8*(4), 36-40.

Lee, E., Kwon, K., & Schumann, D. (2005). Segmenting the non-adopter category in the diffusion of Internet banking. *International Journal of Bank Marketing, 23*(5), 414-437.

Lee, H. L. & Amaral, J. (2002). Continuous and sustainable improvement through supply chain performance management. Stanford Global Supply Chain Management Forum, SGSCMF-W1-2002 (October).

Lee, H. L. & Whang, S. (2001). E-business and supply chain integration. Stanford Global Supply Chain Management Forum, SGSCMF-W2-2001 (November).

Leff, N. (1984). Externalities, information cost, and social benefit-cost analysis for economic development: An example from telecommunications. *Economic Development and Cultural Change, 32*(2), 255-276.

Lehr, B., & Lichtenberg, F. (1999). Information technology and its impact on productivity: Firm-level evidence from government and private date sources, 1977-1993. *The Canadian Journal of Economics, 32*(2), 335-362.

Lentz, R.G. (2000, August). The e-volution of the digital divide in the U.S.: A mayhem of competing metrics. *Info, 2*(4), 355-377.

Levine, R. (1996). Stock markets: A spur to economic growth. *Finance & Development.* Retrieved July 26, 2006, from http://www.imf.org/external/pubs/ft/fandd/1996/03/pdf/levine.pdf#search=%22stock%20market%20and%20economic%20development%22 & http://jed.econ.cau.ac.kr/newjed/full-text/29-1/02_J665_.PDF#search=%22stock%20market%20and%20economic%20development%22

Levine, R. (1997). Stock market, economic development, and capital control liberalization. *Perspective, 3*(5), 1-8.

Li, L., & Engle, R. (1998). *Macroeconomic announcements and volatility of treasury futures* (Discussion Paper). San Diego, CA: University of California, San Diego.

Li, Y., & Chen, D. (2006). The development and trend of mechanical CAD technology in China. *Journal of Wuhan University of Technology, 3*, 73-76.

Li, Z. l. (2005). *Promote e-government, service to environmental management, construct harmonious society.* Paper presented at the Second Meeting of the National Environmental Information Management and Technology's Application, Beijing, China.

Light, J. (2001). Rethinking the digital divide. *Harvard Educational Review, 71*(4), 709-733.

Lipscy, P. (2003). Japan's Asian Monetary Fund proposal. *Stanford Journal of East Asian Affairs, 3*(1), 93-104.

Litan, R. E. & Rivlin, A.M. (2001). Projecting the economic impact of the Internet. *American Economic Review, 91*(May), 313-317.

Liu, H. Z. (2005). *Motif address of deputy director-general of Department of Science and Technology in the State Environmental Protection Administration of China.* Paper presented at the Second Meeting of the National Environmental Information Management and Technology's Application, Beijing, China.

Lockett, A., & Litter, D. (1997). The adoption of direct banking services. *Journal of Marketing Management, 13*, 791-811.

Lohrke, F. T., McClure Franklin, G., & Frownfelter-Lohrke, C. (2006). The Internet as an information conduit: A transaction cost analysis model of US SME Internet use. *International Small Business Journal, 24*(2), 159-178.

Lucking-Reiley, D. & Spulber, D.F. (2001). Business-to-business electronic commerce. *Journal of Economic Perspectives, 15*(Winter), 55-68.

Macháček, J. (2001, April). *Social and economic integration of Cultural Heritage Advanced Research Initiation assisting and developing networks in Europe.* Paper presented at Workshops ARIADNE, Praha, the Czech Republic.

Maeda, T. (1996). Daigaku no rikei-kyoiku to joshigakusei. In Y. Muramatsu (Ed.), *Josei no rikei-noryoku wo ikasu: Senko-bunya no jenda-bunseki to teigen* (pp. 125-147). Tokyo: Nihonhyoron-Sha.

Mahathir, M. (1998). *Excerpts from the speeches of Mahathir Mohamad on the multimedia super corridor.* Selangor, Malaysia: Pelanduk Publications.

Makino, N. (2004). Joshidaigaku no saikin no doko nikansuru kenkyu: Amerikagasshukoku to Chugoku wo chushinni, Nihon joshidaigaku kyoiku gakka-no-kai. *Nigen-Kenkyu, 40,* 71-81.

Makiuchi, K. (2000, May). *Digital archive: The infrastructure for 5th contents segment. New technology for culture: MITI approach.* Paper presented at the Ninth International World Wide Web Conference. The Web: The next Generation, Amsterdam.

Malaysian Industrial Development Authority (MIDA). (2005). *Performance of the manufacturing & related services sectors 2004.* Kuala Lumpur, Malaysia: Author.

Malhotra, Y. (2000). *Knowledge management and virtual organizations.* Hershey, PA: Idea Group Publishing.

Manning, K. (1994). Metaphorical analysis in a constructivist study of college rituals. *Review of Higher Education, 18*(1), 45-60.

Manning, K. (2000). *Rituals, ceremonies, and cultural meaning in higher education.* Westport, CT: Bergin & Garvey.

Margherio, L. (1998). *An abridgement of "The Emerging Digital Economy."* Retrieved August 13, 2006, from https://www.esa.doc.gov/Reports/EmergingDig.pdf

Mariscal, J. (2005). Digital divide in a developing country. *Telecommunications Policy, 29,* 409-428.

Market surveillance. (n.d.). Retrieved July 4, 2006, from http://www.set.or.th/en/operation/supervision/surveillance_p1.html

Marshall, J. J., & Heslop, L. A. (1988). Technology acceptance in Canadian retail banking: A study of consumer motivations and the use of ATMs. *International Journal of Bank Marketing, 6*(4), 31-41.

Maru, J. (1997). The role of institutional investors in the development of Asian stock markets: Singapore, Malaysia, and Thailand (Part 1). *Newsletter, 7,* 1-4. Retrieved August 2, 2006, from http://www/ier.hit-u.ac.jp/COE/japanese/Newsletter/No.7.english/junko.html

Massachusetts Institute of Technology (MIT). (2005). *2004 Program Evaluation Findings Report.* MIT OpenCourseWare. Retrieved July 28 from http://ocw.mit.edu/OcwWeb/Global/AboutOCW/evaluation.htm

Matambalaya, F., & Wolf, S. (2001). The role of ICT for the performance of SMEs in East Africa: Empirical evidence from Kenya and Tanzania. *ZEF Discussion Papers on Development Policy, 42.* Retrieved September 8, 2006, from http://www.zef.de/711.0.html

Matsuzawa, K. (2000). Ima naze joshidaigaku ka? Joshidaigaku no sonzoku-igi. In Heianjogakuin (Ed.), *Kokusai-shimpoziumu no kiroku: Ima naze joshidaigaku ka? Joshikotokyoiku no atarashii yakuwari* (pp. 18-27). Kyoto, Japan: Heianjogakuin.

Mattila, M., Karjaluoto, H., & Pento, T. (2003). Internet banking adoption among mature customers: Early majority or laggards? *Journal of Service Marketing, 17*(5), 514-528.

McClelland, D. C. (1961). *The achieving society.* New York: van Nostrand Publishers.

McConnell, M. M. & Perez-Quiros, G. (2000). Output fluctuations in the United States: What has changed since the early 1980s? *American Economic Review,* 90(December), 1464-1476.

McFarlan, F. (1984). Information technology changes the way you compete. *Harvard Business Review, 62*(3), 98-103.

McKinsey Global Institute (2005c). *The emerging global labor market. Part III: How supply and demand for offshore talent meet.* Retrieved August 2006 from http://www. mckinsey.com/mgi/publications/emerginggloballabor-market/index.asp

McKinsey Global Institute. (2003). *Offshoring: Is it a win-win game?* Retrieved June 25, 2006, from http://www. mckinsey.com/mgi/publications/win_win_game.asp

McKinsey Global Institute. (2005a). *The emerging global labor market. Part I: The demand for offshore talent in services.* Retrieved June 2006 from http://www.mckinsey. com/mgi/publications/emerginggloballabormarket/index. asp

McKinsey Global Institute. (2005b). *The emerging global labor market. Part II: The supply of offshore talent in services.* Retrieved June 2006 from http://www.mckinsey. com/mgi/publications/emerginggloballabormarket/index. asp

Metros, S. (2003). *E-learning implementation strategy and plan.* Retrieved April 21, 2006, from http://telr.osu. edu/resources/ITelearning.pdf

Miller, D.C. (1991). *Handbook of research design and social measurement* (5th ed.). Sage Publication.

Mills College. (2006). *Mills College.* Retrieved September 14, 2006, from http://www.mills.edu/

Minaki, T. (2005). Volatility, spread, volume of JGB futures and macroeconomic announcements. *The Hitotsubashi Review, 134*(5), 231-255.

Minaki, T. (2006). The efficiency test of JGB futures market: Evidence from TSE and SGX. *Journal of Personal Finance and Economics, 22-23,* 177-193.

Minges, M., & Gray, V. (2002). *Multimedia Malaysia: Internet case study.* International Telecommunication Union (ITU).

Ministry of Commerce. (1999, April). *Statistics on information technology in New Zealand.* Wellington.

Ministry of Economy, Trade, and Industry (MEIT). (2006). *2006 white paper on international economy and trade.* Retrieved August 31, 2006, from http://www.meti.go.jp/

Ministry of Education, Culture, Sports, Science and Technology. (2003). *FY2003 white paper on education, culture, sports, science and technology.* Tokyo: Gyosei Corporation.

Ministry of Finance. (2001). *Economic report 2001/2002.* Kuala Lumpur, Malaysia: Percetakan Nasional Malaysia.

Ministry of Finance. (2002). *Economic report 2002/2003.* Kuala Lumpur, Malaysia: Percetakan Nasional Malaysia.

Ministry of Finance. (2006). *Economic report 2006/2007.* Kuala Lumpur, Malaysia: Percetakan Nasional Malaysia.

Ministry of Internal Affairs and Communications. (2003). *2003 white paper information and communications in Japan.* Tokyo: Gyosei Corporation.

Ministry of Internal Affairs and Telecommunication. (2006). *2006 White paper on information and communications in Japan.* Retrieved August 31, 2006, from http://www.soumu. go.jp/menu_05/hakusyo/index.html

Ministry of International Trade and Industry. (2004). *Malaysia international trade and industry report 2004.* Kuala Lumpur, Malaysia: Ampang Press.

Miyake, E. (2003). Josei-kotokyoiku to empowament no kanosei: Doshishajoshidaigaku-sotsugosei nimiru joseizo, doshishajoshidaigaku. *Doshishajoshidaigaku Gakujut-sukenkyu Nempo, 54*(2), 21-57.

Mockaitis, A. (2002). *The influence of national cultural values on management attitudes: A comparative study across three countries.* Unpublished doctoral dissertation, Management and Administration, Vilnius University, Vilnius, Lithuania.

Mody, A., & Dahlman, C. (1992). Performance and potential of information technology: An international perspective. *World Development, 20*(12), 1703-1719.

Mohannak, K., & Turpin, T. (Eds.). (2002). *Innovation knowledge systems and regional development*. Edward Elgar Publishing.

Mols, N. P. (1998). The behavioural consequences of PC banking. *International Journal of Bank Marketing, 16*(5), 195-201.

Mols, N. P. (2000). The Internet and services marketing: The case of Danish retail banking. *Internet Research: Electronic Networking Applications and Policy, 10*(1), 7-18.

Money and Financial Section Department of Economic Research Bank of Thailand. (1980). Financial institutions in Thailand. *Bank of Thailand Quarterly Bulletin, 3*, 22.

Moon, J. M. (2002). The evolution of e-government among municipalities: Rhetoric or reality? *Public Administration Review, 62*(4), 424-433.

Moschella, D., & Atkinson, R. D. (1998). *The Internet and society: Universal access, not universal service*. Washington, DC: Progressive Policy Institute.

Mount Holyoke College. (2006). *Mount Holyoke College*. Retrieved September 15, 2006, from http://ww.mtholyoke.edu/

Mukherjee, A., & Nath, P. (2003). A model of trust in online relationship banking. *International Journal of Bank Marketing, 21*(1), 5-15.

Müller-Falcke, D. (2002). Use and impact of information and communication technologies in developing countries' small businesses: Evidence from Indian small scale industry. In *Development economics and policy*. Frankfurt am Main, Germany: Peter Lang Pub.

Multimedia Development Corporation (MDC). (1996). *Investing in Malaysia's MSC: Policies, incentives & facilities*. Kuala Lumpur, Malaysia: Author.

Multimedia Development Corporation (MDC). (2003). *National report on the ICT sector in Malaysia*. Unpublished manuscript.

Muramatsu, Y. (1996). Preface: Senko-bunya no jeda-bunseki no igi to kenkyu no gaiyo. In Y. Muramatsu (Ed.), *Josei no rikei-noryoku wo ikasu: Senko-bunya no jenda-bunseki to teigen* (pp. 1-16). Tokyo: Nihonhyoron-Sha.

Mutula, S. M., & van Brakel, P. (2006). An evaluation of e-readiness assessment tools with respect to information access: Towards an integrated information rich tool. *International Journal of Information Management, 26*, 212–223.

Myers, M. D., & Tan, F. B. (2002). Beyond models of national culture in information systems research. *Journal of Global Information Management, 10*(1), 24-32.

Napier, A., Rivers, O., Wager, S., & Napier, J. B. (2006). *Creating a winning e-business* (2nd ed.). Thomson, Course Technology.

Nara Women's University. (2004). *Nara Women's University*. Retrieved September 14, 2006, from http://www.nara-wu.ac.jp/

Nath, R., & Murthy, V. N. R. (2003). An examination of the relationship between digital divide and economic freedom: An international perspective. *Journal of International Technology and Information Management, 12*(1), 15-23.

Nath, R., & Murthy, V. N. R. (2004). A study of the relationship between Internet diffusion and culture. *Journal of International Technology and Information Management, 13*(2), 123-132.

National Computer Board, Singapore. (1998). *IT Focus.*

National Electronics Computer and Technology Center (NECTEC). (2006). *The number of Internet users in Thailand*. Retrieved July 28, 2006, from http://www.nectec.or.th/Internet/#iu

National Environmental Monitoring Center of China. (2006). *Data delivering and interface standard technological criterion of pollution sources on line automatic monitoring systems (exposure draft)*. Retrieved July 20, 2006, from http://www.zhb.gov.cn/epi-sepa/zcfg/w3/download/banhan2005-344-2.doc

National Environmental Monitoring Center of China. (n.d.-a). *Brief introduction of water quality auto-monitoring weekly report*. Retrieved from http://www.cnemc.cn/emc/indexs.asp?id=2&cid=26

National Environmental Monitoring Center of China. (n.d.-b). *Construction of urban air quality auto-monitoring system.* Retrieved from http://www.cnemc.cn/country/index.asp?id=1&cid=6

National Telecommunication Information Administration (NTIA). (2000). *Falling through the Net: Towards digital inclusion.* Washington, D.C.: U.S. Department of Commerce.

National Telecommunication Information Administration (NTIA). (2002). *A nation on line: How Americans are expanding the use of Internet.* Washington, D.C.: U.S. Department of Commerce.

National Women's Education Center (NWEC). (2006). *Number of universities and junior college.* Retrieved September 25, 2006, from http://www.nwec.jp/

Nelson, D. B. (1991). Conditional heteroskedasticity in asset returns: A new approach. *Econometrica, 59,* 347-370.

Nelson, D. J., & Rogers, D. C. (2004). *A national analysis of diversity in science and engineering faculties at research universities.* Retrieved September 5, 2006, from http://www.org/issues/diverse/diversity_report.pdf

Neter, J., Kutner, M.H., Nachtsheim, C.J., & Wasserman, W. (1996). *Applied linear statistical models.* Boston: WCB/McGraw-Hill.

New momentum for an Asian Monetary Fund. (2005, May 13). *Asia Pacific Bulletin.*

New Zealand Company Registrar 1996-97 (35th ed.). (1999, April). Prepared by Headliner Publishing Co. Published by Mercantile Gazette Marketing Ltd., Christchurch.

Nichell, S., & Nicolitsas, D. (2000). Human capital, investment and innovation: What are the connections? In R. Barrell, G. Mason, & M. O'Mahony (Eds.), *Productivity, innovation and economic performance.* Cambridge University Press.

Niddifer, J., & Bashaw, C. T. (2001). *Women administrators in higher education.* Albany, NY: Sate University of New York Press.

Nie, Q. H. (Ed.). (2005). *Digital environment.* Beijing, China: Science Press.

Nielsen/Netratings. (2006). *Global Internet trends.* Retrieved July 26, 2006, from http://www.nielsen-netratings.com

Nihonjoshidaigkau Sogokenkyusho. (1999). *Daigaku-sotsugyo 20 nengo no josei no seikatu/seikatsuishiki/daigakuhyoka nikansuru chosa-hokokusho: Joshidaig-kaushusshin/kyogakudaigakushusshinbetsu-bunsekikekka.* Tokyo: Nihonjoshidaigkau.

NINCH Working Group. (2002). *The NINCH guide to good practice in the digital representation and management of cultural heritage materials.* Humanities Advanced Technology and Information Institute, University of Glasgow, & National Institute for a Networked Cultural Heritage. Retrieved July 9, 2006, from http://www.nyu.edu/its/humanities/ninchguide/III/

Nisar, T. (2002). Organizational determinants of e-learning. *Industrial and Commercial Training, 34*(7), 256-262.

Nishimura, K., Hirata, J., Yagi, M., & Urasaka, J. (2001). Sugaku-kyoiku ga jinzai wo tsukuru. In K. Nishimura (Ed.), *"Honto no ikiru chikara" wo ataeru kyoiku towa* (pp. 38-58). Tokyo: Nihon-Keizai-Shimbunsha.

Noll, R.G., Older-Aguilar, D., Ross, R.R., & Rosston, G.L. (2001). The digital divide: Definitions, measurements, and policy issues. *Bridging the digital divide* (pp. 1-12). Sacramento, CA: California Council on Science and Technology.

Nordhaus, W.D. (2002). Productivity growth and the new economy. *Brookings Papers on Economic Activity*, 2, 211-266.

North, D. (1995). The new institutional economics and third world development. In J. Harriss, J. Hunter, & C. Lewis (Eds.), *The new institutional economics and third world development.* London: Routledge.

Norton, S. (1992). Transaction cost, telecommunications, and the microeconomic growth. *Economic Development and Cultural Change, 41*(1), 175-196.

Nuki, T., & Ishii, S. (1999). *Kamakura Bukyo* [Kamakura Buddhism]. Yokohama, Japan: Yurindo.

Nygard, A.M., & Kunnas, T. (1998). *Computer networking hardware/software.* Finland: Int. Trade Administration.

Nysween, H., & Pedersen, P. E. (2002). An exploratory study of customers' perception of company Websites offering various interactive applications: Moderating effects of customers' Internet experience. *Decision Support Systems, 10*(46), 1-14.

NZ Computer Industry Directory 1999. (1999) A Computerworld publication. Published by IDG Communications.

Oates, M. J., & Wiliamson, S. (1978). Women's colleges and women achievers. *Signs: Journal of Women in Culture and Society, 3,* 795-806.

Ochanomizu University. (2006). *Ochanomizu University.* Retrieved September 14, 2006, from http://www.ocha.ac.jp/

OECD. (2000). *OECD small and medium enterprise outlook.* Paris.

Ogawa, M. (2001). *Feminizumu to kagaku/gijutsu.* Tokyo: Iwanami-Shoten.

Oliner, S. D., & Sichel, D. E. (1994). Computers and output growth revisited: How big is the puzzle? *Brookings Papers on Economic Activity, 2,* 273-334.

Oliner, S.D. & Sichel, D.E. (2000). The resurgence of growth in the late 1990s: Is information technology the story? *Journal of Economic Perspectives,* 14(4), 3-32.

Organismo Supervisor de Inversión Privada en Telecomunicaciones (OSIPTEL). (2005). Cabinas públicas de acceso a Internet por modalidad de acceso. *OSIPTEL Statistics.* Retrieved September 8, 2006, from http://www.osiptel.gob.pe/InfoEstadistica/Internet%(6)_C6.7.xls

Organization for Economic Cooperation and Development (OECD). (2004). *Science, technology and industry: Outlook 2004.*

Organization for Economic Cooperation and Development (OECD). (2004). *ICT, e-business and SMEs.* Retrieved

September 8, 2006, from http://www.oecd.org/dataoecd/32/28/34228733.pdf

Organization for Economic Cooperation and Development (OECD). (2004). *Education at a glance: OECD indicators 2004.* Paris: Author.

Otto, A. (2003). *Handbook of international banking.* MA: Edward Elgar Publishing.

Pagiola, S. (1996). *Economic analysis of investments in cultural heritage: Insights from environmental economics.* World Bank, Environment Department.

Palumbo, G. (2002). Threats and challenges to the archaeological heritage in the Mediterranean. In J. M. Teutonico & G. Palumbo (Eds.), *Management planning for archaeological sites: An international workshop organized by the Getty Conservation.* Los Angeles, CA: Getty Conservation Institute.

Payne, R. J., & Nassar, J. R. (2003). *Politics and culture in the developing world: The impact of globalization.* New York: Longman Publishers.

Piek, H. (1998). *Technology development in rural industries.* London: Intermediate Technology Publications Ltd.

Pikkarainen, T., Pikkarainen, K., Karjaluoto, H., & Pahnila, S. (2004). Consumer acceptance of online banking: An extension of the technology acceptance model. *Internet Research: Electronic Networking Applications and Policy, 14*(3), 224-235.

Polatoglu, V. N., & Ekin, S. (2001). An empirical investigation of the Turkish consumers' acceptance of Internet banking services. *International Journal of Bank Marketing, 19*(4), 156-165.

Porter, M., & Millar, V. (1985). How information gives you competitive advantage. *Harvard Business Review, 63*(4), 149-160.

President-Sha. (2006). *President.* Tokyo: Author.

Pringle, R., & Weller, B. (1999). *Reserve management and the international financial system.* London: Central Banking Publications.

Prugh, T., Costanza, R., Daly, H., & Goodland, R. (1999). *Natural capital and human economic survival*. Boca Raton, FL: CRC Press-Lewis Publishers.

Rao, S. S. (2005). Bridging digital divide: Efforts in India. *Telematics and Informatics, 22*, 361-375.

Robinson, K. K., & Crenshaw, E. M. (1999). *Cyber-space and post-industrial transformations: A cross-national analysis of Internet development*. Retrieved May 10, 2004, from http://www.soc.sbs.ohio-state.edu/emc/RobisonCrenshawCyber1a.pdf

Romer, P. (1986). Increasing returns and long run growth. *Journal of Political Economy, 94*, 1002-1037.

Romer, P.M. (1990). Endogenous technological change. *The Journal of Political Economy, 98*(5), Part 2, S71-S102.

Rosenberg, M. J. (2001). *E-learning: Strategies for delivering knowledge in the digital age*. New York: McGraw-Hill.

Rubin, A. M., & Perse, E. M. (1988). Audience activity and soap opera involvement. *Human Communication Research, 14*(2), 246-268.

Ruengsrichaiya, K. (2004). On the effects of e-commerce: Equilibrium and existence of markets. *Thammasat Economic Journal, 22*(2), 139-181.

Rules & regulation. (n.d.). Retrieved July 6, 2006, from http://www.set.or.th/en/rules/rules.html

Saeed, K. A., Grover, V., & Hwang, Y. (2005). The relationship of e-commerce competence to customer value and firm performance: An empirical investigation. *Journal of Management Information Systems, 22*(1), 223-256.

Sagebiel, F., & Dahmen, J. (2006). Masculinities in organizational cultures in engineering education in Europe: Results of the European Union project WomEng. *European Journal of Engineering Education, 31*(1), 5-14.

Şahin, S. (1997). *Türkiye'de bilim ve teknoloji politikası*. Istanbul, Turkey: Gocebe Press.

Salvatore, D. (2004). *Managerial economics in a global economy* (5th ed.). South-Western, Thomson Learning.

Şanlısoy, S. (1999). Bilgi toplumunda ortaya çıkabilecek sorunlar. *D.E.Ü. İktisadi ve İdari Bilimler Fakültesi Dergisi, 14*(2), 169-184.

Sathye, M. (1999). Adoption of Internet banking by Australian consumers: An empirical investigation. *International Journal of Bank Marketing, 17*(7), 324-334.

Schultz, T. W. (1961). Education and economic growth. In N. B. Henry (Ed.), *Social forces influencing American education*. Chicago: University of Chicago Press.

Schumer, C. E., & Graham, L. O. (2005, June 8). Will it take a tariff to free the yuan? *The New York Times*.

Schumpeter, J. A. (1950). *Capitalism, Socialism, and Democracy* (third ed.). New York: Harper and Brothers.

Schumpeter, J.A. (1939). *Business Cycles: A Theoretical, Historical, and Statistical Analysis of the Capitalist Process*. New York: McGraw-Hill.

Section 14 of Securities and Exchange Act B.E. 2535. (1992). Retrieved July 27, 2006, from http://www.sec.or.th/en/enforce/regulate/secact1_e.shtml#sect8

SET Group. (n.d.). Retrieved July 1, 2006, from http://www.set.or.th/en/about/setgroup/setgroup_p1.html

Seymour, E. (1995a). Guest comment: Why undergraduates leave the sciences. *American Journal of Physics, 63*(3), 199-202.

Seymour, E. (1995b). The loss of women from science, mathematics, and engineering undergraduate majors: An explanatory account. *Science Education, 79*(4), 437-473.

Sharma, S. K., & Gupta, J. D. N. (2003). Building blocks of an e-government: A framework. *Journal of Electronic Commerce in Organizations, 1*(4), 1-15.

Shimizu, K. (2003a). Digital archives shin-senryaku [The New Strategies for Digital Archives].

Shimizu, K. (2003b). Digital Shisan Katsuyo Senryaku Kaigi [The Strategic Council on Digital Properties].

Shimizu, K., & Miyahara, N. (2003). *Cultural heritage online plan and regional digital archives* (Tech. Rep. No. 2003-EIP-21). Japan: Information Processing Society of Japan.

Shimizu, K., & Osada, Y. (2003). *Implementation of digital archives and challenges for the future* (Tech. Rep. No. 2003-CH-60). Japan: Information Processing Society of Japan.

Shirai, E. (1999). *Kamakura jiten* [The dictionary of Kamakura]. Tokyo: Kozaido.

Shirhattikar, G. (2005). Future winners and losers in global outsourcing. *Journal of International Business*. Retrieved June 2006 from http://www2.gsb.columbia.edu/journals/files/chazen/Global_Outsourcing_CWJ_Final

Sidaoui, J. J. (2005). *Policies for international reserve accumulation under a floating exchange rate regime: The experience of Mexico (1995-2003). Globalization and monetary policy in emerging markets* (BIS Paper No. 23). Basle: Bank of International Settlements.

Sidorenko, A., & Findlay, C. (2001). The digital divide in East Asia. *Asia-Pacific Economic Literature, 15*, 18-30.

Siems, T. F. (2001b). B2B e-commerce and the search for the holy grail. *Journal of e-Business and Information Technology*, (Fall), 5-12.

Siems, T.F. (2001a). B2B e-commerce: Why the new economy lives. *Southwest Economy*, Federal Reserve Bank of Dallas, 2(July/August), 1-5.

Simens, G. (2004). *Learning management systems: The wrong place to start learning*. Retrieved June 20, 2006, from http://www.elearnspace.org/Articles/lms.htm

Slowinski, J. (2000). Workforce literacy in an information age: Policy recommendations for developing an equitable high-tech skills workforce. *First Monday*, [Online], *5*(7). Available: www.firstmonday.org

Smith College. (2006) *Smith College*. Retrieved September 14, 2006, from http://www.smith.edu/

Smith, A. (1776). *An Inquiry into the Nature and Causes of the Wealth of Nations*. Reprinted in 1937, edited by Edwin Cannan. New York: The Modern Library, 423.

Smiths, D. G. (1990). Women's colleges and coed colleges: Is there a difference for women? *Journal of Higher Education, 61*(2), 181-195.

Smiths, D. G., Wolf, L. E., & Morrison, D. E. (1995). Paths to success: Factors related to the impact of women's colleges. *Journal of Higher Education, 66*(3), 245-266.

So, A. (1991). *Social change and development*. Newbury Park, CA: Sage Publications.

Solow, R. M. (1987, July 12). We'd better watch out. *The New York Times Book Review*, p. 36.

Song, X. (2000). Comprehensive introduction of CAD for machine. *Metallurgical Collection, 6*, 43-45.

Song, Y., & Gao, S. (2005). Networked in manufacturing technology and application in metalforming machinery. *China Metalforming Equipment Manufacturing Technology, 6*, 19–22.

Sookmyng Women's University. (2004). *Sookmyng Women's University*. Retrieved September 14, 2006, from http://e.sookmyng.ac.kr/

Sørnes, J.-O., Stephens, K. K., Sætre, A. S., & Browning, L. D. (2004). The reflexivity between ICTs and business culture: Applying Hofstede's theory to compare Norway and the United States. *Informing Science: International Journal of an Emerging Discipline, 7*, 1-30.

Soyak, A. (1996). *Teknolojik gelişme ve özelleştirme*. Istanbul, Turkey: Ekonomiye Yaklaşım.

State Institute of Statistics (DIE). (2002). *Yoksulluk çalışması: 2002*. Ankara, Turkey.

Statistics Finland. (1999a). *On the road to the Finnish information society - Summary*. Retrieved from http://www.stat.fi/tk/yr/tttietoti_en.html

Statistics Finland. (1999b). *Production and foreign trade of high-technology products*. Retrieved from http://www.stat.fi/tk/yr/tthuippu1_en.html

Statistics New Zealand. (1998). *New Zealand official yearbook* (101st ed.). Wellington, NZ: Department of Statistics.

Steven, L. K., & Session, D. N. (2005). *The relationship between poverty, economic growth, and inequality revisited* (ewp-ge/0502002). Retrieved March 15, 2006, from http://econwpa.wustl.edu/eprints/ge/papers/0502/0502002. abs#viewing

Stiglits, J. E., & Walsh, C. E. (2002). *Economics* (3rd ed.). New York: W. W. Norton & Company.

Stiroh, K. J. (2002). Information technology and the U.S. productivity revival: What do the industry data say? *American Economic Review, 92*(5), 1559-1577.

Strauss, J., El-Ansary, A., & Frost, R. (2003). *E-marketing* (3rd ed.). Prentice Hall.

Strauss, J., El-Ansary, A., & Frost, R. (2006). *E-marketing* (4th ed.). Pearson Prentice Hall.

Streeten, P. (1982). Approaches to a new international economic order. In *World development report*. New York: Oxford University Press.

Suganthi, B., Balachandher, K., & Balachandran, K. (2001). Internet banking patronage: An empirical investigation of Malaysia. *Journal of Banking and Commerce, 6*(1). Retrieved May 22, 2001, from http://www.arraydev.com/commerce/jibc/0103_01.htm

Sugita, T. (1996). Nihonshakai to joshigakusei. In N. Toshitani, Y. Yuzawa, T. Sodei, & E. Shinozuka (Eds.), *Kogakurekijidai no josei: Joshidaigaku karano messeji* (pp. 22-39). Tokyo: Yuhikaku.

Sundarraj, R., & Wu, J. (2005). Using information-systems constructs to study online and telephone-banking technologies. *Electronic Commerce Research and Applications, 4*, 427-443.

Suresh, J. K., & Mahesh, K. (2006). *Ten steps to maturity in knowledge management: Lessons in economy*. Oxford: Chandos.

Takemura, M. (2001). Digital archives and cultural memory. *The Technical Report on the Institute of Image Information and Television Engineers, 55*(1), 62-69.

Tel-Aviv Stock Exchange. *Electronics and computer listings*. Retrieved November 17, 1999, from http://www.tase.co.il/qsystem/index.cgi?subsection

The Economist. (1999). *Pocket world in figures*. London: Profile Books.

The Economist. (2000, April 29-May 5). *Asian capitalism: The end of tycoons*.

The Stock Exchange of Thailand annual report 1999. (2000). Retrieved July 13, 2006, from http://www.set.or.th/en/about/about.html

The Stock Exchange of Thailand annual report 2000. (2001). Retrieved July 13, 2006, from http://www.set.or.th/en/about/about.html

The Stock Exchange of Thailand annual report 2001. (2002). Retrieved July 13, 2006, from http://www.set.or.th/en/about/about.html

The Stock Exchange of Thailand annual report 2002. (2003). Retrieved July 13, 2006, from http://www.set.or.th/en/about/about.html

The Stock Exchange of Thailand annual report 2003. (2004). Retrieved July 13, 2006, from http://www.set.or.th/en/about/about.html

The Stock Exchange of Thailand annual report 2004. (2005). Retrieved July 13, 2006, from http://www.set.or.th/en/about/about.html

The Stock Exchange of Thailand annual report 2005. (2006). Retrieved July 13, 2006, from http://www.set.or.th/en/about/about.html

The Thailand Securities Depository. (n.d.). Retrieved July 27, 2006, from http://www.tsd.co.th/

Thomas, C. (2000). E-markets 2000. In G. Saloner & A.M. Spence (Eds.), *Creating and Capturing Value: Perspectives and Cases on Electronic Commerce* (pp. 253-285). New York: John Wiley & Sons.

Thomas, M. (2005). *E-learning on the move, May 2005*. Retrieved April 25, 2006, from http://education.guardian.co.uk/elearning/comment/0,10577,1490476,00.html

Tidball, M. E. (1973). Perspective on academic women and affirmative action. *Educational Record, 54*(2), 130-135.

Tidball, M. E. (1985). Baccalaureate origins of entrants into American medical schools. *Journal of Higher Education, 56*, 385-402.

Tidball, M. E. (1986). Baccalaureate origins of recent natural science doctorates. *Journal of Higher Education, 57*, 660-620.

Todaro, M. P. (1989). *Economic development in the third world.* Longman Group Ltd.

Toyokeizaishimpo-Sha. (2006). *Yakuin shikiho data text.* Tokyo: Toyokeizaishimpo-Sha.

Trading system. (n.d.). Retrieved July 4, 2006, from http://www.set.or.th/en/operation/operation.html

Trinity College. (2006) *Trinity College: Education for global leadership.* Retrieved September 24, 2006, from http://www.trinitydc.edu/

Trompenaars, F. (1994). *Riding the waves of culture.* London: Nicholas Brealey.

Trow, M. (1991). *University and society: Essays on the social role of research and higher education.* London: Jessica Kingsley Publishers.

Tsuda College. (2006). *Tsuda College.* Retrieved September 24, 2006, from http://www.tsuda.ac.jp/

Tunca, M. Z., & Sutcu, A. (2006). Use of statistical process control charts to assess Web quality: An investigation of online furniture stores. *International Journal of Electronic Business, 4*(1), 40-55.

Tunca, M. Z., Ipcioglu, I., & Zairi, M. (2004). Barriers to online retail activities in emerging economies: The case of Turkey. *International Journal of Applied Marketing, 1*(1), 1-10.

Turpin, T., Xielin, L., Garrett-Jones, S., & Burns, P. (Eds.). (2002). *Innovation, technology policy and regional development.* Edward Elgar Publishing.

U.S. Bureau of the Census. (1999). Report WP/98. *World population profile, 1998.* Washington, D.C.: U.S. Government Printing Office. Retrieved from http://www.census.gov/ftp/pub/ipc/www

U.S. Census Bureau. (2006). *Quarterly retail e-commerce sales 2nd quarter 2006.* Retrieved July 28, 2006, from http://www.census.gov/mrts/www/data/html/06Q2.html

U.S. Census. (2001). *City and county data book.* Washington, D.C.: U.S. Census.

U.S. Census. (2003a). *U.S. census of population, 2000.* Washington, D.C.: U.S. Census. Available: www.census.gov

U.S. Census. (2003b). *County business patterns. Detailed NAICS classified data.* Washington, D.C.: U.S. Census. Available: www.census.gov

Udogu, I. E. (2004). African development and the immigration of its intelligentsia: An overview. *A Journal of African Migration, 3.* Retrieved September 2, 2006, from http://www.africamigration.com/

Uesugi, K. (2003). *Minamoto Yoritomo to Kamakura Bakufu* [Minamoto Yoritomo and Kamakura Shogunate]. Tokyo: Shin-Nihon Press.

Ul-Haq, M. (1972). Employment and income distribution in the 1970s: A new perspective. *Development Digest, 9*(4), 3-8.

UNCTAD. (1972). *Guidelines for the study of the transfer of technology.* New York: United Nations Press.

UNCTAD. (2003). *E-commerce and development.* New York.

UNCTAD. (2004). Handbook of statistics. New York.

UNESCO Institute for Statistics. *Public expenditure on education as percentage of gross national product and as percentage of government expenditure.* Retrieved September 28, 2000, from http://unescostat.unesco.org/i_pages/IndPGNP.asp

UNESCO Institute for Statistics. *UNESCO statistical yearbook 1999.* Science and technology: III.1 Selected R&D indicators. Retrieved from http://unescostat.unesco.org/statsen/statistics/yearbook/tables/

UNESCO Institute for Statistics. *UNESCO statistical yearbook 1999. Science and technology: III.3 Percentage distribution of gross domestic expenditure on R&D by source of funds.* Retrieved from http://unescostat. unesco.org/statsen/statistics/yearbook/tables\SandTec\

United Nations Development Program. (1999). Human Development Index (HDI). *Human development report 1999*. Retrieved July 7, 2000, from http://www.undp.org/hdro/HDI.html

United States Agency for International Development (USAID). (2000). *Croatia ICT assessment*. Retrieved September 8, 2006, from http://unpan1.un.org/intradoc/groups/public/documents/UNTC/UNPAN013159.pdf
United States Government Accountability Office. (2004). *International trade: Current government data provide limited insight into offshoring of services*.

UNPAN. (2005). *UN global e-government readiness report 2004*. Retrieved July 25, 2005, from http://www.unpan.org/egovernment4.asp

Urdan, T., & Weggen, C. (2000). *Corporate e-learning: Exploring a new frontier*. Equity Research. Retrieved November 15, 2005, from http://www.spectrainteractive.com/pdfs/CorporateELearingHamrecht.pdf

van Ark, B. (2002) Measuring the new economy: An international comparative perspective. *Review of Income and Wealth, 48*(1), 1-14.

van Ark, B., Inklaar, R. & McGuckin, R. (2002). 'Changing gear' productivity, ICT and service industries: Europe and the United States. Groningen Growth and Development Centre, Research Memorandum GD-60 (December).

Van Birgelen, M., De Ruyter, K., De Jong, A., & Wetzels, M. (2002). Customer evaluations of alter-sales service contact modes: An empirical analysis of national culture's consequences. *International Journal of Research in Marketing, 19*, 43-64.
Varian, H. R. (2003). *Intermediate microeconomics: A modern approach*. New York: W. W. Norton & Company.

Varian, H., Litan, R.E., Elder, A. & Shutter, J. (2002). The net impact study. Retrieved in January at: http://www.netimpactstudy.com/NetImpact_Study_Report.pdf.
Waller, V., & Wilson, J. (2001). *A definition for e-learning*. Open and Distance Learning Quality Council. Retrieved October 11, 2005, from http://www.odlqc.org.uk/odlqc/n19-e.htm

Wang, P., Wang, P., & Liu, A. (2005). Stock return volatility and trading volume: Evidence from the Chinese stock market. *Journal of Chinese Economic and Business Studies, 3*(1), 39-54.

Wang, Y. Q. (2006). *The discussion of environment informatization task by deputy director general of the State Environmental Protection Administration of China*. Retrieved July 20, 2006, from http://www.gov.cn/ zfjs/2006-06/01/content _297619.htm

Warf, B. (2001). Segueways into cyberspace: Multiple geographies of the digital divide. *Environment and Planning B: Planning and Design, 28*, 3-19.
Watson, R., & Myers, M.D. (2001). IT industry success in small countries: The case of Finland and New Zealand. *Journal of Global Information Management, 9*(2), 4-14.

Wellesley College. (2005). *Wellesley College*. Retrieved September 14, 2006, from http://www.wellesley.edu/

Welsh, E. T., Wanberg, C. R., Brown, K. G., & Simmering, M. J. (2003). E-learning: Emerging uses, empirical results, and future directions. *International Journal of Training and Development, 7*(4), 245-258. Retrieved April 21, 2006, from Blackwell Synergy database.

Wen, X. C., Liang, N., & Wen, X. M. (2005). Informatization thinking and target of environmental monitoring. In F. C. Xu (Ed.), *The application and management of environmental information technology* (pp. 30-34). Beijing, China: Chemical Industry Press.

Werner, P., Werner, G., & Kristina, V. (2006). Survey of environmental informatics in Europe. *Environmental Modelling & Software, 20*, 1-9. Retrieved June 30, 2006, from http://www.sesevier.com/locate/envsoft

West, D. M. (2000). *Assessing e-government: The Internet, democracy and service delivery by state and federal governments*. The World Bank. Retrieved September 10, 2006, from http://www.Worldbank.org/publicsector/egov/EgovReportUS00.htm

White, B. A., Tastle, W. J., & Fox, D. (2003). Barriers to e-learning in information systems. *Proceedings of the*

Information Systems Education Conference (ISECON 2003). Retrieved February 10, 2006, from http://isedj.org/isecon/2003/3523/

Whitt, E. J. (1994). "I can be anything": Student leadership in three women's colleges. *Journal of College Student Development, 35*(3), 198-207.

Wilson, T. D. (2002). The nonsense of "knowledge management." *Information Research, 8*(1). Retrieved from http://InformationR.net/ir/8-1/paper144.html

Wimmer, M., & Traunmuller, R. (2001). Trends in electronic government: Managing distributed knowledge. *Proceedings of the 11th International Workshop on Database Expert Systems Applications.*

Wind, J., & Mahajan, V. (2001). *Digital marketing: Global strategies from the world's leading experts.* John Wiley and Sons, Inc.

Wolf-Wendel, L. E. (1998). Models of successful African-American, European American and Hispanic women. *Journal of Higher Education, 69*(2), 144-172.

Women's University Coalition. (2006). *Members of the Women's College Coalition.* Retrieved September 25, 2006, from http://www.womenscolleges.org/members.html

Wong, P. K. (2002). ICT production and diffusion in Asia: Digital dividends or digital divide? *Information Economics and Policy, 14,* 167-187.

World Bank & MIGA. (2003). *Benchmarking FDI competitiveness in Asia.* Retrieved June 2005 from http://www.miga.org/miga_documents/asiareport.pdf

World Bank world development indicators 2006. (2006) Retrieved July 13, 2006, from http://devdata.worldbank.org/wdi2006/contents/Section5.htm

World Bank. (1999). *World development report 1998/99: Knowledge for development.* Washington: World Bank. Retrieved from http://www.worldbank.org/wdr/wdr98/

World Bank. (2005). *Development data and statistics.* Retrieved December 10, 2005, from http://web.worldbank.org/

World Bank. (2005a). *Sri Lanka: Improving the rural and urban investment climate.* Retrieved June 28, 2006, from http://www.worldbank.lk/

World Bank. (2005b). *Treasures of the education system in Sri Lanka: Restoring performance, expanding opportunities and enhancing prospects.*

World Economic Forum. (1999). *The global competitiveness report 1999.* Geneva, Switzerland.

Wu, X. Q. (2005, November). *Enhancing pollution sources auto-monitoring work improving the efficiency of executing the environmental laws.* Paper presented at the Meeting on the Spot of National Pollution Sources Auto-Monitoring Work. Retrieved from http://www.sepa.gov.cn/hjjc/jcxx/200601/t20060116_73517.htm

Wu, Y. (1996). *Productive performance in Chinese enterprises.* St. Martin's Press, Inc.

Xu, F. C. (2005). *Environment informatization and innovation.* Paper presented at the Second Meeting of the National Environmental Information Management and Technology's Application, Beijing, China.

Yamada, S. (2005). *Conflicts between the cultural diffusion and the intellectual properties protection* (Tech. Rep. No. 2005-EIP-27). Information Processing Society of Japan.

Yamamoto, K., & Fujimura, K. (2000). Joshidaigaku no sonzaiigi nikansuru hikaku-kenkyu: America/Igirisu/Kankoku/Nippon. Toyoeiwajogakuindaigaku. *Jimbun/Shakaikagaku-Ronshu, 18,* 121-189.

Yang, T. (2005). Using computer simulation technology for mechanical design. *Mechanical Research Application, 4,* 14.

Yusuf, M., & Radzi, M. (2003). *A national initiative: Presenting a success story.* Unpublished manuscript, MSC Technology Center, Cyberjaya, Malaysia.

Zeng, X. Y., Chen, K. A., & Li, H. Y. (2005). *Environmental information systems.* Beijing, China: Science Press.

Zhang, D., Zhao, J. L., Zhou, L., & Nunamaker, J. F., Jr. (2004). Can e-learning replace classroom training? *Communications of the ACM, 47*(5), 75-79.

Zhang, Q. Y., & Tian, W. L. (2005). *Environmental management information system.* Beijing, China: Chemical Industry Press.

Zhang, Y. (2003). CAD/CAM/CNC technologies for machining. *Coal Mine Machinery, 12*, 49-51.

Zheng, T., & Chen, C. Y. (2003). *Mathematical models of environmental system.* Beijing, China: Chemical Industry Press.

About the Contributors

Yutaka Kurihara is a professor of international economics at Aichi University, Japan. He was a lecturer and associate professor at Koryo International College in Japan. He has taught economics courses at both the graduate and undergraduate levels. He majored in international economics, finance, and digital economy. He has published about 120 papers and some of them are in refereed international journals. His recently published books are *Global Information Technology and Competitive Financial Alliances* (2006, IGI Publishing), *Economics Declaration* (2006), *Business & Policy Design in the Globalization* (2003), and *Intellectual Skills for Freshman* (2003, in Japanese). He was a visiting fellow at the National Institute of Multimedia Education and the Institute for Advanced Research at Nagoya University, Japan. He has been the executive director of the Japan Association of Monetary Economics since 2006.

Sadayoshi Takaya was educated at Kobe University, Japan, where he graduated in 1986 with a BA in economics, and graduated from the graduate course of economics in 1991. He also gained a PhD in 1998 from there. Between 1991 and 2003, he taught international macroeconomics and finance at Kinki University, Osaka, and since 2004, he has been a professor of international monetary systems and macroeconomics with the Faculty of Commerce, Kansai University, Osaka, Japan. His recent studies are in macroeconomic policies in Europe, monetary policies of European Central Bank, and the budgetary policies of member countries represented by the Stability and Growth Pact. He also conducts research in international financial architectures and the currency turmoil. He is coeditor of the book *Global Information Technology and Competitive Financial Alliances* (2006, Idea Group).

Hisashi Harui, PhD, is a professor of monetary economics in the School of Economics at Kwansei Gakuin University (KGU) in Japan and has served as a senior executive director of the Japan Association of Monetary Economics since 2004. He teaches monetary economics and open macroeconomics at both the postgraduate and undergraduate levels. His current research interests are in the independence and transparency of central banks, lenders of last resort in relation to financial stability, financial literacy education and consumer protection, as well as international financial crises and the IMF's (International Monetary Fund) function as the international lender of last resort. He has a wide teaching experience at the graduate school of the University of Lille 1 in France as well as at KGU for overseas students in open macro- and monetary economics, such as that in Japan's economy, its international transactions, and its financial instability in 1990s.

Hiroshi Kamae, PhD, is a professor of finance in the Graduate School of Commerce and Management at Hitotsubashi University, Japan. He teaches research methods and financial economics at the postgraduate level. Microstructure and time-series modeling of Japanese government bond (JGB) markets are some of his current research interests. He has a large number of publications in the econometric analysis of the cointegration of JGB markets, and in the efficiency of JGB futures markets. He published the books *The Japanese Government Bond Secondary Markets* (1993), *Efficiency of the Japanese Financial and Monetary Markets* (1999), and *The Japanese Government Bond Markets and Information* (2005). He is now a president of the Japan Society of Household Economics.

* * * * *

Frederic Andres has been an associate professor at the National Institute of Informatics since 2000 and at the Graduate University for Advanced Studies since 2002. He received his PhD from the University of Paris VI in 1993 and HDR from the University of Nantes in 2000. He was a researcher at Bull in France from 1989 to 1993, and a system architect at Ifatec and Euriware in France between 1993 and 1994. His research interests focus on distributed semantic information management for geomedia and cultural applications. It is vertical research on an advanced platform including specific research on a large-cluster information engine, advanced cooperative portal, ontology-based metadata management, and multilingual, multicultural, cross-disciplinary ontology management. Part of this research, the image-learning ontology engine, is emerging as a key technology. Furthermore, he is currently working on a topical-maps-based digital semantic management project (Myscoper project) in the Digital Content and Media Sciences Research Division. Finally, he has been serving as referee for the *Canadian Journal of Economics* since early 2006.

Mohamed Aslam is a senior lecturer with the Department of Economics, Faculty of Economics and Administration of University of Malaya, Kuala Lumpur. He has written articles on various subjects of Malaysia economy and has consulted the Malaysian government on a few development projects. He specializes in international trade policy, regional economic integration, international macroeconomics, and post-Keynesian economics.

Selahattin Bekmez earned his BS degree in public finance from Ankara University, Faculty of Political Science, in 1992. He earned his MS degree in economics in 1996 from Louisiana State University, USA. He received his PhD from the same university in 2001 with a dissertation titled *Budgetary Impacts of European Integration: A General Equilibrium Analysis of Turkish Accession into the European Union*. Between 2000 and 2003, he worked at the University of Idaho, National Institute for Advanced Transportation Technology (NIATT), USA, as a postdoctoral research associate. Dr. Bekmez currently works for the Mugla University, Mugla, Turkey, as an associate professor, and as a researcher for the Fondazione Eni Enrico Mattei (FEEM), Venice, Italy. His main areas of interest are general equilibrium modeling, economic development, and the game theory. He teaches mathematics, game theory, and economic development and growth.

Luis Enrique Bernal Vera is an industrial and system engineer at the University of Piura, Peru. He received his master's in small-business studies from the International SEPT (Small Enterprise Promotion and Training) Program at the University of Leipzig. He is experienced in international cooperation projects and entrepreneurship promotion as a supervisor and consultant in the themes of business strategy and information technology. Currently, he is a PhD candidate at the University of Leipzig with a dissertation titled *The Theory of Transaction Costs and Their Impact on Innovation Processes in Knowledge Intensive Business Services*. His research interests include information technology, small-business economy, and business strategic planning.

Raymond Chiong is a lecturer of information technology at Swinburne University of Technology (Sarawak Campus), Malaysia. He obtained an MS in advanced computer science from the University of Birmingham, and a first-class bachelor's degree with honors in computer science from Universiti Malaysia Sarawak. He is a member of IEEE and the British Computer Society (BCS). His research interest mainly lies in the field of artificial intelligence, and he is directed at investigating the principles of dynamic modeling and analysis of behavior of complex systems. He is currently involved in a number of projects using artificial intelligence techniques and advanced technology for learning purposes. Raymond has published numerous papers in the areas of computational intelligence and information retrieval and extraction. He has also won various awards, scholarships, and prizes throughout his academic career.

Utz Dornberger is the director of the International SEPT Program of the University of Leipzig and CEO (chief executive officer) of the consulting firm INNOWAYS Inc. He is the director of the technological start-up support program at the University of Leipzig. He studied biotechnology and biology at the University of Jena (Germany), University of Basque Country (Spain), and University Paris Du Nord (France). He holds a master's in small-business studies from the University of Leipzig. Dr. Dornberger realized a large number of value-chain and cluster analysis projects in developing countries, including Chile, Colombia, China, Mexico, and Vietnam. His special focus is on regional innovation systems and the development of technology-intensive suppliers in global value chains.

Zheng Fahong was born in 1973. She is working as a lecturer at Kunming University of Science and Technology, Kunming, China. She graduated from Kunming University of Science and Technology in 1996 and got her bachelor's degree in geology. After she graduated, she went to Kunming University of Science and Technology as a graduate student in computer application. She got her master's degree in 1999. Fahong kept working in the Department of Computer Science in Kunming University of Science and Technology after her graduation as an assistant the first 2 years, and then as a lecturer.

Michael Gapen is an economist at the IMF. Prior to joining the IMF, he held positions in the Mendoza College of Business at the University of Notre Dame and Van Kampen Investments, a Chicago-based investment company. He holds a PhD in economics from Indiana University.

Kennedy D. Gunawardana (PhD, Assumption University, Thailand) is the senior lecturer at the University of Sri Jayewardenepura, Nugegodda, Sri Lanka. He has also held faculty positions at Assumption University, Bangkok, Thailand. Dr. Kennedy's teaching and research interests are concentrated in the areas of information and communication technology in developing countries. His current research centers on the e-commerce and e-business in developing countries. Dr. Kennedy's research has been published in the *Journal of Computer and Engineering Management, Sabaragamuwa University Journal*, and various international conferences proceedings, such as IEEE management conferences. He is also the author and coauthor of various books and chapters.

Dr. **Ing-wei Huang** is a member of the faculty of the School of Management at Assumption University, Thailand. At present, she is the chairperson for the Department of Business Economics and specializes in microeconomic theory and international trade. She obtained her PhD from Nagoya University and has held a teaching career since 2004.

Princely Ifinedo is a PhD candidate at the Department of Computer Science and Information Systems at the University of Jyväskylä, Finland. He holds an MBA in international management from Royal Holloway College, University of London, an MS in informatics from Tallinn Technical University, Estonia, and a bachelor's degree in mathematics and computer science from the University of Port-Harcourt, Nigeria. His current research interests include e-government, socioeconomics theories, ERP (enterprise resource planning) success measurement, and the diffusion of IS in the transitioning and developing economies of Eastern Europe and Africa. He has published in international IS conference proceedings and journals, including *Electronic Government: An International Journal, Journal of E-Government*, and *Journal of Global Information Technology Management*.

Isa Ipcioglu is an assistant professor at the Dumlupinar University in Turkey. He received his MBA degree from Fairleigh Dickinson University in the United States. He holds a PhD degree from Dumlupinar University. His current research interests include knowledge management, intellectual capital, management information systems, and e-commerce. He has published numerous papers and proceedings in the areas of knowledge management and ICTs.

Biju Issac is a lecturer in information technology at Swinburne University of Technology (Sarawak Campus), Malaysia. He has a BEngr (electronics and communication engineering) degree along with an MCA (master of computer application) with honors from Calicut University, India. He is an IEEE, IEEE Computer Society, and IEEE Communication Society member. His research interests are mainly in computer networks and education. Specifically, his research is in wireless and network security, wireless mobility, IPv6 networks, and education and e-learning. He is currently doing part-time PhD work (network and mobile communication) in Universiti Malaysia Sarawak, Malaysia. He is also the head of network security research in Swinburne. He has a number of refereed publications and has presented papers at various conferences.

Yuko Iwasaki is an associate professor of Yokkaichi University. She worked for the Bank of Tokyo (now Bank of Tokyo-Mitsubishi UFJ), and specialized in international finance businesses as a researcher. She published some manuscripts in the fields of international trade, international businesses, and international finance in the bank's journals. Now she teaches international finance, securities, and financial institutions at the undergraduate and postgraduate levels. She specializes in Asian economics and finance. She has recently been interested in the Vietnamese economy. Iwasaki has published manuscripts on various topics, such as Vietnam's economic conditions and foreign direct investments, in academic journals, and has made several presentations at academic conferences. She is a member of the Japan Society of Monetary Economics, Japan Society of International Economics, and Japan Economics Policy Association.

Seibu Mary Jacob is a lecturer in the School of Engineering at Swinburne University of Technology (Sarawak Campus), Malaysia. She holds an MS in mathematics and a BS in mathematics from

Mahatma Gandhi University, India. She has also obtained a bachelor's degree in education, along with a postgraduate diploma in computer applications. Her research interests mainly lie in the fields of applied statistics, math, and education. She has done some work in assessment and learning methods under educational research. She has published a number of research papers in education and has presented papers at conferences.

Muhammed Karatas earned his BS degree in the Department of Economics at Dokuz Eylul University, Turkey, in 1993 in Izmir. He earned his MS degree in economics in 1996, also from Dokuz Eylul University. He received his PhD from Mugla University in 2002 with the dissertation titled *The Role of Universities in Socio-Economic Development and the Case of Mugla University.* Between 2004 and 2006, he worked at the Dumlupinar University, Turkey. Dr. Karatas currently works as an assistant professor for Mugla University, Turkey. His main areas of interests are economic development, socioeconomic development, human capital, natural resources and the economy of the environment, the European Union, and innovation and technology. He teaches on the topics of natural resources and the economy of the environment, economic development and growth, economics, international economic integration and the European Union, international institutions, and the economics of innovation.

Sachiko Kishino received her MA in history from Ochanomizu University in 1997 and an MA in managing archaeological sites from the University of London in 2005. She was an intern at the National Institute of Informatics from 2005 to 2006. She is currently working as an associate fellow at Ochanomizu University. Her research interests are in the areas of digital representation and the management of cultural assets.

Carlos Lassala Navarré is an associate professor in the Department of Finance at the University of Valencia (Spain). He received his PhD from the University of Valencia. He is the author of several textbooks and papers on financial subjects and collaborates as a reviewer for journals. He directs specialization courses and teaches doctorate programs. Currently, he is directing a research project on online banking at the University of Valencia. His primary research interests include e-banking, mutual funds, and financial markets.

Lu Lei was born in 1971. She is working as a lecturer at Kunming University of Science and Technology, Kunming, China. She graduated from Xi'an University of Architecture and Technology in 1993 and got her bachelor's degree in water engineering. After she graduated, she worked at Kunming University of Science and Technology as an assistant engineer. She then went on to work in the Department of Municipal Engineering at Kunming University of Science and Technology in 2003 and is still working there as a lecturer.

Jian-Xiong Liu is an associate professor with the Faculty of Mechanical and Electrical Engineering at Kunming University of Science and Technology in China. He teaches mechanical CAD (computer-aided design) and CAM (computer-aided manufacturing) at both the postgraduate and undergraduate levels. His current research interests are mechanical optimum design and economic design.

Chollada Luangpituksa is an associate professor of economics in the Department of Economics, Faculty of Economics, at Kasetsart University in Bangkok, Thailand. She was born and raised in Bangkok. She earned her undergraduate degree from Chulalongkorn University, Thailand, both in education in business administration and economics. Her graduate degrees in economics are from Wakayama University and Keio University Japan under the Japanese Government Scholarship. In the area of academic research, Dr. Luangpituksa has published numerous articles and has presented papers that have dealt with financial development in Thailand. She is also interested in Japanese economic history and macroeconomic models.

Zhao Meng was born in 1972. He is working as a lecturer at Kunming University of Science and Technology, Kunming, China. He graduated from Nanjing University of Science and Technology in 1996 and got his bachelor's degree in environmental monitoring. After he graduated, he went to Kunming University of Science and Technology as a graduate student in environmental engineering. He got his master's degree in 1999. He kept working in the Department of Municipal Engineering of the Faculty of Civil Engineering and Architecture at Kunming University of Science and Technology since his graduation as an assistant the first 2 years, and then as a lecturer.

Jasmine Mering is a lecturer in the School of IS and Multimedia, Swinburne University of Technology (Sarawak Campus), Malaysia. She obtained her master's degree in e-business and communication from Swinburne University of Technology, and a bachelor's degree in information technology in computer networking with honors from Universiti Utara Malaysia. Her research interest is in the area of educational technology, focusing on creating an immersive environment for e-learning platforms. Jasmine has numerous publications in the field of educational technology. She is also involved in a number of intercampus collaborations that oversee the management of the university's e-learning initiative.

Takeo Minaki, PhD, is a lecturer in finance at the Department of Economics, Hokusei Gakuen University, Japan. He teaches finance, macroeconomics, and research methods at the undergraduate level. His fields of research are empirical finance, behavioral finance, and market microstructures, for which he used time-series analysis. Some of his publications are on the econometrics of the financial markets of JGB, which are analyzed regarding market efficiency and market microstructures.

Rika Nakagawa, PhD, is a full-time research fellow at the Institute of Developing Economies, Chiba, Japan. She also teaches economics at Chuo Gakuin University. She earned her MA and PhD in international development from Nagoya University. She has conducted research on economic development in Southeast Asia, mainly Malaysia. She is the author of *The Asian Crisis and Monetary Policy in Malaysia* (in Japanese), and has published extensively and given presentations at various conferences, both in Japan and internationally, on the issues of economic development. Her current interest is IT and its role for economic development.

Akiko Nishio is a part-time lecturer in the Department of English at Mukogawa Women's University, Japan. She obtained her MA in women and education and PhD in education from the Institute of Education, University of London. Her interest area is higher education and gender. Her recent work is a chapter titled "Gender Issues in the Globalization of Higher Education: A Study of the Impact of the Prime Minister's Initiative in the UK" in the book *Gender Inequity in Academic Profession and*

Higher Education Access: Japan, the UK, and the US (2006, Research Institute for Higher Education, Hiroshima University).

Michael Papaioannou is a senior economist at the International Monetary Fund. While at the IMF, he served as a special advisor to the governor of the Bank of Greece. Prior to joining the IMF, he was senior vice president at Wharton Econometrics Forecasting Associates. He holds a PhD in economics from the University of Pennsylvania.

Jayanth Paraki graduated with a degree in medicine (1984) from the Kasturba Medical College, Mangalore, India, and acquired immense experience in general surgery during the following 10 years (1994-2004) at various hospitals in India. The decade of 1994 to 2004 was devoted to applied research on the Deming Profound System of Knowledge in the areas of alternative and complementary medicine, telemedicine, and allied fields in biomedical ontology. He is currently expanding on his research work through collaborations with various research groups in the USA, Japan, and Australia. He is proposing to edit a book series titled *Knowledge Management in Telemedicine* to facilitate advanced research in telemedicine. He is also in the process of gathering global support for the International Institute for Knowledge Management to foster trade and commerce activity between private organizations in India, the USA, and Japan.

Carla Ruiz Mafé is an assistant professor in the Department of Marketing at the University of Valencia (Spain), and the coordinator of postgraduate training programs in the Chamber of Commerce of Valencia. She received her PhD from the University of Valencia. She is the author of international publications on e-commerce. Her primary research interests include e-commerce, communication, interactive marketing, and consumer behavior.

Silvia Sanz Blas is an assistant professor in the Department of Marketing at the University of Valencia (Spain). She received her PhD from the University of Valencia. She is the author of international publications on distance shopping. Her primary research interests include communication, sales, e-commerce, interactive marketing, and consumer behavior.

Alejandro Sosa Noreña received an MBA at the University EAFIT, Medellín, Colombia. He is currently a PhD candidate under the Faculty of Economics at the University of Leipzig in the areas of marketing and strategy, and a graduate research associate of the International SEPT Program at the University of Leipzig, particularly in the self-management initiative project. His research interests are in the areas of marketing, strategy, SME (small and medium-sized enterprise) development, entrepreneurship, innovation, and patents in developing countries.

Patrick Then is a lecturer in information technology at Swinburne University of Technology (Sarawak Campus), Malaysia. He is active in research and development as well as in lecturing. After graduating with a bachelor's in information technology in 1999, he was involved in research in the fields of artificial intelligence, remote sensing, phase unwrapping, and fuzzy clustering until the completion of his MS (information technology) in August 2001. He is currently completing his PhD at Universiti Malaysia

Sarawak in the areas of digital watermarking and artificial intelligence. Despite being MIEEE and an active reviewer for some refereed journals, he is enthusiastic in disseminating his knowledge on Web development and e-learning methods.

Mustafa Zihni Tunca is an assistant professor at the Suleyman Demirel University in Turkey. He earned his MBA degree from Fairleigh Dickinson University. He received his PhD degree from the University of Lancaster. His current research interests include e-commerce, total quality management, and supply chain management. He has published papers in *Management Decision*, *International Journal of Applied Marketing*, and *International Journal of Electronic Business*. He has also published two book chapters as well as a number of papers in proceedings.

Ichihiro Uchida was educated at Ritsumeikan University, Japan, where he graduated in 1991 with a BA in economics and in 1997 with a graduate degree. He also gained his PhD there in 2001. Since 2000, he has taught econometrics as an associate professor at Aichi University, Japan. His recent studies are in the monetary policy of BOJ, regional banking systems, and spatial econometrics.

Dr. **Songsak Vanichviroon** is a member of the faculty of the School of Management at Assumption University, Thailand. At present, he is the chairperson for the Department of Business Information Systems and specializes in e-commerce and Internet marketing. He obtained his DBA from the University of South Australia and has held a teaching career since 2000.

Yu-Fei Wu is an engineer. Her current research interest is the application of IT.

Zheng-Ming Xiao is a lecturer with the Faculty of Mechanical and Electrical Engineering at Kunming University of Science and Technology in China. He teaches mechanical design at the undergraduate level. His current research interests are mechanical reliability and molding economic design.

Cha-Biao You is a postgraduate student under the Faculty of Mechanical and Electrical Engineering at Kunming University of Science and Technology in China. His current research theme is mechanical CAD, CAM, and CAE (computer-aided engineering).

Index